'Willcocks and Lacity have been studying and reporting on outsourcing for more than 19 years, and with clarity unmatched by others.... . This new book reinforces their earlier work – outsourcing can produce great results but only when outsourcing professionals ensure great execution.' – **Michael Corbett**, *Executive Director, International Association of Outsourcing Professionals*

'A compelling narrative of personal and professional discovery packed with 20 years of insight and wisdom. Essential reading for students and practitioners at any stage of their career. Willcocks and Lacity are at the top of their game.' – **Dr. John Hindle**, *Outsourcing Research Lead, Accenture*

'The leading researchers on IT and business process outsourcing have collected, updated, and extended some of the most insightful work written on the topic. This and its companion volume *Information Systems and Outsourcing* form a treasure trove of outsourcing knowledge for both academics and practitioners.' – **Jeanne W. Ross**, *Director and Principal Research Scientist MIT Center for Information Systems Research, Sloan School of Management*

'Lacity and Willcocks have enriched us with two decades of extensive research and prolific publications that they build upon in this book. The articles and chapters are written by the co-authors and other highly experienced contributors, who masterfully articulate and integrate outsourcing methodologies, successes, failures, opportunities, trends and lessons learned. The book paints an integral global picture for our time. Readers with no prior outsourcing experience are likely to irrevocably transform their world view, while outsourcing veterans will gain valuable new insights and a broader perspective. Both are destined to forever view the world through a multi-cultural, global lens.' – **Wendell Jones**, *Former VP, Compaq, SVP, NASD/NASDAQ, and outsourcing pioneer*

'Well written, thought provoking and directive.... . By drawing on their unique research base, Willcocks and Lacity provide insight into the development and future of outsourcing which would otherwise take practitioners and academics many years of learning to acquire. This book and its companion volume are essential reading for unlocking and understanding the complex business of sourcing.' – **Simon Ormston**, *Head of Strategic Sourcing Propositions and Marketing, BT Global Services*

'Willcocks and Lacity have assembled and participated with a team of pre-eminent scholars and renowned leaders in IT outsourcing and offshoring to provide a clear and comprehensive practical perspective on a subject that is on everyone's mind, but few truly completely understand.... . Thoughtful managers and executives will find the ideas in this book insightful.... . Willcocks and Lacity make a significant contribution to our ability to derive and leverage an effective IT sourcing portfolio.' – **Jerry Luftman**, *Executive Director and Distinguished Professor, Stevens Institute of Technology*

Also By Mary C. Lacity and Leslie P. Willcocks

INFORMATION SYSTEMS AND OUTSOURCING
Studies in Theory and Practice

GLOBAL SOURCING OF BUSINESS AND IT SERVICES

Also By Leslie Willcocks

OUTSOURCING GLOBAL SERVICES
Knowledge, Innovation and Social Capital (*with Ilan Oshri and Julia Kotlarsky*)

Also By Mary C. Lacity

OFFSHORE OUTSOURCING OF IT WORK
Client and Supplier Perspectives (*with Joseph Rottman*)

The Practice of Outsourcing

From Information Systems to BPO and Offshoring

Leslie P. Willcocks
London School of Economics and Political Science

and

Mary C. Lacity
University of Missouri, St. Louis

palgrave
macmillan

First published 2009 by
PALGRAVE MACMILLAN

Palgrave Macmillan in the UK is an imprint of Macmillan Publishers Limited,
registered in England, company number 785998, of Houndmills, Basingstoke,
Hampshire RG21 6XS.

Palgrave Macmillan in the US is a division of St Martin's Press LLC,
175 Fifth Avenue, New York, NY 10010.

Palgrave Macmillan is the global academic imprint of the above companies
and has companies and representatives throughout the world.

Palgrave® and Macmillan® are registered trademarks in the United States,
the United Kingdom, Europe and other countries

ISBN-13: 978-0-230-20541-3   hardback
ISBN-10: 0-230-20541-0   hardback

This book is printed on paper suitable for recycling and made from fully
managed and sustained forest sources. Logging, pulping and manufacturing
processes are expected to conform to the environmental regulations of the
country of origin.

A catalogue record for this book is available from the British Library.

Library of Congress Cataloging-in-Publication Data
The practice of outsourcing : from information systems to BPO and
offshoring / [edited] by Leslie P. Willcocks and Mary C. Lacity.
    p. cm.
Includes bibliographical references and index.
ISBN 978–0–230–20541–3 (alk. paper)
    1. Contracting out. 2. Offshore outsourcing. I. Willcocks, Leslie.
II. Lacity, Mary Cecelia.
HD2365.O9423 2009
658.4′058–dc22   2009013658

10   9   8   7   6   5   4   3   2   1
18   17   16   15   14   13   12   11   10   09

Printed and bound in Great Britain by
CPI Antony Rowe, Chippenham and Eastbourne

Contents

v

List of Figures

List of Tables

List of Contributors

Leslie P. Willcocks is Professor of Technology Work and Globalization at the London School of Economics and Political Science, head of the Information Systems and Innovation group and director of The Outsourcing Unit there. He is known for his work on global sourcing, information management, IT evaluation, e-business, organizational transformation as well as for his practitioner contributions to many corporations and government agencies. He holds visiting chairs at Erasmus, Melbourne and Sydney universities and is Associate Fellow at Green Templeton College, University of Oxford. He has been for the last 18 years co-editor-in-chief of the *Journal of Information Technology*, and is joint series editor, with Mary Lacity, of the Palgrave Series *Technology, Work, and Globalisation*. He has co-authored 32 books, including most recently *Major Currents in the IS Field* (2008 – 6 volumes), and *Global Sourcing of Business and IT Services* (2006). He has published over 180 refereed papers in journals such as *Harvard Business Review, Sloan Management Review, MIS Quarterly, MISQ Executive, Journal of Management Studies, Communications of the ACM,* and *Journal of Strategic Information Systems.*

Mary Cecelia Lacity is Professor of Information Systems and International Business Fellow at the University of Missouri-St Louis, USA. She has written ten books, including Offshore *Outsourcing of IT Work* (2008; co-author Joe Rottman) and *Global Sourcing of Business and IT Services* (2006; co-author Leslie Willcocks). Her 40 journal publications have appeared in the *Harvard Business Review, Sloan Management Review, MIS Quarterly, IEEE Computer, Communications of the ACM* and many other academic and practitioner outlets. Her work has been cited more than 3,500 times. She is US Editor of the *Journal of Information Technology*, and co-editor of the Palgrave Series: *Technology, Work, and Globalisation* and on the Editorial Boards for *MIS Quarterly Executive, Journal of Strategic Information Systems, Journal of the Association for Information Systems and Strategic Outsourcing.*

Notes on co-authors

Chong Ju Choi is Visiting Professor of International Business at Cass Business School (Department of Shipping, Trade and Finance), City University, London, UK and at the Kingold Business School, Jaitong University, China. His past academic career has spanned many continents, with earlier appointments at the Universities of Oxford, Cambridge and City University in the UK, Duke University, Fuqua School of Business in the USA, the University of Bologna, Italy, the Australian National University, Australia and Waseda University,

Japan. He has published over 100 papers in international journals and is the author of a number of books, including *Emergent Globalization* (2004).

Sara Cullen is the Managing Director of The Cullen Group and a Fellow at Melbourne University. She has a leading profile in Asia Pacific having consulted to over 110 private and public sector organizations, spanning 51 countries, in over 130 projects with per annum contract values up to $1.5 billion. Her research in outsourcing has been published in *MISQE* and the *Journal of Strategic Information Systems*. Previously she was a national partner at Deloitte (Australia).

Wendy Currie is Professor of Information Systems at Warwick Business School at the University of Warwick. Principal Investigator of EPSRC and ESRC (Paccit/Link) funded research into e-business models and emerging technologies. She is currently serving on the editorial boards of the *Journal of Information Technology, Journal of Strategic Information Systems, Journal of Change Management* and the *Journal of Enterprise Information Management*. She has also served on the editorial boards for special issues in *MISQ* and *Information Systems Research*. She served as European, Middle East and Africa representative for the Association for Information Systems, and is currently joint Conference Chair for the International Conference on Information Systems to be held in Arizona in 2009. Her research is published in the information systems and management journals and she works with several "blue chip" companies on various research projects.

David Feeny is Professor of Information Management, and Fellow at Green Templeton College, University of Oxford. He has published widely on CIO and retained capability, strategy and the management of Information Technology, especially in *Harvard Business Review* and *Sloan Management Review* as well as many highly ranked IS journals. His current research interests are in the evaluation of executive education and innovation. Previously he was a senior executive for over 20 years at IBM.

Guy Fitzgerald is Professor of Information Systems in the Department of Information Systems and Computing (DISC) at Brunel University. Before this he was the Cable & Wireless Professor of Business Information Systems at Birkbeck College, University of London, and prior to that he was at Templeton College, Oxford. He has also worked in the computer industry with companies such as British Telecom, Mitsubishi and CACI Inc, International. His research interests are concerned with the effective management and development of information systems and he has published widely in these areas. He is founder and co-editor, with David Avison, of the *Information Systems Journal* (ISJ) from Blackwell/Wiley, is author of a well-known text book on information systems development methodologies, and is currently the elected Vice-President of Publications for the Association for Information Systems (AIS).

Jim Fox is Chief Financial Officer for Mobile Armor, a company that offers products and services to protect data on mobile devices. Prior to his current position, Fox was a partner with DataServ LLC, a market leader in technology-enabled business services for finance and administrative functions. Before joining DataServ in 2005, he served as senior vice president of finance for Reuters Ltd. In this role, he was responsible for developing and managing the Americas Finance Shared Service function, as well as driving the overall implementation of Reuters' world-class finance strategy. His experience at Reuters included establishing an offshore service capability in Bangalore, India, outsourcing various activities and designing "best-in-class" finance management capabilities. Prior to Reuters, he was a corporate controller for Bridge Information Systems. He is also a ten-year veteran of Deloitte and Touche, LLP, where he served as a senior manager of global multinationals in St Louis, New York and Brussels, Belgium. Fox holds bachelor's degrees in accounting and finance from the University of Tulsa. He is also a certified public accountant. As an active member in the St Louis community, he serves on the boards of Junior Achievement and the Juvenile Diabetes Research Foundation. In 2004, he was honored as one of *St. Louis Business Journal*'s 40 Under 40.

Rudy Hirschheim is the Ourso Family Distinguished Professor of Information Systems at Louisiana State University. He has previously been on the faculties of University of Houston, Templeton College, Oxford, London School of Economics and McMaster University. He obtained his PhD from the University of London. He was awarded an honorary doctorate by the University of Oulu (Finland) and is Fellow of the Association for Information Systems. He is co-consulting editor of the Wiley Series in Information Systems. He is senior editor of *Journal of the Association for Information Systems*; on the editorial boards of the journals: *Information and Organization, Information Systems Journal, Journal of Strategic Information Systems, Journal of MIS* and *Journal of Information Technology*.

Thomas Kern is CIO & Executive Manager of KERN Global Language Services (www.e-kern.com). His areas of expertise are operational management of centralized and decentralized ICT services for more than 40 branches across the world. He has a strong background in ICT outsourcing, application service provision, ICT strategy and relationship management. He received his DPhil in Management Information Systems from Said Business School, University of Oxford. He has published more than 30 articles in journals and European and International Conferences. He is co-author of two books, *The Relationship Advantage: Sourcing, Technologies, and Management* (2001) and *Netsourcing: Renting Business Applications and Services over a Network*, Financial Times (2002). E-mail: thomas.kern@e-kern.com

Kuldeep Kumar is Professor at the Alvah H. Chapman Graduate School of Business, College of Business, Florida International University and is also a visiting professor at City University, Hong Kong. He has been Professor of Information Systems Research at The Rotterdam School of Management (RSM), Erasmus University, The Netherlands. In addition to his teaching in North America (FIU, Miami), Georgia State (Atlanta), University of Waterloo (Canada), he has taught in executive and graduate programs at leading business schools in Europe (sda Bocconi, Italy), ESADE (Spain), RSM (The Netherlands) and Asia (MDI, India), AIT (Bangkok) and NTU (Singapore). Further to his early professional IT work background, his research, executive education, and consulting includes working with major IT vendors such as TCS (Tata Consultancy Services), Mphasis, and BaaN. For two years, Professor Kumar was a part-time employee and advisor to the BaaN Institute working to develop scenarios for business use of IT and evolution of enterprise wide systems, He has also worked with and taught senior executives for TCS and RaboBank. Professor Kumar's areas of expertise include global and offshore outsourcing, management of offshore distribution of work, management and governance of IT in organizations, IT Strategy, enterprise systems, and use of ICT in supply chains.

Joseph Rottman is Associate Professor of Information Systems at the University of Missouri-St Louis. He has conducted research and has spoken internationally on global sourcing, innovation diffusion and public sector IT. He has been engaged by Fortune 500 companies to assess their global sourcing strategies as well as public sector organizations seeking strategic leadership. He is author of *Offshore Outsourcing of IT Work* (2008; co-author Mary Lacity). His journal publications have appeared in the *Sloan Management Review, IEEE Computer, MIS Quarterly Executive, Journal of Information Technology,* and *Information and Management.*

Peter Seddon is Associate Professor in the department of Information Systems at the University of Melbourne. His teaching and research focuses on helping people and organizations gain greater benefits from their use of information technologies. His major publications have been in the areas of evaluating information systems success, packaged enterprise application software, IT outsourcing and accounting information systems. He is a senior editor of *MIS Quarterly* and is on the editorial board of *Journal of Information Technology.* E-mail: p.seddon@unimelb.edu.au

Professional Credits

Over the course of a 20 year publication record on outsourcing, the authors comment on which findings remain robust and which findings have significantly changed since initial publication. The authors have thus significantly updated and revised material for this book, including placing the findings in a broader historical and evolutionary context. The authors and publishers are grateful for permission to reproduce in full or in part versions of our work initially published elsewhere.

Chapter 2 – an initial version of this chapter was published as Lacity, M., Hirschheim, R., and Willcocks, L. (1994) "Realizing Outsourcing Expectations: Incredible Promises, Credible Outcomes", *Journal of Information Systems Management*, 11, 4, Fall, 7–18.

Chapter 3 – an initial version of this chapter was published as Willcocks, L. and Fitzgerald, G. (1994) "Contracting for IT Outsourcing: Recent Research Evidence", *Proceedings of the Fifteenth Annual International Conference in Information Systems*, Vancouver, December 13–16, 91–98, AIS, USA.

Chapter 4 – an initial version of this chapter was published as Willcocks, L. and Choi, C. (1995) "Cooperative Partnership and 'Total' IT Outsourcing: From Contractual Obligation To Strategic Alliance?", *European Management Journal*, 13, 1, 67–78.

Chapter 5 – an initial version of this chapter was published as Kumar, K. and Willcocks, L. (1996) "Offshore Outsourcing: A Country Too Far?" *Proceedings of the Fourth European Conference in Information Systems*, Lisbon, July 2–4.

Chapter 6 – an initial version of this chapter was published as Willcocks, L. and Currie, W. (1997) "IT Outsourcing in Public Service Contexts: Towards The Contractual Organization?", *British Journal of Management*, 8, S107–120, June.

Chapter 7 – an initial version of this chapter was published as Lacity, M. and Willcocks, L. (1997) "Information Systems Sourcing: Examining the Privatization Option in US Public Administration", *Information Systems Journal*, 7, 1–24.

Chapter 8 – an initial version of this chapter was published as Currie, W. and Willcocks, L. (1998) "Analysing IT Outsourcing Decisions in the

Context of Size, Interdependency and Risk", *Information Systems Journal*, 8, 2, 120–138.

Chapter 9 – an initial version of this chapter was published as Hirschheim, R. and Lacity, M. (2000) "Information Technology Insourcing: Myths and Realities", *Communications of the ACM*, 43, 2, 99–108.

Chapter 10 – an initial version of this chapter was published as Kern, T. and Willcocks, L.P. (1999) "Contracts, Control, and Presentiation in IT Outsourcing: Research in Thirteen European Organizations Organisations". Proceedings of *The International Conference in Information Systems*, December, AIS, USA.

Chapter 11 – an initial version of this chapter was published as Cullen, S., Seddon, P. and Willcocks, L. (2006) "ITO Configuration: Research into Defining and Designing Outsourcing Arrangements", *Journal of Strategic Information Systems*, March.

Chapter 13 – an initial version of this chapter was published as Feeny, D., Willcocks, L. and Lacity, M. (2003) *Business Process Outsourcing: The Promise of the Enterprise Partnership Model*, Templeton Executive Briefing, Templeton College, Oxford University, ISBN 1 873955162.

Chapter 14 – an initial version of this chapter was published as Lacity, M. and Rottman, J. (2007) "Project Attributes and Contextual Explanations of Offshore Outsourcing Outcomes: Evidence from a Client's Perspective", *Proceedings of The Third International Conference on Outsourcing of Information Systems*, Heidelberg, May 30.

Acknowledgments

First and foremost, as with our companion volume *Information Systems and Outsourcing: Studies in Theory and Practice,* we sincerely thank the now over 1,700 executives across the globe who participated in our research over the past 20 years. Without them our work just would not have been possible. Due to the sensitive nature of outsourcing, many participants requested anonymity and cannot be individually acknowledged. Participants who did not request anonymity are acknowledged in the appropriate places throughout this book. We also wish to acknowledge the supportive research environments from our respective institutions. During the 1990s we both found Templeton College, University of Oxford a special place to work and offer grateful thanks to all the staff and colleagues there who made research and study such a pleasure.

Leslie is very grateful to all his colleagues at Oxford and Warwick Universities and now London School of Economics for their tolerance and support over the years. Special thanks to Julia Kotlarsky and Ilan Oshri for rescuing him from ultimate busyness and making sure the important work got done – it so easily could have been otherwise. Also to Sara Cullen, Peter Reynolds and Peter Seddon for providing the happiest of Australian work climates year in year out as the research progressed.

Mary thanks Vice Chancellor Nasser Arshadi at the University of Missouri-St Louis because his Office of Research provided or facilitated three research grants to support Mary's work. She also thanks her colleagues in the IS department at UMSL, including Dr Marius Janson, Dr Kailash Joshi, Dinesh Mirchandani, Dr Rajiv Sabherwal, Dr Vicki Sauter, Dr Ashok Subramanian, and Dr Joseph Rottman.

Obviously research work of this scope over such a long period is not just a two-person effort. Several colleagues who became friends made significant contributions and published with us in the earlier period, in particular Rudy Hirschheim, Wendy Currie, and Guy Fitzgerald. Latterly we have thoroughly enjoyed researching, digesting and writing with Thomas Kern, Joseph Rottman, Eric van Heck, Sara Cullen, Peter Seddon, Julia Kotlarsky, Ilan Oshri, Jim Fox and John Hindle. They provided intelligence, inspiration and hard work in equal measure and have been a joy to be with. Amongst all David Feeny stands out as the person with whom we owe the most. His insight and wisdom have been guiding lights.

We would like to thank our circles of family and friends for their forbearance and humor. Mary thanks her son, Michael Christopher, her parents, Dr and Mrs Paul Lacity, and her three sisters: Karen Longo, Diane Iudica, and Julie Owings. She thanks her closest friends, Jerry Pancio, Michael

McDevitt, Katharine Hastings, Beth Nazemi, and Val Graeser. Leslie would like to thank Chrisanthi, Catherine, and George for nights at the opera, ballet and all the sustaining things, and Damaris for making life what it should be.

As a further testimony to the value of global sourcing, we are delighted to acknowledge the great contribution of our global publishing team, and in particular Stephen Rutt and Emily Bown of Palgrave, and Shirley Tan, our copy editor and coordinator.

Part I

Introduction

1
Outsourcing Practice: The Search for Flexibility and Control

Leslie Willcocks and Mary Lacity

Introduction

This book has an earlier companion volume in *Information Systems and Outsourcing: Studies in Theory and Practice* (Palgrave, 2009). There we gathered together our major papers and subsequent reflections on two themes: the theoretical perspectives utilized for studying outsourcing; and the learning that has emerged from our research, cast in the form of lessons for practice. In the present book we take the journey further, looking to give insight into the evolution of our research, and of outsourcing practices themselves, as they have developed from 1988 through to the present day. Here we build from a primary concern with Information Technology (ITO) through to the burgeoning market for business process services (BPO), and the moves to offshore, nearshore and hybrid models typical of the late 2000s.

Details of the research base we draw upon can be found in each chapter of the book. But combined, our work as at 2009 formed a 630 (and growing) case research base held by researchers at the London School of Economics Outsourcing Unit, and the Universities of Melbourne and Missouri, St Louis information systems departments. Including survey work, the research base by 2009 represented data from 1,600 plus organizations. It covered all major economic and government sectors, including financial services, energy and utilities, defence/aerospace, retail, telecoms and IT, oil, transportation, central state and local government, health care, industrial products and chemicals, and has been drawn from medium, large and multinational organizations based in Europe, USA and Asia Pacific. Most importantly, as will emerge in this book, we have been able to track many of our cases over the life of their outsourcing contracts, and indeed into their second and third generation, thus providing us with unique insights into clients' and suppliers' *a priori* expectations juxtaposed against actual outcomes (see in particular Chapters 2 and 12 of the present volume).

In this chapter we will assess the evolution of our research and our findings, as well as the major changes in the outsourcing market and how clients have shaped and used the ever expanding service base. Our focus is from 1989 through to the present day, with some comment on present and future trends, especially in the light of the global economic downturn beginning from 2007, and deepening into 2008/9.

Outsourcing's rise to prominence: 1990s IT trends, practices, and lessons

Ever since Kodak's landmark decision to outsource the bulk of their IT functions to three suppliers in 1989, IT outsourcing has been a widely-publicized practice. Most of us are familiar over the years with a number of other high-profile IT outsourcing mega-deals besides Kodak. Companies and public sector organizations that have, since the 1990s, outsourced significant portions of their IT functions by transferring their IT assets, leases, licenses, and staff to outsourcing vendors include (often with name changes along the way): British Aerospace, British Petroleum, Chase Manhattan Bank, UK Inland Revenue and Department of Social Security, Continental Airlines, Barclays, DuPont, First City, General Dynamics, Commonwealth Bank, McDonnell Douglas, and Xerox. When such mega-deals were first signed, the trade press tended to report *expected* outcomes, including reduced IT costs, better service, access to new technology, and an ability to refocus in-house staff on higher-value work. But, even in the 1990s there was substantial debate about the long-term consequences of such deals.

Proponents pointed out that: *"IT outsourcing is a harbinger of the transformation of traditional IT departments and provides a glimpse at the emerging organizational structures of the information economy"* (McFarlan and Nolan, 1995, p. 11). Opponents argued that companies that signed long-term contracts lost control of their IT assets and capabilities. Critics admonished: "Outsourcing, the Scam May Be on You" (Gantz, 1994), "Outsourcing, a Game for Losers" (Strassmann, 1995), and "Selling One's Birth Right" (Dorn, 1989). Despite that debate that is ongoing to this day (the contemporary version includes questions of consolidating supplier numbers down to as few as possible) the growth of the IT outsourcing market during the 1990s was undeniable. For example, IDC estimated the global outsourcing market for 1995 at $76 billion. By 2002 the global market revenues from IT outsourcing were probably $US120 billion (Lacity and Willcocks, 2001).

An interesting fact lost in the focus on mega-deals was that the dominant trend was quite otherwise, even in the 1990s. By 2000, worldwide, there were only about 140 such deals. Our research shows consistently that, in the lead markets of USA and UK, over 75% of organizations outsource 15–50% of their IT budgets, typically with multiple suppliers (Lacity and Willcocks, 2001; Willcocks and Lacity, 2006). A mega-deal, especially with a single supplier, always has been a distinctly minority pursuit. As we will see later in the book, one explanation relates to organizations seeking to lower the high risk profile inherent with large-scale outsourcing to third party suppliers (see especially Chapters 6 and 8). One should also not forget that by 2000 many organizations (USA 10%, UK 23%, other countries much higher) had no significant IT outsourcing contracts (Kern and Willcocks, 2001). Chapters 8 and 9 of this book will detail why in-house provision has often been seen as the economically, operationally and strategically effective option for at least part of any organization's IT portfolio.

As companies accumulated experience with IT outsourcing through the 1990s, we took the opportunity to assess the practices that differentiated success from failure. A major synthesis of our thinking and research appeared in Lacity and Willcocks (1998). This looked at 61 sourcing arrangements over the 1991–98 period (expanded to 116 in Lacity and Willcocks, 2001). There we recorded seven major findings and developed our thinking on three contracting models being utilized by outsourcing practitioners. To position the evolution of outsourcing practice and of our own research, these are worth revisiting, albeit briefly. First, the major findings:

Finding 1: Selective outsourcing decisions achieved expected cost savings with a higher relative frequency than total outsourcing or total insourcing decisions.

We defined the three main sourcing options in play as:

Total Outsourcing: The decision to transfer the equivalent of more than 80% of the IT budget for IT assets, leases, staff, and management responsibility to an external IT provider.

Total Insourcing: The decision to retain the management and provision of more than 80% of the IT budget internally after evaluating the IT services market.[1]

Selective Outsourcing: The decision to source selected IT functions from external provider(s) while still providing between 20% and 80% of the IT budget internally. This strategy may include single or multiple vendors.

Selective outsourcing decisions achieved expected cost savings more frequently (85%) than all-or-nothing approaches (29%). Few vendors or internal IT departments possessed the expertise to perform all IT activities most efficiently. With selective outsourcing, organizations could select the most capable and efficient source – a practice some participants referred to as "best-of-breed" sourcing. Sometimes, the ability to focus in-house resources

---

[1]Included in our definition of insourcing is the buying-in of vendor resources to meet a temporary resource need, such as the need for programmers in the latter stages of a new development project or the use of management consultants to facilitate a strategic planning process. In these cases, the customer retains responsibility for the delivery of IT services – vendor resources are brought in to supplement internally-managed teams.

to higher-value work also justified selective outsourcing. In most total out-sourcing cases, participants encountered one or more of the following problems realizing expected cost savings:

- excess fees for services beyond the contract or excess fees for services participants assumed were in the contract;
- "hidden costs" from both client (such as IT spend hidden in decentral-ized budgets) and suppliers (such as costs to transfer software licenses);
- Inflexible contracts that are poorly adapted to changes in technology, market prices, business processes, and business direction.

Exclusive sourcing by an internal IT department was generally successful (67%). However, in some of our cases, internal IT "monopolies" promoted complacency and erected organizational obstacles against continuous improvement.

Finding 2: Senior executives and IT managers who made decisions together achieved expected cost savings with a higher relative frequency than when either stakeholder group acted alone.

It appears that successful sourcing decisions require a mix of political power and technical skills. Political power helped to enforce the larger busi-ness perspective – such as the need for organization-wide cost cuts – as well as the "muscle" to implement such business initiatives. Technical expertise on IT services, service levels, measures of performance, rates of technical obsolescence, rates of service growth, price/performance improvements, and a host of other technical topics were needed to develop requests-for-proposals, evaluate vendor bids, and negotiate and manage sound con-tracts. The need for joint sponsorship is most apparent when outsourcing and insourcing decisions are analyzed separately because we found that senior business executives realizing their expected cost savings only 40% of the time when they *outsourced* IT. Meanwhile, IT managers realized their expected cost savings only 56% of the time when they *insourced* IT.

Finding 3: Organizations that invited both internal and external bids achieved expected cost savings with a higher relative frequency (89%) than organizations that merely compared external bids with current IT costs (71%), or that had an informal bid process (50%).

We believe this was because formal external vendor bids were often based on efficient managerial practices that could be replicated by internal IT managers. The question was: If IT managers could reduce costs, why didn't they? Some of this was due to internal political barriers. The issue is pursued in detail in Chapter 9 of this book.

Finding 4: Short-term contracts (up to four years, 83%: 4–7 years, 70%) achieved expected cost savings with a higher relative frequency than long-term contracts over seven years, 40%).

Short-term contracts involved less uncertainty, motivated vendor performance, allowed participants to recover from mistakes quicker, and helped to ensure that participants were getting a fair market price. Another reason for the financial success of short-term contracts was that participants only outsourced for the duration in which requirements were more stable, thus participants could adequately analyze the cost implications of their decisions. Also, some participants noted that short-term contracts motivated vendor performance because vendors realized customers could opt to switch vendors when the contract expired.

Finding 5: Detailed fee-for-service contracts achieved expected cost savings with a higher relative frequency than other types of fee-for-service contracts.

Many different types of contracts are used to govern IT outsourcing relationships. We deal with this issue in detail in Chapters 3 and 10. However, it is useful at this point to outline the main contracting forms we encountered in the 1990s. In general, these IT sourcing contracts can be categorized as follows:

1. *Fee-for-Service Contract:* A customer pays a fee to a supplier in exchange for the management and delivery of specified IT products or services. This can take many forms, including:
   a) Standard Contract: The customer signs the vendor's standard, off-the-shelf contract.
   b) Detailed Contract: The contract includes special contractual clauses for service scope, service levels, measures of performance, and penalties for non-performance.
   c) Loose Contract: The contract does not provide comprehensive performance measures or contingencies.
   d) Mixed Contract: For the first few years of the contract, requirements are fully specified, connoting a "detailed" contract. However, subsequent requirements are only loosely defined, connoting a "loose" contract.
2. *Strategic Alliance/Partnership:* Collaborative inter-organizational relationships involving significant resources of two or more organizations to create, add to, or maximize their joint value. In the contract, the partners agree to furnish a part of the capital and labor for a business enterprise, and each shares in profits and losses.

3. *Buy-in Contract:* A customer buys in vendor resources to supplement in-house capabilities, but the vendor resources are managed by in-house business and IT management.

Detailed, fee-for-service contracts achieved expected cost savings in 91% of cases compared with 50% for standard, 40% for mixed, and 0% for loose contracts. These organizations understood their own IT functions very well, and could therefore define their precise requirements in a contract. They also spent significant time negotiating the details of contracts, often with the help of outside experts. In contrast to the success of the detailed contract, all the loose contracts in our sample were disasters, not only in terms of not achieving expected cost savings, but in terms of service. In our sample there was only one strategic alliance, namely that of Phillips with the Dutch software company, that emerged over time as successful. Strategic alliances are discussed in more detail below and in Chapter 4.

Finding 6: More recent contracts had higher success rates than older contracts.

We offer two explanations – learning curve effects and increased sourcing options. First, customers were accumulating experience with IT outsourcing and were thus getting better at negotiating deals. In fact, some of our participants adopted incremental outsourcing precisely to develop an in-house knowledge base learnt from the outsourcing experience. Second, more recent contracts may have achieved expected cost savings more frequently because the outsourcing market was changing in the customer's favor. Once dominated by a few big players, such as EDS, Andersen, CSC, and IBM, the IT outsourcing market in the 1990s fragmented into many niche services. As competition in the global outsourcing market has increased generally throughout the 1991–2008 period, companies and public sector agencies have had more power to bargain for shorter contracts, more select services, and better financial packages. At the same time, of course the complexity and size of IT outsourcing has expanded considerably into the 2000s, so findings on contract success will always be time and context bound.

Finding 7: Size of IT function did not usefully differentiate financially successful decisions from financially unsuccessful decisions. Managerial practices were emerging to be more important than economies of scale associated with size when seeking IT cost reductions.

We were interested in the size of IT function because of the theoretical argument that external service providers have lower average costs than internal IT functions due to mass production and labor specialization efficiencies. We would expect that organizations with small IT functions would gain significant savings by accessing a vendor's economies of scale through outsourcing. We would also expect that organizations with large IT functions would have equivalent economies of scale as a vendor, and therefore could achieve cost savings on their own through insourcing. This prompts the question: Do companies with small IT functions successfully outsource, while companies with large IT functions successfully insource?

In this study, the findings were apparently contrary to expectations based on the theoretical arguments. Large IT insourcing cases did not achieve expected cost savings with greater frequency than small IT insourcing cases. In general, all the size indicators suggested, as the theory of economies of scale predicts, that small IT cases were able to reduce costs through outsourcing. However, small IT outsourcing cases did not achieve expected cost savings with greater frequency than large IT outsourcing cases. When all indicators of size are considered, size does not usefully differentiate an organization's ability to achieve expected cost savings. We suggest the following interpretation of this finding: *In practice, the ability to reduce IT costs may depend more on IT managerial practices than inherent economies of scale associated with size.* This issue is pursued in much more detail in Chapter 9 (see also Lacity and Hirschheim, 1995).

Management lessons from the 1990s: "fee-for-service" or "strategic alliance"?

In the 1990s IT outsourcing was, as it still is, a widely publicized and much debated practice. In particular, practitioners and academics have argued about the validity of long-term, "total" outsourcing. The debate is clarified by our classification of three types of IT outsourcing contracts: fee-for-service contracts, strategic alliances/partnerships, and buy-in contracts. By highlighting the critical elements of various contracting models, we can perhaps reconcile some of the apparent discrepancies on the best ways to outsource IT.

Fee-for-Service Contracts. We found that such relationships required *detailed contracts* that fully specify requirements, service levels, performance metrics, penalties for non-performance, and price; and *short-term contracts* that last only for the duration for which requirements are known. Such contracts were best suited for IT activities where companies could clearly define their needs in an air-tight contract. Fee-for-service contracts were not suited for IT activities in which the technology was ill-defined, immature, or unstable. In these cases, the customer's inability to define baseline requirements together with subsequent unreasonable expectations that additional/undocumented services would be provided without additional costs, caused relationships to deteriorate.

An important insight from our work of this period is that several of our case companies signed fee-for-service contracts, but mis-labeled them as strategic alliances or strategic partnerships (see also Chapters 3 and 4). The rhetoric of a "partnership" prompted the signing of loosely-defined, fee-for-service contracts (perhaps more aptly labeled "flimsy" contracts). Vendors' bids were based on the ill-defined baseline services the customers originally specified. Customers believed vendors would provide additional services free or at reduced prices under the spirit and trust of the "partnership". In reality, additions or changes to the fee-for-service contract triggered additional vendor costs that were recovered through excess fees. Such excess fees contributed to the customer's inability to realize expected cost savings.

Strategic Alliances/Partnerships. In the context of IT, the idea that outsourcing vendors should be treated as "strategic partners" may be attributed to Eastman Kodak. A Kodak manager overseeing the contracts told an audience of practitioners, *"We think of our alliances as partnerships because of their cooperative and long term qualities"* (Lacity and Hirschheim, 1993ab). Kodak's original contracts were only a dozen or so pages long. The importance of Kodak's IT outsourcing model cannot be over-stated – statistical analysis shows that the early 1990s IT outsourcing trend can be attributed to imitative behavior of Kodak's decision (Loh and Venkatraman, 1992; Applegate and Montealegre, 1991).

Kanter (1994) found eight essential factors for successful alliances:

1. *Individual Excellence:* both partners are strong and have something of value to contribute
2. *Importance:* the relationship plays a key role in both partners' long-term strategic plans
3. *Interdependence:* neither can accomplish alone what both can do together
4. *Investment:* partners invest in each other
5. *Information:* communication is reasonably open
6. *Integration:* partners develop organizational linkages so they work together smoothly
7. *Institutionalization:* the relationship extends beyond the deal-makers and cannot be broken on a whim
8. *Integrity:* the partners behave in honorable ways toward each other

Given these criteria, only one of our 1990s cases could really be described as a joint venture, namely Phillips' relationship with a Dutch software company. Phillips provided 1,000 IT employees and owned over 30% of the venture. The Dutch software company provided sales and marketing capabilities. The partners developed and supported application software for external customers, as well as delivering service back to Phillips. Outside of the cases we studied, including the ones described in Chapter 4, there were, in the 1990s, a number of reported IT strategic alliances that may meet most of Kanter's criteria. In principle, these strategic alliances combine strengths to add value by selling jointly-developed IT products and services to the external marketplace. Because each party shared in the revenue generated from external sales, the deals were not based on fee-for-services, but rather on shared risks and rewards, often accompanied by joint investment. Some examples of strategic alliances announced in the 1990s trade press included:

- The Xerox-EDS contract – provided for future shared revenues from the development and sale of a global electronic document distribution service. At the time of the contract signing, the President of EDS and CEO of Xerox announced:

  "We realized that each of our companies brought to the table specific best-in-class capabilities that enabled a level of performance that neither could achieve independently. This is a case of two technology companies enabling one another to achieve a shared vision for adding value for their customers." (reported on October 10, 1996 on WWW at http://www.xerox. com/PR/NR950321-EDS.html)

- Andersen Consulting and Dow Chemical formed a strategic alliance in which the partners planned to sell any systems developed for Dow to external customers (Moran, 1996).
- Swiss Bank signed a 25-year outsourcing deal with Perot Systems worth $6.25 billion. The partners planned to sell client/server solutions to the banking industry (Schmerken and Goldman, 1996).
- In Australia, when Lend Lease outsourced all its information systems to ISSC, it took a 35% holding in ISSC Australia (Lacity and Willcocks, 2001).
- Telstra (Australia's telecommunications company) outsourced its IT to ISSC, which in turn outsourced its network operations and management to Telstra. Additionally, Telstra took a 26% stake in ISSC (Kern and Willcocks, 2001).

Such deals had high expectations for success, but the partners had to truly add value by offering IT products and services demanded by customers in the market. Looking back at these deals from 2006 we concluded that several of these really did not deliver on their promise, and most have had the formal joint venture component in the deal terminated (Willcocks and Lacity, 2006) One widely-publicized deal that failed this litmus test in the 1990s was Delta Airlines and AT&T(NCR) forming TransQuest to provide IT solutions to the airline/travel industry. Their goal was to generate $1 million a year for the 50-50 partnership. Under the $2.8 billion, ten-year agreement, Delta transferred 1,100 employees and 3,000 applications to Trans-Quest while NCR contributed 30 employees, software, and cash. In 1996, however, the joint venture was terminated and Delta brought everything back in-house. An article of the time speculated that NCR's inexperience with large-scale professional service deals was a major contributing factor to the early termination (Hoffmann, 1996). The issue of why such deals succeed or fail is dealt with in much more detail in Lacity and Willcocks (2001). We provide more extensive treatment of the debate and outcomes in Chapter 13 where Xchanging used the model in the 2000s for setting up and running business process outsourcing arrangements.

Buy-in Contracts. One contract model that emerged from our study was the buying-in of vendor resources to supplement in-house abilities. We labelled this an insourcing option because the customers managed the IT activity and vendor resources internally. This strategy was most successful for the development of applications dependent on new technologies. In these cases, companies wished to access the vendor's technical expertise but could neither negotiate a detailed contract (because they didn't fully understand requirements), nor could they afford to miss a learning opportunity. In such cases the best use of the market was found to be to buy in external resources to work under internal management control.

The three general contract models identified above provide a good starting point for understanding customer/supplier relationships. These definitions also reconcile some of the apparent debates in the literature. For example, McFarlan and Nolan (1995) studied over a dozen total outsourcing contracts. Their findings were contrary to our own on a number of points, including their assessment of the viability of long-term IT outsourcing and a call for flexible contracts. The differences in their findings and ours may be attributed to the types of deals we each studied. McFarlan and Nolan primarily studied strategic alliances; we studied fee-for-service contracts.

By 2000, we could conclude that sourcing information technology capability remained a problematic area. The increasing number of vendors and services available in the marketplace were providing more opportunities, but were also complicating decision-making, contracting, and management issues. Our case studies, and the work represented in Part I of this book, contributed to the mounting experience base, particularly in the area of fee-for-service contracts, and especially for contracts directed at cost reduction. We were finding that detailed, short-term contracts worked well for the firms we studied if participants clearly defined their requirements. This ensured they were paying market prices, motivated vendor performance (perhaps with a threat to switch suppliers when the contract expired), allowed organizations to gradually learn how to competently outsource, and, in some cases, allowed organizations to recover from their mistakes more quickly. Our ongoing research was finding a number of emerging practices that in principle would achieve success through other means. These practices included flexible pricing, competitive bidding beyond the baseline contract, beginning long-term relationships with a short-term contract, and performance-based contracts.

In practice into the 2000s, the first three of these options have been regularly adopted by clients. The fourth has been altogether more difficult to operationalize. In the fee-for-service contracts we studied, performance measures focused on ensuring the vendor's technical performance, such as on-line availability and response time. However, we found some contracts relying more on the vendor's business performance. However, even by end of 2008, performance-based contracting was still a relatively untried concept, accounting for only a small percentage of ITO, and even BPO, revenues.

In the 1990s, then, we found practitioners wanting to source their IT portfolios to minimize costs, maximize service, and leverage resources to deliver real value, today and in the future. The practices we identified helped organizations significantly, particularly when reduced IT costs were the primary objective. These practices were selective outsourcing, joint IT/senior executive sponsorship, comparing external bids with newly-prepared internal bids, short-term contracts, and detailed fee-for-service contracts. Our research also provided insights into why practices such as strategic alliances and variations of fee-for-service contracts were emerging. Emerging practices stemmed from organizational learning about the benefits and pitfalls of past IT outsourcing experiences. Our post-2000 research represented in Part III of this book uncovered additional practices that helped sourcing expectations to be met in an ever changing outsourcing environment.

During the 1990s then, in the course of our research, we had identified some individual better practices for sourcing IT. No one company, however, had combined all such practices into a blueprint that others could use. Equally, if not more important, none had constructed an analytical framework explaining why such practices worked. What would such a blueprint and such a framework look like? To show how a company's decision-making process could evolve from conventional approaches to the one we were beginning to advocate, in the mid-1990s we offered the story of Energen, a fictitious petroleum company based in Houston, Texas, that represented a composite of many of the organizational practices identified in our studies to that date. The Energen case is found in Appendix A and illustrates how a client company may answer nine key outsourcing questions:

1. Is this IT system or activity truly differentiating?
2. Are we certain that our IT requirements won't change?
3. Even if an information system activity is a commodity, can it be disaggregated from other IT and business activities?
4. Could the internal IT department provide this IS activity more efficiently than an outside provider could?
5. Do we have the knowledge to outsource an unfamiliar or emerging technology?
6. What pitfalls should we be on the lookout for when hammering out the details of a contract?
7. How can we design a contract that minimizes our risks and maximizes our control and flexibility?

8. What in-house staff do we need to negotiate strong IT contracts?
9. What in-house staff do we need to make sure that we get the most out of our IT contracts and keep control of our IT destiny in the face of changing technologies?

From IT to business process and offshore outsourcing: 2000 and beyond

Our findings and stipulations have tended to hold up well to comparison against outsourcing experiences and outcomes during the first decade of the new century. During 2000–05, IT sourcing strategies, practices and the staffing configuration of client organizations were shifting as clients and suppliers moved up the outsourcing learning curve. This has been a necessary development in the face of growing use of the IT and (since 1998) BPO services market – more organizations increasing their individual ITO and back office (BPO) budget spend, and doing so on a multiple supplier basis. Indeed by around 2005 it was widely portrayed that "multisourcing", as it came to be called (Cohen and Young, 2005), was the main game in town when it came to ITO and business process outsourcing. Unfortunately, practitioners' application of this concept often sometimes left out the key notion inherent of selective sourcing, not just of external supply, but also of internal supply where warranted. There was also the vital question: what number of suppliers is optimal? Clearly the transaction costs of dealing with multiple suppliers could build to formidable levels, and the complexities of contracts and managing relationships could become daunting.

If the global IT outsourcing market was approaching $US250 billion by 2008, then the new decade also saw the rapid growth of two related phenomena, namely business process outsourcing and offshoring. We have estimated that the market for mainstream BPO expenditure was likely to grow worldwide by 10% to 20% a year from $140 billion in 2005 to potentially $350 billion by 2010 (Lacity and Willcocks, 2009). Meanwhile offshore outsourcing revenues have been rapidly rising averaging more than 20% per annum compound growth since 1998 to reach well over $US30 billion by 2010. The question about offshoring inherent in the title of our Chapter 5: "A Country Too Far?" has been answered by the obvious advantages in terms of cost, quality and speed often experienced using offshore providers, initially often for Y2K work leading up to the new decade. Subsequently the boom in IT and BP service provision in India, and, on our count, over 120 other locations worldwide has also made offshoring in both outsourcing and captive forms attractive. At the same time the caveat in that chapter has continued to haunt events and findings through 2000–09: like any outsourcing, offshore outsourcing needs very careful management, but it also throws up distinctive issues and challenges that can be very problematic.

In Part III of this book we provide six chapters that reflect such developments in the ITO, and the newer BPO and offshoring, spaces. On IT, Chapter 11 introduces and elaborates our concept of configuration, defined as: *a high-level description of the set of choices the organization makes in crafting its IT outsourcing portfolio.* The concept is derived from research into 49 ITO arrangements studied over time. We identify seven attributes – Scope Grouping, Supplier Grouping, Financial Scale, Duration, Pricing, Resource Ownership, and Commercial Relationship – as key descriptors of an organization's ITO configuration. The contribution of the chapter is its articulation of the concept of configuration as a taxonomy of ITO structural characteristics, the key attributes, and demonstration that configuration is an important concept for understanding, comparing, and managing ITO arrangements.

In Chapter 12 we revisit the issue of IT outsourcing intentions, outcomes and degrees of success, updating our perspective with new data. Based on results from three ITO surveys conducted during 1994–2000, a review of the literature, and data from 49 in-depth ITO cases, it is argued that although some organizations may, at times, seek outcomes from outsourcing similar to other organizations, fundamentally what each firm seeks from outsourcing is different. Accordingly, it is argued, studies that recognize the idiosyncratic and changing nature of outcomes sought are likely to offer greater insight into what comprises successful outsourcing. Developing this idea, the chapter proposes an ITO outcomes framework consisting of a comprehensive list of 25 goals that organizations, frequently pursue when outsourcing IT. In practice, we found organizations typically pursuing between three and seven such goals, in various combinations and with different emphases, but invariably with cost saving as one of them. Despite over 20 years of research the independent variable – IT outsourcing success – is surprisingly under-researched. Our key argument is that ITO success should be assessed by, first, asking organizations to nominate the outcomes that were/are most important to them at various times in the life of the contract, then second, gauging the extent to which each organization has achieved its nominated outcomes during the period when those outcomes were being pursued.

We provide an overview of developments in business process outsourcing in Chapter 13, which also then investigates in considerable depth the promise of the joint venture model, discussed above in the context of ITO, but this time in the post-2000 context of delivering BPO services. The particular company is a pure play BPO start-up called Xchanging which gained its first contract in 2001 and has since been particularly successful in getting additional clients, but also delivering service.

Two chapters follow that provide overviews and case studies of offshoring outsourcing practices. In Chapter 14, the offshore outsourcing journey of a US-based biotechnology multinational is detailed and lessons drawn from its experiences. Meanwhile in Chapter 15 the research investigates how practitioners can invest the *right amount* of social capital to ensure that they get overall value from offshore outsourcing. In looking at a US Fortune 100 manufacturer of industrial equipment with over 75,000 employees spread across 20 countries, the chapter reports that, at a minimum, clients must invest in social capital by laying the foundation for trust (called the relational dimension of social capital), creating shared language, codes, and systems of meaning among parties (called the cognitive dimension of social capital), and designing social linkages among people (called the structural dimension of social capital). However, the research points to one important caveat: if clients invest too much in social capital, they will erode cost savings.

Our final chapter returns to our theme of operating a truly selective sourcing regime. The study in question looks at shared services as an in-house sourcing option, in this case as adopted at Reuters. Creating shared services requires a coordinated integration of four change programs: business process redesign, organizational redesign, technology enablement, and sourcing redesign. If managed properly, shared services reduce costs, improve services, and can even generate revenues. However, surveys show that many executives fail to achieve the promised results. In this last chapter, we present the lessons Reuters learned during a five year journey to create global shared services within their finance organization. Lessons address the right transformation approach, how to identify processes for shared services by analyzing the costs, attributes and readiness of process activities, and getting business unit clients and internal staff to cooperate and embrace the shared services initiative. It is a good way to conclude the documentation of a 20-year research program that has focused on outsourcing practice as part of larger concern for developing sourcing strategy aligned with business objectives.

Trends 2009 to 2014

To give more context to the chapters and studies that this book contains, it is useful to suggest the larger trends we are seeing, and that our research reflects. Based on recent work we pinpoint the following 12 emerging trends.

Trend 1: Spending will continue to rise in all global sourcing markets, but BPO will overtake ITO. The global IT outsourcing (ITO) market has increased each year since we have been tracking it. Back in 1989, global ITO was only a $9 to $12 billion market (Krass, 1990; Lacity and Hirschheim, 1993ab). In 2007, the global ITO market was estimated to be between a $200 to $250 billion market (Blackmore *et al.*, 2005; Willcocks and Lacity, 2006). The BPO market in 2008 was less than the ITO market, but growing at a faster rate. We estimate that the market for mainstream BPO expenditure is likely to grow worldwide by 10% to 20% a year from $140 billion in 2005 to potentially $350 billion by 2010. BPO expenditure will be in areas such as the human resource function, procurement, back office administration, call centers, legal, finance and accounting, customer facing operations and asset management.

BPO is outpacing ITO because many executives recognize that they under-manage their back offices, and do not wish to invest in back office innovations. Suppliers are rapidly building capabilities to reap the benefits from improving inefficient processes and functions. IT provides major underpinning for, and payoff from, reformed business processes. Thus, many of the BPO deals will swallow much of the back office IT systems. This is also evidenced by the shift in strategy of traditional IT suppliers like IBM, HP, and EDS to provide more business process services. Suppliers will increasingly replace clients' disparate back office IT systems with web-enabled, self-serve portals.

There have been some high profile backsourcing (returning services in-house) cases in recent years, for example Sears (1997), The Bank of Scotland (2002), JP Morgan Chase (2004) and Sainsbury (2005). Although media-worthy, these cases have never represented a dominant trend towards backsourcing. Based on our case studies and surveys, *the most popular course of action at the end of a contract will continue to be contract renewal with the incumbent supplier.* We also estimate that a quarter will be re-tendered and awarded to new suppliers, and only a tenth back-sourced.

Trend 2: The ITO and BPO outsourcing markets will continue to grow through multi-sourcing. Although ITO and BPO spend is increasing, the average size of individual contracts and the duration of contracts is decreasing. For example, the Everest Group found that among the ITO contracts signed in 1998, 24% of contracts were worth more than $400 million and 33% of contracts were worth between $50 and $100 million. In 2005, only 11% of contracts were worth more than $400 million and 57% of contracts were worth between $50 and $100 million. Concerning contract duration, the Everest Group found that 37% of contracts signed in 1998 were more than nine years in duration compared to 18% in 2005 (Tisnovsky, 2006).

How can we reconcile smaller, shorter deals with an overall increase in the ITO/BPO markets? All these figures suggest that client organizations are actively pursuing more multi-sourcing. Multi-sourcing has always been the dominant practice and the overall growth is driven by client organizations signing *more* contracts with *more* suppliers. While multi-sourcing helps clients access best-of-breed suppliers and mitigates the risks of reliance on a single supplier, it also means increased transaction costs as clients manage more suppliers. Multi-sourcing also means that suppliers incur more transaction costs – suppliers must bid more frequently because contracts are shorter, suppliers face more competition because smaller-sized deals means that more suppliers qualify to bid, and suppliers need to attract more customers in order to meet growth targets.

Trend 3: Global clients will stop viewing India primarily as a destination to lower costs, but rather as a destination for excellence. Within our case studies, we saw considerable evidence that US clients initially engaged Indian suppliers to provide technical services such as programming and platform upgrades. But as these relationships matured, US clients assigned more challenging work to Indian suppliers. For example, a US retailer first engaged their Indian supplier to help with Y2K compliance. As the relationship matured, the retailer assigned development and support tasks for critical business applications to the supplier. From this retailer and other satisfied clients we heard, *"We went to India for lower costs, but we stayed for quality"* (Lacity and Rottman, 2008). Supplier executives we interviewed from three of the large Indian suppliers all mentioned their desire to assume higher-value tasks for their clients, like research and development.

Trend 4: China's investment in ITO/BPO services signals promise, but Western clients will still be wary. Within China's ITO and BPO markets, China invested $142.3 billion in information and communication technologies (ICT) in 2006 (Lacity and Rottman, 2008). China hopes that its huge investment in ICT will pay off in terms of its ability to compete globally in the offshore services market. China's long-term ITO/BPO future is expected to be strong. For example, The Everest Group estimated that the Chinese offshore services market was only $2 billion in 2006, but it predicts that China's market will grow 38% annually to reach $7 billion by 2010 (Bahl *et al.*, 2007).

So far, the main ITO/BPO suppliers in China are either large US-based suppliers like Accenture, Cap Gemini, Dell, EDS, HP and IBM, or large Indian-based suppliers like Genpact, Infosys, Satyam, and TCS. Like Indian suppliers, many Chinese suppliers do not want to compete solely on low-level technical skills. Chinese suppliers are trying to show they can fill the needs for product development, systems design and consulting services.

Despite the optimism, many Western client organizations are wary of China's ITO and BPO services. Language barriers, cultural barriers, and fears over losing intellectual property remain significant obstacles for the companies we talked to in North America and Western Europe. The Chinese government and Chinese business sectors are well aware of these barriers and are actively seeking ways to address them. For example, the Chinese government is investing $5 billion in English-language training to target the ITO/BPO markets (Lacity and Rottman, 2008).

Trend 5: Developing countries beyond India and China will become important players in the global business and IT services market. In addition to India and China, suppliers from all six continents will develop centers of excellence. Many US clients already use Central American suppliers for Spanish-speaking business processes like help desks, patient scheduling, and data entry. Synchronous time zones are another favorable factor for US firms looking to source in Central or South America.

In Western Europe, organizations will increasingly source IT and businesses services to providers located in Eastern Europe. For example, the Visegrad-Four Countries (Czech Republic, Hungary, Poland and Slovakia) offer Western European firms closer proximity, less time zone differences, and lower transaction costs than Asian alternatives. Even in Africa, many countries are actively seeking to become players in the global ITO and BPO markets. North Africa already exports IT services to Europe. One interesting study examined five Moroccan IT suppliers that provide services to clients in France (Bruno *et al.*, 2004). The common language, similar time zone, and cultural capability make Morocco an attractive destination for French organizations. South Africa is also exporting IT and BP services, primarily to UK-based clients. South Africa appeals primarily to UK-based clients because of the similar time zone, cultural similarities, English-speaking capabilities and good infrastructure. Even some sub-Saharan countries are building their future economies on IT.

Trend 6: Large companies will give application service provision (ASP) a second look. When we first published our book on ASP called *Netsourcing* in 2002, we noted that many large companies were not interested in ASP because they already had ASP product offerings and expertise in-house, they wanted customized services, and they wanted to source to stable providers, not risky start-up ventures (Kern *et al.*, 2002). Many thought that ASP died with the dot.com bust. But there are several reasons to believe that large organizations will reconsider ASP for targeted activities. First, large organizations will want net-native applications (proprietary applications designed and delivered specifically for Internet delivery) that are only available through ASP delivery (e.g., Salesforce.com). Second, large organizations may finally be ready to abandon their expensive proprietary suites, for cheaper ASP alternatives. Third, ASP providers got the message: clients want customized services, even if the products are standardized. The need for customized services actually increases the service providers' viability because they can generate profits by charging for value-added services.

Trend 7: Outsourcing will help insourcing. As organizations become smarter at outsourcing, they also become smarter at insourcing. In-house operations are facing real competition in nearly every area and can no longer assume they will retain their monopoly status with the organization. As a result, in-house operations are adopting the techniques of the market. However, insourcing will be impeded by a supply shortage of talent within developed countries, particularly for IT skills. The USA is not alone in this. Nearly every research report suggests that other developed countries will suffer a shortage of domestic IT workers within the next five to ten years. In the United Kingdom, for example, some research found that the UK will experience a shortage of 714,000 IT workers by 2010 (Aggarwal and Pandey, 2004). The shortages in developed countries will be caused by the gap between a strong demand for domestic IT workers and a dwindling supply of domestic IT workers due to the lingering effects of declining enrolments today and future effects of "baby boomers" retiring from IT. **Trend 8: Nearshoring will become more prevalent.** We define "nearshoring" as outsourcing work to a supplier located in an adjacent country. Compared to offshore outsourcing, the benefits of nearshoring include less travel costs, less time zone differences, and closer cultural compatibility. Canada, for example, is a significant nearshore destination for US clients. Some analysts argue that US clients can have lower total costs with nearshoring to Canada than with offshoring to India.

The Czech Republic, Poland, and Hungary are significant nearshore destinations for Western Europe. According to a report by Deutsche Bank Research (Meyer, 2006), imports of IT-based services from Central and Eastern Europe to Western Europe rose an average of 13% per year between 1992 and 2004. This growth rate is nearly comparable to the import of IT services from India, which averaged 14% per year over the same time period. Clients in Western Europe are attracted to Central and Eastern European suppliers for many of the same reasons that the USA is attracted to Canadian suppliers: common language, cultural understanding, minimal time zone differences, and low labor costs. However, Central and Eastern Europe may be more attractive for BPO than ITO because these countries provide excellent general education, but have not graduated IT students at near the pace of India. For that reason, IDC predicts that Western Europe's growth in BPO will increased annually by 14.6% compared to 7.2% for ITO.

Trend 9: Knowledge process outsourcing will increase. Knowledge process outsourcing (KPO) is the outsourcing of business, market, and/or industry research. KPO requires a significant amount of domain knowledge and analytical skills. KPO suppliers design surveys, collect new data, mine existing data, statistically analyze data, and write reports. Although the KPO market was, in 2008, quite small, industry analysts expected a huge growth in this sector over the next five years. Evalueserve (2007) estimated that the KPO market in 2007 was $3.05 billion and will grow annually by 39%. They expected the KPO market to be $16 billion by 2010 or 2011, employing approximately 350,000 professionals globally.

The increase in KPO is directly related to our previous observation that offshore suppliers are moving up the value chain. As client/supplier relationships mature, the suppliers have gained an enormous amount of knowledge about the client's business domain as well as the expertise to find, analyze, and report on domain knowledge. US, Canadian, and UK clients value this deep knowledge and will pay Indian suppliers $20 to $100 per hour for KPO services, compared to onshore rates of $80 to $500 per hour. Offshore suppliers are struggling to find enough workers with advanced degrees to fill the demand. But once hired, we anticipate that supplier employee turnover in this space will be lower because professionals finally

Strassmann, P. (1995) "Outsourcing, A Game for Losers", *Computerworld*, 29, 34, August 21, 75.

Tisnovsky, R. (2006) "IT Outsourcing in SME Businesses", An Everest Research Institute White Paper. See www.everestresearchinstitute.com.

Willcocks, L. and Lacity, M. (2006) *Global Sourcing Of Business and IT Services*, Palgrave, London.

Appendix A: "Energen": the future shape of IT sourcing?

About the case: We created this fictitious organization based on the actual experiences of several client firms we studied. The purpose of the case is to illustrate how client organizations may competently answer nine key questions on ITO:

1. Is this IT system or activity truly differentiating?
2. Are we certain that our IT requirements won't change?
3. Even if an information system activity is a commodity, can it be disaggregated from other IT and business activities?
4. Could the internal IT department provide this IS activity more efficiently than an outside provider could?
5. Do we have the knowledge to outsource an unfamiliar or emerging technology?
6. What pitfalls should we be on the lookout for when hammering out the details of a contract?
7. How can we design a contract that minimizes our risks and maximizes our control and flexibility?
8. What in-house staff do we need to negotiate strong IT contracts?
9. What in-house staff do we need to make sure that we get the most out of our IT contracts and keep control of our IT destiny in the face of changing technologies?

Energen's senior managers ran up against the limitations of an all-or-nothing, strategic-versus-commodity approach to IT, came to see that maximizing flexibility and control should drive their sourcing decisions, and then pursued a course that they were able to change along the way. A version of this case originally appeared in *Harvard Business Review* in 1995, as a way of indicating the direction client organizations would take were they to adopt the many better practices we had already uncovered in our research. The case forms a useful attempt to predict where outsourcing practice could, and should, lead to in the following decade. As such we will use it as a baseline later in this Appendix for assessing what actually happened from 2000–08 as documented by our research in Part III of this book.

Energen: decisions, decisions...

In 1992, the CEO of Energen began to question the company's huge investment in information systems. Over the previous three years, almost every division of Energen had reduced costs by 10% as a result of a major restructuring effort. The glaring exception was IT, whose costs had risen by 20%.

To Richard Andrews, the CEO, most of IT seemed like a commodity service. He began to wonder whether the company really needed to own and operate its huge data centers in Houston, Dallas, and New York; its private telecommunications network; and its 2,000 personal computers. When a company he contacted offered to buy Energen's IT assets for $75 million and claimed that it could provide the same service as Energen's IT department for 9.0% less, Andrews was tempted.

Not surprisingly, Donald Peregrine, the vice president of information systems, tried to change Andrews's mind. He argued that IT was not just an expense: other departments had been able to cut costs or increase their business because of IT. Andrews conceded that Peregrine had a point and agreed not to make a hasty decision. He assigned John Martin, Energen's CFO and Peregrine's boss, to head a task force to explore the company's outsourcing options.

The task force, which included Peregrine and the vice presidents of the major functional areas, decided to start by dividing Energen's IT operations into two categories: commodity systems and "strategic" systems. Minimizing costs would be the paramount consideration in deciding whether to outsource the commodities. The commodities that an outside supplier could probably provide as well as and more cheaply than Energen could were the private telecommunications network, the three data centers, support for personal computers, central accounting systems such as payroll, and electronic data interchange.

For the strategic systems, maintaining high levels of service would be the priority. Certain activities were too critical to Energen's business to entrust to an outsider: analyzing seismic data, monitoring quality control in the refineries, and scheduling and tracking oil from the wells, ships, and pipelines. The task force decided to keep those systems in-house for the foreseeable future.

But as the task force members discussed how to proceed, the shortcomings of tackling IT in this fashion became apparent. For instance, they recognized that there were a variety of unknowns – in terms of both technology and issues facing Energen's business – that somehow had to be factored into their decisions.

For example, it was already clear that client-server technology was replacing mainframes and would change the way Energen deployed personal computers. The last thing Energen wanted was to be stuck with outdated technology. So the task force decided that the company should seek only a two-year outsourcing contract for its personal computers.

Another uncertainty was the payroll department. Energen was just beginning to consider whether to outsource the entire department, and Martin, the CFO, thought the company needed to make that decision before it could think about outsourcing the IT system that supported the function.

He had not forgotten what had happened several years earlier. Energen had signed a five-year contract with a supplier that would take over a significant piece of the IT system for the company's warehouses even though there was talk about closing some warehouses. Two years into the contract, Energen's management did decide to close the warehouses and had to pay the supplier a large fee to terminate the contract. Not wanting to repeat the same mistake, the task force postponed the decision about outsourcing the payroll department's IT system until the department's future was clear.

The task force also recognized that although an IT system might be a commodity, it could still be too critical to hand over to an outsider. One example was the telecommunications network that connected Energen's gas stations to headquarters. When Energen's managers had first considered outsourcing the network, seven years earlier, they hadn't felt confident that any of the existing suppliers would be able to keep the system up and running. But the problems that had prompted the company to consider outsourcing at that time had not gone away. The infrastructure was costly to manage, and Energen had had trouble retaining topnotch people: Several employees had left for more promising careers at communications companies. In the end, the task force agreed that Energen should see if there were now more qualified suppliers out there.

The telecommunications discussion sparked a realization: An IT system could be critical but not differentiating. Perhaps the word "strategic" was misleading language in this context. That is, a system could be crucially important without differentiating Energen from its competitors. In this light, the task force saw that of the three systems originally labelled "strategic", only one – the system for analyzing seismic data – truly was. Although many oil companies that engaged in exploration and production had such systems, the task force thought that Energen's enabled the company to excel in analyzing reserves.

The task force then realized something else: just because an IT activity was business-critical or even "strategic" did not mean that all its elements had to be kept in-house. Take the system for scheduling and tracking oil. It was clearly critical and had to be kept in-house, but did the same apply to a major upgrade of the system's software? This question was especially pertinent because Energen wanted to update the software and was going to hire an outside developer for the project. Martin argued that although state-of-the-art software was critical, the software itself would not give Energen a competitive edge, because the company's rivals maintained similar systems. He convinced everyone that Energen would have a better chance of getting the best possible software if the developer was allowed to sell it to other companies.

How to choose suppliers?

Having decided what to outsource, the task force then turned to the job of choosing suppliers. The first step was designing a process. The group concluded that seeking relatively short contracts was a good idea. It also decided that Energen should solicit separate bids for each service. Adopting this approach would ensure that the company could tap suppliers' particular strengths and would prevent any one supplier from ending up with too much power. Peregrine, the vice president of information systems, knew of several organizations that had come to regret their decision to outsource large portions of their IT operations to only one or two suppliers. In one instance, a supplier had charged extra for dozens of services that the company had assumed were covered in the base price and had dragged its feet in introducing new technology.

The members also agreed that they could not automatically assume that a supplier would outperform their own IT department and decided that the department should be allowed to compete when such doubts arose. Peregrine said the data centers were a case in point. The centers had long been forced to satisfy individual users' idiosyncratic needs, resulting in inefficient practices. If his department had the authority to institute best practices, it might be able to operate the centers more cheaply than a supplier, which had to earn a profit. Further, he said, until the department found out how inexpensively the centers could be run, it wouldn't be able to negotiate a good contract with an outside provider.

After the task force agreed on the basic approach to outsourcing, teams consisting mostly of IT managers were formed to request proposals for bids for each contract. With their deep technical knowledge, the managers had the clearest understanding of the company's IT needs. But, fearing that it would be difficult for them to weigh internal and external bids objectively, the task force decided to make the final decisions itself.

The company then started negotiating bids. It found a supplier willing to sign a two-year contract for the personal computers; the deal promised to cut Energen's PC-related costs by 10%. And when Energen negotiated the contract to develop the scheduling and tracking software, it gave the supplier the copyright in exchange for a discount.

The IT department's bid for the data centers was based on a plan for consolidating the three centers into one, thus cutting costs by 30%. That bid was lower than both external bids. One outside bidder then proposed a joint venture with Energen's IT department. Peregrine rejected it. He feared that the combined challenges of consolidating the centers and getting the joint venture on its feet would be overwhelming and that service to Energen would suffer. The department's bid prevailed.

When the task force turned to the telecommunications network, it discovered that there were now qualified providers. Energen awarded a four-year contract for its network to a respected manufacturer of midsize computers that had acquired expertise running its own world-class private telecommunications network. The task force transferred all the employees that had supported Energen's network to the supplier except for two experts, whom it retained to manage the contract.

Because Energen knew what it took to run the network, it was able to hammer out a detailed contract aimed at ensuring that the supplier met Energen's demanding performance requirements. The supplier would have to pay $50,000 the first time network availability fell below 99%, and the penalties would escalate with each subsequent lapse. In addition, if Energen decided not to renew the contract, the supplier would have to cooperate in making the switch to a new supplier. For example, it would have to furnish copies of all programs, data, and technical documentation and also provide installation assistance.

Continuous learning

The process of outsourcing the personal computers and consolidating the data centers went smoothly. But other transitions were rockier. One lesson Energen learned was that technical people accustomed to running an internal IT operation could not necessarily make the leap to managing an outsourcing contract.

For example, the two Energen experts retained to manage the telecommunications contract had difficulty understanding that their job had changed. Instead of actually operating and maintaining the network, they were now responsible for interpreting users' needs and communicating them to the supplier. When a technical problem arose, the two experts still wanted to solve it themselves rather than just report it to the supplier's account manager, who argued that technical matters were his domain. Peregrine intervened and recruited one of his data-center managers, who had overseen Energen's hardware leases. The two experts were retained as consultants.

Separately, the company clashed with the telecommunications supplier over the interpretation of the service levels outlined in the contract. For example, Energen had assumed that the 99% availability requirement meant that all nodes on the network had to be up and running 99% of the time. The supplier, however, interpreted it to mean that the host node had to function 99% of the time. When links to 20 of its service stations went down, Energen demanded a cash penalty, which the supplier refused to pay.

Six months into the contract, Energen discovered that it could pressure the supplier by offering a carrot. Energen had expanded into the Midwest by buying a regional oil company's service stations in five states. The supplier, which wanted to get the contract for the stations' network, agreed to renegotiate the service requirements. Energen awarded the new contract to another supplier but told the first supplier that if its performance improved substantially, it might win the contract for the new subsidiary in two years, when that contract came up for renewal.

Finally, with the emergence of client-server technology as a cheaper, more flexible alternative to large mainframe operations, Energen eventually decided to outsource the data center. The company was no longer fully utilizing its mainframes, but it didn't want to invest the time and energy to find outside customers for its excess capacity. Another reason to outsource the data center was to free up the company's applications experts to develop programs for the client-server networks. It was unreasonable to expect the programmers both to continue supporting the mainframes and to develop client-server applications.

Did the company regret not outsourcing the center originally? No. As Peregrine had argued at the time, his department had found the most efficient way to run the center, and the company's knowledge of the operation enabled it to negotiate a strong contract later.

Commentary on Energen

In confronting whether and how to outsource their IT operations, Energen's senior managers acknowledged what they knew and what they didn't or couldn't know about their business, the course of technology, and the capabilities of outside providers, and of the company's own IT department. Then, with the goal of maximizing flexibility and control, the managers sought bids from many suppliers, let the IT department compete for parts of the business, negotiated short-term contracts, postponed some outsourcing decisions, and retained managerial control of business-critical operations. Finally, they realized that deciding to outsource an IT activity was not the end of the manager's work. The case points to ten valuable questions practitioners need to ask, in order to formulate and deliver IT sourcing strategy:

1. Is this IT system or activity truly differentiating? We found that most IT systems or activities that managers consider differentiating actually are not. In the 1990s research we found very few systems differentiating companies from their competitors. There is a difference between IT that is a "critical differentiator", i.e., gives your business competitive advantage in the marketplace, and one that is a "critical commodity", i.e. underpins your business strategy, and is a minimum entry requirement to operate in the sector, but gives no competitive advantage. By way of illustration Lacity and Willcocks (2001) cited British Airways airline reservation system in the 1990s as a critical differentiator, but its aircraft maintenance systems as a critical commodity. The former should be retained in-house, the latter is in principle outsourceable. Many managers try to make a system differentiating by investing in fancy equipment and customized software. All too often, however, they find that even after they spend lots of money, their systems still do not differentiate the company from its rivals, especially given the pace at which rivals can develop similar systems of their own.

2. Are we certain that our IT requirements won't change? The rise of new technology, of course, will change a company's IT needs. By the late 1990s organizations were experiencing two generations of technology every five years. How can you contract for the implications of such change?

In addition, whenever a company plans to move into a new market or faces potential changes in its existing market, or is involved in a merger or acquisition, its IT requirements may change.

3. Even if a system is a commodity, can it be broken off? Many senior executives think of IT as something that can be plugged and unplugged, like an appliance. But most systems are integrated parts of the businesses they support and cannot be so easily separated. For example, decisions concerning the payroll data center cannot be made independently from those concerning the payroll function. Many IT systems require data from or feed data to other systems and therefore cannot be successfully isolated and handed over to an outside provider. As obvious as it may sound, many managers do not seem to consider that when they make outsourcing decisions.

4. Could the internal IT department provide this system more efficiently than an outside provider could? As argued above, one challengeable assumption is that inherent economies of scale, highly skilled people, and superior practices allow external suppliers to provide IT commodities more efficiently than an internal IT department ever could. We found, however, that many IT departments have equally sophisticated technology and adequate economies of scale but aren't allowed to adopt the best practices that would help them match or beat a supplier's bid. By inviting their IT departments to bid for the contracts, companies accomplish two things. First, they motivate their employees to find ways to provide good service at a lower cost. Second, such companies gain a much deeper understanding of the costs of a given service and the best way to provide it.

5. Do we have the knowledge to outsource an unfamiliar or emerging technology? A company cannot control what it does not understand. Many managers think that because no one in the company has enough technical expertise to assess new technologies, they should hand the job over to an outsider. After all, why devote internal resources to acquiring "esoteric" knowledge? Most of the companies in our studies that outsourced emerging technologies experienced disastrous results because they lacked the expertise to negotiate sound contracts and evaluate suppliers' performances. One alternative is to hire a supplier to team up with a company's IT staff on the project. Such an arrangement enables the company to learn enough about the new technology that it can negotiate a contract from a position of strength if it does decide to outsource.

6. What pitfalls should we be on the lookout for when hammering out the details of a contract? One of the biggest mistakes companies make is signing suppliers' standard contracts. Although large client organizations rarely make this mistake, smaller client organizations sign supplier written agreements to reduce transaction costs or because they trust the supplier. Such contracts usually contain details that not even a company's legal staff can understand or unravel, especially if the company is outsourcing a technology with which it is not familiar. Among those details might be a lot of hidden costs. We also have seen numerous instances in which hidden clauses severely limited companies' options. In addition, many suppliers will try to maximize profits by charging exorbitant fees for services that customers assume are included in the contract, such as personal-computer support, rewiring for office moves, or even simple consultations about which equipment to purchase. But even companies that spell out every imaginable detail in a contract have often been frustrated by the unimaginable.

7. How can we design a contract that minimizes our risks and maximizes our control and flexibility? One way to hedge against uncertainty and change is by creating what we call a measurable partnership, in which the company and the supplier have complementary or shared goals. If a supplier is being hired to develop a new application, for example, the contract might stipulate that the company and the supplier will share any profits that come from selling the application. Another way to maintain control over outsourcing arrangements is to withhold a piece of the business from a supplier and use that potential contract as a carrot, as Energen did with the telecommunications contract for its subsidiary. Or a company can split an IT operation between two suppliers, thus establishing a threat of competition. A company should also try, whenever possible, to sign short-term (3–5 year) contracts. Short-term contracts are desirable because they ensure that the prices stipulated will not be out of step with market prices, technology will change less, staff turnover would be less, and they sharpen supplier concerns about contract renewal.

8. What in-house staff do we need to negotiate strong IT contracts? A negotiating team should be headed by the top IT executive and include a variety of specialists. Many of the worst contracts we saw were broad agreements negotiated by just the CEO with the help of corporate lawyers who were equally unschooled in technical details. However, although the CEO might not be involved in actual negotiations, he or she must provide the team with a mandate and thus authority with both internal groups and the supplier.

The specialists on the negotiating team should include at a minimum in-house technical experts with a deep understanding of the company's IT requirements; operational people who will have to deliver the contract; an IT outsourcing expert who can translate those internal requirements into the supplier's requirements; and a commercially-minded contract lawyer specializing in IT who can detect hidden costs and clauses in contracts. In our research, we found that many companies fail to include one or more of those specialists – usually the IT lawyer or the outsourcing expert – on their negotiating teams.

9. **What in-house staff do we need to make sure that we get the most out of our IT contracts and keep control of our IT destiny in the face of changing technologies?** Few of the companies we studied staffed their teams sufficiently; some had only one or two persons. In addition, many companies underestimated the importance of contract management. Some mistakenly believed that overseeing the contract required little more than assigning someone to review the supplier's monthly bill. And many assigned a technical expert without considering whether that person could manage the complex relationships involved. In subsequent work Feeny and Willcocks (1998) codified in more detail the basis of core in-house IT capability. The research suggested that the future IT function had four tasks – eliciting and delivering on business requirements; ensuring technical capability; managing external supply; and governance, coordination and leadership. The key in-house capabilities are:

IS/IT Governance – "integrating IT effort with business purpose and activity".
Business Systems Thinking – "ensuring that IT/e-business technologies capabilities are envisioned in every business process".
Relationship Building – "getting the business constructively engaged in IT issues".
Designing Technical Architecture – "creating the coherent blueprint for a technical platform which responds to present and future business needs".
Making Technology Work – "rapidly trouble-shoot problems which are being disowned by others across the technical supply chain".
Informed Buying – analysis of the external market for IT/e-business services; selection of a sourcing strategy to meet business needs and technology issues; leadership of the tendering, contracting, and service management processes.
Contract Facilitation – "ensuring the success of existing contracts for IT services".
Contract Monitoring – "holding suppliers to account against both existing service contracts and the developing performance standards of the services market".
Vendor Development – "identifying the potential added value of IT/e-business service suppliers".

Part of this is an organization needing a team of technical experts to help them stay on top of changing technology, changing business needs, and the changing capabilities of available IT providers (both internal providers and suppliers competing in the marketplace). This team can play a significant role in uncovering business opportunities by helping a company understand new ways to use IT. Very few companies have such a group. But without such teams, companies often pay more than they should because suppliers are constantly trying to sell services or technologies that are not included in the basic contract.

One of the team's missions is to look for gaps between the IT the company has and what it needs. With that goal in mind, the team should constantly benchmark the company's IT resources and providers, and should help the company decide whether to change course when an IT contract comes up for renewal. Another of the team's primary responsibilities is to assess emerging technologies. New technologies such as client-servers, object-oriented systems, and multimedia may sound very tempting, but will the company really be able to take advantage of them? The answer is no or not yet in a surprising number of instances. Of course, companies can hire consultants to carry out some of this work, but consultants may have their own agendas. For this reason, we think the team should consist of a core of in-house people who can assess suppliers' capabilities and determine which new technologies can best be applied to the company's businesses.

Part II

Studies of Outsourcing's Rise to Prominence

2
Realizing Outsourcing Expectations: Incredible Promises, Credible Outcomes

Mary Lacity, Rudy Hirschheim and Leslie Willcocks

Introduction

Drawing from the firsthand experiences of senior executives and Information Technology (IT) managers in North American and British companies, this chapter summarizes the expectations they had for outsourcing and explains what went wrong – and why – when expectations were not met. Successful outsourcing experiences are then used to outline a prescription for ensuring that expected benefits are fully realized. All too often outsourcing success is declared even before the ink on the contract is dry. This study has key, perennial things to say on expectations, and on realism about outcomes from outsourcing. It is also an important precursor to our follow-up study on outcomes and success detailed in Chapter 12.

When Kodak outsourced its IT operations to IBM Corp., Businessland, and Digital Equipment Corp. in 1988, it triggered a renewed interest in outsourcing. Although selective outsourcing of certain IT functions – programming, training, documentation, and disaster recovery – had existed since the beginning of data processing, Kodak legitimized the use of "total" outsourcing in which companies dismantle internal IT departments by transferring most of their IT employees, facilities, hardware leases, and software leases to third-party vendors.

Kodak's success sent a message to senior executives that IT had matured into a commodity service best managed by an external supplier. As Lacity and Hirschheim (1993ab) documented, a bandwagon effect resulted as other senior executives sought to duplicate the strategic alliances enjoyed by Kodak and its IT outsourcing vendors. Other large companies, among them Enron, Freeport-McMoran, Continental Airlines, General Dynamics, British Aerospace and Continental Bank, signed long-term outsourcing contacts and publicly announced the anticipated benefits: 10% to 50% cost reductions, increased service levels, and access to new technologies and technical expertise.

Six years after that surge of outsourcing interest, companies that leapt on the outsourcing bandwagon had had time to evaluate whether their expectations were realized. Did IT costs drop by as much as 50%? Did service levels increase? Did vendors introduce new technologies? In 1994 we sought to answer these perennial outsourcing questions by interviewing senior executives, IT managers, and vendor account managers from 14 North American and 15 British companies involved in outsourcing decisions.

The outsourcing study in brief

In all, more than 100 interviews were undertaken. Each interview (typically lasting between one and two hours) was tape-recorded, transcribed, and analyzed. In each company we attempted to interview at least two people in different roles (e.g., CEO, CFO, business unit manager, IT director, account manager, or IT staff member) who might have different perspectives on the outsourcing decision process.

The companies we visited were from a variety of industries. Our study included a broad spectrum of outsourcing arrangements: selective (partial) versus total outsourcing; use of multiple vendors versus a single vendor; short-term versus long-term contracts; detailed versus non-detailed contracts. We also included organizations that had been involved with outsourcing for a considerable length of time (three to ten years) as well as those that had more recently signed outsourcing deals that were less than three years old. In total, we looked at 40 outsourcing decisions (several companies evaluated outsourcing on multiple occasions). Of these, 14 decisions resulted in total outsourcing where at least 80% of the total IT budget was outsourced; 26 decisions resulted in selective outsourcing where 5% to 30% of the IT budget was outsourced.

Although it is dangerous to make sweeping generalizations based on only 40 outsourcing decisions, a number of patterns emerged, common to both sides of the Atlantic. In this chapter, we discuss these patterns by:

- Summarizing the expectations people had before outsourcing;
- Explaining what went wrong – and why – when the expectations were not met;
- Suggesting mechanisms, based on successful outsourcing experiences, to help ensure that all parties have sensible outsourcing expectations that can be realized.

Before going into detail on these three points, one broad theme arises from the data that needs to be expressed at the outset. Based on the participants' outsourcing expectations and experiences, the participants who were most disappointed with outsourcing followed a "total" outsourcing strategy, whereas participants most pleased with outsourcing generally pursued a less publicized – yet more controllable – selective sourcing strategy. This was a strong finding from our subsequent studies throughout the 1995–2008 period (see Lacity and Willcocks, 1998, 2001; Willcocks and Lacity, 2006 and later chapters in this book). Although some companies have been satisfied with their "total" outsourcing arrangements (mainly those that had signed airtight contracts), the same could not be said for a significant portion in our study (particularly those that did not sign detailed contracts). Companies that engaged in "total" outsourcing often suffered service degradation and, in some cases, increased IT costs. Indeed, some companies threatened to sue their outsourcing vendors for non-performance. Three companies proclaimed their "total" outsourcing decisions to be outright failures – they terminated their contracts early despite significant penalties and rebuilt internal IT departments from scratch.

While it might be too strong to say these outsourcing disappointments offer evidence that "total" outsourcing is a fad surrounded by hype, false hopes, and empty promises, it at least appears that there was, in 1994, some semblance of truth to this criticism. As discussed in this book's Introduction, our subsequent study (Lacity and Willcocks, 2001) showed a high failure rate in "total" outsourcing arrangements. While many of these disappointments could be put down to a 1990s learning period for many organizations, the 2000–08 record has not suggested to us a slow-down in disappointed expectations, nor do we predict such a slow-down into the 2008–13 period either (Willcocks and Craig, 2007) In contrast, companies that engaged in selective outsourcing often realized their outsourcing expectations. With selective outsourcing, however, initial expectations were often much more modest than the 50% savings hoped for by the total outsourcing participants. However modest, selective outsourcing participants were generally able to avoid the potentially negative consequences of outsourcing by signing tight, short-term contracts for a definable subset of IT services. A comment here, looking at 2000–08 experiences, would be that taking on a lot of suppliers in selective, multi-sourcing arrangements can also create its own problems, not least of high management time and transaction costs (Willcocks and Oshri, 2009).

Where do expectations come from?

The main goal of this chapter is to contrast participants' expectations before outsourcing with their actual outsourcing experiences. How did their expectations originate? The trade press, discussions with peers, and consultants' forecasts continue to portray outsourcing in a highly rational way – managements look for the best way to deliver a cost-efficient IT service to the organization. In evaluating outsourcing, managements use objective criteria assuming a common (agreed) set of beliefs and values about the need for having the best IT service at the lowest possible cost. But is this the way outsourcing evaluation has actually ever been carried out?

In addition to the typical financial, business, and technical expectations about outsourcing, we uncovered several political motivations for outsourcing (see Table 2.1). More than a few participants viewed outsourcing as a way to demonstrate their corporate citizenship, to enhance their careers, or to eliminate a troublesome IT function. We recorded numerous cases where an outsourcing decision was perceived as a political battle to justify the existence of IT. When IT was perceived by senior management as a cost pit, it often initiated outsourcing evaluations. Similarly, IT managers often used outsourcing evaluations to justify their existence – either to demonstrate that in-house performance was superior or to show a business orientation to senior managers – by outsourcing "commodity" IT functions in order to reduce costs or focus on higher value-added IT work.

Outsourcing becomes a vehicle for subtly managing (some might say manipulating) perceptions about the value of IT. The inclusion of political expectations and behaviors with more "rational" expectations provides a more realistic assessment of sourcing decisions.

Financial expectations

Many participants, especially senior managers, cited financial reasons for outsourcing, usually to cut costs, improve cost control, and restructure the IT budget. Evidence in Chapter 12 and experiences of the 2008 recessionary climate suggest that these are perennial concerns and not restricted to the early 1990s.

Cost reductions

Many participants expected that outsourcing would save them money. They perceived vendors to enjoy economies of scale that enable them to provide IT services at a lower cost than internal IT departments. In particular, participants believed that a vendor's unit costs are less expensive because of mass production efficiencies and labor specialization. One participant summarized this perception as follows:

> "One thing is the economies of scale of the processing. [Vendors] leverage software by running a lot of customers from that utility.... And because of the depth of their organization, they are able to support us with a smaller staff".

This perception was based on the fact that vendors submitted lower bids than current IT costs. After participants engaged in outsourcing, however, many failed to fully realize their anticipated savings, and indeed, IT costs rose in some cases. The participants who failed to realize cost savings were surprised by hidden costs in the contracts. The disappointments were associated with loose contracts that merely stipulated that vendors perform the same services previously performed by the internal IT department. Consequently, the vendor billed participants for services the participants assumed were in the contract. In one case, a participant was charged $500,000 for "extra" services. Another participant warned that exceedingly low bids may indicate hidden costs:

"There usually are some residual costs that the vendor is not picking up in the contract, which [we] have to provide for.... If we see an underpriced bid, that's the first alarm that goes off."

Another source of hidden costs were the vendors' standard "change of character clauses." For example, if a participant changed from one electronic spreadsheet package to another, the vendor charged them an excess fee to support the new package. From the participant's perspective, an electronic spreadsheet is an electronic spreadsheet; why should there be a charge for changing packages? From the vendor's perspective, a new spreadsheet package triggers a need to retrain staff and also creates more customer queries as new users adapt to the package. Participants who realized cost savings generally had signed airtight contracts that fully documented the services and service levels performed by the previous IT department. In some cases, they prudently demanded that the vendors demonstrate how they planned to reduce costs by identifying where exactly the economies of scale exist. Although some vendors could clearly demonstrate economies of scale, others provided intangible reasons, such as "We are technical experts."

Some vendors refused to divulge their cost structures because it would potentially sabotage future bids with other customers. In general, those participants whose cost expectations were met were able to fully define their IT needs and were able to assess the vendor's true cost advantage over the internal IT department.

Improved cost control

Another financial rationale for outsourcing was gaining control over IT costs. As any IT manager can attest to, IT costs are directly related to IT user demands. In most organizations, however, IT costs are controlled through general allocation systems that motivate users to excessively demand and consume resources, and this still remains the case. General allocation systems are analogous to splitting a restaurant tab – each dinner guest is motivated to order an expensive dinner because half the cost will be shared by the other party.

Participants saw outsourcing as a way to contain costs because vendors implemented cost controls that more directly tie usage to costs. In addition, users can no longer call their favorite analysts to request frivolous changes but instead must submit requests through a formal cost control process.

Some participants failed to realize cost control expectations through outsourcing. Instead, users began to use their discretionary budgets to bypass vendor bureaucracy. Users reasoned that they shouldn't have to waste time justifying something that is critical to their job. Rather than control costs, some participants claimed outsourcing created islands of hidden IT costs as users dipped into departmental budgets to satisfy their IT demands. Some participants succeeded in realizing their cost control expectations. In these cases, senior business managers worked with the vendor to prioritize user requests and to prevent users from circumventing cost control mechanisms. Although companies could have theoretically implemented cost control mechanisms without outsourcing, the formal outsourcing relationship bypassed the internal politics that had previously prevented internal IT departments from implementing cost controls. One participant noted:

> "One of the conclusions that we come to is that there is very little that an outsourcer is going to do that you couldn't do yourself. The question is, can you do it? And it's not physically can you do it, it's politically can you do it?"

Restructuring IT budgets

Some participants wanted to use outsourcing to restructure their IT budgets from lumbering capital budgets to more flexible operating budgets. For example, rather than retain a $US15 million mainframe on the books, participants could sell the asset to the vendor and merely buy the number of MIPS they need each year from the vendor. The sale of the asset also generates cash up front, which increases the participants' cash flow. In addition, some vendors will purchase stock and postpone the bulk of IT payments to near the end of the contract, making the overall net present value extremely attractive to participants. In return for these financial incentives vendors require long-term contracts, typically ten years in duration.

Participants often failed to understand the consequences of a long-term contract. How can vendors offer such sweet deals? Vendors know that the unit costs of IT drop exponentially over time. Although IT costs decrease from year-one perspective, over time participants did not share in the benefits of price/performance improvements because they are obliged to pay the same fee for the duration of the contract.

Participants who most fully realized the expectations about restructuring the IT budget signed shorter-term contracts. Although many vendors may fail to submit bids for shorter contracts, participants usually found at least one vendor willing to sign a two- to five-year contract, or a contract incorporating frequent staging points for reassessment. This allowed participants to re-evaluate changes in the underlying cost structure of IT and to renegotiate contracts based on current price/performance ratios.

Business expectations

Participants expressed three business rationales for outsourcing: return to core competencies, facilitate mergers and acquisitions, and start-up new companies.

A return to core competencies

During the 1990s, many large companies abandoned their diversification strategies – once pursued to mediate risk – to focus on core competencies. In other words, executives came to believe that the most important sustainable competitive advantage is strategic focus (i.e., concentrating on what an organization does better than anyone else while subcontracting everything else to vendors). One participant described the focus strategy this way:

"We see the success of the company as doing core things well. It is not an accident that the rest is outsourced. There are a series of outsourced non-core activities with people who we believe are world class at what they do."

As a result of the focus strategy, IT came under scrutiny: Is IT a competitive weapon or merely a utility? Even within the same company, perceptions over IT's contribution to core activities varied. In general, senior executives frequently viewed the entire IT function as a non-core activity, whereas IT managers and some business unit managers contended that certain IT activities were core to the business.

Those participants most disappointed with outsourcing tended to view the entire IT department as a utility and thus pursued a "total" outsourcing strategy. Problems arose, however, when participants realized that certain IT functions – such as strategic planning, development of business-specific applications, support of critical systems – should have remained in-house because they require detailed business knowledge. Although vendors are fully capable of providing technical expertise, they often lack such knowledge (see Feeny *et al.*, 2005).

Those participants most pleased with outsourcing viewed IT services as a portfolio containing both core and non-core activities. Before outsourcing, participants evaluated the contribution of each IT activity. Non-core activities, such as PC maintenance, data center operations, or run-of-the-mill accounting software, were outsourced while core activities, such as development of new strategic applications, remained in-house. In this way, the company's focus strategy was successful – internal IT resources were focused on business-critical applications whereas the more routine IT activities were outsourced.

Facilitating mergers and acquisitions

Because the participants were from large companies, as indicated by their presence on the US Fortune 500 or Europe's Times 1000 lists, many of the companies pursued a growth strategy through mergers and acquisitions. Mergers and acquisitions create many nightmares for IT managers, who are required to absorb acquired companies into existing systems (and sometime extant outsourcing contracts). This can be seen in post-2000 examples too, for example with JP Morgan and Manhattan Chase Bank, and Bank of Scotland's acquisition of ABNAmro bank (in 2007). Participants expected outsourcing to solve the technical incompatibilities, absorb the excess IT assets (e.g., additional data centers), and absorb the additional IT employees generated by mergers and acquisitions.

Some participants found that outsourcing failed to solve their merger and acquisition problems. IT problems associated with mergers and acquisitions can be readily solved by involving IT in the decision process. But because IT departments rarely participate in non-IT strategic decisions, IT managers are usually informed about mergers or acquisitions only after deals are consummated, leaving them with little time to migrate systems. With outsourcing, the IT problems caused by mergers and acquisitions can worsen because senior executives are even less likely to share these plans with vendors than they are with their own IT managers.

One participant, however, successfully used outsourcing to reduce IT problems caused by mergers and acquisitions, having selected a vendor that was an expert at mantling and dismantling data centers. In the outsourcing contract, the participant developed specific service-level measures to accommodate mergers and acquisitions. Because the company in question had acquired 18 companies in a span of two years, it had enough knowledge of the effects of mergers on IT to detail a merger/acquisition clause in the contract. By 2009 one would expect such detailed clauses to be in most outsourcing contracts. And indeed Bravard and Morgan (2006) have also rightly pointed out the similarities between outsourcing arrangements themselves and mergers and acquisitions.

Providing IT for start-up companies

Some participants explained that they outsourced IT when the company was first incorporated. At the time, participants expected that outsourcing was a quicker and less expensive way to provide IT services. Start-up companies simply could not afford the capital investment required to erect internal IT departments because they had neither the technical expertise present nor the business desire to hire such talent internally.

For start-up companies, the primary danger in outsourcing IT is that customers cannot specify their IT needs very well to vendors. Participants were uncertain about the IT services, service levels, and volumes needed to support the new business. Over time, participants realized that they underestimated greatly their IT needs and were tied to a long-term contract that strongly favored the vendor.

To ensure that outsourcing expectations are realized, start-up companies should sign short-term contracts. With start-up companies, customers will always be at a disadvantage when negotiating an outsourcing contract because they have no IT expertise. By signing short-term contracts, start-up companies minimize their outsourcing risks because they are allowed to renegotiate the contract much sooner. Participants stated it took as little as six months to understand their IT needs well enough to sign a fair contract.

Technical expectations

Companies may determine that outsourcing can either improve technical services, allow them to gain access to technical talent not currently available in the organization, or provide access to new technologies.

Improving technical service

Some participants were dissatisfied that their in-house IT departments delivered systems late and over budget and did not respond quickly enough to user requests. They viewed outsourcing as a way to improve technical service, reasoning that outsourcing vendors possess a technical expertise lacking in internal IT departments. Yet some participants were disappointed that outsourcing failed to improve their technical service; in some instances, service levels actually degraded after outsourcing. Participants cited three reasons for failed expectations:

- Service levels were not fully documented in the contract;
- Contention with the vendors' other customers compromised IT service;
- The vendors' staff was overworked and thus often made mistakes.

When service levels were not fully documented in the contact, participants often found severe service degradation. For example, one vendor took 17 working days to implement security requests for new logon IDs and access to data sets. From the vendor's viewpoint, it needed time to verify requests, obtain approvals, and obtain the appropriate signatures. From the customer's perspective, a service that previously took five days to deliver now took 17 days.

Before outsourcing, users could telephone their in-house IT department to get help with IT problems. Because the IT department was a member of the corporate family, it handled requests as best it could. After outsourcing, users' requests were submitted through a centralized procedure that prevented users from directly contacting the vendors' systems analysts. As in the case of cost controls, the new procedures prevent frivolous requests but also tend to slow down the response to legitimate requests. In addition, users became frustrated that the vendors' other customers influenced technical services. For example, some vendors selected technical packages, such as schedulers and security systems, that suboptimized a given customer's service. From the vendor's perspective, it was inefficient to provide multiple packages to perform the same function.

Some participants complained that the level of service degraded because the vendor overworked its staff. Vendor analysts and programmers working overtime were prone to make errors and subsequently provided a level of service that led to lower overall user satisfaction with IT.

The participants' disappointments in technical service stemmed from a lack of understanding of the IT cost/service trade-off. To contain costs, vendors implement cost control measures, such as centralized functions to submit and prioritize user requests, standardized packages to obtain economies of scale, and reduced staff to lower personnel costs. Without these measures, the vendors may not have been able to submit low bids.

Participants who were pleased with the vendors' level of technical service understood the IT cost/service level trade-off. By creating specific service levels in the request for proposals – which are later incorporated into the contract – participants may be willing to accept a more modest savings of 10% to 20% to more drastic savings of 40% to 50%. With high cost savings expectations, participants are more likely to experience service degradation as the vendor attempts to slash internal costs to meet bid specifications. Some senior managers we interviewed specifically said that they understood that IT services would likely degrade through outsourcing but that this was the price they were willing to pay to reduce the costs of IT. Summing up this sentiment, one CEO was overheard to say, *"They [complained] about IT before outsourcing, they [complain] now – but at least it's costing me a lot less."*

Other ways to ensure a quality technical service are (a) to stipulate significant vendor cash penalties for non-conformance of service-levels agreements and (b) to specify the staff size in the contract. For example, some companies stipulate cash penalties for prime-shift downtimes, late reports, or late delivery of newly developed systems. Companies might also specify the number of personnel assigned to specific tasks to ensure service levels. One company specified that five people work the help desk. Another company in our study went so far as to name the vendor account manager it wanted to oversee the account in the contract, choosing an individual who had the respect of senior management, knew the business, and was generally perceived to be critical in making the contract work. The arrangement was highly successful in this particular case but may not be implementable as a general rule.

Access to technical talent

Some participants expected outsourcing to provide access to technical talent. Many of them found it difficult to find or retain staff with the desired state-of-the-art technical skills. This is the primary reason one large UK retailing and distribution company outsourced telecommunications. An international manufacturing company outsourced its systems development work on several projects to gain access to IT expertise not available in-house. Numerous companies consider outsourcing partly for the access to greater IT expertise it would bring, as the following quote suggests:

"We are a relatively small IS department and the spread of skills that's now required for the systems we've got to support, and [the ones] our customers are now asking us to support, is growing. We are not able to keep pace with recruiting those people."

Our study showed, however, that such talent is not all that easy to come by. Many participants complained that the technical expertise remained the same because their internal staff simply transferred to the vendor. One industrial equipment manufacturer outsourced because managers felt that the IT staff did not have the technical skills needed to implement a new computer architecture. The conversion (not to mention the entire outsourcing arrangement) failed because the same IT people (now vendor employees) performed the installation. The company's IT director stated:

"The vendor took over all the people as they usually do, so what happens is that your unqualified IS people become your unqualified vendor people."

In another case, the access to new technical talent was made available to the company but at significant expense. A purchasing manager noted:

"None of it is cheap. There is a perception that once you have [a vendor] locked in, you have a conduit to all this expertise. But you pay."

The only way to ensure that access to technical talent will occur is to have it specifically noted in the contract. Informal understandings and appeals to "strategic partnerships" are ineffectual. Instead, customers should detail the price of additional technical skills they need. We have found that the contract is the only mechanism to ensure wishes are fulfilled.

Gaining access to new technologies

Some participants viewed outsourcing as a way to hedge bets on emerging technologies, providing them with access to the products of the vendors' large research and development departments. (Participants in our 1994 study were most interested in client/server technology, expert systems, new development methodologies, and CASE tools).

Some participants were disappointed that outsourcing did not automatically provide access to new technologies. Rather, contracts often motivated vendors to run older technology as long as possible. For example, one company signed a ten-year contract for all mainframe applications. Even though the company wanted to migrate to client/server technology, this shift – considered a "change in character" – was subject to excess fees. The participant complained that the vendor brought in the desired new technology and the technical skills to use the technology, but at enormous expense. In addition, the contract did not provide a discount for discontinuation of the mainframe applications, thus the customer was contractually bound to old technology. In hindsight, the participant should have signed a shorter contract for the duration of the expected life of the mainframe.

Participants most pleased with their access to new technology created specific contracts for new technologies. One company specifically hired a vendor to help implement its first client/server application. The company maintained managerial control over the development, but used the vendor to provide technical expertise. In this way, the company learned about the technical aspects of client/server technology which enabled it to implement future client/server applications on its own if it wished.

Other participants used outsourcing for just the opposite reason: they outsourced their old technology to a vendor so as to refocus internal resources on new technology. Sun Microsystems, for example, signed a $27 million deal for CSC to handle all of Sun's mainframe operations for up to three years. Meanwhile, Sun rewrote its mainframe-based manufacturing and financial applications to run on a new client/server architecture. The new systems were not outsourced but run by the Sun Microsystems staff.

A third option to ensure that access to new technologies becomes a reality is to include incentives in the contract to share benefits of new technologies. Customers and vendors can collaborate to develop valuable business applications to harness the power of new technologies. For example, one company hired a vendor to create an image-based customer-tracking system that was subsequently sold on the market. Both the customer and vendor shared in the profits.

In short, outsourcing provides access to new technologies only if the contract specifically addresses the issue. A host of contractual options provide access to new technologies: Companies can create a specific contract that requires the vendor to manage, develop, and implement the new technology; companies can manage and develop the new technology themselves and only contract in a vendor's technical expertise; companies can create specific contracts to outsource old systems while they focus internal resources to develop new technologies themselves; or companies can engage in true strategic partnerships, where shared risks and rewards of new technologies are stipulated in the contract. These options also remain meaningful ones in the post-2005 period.

Political expectations

The political dimension of outsourcing involves the behavior of the various parties to the decision-making process, and how they shape senior management's perception about IT and its value. Political rationales for why organizations outsource include: proving efficiency, justifying new resources, duplicating the outsourcing success of others, exposing exaggerated claims, eliminating a troublesome function, and breaking the so-called glass ceiling.

Proving efficiency

Because many companies account for IT as an overhead function, senior managers frequently evaluate the function solely on cost efficiency. Because no concrete measures of actual efficiency exist, senior managers formulate only a perception of efficiency. Some participants in our study, especially IT managers, expected that an outsourcing evaluation would demonstrate to senior management that the internal IT department was cost-efficient. By comparing internal IT costs with vendor bids, IT managers could hold up their reports and say, "See, no one can provide services cheaper than us." The hard numbers appear objective and, therefore, add credibility to their efficiency claims.

Some IT managers were disappointed that their senior managers viewed the outsourcing evaluation results with skepticism. Senior managers may suspect that IT managers biased the evaluation by selectively picking functions that they knew vendors could not underbid – that is, IT managers select one of their best-managed functions as a candidate for outsourcing while eliminating poorly managed functions from the scope of the evaluation. One IT manager conducted an outsourcing evaluation for data center operations that had exceedingly low costs and excellent service levels. The IT manager's real problem was with systems development – users were complaining that new systems were late, over-budget, and defective. By limiting the evaluation to what IT performed well, the IT manager hoped that the positive outsourcing evaluation would have a knock-on effect for the whole IT department.

Another source of skepticism came from vendors. Some vendors view outsourcing requests initiated by IT managers with suspicion, claiming that many IT managers merely inquire about outsourcing for a free assessment. In the early 1990s some vendors responded by charging as much as $20,000 to submit a bid. Other vendors may bypass the IT manager by contacting a more senior manager in the company.

Some IT managers have, however, successfully used an outsourcing evaluation to prove efficiency. One IT director at a start-up company conducted an outsourcing evaluation to demonstrate to senior management that it was cheaper to build a data center than outsource. The director stated:

"In a start-up operation I had to satisfy my management that I was not building an empire."

By showing that outside vendors could not provide the service less expensively, the IT director "proved" his data center plans were efficient.

But such control over the evaluation process may have biased the outcome in the IT director's favor – for example, the internal bid failed to include specific personnel costs. Because the vendors bid included personnel costs, the bids were not commensurable. Such behavior, however, may not go unnoticed by senior management.

The most effective way to ensure credibility of IT efficiency is to involve senior management in the evaluation process. Senior management may serve to verify the scope of the evaluation, help develop bid criteria, and review the bid analysis. IT, however, must be integrally involved in the evaluation and is needed to specify the technical (and often financial) details in the request for proposal and to interpret the technical aspects of the external bids. Senior management sponsorship does not replace IT involvement, but may serve to minimize politics, or at least some forms of politics.

Justifying new resources

Some IT managers initiated outsourcing evaluations in order to acquire new resources, such as machine upgrades and additional personnel. Because senior managements all too many times view the IT department as a cost burden, they may be reluctant to provide additional funds for new IT investments without substantial justification. By showing that growth cannot be satisfied more efficiently through outsourcing, the IT managers in the study expected that their resource requests would be granted.

One IT director wanted to upgrade to a more sophisticated operating system on the AS/400 and move to relational data bases. Knowing that senior management would question whether the additional capacity could be acquired without purchasing a new machine, the IT director bundled resource requests with the results of an outsourcing evaluation that demonstrated it was cheaper to purchase the machine than to outsource. The IT director stated:

> "I was building a base to upgrade to a CPU with a 5-year lease on it. That was my thought process at the time. While it was an outsourcing study, it was also designed to enhance my personal credibility when it came time to ask for bucks."

Such a request may be perceived to be biased. Senior management may be reluctant to buy in to the "need for additional resources" argument, choosing instead to view the justification as not credible. Management may simply continue to fund IT at the minimum level possible. In one case we looked at, the IT manager initiated what might be termed a cursory outsourcing evaluation. Without any formal bidding process, the IT manager claimed that outsourcing was not a viable alternative and that the IT department needed the money for hardware and software upgrades. In this case, senior management was not persuaded. Less than a year later, it outsourced all of the IT department.

It must be re-emphasized that, in this and subsequent studies, we have found that the most effective way to handle such a crisis in believability is to have senior management involved in the outsourcing evaluation exercise. In addition, the involvement of outside experts may help the evaluation of IT alternatives.

Duplicating success

Favorable outsourcing reports trigger managers, particularly senior managers, to initiate outsourcing evaluations to duplicate the success stories at other companies. Because these senior managers often do not truly value the IT function anyway, they hope to at least reduce costs to the levels their competitors allegedly achieved through outsourcing. These managers jump on the bandwagon after hearing good reports from other companies, even though these early successes are usually reported during the so-called honeymoon phase of the contract. Actual savings often fall short of anticipated savings (Lacity and Hirschheim, 1993ab).

Nonetheless, several participants initiated outsourcing evaluations because they wanted to duplicate the outsourcing success stories they read in the trade press or heard about at seminars or from colleagues. A senior vice-president of operations at a bank who participated in our study considered outsourcing after talking to several colleagues in other banks that had outsourced and reported significant anticipated savings. With little formal analysis and little understanding of outsourcing, the bank selected a vendor and hastily signed an agreement in hopes that outsourcing would bail it out of its financial troubles. As in many cases, the anticipated savings were not realized. The vice-president of IT described the motivation for the outsourcing decision this way:

> "The operations vice-president really felt, and I think correctly, that outsourcing was something people were talking about. Other organizations had done it, especially banks that were the same size as us."

The only way to guard against such optimism is to educate senior management about the often exaggerated claims made in the outsourcing stories. This can be done by analyzing the real experiences of these so-called success stories. Our evidence is that the successes continue to be neither as prevalent nor as dramatic as reported (Willcocks and Lacity, 2006). Bringing in outside (and hopefully neutral) experts to help temper expectations is one successful strategy we have seen employed in some of our case participants in the present, and subsequent, studies.

Exposing exaggerated claims

IT managers, on the other hand, usually fear that the favorable reports will seduce their managers into outsourcing. By taking the initiative, IT managers expect outsourcing evaluations to temper the many exaggerated claims made in public information sources.

IT managers face a major risk if they conduct a cursory outsourcing evaluation simply to expose exaggerated claims: senior management may perceive that the IT department is unwilling to make a rationale decision. As a result, senior management may conduct its own outsourcing evaluation without including the IT department in the process. For example, one IT manager in our study commissioned the IT staff to generate a white paper on outsourcing after hearing senior management quote a business magazine article on the subject. The manager explained:

> "A lot of the industry is nervous. Industry observers for the last couple of years have been saying, 'If you don't look at outsourcing, somebody will do it for you.' So we have undertaken a review of what the outsourcing market looks like."

The white paper, which contained warnings from one outsourcing consultant, was virtually ignored by senior management. The IT department failed to formally evaluate whether outsourcing was feasible for the company. Less than a year later, senior management outsourced systems development.

In summary, if senior management perceives that the IT manager is only trying to buy time by "researching" outsourcing claims (i.e., trying to disprove them), it may simply move ahead while hiding the evaluation from the IT group. Once again, the only way to guard against such negative interaction is to conduct a formal evaluation process involving benchmarking, often against best-of-breed companies.

Eliminating a troublesome function

It is not uncommon for IT to be perceived by senior management as a troublesome function – in a word, a headache. IT administrators receive few accolades for managing the function. When the function runs smoothly, senior executives do not notice. When the function experiences problems, senior management screams. Some people wonder, who needs the aggravation? Why not outsource the function and let the vendor worry about it?

The controller at one company in the study claimed that outsourcing reduced costs and that its vendor primarily achieved economies of scale for the data center. Yet applications were also outsourced. During the interview, the controller identified another motive:

> "People say you should keep applications. I ask them, Why would you want to do that? That's the biggest headache. Anybody can run a machine, it's the applications that are a headache."

Through outsourcing, the controller believed the company no longer had to worry about IT. Some senior managers may consider outsourcing as a way to eliminate a burdensome function. Although this intention appears pejorative, it captures a very human element. We all wish some portion of our job responsibilities would disappear. On the other hand, is it really possible to outsource the management of IT? It is likely that by eliminating one headache, all that management may be doing is exchanging one headache for another?

Clearly, if outsourcing is considered, it must be evaluated from a position of strength. You cannot successfully outsource a problem. The successful outsourcing cases that we saw involved outsourcing well-understood IT environments. Similarly, most unsuccessful outsourcing cases involved management turning over to an outside vendor something that they did not understand or want to understand. The latter case was a recipe for disaster, and remains poor practice to follow (Lacity and Willcocks, 2009).

Breaking the glass ceiling

Sometimes IT directors see the purpose of outsourcing as a means to enhance their personal or departmental credibility of the IT director. Because senior managers appear not to value fully the services of the IT department, they may not value the contribution of the people who run the function. To this day, in all but the high-tech sector, IT personnel rarely break into the upper echelons of management. Hence, IT managers may initiate outsourcing decisions for the purpose of enhancing their credibility. By showing that they are willing to outsource their kingdom for the good of the company, they prove to senior management that they are corporate players.

We saw numerous examples in our study where IT managers specifically undertook outsourcing evaluations to alleviate the misconception that IT managers are myopic. They demonstrate to senior management that they are business professionals committed to corporate goals, not technocrats attempting to build technology empires. According to IT managers, increasing their personal credibility benefits the entire IT organization – upper management support means support for the entire IT team, not just the department head.

The fact that IT directors are willing to sell off their empire for the good of the company appeared to have very little bearing on credibility. On the other hand, it seemed very clear that IT managers had to become more business-minded or would become vulnerable to outsourcing. Internal IT managers' knowledge of the business may be the only factor that differentiates them from outsourcing vendors. In order for IT directors to become part of the true corporate team, they must be, first and foremost, business savvy (Lacity and Willcocks, 2001).

Guidelines for success

Our study produced a lot of learning on what makes for failure. Table 2.1 provides a succinct summary of the main practices to avoid.

But what makes success? Although it is imprudent to make superficial generalizations, several guidelines can be inferred on the relative success of certain outsourcing practices. We would contend that those detailed in Table 2.2 and below continue to stand to this day as useful guidelines for the management of outsourcing.

Table 2.1   Determinants of Failed Outsourcing Expectations

Initial Expectations/ Reasons for Outsourcing	Determinants of Failed Expectations
Financial	
Reduce Costs	Hidden costs
Improve Cost Controls	Users by-passed vendor bureaucracy
Restructure IT Budgets	Over time, IT unit costs out of sync with price/performance improvements
Business	
Return to Core Competencies	Loss of business expertise resulting from treating the entire IT department as a utility
Facilitate Mergers and Acquisitions	Vendor unable to absorb new assets and people because of short notification
Start-up Companies	IT costs and service expectations not met because of the new company's inexperience with IT
Technical	
Improve Technical Service	Service degrades because of lack of service-level agreements, contention with the vendor's other clients, overworked vendor staff
Access to Technical Talent	No change in technical talent when staff transfers to the vendor; new vendor talent is possible but expensive
Access to New Technologies	Possible but expensive; vendors motivated to run old technologies as long as possible
Political	
Prove Efficiency	Senior management views evidence of IT efficiency with skepticism
Justify New Resources	Senior management views justification of new resources with skepticism
Duplicate Success	Senior management initiates outsourcing based on exaggerated claims appearing in the literature
Expose Exaggerated Claims	IT manager sponsors outsourcing evaluation to expose exaggerated claims, but it is perceived by senior management as a ploy to simply buy additional time; IT manager fails to establish credibility
Eliminate Troublesome Function	Cannot outsource the **management** of IT
Break the Glass Ceiling	Initiating of outsourcing evaluation perceived as ploy to enhance reputation of IT manager

Table 2.2   Determinants of Realized Expectations

Initial Expectations/ Reasons for Outsourcing	Determinants of Realized Expectations
Financial	
Reduce Costs	Create specific contracts
Improve Cost Controls	Involve business managers in rating/ranking user requests
Restructure IT Budgets	Sign short contracts
Business	
Return to Core	View IT as a portfolio of core and non-core activities Competencies
Facilitate Mergers and Acquisitions	Select a vendor with expertise in mantling and dismantling systems
Start-up Companies	Sign short contracts that are renegotiable as soon as IT needs are better defined
Technical	
Improve Technical Service	Specify service-level agreements, vendor account manager, and penalties for non-performance in contract
Access to Technical Talent	Make explicit what technical talent is desired in the contract and its cost
Access to New Technologies	Sign contracts for duration of the expected life of current technology and renegotiate as new technologies emerge; for longer contracts, include incentives to share the benefits of new technologies, negotiate planned obsolescence and replacement of technology
Political	
Prove Efficiency	Ensure credibility of IT efficiency through senior management buy-in; senior management sponsors outsourcing evaluation
Justify New Resources	Ensure the justification for new resources through senior management buy-in; senior management sponsors outsourcing evaluation
Duplicate Success	Involve outside expertise to help temper expectations; analyze the "real" experiences of outsourcing successes
Expose Exaggerated Claims	Involve outside experts in developing objective evaluation criteria and site visits to best-of-breed companies
Eliminate Troublesome Function	Outsource IT only from a position of strength (i.e., a company should not outsource a problem)
Break the Glass Ceiling	IT manager must possess business savvy rather than just technical capabilities

Both Senior Management and IT Management Involvement is Required to Conduct a Rational Outsourcing Evaluation. Otherwise, politics from either side may drive an outsourcing evaluation, with senior management possibly attempting to negotiate with a vendor without IT involvement and IT managers attempting to conduct a cursory evaluation to temper exaggerated claims, justify new resources, or prove efficiency. When both senior management and IT management are involved, each assumes a role that helps reduce political behavior. Senior management assumes the role of defining the objectives – whether they are financial, business, or technical – defining the scope of the outsourcing evaluation, developing bid analysis criteria, and verifying the bid analysis. IT assumes the critical role of creating the detailed request for proposal, evaluating the legitimacy of vendor economies of scale, estimating the effects of price/performance improvements, and providing insights on emerging technologies that may effect the business.

Selective Outsourcing is More Often the Right Preference. Participants' successful experiences with "total" outsourcing were usually limited to cases in which the company's internal politics prevented the IT department from initiating cost savings; the company needed to focus energies on more strategic issues than IT; or the company needed the cash infusion from the sale of information assets (but see also Chapter 4). In most cases, however, selective sourcing was the preferred option. Although vendors may be technical experts, critical business skills are required to align IT with overall business strategy. Participants agreed it is unwise to outsource IT activities that require extensive knowledge of business needs, such as the development and support of strategic systems, IT planning and strategy, and IT architecture. In addition, it is unwise to outsource any IT activity that is perceived as a problem. Outsourcing IT activities that are not understood leaves the customer in a poor position to negotiate a sound contract. Companies cannot get rid of problems by outsourcing – instead they tend to exchange one set of problems for another.

If Outsourcing is the Preferred Mechanism for Meeting Sourcing Objectives, Companies Need a Solid Contract. Depending on the precise sourcing objectives, customers should negotiate the appropriate contract type, contract length, and contract detail. In general, customers can sign one of three types of contracts:

1. Resource buy-in, in which the customer retains managerial control;
2. Resource buy-out, in which the vendor assumes management control;
3. Strategic partnership, in which the customer and vendor jointly manage IT and share in the risks and rewards (see Chapter 4).

In general, customers preferred short-term contracts because it was very difficult to predict future IT demand and supply – few participants felt confident predicting their own IT needs or the impact of future technologies past five years. This remains the case in the post-2005 period. Vendors prefer long-term contracts for precisely this reason. The longer the contract, the more likely the vendor can exploit price/performance improvements to increase their profits and sell additional products and services. In general, specific contacts with detailed service level requirements and penalties for non-performance are preferable to non-specific contracts (see also Chapters 3 and 10). If customers follow the prescription to outsource only what they already understand, then creating a detailed contract should not be a problem.

Conclusion

All organizations will undertake outsourcing evaluations – outsourcing was not a passing fad even in 1994. It is simply common sense for organizations to consider whether outside vendors can better meet sourcing objectives. If they can, then outsourcing may make sense. This, of course, assumes that IT is a commodity and that there is no intrinsic difference between the provision of an IT service from outside or inside. The arguments used to support the alternative positions are equally convincing and strongly held. Yet irrespective of the opinion you hold, it is interesting to speculate why in-house IT departments could not reduce their costs to be competitive with an outside vendor.

First, an internal IT department does not have to make a profit. Vendors not only have to make a profit, but they have significant overhead expenses that increase their costs. Second, an in-house IT department has knowledge of the business (and industry) that the vendor will likely not have. If an outside vendor can provide service less expensively than an internal IT department, then why does the in-house department not adopt its strategies? So-called insourcing arrangements can work very effectively if the in-house IT unit can cut costs – for example, through data center consolidation, the implementation of improved chargeback systems, worker empowerment, the purchase of used equipment, and offering a reduced software portfolio. Although insourcing is not necessarily the preferred solution, it should be considered alongside the options of "total" and selective outsourcing. This is an argument we return to in Chapter 9.

References

Bravard, J-L. and Morgan, R. (2006) *Smarter Outsourcing*, Prentice Hall, London.
Feeny, D., Willcocks, L. and Lacity, M. (2005) "Taking The Measure of Outsourcing Providers", *Sloan Management Review*, 46, 3, 41–48.
Lacity, M. and Hirschheim, R. (1993a) "The Information Systems Outsourcing Bandwagon: Look Before You Leap", *Sloan Management Review*, 35, 1, 72–86.

Lacity, M. and Hirschheim, R. (1993b) *Information Systems Outsourcing: Myths, Metaphors, and Realities,* Wiley, Chichester.

Lacity, M. and Willcocks, L. (1998) "An Empirical Investigation of Information Technology Sourcing Practices: Lessons From Experience", *MIS Quarterly,* 22, 3, 363–408.

Lacity, M. and Willcocks, L. (2001) *Global Information Technology Outsourcing: Search For Business Advantage,* Wiley, Chichester.

Lacity, M. and Willcocks, L. (2009) *Information Systems and Outsourcing: Studies in Theory and Practice,* Palgrave, London.

Willcocks, L. and Craig, A. (2007) *The Outsourcing Enterprise 4 – Building Retained Core Capabilities,* Logica, London.

Willcocks, L. and Lacity, M. (2006) *Global Sourcing of Business and IT Services,* Palgrave, London.

Willcocks, L. and Oshri, I. (2009) The Effective Buying of IT and Business Process Services. LSE Outsourcing Unit Executive Brief, LSE, London.

3
Contracting and Relationships in IT Outsourcing

Guy Fitzgerald and Leslie Willcocks

Introduction

This chapter is based on a research study on the outsourcing of information technology activities in the United Kingdom. This involved a large survey and a set of detailed case studies based on large and medium-sized organizations. This chapter uses findings from the survey and cases to address the two key issues of contracting and partnering. We show the variety of approaches and perceptions that exist concerning these issues, and conclude that there is much misunderstanding, particularly in relation to partnership. We conclude by creating a framework for helping to identify and examine the interrelationship between contractual arrangements, the required degree of contractual definition, and the characteristics of the area being outsourced. These themes are perennial and continue to be addressed in our subsequent work, particularly in Chapters 4, 10, and 13, our 2001 book that focuses on "the relational advantage" (Kern and Willcocks, 2001), and our 2006 paper on the power of relationships. A collection of papers on relationships also appears in Volume 2 of Willcocks and Lacity (2009).

By 1994 the outsourcing of Information Technology (IT) and associated services was a rapidly growing phenomenon in the United Kingdom (UK), the market expanding at 12% per annum to a predicted 1995 revenue of £1.08 billion (Willcocks and Fitzgerald, 1994). A large 1993 example of this continuing trend was the announcement by British Aerospace (BAe) to outsource its Information Technology to Computer Sciences Corporation (CSC) in a ten-year deal worth £900 million, and involving the transfer of over 1,000 IT staff (Evans, 1993). Additionally most of public sector IT was being opened up to market testing, the outcomes from which greatly increased this figure (See Willcocks, 1994; Cordella *et al.*, 2008).

By 1994 outsourcing had been the subject of a number of academic studies, particularly in the USA (as examples only see Apte, 1990; Apte and Mason, 1993; Clark and Zmud, 1993; Klepper, 1993; Lacity and Hirschheim, 1992, 1993; Loh and Venkatraman 1992abc). A number of detailed case studies had been produced on US corporations (for example Buck-Lew, 1992; Huber, 1993; Moad, 1993). There had been a series of case studies produced from various European countries (for example Auwers and Deschoolmeester, 1993; Griese, 1993; Heinzl, 1993; Saaksjarvi, 1993). Outsourcing IT had also been the subject of considerable debate, not only at the level of how best it can be done, but also in terms of its implications for organizational forms and management (Grant, 1992; Huber, 1993, Quinn, 1992).

Our overall aim was to complement such work by investigating, by an empirical study, the relatively neglected area of outsourcing of IT activities in the United Kingdom. In particular, we sought to identify patterns of outsourcing in terms of resources, decisions and activities outsourced, the reasons for, and risks of outsourcing, criteria for success, the difficulties being experienced, and how they are handled. The findings were extensive and detailed and many categories are not discussed here, including important findings in the areas of outsourcing economics, human resource and staff issues, vendors, decision-making criteria, and post-outsourcing organizational shapes (see Willcocks and Fitzgerald, 1994). This chapter presents a subset of the findings and in particular focuses on contracts, outsourcing relationships, and partnerships.

We define outsourcing as the commissioning of a third party to manage a client organization's IT assets, people and/or activities to required results. This may involve a degree of transfer of assets and staff to the third party organization. A key distinction can be made between contracts that specify a service and result which the market is to provide and manage ("outsourcing"); and contracts which call for the market to provide resources to be deployed under the buyer's management and control. Elsewhere (Feeny *et al.*, 1993) we have described the latter as "insourcing" or "contracting in" contracts. We use the term IT (Information Technology) to refer to the supply of information-based technologies, and IS (Information Systems) as organizational applications, more or less IT-based, designed to deliver on the information needs of the organization and the defined stakeholders. These definitions hold throughout this book.

Research methodology

Following Mintzberg (1979), the researchers adopted a research methodology that attempted to collect both hard and soft information, the hard to uncover relationships, and the soft to help explain such relationships. It was decided that the study should integrate a variety of investigative techniques. A series of 16 telephone interviews was undertaken, based on a relatively open ended set of questions, the major objective being to establish whether the assumptions that we made about outsourcing, based on our own experiences, and from the literature, were viable in the context of the UK. We concluded that broadly our assumptions were appropriate but that we needed an amended focus in certain areas. One major conclusion was that we should investigate more thoroughly issues of contracts and partnerships. It is this final issue that forms the subject of this chapter. The second stage of the research was a survey of experience based on a detailed postal questionnaire. The questionnaire was devised to establish the quantitative issues and give a picture of what the situation concerning outsourcing was like in the UK. We also attempted to investigate a few softer issues of perception concerning success, key issues, and reflections. The questionnaire was piloted on a small group of senior managers, and revised as a result of the pilot. It was then dispatched to over 1,000 senior managers/directors, the majority being IT managers/directors, in both medium and large sized organizations in the UK (and a small proportion to European countries as well). The survey elicited a response of 16.2%. The third aspect of the research comprised a series of semi-structured interviews with a range of participants involved in outsourcing in organizations. This formed the basis of 30 case studies that were backed up by the collection and analysis of relevant documentation, including copies of outsourcing contracts. Fourthly the study added a number of further interviews with other major players in the outsourcing arena, including outsourcing vendors and legal experts. The methodology sought to gain triangulation at two levels. Firstly, from the range of techniques employed, and secondly, in the interviews, from the range of respondents, including senior general management, IT management, and user management.

In this chapter we first highlight some of the findings from the 1994 survey before considering the issues of contracts, outsourcing relationships and partnership in more detail.

Survey findings

Some 81% of respondent organizations were UK-located, reflecting to some degree the original bias in the survey, but also the much higher response rate from UK-located organizations. Remaining respondents were from Belgium (8%), Germany (4%), France (3%), Netherlands (2%), with the others located in Switzerland, Finland and Luxembourg. One suggestive finding from the sample was that the UK-located organizations were much more likely to be outsourcing IT than organizations in other European countries – a trend that has continued ever since (Willcocks and Lacity, 2006).

Sectors and types of organization

The sectors represented in the sample were Manufacturing 30%, Banking and Finance 21%, Public Sector 13%, Retail, Distribution and Sales 9%, Services 7%, IT/Telecommunications 8%, "Other" 12%. In our survey we found that Finance/Insurance, Manufacturing and Public Sector organizations accounted for more than half of the outsourcing market. The

Public Sector represented a special case in the UK as the growth in outsourcing here was not simply a matter of market forces in operation but was strongly influenced by the UK Government policies such as Compulsory Competitive Tendering (CTC). This compelled most public sector organizations to test and evaluate up to 80% of their services in the marketplace (Cordella *et al.*, 2008).

Extent of outsourcing

The survey revealed that, on the face of it, outsourcing IT had been a popular preoccupation in the 1990s, as 47% of the organizations surveyed outsourced some or all of their IT activities. Another 33% had considered outsourcing but rejected it. Thus nearly 80% of organizations had IT outsourcing experience or had at least considered outsourcing, if only to reject it (This figure is relatively high compared to other surveys at the time).

Organizations that had outsourcing contracts by 1994 were spending on average 24% of their IT budgets on outsourcing. To some extent this qualifies the higher figures mentioned in a range of other surveys. To provide further qualification, we found that, of the organizations outsourcing IT, only one-fifth were spending more than 50% of their IT budget specifically on outsourcing, while just over two-thirds were spending 20% or less on outsourcing.

Future plans

Looking at projections for five years' time, 3% of organizations outsourcing in 1994 believed that they would be not be outsourcing in 1998. Another 17% felt unable to predict what they would be doing in five years time. Amongst the other responses two main patterns in projected spend emerged. Two-thirds showed a steadily rising trend in outsourcing expenditure as percentage of the IT budget over the 1993–98 period. Interestingly, the other one-third show a slowly decreasing expenditure on outsourcing as a percentage of total IT spend over the five years. There were no great predicted changes in the size of spend on outsourcing as a percentage of the total IT budget. By 1998 16% felt they would be spending 70% or more of their IT budget on outsourcing (1993: 12%). In 1998 45% felt they would be spending 20% or less of their IT budget on outsourcing (1993: 67%). Organizations outsourcing IT in 1994 were predicting that IT outsourcing as a percentage of their total IT budgets would increase on average by 12% between 1993 and 1998 – this subsequently proved to be quite a good estimate! (Lacity and Willcocks, 2001).

20% of all organizations in the sample had not contemplated outsourcing IT, and the question was asked concerning their likelihood of outsourcing in the future. Of the 20%, only 3% positively indicated that they were likely to be outsourcing IT in the near future and the remaining 17% indicated they were unlikely to outsource IT. The most likely candidates to outsource were to be found amongst the 33% of organizations that had contemplated outsourcing before, but rejected it at present.

Activities and services outsourced

Figure 3.1 indicates the spectrum of IT and related activities that organizations were outsourcing in 1994. The left hand axis only takes into account organizations that had outsourced. The major outsourcing activity was in what we have defined as Operations and organizations seemed much more confident in outsourcing in this area, especially with regard to hardware maintenance, mainframe/data center management and PC support. It is also interesting to note the high figures for outsourcing all as opposed to some networking activities, like planning and design, LANs and network management.

In the "Other" category it is clear that organizations were fairly confident about outsourcing user training and education, though relatively less so about the training and education of management. It is slightly surprising to find nearly 13% of organizations outsourcing all, and another 11% some, of their IT strategy and planning activities. (A small amount (3%) was accounted for by the contracting out of work to a related company.) The indications from outsourcing theory and our case study work at the time indicated (and

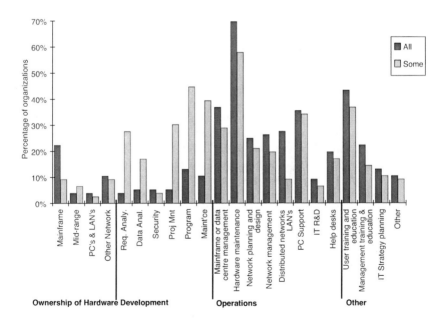

Figure 3.1 What IT are Organizations Outsourcing

continue to indicate) that IT planning and strategy should remain in-house (Lacity and Willcocks, 2009).

Looking at ownership of hardware, there seemed to have been no great move to change ownership through outsourcing. Mainframes were the main items likely to switch ownership in an outsourcing deal with 29% of organizations selling some or all of their mainframe hardware. It is interesting to note that while many organizations outsourced much on the operations side of networks, they seemed much less reluctant to outsource ownership of the related hardware. With respect to the outsourcing of systems development activities, programming was the most popular (12% of organizations), followed by maintenance (10%) followed by project management and requirements analysis. However, in general, there appeared to be a reluctance to outsource all development work. Our other work at the time suggested that the more effective policy is to outsource development only where the work can be clearly defined, with clearly identifiable deliverables, where the technology is stable and where the organization does not feel the area to be a problem (Willcocks and Fitzgerald, 1993). Otherwise the wiser approach is to "insource", that is buy in expertise and/or use contractors as part of the team, with a view to building in-house capability. Later work confirms the relevance of this stipulation (Lacity and Willcocks, 2009).

Of the 33% of organizations that had considered outsourcing but rejected it by far the most important reasons were firstly worries concerning loss of control, secondly the lack of identifiable benefits, and thirdly the conviction that IT was strategic to the business and therefore should not be outsourced. Indeed 43 out of the 55 organizations that rejected outsourcing mentioned at least two of these factors.

Problems encountered

The survey differentiated between problems experienced when making decisions about outsourcing and problems arising during the progress of an actual contract. Obviously questions on the latter were restricted to organizations that had actually outsourced IT. We also asked organizations separately whether they experienced problems with the vendor. Respondents indicated many problem areas that emerged during their actual outsourcing experiences but the top five ranked as "very difficult" were, in order:

1. Defining service levels;
2. Managing the contract and its details;
3. Getting different contractors and vendors to work together;
4. Vendor's lack of flexibility;
5. Vendor's lack of responsiveness.

Thus the major problems related to the details of the contract; including the definition of service levels, and the client's ability to manage the contract. The next three areas of some or more difficulty related to problems experienced with the vendor, namely lack of flexibility, staffing of contract and lack of responsiveness. Given that difficulties with the vendor were a prominent problem area, we explored whether these difficulties turned into disputes and found that half of the organizations that outsource IT have experienced disputes with their vendor(s). Disputes centred around one or more of:

- Failure of vendor to meet service levels (37% of the cases mentioned);
- Unclear contractual issues (23%);
- Changing requirements (21%);
- Unforeseen charges (18%).

Of the organizations experiencing disputes, 69% had encountered two or more of these issues. When asked if they would have done anything differently when they outsourced most (over four fifths) referred explicitly to tightening service contracts, more detailed measurement, and making more clear what was covered by the contract and what was not. Another frequent comment was that they would strengthen their ability to manage the vendor. Our later work (Willcocks and Craig, 2007) continues to find all too frequently such experiences and learning.

Contractual issues

The survey covered some 226 contracts. The vast majority (95%) were of less than five years in duration and organizations in general appeared reluctant to enter into the more highly publicized long-term relationships such as, for example Eastman Kodak, and General Dynamics in the USA, and British Aerospace and the Inland Revenue in the UK (see also Chapter 4). The trend toward shorter-term contracts was often expressed as being driven by the current high degree of business uncertainty, in terms of both the business environment, and internal organizational change.

Outsourcing was also revealed by the survey as a dynamic process. Against general projections of a rising trend in outsourcing, nearly a third of organizations who had experienced outsourcing had in the past five years cancelled contracts as opposed to straightforwardly renewing them. In one half of these cases the contract was subsequently re-negotiated, but a further 28% of the cases involved a change of vendor, while the remaining 22% saw the IT work brought back in-house. Later work (Willcocks and Lacity, 2006) suggests that subsequently in Europe and the USA there has been no substantial "backsourcing" trend occurs with only about 10% of contract terminations.

The survey also suggested that the relationship that clients adopted with vendors were increasingly contractually based. Three of the identified types were what might be termed partnership-based arrangements, one was a flexible agreement based on trust, the other was based on a more formal contract, and the third was defined as a strategic alliance. The other types were a short, flexible service contract, and a tightly defined service contract. We see that 53% of the relationships were in some way "partnership" based, whilst 47% were defined as contractually based. Thus a greater proportion of respondents considered important the partnering aspects of the outsourcing relationship. However, strategic alliances, or risk/reward relationships, accounted for only 7% of those partnering arrangements, a trend that continues to this day (Lacity and Willcocks, 2009).

An interesting comparison is with what these organizations were doing two years before (in 1991/92). The survey showed a trend over the two years away from flexible partnering based on trust (down 9%) towards partnering based on more formal contracts. This suggests a learning curve in operation with organizations, as a result of their experiences, slowly realizing the need to get into a more clearly defined contractual relationship with vendors. However, even though there was a trend towards more contractually based relationships there was strong evidence that the contracts, and their definition, could be improved. Legal experts on outsourcing were suggesting at the time that as a minimum contracts should include four elements:

- specified service level agreement;
- penalty clauses;
- specific arrangements for adapting to changing circumstances in the future;
- early termination provisions.

However we found that only 26% of outsourcing organizations actually provided all four contractual items. Some 82% of organizations operated service level agreements, but then there was a fall-off with 53% including penalties, and only 49% including early termination provisions. A rather surprising 78% did not include clauses in their contracts on arrangements for adapting to changing circumstances in the future. Yet nearly 80% of all organizations admitted to experiencing some or more difficulty in anticipating future business directions when outsourcing – again a difficulty that continues to be experienced to this day (Lacity and Willcocks, 2009).

Types of contract

Outsourcing contracts are perhaps more complicated than some other business contracts as many of them also involve the transfer (or sale) of assets, such as, hardware, software, buildings, sites, people, etc., to the vendor. In such cases the contract can involve significant payments from the vendor company to the client. This may be an up-front payment by the vendor to the client and then an ongoing payment from the client to the vendor for provision of services over the period of the contract, or the initial payment may include the cost of the services over the period. The selling of IT assets to the vendor is what sometimes makes the deal worthwhile to the client but the contract is also, importantly, about the provision of services over the ongoing contract period.

We identified six types of contract in the research. The first category was the basic time and materials type of contract, familiar to most IT management from the area of systems development, where it has been common to contract in development skills from vendors in this way (this is really more akin to what we defined above as insourcing). Secondly, the fixed fee (or lump sum) contract, often used in situations where the workload or service is well understood and easily definable, enabling the costs and pricing to be relatively accurately calculated at the outset. The fee may be paid at the initiation of the contract or distributed over the duration of the contract. The third type was a variation of the fixed fee contract which additionally has a number of factors that may vary the level of payments over time depending on, for example, work loads, easily predicted changing business circumstances, new technology.

A fourth type of contract was the cost plus deal which involves a fee based on the actual costs of providing the facility or service (calculated on a periodic basis over the life of the contract) plus a percentage or management fee. This is similar to other fee type of contracts except that, rather than a market fee for the service, all the costs are the real costs incurred by the vendor and are usually of necessity open to inspection. Fifthly, there were a number of contracts that contained some performance, or other, incentives for the vendor. This might involve the sharing of some of the benefits or savings that accrued to the client company as a result of the deal, or it might be the rewarding of good service or performance over and above an agreed baseline. Such contracts may also involve reductions to the vendor if performance fell below a certain level. Sixthly, the full profit (and loss) sharing contract, where the return might be based on how well the client company performs (defined in some way) or how well a particular product or service sells in the marketplace, (for example in the insurance industry there are deals where payment depends on how many policies are sold), or the sharing of risks and rewards from a specific joint venture. The issue of types of contract, and contract "fit" in the larger picture of how an outsourcing arrangement can be configured has been detailed further in Chapter 11.

Outsourcing relationships

We now turn to some findings from the case study component of the research where the trend toward more tightly defined contract was also evident. For example in one case it took some 18 months of vigorous contract management finally to get the performance measures right and end disputes on service. The manager described the situation as follows:

> There was a contract, a legal one with our signatures on it, with various sections in it, but really it did not define what the service was going to be...the section in the contract that talked about the penalty clauses was

so ambiguously written that we had a fight for nearly 6 months over it…we needed to get out of this partnership issue and back into a proper business contractual relationship and that is what really set us off, I think, down the right road. (Contract manager, Retail and Distribution Company)

Thus a common response to problems with the vendors was to try to define and specify the contract more rigorously. For many this had become the established principle in the outsourcing business as a way of overcoming problems, and subsequently has led to a focus on contracts and the involvement of both internal and external legal expertise in contract negotiation.

Another way of overcoming problems with vendors is to enter only short-term contracts, and, as we saw above from the survey, this also appeared to be an important trend. However there was another important group of organizations advocating the establishment of "partnership" relationships between client and vendor. It was argued that partnering becomes the basis of the relationship and so overcomes all the potential legal contractual wrangles associated with contracts. This suggests that anything not specifically mentioned in a contract would not cause problems, that disputes would be discussed and resolved in a spirit of partnership, that the contract does not have to be a watertight document, and that a degree of flexibility is achieved:

There's got to be flexibility, and that comes back to trust. You can't put everything in a contract, you can't tie everything down. In fact one shouldn't aim to put everything in a contract because I wouldn't employ someone I didn't trust and I think the trouble was we didn't know enough about them (the vendors). They have not turned out to be bad people, but we got what we deserved. I have been involved in this industry a lot of years, and there are people you know you could bring in and turn your back on and people that you don't, I know it's daft, but it really is about that relationship….. Now that relationship is developing, much better than at the beginning. (IT Manager, Aviation Authority)

"Partnership" was certainly a frequently used word for describing the relationship between vendor and client and was clearly a feature often looked for by client companies. This notion of partnership was often expressed as "cultural understanding" between client and vendor. For some this was the most important single factor in selecting a vendor, although it was not always an easy quest. Another interpretation of the term partnership was the give and take that this implied, often expressed as not having to debate every issue that arose. The hope was that the vendor would just get on and do whatever was necessary and would not say that this was not in the contract and we want to be paid extra, every couple of weeks. Only when there were major mismatches would extra payment be negotiated. On the other side this would mean that if something that was supposed to be provided by the vendor was not, or there was an element of slippage, this would be overlooked by the client, or if not overlooked it would not become a big issue and trigger penalties and damages. This give and take element was closely related to the perception that this was best achieved if the vendor was allowed to make a "fair" profit.

The notion of a fair deal for both sides was frequently stressed as an important criteria for successful outsourcing. This was initially a rather surprising finding as it might be expected that the client would try and negotiate for the lowest possible deal and be only too pleased if the vendor gets it wrong or under-prices. After all, for many, one of the main incentives for considering outsourcing deals is to reduce costs, and therefore presumably the cheaper the deal the better.

We identified two main reasons why client companies may prefer the vendor to make a profit on the deal. Firstly, client companies were clearly very worried by the possibility of their vendor running into financial difficulties and failing; it was seen as counter-productive for the contract to help drive them into trouble. The consequences of the vendor ceasing to be able to provide service for the duration of the contract, and the effect on the well-being of the client organization, was generally seen as much more serious than any short-term contract pricing gain that could be available. However the research did not provide any examples of vendor collapses at the time so this appeared to be a basic fear rather than hard experience.

The second reason expressed for not driving too hard a bargain on the contract price was the effect it had on the behavior of the vendor. It was perceived that the vendor would attempt to overcome their "losses" on the initial contract by seeking every opportunity to contest the detail of what was, and what was not, included in the contract and to try and bill for every possible addition. This was certainly borne out in the research, for example:

> I think that within the vendor this deal was struck for strategic reasons. When the senior vendor guy asked his subordinates "Can we make money at £8 million?" and they said "No", his response was "Well you'd better!" So with a tight contract they looked for every opportunity to increase their margins and that was not conducive to a happy relationship. (IT Director, manufacturing company)

The perceived wisdom was to agree a "fair and reasonable" deal for both sides, thought by several client companies to be a profit on the deal of between 15 and 20%. As one IT Director remarked:

> If the outsourcer could make a 15% profit and I could save 15% of IS expense, then we'd probably get pretty close to a deal.

It was also thought important for client companies to understand where and how the vendor was making their profit – indeed this was viewed as essential for arriving at a "fair" deal. Although the vendor had experience on their side in calculating the value of a deal they did sometimes get it wrong and take on an unprofitable deal. Occasionally vendors were forced to quote on relatively little information in short time-scales. We found situations where the deal was potentially very sensitive (e.g., where the employees were in dispute) and the vendors were not allowed access, and other examples where they were not provided with all the necessary information until just before the deal was made. All these findings are interesting in the light of our subsequent research culminating in a paper on "the Winner's Curse" in outsourcing (Kern *et al.*, 2002). The "winner's curse", we found, occurred in nearly one-fifth of deals researched. In such a deal, not only does the vendor not make its margins, but the client also stand a strong chance of having a very adverse outsourcing experience.

"Partnership" was also often expressed not just as involving trust, as was noted above, but commonly as being able to work with the vendor, and particularly important was that the vendor understood the client's business and culture. The notion of cultural fit was not always very well explained but it sometimes appeared to manifest itself as a concern that the vendor should treat the staff to be transferred well:

> We never use the word outsourcing here we always use the word partnership, but a lot of that sensitivity is because we are transferring 100 people, we felt the key criteria was the culture and philosophy of business had to be compatible. (Systems manager, brewing company)

In summary, outsourcing "partnership" was usually seen as embodying the following:

- a non-reliance on the contract as the basis of the relationship;
- a mutual desire to work things out, and a give-and-take philosophy;
- a fair profit for the vendor, so that they do not seek to resort to what may be an inadequate contract;
- the ability to work together in personal relationship terms;
- the existence of a cultural fit between the client and vendor organizations;
- good treatment of the clients transferred staff;
- a perception that the vendor understands the client's business and problems.

This type of partnership was often stated as an ideal and some client companies felt they had actually achieved this. Obviously such relationships work best where the service being provided is viewed by the client as at least up to the standard of the previous (usually in-house) service, and where in general the perception of service, and level of satisfaction, was high. In our view, in such situations this give-and-take notion of partnership can flourish.

Business-based partnership

There is, however, an alternative view of partnership. This view dismisses the viability of the give-and-take type of partnership in outsourcing. It is argued that it is not really a business partnership at all but a cosy working relationship which relies on an over-generous profit for the vendor to make it work. On this view, partnership is unlikely to sur-vive severe problems and will only work when times are good; for example it is unlikely to survive where, as we found in several contracts, the vendor service declined in the later stages of longer-term contracts, as vendor staff and vendor-client relationships changed or the vendor opportunistically attempted to retrieve its investment in the early years of the contract. On this view, for the client to talk of partnerships is foolish and liable to lead to them being taken advantage of in the long term.

Furthermore, the above sense of the term partnership is not the one commonly used in many business relationships. Henderson (1990) suggests that corporate strategy researchers have focused on the concept of partnership as a general management strategy which specifically includes "... shared risk and benefits, and other qualities consistent with concepts and theories of participatory decision making." In a business sense, partnership is not primarily about a cosy give-and-take relationship (although hopefully this would exist) but more about the sharing of risks and rewards, and mutual incentives for success, which most of the above uses of the term partnership do not embody. Consider the following:

> They (vendors) talk all that partnership stuff but they behave like a monopoly... they try and screw you into the ground.... You want them to be sharp and aggressive but you want them to work for you. (Logistics Director, Retail company)

> There is a lot of rubbish talked about partnerships.... I think its nice to work together but its never a true partnership, unless you have a joint financial venture. (IT Director, Retail and distribution company)

There can be real problems arising from differing perceptions of the meaning of the term partnership. In one example the vendor interpreted partnership to refer to a good working relationship with client staff backed up by a literal interpretation of the contract details. The client believed it meant the willingness to work together to resolve issues that were not anticipated, that were not covered or were ambiguous in the contract. Our central finding here, as in several cases, was that a good relationship quite easily degraded into a poor one if the contract was not properly comprehensive and specific about the expectations and obligations of all parties. As one vendor representative commented:

> Outsourcing contracts are agreed in concept and delivered in detail, and that's why they break down.

One way of handling this potential set of problems was described by a systems director in a respondent brewing company:

> Basically we negotiated a tight contract and then put it to one side, which was the intention, so that we could run the thing as a partnership. But you've got to be protected.

For some organizations, partnership was indeed something more akin to the business definition of partnership, where there was a more up front, well defined, element of shared risk and reward:

> Basically they (the vendor) are rewarded on financial targets, if they beat them we share the rewards 50:50. If they say they will provide that service for the year for $X and they manage to knock $500,000 off $X that's $250,000 to them and for us. There are also quality targets, measured through customer satisfaction surveys, if it reaches particular points this triggers additional reward for them, and again if it falls below those points it gives a reduction in the base margin. They have a very low base margin, the majority of their remuneration is made up on the risk reward calculation. (IT manager, Oil company)

Sometimes even policy making was shared with the vendor:

> We manage policy through a particular board which has representatives from each of the partners on it. We retain the right to set IT policy but generally will formulate it in collaboration with our partners through this particular board, which is valuable, you can get some good external views on what's sensible to consider achieving and what isn't sensible. (Contract manager, Oil exploration company)

For a very few the concept of partnership extended beyond incentives and embraced full risk reward arrangements and joint participation in potential business making ventures:

> We have got a lot of data models that we built of our business, and which they (the vendor) confirm are quite good so they are putting together a marketing package to sell them.

... They (the vendors) are (currently) trying to sell something to a Council, they know we have got spare space in our warehouse offices, can they look at it because they might be able to let it for us. And I thought well that's good because that just shows they have got to know our business, they have understood the distribution centre, and if I pick up a hundred grand a year like that then that partnership has yielded something. (Logistics director, Retail company)

The above examples of business partnership were relatively rare and restricted to the private sector. There were no examples of this business concept of partnership in the public sector, indeed we found a degree of skepticism as to its possibility:

The only real partnership is if you share the company profits or losses,.... It's very difficult to do this in the public sector because you haven't got the freedom to make offers like that and you are getting into a whole lot of unconventional finance arrangements. So I would be very surprised if anyone really can (have strategic partnerships) in the public sector, although rules on joint ventures are opening up a little. (IT manager, public sector organization)

A contractual and relationship framework

Thus there seemed to be a number of somewhat conflicting trends in outsourcing arrangements and a significant degree of misunderstanding. Firstly, as we have seen, the concept of partnership was not well understood. Secondly, we believe notions of partnership cannot be divorced from that of the type of contract. Thirdly, the preferred type of contract would seem to depend on the type of outsourcing under consideration.

In order to facilitate and explore these issues we have developed a framework that is provided in Figure 3.2. Here we plot the degree of contractual definition along the bottom on a continuum between loose and tight. A loose contract is one where only the bare bones of the service requirements are enshrined in the contract and where other elements of the contract such as what happens when circumstances change, are absent or not fully defined. A tight contract is the opposite, where all aspects of the service level required and the other elements are very specifically defined, including what is to happen in changing technical and business circumstances.

The vertical dimension in Figure 3.2 represents the context in which a specific type of outsourcing takes place. The degree of business and technical uncertainty feeds into how far the requirements of the client can be fully defined and specified. This includes the initial definition, requirements over the duration of the contract, and the requirements on termination of the contract. This is also expressed as a continuum between

Area of Concern

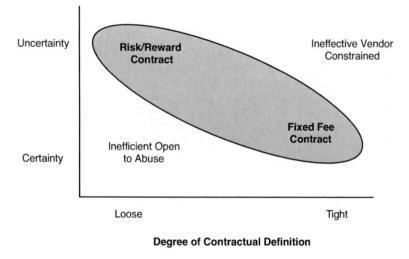

Uncertainty

Certainty

Loose   Tight

Degree of Contractual Definition

Figure 3.2   Type of Contract/Relationship

requirements that are fully known and understood, and those that are substantially unknown and unknowable. Typical of those that are known are the transaction processing/mainframe type of outsourcing that many companies have entered into. The client companies have a wealth of experience over a number of years of what is required and know for the duration of the contract how and in what ways these are likely to change. This does not always mean that the specification of the requirements is an easy task, but in principle, with the necessary effort, they are definable.

The other end of the continuum is the type of outsourcing that is difficult to specify because of the range of uncertainties both current and future. Significantly, in our 1994 research we found that 95% of respondents who outsourced IT did so on contracts of four years or less duration (the trend toward shorter contracts has continued to this day, for the reasons discussed below). A major reason related to the high degree of business and technical uncertainty organizations were experiencing and predicting. Typical of the type of activity we uncovered that fell into the "uncertainty" end of the continuum at the time were moves to client-server architectures, or open systems, the design and development of new business functions, and business process redesign activities. Elsewhere we have argued that it is unwise and risky to outsource in situations of high technical uncertainty, especially where the organization is dealing with a new and unstable technology, or an old technology being applied to a new application, or where there is a lack of in-house expertise relating to the technology in question. A buying-in of expertise to work with the in-house team is a more effective approach (Feeny *et al.*, 1993). However, it is clear that some organizations did (and still do) outsource in such circumstances, though more in situations of high business, than technical uncertainty. Those who do so effectively make explicit the risks of doing so, in order to manage them down. Where they do outsource, it is also clear that standard fixed fee type contractual arrangements are not relevant because, by definition, the full requirements cannot be specified. Such circumstances are best dealt with via a contractual arrangement that shares the risks and rewards arising from the uncertainty. There exist various intermediate positions of lesser or greater uncertainty that might involve the variety of incentive type contractual arrangements discussed earlier.

The purpose of Figure 3.2 is to illustrate that certain positions in the diagram are more likely to lead to successful and sustainable outsourcing, whilst other positions are more likely to be situations of risk or inefficiency. For example, we argue that situations of relative certainty should and can be accompanied by a very tightly defined contract for best results. The tight specification means that the contract is relatively easily and accurately priceable and that vendors can be compared. Such situations are best organized via a fixed fee type of contract, and the result is likely to be a keen and realistic contract price. To be in a loose contract in this position on the diagram exposes the client organization to unnecessary risk, i.e., where the vendor can charge extras for anything not fully specified in the contract. For the vendor not to be tempted to do this, they would have to feel that they were making enough money from the contract not to wish to jeopardize the situation. This is likely to mean that the client is not getting the best deal potentially obtainable.

In situations where the contractual arrangement is a sharing of risk and reward, i.e., in conditions of uncertainty, a tight contract is very difficult to achieve, and indeed is likely to be counter-productive. A tight contract will be making various assumptions about the future which are unlikely to be true as we are talking here about possibly fundamental and unpredictable situations, perhaps quantum change, rather than incremental developments. The essential requirement is for flexibility, and a tight contract is likely to constrain the vendor from reacting in the way that the client may wish. A tight contract can also leave the way for vendor opportunism on price, when unanticipated services are identified as required, the client is dependent on the vendor, and so the latter finds itself in a semi-monopoly position for providing these. Nevertheless, the client cannot just leave the situation open and hope that the vendor will perform in the right way simply on trust (or the type of partnership described above). It would be too risky. Therefore the risk must be minimized by the use of the sharing of risk/reward type of contractual arrangement but with a looser contract definition, in terms of service levels and penalty clauses, etc, to ensure flexibility. The incentive for the vendor to do what is best for the client is for them to share the rewards resulting from the combined vendor/client performance (or to minimize the losses), almost irrespective of the original contract definition. This is perhaps closer to the normal business definition of partnership, as discussed above and also in Chapter 4.

One interesting finding from our case research relates to transaction cost theory as proposed by Williamson (1975). He suggests that where a transaction is recurrent and involves both specific and idiosyncratic assets and activities, then the most appropriate mechanism, other things being equal, is a relational contract with an external provider. With Lacity and Hirschheim (1993), however, we found that the IT outsourcing cases where relational contracts had been operating for several years were regarded by client participants as failures rather than successes. There tended to be two more effective responses where clients were contracting for mixed assets/activities on a recurrent basis. One was to develop comprehensive, detailed performance measures for everything possible in the contract, then leave the residue to be the subject of a relational form of contracting. We can call this, in Williamson's language, a neo-classical contract with relational aspects. A critical aspect here was that, in tandem with such contracts, client companies also sought to retain leverage over the vendor by non-contractual means, for example keeping the vendor sharp by operating a multi-vendor site, or the promise of further work if the contract went well.

The second response also involved detailed measurement and monitoring of the vendor, together with risk/reward deals for both elements that could be specified and for those that were difficult to specify, but where the financial gain achieved could be recognized and shared on a pre-agreed basis. From this perspective, it may well be that the relational type of contract, at least in its pure form, is particularly inappropriate in IT outsourcing (see also on this topic Lacity and Willcocks, 2001). Our evidence is that the expectations engendered by the rhetoric of partnership, and by good personal relations established with vendors in the early "honeymoon" period of a contract or when things are going well, need to be underpinned by neo-classical contracts and risk-reward deals in order to make those relationships binding (see also Chapter 10 and Lacity and Willcocks, 2009).

Conclusion

This chapter shows the variety of approaches and perceptions that exist concerning contractual and vendor relationship issues, and we conclude that there was (and still is) much misunderstanding, particularly in relation to the concept of partnership. It is suggested that a great deal of serious thought concerning partnership is required by organizations entering into outsourcing deals, but that, although, at the time of our original study, there was an identified trend to move to more tightly defined contracts, this approach may not be appropriate in all circumstances and there are situations where it may be counter-productive. Chapter 13 discusses this issue further in the light of the development of "enterprise partnerships" as forms of joint venture in business process outsourcing arrangements. But equally, a move toward a partnership relationship may not be appropriate and even dangerous where this is simply an excuse for not fully defining and specifying the contract. In each situation the type of contract is crucial and for situations of uncertainty the shared risk/reward contract may be the only appropriate arrangement. These issues are explored further in the case studies of the next chapter.

References

Apte, U. (1990) "Global Outsourcing of Information Systems and Processing Services", *The Information Society*, 7, 287–303.

Apte, U. and Mason, R. (1993) Global Disaggregation of Information Intensive Services. Paper at *the Outsourcing of Information Systems Services Conference*, University of Twente, The Netherlands, May 20–22.

Auwers, T. and Deschoolmeester, D. (1993) The Dynamics of an Outsourcing Relationship: A Case in the Belgian Food Industry. Paper at *the Outsourcing of Information Systems Services Conference*, University of Twente, The Netherlands, May 20–22.

Buck-Lew, M. (1992) "To Outsource Or Not?", *International Journal of Information Management*, 12, 3–20.

Clark, T. and Zmud, R. (1993) The Outsourcing Decision Structure: A Dynamic Modelling Approach. Paper at *the Outsourcing of Information Systems Services Conference*, University of Twente, The Netherlands, May 20–22.

Cordella, A. Willcocks, L. and Mola, L. (2008) ICTs, Marketization and Bureaucracy in the UK Public Sector: Critique and Reappraisal. Paper at the *Second Global Sourcing Conference*, Val D'Isere, France March.

Evans, D. (1993) "BAe Offloads 1,000 Staff in £900 Million Deal with CSC", *Computer Weekly*, November 18th, p. 1.

Feeny, D., Willcocks, L., Rands, T. and Fitzgerald, G. (1993) "Strategies for IT Management – When Outsourcing Equals Rightsourcing", Rock, S. (ed.) *Directors Guide to Outsourcing*, Institute of Directors/IBM, London.

Fitzgerald, G. and Willcocks L. (1994) Information Technology Outsourcing Practice: A UK Survey, Business Intelligence, London.

Grant, R. (1992) "The Resource-based Theory of Competitive Advantage: Implications for Strategy Formulation", *Sloan Management Review*, 33, 3, 114–135.

Griese, J. (1993) Outsourcing of Information Systems Services in Switzerland – A Status Report. Paper at *the Outsourcing of Information Systems Services Conference*, University of Twente, The Netherlands, May 20–22.

Heinzl, A. (1993) Outsourcing the Information Systems Function Within the Company – an Empirical Survey. Paper at *the Outsourcing of Information Systems Services Conference*, University of Twente, The Netherlands, May 20–22.

Henderson, J.C. (1990) "Plugging into Strategic Partnerships: The Critical IS Connection", *Sloan Management Review*, Spring, 7–18.

Huber, R. (1993) "How Continental Bank Outsourced its Crown Jewels", *Harvard Business Review*, January – February, 121–129.

Kern, T. and Willcocks, L. (2001) *The Relationship Advantage: Information Technologies, Sourcing and Management*, Oxford University Press, Oxford.

Kern, T., Willcocks, L. and Van Heck, E. (2002) "The Winner's Curse in IT Outsourcing: Strategies for Avoiding Relational Trauma", *California Management Review*, 44, 2, 47–69.

Klepper, R. (1993). Efficient Outsourcing Relationships. Paper at *the Outsourcing of Information Systems Services Conference*, University of Twente, The Netherlands, May 20–22.

Lacity, M. and Hirschheim, R. (1992) The Information Systems Outsourcing Bandwagon – Look Before You Leap. *Paper at the OXIIM/PA Conference*, Templeton College, Oxford.

Lacity, M. and Hirschheim, R. (1993) *Information Systems Outsourcing*, Wiley, Chichester.

Lacity, M. and Willcocks, L. (2001) *Global Information Technology Outsourcing: Search for Business Advantage*, Wiley, Chichester.

Lacity, M. and Willcocks, L. (2009) *Information Systems and Outsourcing: Studies in Theory and Practice*, Palgrave, London.

Loh, L. and Venkatraman, N. (1992a) Diffusion of Information Technology Outsourcing: Influence Sources and the Kodak Effect. *CISR Working Paper No. 245*, October, Massachusetts Institute of Technology, Cambridge, USA.

Loh, L. and Venkatraman, N. (1992b) "Determinants of Information Technology Outsourcing: A Cross Sectional Analysis", *Journal of Management Information Systems*, 9,1, 7–24.

Loh, L. and Venkatraman, N. (1992c) Stock Market Reactions to Information Technology Outsourcing: An Event Study. *Working Paper No. 3499–92BPS, Massachusetts Institute of Technology*, Cambridge, USA.

Mintzberg, H. (1979) "An Emerging Strategy of 'Direct' Research", *Administrative Science Quarterly*, 24, 4, 582–589.

Moad, J. (1993) Inside an Outsourcing Deal. Datamation, 15 February, pp. 20–27.

Quinn, J. (1992) "The Intelligent Enterprise: A New Paradigm", *Academy of Management Executive*, 6, 4, 44–63.

Saaksjarvi, M. (1993) Outsourcing of Information Systems: Matching Organizational Forms and Organizational Roles. Paper at *the Outsourcing of Information Systems Services Conference*, University of Twente, The Netherlands, May 20–22.

Willcocks, L. (1994) "Managing Information Systems in UK Public Administration: Issues and Prospects", *Public Administration*, 72, 1, 13–32.

Willcocks, L. and Craig, A. (2007) *The Outsourcing Enterprise 4 – Building Retained Core Capabilities*, Logica, London.

Willcocks, L. and Fitzgerald, G. (1993) "Market as Opportunity? Case Studies in Outsourcing Information Technology and Services", *Journal of Strategic Information Systems*, 2, 3, 223–242.

Willcocks, L. and Fitzgerald, G. (1994) *A Business Guide to Outsourcing IT: A Study of European Best Practice in the Selection, Management and Use of External IT Services*, Business Intelligence, London.

Willcocks, L. and Lacity, M. (2006) *Global Sourcing of Business and IT Services*, Palgrave, London.

Willcocks, L. and Lacity, M. (eds) (2009) *Research Studies in Information Technology Outsourcing: Perspectives, Practices and Globalization*, Sage, London, Three volumes.

Williamson, O. (1975) *Markets and Hierarchies*, Free Press, New York.

4

Cooperative Partnerships and IT Outsourcing: From Contractual Obligation to Strategic Alliance?

Leslie Willcocks and Chong Choi

Introduction

This chapter has two primary purposes. The first is to think through the concept of cooperation and its relevance for strategic alliances. The second is to analyze the potential role of information technology in such alliances. Specifically in the latter we focus on examples of "total" IT outsourcing – often cited as forms of "strategic alliance" – to examine the structure of cooperation, the relationships formed, how structure and relationships evolve, and the degree to which they might be sustainable. Here, as in all our chapters, "total" IT outsourcing is taken to be where 80% or more of an organization's IT budget is spent on third party management of IT assets, people and/or activities to required/agreed results (Lacity and Willcocks, 1998). In the mid-1990s, when an earlier version of this chapter was published, the topic of cooperation in strategic alliances, especially in the specific area of IT outsourcing, was relatively undeveloped in the academic management studies literature. "Undeveloped" refers to a lack of agreement on definitions of fundamental concepts; wide differences in use of terms such as "partnership", "strategic partnership" and "strategic alliance"; and a lack of academically researched case material to work through such problems, as opposed to an uncritical adoption of cases and vocabulary described in trade journals, the press, and business magazines. Subsequently the strategic alliance literature has developed immensely (for overviews see Child *et al.*, 2006; Faulkner and Campbell, 2005). However, strategic alliances remain understudied in the IT literature (exceptions include DiRomualdo and Gurbaxani, 1998; Barthélemy and Geyer, 2004). We have suggested elsewhere that this is because, when it comes to outsourcing, strategic alliances exist more at the rhetorical level than in practice (Lacity and Willcocks, 2001, 2009).

There are many extant definitions of "strategic alliance" in the literature. For the purposes of this chapter our working definition is as follows:

> Strategic alliances are about inter-organizational relationships involving voluntary, collaborative efforts of two or more firms to create and add to, if not maximize, their joint value.

This definition does not say that the collaborators display altruistic behavior, but it does assume that neither would wish the relationship to be terminated prematurely as a result of one side's dissatisfaction. There are two hidden assumptions on which the above definition is based: firstly, organizations consciously enter into relationships for explicitly formulated purposes; and secondly, there are certain determinants that actually motivate organizations to establish relations (Oliver, 1990). An underlying concept is that of partnership. This chapter will build on the discussion in the previous chapter and reveal the different senses in which this term is used amongst both practitioner and academic communities, moving from a concern on the process and quality of a relationship through to structural characteristics. In practice, most uses of the term neglect the key characteristic that in our view links it with that of strategic alliance, namely a contracted relationship in which a dominant, rather than minor, feature is that of sharing of risk and reward (see Chapter 3). A further, overriding characteristic of a strategic alliance would seem to be that the joint activity is orientated in its ends toward the external marketplace rather than focused predominantly on internal efficiencies.

Transaction costs and strategic alliances

Before exploring in more detail the concept of inter-organizational relationships one has to be aware of the other alternative forms for governing transactions, namely market-based and hierarchical or managerial modes (Ring and Van de Ven, 1992; Choi, 1994; Choi *et al.*, 1994). In the first case the competitive marketplace and classical contract law provide efficient safeguards to the parties for governing those transactions. In addition, social relationships are not important and can be largely ignored. The second scenario deals with the production of wealth or the rationing of resources among superiors and subordinates. Power and control issues are relevant in this situation.

Transaction cost theory has been usefully employed elsewhere for examining IT outsourcing arrangements (see for example Beath, 1987; Klepper, 1993; Lacity and Hirschheim, 1993; Lacity and Willcocks, 2009). However, based on the definition of inter-organizational relationships that the chapter adopts, it appears inappropriate to try and apply the transaction cost perspective, as represented in for example Williamson (1975, 1985), to the type of inter-organizational relationships we wish to study. One may also point out that a review of the very wide literature on the subject reveals at least two main limitations of transaction cost theory as applied to inter-organizational relationships, namely:

- a focus on cost minimization of the focal company which neglects the interdependent relationship between exchange partners in their effort of value maximization; and
- a focus on the structural features of the exchange act that neglects significant processual issues.

For examples of critical reviews see Blois (1990), Dietrich (1994), Lacity and Willcocks (2009) and Masten (1994).

Alliances and inter-oganizational relationships

Before attempting to analyze the particular stages of an inter-organizational relationship in strategic alliances, let us cast some light on the reasons for, and contingencies of, relationship formation. Oliver (1990) usefully argues that there are six determinants, namely necessity, asymmetry, reciprocity, efficiency, stability, and legitimacy.

1) **Necessity** – an organization often establishes relationships with other organizations in order to meet legal or regulatory requirements. These relationships can be voluntary (which represent the pivotal point of our discussion) or mandatory (i.e., hierarchies).
2) **Asymmetry** – as a result of the gap between the amount of information possessed by various organizations, a need or wish for control will occur accompanied by the reluctance of the other firms/organizations to relinquish control. This is a strong motivator in organizational decisions in favor of interaction.
3) **Reciprocity** – organizations might consider that cooperation and collaboration will be more appropriate than dominance, control and competition. In this case, they will seek harmony, balance, equity and mutual support as a means for achieving shared or complementary goals and maximizing joint value.
4) **Efficiency** – organizations might establish relationships with other organizations in their pursuit for improving their internal input/output ratio (in Williamson's terms, in order to economize on the cost of transaction).
5) **Stability** – the complexity and uncertainty of the external environment drive organizations into inter-organizational relationships which are supposed to serve as coping strategies to forestall, forecast and absorb uncertainty. In more detail, uncertainty can refer to either a future state of nature or to the parties' ability to rely on trust as a counter to the

problem of adverse selection and moral hazard. This has hidden implications for the type of trust parties will chose to rely upon. A theorization on trust will be offered in the fourth section of this chapter.

6) **Legitimacy** – inter-organizational relationships can be the result of a firm's desire for an increase in their legitimacy and for the demonstration or improvement of their reputations.

Other authors talk about further contingencies. Equity, for example is defined as a process in which individuals seek to reconcile their self interests with the need to maintain social relationships (Blau, 1964; Homans, 1961). Equity goes beyond reciprocity, since equivalence of benefits amongst parties includes also sociological indebtedness. Scott (1987) argues that potential variations from equity and fair dealing tend to be limited by cultural or institutionalized norms of acceptable behavior in organization and/or society.

A further dimension here is what organizations wish to cooperate on. Krubasik and Lautenschlager (1993) are useful here in categorizing types of cooperation. These range from merger/acquisition to core business joint venture, sales joint venture, production joint venture, product swap, production licence, technology alliance, development licence. Typical objectives may be to develop new product markets, share up-stream risks or development costs, leapfrog product technology, increase capacity utilization, exploit economies of scale, fill a product-line gap, or penetrate a new geographic market. While this list is hardly exhaustive it is interesting to note how few IT outsourcing agreements, in their essentials, could be read into these categories. Further dimensions of a "strategic alliance" as mentioned by Lorange and Roos (1992), include interdependence and degree of vertical integration. Again, to this day, few IT outsourcing deals, even of the "total" type, would register highly on these variables (Lacity and Willcocks, 2009).

Cooperation

A review of the literature suggests that little scholarly attention has been given to the study of the processual aspects of inter-organizational relationships. This has been rectified in recent years (see for example Child *et al.*, 2006; Kern and Willcocks, 2001). Ring and Van de Ven (1994) argue that knowing the developmental processes in relationships has an impact on three major aspects. Thus, processes include and influence:

- the way agents negotiate, execute and modify the characteristics and terms of the relationship;
- their motivation to continue or terminate a relation;
- the means by which they settle conflicts.

We have so far emphasized business strategy aspects of cooperation. Let us now try to bring in organizational behavior aspects in order to enhance the understanding of organizational relationship from a processual viewpoint. The importance of these aspects is paramount since these relationships emerge, develop and terminate over time as a consequence of individual activities. Ring and Van de Ven (1994) and Choi (1994) argue that cooperative inter-organizational relationships are mechanisms for collective action, which are continually shaped and restructured by actors and by symbolic interpretations by and of the parties involved.

We shall now attempt to explore the organizational behavior aspects of the relationships. Cooperation require that the two parties can make congruent choices. People will make commitments to engage in uncertain and ambiguous courses of action only if they believe that terms are congruent and will be enforceable. Motivation theory gives us a potential explanation for why social actors engage in relationships. Turner (1987) argues that identity and inclusion are fundamental forces that motivate them. On the one hand, social actors can identify themselves better with respect to others and on the other hand, they need to feel included in a potential relationship. Sense-making (Weick, 1979) is the process by which organizational participants/social actors come to understand the potential for transacting with others by clarifying, reshaping, negotiating, and enacting their own identity.

In the "**commitment stage**" the parties reach an agreement on the rules that will be guiding their future relationship. The psychological contract is now backed up by a formal contract which spells out clearly in written form the terms of the relationship. Over time this instrumental transaction will become a socially embedded relationship through an institutionalization process. In fact, as a result of socialization, the relation will be infused with norms and values that permit its reproduction beyond the immediate tenure of its founders (Berger and Luckmann, 1966). Institutions are seen to impact on interactions between individuals or firms, transforming them into more predictable endeavors as a result of structuring incentives into human exchanges (whether intellectual, political, social or economic). In other words, institutions are socially constructed constraints on transactions and interactions between individuals and firms. This is especially the case in Asian countries and corporations, as analyzed by Choi and Wright (1994). There are also cultural differences towards the sharing of information, such as that of intellectual property. Asian cultures can believe that "copying" something or someone is a sign of respect, a stark contrast to the Anglo-Saxon societies where intellectual property rights are severely enforced (Choi, 1994).

Formal and psychological contracts often mirror each other and ideally they should support each other. The necessity for formal contracts is supported by three factors (Ring and Van de Ven, 1994):

- psychological contracts get established firstly at the individual level; however, cooperative relationships between firms imply psychological contracts that are more widely organizationally imbedded;

- these relationships require some sort of documentation in order for them to be recognized beyond the time span of the individuals who negotiated the relationship;
- the process of institutionalization can often transform informal relationships into habits and routines that are very resistant to change.

It is both the formal and relational aspects enunciated above that feed into three critical features and stages of any cooperative venture: cooperation as we conceive it here requires negotiation, enforcement and maintenance of the relationship.

Organizational culture

A major dilemma facing a strategic alliance relates to the cultural compatibility of the constituent organizations. For the case of IT outsourcing this issue is worked through in more detail in the Philips-Origin case below. In the more general strategic alliance literature the issues have received attention at the level of national, industry and organizational cultural differences amongst allies. Over the last three decades two trends can be identified in the literature, one highlighting the differences between cultures and one focusing on similarities. On the one hand, it is argued that cultural differences can be so critical and radical that they inhibit the process of synthesizing. Two authors trying to make this point over the years, mainly in looking at cultures at the societal level, have been Hofstede (1980), and Trompenaars (1993). The measures of difference between societies vary with author but there are apparently crucial differences in the way nations do business and respond to strategic challenges. However, theories of culture that suggest that management practice and discourse developed in one country will not operate in another (e.g., Hofstede, 1980; Haggerty, 1990; Waxler and Higginson, 1990) or theories that suggest that every country has an inertial culture (e.g., Trompenaars, 1993) have tended to be questioned, not least on methodological grounds (Child *et al.*, 2006). At the same time, such cultural differences have also been found in extreme form within specific industries and individual organizations. As one example, this has been demonstrated within the rapid changes in the multi-media industries. Multi-media industries have the additional complication of a working environment that combines the creative, or "arts" oriented managers along with the more business, or practical driven managers (Choi and Hilton, 1995).

In addition, we are told that national cultural differences militate against communication and best-practice sharing, and we should search for and highlight the covert differences between countries in order to ensure that managers get accustomed to them through appropriate training. On the other hand, a further approach highlights the similarities that exist between nations and the possibility of synthesizing the differences. This trend regards national differences as opportunities, not threats and such differences are by no means impermeable or indecipherable. Therefore they can be emulated, imitated and imported as cross-cultural competencies that will work in any environment. From this line of thinking emerges the notion of corporate allies having not similar, but, more importantly, distinctive and complementary cultures and competencies, In this context, organizations will be able to cooperate successfully which each other, and their joint effort to manage diversity will result in the attainment of all their strategic goals.

Collaborating to compete: towards strategic IT partnerships?

This brief review highlights dimensions of cooperation taken from the strategic management and organizational behavior literature. A major premise of much of the late 1980s research into organizational networks and alliances has been that the Porter (1980, 1985), "Anglo-Saxon" model of competition is either outmoded, or at best one-sided, and that cooperating/collaborating to compete has become a fundamental, not a marginal way forward in many economic sectors (Child *et al.*, 2006; Huber, 1993; Pralahad and Hamel, 1991; Quinn, 1992). In fact since the 1990s there has been in the modern organization as well as in the academic literature a major focus on two developing aspects: one is the notion of core competence, and the development of a core-periphery model of organizing and managing; the second and related issue is that of the possibilities for and dimensions of cooperation. The case of IT outsourcing can be read easily into these two central concerns (Willcocks and Craig, 2009).

Most long-term total IT outsourcing deals are almost automatically ascribed the title "strategic alliance" or "strategic partnership". This is certainly the case in the USA in the 1989 Eastman Kodak outsourcing deals for example, and in other subsequent high profile deals as at Continental and First Fidelity banks, and at General Dynamics. As we discovered in Chapter 3, a 1994 survey found some 7% of IT outsourcing deals labelled by the participants as "strategic alliances", possibly reflecting how few "total" IT outsourcing deals there were in the UK at that time. However, it has often been difficult to read into the US and European cases we have studied over the years the dimensions and characteristics of cooperation and alliance detailed in literatures outside the information technology/management fields. One of the few papers within information systems studies to attempt to delineate the dimensions of what is called "strategic partnership" has been that of Henderson (1990). Here, based on respondent perceptions and experiences, a model of the determinants of successful IS partnership is developed. Briefly, the model suggests that predisposition, commitment and mutual benefits are three determining factors in the environment in which the partnership functions. Three further determinants of success feed into the day-to-day management of the partnership, namely shared knowledge, distinctive competency and resources and organizational linkage. The model is persuasive and comprehensive, matches with many of the case study experiences of other researchers, and matches with many of the intentions and comments addressed in the three case studies below.

However, based on recent research, several comments need to be made about Henderson's work:

1. The paper underplays the role of the contract and of measurement in influencing practice. Willcocks and Fitzgerald (1994), in looking at 226 contracts and a further 30 case studies, found the contract to be a critical foundation stone for all subsequent relationships whether the organization was selectively or totally outsourcing (see also Chapter 3). The experiences of respondents also suggested that partnership concepts could not substitute for detailed measurement and monitoring of vendor performance. In practice, contract and measurement arrangements influenced greatly the quality of the relationship. Relationships developed over time and could not be assumed to be in place or that they would develop into the type of partnership described by Henderson unless there was a motivating contract and measurement framework also in place.
2. Against the weight of Henderson's framework, in practice, in IT outsourcing situations, organizations find it difficult to build mutual as opposed to asymmetric dependence on distinctive competency and resources of the vendor (see Kern and Willcocks, 2001; Lacity and Hirschheim, 1993 and Willcocks and Fitzgerald, 1994 for case examples).
3. This may well be one reason why Henderson himself admits that building strategic partnerships involves "significant" costs, difficulty and effort.
4. While Henderson records the importance of shared risk in partnership arrangements for IT outsourcing, his paper tends to downplay the criticality of structured risk-reward arrangements, as found in the British Home Stores, BP Exploration and Philips-Origin cases described below.
5. Henderson's respondents stressed the importance of shared goals. The strategic alliance literature is more sophisticated, and perhaps more realistic in talking also of complementary goals, or a common understanding of what the goals of each participant are.
6. The "strategic partnership" framework understates the influence of external factors not only on why such partnership type arrangements are formed, but also on their subsequent evolution. External business pressures, for example, clearly and heavily influenced the cooperative arrangements in the three case studies described below.

These points, together with the earlier discussion on cooperation and strategic alliances, would suggest that a revised model for "strategic partnerships" would be needed to make sense of why such IT outsourcing partnerships form, how they evolve and whether the participants experience success and failure. We now explore the "alliance/partnership" dimensions of three cases of total IT outsourcing, in order to provide an empirical base for the discussion so far. The cases have been selectively developed from work initiated in Willcocks and Fitzgerald (1993, 1994), and provide important learning for organizations looking to undertake close partnering relationships with ITO and BPO vendors.

Case 1 – British Home Stores and CSC 1993–2003

In 1993 British Home Stores signed an IT outsourcing deal for ten years that would cost BHS approximately £10 million a year. Expected savings were a minimum of £33 million. CSC took over the data processing centres, computers and some 120 IT staff. The vendor became responsible for management of computerized cash registers, electronic information to suppliers, PCs, the data network, management and accounting systems. The stated aim was to:

> ally the company with a world class computer group capable of developing the most advanced technology...it is not about saving a few bob on the IT in the short term, it is about long-term commitment. (Logistics Director, quoted in Willcocks and Fitzgerald, 1994)

Business pressures and a core competence focus helped to explain the move to total IT outsourcing. In 1989 this company was heading for a financial loss and was deemed to have lost strategic direction. The business formula that had proved successful in the 1970s and 80s was no longer proving effective. A new chief executive was appointed to turn the company around. He put into effect a threefold strategy. Firstly, he removed levels in the hierarchy; secondly, he decentralized the organization; and thirdly, and in this context most importantly, he focused on the core competencies or skills of the business. These core skills were identified as essentially buying and selling, and from this analysis the philosophy of outsourcing was developed. The argument put forward was that the core activities have to be world class and that the organization must strive to achieve this. You also need world class support, i.e. non-core activities, but that this is difficult, if not impossible to achieve in-house. This is because you need to use people who are working in the forefront, or the core, of that industry, and that, by definition, your people are not in the forefront because it is a non-core activity.

In relation to IT, the feeling of senior management was that IT was performing reasonably well in an operational sense but not really delivering its potential for the business:

> Well it fitted into the philosophy but I wouldn't have done it if I didn't think I was going to get a better service by it. What I actually feel about

our IT is that we have never really leveraged what is a pretty good platform. We had EPOS 10 ten years ago and we have just replaced it. The
actual operation of the IT works very well but to be frank it needed
shaking up. (Logistics Director)

The selected vendor was the one that was felt to best understand the philosophy and objectives of the company, especially in the area of development. The ones that treated it as basically a large data center deal with
a few extras were felt to have misunderstood the companies real
requirements:

... they (one of the vendors) just really didn't grasp the bit about partnership and understanding the culture stuff... They just didn't listen to
what we had told them... They talked all the partnership stuff but they
didn't behave as if it was important... and that irritated me intensely.
(Company respondent)

The selection was made on the basis of a compatible partner as well as competence. The company was very keen to enter a true partnership with their
vendor:

I mean essentially we believe, and they do too, that you are better
working together to make the profit pile bigger rather than just arguing
over the thing. (Company respondent)

The notion of partnership based on sharing of risks and rewards sense is
encapsulated in two developments:

They (the vendors) are trying to sell some space in our warehouse
...that just shows they understand us, and if I pick up a hundred grand
a year like that then that partnership has yielded something...we have
got a lot of data models...so they (the vendor) are putting together a
marketing package to sell them. (Company respondent)

Almost all the details of the company's performance requirements in IT
had already been defined in detail over the previous three years, especially
the key requirements of their stores and for buying and merchandising.
This was felt to be an essential pre-requisite. A series of hard negotiations
were completed and the contract agreed and drawn up with help from
outside legal specialists, the in-house legal activities having already been
outsourced. The contract was a long one, 11 years, and obviously over this
period needed to be flexible. There were some penalty clauses for failure to
meet service levels but there were also benefit clauses which trigger extra
payments if they beat service levels significantly. There were guarantees

of certain levels of spend in the area of systems development, the level of which declines over the period of the contract. If more people were required this could be increased provided it was planned, i.e., six months notice, otherwise extra people were charged at market rates. The planned rate was very much cheaper but this provided for flexibility and was an incentive for good planning. The company felt that pre-existing outsourcing experiences within the organization had helped to smooth the way for IT outsourcing. It enabled them to understand the importance of putting the effort into building the contract and getting it right. It gave them the confidence to go for a long contract and seek a partnership rather than base everything on price considerations.

Case 2 – BP Exploration: multiple alliances 1993–98

By the late 1980s, through business pressures, senior management in BP and BP Exploration identified the need to greatly reduce costs and radically change both organization and performance. As in the previous case, core competence notions were uppermost in senior management minds. This connected again with outsourcing non-core IT and non-IT activities:

> ... for us to remain, and in fact become an even stronger player in the exploration production market in the next 10 years, we are going to need the skills of not just an in-house traditional organisation, but we need to move towards, what we would probably call, a constellation of partners. (Contract manager, BPE)

> Failure to outsource our commodity IT will permanently impair the future competitiveness of our business. (John Browne, MD/CE of BPE)

Closely allied to this general strategy was that the company also faced a change in its core business from a relatively narrow focus that existed from the mid-70s through to the 1990s, to a much more diversified production company. They now required a presence in a number of areas they were not previously identified with, and these were areas in which they did not really have the necessary in-house experience and skills. They could, of course, have attempted to develop them but the feeling was that a better solution was to identify partnerships with organizations that had the relevant experience and skills and work together. An example from the IT area of this concept was in the field of Wide Area Networking (WAN) where the company felt they were lacking but nevertheless identified it as a key strategic requirement:

> ... the identification of a partner who could assist us in the application of telecommunications from quite immature telecoms infrastructures, is

pretty key to us. That partner could add a lot of value to us in terms of cost efficiency, improvements in service, in the traditional telecoms world, but also could be a significant partner to us in the new areas we are seeking to exploit. (Contract manager, BPE)

BP Exploration sought a consortium of outsourcing partners to handle their IT. At the end of 1992 they identified three major partners and signed five-year contracts worth a total of roughly $35 million per year. All the partners were identified as capable of covering the company's requirements globally, which was identified as an important criteria. One partner was to handle the data center operations, etc., the second was to develop and innovate in client server type systems, and the third was for telecommunications and WANs. They concluded that they needed different partners for different activities requiring differing skills, but all with the ability to work together so eliminating the "cracks" that had caused such problems earlier. They wanted them to work together as a kind of consortium to present a united interface to the company, and deal with any issues amongst themselves, minimizing the companies involvement. Part of the selection procedure was that the vendors get together and agree to this and establish how they would achieve it. The key to this was partnership not only between the client and the vendor but also between the vendors themselves. This was quite a challenge for the vendors involved, who in other situations were competitors. It took a great deal of arranging and negotiating, and took longer than the company originally expected but in the end the company was satisfied. The objective was not to simply reduce costs but to put the whole of the IT in the company on a different and more effective footing:

> We were looking for those partners not just to save us some money, that's not really been the dominant feature. It's important that they add value with their skills, and it is the sharing of risks and rewards that will help to achieve this. I think if you pursue outsourcing purely and simply as a short term cost saving measure, you are going to be disappointed. (George Fish, BPX)

The partnership extended to IT policy which was managed through a particular board which had representatives from each vendor. Generally policy was set in collaboration. Some further sense of the practical control and practice underpinning the partnering arrangements can be gained from the following quotes:

> We put people in the vendors' organisations for months even years to help them understand our needs.... They (the in-house staff) changed from a system delivery group to a consulting group which would ques-

tion the need to have a system to begin with. They're expected to work from a global perspective. It took massive reskilling. (Larry Gahagan, Principal consultant)

Basically they are rewarded on financial targets, if they beat them we share the rewards 50-50... they have a very low base margin, most of their remuneration is made up on the risk reward calculation. (Contract manager)

We retain with our outsourcing partners an agreement about benchmarking their performance, and also a requirement for them to employ best-in-class subcontractors...if you can demonstrate through benchmarking that somebody else can do the job better, they will incorporate them as a sub-contractor. (Contract manager)

Clearly the-risk reward basis of the remuneration together with detailed monitoring were critical features of the partnership as well as mutual understanding of needs and, as found in the other two cases in fact, the retention of sufficient appropriately skilled people in-house to manage the different aspects of the outsourcing arrangements, not least vendor relations.

Case 3 – NV Philips and BSO-Origin

The case of NV Philips and its alliance with BSO, a Dutch software house, represents some similar, and some different, forms of cooperation from those exhibited in the BHS and BPX examples discussed above. In 1988 most of NV Philips IT was managed and delivered by an in-house group. A consolidation and rationalization of IT had taken place, with business systems and analysis moved into business units, and the rest of IT organized into two main sections: software development and support (SDS) and Communications and Processing (CandP). This represented a separation of the demand for IT from its supply, though IT was still managed and delivered in-house. Subsequently an alliance was sought with BSO. In April 1990 SDS and BSO formed a joint venture, with 1,000 Philips IT staff transferring to the newly formed company of BSO-Origin. NV Philips took a 15% share in BSO. In April 1991 NV Philips surrendered its 50% share in BSO-Origin but increased its shareholding in BSO to 30+%.

Philips undertook the joint venture for a number of reasons. It looked for present and future cost reductions in a difficult business climate; its internal IT customer base was too narrow, however it had no sales/marketing skills to sell IT services on the external market; it was moving to greater use of software packages internally, but wished to secure IT staff jobs; at the same time it wanted a relatively secure supply for software and support.

BSO had a number of complementary objectives. It faced severe competition in its Dutch home base, and a joint venture with NV Philips would give immediate presence in 14 countries; it also needed a lot more staff, with the capability to deal with multinational client needs.

The alliance experienced a number of early problems. The cultural mix was different, with ex-BSO staff previously working in small units in local markets, and ex-Philips staff used to a large-company, paternalistic culture operating in global markets. For ex-BSO staff the new organization meant more travel and working for an international organization; while ex-Philips staff faced challenges on deficiencies in commercial awareness and technical skills, and with working in a new structure. The joint venture implied changing skill bases and changed ways of working for both groups of employees. These proved lengthy processes, and there was resistance to mobility and difficulties in attempting to move to dealing in more customer-focused ways with clients. The existing "cell" structure of organization inherited from BSO – small units of up to 30 people – tended to inhibit communication and engendered unnecessary competition between the cells in the new environment. At the same time the organization had to compete in a highly competitive marketplace, even though it had a low profile, small budgets and no country level roles with marketing responsibilities. A further difficulty was experienced in NV Philips itself which continued to see BSO-Origin as preferred supplier/contractor, even though from 1991 there was subsequent decline in the Philips demand. NV Philips found it difficult to sustain the professionalism of in-house IT management relative to its IT supplier, and this caused some difficulties in the partnering relationship and in IT delivery.

These were early issues in the Philips-BSO-Origin alliance, and were worked through in the 1991–94 period. Philips took a further step in separating IT supply from business demand in this period by changing the status of C. and P. to a wholly owned company able to sell its services on the external market. The main reasons for this related to the imminence of downsizing and general change in hardware platforms, concern about the cost of mainframe processing, and about the stability and viability of an internal-only global communications and processing group. This form of outsourcing also created a range of emerging issues. The need for culture change on several dimensions became evident, for example a lack of "business" attitudes and disciplines, and the tendency to take Philips customers for granted. At the same time, there emerged the need to develop a sales and marketing capability. In Philips itself the separation highlighted concern about losing direct control of the global network, and raised questions about the isolation of IT people left in the business units. How would their careers develop, what succession planning was there, was there too much fragmentation of existing in-house IT expertise? At the same time there was a widespread, initial belief in the businesses that outsourcing had somehow solved the Philips IT management problem, that is it was up to Philips C. and P. services to look after those. A further emerging issue in the 1992–94 period was the difficulty, felt in more extreme form in the case of C. and P. than BSO-Origin, of low profile and inexperience in the marketplace. By 1994 much of the work was still with the Philips host company. In fact, faced with a highly competitive marketplace, and a move amongst suppliers for offering wider service levels, and the need for size in achieving this, one emerging possibility could be renewed links between Origin and Philips Communication and Processing services.

Discussion and conclusions

To start our discussion it is useful to revisit Oliver's six determinants of strategic alliance formation. In the three cases studies, necessity related not to legal or regulatory requirements but managerial judgments based on business pressures in highly competitive environments. A major effect here related to Oliver's fourth determinant, namely the need for internal efficiencies. Following this line further, a major determinant in all three cases was cost control/reduction. Elements of asymmetry also exist in the three cases, though not on information holding, but in terms of resources available within the cooperating parties, and what client companies identify as the resources they need to retain for future operations, and what they can get from third parties. A major element in achieving this in total outsourcing situations is the achievement of stability, and one can see in the case studies powerful forces at work to push vendor-client relations in the "strategic partnership" direction, though it is probable over time that the power balance shifts in favor of the vendor, unless client organizations maintain countervailing leverage to support the basis of the partnership (Lacity and Willcocks, 2001). On this point, it is interesting to note that, as described, all three case studies represent organizations at early stages of their partnering arrangements and that Symons (1994) and Lacity and Hirschheim (1993) both note from their case work that long-term deals of the total outsourcing type have tended to deteriorate after five years in their partnering dimensions. Certainly this was found in the BHS-CSC case in the later 1990s. In subsequent work we also found the BPX multiple partnering arrangements needing a lot of refereeing by the internal function, and suppliers rarely shared learning and best practices with each other (Kern and Willcocks, 2001).

The findings of Willcocks and Fitzgerald (1994) support the case for providing a detailed contract and measurement base to the outsourcing relationship in such deals; in practice this can be seen operating in both the BHS and BP Exploration cases. The other dimension emerging from the cases is shared risk-reward structured into the fundamentals of the relationship. This is less of a characteristic in the BHS-CSC and Philips-PCandPS examples, but can be clearly observed in the BPX-multiple vendor arrangements, and also in the joint ownership of BSO-Origin by Philips and BSO.

From our review, the Henderson (1990) model would seem to be a good starting place for understanding the basis by which "total" IT outsourcing relationships can be formed and developed. However, we have already noted a number of features of the framework that further research and our case studies suggest need to be addressed if the "strategic partnerships" that Henderson refers to are to evolve and be sustained. What often compromises such partnership arrangements in practice is asymmetrical resources, dependence, and power relations developing over time in favor of the vendor. The mutual dependence element in such partnerships, and indeed strategic alliances would seem to be fundamental. It is important to note that selective IT outsourcing cases are rarely referred to in "strategic partnership" terms, and yet often total outsourcing cases have very much the same characteristics, except for an even greater reliance on the vendor, who holds the resources, and there are very high costs attached to reversing the decision. It may well be that as far as IT is concerned a characteristic of strategic alliance may be where two or more organizations share the use of IT as part of their ongoing businesses, rather than their being a vendor who provides IT services for clients, that is there is a much greater interdependence in terms of sharing and using IT resources in prime areas of their businesses. In this respect a further productive area for investigating strategic alliances where IT is concerned may be that of inter-organizational systems.

A further defining characteristic of strategic alliance might be where the relationship does not merely represent a contract for services which deals with the internal efficiencies of a client organization, but represents a shared development and use of IT focusing on marketplace activity. Again, this would see the risk-reward structure as being raised above the sharing of achieved cost savings on IT use, as in the BPX case, or the saving of warehouse space, as in the BHS example. It would see risk-reward as shared where the IT service or product is sold on the marketplace as a major reason for the alliance being in place. This would seem to be more the case in the BSO-Origin venture, and was developing in the PCandPS example at the time of study. The Xchanging set of cases detailed in Chapter 13 serve to continue this debate in the context of the developing market for IT-enabled business process outsourcing.

References

Barthélemy, J. and Geyer, D. (2004) "The Determinants of Total IT Outsourcing: An Empirical Investigation of French and German Firms", *The Journal of Computer Information Systems*, 44, 3, 91–98.

Beath, C. (1987) Strategies for Managing MIS Projects: A Transaction Costs Approach. *Proceedings of the Fourth International Conference on Information Systems*, December, 72–80.

Berger, P.L. and Luckmann, T. (1966) *The Social Construction of Reality*, Doubleday, New York.

Blau, P.M. (1964) *Exchange and Power in Social Life*, Wiley, New York.

Blois, K. (1990) Transaction Cost Analysis: Is It Being Used Out of Context? *Working Paper MRP/94/6*, Templeton College, Oxford University, Oxford.

Child, J., Faulkner, D. and Tallman, S. (2006) *Cooperative Strategy: Managing Alliances, Networks and Joint Ventures*, Oxford University Press, Oxford.

Choi, C.J. (1994) *Generic Cultural Competencies: Managing Co-operatively Across Cultures*, Dartmouth Publishers, London.

Choi, C.J. and Wright, N. (1994) *Achieve Business Success in Korea*, Macmillan Publishers, London.

Choi, C.J., Grint, K., Hilton, B. and Taplin, R. (1994) "Achieving Co-operation", *Journal of Interdisciplinary Economics*, 3, 190–212.

Dietrich, M. (1994) *Transaction Cost Economics and Beyond*, Routledge, London.

DiRomualdo, A. and Gurbaxani, V. (1998) "Strategic Intent for IT Outsourcing", *Sloan Management Review*, 39, 4, 67–80.

Faulkner, D. and Campbell, A. (2005) *The Oxford Handbook of Strategy*, Oxford University Press, Oxford.

Haggerty, A.G. (1990) "Foreign Cultural Awareness Stressed", *National Underwriter*, 94, 49, 21–30.

Henderson, J. (1990) "Plugging into Strategic Partnerships: The Critical IS Connection", *Sloan Management Review*, Spring, 7–18.

Hofstede, G. (1980) *Cultures Consequences: International Differences in Work-related Values*, Sage, Beverly Hills.

Homans, G. (1961) *Social Behaviour: Its Elementary Forms*, Harcourt, New York.

Huber, R. (1993) "How Continental Outsourced Its Crown Jewels", *Harvard Business Review*, Jan–Feb, 121–129.

Kern, T. and Willcocks, L. (2001) *The Relationship Advantage: Information Technology, Sourcing and Management*, Oxford University Press, Oxford.

Klepper, R. (1993) Efficient Outsourcing Relationships. *Paper at the Outsourcing of Information Systems Services Conference*, University of Twente, The Netherlands, May 20–22.

Krubasik and Lautenschlager (1993) in Bleeke, J. and Ernst, D. *et al.*, *Collaborating To Compete*, Free Press, New York.

Lacity, M. and Hirschheim, R. (1993) *Information Systems Outsourcing: Myths, Metaphors, and Realities*, Wiley, Chichester, England.

Lacity, M. and Willcocks, L. (1998) "An Empirical Investigation of Information Technology Sourcing Practices: Lessons from Experience", *MIS Quarterly*, 22, 3, September, pp. 363–408.

Lacity, M. and Willcocks, L. (2001) *Global Information Technology Outsourcing: Search For Business Advantage*, Wiley, Chichester.

Lacity, M. and Willcocks, L. (2009) *Information Systems and Outsourcing: Studies in Theory and Practice*, Palgrave, London.

Lorange, P. and Roos, J. (1992) *Strategic Alliances*, Blackwell, London.

Masten, S. (1994) Empirical Research in Transaction-cost Economics: Challenges, Progress, Directions. Paper presented at the *Conference of Transaction Cost Economics and Beyond*, Erasmus University, Rotterdam, The Netherlands, June.

Oliver, C. (1990) "Determinants of Interorganisational Relationships: Integration and Future Directions", *The Academy of Management Review*, 15, 2, 88–102.

Porter, M. (1980) *Competitive Strategy*, Free Press, New York.

Porter, M. (1985) *Competitive Advantage*, Free Press, New York.

Pralahad, C. and Hamel, G. (1991) "The Core Competence of the Corporation", *Harvard Business Review*, 63, 3, 79–91.

Quinn, J. (1992) *Intelligent Enterprise*, New York, Free Press.

Ring, P.S. and Van de Ven, A.H. (1992) "Structuring Cooperative Relationships Between Organisations", *Strategic Management Journal*, 13.

Ring, P.S. and Van de Ven, A.H. (1994) "Developmental Processes of Cooperative Interorganisational Relationships", *The Academy of Management Review*, 19, 1, 20–33.

Scott, W.R. (1987) "The Adolescence of Institutional Theory", *Administrative Science Quarterly*, 32, 3 , 218–236.

Symons, C. (1994) Reorganising IT for Business Value. *Presentation at Templeton College, Oxford*. Private correspondence.

Trompenaars, F. (1993) *Riding on the Waves of Culture: Understanding Cultural Diversity in Business*, Economist Books, London.

Turner, J. H. (1987) "Towards a Sociological Theory of Motivation", *American Sociological Review*, 52.

Waxler, R.P. and Higginson, T.J. (1990) "Leadership, Communication and Integrity in the 1990s", *Industrial Management*, 32, 4, 104–110.

Weick, W. (1979) *The Social Psychology of Organising*, Addison-Wesley, Reading MA.

Willcocks, L. and Craig, A. (2009) *The Outsourcing Enterprise 5 – Step Change: Collaborating To Innovate*, Logica, London.

Willcocks, L. and Fitzgerald, G. (1993) "Market as Opportunity? Case Studies in Outsourcing Information Technology and Services", *Journal of Strategic Information Systems*, 2, 3, 223–242.

Willcocks, L. and Fitzgerald, G. (1994) *A Business Guide to Outsourcing IT: A Study of European Best Practice in the Selection, Management and Use of External IT Services*. Business Intelligence, London.

Williamson, O.E. (1975) *Markets and Hierarchies*, Free Press, New York.

Williamson, O.E. (1985) *The Economic Institutions of Capitalism*, Free Press, New York.

5
Offshore Outsourcing: A Country Too Far?

Kuldeep Kumar and Leslie Willcocks

Introduction

The Yankee Group estimated the 1994 global IT outsourcing market as exceeding $US49.5 billion with an annual 15% growth rate. As at 1995 the US market was the biggest, estimated to exceed $US18.2 billion (Patane and Jurison, 1994). Offshore outsourcing formed a very small part of this growing outsourcing phenomenon. Its main appeal up to this date had been in the systems/software development area, and resided in four critical factors: low salaries in foreign countries, access to a larger group of trained professionals, reduced cycle time for systems development, and improved access to global markets (Ravichandran and Ahmed, 1993. For subsequent developments see also Chapters 14 and 15). As such, offshore outsourcing by this date would seem to have been mainly a response to the need to contain costs (though, according to the research by Sobol and Apte (1995), the median cost saving in 1995 needed to be 30% to make offshore out-sourcing attractive). A further factor would seem to be dissatisfaction with the quality and speed of software/systems development in the developed economies.

At this time, companies in the USA and other developed economies were increasingly shifting software/applications development to offshore sites like India, Israel, Singapore, Ireland, Mexico, China, Hungary and the Philippines (Infotech Consulting, 1992; Nidumolu and Goodman, 1993). Of course, by 2008 the offshore outsourcing of IT had become a $30 billion plus market, involved over 120 locations around the world, and the activities offshored had moved increasingly up the value chain to include call centers, business processes and knowledge process outsourcing (Oshri *et al.*, 2008). Moreover, the academic study of the phenomenon has greatly advanced along with this pattern of growth (see for example Carmel and Abbott, 2007; Lacity and Rottman, 2007; Willcocks and Lacity, 2009). However, in the mid-1990s academic studies of this phenomenon were pre-liminary in nature, either reviewing the general position or carrying out

97

exploratory surveys, for example Jones (1994). The trade press contained background detail and some brief case studies, for example Anthes (1993) and Krepchin (1993). This lack of attention belied the size and growth rate of the phenomenon. Meta Group estimated that the market for overseas programming for US companies alone exceeded $US500 million in 1993 and was growing 50% annually (Anthes, 1993). The main focus of this chapter, probably the first academic study of the rising IT offshoring phenomenon in the 1990s, will be on India as an offshore site for US companies. India's software exports grew from $US24 million in 1985 to $US350 million in 1994. Of this, nearly 59% came from on-site programming, while much of the rest came from offshore services – typically systems analysis and design, installation and testing performed at the customer's site while programming services were provided from India (Kohli, 1994; Sobol and Apte, 1995).

The mid-1990s saw the growth of the Indian software industry, represented by some major firms such as Tata Consultancy Services, InfoSys Consultants, HCL America, and Wipro Systems Limited US, together with hundreds of small entrepreneurial firms pursuing niche markets (Nidumolu and Goodman, 1993). According to several sources, these firms also had the experience and expertise to work on most platforms and software (Soota, 1994; see also Chapters 14 and 15). US companies tended to choose from several offshore outsourcing strategies. One was direct outsourcing to India, with the Indian company maintaining a small marketing and personnel base in the USA. Another was sub-contracting to a US agent of the Indian company, for example Mastech, based in Pittsburgh. Thirdly, several companies, for example IBM, set up wholly owned Indian subsidiaries. Fourthly, some companies, like Hewlett Packard, set up joint ventures or strategic alliances with Indian firms. Since then, these strategies have developed into a rich diversity of offshore practices, including the development of "best-shoring" – locating work onshore (with the client) nearshore (close to the client) and offshore (in a distant geographical location) – by many of the top six Indian firms, as we found when studying Tata Consultancy Services' relationship with its client ABNAmro bank (Oshri *et al.*, 2007).

What we did not know in detail from academic studies in the mid-1990s were: how offshore outsourcing was conducted, with what degree of success, what barriers were encountered, the degree to which offshore outsourcing was a special case, different from other types of IT outsourcing, so raising fresh issues, and challenging existing theoretical perspectives. To further understanding, we carried out a detailed longitudinal case study of a US company, Holiday Inns, outsourcing offshore to India-based CompTech Consultants. The case was selected because it moved quickly from an initial "body-shopping" on-site software development operation, to a fully fledged direct outsourcing arrangement. This chapter assesses critically the IT outsourcing literature relevant to providing insight into the case history. A description of the case then follows. The subsequent analysis of events points to important technical, economic, relationship, cultural, regulatory/ environmental and temporal issues raised by offshore outsourcing, that have proven to be perennial (see for example Carmel and Abbott, 2007). An assessment is also made of the degree to which IT use can itself offset barriers, and facilitate this form of outsourcing.

Outsourcing IT – theory and practice

In this section we review the extant theory and recorded experience on off-shore outsourcing and interweave this with a general review of six relevant areas for analysis. These are: decision factors, types of contract, economic issues, relationship building and maintenance, the role of IT as a coordinating technology, and offshore issues such as country infrastructure, culture and regulatory environment. The discussion focuses mainly on systems/ software development, which is the main subject of the case study detailed below.

Decision factors

This subject has been much developed since the mid-1990s. Reviews appear in the first volume of Willcocks and Lacity (2009), and more recent case studies appear in Chapters 14 and 15 of the present volume (see also Lacity and Rottman, 2007). By the mid-1990s Ravichandran and Ahmed (1993) had produced a useful, though not researched, decision-making framework for offshore development. In addition to the often stated advantages of lower cost, and faster, high quality software development, they argued that the circumstances were favorable for any offshore development activity when number of users, user interaction and number of organizational units in which end users are located were all low, while level of professional users was likely to be high. They also suggested that an application needs to be complex and large to merit the cost of setup time involved in communication and coordination offshore. This is only partially supported by the Unum Insurance offshore experience (Anthes, 1993). Respondents there concluded that the ideal job to be sent offshore would cost more than $US250,000, but be straightforward in scope, for example moving a legacy mainframe application to a client-server environment without re-engineering the underlying business practices. Case research into IT projects also suggests that risk increases with size and complexity. Offshore should also be considered when systems specification is highly detailed and structured, and a low number of changes to systems specification are anticipated. Notoriously, of course, the latter is difficult to predict.

Ravichandran and Ahmed (1993) also suggested a range of technological, geo-political and managerial factors to help in evaluating a specific offshore site, and point out that a multi-criteria approach sensitive to trade-offs should be used. For example, cost savings from lower programmer salaries should offset setup, communication and coordination costs, but strategic considerations, for example a shortage of domestic programmers, may make such trade-offs a moot issue. Rajkumar and Dawley (1996) endorsed much of this but added several key issues for both supplier and customer: necessity of face-to-face contact; commitment to long-term relationships; standardization of international data flows; unfamiliar technology can lead to disastrous results; the need to break down large projects into deliverables that are manageable and measurable; and contracting clearly on product definition, intellectual property protection and payment structure.

The literature on making sourcing decisions has always tended to be more developed than this (see Chapter 8. Also Willcocks and Lacity, 2009 volume 1 for a review). By the mid-1990s several frameworks had been partly developed out of the software make/buy literature (for example Apte and Mason, 1995), but were also based on empirical research. McFarlan and Nolan (1995) developed a strategic grid using two dimensions: current dependence on information and importance of sustained innovative information resource development. Outsourcing is a preferred option when the latter is low. However, the decision matrix has not proved that helpful because the sourcing presumption in each quadrant is clearly stated but then highly qualified. The authors also presume long-term outsourcing alliances as the norm. Empirical research elsewhere suggest this is incorrect for most outsourcing deals (Lacity and Willcocks, 1995, 2001, 2009; Willcocks and Fitzgerald, 1994). This caveat probably also applies to most offshore arrangements to this day except where there is a joint venture or an offshore subsidiary.

Lacity *et al.* (1996) used survey evidence and 40 US and European case studies to develop the business, technical and economic factors influencing outsourcing decisions. Outsourcing is preferred where an IT activity is a commodity, not a business differentiator; is useful but not strategic; represents a discrete set of operations rather than is highly integrated with other systems or with many business interfaces; is high in "technological maturity"; where production/labor specialization economies of scale can be achieved offsetting transaction costs incurred; where in-house IT managerial practices are lagging; and where the market can offer a better price for the service quality required. In practice trade-offs have to be made between these factors. Willcocks and Fitzgerald (1994) also pointed to a subset of influencing factors emerging from research: degree of business uncertainty, rate of technological change, availability and suitability of vendor, people and ownership of assets, in-house management capability for running the contract; and in-house human resource issues resulting from outsourcing.

These factors have relevance for offshore development decisions, and will be tested in the case study below. At this stage a particularly important factor to be clear about is that of "technological maturity". Feeny *et al.* (1996) found that systems development should proceed with a "user" focus rather than a "specialist" focus where any or all of the following conditions pertained: the technology exhibits a high rate of change in terms of function provided, technical specification and performance; the technology is established but is being used in a radically new way; and/or when the implementing organization has little prior experience of the application or technology. In such cases the prescription is to build learning in-house through user led development, teamworking and focusing on business benefits. Only in conditions of technological maturity, when the technology no longer represents a problem, and detailed, stable specifications can be provided should systems development be left to IT specialists or outsourced. Saarinen and Vepsalainen (1994) provide some further empirical support for this. The theory also represents closely what commentators and practitioners have urged ever since when making offshore outsourcing decisions (see Krepchin, 1993; Anthes, 1993; Lacity and Rottman, 2007 for case examples), and can be tested further in the case below.

Types of contract

Williamson (1975, 1979, 1985, 1991) is the most cited source in outsourcing studies for understanding contract issues. A critique appears in Lacity and Willcocks (2009). Briefly, Williamson posits three types of contract: classical, neo-classical and relational. The classical or standard contract is most appropriate for exchange of non-specific assets (e.g., a PC purchase), whether the transaction is occasional or frequent. Transaction costs are minimal because the buyer does not need to monitor the vendor. A neo-classical, highly detailed, contract is needed where asset specificity is mixed or idiosyncratic, and where the transaction is occasional. The detailed contract covers all foreseen contingencies and minimizes transaction costs and risk. For transactions that are frequent and involve assets of mixed specificity a relational contract with the vendor is suggested. A long-term relationship is sustained because both parties have incentives – a steady supply on one hand, a steady revenue for the vendor. Transaction cost theory (TCT) recommends that frequent transactions for idiosyncratic should be carried out in-house. The transaction costs of contracting tend to be prohibitive, and few economies of scale will be available to the vendor.

Many outsourcing studies assume the efficacy of TCT when applied to the IT outsourcing context (see for example Jurison, 1995; Nam *et al.*, 1995). However, in an empirical study Lacity and Willcocks (1995) found TCT less efficacious in explaining successful and less successful contracting. Only three of 33 sourcing successes and two of seven sourcing failures were readily explained by TCT, resulting in 87.5% anomalies. We found these anomalies could be explained only by appealing to ambiguities in language or by the TCT exceptions of high uncertainty, recurrent-idiosyncratic transactions or small number of suppliers raised by the special case of Information Technology outsourcing. In particular, when the IT services market was used we found neo-classical contracting the most successful form. In the context of offshore outsourcing not involving joint ventures and wholly owned subsidiaries, commentators tend to support this finding (Rajkumar and Dawley, 1996; Ravichandran and Ahmed, 1993). Respondents in cases of offshore outsourcing at Unum Life Insurance, Country Companies and Turner Broadcasting in the USA also all stressed the need for rigor in providing detailed specifications, keeping business change minimal, and maintaining tight monitoring and change control (Anthes, 1993; Krepchin, 1993). The case study provides an opportunity to explore further the applicability of TCT in a systems development outsourcing context.

Economic issues

TCT as presented by Williamson (1975) has also been widely adopted or suggested as one major perspective for examining the economics of IT outsourcing (see for example Cheon *et al.*, 1995; Jurison, 1995; Klepper, 1995; Lacity and Hirschheim, 1993; Lacity and Willcocks, 2009). In the wider economics literature the applicability of TCT has often been questioned (for example by Blois, 1994; Dietrich, 1994; Hodgson, 1994; Masten, 1994; Pitelis, 1991). In offshore outsourcing the applicability of TCT concepts of production/labor specialization economies of scale and transaction costs would seem readily apparent. Williamson argues that when the former exceed the latter then the use of the market becomes attractive. A particular issue in offshore systems development in the 1990s was the high and rising cost of US domestic software development, sometimes representing more than half of organizational IS budgets (Ravichandran and Ahmed, 1993). Moreover, software development is generally very labor intensive but with limited capital requirements. Additionally there were (and still are) large discrepancies between comparative pay of US and Indian programmers. Lower offshore production costs could offset higher transaction costs and even achieve net savings of between 30–50% compared with US-based development. Taking another route, One US firm at the time – The Travelers Corp. – set up a subsidiary in Ireland and achieved 12% savings on offshore work (Anthes, 1993).

In the domestic IT outsourcing context empirical work has questioned the Williamsonian assumption of superior production/labor specialization economies of scale pertaining to the vendor (Lacity and Hirschheim 1995; Lacity and Willcocks, 1995). The work found that even some small in-house IT installations could often compete with vendors, and that lagging in-house IT managerial practices were a greater determinant of in-house versus market cost difference. The case study provides an opportunity to investigate further the role of size of operation, managerial practices, production and transaction costs relating to in-house, domestic and offshore systems development.

Further, beyond Williamson, it enables a more detailed analysis of costs pertaining to IT sourcing decisions. Developing the work of Lacity and Hirschheim (1995), one can posit that an offshore outsourcing vendor can offer cheaper options to a US company through economies of scale on data center running, hardware and software acquisition, cost of technical expertise, research and development costs, lower opportunity costs for the client, and possible gains from financial, accounting or tax opportunities relating to the outsourcing deal. However, in theory a large in-house department has the cost advantage over a vendor in business expertise, transaction costs, shareholder costs, and marketing costs. It may also have equivalent economies of scale on data center running, hardware and software acquisition (Lacity and Hirschheim, 1993, 1995). These economics prevail to this day (Lacity and Willcocks, 2009).

Relationship building and maintenance

These elements are regarded as important in the IT outsourcing literature, and as critical in large-scale, long-term "preferred supplier" or "strategic alliance" type deals where management through detailed formal contract alone is often deemed less effective (Applegate and Montealegre, 1991; Huber, 1993; McFarlan and Nolan, 1995). A recent review of the subject appears in the second volume of Willcocks and Lacity (2009). As discussed earlier, in Chapter 4, Henderson (1990) developed a model of the determinants of successful IS partnerships suggesting that predisposition, commitment and mutual benefits must be present. Further determinants of success feed into the day-to-day management of the partnership, namely shared knowledge, mutual dependence on distinctive competency and resources, and organizational linkage.

It is useful to test the applicability of the model in an offshore outsourcing context. Willcocks and Choi (1995, and in the previous chapter) already suggested a number of modifications that can also be assessed in our offshore outsourcing case. From research by Willcocks and Fitzgerald (1994), the Henderson model would seem to underplay the central role of the contract and of measurement in influencing practice (see Chapter 4). In practice, organizations find it difficult, at least in long-term "total outsourcing" deals, to build mutual as opposed to asymmetric dependence on distinctive competency and resources of the vendor. The criticality of structured risk-reward arrangements are downplayed, as are the influence of external factors on partnership formation and evolution. The Henderson model also lacks a discussion of the staffing, skills and role implications for both vendor and client organizations for sustaining the relationship over time. Willcocks and Fitzgerald (1994) identified seven major capabilities for the client organization to develop in-house, while Feeny and Willcocks (1998) suggested nine. This raises the question as to what capabilities are required to maintain and develop the relationship in offshore outsourcing arrangements. A recent discussion of this appears in Ranganathan and Balaji (2007). Several other models might be appropriate for examining offshore outsourcing relationships. Klepper (1995) has suggested the use of the Dwyer *et al.* (1987) model for studying outsourcing relationships and their development over time. The sequential stages of relationship development are awareness, exploration, expansion and commitment. Several sub-processes are posited to influence the subsequent development or otherwise of the relationship, namely attraction, communication and bargaining, power, norms and expectations: *"These are levers that managers can use to actively manage the development of partnerships."* (Klepper, 1995). Two sets of models hardly explored in the IT outsourcing literature but that have considerable promise are provided from empirical studies in the strategic alliance literature (see Faulkner, 1995) and the industrial networks literature (for example IMP Group, 1990). In the former case a three stage model of relationship evolution is posited. An alliance needs strong motivation and external influence to form. Partners need to have complementary assets, synergies, a balance in size and strength and compatible cultures. Relationship management involves setting up and running appropriate systems – for control, dispute resolution, authority channels, divorce procedure, and information dissemination. There also need to be congruent goals and positive partner attitudes involving mutual trust, commitment and cultural sensitivity. Alliances evolve where the partners are flexible, bonded by external challenge, there is balanced, not unequal development, learning is disseminated and reviewed, and strategic advantage is balanced between the partners, as are ongoing benefits.

The IMP Group (1990) supplement this three stage framework of factors with an interaction approach. Between buyer and seller there are four elements that are exchanged and that need management: product/service exchange, information exchange, financial and social exchange. The last mentioned becomes particularly important where there exists spatial or cultural distance between the two parties – the circumstances pertaining in offshore outsourcing (IMP Group, 1990; Ravichandran and Ahmed, 1993). Over time these exchanges build up into patterns and expectations become institutionalized. Any adaptations in the elements exchanged or the process of exchange must be fully understood by both parties for the relationship to be maintained. Characteristics of the parties – in terms of technology, organizational size, structure and strategy, individuals involved, and organizational experience – also influence the relationship and process of interaction. Likewise the interaction environment, in particular the market structure, degree of dynamism and internationalization involved, position in the manufacturing channel, and social system.

Interaction also creates atmosphere, that can be defined by power/dependence, and degree of cooperation, closeness and shared expectation.

Atmosphere may also support or damage the relationship over time. The case provides an opportunity to examine the applicability of these models to the IT outsourcing context. The interaction approach is discussed in more detail in Lacity and Willcocks (2009).

IT as a coordination technology

How far can IT use itself to facilitate an IT outsourcing arrangement, and at what cost? With its inbuilt need to communicate at a distance, offshore systems development provides a particularly interesting case for examining these two questions. The IT literature has always tended to report favorably on the ability of IT to achieve coordination between remote parties speedily and at reduced cost (Bensaou, 1993; Malone *et al.*, 1987). In studying inter-organizational systems, Kumar *et al.* (1995) pointed to the possibilities of both cooperation and conflict induced through use of coordination technologies. Clemons and Row (1992) added to this picture. They sought to develop TCT analysis by suggesting that transaction costs can be decomposed into coordination costs and transaction risks. They then argued that: *"by reducing the costs and the risks of explicit coordination, IT can facilitate the development of stable, tightly coupled relationships among firms"* (p. 10). Several examples of how IT reduces transaction costs are then cited, and the theory and examples can be directly read into the offshore outsourcing arrangements. However, Clemons and Row also suggested that there may be limitations to IT's ability to reduce transaction risk. Such risks develop where one party makes a capital investment in IT which has no transferable value from the specific interaction undertaken; where there are asymmetries in information, making monitoring of performance and assignment of responsibility in integrated decisions and operations difficult; or where there is loss of resource control, including information or know-how. The latter is a particular concern in offshore arrangements, including loss of intellectual property rights and of IT know-how, especially as expertise codified in IT is much easier to duplicate and transfer than is human expertise (Rajkumar and Dawley, 1996; Sobol and Apte, 1995). At the same time IT such as electronic mail and forums, fax machines, teleconferencing, telecasting, satellite links, may well facilitate relatively easy explicit coordination (Ravichandran and Ahmed, 1993). Subsequently it has become clear that IT coordination, together with lower labor costs, have been key facilitators of the development of global outsourcing (Lacity and Rottman, 2007) These issues are pursued further in the case study below.

"Domestic versus global" issues

These represent the more obvious issues that can be explored in an offshore outsourcing case. Sources indicate a range of possible barriers to offshore development. For the mid-1990s Sobol and Apte (1995) suggested, from research in US companies, that these include: unclear government attitudes toward trans-border data flow and trade in IS services; data and verbal communications difficulty with foreign vendors; risk to intellectual property rights; time zone differences affecting working hours (though these may in fact be advantageous – see below); and cultural differences. The latter are particularly well researched in the general literature (see for example Hofstede, 1980; Trompenaars, 1993 and their subsequent work). Our Chapter 4 focused on these in the context of IT outsourcing alliances. Other sources also cite differences in laws and regulations, infrastructure problems in developing economies and political uncertainties as additional potential barriers (Carmel and Abbott, 2007; Jones, 1994; Nidumolu and Goodman, 1993; Ravichandran and Ahmed, 1993). The significance of such factors as barriers, or even as facilitators need to be assessed in the case study we detail below.

Holiday Inns: a passage to India[1]

Acquisition and the move to Atlanta

In 1992, United Kingdom based Bass plc, as a part of its ongoing strategy of diversification and expansion, acquired the Memphis, Tennessee based Holiday Inns hotel chain. Immediately after the acquisition, Bass plc decided to move Holiday Inn head offices from Memphis, Tennessee to Atlanta, Georgia. There were a number of reasons for this move. First, Atlanta's location as a central airlines hub with direct connections to most of the international and US cities provided Bass and Holiday Inn executives convenient and direct access to their world wide locations. Second, the highly developed telecommunications infrastructure in Atlanta provided Holiday Inn with a suitable technological base for developing their own world wide communication network. Third, with a vigorous business climate, large number of corporate head offices, a large business applications software industry and four world class universities, Atlanta provided a ready pool of trained business and technical talent.[2] Fourth, the availability of high quality office space in Atlanta at reasonable prices meant that appropriate office space could be acquired. Finally, Atlanta's growing reputation as a cosmopolitan, inter-

---

[1]A note on the research approach and use of pseudonyms in the case appears at the end of the chapter.
[2]The Hartsfield Airport in Atlanta was considered at the time to be the busiest airport in the US. Major international airlines fly in and out of Atlanta. It has direct connections to most major European and Pacific Rim cities. Furthermore, as a consequence of large investments by Bell South and the State Government and the location of headquarters of major international corporations such as Coca-Cola and United Parcel Service (UPS), and news services such as Turner Broadcasting (CNN), Atlanta has developed an excellent telecommunication infrastructure. Finally, the location of a number of major software houses and IS/IT based businesses has made Atlanta the business application software capital of the US.

national city meant a high quality of life for Holiday Inn's local and international executives and employees.

To house its corporate headquarters in a building befitting its image as an international corporation, Holiday Inn acquired a major property on the North Side of the city. The property – called the Ravinia – consisted of a complex of modern office buildings among a forest of tall green trees. This complex included the former Hyatt Regency Ravinia hotel which was converted into the flagship Holiday Inn Crowne Plaza Hotel. The new Holiday Inn executive offices were in the next building.

Despite, the attractiveness of the new locale, about 80% of the IT staff from Memphis decided not to relocate to Atlanta. No specific reasons for the unwillingness of this large number of people to move are available. However, it is our conjecture that despite Memphis being larger than Atlanta, the latter had a reputation as a big city (rated world's fourth best city for international business by Fortune magazine in November 14th 1994), and Memphis employees were reluctant to leave a relatively cosy smaller-city atmosphere and also face higher cost of living and real estate prices. Most of the operational staff (operators, programmers, analysts) and the senior staff (CIO and assistant vice-presidents) did not relocate to Atlanta.

Consequently, Holiday Inn hired a number of new senior and lower level IT staff. At the senior executive level, they recruited Dick Smith from Memphis-based Federal Express and appointed him as the Sr VP/CIO of Information Systems. Dick Smith brought Greg Tollander with him from Federal Express and appointed him as the Holiday Inn vice-president of technology and operations. Michael Kennedy, an executive from the Holiday Inn user community was recruited as the vice-president in-charge of applications and strategic systems. Through an appointment to the Bass plc executive committee, and in keeping with his role as the CIO, Smith was connected closely to the Bass decision-making structure. Consequently a large percentage of his time was spent in working with the Bass headquarters. At the same time he had considerable autonomy in running the Holiday Inn IT operation. Most of the day-to-day operational and tactical IT decisions were made by Mike Kennedy and Greg Tollander.

Unlike the senior and operational staff, most personnel at the middle management level did relocate from Memphis to Atlanta. Holiday Inn hired one new middle-level manager, Daniel Newton, from outside Holiday Inn. Originally, hired as the Senior Manager of Databases, in 1994 Daniel was promoted to the position of Director of Strategic Systems. The case concerns his group's experiences of outsourcing. A brief discussion of his background is provided as a context for understanding his decisions. He was recruited in 1993 from Lithonia Lighting, another Atlanta company. At Lithonia he had been a key player in the development and implementation of the innovative LightLink System. Thus he was experienced in building and implementing high profile strategic systems using advanced technologies. Prior to working at Lithonia Lighting, he had worked and studied in the United Kingdom. Daniel was originally from Sri Lanka, a fact which could have been a factor in his willingness to experiment with offshore outsourcing.

Dealing with legacy issues: 1993–Summer 1994

As indicated, the move from Memphis to Atlanta was a consequence of Holiday Inn being acquired by a UK firm – Bass plc. Moreover, 80% of the IT staff and most of the top IT management were recruited from outside immediately after the move. However, the middle management, along with the legacy systems and legacy data did move from Memphis to Tennessee. This made for a complex dynamic. While the people brought in from outside brought in new ideas and practices, they had to function within an established framework of day-to-day management practices and technology brought over from Memphis.

An analysis of the Holiday Inn data very quickly established that the usual problems of legacy data, data fragmentation, data redundancy, lack of data integration, and lack of consistency in data quality, access, and security standards also existed in the Holiday Inn data files. As a result of this analysis, Daniel initiated a new Database Re-Engineering project. The objective of this project was to develop an enterprise data model for Holiday Inn World-Wide. Based upon this data model the existing corporate data would be converted to a relational (DB2) database. This would be followed by modification/rewriting of all legacy software interfacing with the relational database. Given the strategic and operational importance of data to Holiday Inn, Daniel also set a very high ambition level for the project by establishing a goal of completing the re-engineering in a one year timeframe. It is our conjecture that this ambitious timeframe was partly motivated by Daniel's desire to prove himself in a new job.

However, it should be recognized that the project did not involve any re-engineering of the underlying business practices. It was conceived primarily as a technical conversion project in which existing files and databases were to be redesigned and implemented as an integrated relational database. Daniel developed a database re-engineering strategy in which data-models were to be reverse engineered from existing file and database definitions, fragmented data views integrated, and the relational databases forward engineered from these integrated data models. In addition, all legacy programs accessing these files were to be identified, and their data interfaces modified to accommodate the move to relational databases.

Very soon it became clear that except for Daniel and a few people in his group, the IT department at Holiday Inn had neither expertise nor headcount to undertake a project of this magnitude. The high labor turnover due to the move had left Holiday Inn critically short-handed. Furthermore, data modeling and database redesign skills crucial to the project were lacking in the remaining in-house staff.

It was apparent that creative strategies were needed to cope with this lack of expertise and manpower and the ambitious self-imposed deadline. A two-part strategy was developed to meet these challenges. First, a set of computer-aided software engineering (CASE) tools were acquired to support the database re-engineering methodology. Originally Holiday Inn had acquired the Bachmann reverse engineering tool. However, the limited scope of the Bachmann tool (it did not address the software re-engineering component of the project), coupled with the perceived high learning curve resulted in it being supplanted by the LBMS CASE tool. The LBMS CASE tool was based upon the SSADM development methodology developed by LBMS. At that time the SSADM was considered to be the *de facto* development standard in the UK data processing industry. It is likely that Daniel's UK based training and experience, and the parent company Bass plc's UK roots had some influence on this decision.

The second part of the strategy was to rely on outside consulting firms to supply the necessary expertise and labor. Accordingly, after a short search, two firms, California based Codd and Date Associates, and Bangalore India-based CompTech were engaged to support the project. Codd and Date Associates, a consulting firm founded by the two relational database pioneers E.F. Codd and Chris Date, was hired based upon the reputation of its principals. CompTech, an Indian DP consulting firm founded in 1982 by seven Indian IT professionals, was hired based upon its cost estimates and an excellent reputation with offshore clients. CompTech had clients and offices in Tokyo, Sydney (Australia), Maastricht (The Netherlands), Boston, and San Francisco. They also had a local Atlanta presence through half ownership of a joint venture firm with another Atlanta management consulting company, Kurt Salmon Associates. Kris, one of the seven founding partners of CompTech, represented CompTech in this joint venture firm and also provided high level liaison between Holiday Inn and CompTech.

While Codd and Date Associates were to supply database programming as well as logical database analysis and design expertise, CompTech's original role was to supply programmers for modifying and/or re-writing the legacy programs. Classic "body-shop" or "insourcing" arrangements characterized both consulting contracts. Codd and Date and CompTech were to supply the necessary labor which would then be deployed under the Holiday Inn (Daniel's) management and control. CompTech, however, did supply an on-site project-manager/coordinator to coordinate with Holiday Inn's requirements and to help manage their CompTech's staff.

The contracts themselves were not very specific as to the services to be provided by the vendor. Daniel reasoned that given the complex and reciprocal nature of the re-engineering task, and the relative uniqueness of the re-engineering process, specific and detailed requirements could not be developed in advance. He expected that by developing a working relationship with the vendors, Holiday Inn and the vendors should be able to mutually adjust to the evolving requirements. At this point it should be recognized that while each of the parties brought complementary expertise to the project, none of them had any actual experience in integrating all these components of the strategy into a database re-engineering project of this magnitude and ambition. While Daniel had devised the overall strategy, methodology, and CASE tools to support the project, the details of the methodology and project tasks could only be filled in as the project evolved. Thus, rather than using pre-specified outcome standards or process standards as coordination mechanisms, he decided to rely upon mutual adjustment and personal supervision as the primary coordination strategies.[3]

Evolving and deteriorating relationships: 1994

The working relationship with Codd and Date went quickly downhill. Codd and Date Associates were not accustomed to working in an evolving reciprocal environment and insisted upon detailed pre-specification of all work. Furthermore, Daniel felt that Codd and Date were not supplying adequately trained people for the project. His impression was that the quality of effort and work delivered by Codd and Date was below par. Though contracted with and paid for in advance – he felt that Codd and Date was unable to deliver on promises. The relationship was dissolved.

On the other hand, as the working relationship with CompTech matured, Holiday Inn (Daniel) realized that CompTech had design and project management expertise beyond straight programming skills. The CompTech project manager was brought into the DB design process. The actual database redesign and software re-engineering process was interleaved. While the components of the relational database were being redesigned, specifications were produced on an ongoing basis for program redesign, and programs were modified or re-written as needed. The close working relationship between Daniel's group and on-site CompTech personnel, coupled with the CompTech project manager's involvement with the logical design team meant that CompTech could anticipate Holiday Inn's needs and adjust its services and staff assign-

---

[3]Mintzberg (1993) identifies five key coordination strategies: mutual adjustment, direct supervision, outcome standards, process standards, and personnel standards. In addition, Simon (1976) identifies the use of detailed plans and programs also as coordination strategies. Standards and plans are considered appropriate in the case sequential interdependence where one party clearly passes work onto another party in a sequential manner. But in the case of reciprocal interdependence, where parties pass work back and forth among themselves (as was the case here) mutual adjustment and direct supervision are considered to be the primary coordination mechanisms.

ments on an ongoing basis. CompTech pulled out all stops to service the Holiday Inn account. They brought in a number of experienced and qualified programmers and analysts from India to support the re-engineering effort. Daniel's satisfaction with and trust in CompTech had grown to the point that he started talking of the CompTech's project manager as if he were his own employee.

New problems

However, by this time some new problems were becoming evident. First, CompTech realized that while the cost of Indian programmers in India was low, when they were brought to the US, the cost of transportation, housing, and per diem expenses quickly increased these costs to be at par with the costs of local consulting firms. Thus competing on costs alone was not feasible. Next, about this time there was a tightening of US regulations on issuing visas to foreign professionals. US professional associations were lobbying against the entry of foreign programmers. As a result the US embassy in India made it very difficult for Indian IT firms to obtain work permits for Indian professionals to work in the United States. Finally, some signs of tensions were beginning to appear between the regular Holiday Inn staff and the Indian expatriates. These tensions seemed to be the result of cultural differences between the two groups.

While the Indians' knowledge of English has been mentioned in the literature as a key advantage for the Indian Software Industry, the cultural differences between the US and Indian IT professionals became apparent when they met face-to-face. First, the work style of Indian programmers and analyst was very different from that of their American counterparts. Compared to most US professionals who had acquired their expertise on the job, most of the Indian professionals had formal, graduate level training in development methodologies (Yourdon, 1992). Thus, while the work style of the Americans relied upon informally learnt practices and improvization,[4] the Indian work style reflected a greater degree of methodology formalism. Second, the Indians being away from home, did not have as many day-to-day living concerns as their US counterparts. Thus they tended to devote longer hours to work and in general worked harder. One of the senior Holiday Inn executives remarked that a new plantation culture seemed to be developing at Holiday Inn. Finally, with their foreign accents, habits, and color, the Indians seemed a very visible reminder of the foreigner taking away US jobs.

---

[4] Ed Yourdon has called the American Programmer's work style the "Cowboy Programmer" work style.

From insourcing to offshore outsourcing: passage to India

The increasing costs of maintaining a staff in the US and the problems associated with obtaining visas for its staff prompted CompTech to seek alternatives to bringing Indian professionals into the US. With Holiday Inn's concurrence they decided to move their programming staff back to CompTech headquarters in Bangalore India and work on the programming tasks from India.

Four issues were associated with the move. First, as the process of developing program re-engineering specifications, developing the programs, and testing them was an interactive process involving both Holiday Inn and CompTech staff, mechanisms were needed for the "to and fro" transfer of specifications, software, test data, and test results. Second, as the personnel involved in the process could no longer interact face-to-face, direct clarification of the usual specification ambiguities and incomplete specifications was no longer possible. Third, as the Indian staff was now half way around the world, direct supervision of the staff was no longer feasible. Finally, the ten and one-half hour difference in time-zones between Atlanta and Bangalore meant that the normal working hours at the two locations did not overlap. The coordination procedures needed to take this geographical and time difference into account.

A combination of technical, procedural, and administrative mechanisms were established to resolve some of these issues. First, a high speed data link (a T1 line) was set up between Atlanta and Bangalore to transfer specifications, programs, and test results. To utilize the expensive line capacity, CompTech shared this line with another offshore outsourcing project it was conducting for another major corporation in the US. Second, both Holiday Inn and CompTech decided to use the LBMS CASE tool as a basis for communicating specifications. The use of the CASE tool formalized and standardized the specification process, thereby reducing some of the ambiguities and impreciseness of informal specifications. Finally, a common time window was established such that the Holiday Inn staff in Atlanta could communicate in real-time with CompTech staff in Bangalore India. This communications was usually by telephone, but could also utilize faxes and the high speed data link when necessary.

By summer of 1994 these mechanisms were in place and seemed to be working well. CompTech's manpower costs were under control and the visa regulation problems had been considerably reduced as CompTech no longer needed to bring its personnel into the United States. There was another unexpected bonus. The ten and one-half hour time difference was exploited by the re-engineering team to reduce the delivery time. As the working hours of the American and Indian teams no longer overlapped, each team could pass work to the other to be worked on by the other team overnight, and shipped back next morning via the transmission lines. This in effect meant that project work could now be performed round the clock thereby reducing the delivery times considerably.

Departures and developments: Autumn 1994–Summer 1995

During this period a number of new developments took place at Holiday Inn and CompTech which affected the course of the project. On the Holiday Inn side, a number of senior IT executives left Holiday Inn. Mike Kennedy, vice-president in charge of applications and strategic systems, left Holiday Inn to accept a senior position at a hotel chain in MidWest USA. Greg Tollander, the vice-president of operations also left Holiday Inn. Dick Smith, by now the executive vice-president of IT, was involved primarily in strategic issues and setting up a Holiday Inn IT subsidiary. This left the middle managers, previously from Memphis, very much in charge of day-to-day operation of the IT group.

Daniel Newton decided to form his own consulting firm with Phil Fasone, senior manager of IS quality and methodology at Holiday Inn. He tendered his resignation to Dick Smith who asked him to stay on until the database re-engineering project was completed. For some time Daniel worked in a dual capacity, running his consulting firm and managing the strategic systems group at Holiday Inn. Finally, in the spring of 1995 he resigned from Holiday Inn to manage his company "PowerSolv" on a full-time basis. His clients from that date included some user groups in Holiday Inn.

During this timeframe CompTech was also undergoing major changes. First, CompTech decided to dissolve its Atlanta based joint venture by selling its shares in the joint venture to its former partnering company, Kurt Salmon Associates. Second, CompTech decided to focus on developing and marketing logistics and distribution software packages. It recalled Kris, CompTech's founding partner in Atlanta, to head up the research and product development group in Bangalore. Thus the high level liaison between CompTech and Holiday Inn no longer existed. Third, in the summer of 1994 CompTech went public on the Bombay stock exchange and within a week their stocks were trading at ten times the initial opening price. This surge in stock prices reflected the strong growth in new business for CompTech. This growth was putting additional demands on CompTech's manpower resources. As a result, CompTech reassigned people form the Holiday Inn project to other projects and replaced them with new personnel. Given this rapid growth, the change of focus to package software development, and the closing of its Atlanta office, it is likely that Holiday Inn was no longer a significant account for CompTech.

By early 1995 the situation had started to deteriorate. As Daniel was no longer in face-to-face contact with the Indian team, he was not aware of the personnel changes in Bangalore. Only after a few software conversions blew up did Daniel become aware that the original CompTech staff, experienced with Holiday Inn systems, were no longer working on the project. It had been replaced by relatively inexperienced newcomers. While in the past, Daniel could rely on the Indian project-manager's and team's intimate understanding of the project requirements, the new staff needed detailed specifications. An example mentioned by Daniel illustrates this point. CompTech was given the assignment to create a certain set of relational tables by combining data from a variety of sources. Daniel maintains that persons familiar with the requirements of the re-engineering project would have developed a customized merge utility which would check for duplicate records, inconsistent data, missing data, and unacceptable data before this data was loaded onto the relational database. The inexperienced CompTech staff, instead, used a standard merge utility without these checks to create the relational tables, thereby corrupting the database. The problem was found only after reports based upon this data were distributed to Holiday Inn sites worldwide.

This incident also illustrates another problem. While these staffing changes were being made by CompTech in its Bangalore Holiday Inn team, Daniel and his staff were no longer closely monitoring the work produced by CompTech. Daniel agreed that he became a bit too comfortable with CompTech and therefore started relying upon them for interpreting the specifications and monitoring the quality of the results. It is also likely that during this time Daniel was preoccupied with other priorities and thus was not as careful as he would have otherwise been.

By spring 1995 Daniel had left Holiday Inn to form his own consulting company with Phil Fasone. One of his major clients was the marketing group at Holiday Inn who retained him to develop and implement a Data Warehouse for strategic marketing information. In this case he worked directly with the marketing group and not through the IT department. He still maintained a good relationship with Dick Smith who became increasingly involved with Holiday Inn's plan for spinning off an IT-based subsidiary. As mentioned above, except for Dick Smith, most of the senior staff hired from outside after the move had left Holiday Inn by mid-1995. Daniel's relationships with the remaining IT group at the Holiday Inn were not so cordial. The Database re-engineering project was complete by mid-1995. Glory Cung, Daniel's right hand man, and the key analyst on the database re-engineering project, who was also brought in from outside, had also left Holiday Inn to form his own consulting company. CompTech had been retained by Holiday Inn to maintain the software it helped modify and develop.

Despite his problems with CompTech, Daniel believed that offshore outsourcing had great potential. He suggested that where coordination and monitoring problems were recognized and solved, the combination of lower costs, higher quality, and reduced cycle times would make it profitable for firms to use offshore personnel.

Analysis: offshore and onshore issues

The case provides a rich experience base for investigating offshore versus onshore issues. Furthermore, the longitudinal nature of the case study provides interesting data about the evolution of relationships between the client and vendors. However, before we outline some of these issues we need to differentiate between two dimensions of analysis shown in Figure 5.1. On the first dimension, there are certain issues which arise due to the move from "on-site insourcing" to "off-site outsourcing" of development. In the on-site situation, the development personnel provided by the consulting company are on-site at the client site, usually under the client's direct control, integrated with the client's practices, and interact face-to-face with the client and his staff. On the other hand, in off-site outsourcing the development personnel provided by the consulting company are away from the client site, usually under the direct control of the consulting company itself. The client can exercise control, but only indirectly.

On the second dimension, off-site development may be carried out either "Onshore" (i.e., within the client's country) or "Offshore" (i.e., in a country which is separated from the client's country geographically, nationally, temporal, and culturally). These differences between the Onshore and Offshore environment add an additional layer of complexity to the off-site situation. It is also possible for an Offshore vendor to provide on-site insourced manpower to a client.

This case provides examples of on-site onshore insourcing (Holiday Inn and Codd & Date Associates), on-site offshore insourcing (Holiday Inn & Comp-Tech: 1993–94) and off-site-offshore outsourcing (Holiday Inn & CompTech: 1994–95). As the purpose of this chapter is to examine the use of offshore vendors, the following discussion will focus on the latter two examples.

Physical Location of Development Personnel

		On-Site	Off-Site
Location of	**Onshore**	Insourcing or Body-Shopping HI + Codd & Date	Off-Site Onshore Outsourcing
Vendor			
Employing			
Development	**Offshore**	Imported manpower Body-Shopping HI + CompTech1993–4	Off-Site Offshore Outsourcing HI + CompTech1994–5
Personnel			

Figure 5.1   Holiday Inns Atlanta: Use of the Market

On-site offshore insourcing: 1993–1994

The original insourcing/body-shopping arrangement between Holiday Inn and CompTech was set up on the basis of CompTech supplying low cost and high quality manpower to Holiday Inn. The development project involved a technical conversion from existing file-based systems to an integrated relational database based system. It did not involve any direct changes to the client's business practices, nor did it involve any direct contact between the client's user groups and the vendor's personnel. Thus, according to the conventional wisdom, it was a ready-made situation for offshore outsourcing.

The initial intention of Holiday Inn was to utilize the CompTech personnel purely in a programming capacity. Traditionally this would require the preparation of detailed specifications by the client and "handing them over" to the vendor personnel for programming. Given the innovative and exploratory nature of the re-engineering process, the complex, iterative, and reciprocal nature of the programming task, and the stringent time requirements, it was not possible to develop and provide detailed specifications in a timely manner. Codd & Date Associates were not comfortable with these constraints and thus their relationship with the project could not be sustained over time. On the other hand, CompTech was willing to work under these semi-structured conditions. They coped with the lack of structure by providing highly experienced and qualified labor for the project. Furthermore, they appointed a project manager/coordinator who was willing to understand the project requirements in details, work closely with the design team, and in effect become a member of the design team. This close working relationship resulted in a high level of client satisfaction and trust on part of the client.

It should be recognized that the problems with Codd & Date cannot be generalized to all on-site onshore insourcing. Nor can the positive response of CompTech be generalized to all on-site offshore insourcing vendors. The overriding issue in this situation is the vendor's willingness to adapt to work with the clients requirements and constraints. As long as the vendor is willing and able to devote resources and effort to the client's specific needs the lack of structure in the insourcing/outsourcing can be managed (see Lacity and Rottman, 2007. Also Chapter 15).

The labor cost advantage of offshore vendors has been cited invariably as a key reason for employing on-site, offshore personnel. Our case shows that this cost advantage from the vendor's perspective is greatly eroded when the total cost of bringing these personnel on-site is considered. Furthermore, the increasingly stringent requirements for obtaining work visas for offshore personnel and the potential interpersonal tensions arising due to cultural differences and the visible presence of these workers also made the use of on-site offshore personnel less attractive – in this case at least.

Off-site offshore outsourcing: 1994–95

In this case the above problems led to relocating the offshore personnel back at their home base and the use of IT (telecommunication lines and CASE tools) to mediate the work between the client site and the offshore development site. Initially, this experiment was successful in delivering satisfactory work, while reducing the cost disadvantage and circumventing visa problems. It also had two unexpected bonuses. First, due to round-the-clock work the delivery time was greatly reduced. Second, distance and information technology provided a buffer between the US and Indian personnel thereby reducing the tensions due to cultural differences.

However, in the longer term this also led to an "out-of-sight out-of-mind" attitude developing at both locations. From Holiday Inn's perspective, once the Indians were off-site, the day-to-day interaction and the constant monitoring by the client lapsed considerably. From the CompTech perspective, as a dedicated staff was no longer at the client site, it was much easier to pull out experienced members of the team and replace them with new personnel who were not experienced in the client's needs. Therefore the mutual adjustment process that worked well before was no longer tenable. Again, it needs to be recognized that these problems are not inherent in the move to offshore development. They can equally arise in case of off-site onshore development.

Finally, the changing dynamic of both the client and the vendor also had an effect on the project. From the Holiday Inn side, once the non-Memphis executives started losing their commitment to Holiday Inn, attention needed for ongoing management of the offshore-outsourcing project became less consistent. From the CompTech side, as CompTech experienced rapid growth, they were not willing to give Holiday Inn the same attention they had given it in earlier stages. Furthermore, the departure of the high level liaison person, Kris, further degraded this relationship.

Comparison with theory

On decision factors, much of the theory on business, technical and economic issues outlined earlier is endorsed by the case. Technical issues emerged as particularly critical, however. Following Feeny *et al.* (1996), with system requirements difficult to define in advance and in a situation of low technological maturity the "buy-in" strategy with Codd & Date was *a priori* correct, but the vendor was not prepared to work in a "user" rather than a "specialist" focused manner. Initially, CompTech adapted successfully to such a mode of work, but other factors took them offshore where lack of detailed requirements specification together with less informal working relationships caused the outsourcing arrangement to be less successful.

On **contracting**, it is clear that, following Anthes, (1993), Krepchin (1993), and the arguments and evidence in Lacity and Willcocks (2009), and to some extent against Williamson (1975), offshore outsourcing in this case did require a neo-classical type contract as a fall back against probable changes in relationships. On **economics**, lower offshore production costs did offset the higher transaction costs of offshore, off-site outsourcing. Following Williamson (1975, 1991), to some extent this was due to economies of scale favoring the vendor, but in practice it was much more a reflection of the lower cost Indian labor market. The offshore, off-site experience also supports other research showing the difficulty in **building and maintaining relationships** in outsourcing arrangements, and the high risks prevalent in depending rather more on relationships than contracts to see the work through. The problems with applying the partnership model proposed by Henderson (1990) would seem to be exacerbated in an offshore outsourcing situation, and other commentators' prescriptions on this issue would seem more appropriate for offshore outsourcing (Lacity and Rottman, 2007; Willcocks and Fitzgerald, 1994). However, other work does seem to provide useful frameworks for analyzing the relationship dimension in offshore outsourcing (see for example Oshri *et al.*, 2008), with the interaction approach able to provide the most complete extant framework for analyzing the complex factors and dynamics emerging from the case (IMP Group, 1990; Lacity and Willcocks, 2009).

The case also endorses the use of **IT as a coordination technology** for offshore outsourcing arrangements, both facilitating communication and reducing otherwise prohibitive transaction costs (Bensaou, 1993; Clemons and Row, 1992; Malone *et al.*, 1987). At the same time, adding to the notion of transaction risk put forward by Clemons and Row, while IT set up the possibility of close monitoring, the real problem was Holiday Inn management's reluctance to pursue that possibility, rather than any inherent technological characteristic creating asymmetries in information availability. Finally, on the **domestic versus global issue**, outsourcing to India actually incurred two advantages – from time zone differences, and, ironically, from lessening cultural dissonances through distance.

Conclusions

This case provides a number of interesting insights into the insourcing/outsourcing process. First, it was one of the first studies to recognize that there are situations in which detailed pre-specification and consequently specific performance contracts may not be possible. In these situations the development of a close working relationship between the client and the vendor personnel is essential to the progress of the work. However, this only really worked in the offshore insourcing case, which approximated quite closely to the "user focus" mode of systems development (Feeny *et al.*, 1996).

Next, the case evidence points to the fact that once the logistics, regulatory, and cultural costs of bringing people on-site are recognized, the cost advantages of using offshore personnel are greatly reduced. This lesson had to be learned many times over in the next decade during which offshoring outsourcing grew very fast. On the other hand, the case shows that it is possible to use IT as an enabling technology to move the work off-site-offshore. This move can ameliorate logistics costs and regulatory problems, but can also provide positive benefits in terms of round-the-clock work and a buffer which can reduce interpersonal problems arising due to cultural differences. In 2007 we found the major Indian suppliers working on the assumption that they would start with a 70/30 onshore/offshore ratio but would hope to move this to 30/70 over the contract, thus managing risk/cost trade-offs (Oshri *et al.*, 2007).

However, this move to off-site development cannot work without substantive contract maintenance mechanisms. These include the use of coordination mechanisms which can overcome the "out-of-sight, out-of-mind" problem. Such mechanisms include the use of a customary "overlap" time during which voice or video contact can keep the relationship alive.[5] In addition, both the client and vendor need to establish a regular and frequent pattern of contact, review, and monitoring, through telecommunications and occasionally through personal visits. Finally, in critical projects or projects of sufficient magnitude, this contact may be further strengthened by placing a key coordinating person at each other's site. These issues have been explored in considerable depth by Lacity and Rottman (2007; see also Chapters 14 and 15). Thus, as long as sufficient attention is given to the design and implementation of long distance relationship maintenance and coordination mechanisms, it may be possible to realize the benefits of off-site-offshore development without incurring its negative costs.

Note

1. Data for this case history was gathered through face-to-face interviews with five key managers in both organizations (Holiday Inn and CompTech). Some managers were interviewed multiple times. Interviews lasted one and one-half to two hours with each manager. Given the evolving nature of the relationship and the project, the interviews were conducted using open-ended questions. In addition, key managers from Holiday Inn developed and presented project, descriptions, plans, and summaries to one of the authors and his systems development class.

    The names of some individuals and the outsourcing vendor in this longitudinal case study have been changed to protect the firms and individuals. The case was still evolving as at February 1996. The principal actors continued to relate to

---

[5]For example, Hitachi Corporation uses an overlap window and regular video-conferencing to maintain contact between their Atlanta and Tokyo accounting offices.

and conduct business with each other. The key decision maker at Holiday Inn, Daniel Newton, was no longer working for Holiday Inn. He had set up his own consulting firm and had Holiday Inn as one of his clients. CompTech continued to maintain the software it developed for Holiday Inn. Thus, at this time, it was not appropriate to reveal the names of all of the parties in the story.

References

Anthes, G. (1993) "Not Made in the USA", *Computerworld*, December 6, 123–124, 129.

Applegate, L. and Montealegre, R. (1991) "Eastman Kodak Company: Managing Information Systems through Strategic Alliances", *Harvard Business School Case*, 9–192–030, Harvard Business School Press, Boston.

Apte, U. and Mason, R. (1995) "Global Outsourcing of Information Processing Services", in Harker, P. (ed.) *The Service Productivity and Quality Challenge*, Kluwer Academic, Norwell, 169–202.

Bensaou, M. (1993) Interorganizational Cooperation: The Role of Information Technology. An Empirical Comparison of U.S. and Japanese Supplier Relations. *Proceedings of the Fourteenth International Conference of Information Systems*, Orlando Florida, December, 117–127.

Blois, K. (1994) "Transaction Costs Analysis: Is It Being Used Out of Context?", *Working Paper MRP94/6, Templeton College*, Oxford University, Oxford.

Carmel, E. and Abbott, P. (2007) "Why Nearshore Means That Distance Matters", *Communications of the ACM*, 50, 10, 40–46.

Cheon, M., Grover, V. and Teng, J. (1995) "Theoretical Perspectives on the Outsourcing of Information Systems", in Willcocks, L. and Lacity, M. (eds) *Information Systems Outsourcing: Theory and Practice – Theme Issue, Journal Of Information Technology*, 10, 4, 209–220.

Clemons, E. and Row, M. (1992) "Information Technology and Industrial Cooperation: The Changing Economics of Coordination and Ownership", *Journal Of Management Information Systems*, 9, 2, 9–28.

Dietrich, M. (1994) *Transaction Cost Economies and Beyond*, Routledge, London.

Dwyer , F., Schurr, P. *et al.* (1987) "Developing Buyer-Seller Relationships", *Journal of Marketing*, 51, 11–27.

Faulkner, D. (1995) *International Strategic Alliances*, McGraw Hill, London.

Feeny, D., Earl, M. and Edwards, B. (1996) "Organizational Arrangements for IS Roles of Users and IS Specialists", in Earl, M. (ed.) *Information Management – The Organizational Dimension*, Oxford University Press, Oxford.

Feeny, D. and Willcocks, L. (1998) "Core IS Capabilities for Exploiting IT", *Sloan Management Review*, 39, 3, 9–21.

Henderson, J. (1990) "Plugging into Strategic Partnerships: The Critical IS Connection", *Sloan Management Review*, 33, 1, 7–18.

Hodgson, G. (1994) "Corporate Culture and Evolving Competencies: And Old Institutionalist Perspective on the Nature of the Firm". Paper presented at *The Conference of Transaction Cost Economics and Beyond*, Erasmus University, Rotterdam, Netherlands.

Hofstede, G. (1980) *Culture's Consequences: International Differences In Work-Related Values*, Sage, Beverly Hills.

Huber, R. (1993) "How Continental Bank Outsourced Its 'Crown Jewels'", *Harvard Business Review*, 71, 1, 121–129.

IMP Group (1990) "An Interaction Approach", in Ford, D. (ed.) *Understanding Business Markets: Interaction, Relationships, Networks*, Academic Press, London.

Infotech Consulting (1992) *International Studies of Software and Related Services*, Maxi/Micro Inc, New York.

Jones, C. (1994) "Evaluating Software Outsourcing Options", *Information Systems Management*, Fall, 28–33.

Jurison, J. (1995) "The Role of Risk and Return in Information Technology Outsourcing Decisions", *Journal of Information Technology*, 10, 4, 239–247.

Klepper, R. (1995) "The Management of Partnering Development in IS Outsourcing", *Journal of Information Technology*, 10, 4, 249–258.

Kohli, F. (1994) "A Bonafide Industry with a Long Way to Go", *IEEE Spectrum*, March, 32–34.

Krepchin, I. (1993) "When Offshore Programming Works", *Datamation* July 15, 55–56.

Kumar, K., Van Dissel, H. and Welke, R. (1995) War and Peace: Conflict And Cooperation in Inter-organizational Systems. *Proceedings Of The Third European Conference On Information Systems*, Athens, June 1–3.

Lacity, M. and Hirschheim, R. (1993) *Information Systems Outsourcing: Myths, Metaphors, and Realities*, Wiley, Chichester.

Lacity, M. and Hirschheim, R. (1995) *Beyond The Information Systems Outsourcing Bandwagon*, Wiley, Chichester.

Lacity, M. and Rottman, J. (2007) *The Offshore Outsourcing of IT Work*, Palgrave, London.

Lacity, M. and Willcocks, L. (1995) On Interpreting IT Outsourcing Experiences From a Transaction Cost Perspective. *Oxford Institute of Information Management Research Paper 95/8*, Templeton College, Oxford.

Lacity, M. and Willcocks, L. (2001) *Global IT Outsourcing: Search for Business Advantage*, Wiley, Chichester.

Lacity, M. and Willcocks, L. (2009) *Information Systems and Outsourcing: Studies in Theory and Practice*, Palgrave, London.

Lacity, M., Willcocks, L. and Feeny, D. (1996) "Sourcing Information Technology Capability: A Framework for Decision-making", in Earl, M. (ed.) *Information Management – The Organizational Dimension*, Oxford University Press, Oxford.

Malone, T., Yates, J. and Benjamin, R. (1987) "Electronic Markets and Electronic Hierarchies", *Communications of the ACM*, 30, 6, 484–497.

Masten, S. (1994) "Empirical Research in Transaction-Cost Economics: Challenges, Progress, Directions". Paper presented at *The Conference of Transaction Cost Economics and Beyond*, Erasmus University, Rotterdam, Netherlands, June.

McFarlan, W. and Nolan, R. (1995) "How to Manage an IT Outsourcing Alliance", *Sloan Management Review*, 36, 2, 9–24.

Mintzberg, H. (1993) *The Nature of Managerial Work*, Free Press, New York.

Nam, K., Rajagopalan, S., Rao, R. and Chaudhury, A. (1995) "Dimensions of Outsourcing: A Transaction Cost Framework", in Khosrowpour, M. (ed.) *Managing Information Technology Investment With Outsourcing*, Idea Group, Harrisburg, 232–248.

Nidumolu, S. and Goodman, S. (1993) "Computing in India: An Asian Elephant Learns to Dance", *Communications Of The ACM*, 36, 4, 15–22.

Oshri, I., Kotlarsky, J. and Willcocks, L.P. (2007) "Managing Dispersed Expertise in IT Offshore Outsourcing: Lessons from Tata Consultancy Services", *MISQ Executive*, 6, 2, 53–65.

Oshri, I., Kotlarsky, J. and Willcocks, L. (2008) *Outsourcing Global Services: Knowledge, Innovation and Social Capital*, Palgrave, London.

Patane, J. and Jurison, J. (1994) "Is Global Outsourcing Diminishing Prospects for American Programmers?", *Journal Of Systems Management*, 45, 6–10.

Pitelis, C. (1991) *Market and Non-Market Hierarchies: Theory of Institutional Failure*, Blackwell, Oxford.

Rajkumar, T.M. and Dawley, D.L. (1996) "Designing and Managing Client/Server DBMSs", *Information Systems Management*, 13, 2, 49–57.

Ranganathan, C. and Balaji, S. (2007) "Critical Capabilities for Offshore Outsourcing of IS", *MIS Quarterly Executive*, 6, 3, 147–164.

Ravichandran, R. and Ahmed, N. (1993) "Offshore Systems Development", *Information And Management*, 24, 1, 33–40.

Saarinen, T. and Vepsalainen, A. (1994) "Procurement Strategies for Information Systems", *Journal Of Management Information Systems*, 11, 2, 187–208.

Simon, H., (1976) *Administrative Behavior*, The Free Press, New York.

Sobol, M. and Apte, U. (1995) "Domestic and Global Outsourcing Practices of America's Most Effective Users", *Journal of Information Technology*, 10, 4, 269–280.

Soota, A. (1994) "A Partner on the Other Side of the Globe", IEEE Spectrum, March, 34–36.

Trompenaars, F. (1993) *Riding on the waves of Culture: Understanding Cultural Diversity in Business*, Economist Books, London.

Willcocks, L. and Choi, C. (1995) "Cooperative Partnership and 'Total' Outsourcing: From Contractual Obligation to Strategic Alliance?" *European Management Journal*, 13, 1, 67–78.

Willcocks, L. and Fitzgerald, G. (1994) *A Business Guide to IT Outsourcing: Study of European Best practice in the Selection, Management and Use of External IT Services*, Business Intelligence, London.

Willcocks, L. and Lacity, M. (2009) *Research Studies in Information Technology Outsourcing: Perspectives, Practices and Globalization*. Volume 1 – Making IT Outsourcing Decisions; Volume 2 – Managing Outsourcing Relationships; Volume 3 – Global Outsourcing: Issues and Trends, Sage, London.

Williamson, O. (1975) *Markets and Hierarchies: Analysis and Antitrust Implications. A Study in the Economics of Internal Organization*, The Free Press, New York.

Williamson, O. (1979) "Transaction Cost Economics: The Governance of Contractual Relations", *Journal of Law and Economics*, 22, 2, 233–261.

Williamson, O. (1985) *The Economic Institutions of Capitalism*, Free Press, New York.

Williamson, O. (1991) "Strategizing, Economizing, and Economic Organization", *Strategic Management Journal*, 12, 75–94.

6

IT Outsourcing in Public Sector Contexts: Researching Risk and Strategy

Leslie Willcocks, Mary Lacity and Thomas Kern

Introduction

The origins and history of a single case study of large-scale IT outsourcing in the 1994–99 period is investigated in the United Kingdom Defence sector. Such deals are high risk and we describe types of risk and how the client organization sought to mitigate these. These risks and mitigation approaches are then analyzed against a distinctive risk framework formulated for IT outsourcing. Risks emerging in terms of type and scope of outsourcing, vendor selection criteria and process, the role of the contract, retained capabilities and management processes, and partnering and relationship dimensions are then assessed against other research findings. Two additional distinctive risks are identified from the case history arising from the public sector context and supplier long-term market strategy. A contribution of the chapter is the revised risk framework for analyzing IT outsourcing that is then presented. Finally, we highlight the implications of these findings for future research and practice.

Information Technology (IT) outsourcing grew rapidly to an estimated global market share of $99 billion in 1998 and $120 billion in 2002 with an annual growth rate of 16% in the 1997–2002 period (Walker, 1996; Klepper and Jones, 1998; Lacity and Willcocks, 2000, 2001). This ensured that from the late 1990s IT outsourcing has attained extensive, ongoing, worldwide business attention (see for example Applegate and Montealegre, 1991; Bicknell, 1996; Clement, 1996; Cross, 1995; Huber, 1993; Impact Group, 1999; Kern and Willcocks, 2000, 2001; Moad, 1993; Strassmann, 1998). As the introduction to this book shows, this has remain the case into the late 2000s.

By the late 1990s the growth in significance, and in the size of outsourcing deals, had resulted in an increased concern with the actual management of an outsourcing venture, and in particular with the issue of risk mitigation. This emerged particularly as an issue because of the mixed press and results IT outsourcing regularly received (and still receives) in both the trade and academic literatures (see for example Ang and Straub, 1998; Collins, 1999; Collins and Phillips, 1999; Dempsey, 1999; Lacity and Willcocks, 1996, 1998, 2009; Loh and Venkatraman, 1992; McFarlan and Nolan, 1995; Poston, 1997; Strassmann, 1998; Thomas and Schneider, 1997; Vowler, 1996). Particularly interesting have been the high profile "total" outsourcing deals with a single supplier (see Chapters 2 and 4). As we saw, even proponents point out that it can be a high risk strategy (McFarlan and Nolan, 1995). Such risks, it has been suggested, can be mitigated by adopting a multiple vendor approach (see for example Cross, 1995; Hoffmann, 1996) or by a selective outsourcing approach on shorter-term contracts (Lacity and Hirschheim, 1995; Lacity and Willcocks, 2001; see also Chapter 2). More recently, within the context of large scale single supplier outsourcing, we have seen attempts at more creative and mature approaches to leveraging deals in order to gain business advantage. These include "value-added" outsourcing whereby vendor and client combine their capabilities to market IT products and services; client and vendor taking equity holdings in each other; "co-sourcing", involving "performance-based contracts"; and the creation between the vendor and client of a "spin-off" company selling IT services on to the wider market – see the Philips strategy in Chapter 4 for example (Currie and Willcocks, 1998; Lacity and Willcocks, 2001). There have also been signs of more creative and informed forms of contracting in order to mitigate risks across long-term deals (Willcocks and Lacity, 1998, 1999, 2000). Clearly there have been no shortage of attempts to mitigate risk, but how thoroughly have such risk mitigation approaches and their outcomes been analyzed?

Following Charette (1991) and Willcocks and Margetts (1994), risk is here taken to be a negative outcome that has a known or estimated probability of occurrence based on experience or some theory. In information systems studies risk has been heavily researched in the areas of software development (see for example Boehm, 1991; Charette, 1991; Griffiths and Newman, 1996; Lyytinen *et al.*, 1998; Ropponen, 1999) and project management (as examples only see Morris, 1996; Willcocks and Griffiths, 1996). However, as Willcocks and Lacity (1999, 2006) point out, although many of the case examples researched in this literature have external IT suppliers involved, this has rarely flowed into detailed analyses of risks in IT outsourcing.

In practice, in fact, the authors' detailed review of the 1990s found all too few systematic academic studies of types of IT outsourcing risks, their salience and their mitigation. The main studies were Earl (1996) and Klepper and Jones (1998), both of which are somewhat anecdotal in character; Ang and Toh (1998) with a detailed case history of a failed software development project, and derived guidelines; Jurison (1995) who provided a theoretical risk-return analytical model for making IT outsourcing decisions; Willcocks and Lacity (1999) who investigated risk mitigation tactics in a single case history; and Lacity and Willcocks (1998) and Willcocks (1998) who derived risk reduction guidelines from studying 40 organizations and their IT sourcing practices. Outside these, there have been many other studies that deal with IT outsourcing but did not choose to focus on providing a comprehensive analysis of salient risks and/or risk mitigation approaches (for example Ang and Straub, 1998; De Loof, 1998; McFarlan and Nolan, 1995; McLellan *et al.*, 1998). Given this state of affairs, one primary motivation for the study in this chapter was to build on previous studies and provide much needed empirical and analytical work in an area of burgeoning importance to academics and practitioners alike. Tho (2005) and Osei-Bryson and Ngwenyama (2006) provide more recent reviews of risks in IT outsourcing, but the surprising neglect of this area continues into the late 2000s.

A further motivation was to address the disappointing record on outsourcing IT experienced in the UK public sector. Was there something distinctive about such contexts that made IT outsourcing more, or at least differently, risky? Market testing, compulsory competitive tendering, Private Finance Initiative (PFI) and privatization initiatives were encouraged in the UK public services by the British government from the early 1990s, through successive Conservative and Labour governments to the present day. Market testing proposals made in November 1992, for example, saw ICT activities in 13 government departments cited as an essential part of the increased "businessization" and competition desired by government (Willcocks, 1994). Contracting out could range from selective outsourcing as occurred in many parts of the NHS and local government in the 1990s through to large "total" outsourcing deals as subsequently progressed through to 2008 in the then named HM Inland Revenue and Department of Social Security. Alternatively, these proposals meant the privatization of in-house IT departments, or the hiving-off of IT departments to agency status within the public sector.

However, the 1990s produced a very mixed record where significant contracting out of IT took place in the public services, with Wessex Regional Health Authority, the Child Support Agency and several local authorities being only high profile examples of the kind of difficulties that were experienced (Willcocks, 1994). (Such results were not restricted to the UK of course, as the next chapter reveals). Unfortunately, such results seemed to have continued into the 2000–08 period as recorded by a succession of National Audit Office and House of Commons Committee of Public Accounts reports and academic research studies alike covering NHS, Inland Revenue National Identity Card and many other marketized initiatives (see as example only Davies and Hosein, 2007; Dunleavy *et al.*, 2007; HCCA, 2007abcd; NAO, 2006; Sauer and Willcocks, 2007; Willcocks and Lacity, 2006). Clearly such results make an understanding of risks in IT outsourcing, and how they can be mitigated into a continuing set of public sector challenges, which this chapter seeks to address.

We start by outlining the analytical framework, and the research choices and approach adopted to arrive at the case history. The case study of the Logistics Information Systems Agency (LISA) – its genesis and its "total" outsourcing deal with the IT services vendor EDS – is then detailed covering the 1994–99 period. We then analyze the case history for risk issues and the ways in which LISA managers strove to mitigate the risks associated with the chosen form of outsourcing. In this analysis we utilize evidence from prior research to comment on the levels of risk and efficacy of managerial response. Given that the outsourcing was a long-term one in its first few years, we also discuss in the light of prior research likely future risks, and the potential risks for the wider public sector, over and above, but still likely to impinge on the LISA-EDS deal in the future. From the analysis we develop a new and distinctive risk framework for analyzing IT outsourcing arrangements. Finally, the chapter relates the findings to, and examines the implications for other IT outsourcing contexts.

Research approach

The focus of the research is on risks in IT outsourcing, and more specifically the types of risks emerging in a total IT outsourcing arrangement, whether risk mitigation tactics were successful or otherwise, and the reasons for those outcomes. We were also interested to delineate if there was transferable learning for other IT outsourcing arrangements, and paths forward for future research on IT outsourcing risks. Following Pettigrew and Whipp (1991) and Willcocks and Margetts (1994), we sought to gain an in-depth knowledge of the external and internal contexts, history, content and process of change, and of the interim outcomes represented by a single, rich case study. Key resources here included understandings arrived at through participant observation and from the views of multiple stakeholders collected as the events unfolded across the 1996–99 period. As such the present study falls into the category of interpretive case research, recognizing with Walsham and Sahay (1999) that: *"there are significant differences of methodology, theory and method under the broad interpretive case studies label"*. The study also seeks to address a further issue with some currency in the IS literature, namely that of relevance. While there is some debate about how IS studies can achieve both relevance and rigor (see Benbasat and Zmud, 1999; Davenport and Markus, 1999; Lee, 1999; Willcocks and Lee, 2008), the present chapter is motivated by the criteria for relevance suggested by Benbasat and Zmud – interesting, applicable, current and accessible – with the Davenport and Markus proposals for new models of research and the suggestion of Lee (1999) for moving beyond the approach of positivism alone.

Research choices and methodology

The choice of subject – risks in IT outsourcing – reflects three related observations. The first is that the academic outsourcing literature demonstrates a series of risks connected with IT outsourcing. The second is that such risks are widely commented upon by and a considerable matter for concern amongst practitioners considering or involved in IT outsourcing. The third is that, though risks in IT projects have received detailed and sustained academic attention, there has been to date a surprising lack of academic focus on risks in IT outsourcing. In order to explore the issue of IT outsourcing risks, the research strategy limited itself to a single case that could be explored in detail and longitudinally, and that covered a time period in more recent outsourcing history wherein managers had become more aware and more informed about IT outsourcing risks. We also sought an example of a total outsourcing single supplier deal which our own previous research showed to be a more risky form of outsourcing where the issues were likely to be both more transparent and significant, and so more accessible to study. While the LISA-EDS deal met these criteria, our choice was also partly opportunistic, in that several of the players were known to the researchers, thus making accessibility less of a problem.

As indicated above, our study draws on contextualism as utilized by Pettigrew (1985), Pettigrew and Whipp (1991) and as applied to risk assessment in information systems in a previous study by the authors (for details of the approach see Willcocks and Margetts (1994). Following Pettigrew (1990), we also designed the study as longitudinal, collecting data over three years from the inception of the contract to mid-1999. This enabled us to identify events in this period as they happened and stakeholders reactions to these, as well as providing understandings of their forward and retrospective views, and of the shifting and differing interpretations provided by multiple stakeholders. We also took the study period back to the inception of LISA in 1994 to understand the contexts of, and rationale for the development of the Agency and for IT outsourcing there. For this period we were dependent on historical reconstruction, using published reports, internal documents, including minutes of meetings, and accounts of the past from stakeholders.

Method

We interviewed three senior managers within the vendor, three senior managers in LISA, a staff representative, three operational staff, and two outsourcing consultants involved in supplier selection and contract preparation. The interviews were carried out, and related documents collected, at various times across the February 1996–March 1999 period. Six respondents were interviewed three times, and the others twice, across this three-year period. Interviews were semi-structured, lasted between one and 2.5 hours each and covered the history, context, process, content and outcomes of the IT outsourcing deal, subsequent developments, opinions, and statements and assessments of future plans.

We probed in detail on the specific issues that have emerged from earlier studies as potentially significant areas, in particular: reasons and decision criteria for outsourcing; vendor selection criteria and process; contract details; post-contract management arrangements and issues, risk areas (Kern and Willcocks, 2000; Kern *et al.*, 1999; Lacity and Willcocks, 1998; Willcocks and Fitzgerald, 1994ab). All participants were also asked to assess the outcomes in terms of their perceptions of levels of success/failure. Where respondents expressed a viewpoint they were prompted to provide further supporting evidence, either anecdotal or in documentary form. Each interview was audio-taped, and subsequently transcribed. The transcriptions were checked with the interviewees, and the final versions ran, in total, to 296 pages. The four steps of intentional analysis were used for interpreting transcribed interviews (Sanders, 1982). In step four the researchers assess their own views as to how the accumulated evidence can be interpreted, and whether specific patterns, themes and interpretations emerge from the rich data. This last set of interpretations make up the bulk of the case study as written. As Lincoln and Guba (1985) and Craig Smith (1990) point out, the validity of interpretive analysis defies quantification. However, so far as space constraints allow, we have included excerpts from the transcribed interviews to help readers to judge for themselves the validity of our analysis.

We also used published sources and were given access to a number of internal documents in order to help in the construction of the case history. We attended five review meetings across the three-year period, and made a number of site visits that allowed informal contact with outsourcing participants outside the interviewing process. The case material that follows represents a distillation from these information sources, arrived at from an interpretivist perspective.

Building an analytical framework

A final research choice arrived at by late 1998 was to take advantage of the cumulative experiences of IT outsourcing in the research literature and build an analytical framework for risks in IT outsourcing, that could provide insights, and which, further developed, could be useful to practitioners and other researchers alike. Research into the 1991–99 period had shown that long-term, large-scale single supplier deals were particularly risky (Lacity and Willcocks, 1998, 2000, 2001; Strassmann, 1998). Lacity and Willcocks (2001) for example, analyzing 116 sourcing decisions, found 38% of "total" outsourcing decisions successful. By comparison 77% of selective outsourcing and 76% of in-house sourcing decisions had successful outcomes (see also Chapter 1). Even so, "total" deals, where 80% or more of the IT budget is outsourced, continued to be entered into, with for example the Inland Revenue-EDS, Sears-Andersen Consulting and British Aerospace-CSC arrangements signed since 1993 in the United Kingdom (UK), with similar deals signed elsewhere for example, Xerox-EDS in the USA, Lend Lease-ISSC and Commonwealth Bank-EDS in Australia, and Swiss Bank-Perot Systems in Switzerland.

Although there is a limited literature on which to draw for the identification of salient risk, an exploratory analytical framework can be distilled from case study and survey work by Lacity and Willcocks (1998, 2000) and others (see below). Drawing on this work, the main reasons for failure/negative outcomes in IT outsourcing deals have been various combinations of the factors shown in Table 6.1 (see also Ang and Straub, 1998; Ang and Toh, 1998; Auwers and Deschoolmeester, 1993; Currie and Willcocks, 1998; DiRomualdo and Gurbaxani, 1998; Klepper and Jones, 1998; Kumar and Willcocks, 1999; Lacity *et al.*, 1996; Thomas and Schneider, 1997).

Apart from being built on prior research findings, a pilot of the framework was also utilized and further developed for present use in earlier case work (see Willcocks and Lacity, 1999). A finding there in applying the framework was that it provided sufficient generic coverage of salient risks to allow complementary detail to be explored in an insightful, qualitative manner. Therefore a decision was made to apply the framework to the present study to see if the framework continued to hold up as a useful analytical tool.

Some final observations on applying the research approach and framework. Much of the academic attention in IT outsourcing has focused on two areas we will investigate further in the case study, namely decision-making frameworks and contracting. But when it comes to risk mitigation what has lacked serious academic attention, we will argue, are two critical areas that demand managing, especially in the long-term "total" outsourcing context of a case like LISA. As pointed out by Willcocks and Fitzgerald (1994b) and Feeny and Willcocks (1998) one of these is retained in-house

Table 6.1   Risk Factors in IT Outsourcing

RISK FACTORS
1. Treating IT as an undifferentiated commodity to be outsourced
2. Incomplete contracting
3. Lack of active management of the supplier on contract and relationship dimensions
4. Failure to build and retain requisite in-house capabilities and skills
5. Power asymmetries developing in favor of the vendor
6. Difficulties in constructing and adapting deals in the face of rapid business/technical change
7. Lack of maturity and experience of contracting for and managing "total" outsourcing arrangements
8. Outsourcing for short-term financial restructuring or cash injection rather than to leverage IT assets for business advantage
9. Unrealistic expectations with multiple objectives for outsourcing
10. Poor sourcing and contracting for development and new technologies

capabilities, and this continues to be the case into the second half of the 2000's (Willcocks and Craig, 2007). The second area is the formation, development and sustaining of client-vendor relations. As already explicated in academic research, IT outsourcing agreements eventuate in inter-organizational relationships due to the resulting dependency that arises (Grover *et al.*, 1995; Kern and Willcocks, 2000; Kirkpatrick, 1991; McFarlan and Nolan, 1995). Paradoxically though, as we argued in Chapter 4, with a few notable exceptions (Henderson, 1990; Klepper, 1994, 1995; McFarlan and Nolan, 1995; Willcocks and Choi, 1995), the area in IT outsourcing that had received the least research attention is this relationship issue, and particularly the characteristics that determine effective and ineffective outsourcing relationships. This neglect also continues into the late 2000s (Willcocks and Craig, 2009). The case study offers an opportunity to investigate the content of a specific large-scale outsourcing arrangement, its contractual elements and how these interrelate and are influenced by client-vendor relationships over time.

Case study: IT outsourcing at LISA

History and background

The Logistic Information Systems Agency (LISA) was launched as a UK Defence Agency in November 1994, its stated mission being "to enhance the logistic effectiveness of the (British) Army in peace and war by providing information systems, services and support" (corporate plan document, 1996).

The British Army is divided into three areas – operations, personnel and logistics. From the late 1950s the logistics area had been operating stock control information systems, the third generation Store System III being the main successor in the 1990s. In 1990 a single Directorate of Logistic Information Systems (DLIS) was formed to manage these systems. More broadly, in the early 1990s, a Defence Cost Study followed by a Logistics Support Review led to rationalization of the logistics area into a single Royal Logistics Corps. Meanwhile the Next Steps Review by the UK government generated pressure to create Agencies in the Ministry of Defence. In all, seven were created in the logistics area, one of these being LISA.

Before LISA was set up a formal Prior Options Process was undertaken. The options considered were abolition, privatization, "contractorization", and Agency status. An important part of the analysis was to assess DLIS's core and non-core tasks. Six core capabilities were defined:

- maintain sufficient military capability to support operations;
- responsibility for IS strategy and policy in the logistics area;
- act as regulator on standards, monitoring, guidance, technical approval, IS security and contract specification;

- articulate and define IS requirements as requested by customers;
- provide costed technical options to enable choice of IS solutions; and
- procure, implement, support chosen technical options, changing them as requested.

IT delivery was seen as "non-core", better delivered by a private sector industry with greater flexibility, and access to requisite skills. As at 1996 these activities were defined as:

- "Facilities Management" (for example data preparation and encoding, disaster recovery, help desk, system administration);
- software maintenance and development; and
- consultancy support.

Since there was never an intention to keep non-core IT activities in-house, a formal market-testing of in-house IT delivery capability was eschewed. Instead, ministerial approval was gained to set up LISA and enter into what was called a "strategic partnership" with a private sector vendor offering non-core IT services.

At this stage it was envisaged that the supplier would initially be given a base contract but that the deal would need to have innovative elements. The supplier would have to operate on-site for four reasons: the significant amounts of classified information being processed; the newness of Agency status; the desire to keep visibility and control over the IT activity; and because location had significant staff implications. The main systems were located in Oxfordshire at Bicester, an area with few alternative employment opportunities for 150 IT service delivery staff. To avoid redundancies the vendor would be expected to forego the economies of scale that could be achieved by transferring and consolidating the work and IT equipment elsewhere.

As an incentive the vendor would be offered the opportunity to exploit LISA's capacity, products and services on the wider market on a basis of shared revenues; and the opportunity to be preferred supplier – though subject to competitively priced bids – for subsequent parcels of IT development, project or consultancy work. LISA would retain the right to reject those bids on its own criteria, and use a different supplier if necessary. On this basis LISA was formally allowed to be set up as an Agency. Its main customers in the 1994–99 period were the Directorates General of Equipment and Logistics Support and their supporting new Defence Agencies, and the Quarter Master General's corporate headquarters and central functions.

Selecting a supplier: 1994–95

In late 1994 a Project Management Board was formed to set up a vendor selection process. This consisted of three in-house IT managers, two from the CCTA (government funded IS advisory agency) and two external consultants who had previously advised on large-scale outsourcing at the UK Inland Revenue. The team was a mix of contract expertise, functional expertise with a knowledge of (army) customer requirement, internal service delivery capability, together with external commercial skills and knowledge of the IT marketplace and its vendors. A list of 42 potential suppliers was drawn up. The selection criteria were:

- a sizeable company with a proven outsourcing track record;
- financial viability;
- an understanding of logistics and of the Army;
- some contact with DLIS in the previous five years; and
- the capability to handle classified information.

A questionnaire was issued to the 22 respondents, ten of whom were invited to a bidders conference in December 1994, after which the short list was reduced to six.

A Statement of Requirement was issued in April 1995. A detailed evaluation of responses left two contenders. There followed a 17-week contract evaluation and negotiation phase with each company, with the best and final offers made in Autumn 1995. The winner, in this instance EDS, was chosen on the quality of its final bid, its consistency of approach, cost factors and "partnership" criteria. At LISA "partnership capability" was assessed on-site reference reports and visits and detailed partner profile assessments, based on vendors' values, corporate emphasis, reliability, responsiveness and consistency. The process was necessarily arduous and detailed, not least because it involved subjective assessments, and many participants. In the end there were ten members of the final evaluation team, including internal LISA support directors, while CCTA also carried out a parallel control score:

> "As many referees as possible should be consulted to minimize the potential for bias in the evaluation, and the final scores should be discussed and awarded by the evaluation team as a whole and not by any one individual" (outsourcing consultant for LISA).

This evaluation process was exhaustive because senior management at LISA were concerned about fairness, the strategic importance of securing a single, highly satisfactory partner, and aware of the need to debrief without controversy the unsuccessful candidate. In the event all respondents suggest that these goals were achieved.

1996: moving to contract

An important and difficult part of the evaluation process was drawing up base lines for comparison on cost and services delivery. The difficulties

stemmed from LISA's broad and diverse customer base, and shifting requirements and Defence commitments over time, together with an inflexible
long-term Treasury costing cycle. The latter meant that LISA was cost-capped,
and this constrained its room for maneuver in the contracting process.

The Project Management Board evaluated three areas: functionality
required, service levels and costs. The requirement from EDS was defined and
their bid costed against the putative in-house provision of the same requirement. The bid was also evaluated against the actual cash available. In practice
the final EDS bid represented substantial savings on the cost of the base
service provision. In practice EDS did not stand to recover much of their costs
from base service delivery alone. DLIS had already worked through most of
the in-house inefficiencies, removing 200 posts through reorganization in the
1990–93 period, and operating almost on a "lights-out" basis with four person
rather than the previous 15 person shifts. Clearly, in these circumstances, the
contract had to be made attractive to the supplier in other ways. As a senior
LISA manager commented subsequently:

> "'EDS' perception is much more over the horizon as to what they can
> gain in terms of additional business and revenue which is where they
> foresee the money coming back. That's why they for their part keep up
> continual pressure on us to make sure we are maximising their oppor-
> tunity... they are basing returns on the partnership potential. That's why
> the contract was so constructed that it's quite challenging for them... we
> are actually (by 1997) now starting to see a genuine degree of mutual
> dependence. And that's good because they can't survive without us and
> we can't survive without them."

The contract was constructed so that the vendor inherited the running of
50 systems under £40 million ($US70m), five-year deal, extendable for a
further two years. The highlights are:

- Vendor commitment to savings in excess of £15 million over contract
  length;
- In addition to the base service provision EDS was offered the opportunity
  to exploit LISA's capacity, products, services and sell them into a wider
  market on the basis of shared proceeds assessed on a case-by-case basis;
- EDS was asked to construct their bid on the basis of their confidence in
  such future revenue flows;
- LISA to receive guaranteed minimum revenue returns on an annual rising
  scale based on forecasts of receipts. The guaranteed minimum amounted to
  several million pounds over the life of the contract. It would be supplemented by further revenues if the partnership actually took off;
- LISA would also look to EDS as preferred supplier for all future work,
  including systems/software development, projects, and consultancy.

However, each piece of work would be the subject of a competitively priced bid. This would be formally evaluated on pre-defined criteria and it could be rejected, with EDS having no further participation in that piece of work.

As one vendor manager commented:

> "The idea, I think, was not to try to prevent us from getting work but actively attempt to make sure that we as vendor perform and can deliver."

This additional work could be considerable, the scope for technological change being far greater than LISA's financial and skills capability as an in-house organization to effect that change. The Army itself had rapidly changing IT requirements, not least in the area of "front-line" military systems. Government Private Finance, Quality and Agency initiatives created ever new challenges with IS implications, including automated accounting, resource accounting and management information systems and wider commercial funding and exploitation of IS. New systems were always needed, recent ones being logistics, tracking and workshop management systems, while the main inventory control system required regular software updates.

The partnership element here was conceived as a way of effecting the increasingly demanded technical changes more quickly, exploiting a greater range and depth of technological expertise through a faster procurement process. Also transferred staff would gain career opportunities within the supplier, while commercial skills and practices would rub off on LISA staff. At the same time there were several other potential advantages perceived by both LISA and vendor:

> "As in several other recent deals... we could smooth out the client's IT cost profile with our servicing of the base contract; as vendor we could also build on our investment through these additional contracted out parcels of work" (vendor manager).

Ownership of IT assets was retained on a GOCO (government-owned-contractor-operated) basis, though the contract stipulated that this could be changed at any later date. LISA also retained the intellectual property rights for – and so the ability to exploit – any software or systems developed under the LISA-EDS contract. All these elements were included in the Tranche 1 contract, and also in the Tranche 2 contract (prepared as an adjunct later in 1996).

There followed a three-month transition phase, from January–March 1996, for transfer of personnel in what was called Tranche 1. About 100 civil servants and 29 contractors were transferred, together with about 20 additional unfilled posts. It was envisaged that a further 50 software maintenance and enhancement staff would also transfer in 1997 in Tranche 2, if the EDS bid for that development work proved to be acceptable. Tranche 1 would seem to have been handled uncontentiously with trade union representatives going on record as commending the smooth transfer process.

1996: post-contract management, skills and relationships

The agreement, called the Partnership Contract, came to be managed by a regular, sometimes, monthly board meeting consisting of LISA senior managers, the managing director of EDS defence, the EDS sales director and the EDS account manager. According to respondents, and the minutes, in the first year this proved a cooperative forum, with little or no recourse to the contract. LISA adjusted its management structure to fit with the outsourcing arrangements (see Figure 6.1).

Reporting directly to the Chief Executive was a Director of Quality and Standards, responsible for implementing government initiatives in this area. LISA aimed to be a "one-stop shop" for IT within the Army's Equipment and Logistic Support area. Therefore, to manage the customer interface and actively work on all aspects of systems specification, procurement, usage and replacement three Customer Support Directors were created each to cover one of the business areas of Logistics, Corporate and Infrastructure, and Equipment. There was a separate Director of IS Strategy while corporate services had three Directors covering Finance, Personnel and Partnership Contract Management. These changes supported and reinforced the earlier introduction of Systems Management Boards. Lodged within and run by the businesses, these

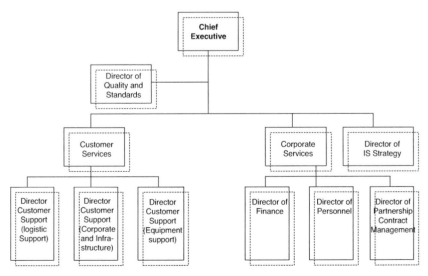

Figure 6.1   LISA Organization and Structure (1996)

were responsible for the "whole-life" management of systems (corporate plan document, 1996).

These arrangements embodied and were underpinned by in-house retention of skills in two main areas. One related to LISA's IT strategic direction, contracting, costing, standards and planning. LISA also retained and developed skills in customer contact and active understanding of the customers' businesses. This was aided by one-fifth of LISA's retained personnel being uniformed, while retained civil service staff all had a long history in military logistics. This second area of skills essentially involved relationship building, identifying customer requirement, and cost justification of LISA's activity through systems/service delivery. Additionally, the retention of some technical skill was also considered important:

> "We can't retain too much... (technical)... skill because we will be paying twice for it, but we are retaining a modicum.... in the systems analysis and requirements definition area... and for rapid application development and prototyping, and hybrid skills for example... There can be a flaw in any outsourcing if you are actually outsourcing your basic skill, that there will come a time when you can no longer call yourself an intelligent customer..." (Alan Pollard, CEO of LISA).

Over the first two years the basic principle for involving LISA personnel was described as "customer backwards, control downwards". LISA's essential remit was twofold: to operate closely and actively with the end customer to elicit and clarify customer demand; and secondly to maintain overall control of the contract and performance, while leaving detailed operational delivery in the hands of the supplier. Project management and customer management skills were retained within LISA for these higher levels. As one example, on a particular systems project LISA supplied the project manager, and EDS the stage manager (a lower element manager within the PRINCE development methodology). A summary of the management approach is shown in Figure 6.2.

Part of LISA's task was to identify customers' information systems' requirements. In the face of an increasingly knowledgeable user base with some history of wanting to branch out on their own, this was not always easy. The Systems Management Boards represented one way forward. These were chaired and led by the business with LISA advisors on each one. Business managers funded and took the ultimate decisions on IS projects, subject to technical and – as a statutory requirement – financial approval by LISA. LISA staff offered project initiation and IS requirement identification, but the business had to commit a project champion with budgetary responsibility. EDS would then be expected to deliver the system, with LISA retaining final responsibility to the customer.

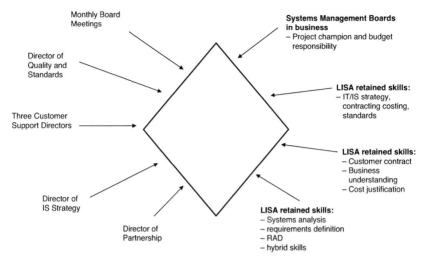

Figure 6.2 LISA Management Approach: "Customer Backwards, Control Downwards"

According to respondents, in the first three years the partnering relationship appeared to be functioning much along the preferred lines outlined by LISA's CEO:

> "We expect the partnership to be expressed as doing first and asking afterwards within given constraints, because obviously one of the key things we are looking for from the private sector is responsiveness and minimising the 'flash to bang' time of getting help to the (user) customer... we therefore expect EDS to apply the resource without too much question... but it's a delicate balance... if they commit too much resource at risk and the formal approval doesn't materialise, then they will be less inclined to commit a risk again. But we are looking for flexibility, a joint understanding of what we are trying to achieve, a sharing of goals and evidence that we are both working to the same game plan."

A final area of note in the first three years was evaluation. DLIS, then LISA, had been involved in evaluation and benchmarking issues for several years before 1996. Outsourcing had served to make LISA and its customers even more cost and resource conscious than before. Additionally there continued to be government pressures to index performance and create, for example, a league table of Agency performances. One valuable series of evaluations emerging at LISA were the pre-delivery justifications of IS investments, now carried out by the user customers, and, because of outsourcing, on a full cost basis.

A second area was LISA's close monitoring of service performance and customer satisfaction against a standard code of practice and service level agreements at end-customer and individual project levels. In effect these evaluations meant that the individual and joint performances of LISA and EDS were always under close review. Given that the vast majority of LISA's customers were Agencies, this meant also that the Partnership Contract came under intense pressure to deliver to Agencies' perceptions of quality, value, and timeliness. Therefore these perceptions also had to be closely tracked and met.

1997–99: service levels, developing applications, building infrastructure

After three years of monthly service review meetings LISA's contractual right to withhold 20% of any monthly payment if EDS had breached 50 negative points on service had never been exercised: As one manager commented:

> "They had met, indeed mostly exceeded the service levels, that were in excess of the ones we had set for ourselves before they came on the scene."

Good working relationships had also been established, with both sides having to learn a different style of operating. Nor had any major contentious personnel issues emerged amongst transferred or in-house staff. Some customers in other Agencies had envisaged large cost rises, but in fact they experienced benefits that were transparent because customer Agencies were charged on a full cost basis.

LISA was meeting its key targets of agreeing and delivering its customer IS programs 95% to cost, 95% to time and 80% to time and cost. The cost savings and minimum guaranteed revenues established in the outsourcing contract were being delivered. Baseline unit costs were established in the second year to ensure year on year cost reductions. Benchmarks and performance indicators had also been developed to enable better management of overall Agency performance against targets. Using the existing evaluation systems and measures, LISA and the EDS were meeting their targets without no major issues arising.

Tranche 1 had included two sample application development projects to assess EDS' ability to take on major applications work in Tranche 2. In the event, Tranche 2 was transferred in mid-1997, together with unforeseen local network development work for which there was a large user demand. One senior manager believed that LISA had paid more than it would have liked for the latter but:

> "At the end of the day if you try and screw them down too much on price it will come back and hit you in the back of the neck because you'll get what you pay for."

One element in early applications development work had not gone well amongst customers. This was Requests For Change (RFCs). Partly the problem was an over-bureaucratization of the process, with LISA sitting between vendor and customer. EDS also felt that LISA was not anticipating requirements as well as they might. Subsequently both LISA and EDS worked on a detailed prioritization mechanism distinguishing between minor (under 1,500 pounds, e.g., less than one day's coding), medium and high priority requests. According to a vendor respondent:

"The innovation here was to offer the low priority requests for free to the customer, the cost being born by EDS and LISA."

The obligations of EDS and LISA to respond as supply and demand managers were also tightened and made retrospectively contractually binding. Complaints about RFC costs were removed after mid-1997 when responsibility for prioritization and spending was taken over by the Quarter-Master General, leaving LISA and EDS dealing only with IT service delivery:

"The effect of these contract innovations was to remove the politics from issues like cost and service credits, a clearer recognition by the user of the quality of service being delivered, and a dramatic reduction in customer complaints throughout 1998" (senior manager, LISA).

From late 1997 LISA was looking to EDS to develop those systems defined as "strategic", while other suppliers were bidding on "non-strategic" development work. By then, however, Army center had developed a new strategic approach, and had identified the need for a corporate network. It was envisaged that this corporate infrastructure, with a 12,000 seat, intranet, data warehousing and electronic commerce capability, would be eventually run by EDS. This prompted the supplier to make an innovative bid to fund the development in its totality, and be paid out of the business savings that resulted. However, such a deal would have dwarfed the original Tranche 1 and 2 contract. It also short-circuited competitive bidding and its incentive element.

The LISA response was designed to give incentive to the supplier, while maintaining control. LISA would pay for the development of the first 2,000 terminals. If EDS could deliver these in time and within cost, then LISA would consider the possibility of EDS funding the rest of the development, and being recompensed out of business benefits. In practice EDS delivered the first stage successfully. By late 1998 the relationship seemed to have taken off. Furthermore, opening work to further competition could put a two-year break on any major systems development. According to the CEO of LISA, EDS were moving into the business strategic area of their customer and out of IT service commodity delivery:

"For the previous three years they have been our IT partner. The climate is changing whereby they are beginning to be the business partner now.

To reflect that, I requested that the final ownership of the partnership be with the Quarter-Master General, not with me.... You could see the IS side wasn't going to take off until the business processes were fully aligned. And therefore EDS had to be in at the groundwork."

Analysis and discussion of the LISA-EDS contract

In this section we will draw upon the analytical framework and prior research to develop comparative material against which case evidence on risk issues and their mitigation can be analyzed. The organizational risk from the LISA-EDS deal – quite quickly becoming a "total" outsourcing contract – was high, and the arrangements as at mid-1999 were still in place, and considered, with some qualifications, still reasonably effective by the diverse parties interviewed. Therefore it becomes valuable to analyze in more detail what and how risks were mitigated, and what risks remained. We achieve this by blocking the analysis into five primary areas that emerge for us from the case, namely outsourcing type and scope, vendor selection criteria and process, the contract, retained management capabilities and processes, and client-vendor partnering and relationships. Two further risk areas, distinctive enough to merit separate treatment, also emerge and are discussed. We subsume the points summarized in Table 6.2 into the analysis that follows, and compare the findings here against other research.

Outsourcing: type and scope

Based on Lacity *et al.* (1996) and Cronk and Sharp (1998), there are major risks when IT is treated as an undifferentiated commodity and becomes the subject of "total" outsourcing. Their research suggests that the low risk option route to using the market is to outsource "useful commodities" as opposed to "critical differentiators" in conditions of low business uncertainty. On the technical front, additionally, it is important to reduce risk by outsourcing discrete, as opposed to integrated systems, in situations of high technology maturity where the market could provide an at least comparable service at a more efficient price. To some extent LISA followed this low risk path. Thus clear distinctions were made between "core" and "non-core" business and IT activities, with only the latter considered as candidates for outsourcing. At the same time some of the IT activities outsourced to EDS were probably "critical" as opposed to "useful", in the sense of significant underpinning to LISA's and its customers' strategies and operations. The retention of certain LISA functions in-house together with the partnering aspect of the deal were designed to mitigate the risks here. One possibility, however, is that some future development work could be for "core" or "differentiating" systems and this may not be picked up in the analysis, or, with the transfer of large amounts of technical expertise, that LISA would not be in a position to control and deliver such systems. With

Table 6.2   LISA – Approaches to Risk Mitigation

Risk Factors	Practices at LISA	Emerging Risk Issues
1. Treating IT as an undifferentiated commodity	• Core/non-core split • Retained key in-house analysis, management and technical skills • Outsourced technology implementation	Ability to develop/retain control of future differentiating systems? (see also 4 below)
2. Incomplete contracting	• Tranche 1 detailed contract • Two-year option after five years • Tranching future work open to competitive bidding	Is future work forthcoming? Effect of giving work to another supplier? Effect of giving all work to EDS?
3. Lack of active management of the supplier on a) contract and b) relationship dimensions	• Detailed active daily management (see customer backwards, control downwards Figure 6.2) • Clear comprehensive management structure (Figure 6.1) • Regular supplier-business reviews • Processes in place to let relationship develop • Co-location • Contract a good foundation for relationship	Degree to which business, not just LISA will take responsibility? What happens to relationship if less optimistic scenarios occur?
4. Failure to build and retain requisite in-house capabilities and skills	• Retained strategy, contract management, standards maintenance, supplier relationship, customer contact, project management, business/ systems analysis and some technical capabilities (Figure 6.2)	Will bringing EDS into core areas (1998 on) erode in-house capabilities over time?
5. Power asymmetries developing in favor of the vendor	• Carefully delineated performance measures • Government ownership of assets • Intellectual property rights retained • Co-location and high security established • Competitive bidding mechanism • LISA acts as "intelligent customer"	Effect of rapid change and supplier/LISA staff turnover on ability to control vendor performance? By 1999 high dependence on a single supplier Very high switching costs Long-term supplier strategy to dominate the vertical market may increase power asymmetries in its favor.
6. Difficulties in constructing and adapting deals in the face of rapid business/technical change	• Staged five-year contract with additional two-year option • Tranching and "parcelling" of work for suppliers • Regular reviews and updates of price/service/requirement • Switching possibilities retained (?)	Inflexibilities in Treasury rules and funding Army procedures introduces inflexibilities Flexibility requires co-dependence not 5. Above LISA/customers possibly overwhelmed by expansion in business and technical requirements from 1998?

Table 6.2   LISA – Approaches to Risk Mitigation – *continued*

Risk Factors	Practices at LISA	Emerging Risk Issues
7. Lack of maturity and experience of contracting for and managing "total" outsourcing arrangements	• Used external consultant advice • Tranching designed to build up to total outsourcing gradually while developing experience • Thorough supplier selection process • Multi-disciplinary group for supplier selection • Careful analysis of need pre-contract • "Soft" factors assessed, not just price/cost	Retained management capability drawn largely from existing in-house resources with little commercial expertise. Turnover amongst in-house management group loses continuity and attained expertise over time Underestimated technical "fixing" capability needed in-house?
8. Outsourcing for short-term financial restructuring or cash injection rather than to leverage IT assets for business advantage	• £15 million to be saved over contract length • Looked to develop a preferred supplier relationship to deal with unanticipated work over the seven years • Multiple objectives, not just IT budget constraint	Over-dependence on supplier may detract from business advantage target Initial cost savings being sidelined by subsequent expansion in demand and dependence on supplier
9. Unrealistic expectations with multiple objectives for outsourcing	• Cost-service trade-offs initially focused and clear • Started with good control mechanisms to realize several objectives • LISA in place throughout as controlling intermediary	Service levels, especially with newly developed systems, more patchy than first two years Increasingly complex arrangements and IT developments to manage
10. Poor sourcing and contracting for development and new technologies	• Initial tranching of development work on potential competitive bids • Retention of technical, RAD and project management capability • 1998 deal motivates supplier using business contribution measurement for development and building infrastructure	Extent of customer/LISA participation in development work? Especially from 1998? Quality of retained in-house project/technical skills? Over-dependence on single supplier for all development needs Supplier capability to service all these needs? At reasonable price?

the further development in 2005 of a ten year £4.9 billion contract for all three services (army, airforce and navy) to be delivered by a consortium led by EDS, this became a particularly key issue in our view, though not discussed much in subsequent official reports (National Audit Office, 2008).

Contract tranching mitigated technical risks, at least at the front end of the contract. The work first handed over was stable, mature technical activities well understood by LISA, and being worked on by knowledge-able ex-LISA staff. However Willcocks *et al.* (1995) show that the outsourcing of immature IT activities – where the technology is new and unstable, or it is a new application of existing technology, or in-house staff do not possess the relevant experience – can be high risk. This would be the case with the Tranche 2 development work at LISA, but even more with the development work coming on-stream from 1998 onwards. Those authors recommend such work should be done in-house, with experienced resources being contracted in to work under internal management control to facilitate mutual learning on the technology and its business applications. There are two points here. LISA mitigated the risk here by expecting the long-term partnering element to pay the dividend of the supplier coming to act as a surrogate insourced resource. However, this dividend would probably take time to develop, and development work was already being considered for outsourcing within the first year of the contract. A more substantial mitigation was likely to come from the arrangements to run IT projects as business projects with the businesses heavily involved and responsible, LISA providing advice and regulation, and EDS acting as junior IT partner. LISA did also retain a level of tech-nical skill to offset technical risks, though how much to retain seems to be always a difficult judgement (Cross, 1995; Feeny and Willcocks, 1998; Reynolds *et al.*, 2007).

Finally, it was clear from all respondents that there was considerable technical and business change expected within LISA and its customers. In such circumstances short term selective outsourcing has been recommended as the lowest risk option (Lacity and Willcocks, 1998). However, the abiding logic at LISA was that uncertainty could be managed by tranching future work and making it the subject of competitively priced bids rather than putting it all out under the same contract conditions that would be difficult to draw up in the face of future uncertainties. This arrangement did also allow for the possibility of using a different supplier at a later date, if it proved necessary, while gaining motivational and learning advantages from developing a long-term relationship with EDS. Subsequently, to late 2000, a different supplier was never called upon for a major piece of work, thus rendering the mechanism designed to give incentive to the supplier while retaining flexibility somewhat redundant.

Vendor selection criteria and process

Several researchers have shown that poor vendor selection practice, misperceptions of vendor capabilities, together with exaggerated expectations as a result of vendor promises have been the source of relative lack of success in IT outsourcing deals (Lacity and Hirschheim, 1993; Michell and Fitzgerald, 1997; White and James, 1996). At LISA the risks were mitigated first of all by a thorough procurement process. This derived partly from military and public sector disciplines, but also because of the large scale of the outsourcing contemplated. Secondly, a range of disciplines were included on the Project Management Board. These included two areas that previous researchers noted as frequently absent from such teams, namely outsourcing contract (as opposed to straightforward legal contract) expertise, and outsourcing experience and marketplace/vendor knowledge (in the form of third party outsourcing consultants). The team reflected the composition of the effective vendor selection process at another public sector site, namely the UK Inland Revenue in 1992–94 (Willcocks and Kern, 1997).

A further weakness in vendor selection has often been an over-focus on price and cost to the detriment of "softer" factors, even though getting these wrong can be a significant risk area (White and James, 1996). In the LISA case this risk area was mitigated by a comprehensive evaluation of "partnership capability" using reference sites, site visits, and involving a range of assessors, including user managers. At the same time, clearly the assessment of cost and service delivery parameters are crucial in a bid process. Looking at 61 sourcing decisions Willcocks *et al.* (1995) showed considerable weaknesses arising in this assessment area with concomitant detrimental affects for the resulting outsourcing arrangements. In practice LISA would seem to have managed this evaluation area comprehensively and effectively, at least for Tranche 1. One sign of this was that two acceptable, competent suppliers emerged from the vendor selection process, and LISA was able to select the preferred candidate on additional superior criteria namely its more commercial, as opposed to the second candidate's more technical, orientation.

The danger would be in allowing success here to lead to cutting down the detailed work on later contracts for other work being put out to the bidding process. Another danger is to allow the competitive bid mechanism to become a routine process for selecting the preferred supplier rather than a motivational device for sharpening evaluation and the preferred supplier's bid. Both features have been observed in several other case histories, and both, according to several respondents, were also partly observable in the LISA-EDS arrangement (Currie and Willcocks, 1998; White and James, 1996).

The contract: substance, compliance and motivational mechanisms

Several researchers have pointed out the centrality of the contract to success or failure in the IT outsourcing deals they have studied (Fitzgerald and Willcocks, 1994; Lacity and Willcocks, 2000, 2009; McFarlan and Nolan, 1995; Shepherd, 1995). Certain weaknesses in contracting can result in significant, unanticipated costs arising. Thus the client may fail to contract completely for present and future requirements, allowing the vendor to charge excess fees at different prices from the contract. Ambiguities and loopholes in the contract, and failure to allow a reasonable profit can all prompt opportunistic behavior on the part of the vendor. Failure to contract properly can also mean a high, unanticipated amount of management activity and dispute resolution once the contract has become operational (Willcocks *et al.*, 1996; Williamson, 1996).

The LISA-EDS contract was an example of the more creative forms of contracting emerging in the outsourcing field in the mid and late 1990s. The comprehensive, and complete contract for Tranche 1 would seem to follow most of the guidelines and prescriptions on risk mitigation emerging from earlier IT outsourcing research. Tranching the future work, and drawing up separate contracts for each parcel, having a two year further option after five years, as well as making each piece of work open to a competitively priced bid – all these features were designed explicitly to mitigate the risks associated historically with having one long-term supplier. These include: power asymmetries developing in favor of the vendor; opportunistic behavior in the second half of the contract term; mid-contract sag as the vendor delivers to contract and nothing more; being locked in to the technologies that are convenient to the supplier rather than focused on client business requirements (Lacity and Hirschheim, 1993; Lacity and Willcocks, 1998, 2009; Willcocks and Lacity, 1998, 2009).

At the same time there could be risks associated with future work. Clearly the vendor was motivated to secure such work, not least because EDS could make little return on the base contract. But if this work had not been as forthcoming as had been anticipated, or the vendor could not make as competitive bid as an alternative supplier would be adjudged to make – in these circumstances the supplier would not have been so motivated, and may also have looked to minimize costs as much as possible on the base contract work. This could have eaten into the supplier's interest in providing the flexibility, fast response and technical access expected to emerge from the partnering dimension of the outsourcing arrangement. In practice these risks did not materialize, at least in the period under study. By 2000 the amount of IT work needing to be done had greatly expanded and EDS were very pro-active in presenting creative proposals to secure the contracts. In practice LISA and its customers perceived no real practical alternative but to give most future work to EDS – but the effect, as evidenced in some other deals, may well be to make the supplier complacent rather than competitive, in costing and service delivery terms (Lacity and Willcocks, 2000, 2009).

The balance for LISA and EDS remained a delicate one. In the initial two years EDS seemed to have been taking most of the risks, with only LISA securing the immediate rewards. The same applied to LISA's contractual right to have guaranteed minimum returns from the potential shared returns from selling mutual products and services on the wider market. Both elements of the contract represented calculated risks for EDS. But subsequently EDS took the opportunity to shift the risk-reward equation in its own favor, resulting in greater risks being experienced by LISA, not least through the higher switching costs and increased dependence on the supplier from 1998 on.

Retained capabilities and management processes

The subject of retained skills in outsourcing arrangements has received surprisingly little attention, and this continues to this day. A common approach, especially observable in the UK public sector has been to keep as few staff as possible in a "residual" function, carrying out IT governance contractual monitoring, and vendor liaison responsibilities (Willcocks, 1994). Other research has pointed to a more in-depth capabilities and skills base for the modern IT function where external suppliers are used on any significant basis (Rockart and Earl, 1996; Willcocks and Fitzgerald, 1994ab; Reynolds *et al.*, 2007). Research by Feeny and Willcocks (1998) showed the need to mitigate risks by staffing the four faces of the IT function – governance, elicitation and delivery of IS requirements, maintaining the technical base and managing external supply – with nine capabilities and their underlying skills. These are leadership and informed buying (governance); relationship building and business systems thinking (business "face"); technical architecture and making technology work (technical "face"); and informed buying, contract facilitation, contract monitoring and vendor development (external supply "face").

LISA's retained skill base mapped quite well on to this conceptualization (see Figures 6.1 and 6.2). The leadership and informed buying capability was clearly in place. The Customer Support Directors and their staff fulfilled the business facing functions, while the Contract Partnership Directorate staff fulfilled the four capabilities for external supply management. And indeed there were signs in the case study of further strengthening occurring on the evaluation and vendor monitoring front. The technical "face" was partly filled by the IS Strategy Directorate staff. Other research shows organizations making different decisions on how much technical skill to retain, though the evidence is that different types and levels of knowledge and "doing" skill need to be spread throughout all the nine capabilities, though in different degrees (Feeny and Willcocks, 1998). The balance and risks are usefully detailed by the comment of LISA's CEO in the case study section of this chapter (see above).

Management processes built on the "customer backwards, control downwards" principle (Figure 6.2) would also appear, on other research evidence, to be an effective risk mitigating approach, with LISA and business managers becoming much more involved in IT the closer it got to the business application area, and the more high level control and monitoring of the supplier was needed (Willcocks and Fitzgerald, 1994ab; Currie and Willcocks, 1998; Lacity and Willcocks, 2009). Particularly important risk mitigating features were the retention in-house of project management skills, and of control over what one respondent called the "business projects with an IT component" staying with LISA and business managers (Feeny *et al.*, 1997). The Systems Management Boards also represented active in-house information management components that served to mitigate risk of loss of in-house control of the critical information systems (business applications) as opposed to the IT (technical supply) area.

The worry in the LISA case is that, though the structure and capabilities remained in place throughout 2000, firstly the staffing of those capabilities were largely from in-house sources with little commercial and market expertise. Secondly, as several respondents commented, as staff turnover occurred, continuity in capability was lost, while the expertise established over time also eroded. A higher risk factor here, observed in other cases (Feeny and Willcocks, 1998; Currie and Willcocks, 1998), was that the in-house core capability would erode as the supplier took over responsibility for an increasing amount of work rationalized as part of "strategic relationship" development as suggested by LISA's CEO in 1998. Again, subsequent developments suggest that this risk was not really managed down, even when the retained capability was amalgamated to run defence information infrastructure for all three armed services (National Audit Office, 2008).

Vendor-client partnering and relationships

The case respondents talked frequently of the partnership between EDS and LISA, and indeed the outsourcing arrangement was formally known as the Partnership Contract. But partnership here was not meant in the strict legal sense, though the contractual agreement to mutually sell products and services on to the wider market embraced some more legal partnership elements. In examining the UK Inland Revenue-EDS total outsourcing agreement Willcocks and Kern (1997) concluded that forming, developing and sustaining relationships over and above the contract were fundamental to the mitigation of risk and to the achievement of the wider objectives of such deals. Other commentators and researchers have come to similar conclusions (Alberthal, 1994; Henderson, 1990; McFarlan and Nolan, 1995; see also Chapter 4). One important element identified is to have processes in place to allow the relationship to develop (Willcocks and Craig, 2009). The regular management board meetings, and often daily meetings between staff of the Partnership Management Directorate and EDS managers facilitated the development of the relationship. Co-location was also found to help in this process and in LISA's case the EDS account manager and staff were all located at the Bicester site.

At the same time, there has been found to be in IT outsourcing a mutual dependence and influence between contract and relationship development. Using case studies Kern and Willcocks (2001) showed that good relationships could not substitute for poor contracting; indeed the impact of the latter was usually to sour relationships. Building working relationships, confidence and a degree of trust takes time, and can deal with problems and difficulties, but only where the contract has been well set up and the vendor stood to make the required profit margins, or was achieving its wider strategic objectives (see below). In the LISA-EDS case the first two years obviously reflected the relationship in its transitional and formative phases. All respondents reported relationship development as a positive influence on the progress of the outsourcing arrangement. The risk element, and the real test of the ability of the relationship to mitigate risk for both parties, must be assessed from what happened subsequently.

Here, by 2000, the formal relationship structure and processes were still in place and over the next year continued to be utilized. Meanwhile, by 1999, EDS had made a strong move to become the major, single supplier of IT to UK army logistics. Its innovative bid to develop infrastructure and networks had considerable relationship implications. It meant that EDS would be responsible for most of IT development in army logistics, and, on EDS respondents' arguments, would need to be much more involved in the "business" aspects of IT planning and delivery. Here one can see a relationship in what Lacity and Willcocks (2001) have called the "middle" to "mature" phase of an outsourcing arrangement. However, while several respondents from both EDS and LISA suggested that this move would further develop the relationship and mitigate risk to mutual advantage, some new risks also emerged. Ironically, one tendency, according to two respondents, was to distance EDS operationally. As EDS subsumed to itself more work so their staff became more self-contained. To some extent, through these developments, LISA technical understanding was also being eroded or superseded over time. Also as EDS staff gained more knowledge of the business, and senior staff attended more in-house meetings, so its ability to facilitate solutions increased but so also did its ability to collect data that could be useful for its own revenue and profit generating purposes. The risk here was that these purposes might not always coincide with that of the client (Lacity and Hirschheim, 1993, 1995; Kern and Willcocks, 2001). According to several respondents, the relationship dimension was not helped in its development by the staff turnover experienced in both the client and the supplier during the expansion phase from 1998 onward.

Distinctive risks (1) the public sector context

Several specific characteristics of the history and context of LISA influenced the risk mitigation undertaken. These are subsumed into Table 6.1, but emerged as sufficiently significant in the case to merit separate comment. The first is the public sector context. Willcocks (1994) and Willcocks and Currie (1998) point to distinctive risks in public sector contexts (see also Chapter 7). In the present case the classified nature of the work for military establishments led to the IT work being carried out on-site at Bicester. This mitigated risk in permitting greater daily overseeing and control of vendor performance, as well as the development of closer relations between staff. Human resource issues were also always going to be sensitive, not least due to the Bicester area not offering opportunities for alternative employment, and the fact that the workforce had a strong voice through a recognized trade union. Siting of the work at Bicester, and the choice of a vendor able to deal with sensitive human resource issues and offer wider career opportunities, helped to mitigate the risks of staff hostility, demotivation or exit. The government's continued ownership of assets and of the intellectual property rights of future developed systems and software was also a public sector requirement that, in fact, served to mitigate LISA's risks in the outsourcing arrangement, by reducing potential switching costs in the event of dissatisfaction with the deal, and by securing rights to possible future revenues.

At the same time, the public sector in this period represented a volatile and uncertain environment in which to carry out a long-term total outsourcing deal, not least because of a range of management initiatives (for example quality improvement, Agency status) coupled with perennial, more traditional inflexibilites (for example Treasury rules on funding, and its Long Term Costing (LTC) plans) impacting on the conduct of any outsourcing arrangement (Willcocks and Currie, 1998). Some comment on how these risks engendered by change and uncertainty were mitigated has already appeared above. All this made any mutual flexibility developed within the Partnership Contract a critical, risk-mitigating feature. As one example, Treasury rules would require cash revenues generated from the EDS-LISA deal to be netted against LISA's annual cash provision from Treasury. The impact would be to reduce that cash provision. LISA wished to work with EDS to secure payment in kind so that a greater application of resource would benefit the LISA customer at no increased cost to the taxpayer. In practice such mutual flexibility, like the relationship itself, was reliant for its development on co-dependence of the parties.

Co-dependence was generated in several ways. Thus, because of tranching, EDS was reliant on LISA for future, additional, possibly more profitable work. LISA for its part had to answer to its business customers for delivering IT requirements at a competitive price – something it could not do without the contracted supplier. Thus LISA needed to motivate EDS and actively secure work for it while trying to ensure that its future margins were attractive. At the same time LISA could be squeezed out over time as the "middle man", with EDS going straight to the end customer for work. In this respect, it was important for LISA to secure a contractual and physical position that ensured it added value to both customers and EDS by its very presence. In so far as these built-in elements created mutual dependence they represented risk mitigating features of the outsourcing arrangements. However, by 1999 there were some question marks about the degree of co-dependence. By then EDS had achieved almost a monopoly on public sector military logistics IT outsourcing (see below). Moreover, army logistics had committed itself to high dependence on EDS for building infrastructure and networks from 1998, with very high switching costs and no practical alternative, given its time-scales and urgent need. In these ways the wider public sector context for IT outsourcing as it was created in the 1990s, together with public sector operational inflexibilities developed distinctive risks in the LISA-EDS outsourcing arrangement.

Distinctive risks (2) supplier long-term market strategy

A related risk area needs to be highlighted, namely the broader market strategy of the supplier, an issue highlighted in an earlier study by Kern and Willcocks (1996). One feature of EDS' business strategy in the mid- and late-1990s was the attempt to dominate vertical markets, including military logistics. Thus in the UK, with the conclusion of the LISA-EDS deal, as at 1997, EDS had the main IT outsourcing contracts for logistics support in all three services – Army, Navy and Airforce. In one respect this may result in a logical development that could have been countenanced by the in-house logistics teams. EDS had placed itself in a position to secure the economies of scale and efficiencies for the military services that some believed should have been achieved by earlier consolidation of the three in-house IT functions. In this way the previous barrier to consolidation – essentially the separate traditions and loyalties of the three Services – could be set aside and the risk of continuing undue expenditure mitigated. Subsequently, of course, a 2005 ten-year contract was let for the whole of the Defence information infrastructure to the Atlas consortium in which EDS was positioned as prime contractor, overseeing also Logica, EADS, General Dynamics and Fujitsu, and other sub-contractors where needed (National Audit Office, 2008).

Given that EDS probably had broader strategic reasons for entering into and supporting the LISA-EDS contract, it might well be that this was the overriding risk mitigation factor throughout the whole case. In this respect one could argue that many of the risk mitigation features implanted by LISA management were, perhaps, not that necessary. With broader objectives, EDS might not be too concerned about five–seven year profit margins in this specific case. There may well be few pressures militating against the development of good relationships between LISA and EDS, simply because the longer EDS stayed in the contract the more likely it was for the switching costs for LISA to rise to prohibitive levels – as indeed did happen. This has especially been the case where EDS also secured most, if not all future contract work, firstly through ensuring its bids were competitively priced, then subsequently pursuing a strategy of bidding innovatively for all future development work, the attraction being it would be paid not immediately but out of subsequent business savings and possibly bigger contracts. On this scenario, EDS price and delivery would remain satisfactory, at least during the first few years. Its broader strategic objective to dominate a vertical market would, in that period, secure an effective outsourcing arrangement for LISA, while EDS itself would begin to gain, as it did, valuable margins from the work and sales outside the base service offered.

There is a potentially longer term and bigger risk for LISA involved in all this, however. As EDS has become a near monopolistic supplier of IT services in the UK military logistics field it would become very difficult to dislodge. As Williamson (1996) points out, sitting suppliers have the advantage over new bidders of knowledge of and relationships with their customers. Moreover, in the IT field switching costs can be highly prohibitive (Lacity and Hirschheim, 1993; Lacity *et al.*, 1995, 1996). Switching costs become even more prohibitive when it is realized that there are no suppliers with any where near comparable experience and expertise in the military logistics market that EDS would have dominated for such a long period. One alternative might be to rebuild the in-house IT delivery function – again a very costly and time consuming process. On the other hand, EDS as a near-monopolistic supplier would not necessarily result in higher prices and lower quality delivery; it might well be satisfied with securing steady long-term profit margins rather than profit maximization. However, the problem for LISA remained that there were risks to it in all this. As suggested by Cross (1995), Currie and Willcocks (1998) and Lacity and Willcocks (1998) in this respect the real risk mitigation factor at LISA may well be to retain EDS's competitiveness by adopting a multi-vendor strategy, something its 1995–2000 contractual arrangements still made possible. As we now know, from 2005 the Department of Defence actually went down the consortium route in order to build on EDS's experience with military logistics, while bringing in a competitive element but on a partnering basis. In this scenario, much depends on the ability of suppliers to work together, otherwise the in-house group will spend a lot of time intervening and managing (Lacity and Willcocks, 2001).

Implications and conclusions

The chapter has presented an exploratory study of risk issues and their mitigation in a long-term total outsourcing arrangement in a UK public sector context. The case study work uncovered overall what might be considered an effective set of arrangements established for the first two years. However, the contextual and longitudinal approach adopted in this research has allowed us to pinpoint features, subsequent developments and risk factors whose risk mitigation might not be so easily contained by those initial arrangements.

We uncovered a range of risks relating to outsourcing type and scope, vendor selection criteria and processes, the contract terms, retained capabilities and management processes, and vendor-client partnering. The analytical framework proved once again to be sufficiently comprehensive to enable us to make sense of much of the rich data, while also allowing further in-depth qualitative, complementary analysis. The research approach enabled the further identification of two distinctive risk areas. The public sector context of the 1990s and the supplier's long-term market strategy emerged as significant distinctive risks. In terms of developing the analytical framework, the evidence from our case analysis is that supplier capability and long-term market strategy could be usefully added as a further distinctive risk area, as could external and organizational contexts for the period contracted for. Both would receive endorsement from work on IT project risks by Willcocks and Griffiths (1996) and by Sauer and Willcocks (2007).

In this chapter we have delineated the ways in which many of these risks were mitigated either by conscious management planning and action or by a combination of circumstances and features. We also pointed to a range of new risks emerging as the outsourcing arrangement, staffing and context shifted over the three years examined. In particular we flagged the importance of a longer-term risk feature in the LISA-EDS deal. This related to the broader vendor strategy of dominating vertical markets, in this case IT, and possibly wider, services to the UK defence logistics sector. We suggested that a multi-vendor strategy is one of the ways of mitigating this long-term risk, though multi-vendor strategies, of course, themselves incur their own risks (Cross, 1995; Currie and Willcocks, 1998) – something that those in charge of running the 2005–10 program for Defence Information Infrastructure outsourced to Atlas would probably be very aware of by 2008 (National Audit Office, 2008).

The implications of this research for practice are several. Firstly, we have utilized productively an analytical framework, that has, as a result of the case, been expanded into a 12 generic factor framework. The research supporting the gestation of this framework is sufficiently strong for its use to guide practice at the start of and during the course of IT outsourcing arrangements. In Figure 6.3 we put together a distillation of previous and current findings on the risks in IT outsourcing that have been emerging

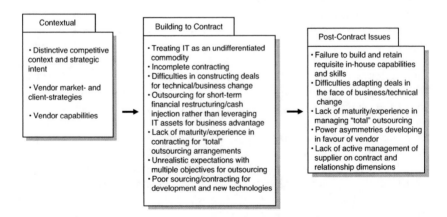

Figure 6.3   IT Outsourcing: Risk Analysis Framework

as distinctive and significant, as a possible guide for practitioners and for further research.

Secondly, how far are LISA's risk mitigation tactics replicable in other IT outsourcing situations? Table 6.1 indicates that many of the tactics were highly useful, especially in the first two years, but as circumstances, demand, and personnel shifted, so there emerged a constant need to re-examine the nature of risks and how they combine, and respond accordingly. There is some evidence in the case that LISA management were slow in doing this, and that emerging risks were both escaping their attention and also eroding their ability to respond. This suggests that in all IT outsourcing risk mitigation needs to be constantly revisited, but also that if understanding supplier long-term market strategy is as widely neglected as some authors suggest (Michell and Fitzgerald, 1997; Kern and Willcocks, 2000) it nevertheless emerges once more as a vital, risk mitigating task.

Thirdly, a key risk mitigating factor emerging from the case is that of building and retaining in-house distinctive core human resource capabilities. The capability to elicit and deliver business requirement, ensure technical capability, manage external supply and coordinate these to ensure control over the organization's IT destiny for business advantage emerges from the case as difficult to achieve, not least because of its public sector context. Feeny and Willcocks (1998) argue for high performers, constant rebuilding of the human resource capabilities needed, succession planning and human resource policies flexible enough to underwrite these requirements. What is observable in the case is that these capabilities need to be present before an outsourcing contract is signed if they are to be alive to risks and how they can be mitigated. Moreover, it becomes critical not to allow subsequent events and supplier strategies to cut across these capabilities and cause them to be eroded, as was, in our analysis, beginning to happen by early 1999 in the present case. Retention of these capabilities provides the primary means by which developing risk can be identified and assessed, and risk mitigating practices devised (Reynolds *et al.*, 2007).

Finally, and relatedly, there may well be common links between risk assessment for major IT projects and IT outsourcing, certainly where the latter also embraces new systems development, as in the LISA case. The issue received some discussion above (see section headed Outsourcing: Type and Scope). Invariably these days external suppliers become involved in large IT projects, and the question is: are there any sourcing principles that can guide how and in what such suppliers should be involved? The basic premise emerges once again from the present case: the lower risk approach is to outsource only mature IT activities that you can write a detailed contract for provided that the vendor is motivated, capable, stands to make a reasonable profit, and can be sufficiently monitored and supported. Furthermore, an organization needs to retain in-house the nine core IS capabilities, together with project management capability (as discussed by Feeny and Willcocks, 1998; see also above).

In the LISA case this was certainly the early intention, but by 1999, with EDS taking over major development work, increasing risks were being generated as retained in-house capability became distanced from such development, and became eroded over time as EDS got involved in more tasks and concerns that in 1995 had been defined as "core" and in-house.

The study has been necessarily an exploratory one but does illustrate the richness of the subject of risk and its mitigation in IT outsourcing arrangements. Hopefully the work here will stimulate other researchers to pursue this underdeveloped, but for both academia and practice, highly important field.

References

Alberthal, L. (1994) *User Satisfaction – The Global Challenge.* Address to the 9th World Computing Services Congress, Yokohama, Japan.

Ang, S. and Straub, D. (1998) "Production and Transaction Economies and IS Outsourcing: A Study of the US Banking Industry", *MIS Quarterly*, December, 535–542.

Ang, S. and Toh, S-K (1998) "Failure in Software Outsourcing: A Case Analysis", in Willcocks, L. and Lacity, M. (eds) *Strategic Sourcing of Information Systems*, Wiley, Chichester.

Applegate, L. and Montealegre, R. (1991) "Eastman Kodak Company: Managing Information Systems through Strategic Alliances", *Harvard Business School Case 9–192–030*, Harvard Business School, Boston, MA.

Auwers, T. and Deschoolmeester, D. (1993) The Dynamics of an Outsourcing Relationship: A Case Study in the Belgian Food Industry. Paper at the *Outsourcing Of Information Systems Services Conference, University of Twente, The Netherlands*, 20–22nd May.

Benbasat, I. and Zmud, R. (1999) "Empirical Research in Information Systems: The Practice of Relevance", *MIS Quarterly*, 23, 1, 3–16.

Bicknell, D. (1996) "Special Report: Contract Dispute: Miami Blues", *Computer Weekly*, 26–27.

Boehm, B. (1991) "Software Risk Management: Principles and Practices", *IEEE Software*, January, 32–41.

Charette, R. (1991) *Application Strategies for Risk Analysis*, McGraw Hill, New York.

Clement, D. (1996) "Big Mac Poised to Sign with Big Blue", *Sunday Business – Computer Age*, London, 2.

Collins, T. (1999) "End of the EDS Dream", *Computer Weekly*, October 28, 1, 22.

Collins, T. and Phillips, S. (1999) "Utility To Pull Plug on Perot Systems Deal", *Computer Weekly*, March 25, 1.

Craig Smith, A. (1990) "The Case Study: A Useful Research Method for Information Management", *Journal Of Information Technology*, 5, 2, 123–133.

Cronk, J. and Sharp, J. (1998) "A Framework for Deciding What to Outsource in Information Technology", in Willcocks, L. and Lacity, M. (eds), *Strategic Sourcing of Information Systems*, Wiley, Chichester.

Cross, J. (1995) "IT Outsourcing: British Petroleum's Competitive Approach", *Harvard Business Review*, May–June, 94–102.

Currie, W. and Willcocks, L. (1998) *New Strategies in IT Outsourcing: Major Trends and Global Best Practice*, Business Intelligence, London.

Davenport, T. and Markus, L. (1999) "Rigor vs. Relevance Revisited: Response to Benbasat and Zmud", *MIS Quarterly*, 23, 1, 19–23.

Davies, S. and Hosein, G. (2007) *Identity Policy: Risks and Rewards*, LSE, London, April.

De Loof, L. (1998) "Information Systems Outsourcing: Theories, Case Evidence and a Decision Framework", in Willcocks, L. and Lacity, M. (eds) *Strategic Sourcing Of Information Systems*, Wiley, Chichester.

Dempsey, M. (1999) "Outsourcing Refusenik Enjoys His Vindication", *Financial Times* – IT Review, August 4, 3.

DiRomualdo, A. and Gurbaxani, V. (1998) "Strategic Intent for IT Outsourcing", *Sloan Management Review*, 39, 4, 1–26.

Dunleavy, P., Margetts, H., Bastou, S. and Tinkler, J. (2007) *Digital Era Governance*, Oxford University Press, Oxford.

Earl, M.J. (1996) "The Risks of Outsourcing IT", *Sloan Management Review*, 37, 3, 26–32.

Feeny, D., Earl, M. and Edwards, B. (1997) "Organizational Arrangements for IS: Roles of Users and Specialists", in Willcocks, L., Feeny, D. and Islei, G. (eds) *Managing IT As A Strategic Resource*, McGraw Hill, Maidenhead.

Feeny, D. and Willcocks, L. (1998) "Core IS Capabilities for Exploiting IT", *Sloan Management Review*, 39, 3, 1–26.

Fitzgerald, G. and Willcocks, L. (1994) Contracts and Partnerships in the Outsourcing of IT. *15th International Conference on Information Systems*, Vancouver, Canada, December.

Griffiths, C. and Newman, M. (eds) (1996) "Risk Management and Information Systems", *Journal Of Information Technology*, Special Issue, 11, 4.

Grover, V., Cheon, M.J. and Teng, J. (1995) Theoretical Perspectives on the Outsourcing of Information Technology. *Working Paper*, University of South Carolina, Columbia, 1–27.

Henderson, J.C. (1990) "Plugging into Strategic Partnerships: The Critical IS Connection", *Sloan Management Review*, Spring, 7–18.

Hoffmann, T. (1996) "JP Morgan to Save $50 million Via Outsourcing Pact", *Computerworld*, 30, 21, May 20, 10.

House of Commons Committee of Public Accounts (2007a) *Central Government's Use of Consultants*, HMSO, London HC309 June 2007.

House of Commons Committee of Public Accounts (2007b) *Delivering Successful IT-enabled Business Change*, HMSO, London HC113 June 2007.

House of Commons Committee of Public Accounts (2007c) *HM Revenue and Customs: ASPIRE – The Re-competition of Outsourced IT Services*, HMSO, London HC179 June 2007.

House of Commons Committee of Public Accounts (2007d) *Department of Health: The National Programme for IT in the NHS*, HMSO, London, HC390 April 2007.

Huber, R.L. (1993) "How Continental Bank Outsourced its 'Crown Jewels'", *Harvard Business Review*, January–February, 121–129.

Impact Group (1999) *Creating New Value from an IT Outsourcing Relationship*, Impact Report, London.

Jurison, J. (1995) "The Role of Risk and Return in Information Technology Outsourcing Decisions", *Journal Of Information Technology*, 10, 4, 239–247.

Kern, T. and Willcocks, L. (1996) "The Enabling and Determining Environment: Neglected Issues in an IT/IS Outsourcing Strategy", *European Conference of Information Systems*, Lisbon, Portugal.

Kern, T. and Willcocks, L. (2000) "Cooperative Relationship Strategy in Global IT Outsourcing: The Case of Xerox Corporation", in Faulkner, D. and De Rond, M. (eds) *Perspectives On Cooperation*, Oxford University Press, Oxford.

Kern, T. and Willcocks, L. (2001) *The Relationship Advantage: Information Technology, Sourcing and Management*, Oxford University Press, Oxford.

Kern, T., Willcocks, L. and Heck, E. (1999) "Relational Trauma: Evidence of a Winner's Curse in ICT Outsourcing", *OXIIM Working Paper 99/2*, Templeton College, Oxford.

Kirkpatrick, D. (1991) "Why Not Farm Out Your Computer?", *Fortune*: 73–78.

Klepper, R. (1994) "Outsourcing Relationships", in Khosrowpour, M. (ed.) *Managing Information Technology with Outsourcing*, Idea Group Publishing, Harrisburg, PA.

Klepper, R. (1995) "The Management of Partnering Development in IS Outsourcing", *Journal of Information Technology*, 10, 4, 249–258.

Klepper, R. and Jones, W. (1998) *Outsourcing Information Technology, Systems and Services*, Prentice Hall, New Jersey.

Kumar, K. and Willcocks, L. (1999) "Holiday Inn's Passage to India", in Carmel, E. (ed.) *Global Software Teams*, Prentice Hall, New Jersey.

Lacity, M.C. and Hirschheim, R. (1993) *Information Systems Outsourcing: Myths, Metaphors and Realities*, John Wiley, Chichester.

Lacity, M. and Hirschheim, R. (1995) *Beyond the Information Systems Outsourcing Bandwagon*, Wiley, Chichester.

Lacity, M. and Willcocks, L. (1996) *Best Practices in Information Technology Sourcing*. Executive Report No 2, June. Templeton College, Oxford.

Lacity, M. and Willcocks, L. (1998) "An Empirical Investigation of Information Technology Sourcing Practices: Lessons from Experience", *MIS Quarterly*, 22, 3, 363–408.

Lacity, M. and Willcocks, L. (2000) *Inside IT Outsourcing: A State-Of-Art Report*, Executive Research Report, Templeton College, Oxford.

Lacity, M. and Willcocks, L. (2001) *Global IT Outsourcing: Search for Business Advantage*, Wiley, Chichester.

Lacity, M. and Willcocks, L. (2009) *Information Systems and Outsourcing: Studies in Theory and Practice*, Palgrave, London.

Lacity, M., Willcocks, L. and Feeny, D. (1995) "IT Outsourcing: Maximize Flexibility And Control", *Harvard Business Review*, May–June, 94–104.

Lacity, M., Willcocks, L. and Feeny, D. (1996) "The Value of Selective IT Sourcing", *Sloan Management Review*, Spring, 37, 3, 13–25.

Lee, A. (1999) "Rigor and Relevance in MIS Research: Beyond the Approach of Positivism Alone", *MIS Quarterly*, 23, 1, 29–33.

Lincoln, Y. and Guba, E. (1985) *Naturalistic Enquiry*, Sage, Beverly Hills.

Loh, L. and Venkatraman, N. (1992) "Diffusion of Information Technology Outsourcing: Influence Sources and the Kodak Effect", *Information Systems Research*, 4, 3, 334–358.

Lyytinen, K., Mathiassen, L. and Ropponen, J. (1998) "Attention Shaping and Software Risk: A Categorical Analysis of Four Classical Risk Management Approaches", *Information Systems Research*, 9, 3, 233–255.

McFarlan, F.W. and Nolan, R. (1995) "How to Manage an IT Outsourcing Alliance", *Sloan Management Review*, Winter, 9–23.

McLellan, K., Marcolin, B. and Beamish, P. (1998) "Financial and Strategic Motivations Behind IS Outsourcing", in Willcocks, L. and Lacity, M. (eds) *Strategic Sourcing Of Information Systems*, Wiley, Chichester.

Michell, V. and Fitzgerald, G. (1997) "IT Outsourcing, Vendor Selection and the Vendor Marketplace", *Journal of Information Technology*, 10, 3, 135–147.

Moad, J. (1993) "Inside an Outsourcing Deal", *Datamation*, 20–27.

Morris, P. (1996) "Project Management: Lessons from IT and Non-IT Projects", in Earl, M. (ed.) *Information Management – The Organizational Dimension*, Oxford University Press, Oxford.

National Audit Office (2006) *Department of Health – The National Programme for IT in the NHS. HC1173*, HMSO, London.

National Audit Office (2008) *Defence Information Infrastructure: Report to the Comptroller and Auditor General HC788 Session*, HMSO, London.

Osei-Bryson, K. and Ngwenyama, O. (2006) "Managing Risks in Information Systems Outsourcing", *European Journal of Operational Research*, 174, 1, 245–264.

Pettigrew, A. (1985) *The Awakening Giant: Continuity and Change In ICI*, Basil Blackwell, Oxford.

Pettigrew, A. (1990) "Longitudinal Field Research on Change: Theory and Practice", *Organization Science*, 1, 3, 267–292.

Pettigrew, A. and Whipp, R. (1991) *Managing Change for Competitive Success*, Blackwell, Oxford.

Poston, T. (1997) "Lloyds Ditches 50 Million Pound Outsourcing Contract", *Computer Weekly*, January 30, 1.

Reynolds, P. Willcocks, L. and Feeny, D. (2007) "Evolving IS Capabilities to Leverage the External IT Services Market", *MISQ Executive*, 6, 3, 127–145.

Rockart, J., Earl, M. *et al.* (1996) "Eight Imperatives for the New IT Organization", *Sloan Management Review*, Fall, 1–25.

Ropponen, J. (1999) "Risk Assessment and Management Practices in Software Development", in Willcocks, L. and Lester, S. (eds) *Beyond the IT Productivity Paradox*, Wiley, Chichester.

Sanders, P. (1982) "Phenomenology: A New Way of Viewing Organizational Research", *Academy of Management Review*, 7, 3, 353–360.

Sauer, C. and Willcocks, L. (2007) "Unreasonable Expectations – NHS IT, Greek Choruses and the Games Institutions Play around Mega-Programmes", in Sauer, C. and Willcocks, L. (eds) NHS Special Issue, *Journal of Information Technology*, 22, 3.

Shepherd, A.J. (1995) *IT Outsourcing Hype and Reality: A Practitioner Perspective*. Oxford Institute of Information Management, RDP85/6: 31, Templeton College, Oxford.

Strassmann, P. (1998) "The Squandered Computer", *Information Economics Press*, New Canaan.

Tho, I. (2005) *Managing the Risks of IT Outsourcing*, Butterworth Heinemann, Oxford.

Thomas, K. and Schneider, K. (1997) "Ernst and Young Scraps 45 Million Pound Model FM Deal", *Computer Weekly*, March 13, 1.

Vowler, J. (1996) "Management: Lessons in Outsourcing", *Computer Weekly*, 26.

Walker, C. (1996) "Giant Contracts Boost UK Outsourcing Growth", *Computer Weekly*, 12.

Walsham, G. and Sahay, S. (1999) "GIS For District-Level Administration In India: Problems and Opportunities", *MIS Quarterly*, 23, 1, 39–65.

White, R. and James, B. (1996) *The Outsourcing Manual*, Gower, London.

Willcocks, L. (1994) "Managing Information Systems in UK Public Administration: Issues and Prospects", *Public Administration*, 72, 1, 13–32.

Willcocks, L. (1998) "Reducing the Risks of Outsourced IT", in *Financial Times* (ed.) *Mastering Global Business*, Financial Times/Pitman, London.

Willcocks, L. and Choi, C. (1995) "Co-operative Partnership and Total IT Outsourcing: From Contractual Obligation to Strategic Alliance", *European Management Journal*, 13, 1, 67–78.

Willcocks, L. and Craig, A. (2007) *The Outsourcing Enterprise 4 – Building Retained Core Capabilities*, Logica, London.

Willcocks, L. and Craig, A. (2009) *The Outsourcing Enterprise 5 – Step Change: Collaborating To Innovate*, Logica, London.

Willcocks, L. and Currie, W. (1998) "Information Technology in Public Services: Towards the Contractual Organization?", *British Journal Of Management*, 8, S107–120.

Willcocks, L. and Fitzgerald, G. (1994a) *A Business Guide To IT Outsourcing*, Business Intelligence, London.

Willcocks, L. and Fitzgerald, G. (1994b) *IT Outsourcing and the Changing Shape of the Information Systems Function: Recent Research Findings*. Oxford, Oxford Institute of Information Management, Research and Discussion Paper, Templeton College, Oxford.

Willcocks, L., Fitzgerald, G. and Feeny, D. (1995) "IT Outsourcing: A Strategic Approach", *Long Range Planning*, 28, 5, 59–70.

Willcocks, L., Fitzgerald, G. and Lacity, M. (1996) "To Outsource IT or Not? Recent Research on Economics and Evaluation Practice", *European Journal of Information Systems*, 5, 143–160.

Willcocks, L. and Griffiths, C. (1996) "Predicting Risk of Failure in Large-Scale Information Technology Projects", *Technological Forecasting and Social Change*, 47, 205–228.

Willcocks, L. and Kern, T. (1997) IT Outsourcing as Strategic Partnering: The Case of the UK Inland Revenue. *Proceedings of the Fifth European Conference in Information Systems*, June, Cork, Ireland.

Willcocks, L. and Lacity, M. (eds) (1998) *Strategic Sourcing Of Information Systems*, Wiley, Chichester.

Willcocks, L. and Lacity, M. (1999) "IT Outsourcing in Insurance Services: Risk, Creative Contracting and Business Advantage", *Information Systems Journal*, 9, 163–180.

Willcocks, L. and Lacity, M. (2000) "Strategic Dimensions in IT Outsourcing", in Davenport, T. and Marchand, D. (eds) *Mastering Information Management*, FT/Pitman, London.

Willcocks, L. and Lacity, M. (2006) *Global Sourcing of Business and IT Services*, Palgrave, London.

Willcocks, L. and Lacity, M. (2009) *Research Studies in Information Technology Outsourcing: Perspectives, Practices and Globalization*. Volume 1 – Making IT Outsourcing Decisions; Volume 2 – Managing Outsourcing Relationships; Volume 3 – Global Outsourcing: Issues and Trends, Sage, London.

Willcocks, L., Lacity, M. and Fitzgerald, G. (1995) "IT Outsourcing in Europe and the USA: Assessment Issues", *International Journal Of Information Management*, 15, 5, 333–351.

Willcocks, L., Lacity, M. and Kern, T. (1999) "Risk Mitigation in IT Outsourcing Strategy Revisited: Longitudinal Case Research", *Journal of Strategic Information Systems*, April, 8, 2, 285–314.

Willcocks, L. and Lee, A. (2008) Series Introduction to *Major Currents In the Information Systems Field*, Sage, London. Six volumes.

Willcocks, L. and Margetts, H. (1994) "Risk Assessment in Information Systems", *European Journal Of Information Systems*, 4, 1, 1–12.

Williamson, O. (1996) *The Mechanisms Of Governance*, Oxford University Press, Oxford.

7
IT Sourcing: Examining the Privatization Option in Public Administration

Mary Lacity and Leslie Willcocks

Introduction

In this chapter the process and content of decision making on sourcing information technology (IT) in two case histories from the United States public sector are examined in detail. We find that outsourcing IT problems, as opposed to tasks, rarely works in either private or public sectors. The findings suggest that both sectors must develop similar IT competencies before considering sourcing decisions. These include fostering relationships with senior management, benchmarking performance, creating shared IT objectives, understanding requirements, diagnosing IT problems, evaluating in-house versus market capabilities, and, in the case of outsourcing, developing competencies in contract negotiation and post-contract management. The major difference between public and private sector sourcing was found to be that public sector agencies faced more environmental constraints, including dictated budgets and requirements, and restrictions on civil servant salaries (see Chapter 6 for a discussion of distinctive public sector contexts).

Privatization is the practice of outsourcing government assets and/or operations to the private sector. In this chapter the focus will be only on decision making and practice on sourcing information technology (IT) equipment and services. In the United Kingdom (UK) the outsourcing of IT to private sector IT service companies was a growing practice in the mid-1990s, leading by 1996 to contracts worth £2 billion (Willcocks, 1996). At the same time, however, the UK government's own Competing For Quality review pointed to long-standing problems with the privatization program, finding it consistently falling short of its financial objectives, while suppliers and in-house IT staff alike were, in this report, highly critical (Hassell, 1994; Collins, 1996). Under the Clinton administration in the 1990s the United States (US) public sector sought to follow the lead of the UK government in several respects with regard to privatization, not least in encouraging large-scale IT outsourcing. In Mintzberg's terminology such public sector privatization and "businessization" in the UK and USA represented a shift from a government-as-machine model to a managerial, performance-control model of government that, taken to its logical conclusion, could result in a virtual-government model being adopted (Mintzberg, 1996).

In many ways the 1990s was a very formative period for public sector IT outsourcing, which in both countries expanded massively, though not always successfully, in the following decade (Cordella *et al.*, 2008; Dunleavy *et al.*, 2007; National Audit Office, 2006). Here we investigate two cases of impending or actual privatization taken from the USA in the 1995–97 period. In addition to developing these case histories, we analyze and compare the findings against our research in both US and UK private and public sectors. In doing so, and in tandem with the previous chapter, we arrive at an assessment of emerging lessons on IT sourcing practice in public sector contexts. The chapter first outlines the US government context in which greater IT privatization was encouraged during the mid-1990s. The case histories follow, then the analysis and lessons.

Information technologies in context: the US government and privatization

In the USA, the growth of privatization in the 1990s may be attributed to Americans' increasing loss of faith in big government. As at 1997 the US Federal government employed three million civilians and two million military personnel and was spending $US1.5 trillion a year. The US federal government had run a deficit every year since 1970, with a federal debt of over $US3 trillion by 1992 (Samuelson, 1995). In 1996, when the federal debt swelled to $US5 trillion,[1] President Clinton briefly shut down the government.

In contrast to the Federal government, the 50 US States experienced budget surpluses in the 1986–96 period. In 1995 the States had a combined budget of $US344 billion and ran a combined surplus of $US20 billion. However, as the federal government began to hand over more programs, such as welfare, to the states, state governments could face a significant crisis (Wysocki, 1996). In January 1997, the US State Governors lobbied Congress to stop additional federal budget cuts.

Overall, by 1997, the US government was spending more than it collected in taxes. Was privatization the solution? During the Reagan Administration (1981–89), the Commission on Privatization was established to help resolve divisions of responsibility between the private and public sectors. The Chairman of the Commission, David Linowes (1996) outlined three arguments for privatization:

1. Government should access the creative talent available in the private sector;

---

[1]The federal debt is almost $20,000 per American citizen.

2. Consumers who require government services should be given a choice (parts of government are perceived as monopolies);
3. Government should not be in the business of business (such as being a $200 billion money loaner to farmers, home owners, and students).

The perceived benefits of privatization have included:

- raising money by selling government assets, such as land (as at 1996 the government owned 50% of the land west of the Mississippi River) and oil reserves (Linowes, 1996);
- lowering the cost of government (presuming the private sector was more efficient due to competitive market forces – a presumption fairly typical amongst senior politicians within the governing parties in both the USA and the UK both in the 1990s and to the present day (Cordella *et al.*, 2008; Willcocks and Currie, 1996).

Under the Clinton Administration, Vice President Gore's National Performance Review in 1993 proposed to re-invent government by measuring results, putting the customer first, introducing competition, and decentralizing (Peters, 1996). The promised results were a budget cut of $108 billion, and a cut of 252,000 civilian jobs, mostly managerial. The Congressional Budget Office promised that the federal outsourcing market – expected to grow at 5% annually – would save taxpayers 20% to 40% (Government Executive, 1996).

By 1996 US public sector IT was considered a prime target for privatization, particularly because government agencies had had trouble attracting and retaining IT professionals due to below-market salaries. By outsourcing IT, government officials were hoping to cut costs, increase service, and access new technologies. For example, in the State of Indiana the governor, Evan Bayh, signed an $80 million dollar contract, affecting 800 state IT employees. In press reports he stated: "*Data processing is not one of the central missions of government, and we believe it can best be done by the private sector*". As we shall see, the County Executive of Westchester commenced an $85 million, seven-year IT outsourcing contract with IBM in January of 1997. Another government agency that was evaluating large-scale outsourcing in the mid-1990s was the US Department of Defense (DOD). In 1995 the DOD had one of the largest IT functions in the world, with over 1.4 billion lines of code just for *non*-combat systems, 1,700 data centers, and an annual budget for maintenance of legacy systems of $9 billion. In addition to its immense size, the DOD had been an IT pioneer – the DOD for example was responsible for creating the Internet. Traditionally, IT was a DOD core responsibility. The Clinton Administration's push for privatization in the mid-1990s questioned that responsibility. For example, Vice President Gore sponsored a National Performance Review which made the following recommendation:

"By contracting out non-core functions, the Department of Defense will be better able to focus on its core responsibilities."

In the light of this interest in IT privatization we conducted two case studies on IT sourcing decisions in the US public sector – the Internal Revenue Service (IRS) and Westchester County (WC) in New York State. Both public agencies were under pressure to reduce IT costs. In the case of the IRS in particular, IT costs had, by 1996, swelled to 20% of the overall budget (and, indeed, became the subject of a congressional committee to restructure the IRS). The cases explore the context, process and content of IS sourcing decisions, with a view to deriving lessons from these case histories.

Research approach

The case studies were prepared from research evidence gathered in a nine month period in 1996, and a follow-up period in January 1997. Recognizing the growing importance of the public sector IT outsourcing phenomenon and the dearth of academic research in this field at the time, the overall research objective was to gain insight into the processes of decision making, and into factors influencing decisions on and management practice concerning IT privatization in public sector contexts. A further objective was to derive lessons from the two case experiences so far, by comparing them against each other and against findings from our previous research into IT sourcing decisions and practices in both the private and public sectors (see Chapters 4, 6 and 7). We pre-selected two cases for analysis: one in central government – the Internal Revenue Service (IRS), and the second in county government administration – Westchester County (WCC). The research sites were chosen because they gave some spread in terms of size of unit being considered for privatization, and type of public sector operation, and both were current cases – as at the beginning of 1996 – in which we could observe events as they unfolded. In the latter respect the selection was opportunistic. We observed principles of triangulation in respect of gaining access to participants with different perspectives and interests, including IT and general managers, politicians and union representatives in each case.

A limitation here is that we interviewed low-level operational employees in the WCC case only (five people), though we did interview union representatives in both cases. A further limitation is in respect of the longitudinal nature of the cases. While we consulted written materials relating to prior periods, essentially our participant observation and analysis was for a ten-month period only. In research into organizational change in the United Kingdom (Pettigrew, 1990) and into IT-enabled business process re-engineering (Currie and Willcocks, 1996) the advantages of a longitudinal case study approach were advanced and demonstrated. In practice, it was intended to continue further research into the cases under review, though the limitations of reporting results from a ten-month study period need to be accepted. A strength of the research approach, however, is the assembly of research evidence in a contemporaneous time period, in public sector contexts, allowing a degree of comparison of results, also facilitated by structuring the research approach along similar lines, as far as practically possible in each case. In practice, the cases produced many similar, but also some necessarily distinctive research materials. It is important to be aware of these in order to substantiate the validity of comparisons between the research findings.

In more detail, the first case was prepared from IRS documentation, press reports, audit reports of the General Accounting Office (an oversight agency of the IRS), discussions with senior policy advisors from the National Commission to Restructure the IRS, and discussions with and evidence presented by the Commissioner of the IRS, the Chief Information Officer of the IRS, the IRS Deputy Chief of Taxpayer Services, a senior IRS union official and a senior administrator of the General Accounting Office. Research in the second case began in 1996 with detailed discussions with senior legislators in Westchester County. Subsequent interviewing and contact with WCC employees observed triangulation principles. Additionally, the following documents were gathered: IT budgets and organizational charts, press articles, the County's strategic and capital plans, report prepared by a consulting firm (hired by the County Executive) endorsing privatization, rebuttal of the Consultant's Report by County IT employees, outside Review of the Consultant's Report by an accounting firm (hired by the Citizen's Advisory Board), and a report prepared by a consulting firm – hired by the legislature – evaluating a draft Request For Proposal document. Additional documents included memos between the administration and the CSEA union, between the administration and IT managers, and documents/presentation materials on the proposed contract.

These diverse research materials gained from a range of stakeholders and perspectives, together with a degree of participant observation in each of the case study sites enabled us to develop a qualitative, interpretative approach to case study construction (Walsham, 1995). So constructed, the case studies will now be detailed in the next two sections.

Case: the US Internal Revenue Service (IRS)

In this case synopsis, we look at IT sourcing issues at the Internal Revenue Service.[2] In the 1990s the IRS lacked the project management capabilities to develop large-scale integrated systems in-house. One such visible failure was a \$US4 billion Tax Modernization System which did not meet cost, budget, or functionality objectives. Outsourcing was perceived as a solution to poor internal system development efforts. The initial faith in outsourcing, however, was tempered by two abandoned IT outsourcing contracts

---

[2]The Internal Revenue Service is the USA's tax administration and collection agency.

– one $285 million contract for an imaging system, and a $17 million contract for an electronic filing system. In 1996, the US Congress created the National Commission to Restructure the IRS to assess, analyze and propose positive reforms to the IRS, particularly for the Tax Modernization System designed to increase efficiency, quality, and compliance.

Background and context

As at 1996 the stated mission of the IRS was as follows:

> The purpose of the Internal Revenue Service is to collect the proper amount of tax revenue at the least cost; service the public by continually improving the quality of our products and services; and perform in a manner warranting the highest degree of public confidence in our integrity, efficiency, and fairness (Internal document).

The IRS's challenge to meet these three competing missions of compliance, service quality, and efficiency necessarily raised the issue of where it should focus resources. On the issue of compliance, in 1996 the IRS collected 86.5% of the taxes due (all figures for 1996 unless otherwise stated). About 83% was through self-assessment, and another 3.5% through compliance (that is, IRS audits). The fact that the IRS regularly had not collected nearly 15% of the taxes due has had profound implications for the federal government, as well as reducing the faith of American taxpayers in the system. As the IRS Commissioner commented in evidence to the Commission on Restructuring the IRS: "no one wants to pay taxes, but people expect that the system is at least fair, that everyone is paying their share."

On the issue of service, the quality of service was regularly perceived by taxpayers as very poor. A survey conducted by the University of Michigan found that the IRS customer satisfaction ratings were the lowest among the 200 companies and government agencies measured on the index. Customer satisfaction also dropped from 55% in 1994 to 50% in 1996.[3] During tax season (January–April), American tax payers who called the IRS to seek assistance in preparing their returns had often encountered a busy signal. For those calls that were answered, IRS case workers had to use as many as seven terminals to access taxpayer information due to the lack of integrated systems, resulting in poor customer service. There was another aspect of customer service that irritated taxpayers: when IRS case workers gave the taxpayer wrong information, the taxpayer remained liable.

On the issue of efficiency, the IRS was widely perceived to be, up to 1996, a large, wasteful bureaucracy. While the IRS' budget rose from $2.5 billion in

---

[3]Reported on National Commission to Restructure the IRS web site http://www.house. gov/natcommirs on February 6, 1997.

1979 to $7.3 billion in 1996, "*tax returns processing has not become significantly faster, tax collection rates have not significantly increased, and the accuracy and timeliness of taxpayer assistance has not significantly improved.*"[4] Much of the criticism on the inefficiency of the IRS to this date focused on information technology – $1.32 billion (18%) of the IRS' budget was spent on IT. With this IT budget, the IRS was trying to maintain the legacy systems ($758 million per year) while at the same time build a Tax Modernization System ($336 million per year). It is this modernization effort that, by 1996, was receiving the most negative attention. For example, the front page of the *New York Times* reported on January 31, 1997 that "*The IRS conceded today that it had spent $4 billion developing modern computer systems that a top official said, 'do not work in the real world.'*" The National Commission to Restructure the IRS found:

"To date, the Tax Systems Modernization program has cost the tax payers $2.5 billion, with an estimated cost of $8 billion. Despite this investment, modernization efforts were recently described by the General Accounting Office as 'chaotic' and 'ad hoc'".[5] (The discrepancy in figures – $4 billion verses $2.5 billion – despite our research efforts, remains unexplained).

Therefore, by 1996, the public *perceived* the IRS as ineffective in meeting the three objectives of compliance, service, and efficiency. The Commissioner of the IRS attempted several times to alter perceptions of the IRS by pointing to its many successes. In evidence to the National Commission to Restructure the IRS she summarized these points. First, the IRS did function – in 1996, for example, it processed all 200 million tax returns and 80 million tax refunds in a timely manner. The IRS annually collected $1.5 trillion in taxes. Second, the IRS had made significant progress in helping taxpayers obtain information, file their returns, and make payments. Specifically, the IRS had successfully implemented the following systems:

• Telefile system, a system that allowed taxpayers to submit their return on the phone. In 1996, this system was used by over 12 million Americans;
• Taxlink, an electronic filing system, was used by 70,000 participants;
• The IRS forwarded 3.2 million returns to 31 states through the Fed/State electronic filing system (to help US states collect state taxes);
• The IRS' world wide web site was assessed 1,000,000 times a day during tax season. The site provided all IRS forms, publications, summaries of regulations, and self-help tools. The IRS' www site had won over 40 awards for its design and ease of use;

[4]*Ibid.*
[5]*Ibid.*

- The IRS developed a FAX-Forms service which faxed over 170,000 pages of tax forms;
- The IRS developed a system to deposit refunds directly into bank accounts, which was used by 10.1 million taxpayers.

Despite these IT successes, the major challenges facing the IRS included project management of (1) in-house, large-scale, systems development and (2) outsourced systems development projects.

Project management of in-house systems development.

The IRS was being severely criticized for its inability to manage large systems development efforts. The most visible of these programs was the Tax Modernization System (TMS). One of the main system development efforts under TMS was the replacement of legacy systems that have multiple, fragmented databases. Typically when a US taxpayer called the IRS for a question, the IRS case worker needed to access several terminals. Even then, as at 1996, only 10% of taxpayer information was accessible. TSM was supposed to replace these legacy systems with an integrated, relational database system. The proposed system was supposed to provide a single interface for IRS case workers to access and update taxpayer information, as well as to improve compliance and financial reporting. According to testimony of the IRS's CIO to the National Commission to Restructure the IRS on January 30, 1997, the development of the system *"never progressed beyond the design stage."* Instead, a less ambitious project was undertaken. Rather than develop a radically new system, the IRS kept the legacy databases and provided a multi-windowed view of data from a single terminal. The pilot system (which was never rolled-out) was a success in that the case workers could access multiple databases from one terminal, but as at early 1997 they did not have update capabilities. It took ten days for updates to be reflected in the databases.

The General Accounting Office (GAO) criticized the IRS for poor results of the $4 billion spent on the Tax Modernization System so far. GAO report AIMD/GGD-96-152 stated:

> The Department of Treasury concluded that IRS has not made progress on TSM as planned because systems development efforts had taken longer than expected, cost more than originally estimated, and delivered less functionality than originally envisioned.

Significant problems on the tax modernization efforts reported by the GAO included:

- Failure to achieve customer service and compliance goals;
- Re-engineering efforts are not integrated;
- IRS information systems projects are poorly managed;

- Software development activities are inconsistent and poorly controlled;
- System architectures, integration, and testing are incomplete;
- No single IRS manager controls all information systems efforts;
- Plans must be defined and capabilities strengthened before obtaining additional contract support.

Managing outsourcing contracts

For several years the GAO believed that the IRS did not have the project management capabilities to develop large-scale integrated systems. This perception led to the outsourcing of a number of system development projects. Several outsourcing contracts, however, also led to failure because the IRS did not have the capabilities to oversee outside contracting. In particular, according to respondents, the IRS lacked the capabilities to properly define requirements, to negotiate, and to manage system development contracts.

In a report prepared by the General Accounting Office, the IRS was criticized for a number of large, expensive outsourcing contracts that were abandoned during systems development. The IRS contracted the development of Cyberfile, an electronic filing system, to the National Technical Information Service (NTIS), part of the Department of Commerce. Development of the system was abandoned after the IRS had spent $17 million dollars. The General Accounting Office (GAO) Report AIMD-96-140 stated:

> GAO reported that IRS's selection of NTIS to develop Cyberfile was not based on sound analysis; nor did IRS adequately analyze requirements, consider alternatives, or assess NTIS' capabilities to develop and operate an electronic filing system, even though the need for these critical prerequisites was brought to management's attention as early as July 1995.

According to a Senior Policy Advisor for the National Commission to Restructure the IRS, another large-scale outsourcing contract for the development of imaging system to process paper returns also failed. The contract, initially signed with IBM but later bought-out by Lockheed-Martin, was cancelled after expenditure of $285 million. The system did not work because error rates for optical character recognition of handwritten returns was too high. Again, the IRS failed to both assess the vendor's capabilities and manage the outsourcing contract.

Despite these failures, as at early 1997 many other IRS information systems functions were likely to be outsourced. Thus the Deputy Chief of the IRS' Taxpayer Service had already called for the outsourcing of the processing of paper returns in testimony to the National Commission to Restructure the IRS on January 30, 1997:

> A primary reason for our interest in outsourcing is that we believe imaging technology must be a large part of the future for efficient processing

activities". (No mention was made of the failed $285 million imaging project).

The Commissioner of the IRS, in testimony to the National Commission on Restructuring the IRS on January 31, 1997 said:

> Implicit in the idea of privatizing government is an idea one often hears these days that government should be operated more like a business. Clearly, an attractive notion, at least superficially...There are constraints in the public sector today not present in the private sector. At the IRS, for example, we do not determine our product lines, nor can we drop those that are unprofitable. We do not choose our customers – we take all comers, even those who are not particularly credit-worthy. We have no control over the rate of employee compensation nor benefits. Sometimes, we cannot even choose a business location." – Margaret Richardson, Commissioner of the IRS.

Other IT issues

In addition to these sourcing issues, as at late 1996 the IRS faced a number of other IT-related challenges, including encouraging taxpayers to submit electronically, and updating the legacy systems for the Year 2000. In the 1996–97 period under review the IRS was trying to encourage electronic submissions because the error rate for electronic submissions was only 1%. With paper returns, the error rate was 20%. Half of the errors were caused by the IRS (such as keypunching errors), and half the errors were caused by taxpayers. Another benefit to the taxpayer for filing electronically was that refunds were processed in two days versus 20–30 days. But taxpayers did not expect refund cheques to arrive quickly, and therefore this benefit had, by early 1997, not enticed them to switch from paper to electronic submission. In addition, taxpayers had been reticent to submit electronically because of a perception that it would increase the likelihood of a personal audit. American taxpayers generally also perceived that paper filing was less expensive, at least initially, for themselves. The cost of postage to mail a paper return was 32 cents, while electronic filing had to go through a tax preparer that charged a minimum fee of $25).[6] Simply put, there were insufficient incentives for Americans to file electronically. As several case respondents described it, the attitude of many American taxpayers tended to be: why make it easier for the IRS to take my money? This is an example of an IT system that was, as at early 1997, a technical success, but failed to gain user acceptance.

---

[6]Testimony of CEO of H&R Block, a private company that prepares over 17 million returns, to the National Commission to Restructure the IRS on January 30, 1997.

As at 1997, the IRS faced serious problems with current systems because of the century date problem. The IRS' legacy systems had 62 million lines of code needing to be reviewed, recoded, and tested by December 31, 1998. A Report by the National Commission to Restructure the IRS concluded that: "*The consequences of not completing this activity on time are catastrophic.*" Issues here included a shortage of personnel to make changes, confounded by poor documentation of legacy systems to even detect date fields.

Future issues and developments

Most of our investigation of the IRS and its ability to manage IT has focused on internal workings of the agency. But a major problem rested with the US Congress regularly setting down tax laws, IRS salaries, and IRS budgets without considering the IRS' ability to function under these constraints. US tax laws were (and are) complex enough for more than 50% of American taxpayers to hire tax professionals to prepare their tax returns. As at early 1997 it seemed that, until tax reform occurred through Congress, the IRS would continue to have to go on reactively managing its ageing systems. But as at 1997 such reform seemed unlikely, and IRS senior management remained under pressure to find a way forward despite the external constraints.

On the issue of dictated salaries, the IRS at this date was unable to recruit and retain an adequate workforce because civil servant salaries were well below market-value. As one example, it took the IRS a year to find a CIO because the salary for the job was not competitive with private sector salaries for similar work. But outsourcing to access vendor talent had not worked well in the past because the IRS had lacked key management capabilities to define requirements, assess vendor capabilities, and negotiate and manage contracts. Without developing these in-house capabilities first, outsourcing in the future could lead to the same outcome: costly termination of outsourcing contracts.

In testimony to the National Commission to Restructure the IRS, Christopher Hoenig, Director of Information Resources Management for the General Accounting Office, suggested that the IRS needed to return to the fundamentals of sound IT management. In his estimation these included: strategic alignment of IT strategy with IRS mission, fostering key relationships between IT and agency management, holding program managers and stakeholders accountable for IT, creating a Board to evaluate and prioritize IT projects, benchmarking current performance, and rigorous measurement and accountability for results. These would, indeed, seem to be the fundamental capabilities the IRS needed to develop, as at early 1997, before further outsourcing could be considered.

Case – Westchester County

In late 1995 the County Administrators began looking at privatizing the IT function together with the majority of the 160 IT employees at Westchester

County. Their evaluation culminated in an $85 million dollar, seven-year contract with ISSC, a subsidiary of IBM on January 1, 1997. However, the contract was subsequently declared illegal by two New York state judges. The judges found that the County Executive failed to obtain a majority approval of the County Legislators to privatize. In early 1997 the County Executive appealed against the decision for a second time, and the court issued "stays" until the appeal process was complete. In the meantime, the County Executive planned to fund the contract by diverting moneys from other departments and services. In this case, we describe the decision process that led to this situation.

Background and context

Westchester County lies 20 miles north of New York City. In 1996 the County had a population size of 875,000. As at 1996 the County Government comprised an elected County Executive (four-year term) and 17 elected County Legislators (two-year terms). The County Legislators approved policy, including the creation/elimination of positions and major budget decisions. Westchester County was staffed by 9,300 employees. Most employees belonged to a civil service union. The budget for the County in 1996 was $948,812,567. In 1996, Westchester County's centralized IT department had an annual budget exceeding $30 million, half of which was charged back to user departments. The centralized IT budget was 3% of the County's total budget.[7] In 1996, Westchester County's IT Department was staffed with 160 employees, whose salaries amounted to $7,615,205 or 0.8% of the County's total budget.[8] On average, the annual budget represented $1,084 per citizen, $34 of which was spent on IT.

Westchester County's IT department was functionally organized to cover Technical Services, Distributed Systems, Client/server Systems, Graphics Services and Customer Liaison. The IT department serviced over 3,500 terminals, handled over one million transactions per day, and printed over 27 million pages annually. The County operated a world-class imaging system for the processing of land records, financial claims, and voter registration. The system had been such a success that various other County departments had requested imaging systems and the IT department was receiving many visits from staff from other Counties.

IT outsourcing decision process

In the early part of 1995, the County had sought advice from the County's business executives in the private sector on cost reduction strategies. Some business executives suggested outsourcing as a possible way to reduce costs.

---

[7]On average, government agencies spend 9% of their budgets on IT (Minoli, 1994).
[8]On average, government agencies spend 3.4% on IS salaries (Minoli, 1994).

Based on this recommendation, the County Executive engaged a consulting firm to assess the County's information systems department and the viability of privatization. The purpose of the study was to review the costs and services of the IT function, including the identification of "procedural improvements and alternative processing." The seven-member consulting team interviewed 45 managers in the County and administered a user satisfaction survey. On June 30, 1995, the consulting firm delivered their final report. In essence, the consulting firm validated the push for privatization, claiming a savings of $3 million to $5 million annually.

The IT County employees refuted the consulting firm's report. They argued that the consulting firm's report was biased because the seven-person team comprised five IT outsourcing vendor representatives. The IT employees identified inaccuracies in the document, such as the claim that outsourcing would avoid spending $6 million on a new data center. Employee representatives argued that the downsizing of technology had allowed enough space in the existing data center to accommodate all machines, without the need for a new data center. The IT employees noted that the projected $3 million to $5 million was calculated by multiplying the usual savings for IT outsourcing of 10% to 20%, and that no concrete cost savings had been identified. The IT employees also contended that the report omitted the IT employees' initiatives and recommendations to reduce costs, including hardware maintenance renegotiation, data center automation (reduces headcount and improves service), data center consolidation (reduces facility costs), and online reporting (reduces printing costs).

The County Administrators defended the report, arguing that the consulting team was not biased and that the $6 million was a legitimate cost saving. The Citizen's Budget Advisory Committee – a committee advising the Legislators – hired an accounting firm to comment on the validity of the report. The accounting firm was already employed by the County and represented a number of city governments in Westchester County. On August 31, 1995 the accounting firm presented their report. The partner from the accounting firm wrote:

> Overall I am surprised [the consulting firm] would deliver such a report. I would expect a higher standard of performance than this report evidences. It generally claims to be a privatization study of the county's Information Systems Department yet it is lacking in many fundamental respects...
> First, a privatization study is essentially a make-vs.-buy analysis which is a comparative study. Is it more cost effective to purchase services compared to the county producing them itself? Yet, the report does not present any comparison to this central issue... Second, the report addresses privatization at an aggregate level and fails to adequately consider alternative provision of services on a disaggregated basis... Third, the report

fails to present other alternatives to privatization... Fourth, there is a general lack of analytical methodology presented in the report... Not only is comparative analysis missing, so too is sensitivity analysis, present value analysis, or any statistically based methodologies... Fifth, the report is long on background and short on analysis. Indeed only 8 of the 101 pages of the report seen to address the central question... Sixth, the eight pages of analysis are lacking in support. The $3 to $5 million savings seems to come from thin air.

After the initial report recommending privatization, the Deputy County Executive wrote a memo to the president of the CSEA[9] announcing the IT outsourcing evaluation and inviting CSEA IT employees to submit a competitive bid. In October 1995, the County Administrators (Deputy Administrator for General Services and a representative for County Executive) and IT managers (IT Manager, Assistant Manager, Director of Applications Development, Director of Technical Support, Director of Telecommunications) began to create the request for proposal. They hired the services of a law firm specializing in IT outsourcing contracts. The RFP was completed in December 1995.

On November 2, 1995, the President of the CSEA responded to the memo. Her memo welcomed the stated goal of tax relief for Westchester County and the invitation to provide cost savings. She requested several items to enable an internal response, including management participation, full access to information, ample time to discuss alternatives. In addition, she requested the assurance that the implementation of changes would result in the avoidance of layoffs because "it would hardly suit our mutual purposes to develop new processes, build trust and partnership and then destroy it with a fresh layoff threat during the next budget season".

On November 21, 1995 the County Administrator of General Services sent a memo that outlined the guidelines for an internal bid submission:

We understand that it is management's requirement that only staff who are a grade 14 and below could participate in this process and that no work on this response could occur during normal working hours or on County owned equipment. We also understand that due to a perceived conflict of interest or the possible appearance of preferential treatment, no assistance in the bid preparation could be received from staff who are above a grade 14 or from our IS management. We further understand

---

[9]The County Administrator's office comments, "It is important to note that both consistent with NYS laws governing labor relations as well as existing collective bargaining agreements that all communications by management involving employer/ employee issues are to be addressed through the CSEA and not the IS employees who are part of the collective bargaining unit."

that in reference to information regarding the scope of the RFP or supporting detail such as baseline of IS operations, staff would only receive materials which are also available to all vendors involved in the bidding process.

There were two perspectives on the proposed process for the creation of an internal bid. The County Administrators noted a conflict of interest if the internal IT managers who took part in the creation of an RFP also took part in the creation on an internal bid. The County Administration also wanted to create a level playing field between internal and external bidders. The rank-and-file IT employees (grade 14 and below) contended that the proposed process severely hampered their ability to create an internal bid because they were denied access to management, resources, or time off to prepare a bid. In the IT department, the titles above grade 14 included all the IT managers. The IT employees invited to make a bid (grade 14 and below) held titles such as Senior Systems Programmer, Senior Systems Analyst, Systems Analyst, and Computer Operator. The IT employees contended that the process did not provide a level playing field because vendors paid their employees and provided resources to respond to a request-for-proposal. In addition, they argued that vendors had full access to their own costs, service levels, and management input to make an informed bid, whereas the internal IT employees did not.

At this time the Legislators also hired a consultant to advise them on the outsourcing decision. One of his tasks was to analyze the RFP. On February 6, 1996, he presented his report. He recommended a supplement to the RFP to address missing policy issues. His primary finding was that: *"In short, the documentation and structure of the outsourcing alone do not assure the County of any cost savings whatsoever."* He specifically recommended that the vendor be required to identify how they propose to achieve cost savings; that processes should be re-engineered before outsourcing them; that current performance levels should be documented; and that the goal should be refocused on accessing new technologies. New technology should be selected based on fit with County objectives, such as integration, costs of later upgrades, training. He also recommended the creation of an IT Review Committee. In his executive summary, the consultant questioned the proposed timescale for outsourcing by May 8 of 1996 due to the approval process. (In practice the contract was not signed until January 1, 1997).

In January 1996, four companies responded to the RFP – Lockheed Martin Marietta, Unisys, ISSC, and SCT (Systems and Computer Technology Corp). Six people from General Services and two independent consultants evaluated the bids. In March, two finalists were selected. Site visits were made to the existing outsourced operations for both finalists. According to a County Administrator, the final evaluation process involved two independent consultant firms with two independent subconsultant firms, the three top management of General Services and the Director of Management and Operations. Input was received from grade 15 and above IT employees. The decision makers unanimously and independently selected ISSC after oral presentations and final bid submissions. Contract negotiations began immediately. The decision was officially announced on July 11.

At this time, communications between the lower-level IT employees and County Administrators and IT managers were severely limited. The IT employees were given a copy of the RFP. The IT employees were prohibited from reviewing any vendor bids, and were provided little information about the contract negotiation (The senior management view here was that internal bid teams should not be privy to vendor bids.) However, the County Executive did promise that all affected IT employees would be offered permanent jobs at equal or higher pay. The IT employees argued that the County would not achieve the promised savings unless a benchmark was done to assess current performance, and that any proposed cost savings must be concretely identified rather than based on a general appeal to "vendor economies of scale". The IT employees began to lobby for support. They met with the Editorial Board of their local newspaper, held press conferences, met with the civil servants union, and constantly contacted the Legislators.

The County Administrators physically moved nine IT employees from the County Offices to a remote site 20 miles away. Subsequently the nine employees served notice of claim for violation of civil liberties, preserving their right to sue at a future date. They argued that they were being illegally discriminated against because of their campaign, in non-work hours, against the privatization plan for their division. The County Administrators contended that the moves were necessary and part of a larger planned relocation of the entire General Services Department, including IT by the end of 1996. The accommodations at headquarters became inadequate due to transfers from the Medical Center.

On July 22, a public meeting was attended by the County Administrators, various consultants, and the IS employees. The agreed subject was that of IT sourcing options. After the meeting, there was a discussion between the Deputy County Executive and the IT employees. No one knows the exact outcome of this discussion, as all subsequent accounts were verbal. One point was agreed upon by both stakeholder groups, namely that the IT employees (grade 14 and below) would have to make a bid on their own without access to IT management.

According to IT employees, the Deputy County Executive supported an internal bid, including the resources necessary to create such a bid after the public meeting. In particular, the IT employees contended that the benchmark was agreed to in principle. But the IT employees also pointed out that the Deputy County Executive subsequently refused to provide any resources, time off, funding for a benchmark, or access to IT management to help the rank-and-file employees to create an internal bid.

According to a County Administrator:

"The Deputy County Executive did not subsequently impede an internal bid offer. What was conveyed to the IS employees through CSEA is that the administration is obliged to preserve a level playing field which means that the IS employees would be accorded access to the same information as was provided to outside vendors and that they would have the same access to the IS managers for support information as was given to the vendors. Since the IS managers were involved in the evaluation of the vendor responses, it could not be possible for them to have a hand in drawing up an internal vendor response".

In a memo dated July 31, 1996, the CSEA employees stated that they would only submit a bid after a benchmarking report and the hiring of a CIO. Different stakeholder groups perceived the implications of this memo differently. One respondent perceived that the CSEA employees imposed two new conditions which were never asked for before, and were not part of the verbal agreement made between the IT employees and the administration in discussions after the July 22 meeting. Several IT employees also contended that there was a history of the legislators requesting a CIO, and that they needed a benchmark to help them understand additional cost cutting opportunities because they did not have access to IT management.

In a memo dated August 6, The Deputy County Executive could not meet the two new conditions because "*the County Attorney has advised that providing such information might unfairly penalize those vendors who timely responded to the RFP when it was written*". He also requested an employee response to the RFP by August 23, 1996. The IS employees did not submit an internal bid by this date.

In early October, the benchmark was finally approved. Compass (a benchmark company) was hired to conduct a benchmark of current costs and performance. Compass found that the County's IT department could be run more efficiently. According to the IT employees we interviewed, they were hoping that the Compass recommendations would provide a basis for their internal bid. The IT employees, suggested however, that the benchmark would be used to further justify outsourcing.

On November 11, the Deputy County Executive presented an overview of the proposed contract, to be given to the Legislators on November 15, 1996. The financial benefits of outsourcing were expected to be $3.5 million in savings in 1997 and $26 million over ten years. Cost savings, it was suggested, would come from data center renovation/relocation ($2.5–$10 million).

On November 25, the rank-and-file IT employees finally created an internal plan for IT which promised savings equivalent to the savings promised by outsourcing. Their savings were based on replacing current contractors with civil servants (civil servants earn significantly less than private sector IT employees), elimination of redundant software, data center automation, and not filling currently open IT slots. For example, the IT employees included a table of current costs per day for civil servants with the costs per day currently paid to two IT outsourcing vendors: Image Works and EDP-Temp. This was the internal bid the County Legislators had been requesting for months. The IT employees also presented their bid to the County Executive. According to the IT employees, he promised to consider their proposal, but the stakeholders did not have enough time to evaluate the proposal because the budget vote was only two weeks away. In addition to the employees' proposal, the County Legislators had to digest the proposed County budget sent to them by the County Executive and the proposed ISSC contract (over 200 pages long). The proposed budget included eliminating 367 jobs through privatization (109 computer jobs, and other jobs in the Medical center), and proposed additional funds for outsourcing contracts (one for IT, one for Medical center).

Subsequent events and issues

On December 13, the County Legislators vetoed the outsourcing budget, and put the 367 employees back in the budget. According to several editorials, the Legislators did not feel that they had enough time to make decisions. The Citizens Advisory Board recommended that the administration should not force the County Legislators to make a decision on the IT outsourcing contract until March (1998), after they had time to evaluate the contract.

On December 17, the County Executive vetoed most of their budget amendments (He agreed to keep 80 medical care positions in-house). By law, he could not put back the funding for the outsourcing contracts, but he vetoed the Legislators' decision to put the IT employees back in the budget. The County Executive's budget went back to the Legislators for one more round of votes on December 20. The Legislators needed 12 votes out of 17 to override the County Executive one last time. Only ten of the legislators vetoed this round. The result seemed to be that the County had no internal IT employees and no money for the ISSC contract. On paper, at least, Westchester County no longer had an IT function. However, ISSC agreed to honor their commitment and begin providing IT services on January 1, 1997. ISSC hired 66 of the targeted 109 IT employees and hired temporary IT employees to fill the remaining positions. According to the Editorial Board of the Gannet, December 20, 1997:

> The County Executive "said he would probably not spend the money as directed [by the budget], but instead use it to fund the privatization the board had clearly rejected..."[The County Executive] said, "he might not spend additional money on day care, as the board of legislators directed, if he finds he needs money elsewhere."

The Civil Servant Union sought a restraining order based on violation of the County Charter. According to the County Charter, the Board of Legislators needs a majority vote to "create, organize, alter, or abolish" county agencies. By using the veto process, the County Executive only needed seven votes, not a majority, to eliminate the IT positions and implement the contract. On January 1, 1997, a State Supreme Court judge found in favor of the union, claiming that the County Executive violated the County Charter, and that County employees would be reinstated with back pay. But because the County Executive indicated he would appeal, the decision was suspended for two weeks until the case was heard by a second State Supreme Court judge. On January 14, a second judge found that the County Executive, *"overstepped his power by signing the ISSC contract and the Medical Center Contract."* But the judge did not reinstate the former County Employees. Instead, the judgment was stayed until another court appeal to the Appellate Division of the State Supreme Court. IBM Spokesperson Fred McNeese said that ISSC would continue to run the County's IT department until the appeal.

Analysis and lessons

The public sector context

In comparing the two cases with our own prior research (Lacity and Hirschheim, 1993, 1995; Willcocks and Fitzgerald, 1994; Willcocks and Currie, 1996), the IRS and Westchester County cases would seem to illustrate several similarities and differences between the private and public sectors in both their contexts and IT sourcing decisions. Both sectors emerged as alike in the following ways, and these similarities can be seen to continue in contemporary sourcing contexts (Lacity and Willcocks, 2009):

- In both sectors, multiple stakeholders often create conflicting expectations for information technology. Senior level executives or officials often set tight IT budgets without considering IT's ability to deliver products and services with such budgetary constraints. Users only see their part of the IT world, and demand quick and effective service without understanding the other demands placed on IT personnel. Because users demand more information technology than can be supplied, IT managers develop a regulatory role by trying to prioritize IT requests. IT personnel subsequently feel pressured by different stakeholder demands.
- In both sectors, organizations struggle to keep up with the dizzying pace of emerging technologies while simultaneously running current systems. While most IT managers want to plan for the future by establishing an IT architecture, they are also highly engaged in maintaining existing systems and dealing with legacy issues, while new requirements also become the responsibility of the IT department. This situation was exacerbated in the late 1990s by the impending century date problem.
- Both sectors must balance trade-offs between low cost solutions like standardization and high-service solutions like customization. Such

practices are political by nature and require senior management sponsorship and support.

However, it emerged from the case studies that, as we saw in the previous chapter, there were several sets of issues distinctive to the public sector, which seemed to make IT sourcing decisions even more difficult. In addition to the comments made by the IRS Commissioner (see IRS case) one can note:

1. The two government organizations had outside agencies dictating budgets, requirements, and salaries. Public sector organizations would seem to have nowhere near the control over their own destinies as private sector enterprises. Thus, in the two cases public sector IT managers needed to cope with external stakeholders and a highly influential political overlay in addition to their internal senior officials and users. In particular, this situation was evident in the IRS. This can have a number of ramifications. Willcocks and Currie (1996) noted that senior politicians in the UK were invariably not knowledgeable of IT (a comment that continues to apply – see Cordella *et al.*, 2008), and were little concerned with the IT implications of their decisions. In the two US cases one can see a similar pattern; for example Congress passed tax laws without considering the IT implications, while Westchester County (WCC) politicians seemed eager to outsource with little analysis of the IT service levels that might result.

2. In the two cases senior government officials and politicians seemed to have a pre-conceived view that outsourcing would automatically save money – a pre-conceived view also found in several of our studies into IT outsourcing in the UK (See Cordella *et al.*, 2008 for a summary). These pointed to a widespread belief in government that private sector companies tended to be more efficient (Dunleavy *et al.*, 2007; Willcocks, 1994; Willcocks and Currie, 1996). Our own research has consistently shown that in-house IT functions can often achieve the same sort of savings and efficiencies as external IT suppliers (Lacity and Hirschheim, 1995; Lacity *et al.*, 1996; Willcocks and Lacity, 2006 – see also Chapter 9). Mintzberg has argued that in the USA privatization has often been based on a misplaced faith in private sector management. "We are so enamoured of the cult of heroic leadership, that we fail to see its obvious contradictions." (Mintzberg, 1996, p. 80). Such a pre-conception can be dangerous, because it may lead some officials to outsource without a proper evaluation. This happened in both cases; it is also noticeable how cost reduction seemed to be a dominant factor in those decisions, rather than multiple objectives, though in the IRS improved compliance and customer service, along with access to technical talent, were also coming to the fore in the later debate. A focus on cost reduction has been distinctive to the UK public sector and clearly

influenced the evaluation and decision-making processes in both US cases. A major distinctive factor has been cost pressures due to high public budget deficits in both US and UK public sectors in the 1990s.

The evaluation process

It is useful to compare the evaluation processes in the two cases against what other research has identified as effective practice. According to Lacity and Hirschheim (1995) and Willcocks *et al.* (1996), in-house improvements should be pursued first. Performance benchmarks then need to be established and full costs identified, performance improvements again sought, then an in-house/outsource comparison made. Where a decision to keep IT in-house is made the loop should be repeated and the outsourcing reassessed at up to two-year intervals. If an outsourcing decision is made specific measures need to be developed, though existing metrics and benchmarks may prove helpful. There needs to be regular monitoring and searches for how vendor performance can be improved. Organizations following this route into outsourcing generally reported anticipated or above-anticipated benefits several years into their contracts (Lacity and Willcocks, 2001).

At IRS there were clear weaknesses in the earlier outsourcing contracts. These related to the failure to adequately assess vendors' technical capabilities. The assumption was that in-house technical expertise was highly deficient, and that a private sector vendor was much more likely to give access to the necessary technical talent. However, the failure was, in our analysis, not just on this evaluation but also on the assessment of retained capabilities, and the sort of relationship needed to run innovative systems development projects (see below). In the WCC case there were early moves to short-circuit a full evaluation process, with a consultancy report seemingly used to legitimate a *de facto* decision to outsource IT – a not uncommon occurrence in other cases (Lacity and Hirschheim, 1993). At WCC, originally no in-house assessment, comparison of in-house against vendor bid, benchmarking or alternative sourcing options were contemplated (see Chapter 9 for why these are important). At WCC it was noticeable how it was the in-house IT group that constantly insisted on a full and detailed evaluation process as outlined above, and how these efforts were continually undermined by senior officials. This underlines the political aspects of evaluation often uncovered in other cases we have researched in both private and public sectors (see Chapter 2). Our own research shows that allowing a competitive in-house bid can often achieve considerable cost savings (Willcocks *et al.*, 1995; see also Chapter 9). Ironically, in the WCC case, this was a forced rather than a preferred option for senior officials.

A significant lesson from other research is the need to properly diagnose IT problems before making a sourcing decision. The notion that there exists outside an organization instant solutions that can make IT problems disappear has been shown to be all too often illusory (Feeny *et al.*, 1997; Willcocks and Lacity, 2006). Organizations need to diagnose the right problem and then determine how best to fix it; this would necessarily involve contemplating several sourcing options rather than the straightforward one of outsourcing the problem (Lacity *et al.*, 1996). In the IRS case the original outsourcing contracts were entered into for development projects without assessing the need for re-engineering processes, and providing adequate project management in-house business expertise to support the vendors. By late 1996 the IRS Commission was moving closer to a more informed view of the problems, of the in-house capabilities needed, and of the possible role of external IT vendors. At WCC decision makers were driven by a cost reduction concern that pushed for a "total" outsourcing arrangement and overrode proper analysis of what service was actually being achieved in-house and what were appropriate aspects of IT to consider outsourcing.

Proper diagnosis of the problem first requires a measurement of current IT costs and performance levels, perhaps through a benchmarking service (Lacity and Hirschheim, 1996). We have found that a good benchmark documents current performance in terms of costs and service levels, and compares these to the performance of best-of-breed companies. Furthermore, where performance is weak, benchmarking companies identify cost saving tactics practiced by the best-of-breed companies. Our research has uncovered 11 categories of cost reduction tactics:

- Automation;
- Better Chargeback Systems;
- Consolidation;
- Departmental Reorganization;
- Employee Empowerment;
- Tougher Hardware Negotiations;
- Just-in-time Resources;
- More Efficient Resource Use;
- Service Elimination;
- Tougher Software Negotiations;
- Software Standardization.

These are the practices that vendors themselves often use to reduce costs. Internal IT managers may replicate many of these tactics if empowered by senior management to do so (see Chapter 9 for more details). The real value of such benchmarks prior to a sourcing evaluation is that it focuses decision makers on the IT cost drivers, rather than on general appeals to a vendor's superior expertise. In both IRS and WCC the need for such benchmarks would seem paramount before any further outsourcing was contemplated.

Once an organization properly diagnoses their IT problems, they can then intelligently evaluate sourcing options. In cases we have studied, the most successful decisions involved two separate teams: a decision-making team and an internal bid team (Lacity and Hirschheim, 1995; Lacity and Willcocks, 2001). The successful decisions appointed a decision-making team comprised of senior level managers and IT managers. Senior level managers provided the larger business perspective – such as the mandate to reduce costs – and the power to enforce decisions. IT managers provided the necessary technical expertise to develop requests for proposals, to evaluate vendor bids, and to negotiate, and manage sound contracts.

The internal bid team needs to be a separate group of IT specialists and IT managers that submit a competitive bid along with external vendor bids. Some senior executives in organizations we studied were reluctant to allow internal bid submissions, believing that the internal staff were incapable of improving their performance (Lacity and Hirschheim, 1995). But in many cases we studied, IT managers did not have the power to enforce change or implement best practices due to organizational politics. Users may not want practices that reduce costs because they think it will lower service. But outsourcing evaluations empower internal IT managers to behave like vendors. Senior managers communicate the mandate for change to users, whether it is implemented by external providers or their own IT staff (see Chapter 9).

At Westchester County, we saw that the internal IT employees were consistently invited to make a bid. But senior management must also staff the in-house team with senior level IT managers and provide resources to make an internal bid, such as access to consultants, lawyers, equipment, and time off to create the bid. In the end, the Westchester County IT employees put together a budget proposal, but this was not a legal response to a request-for-proposal, but rather a laundry list of cost-saving ideas. In contrast, other organizations we have researched that allowed internal bids, such as Occidental Petroleum, developed a team of high-level IT managers, rented them office space off-site (to eliminate conflict of interest and insider information), provided equipment, hired a benchmarking consultant to help identify improvements, and provided access to other needed experts (Lacity and Hirschheim, 1995). In contrast to the WCC case, such internal bid teams were treated the same as external bidders, such as requiring all questions in writing.

IT sourcing decisions

Turning to the decisions which lead to outsourcing, what differentiates outsourcing successes from failures? In the majority of successful outsourcing decisions we have identified in previous research the organization knew exactly what they wanted from their IT provider (Lacity and Willcocks, 1996, 2001; see also Chapter 8):

• The organization selected activities which were well understood and they could therefore negotiate a sound contract;

- The organization signed contracts only for the duration for which requirements were known;
- The organization practiced hands-on management of the contract, rather than abandoning it to the vendor (Willcocks and Fitzgerald, 1994).

Returning to the example of the IRS, their unsuccessful outsourcing contracts failed to meet these points. First, the IRS did not understand their requirements for the $285 million imaging system or the $17 million electronic processing system. Second, the IRS did not understand how to evaluate vendor bids, negotiate sound contracts, or manage the relationship. The attitude that superior vendor expertise would lead to improved performance, and that they were best left alone, was in fact a major contributing factor to the failures. In the WC case there seemed to be no real differentiation of the type of IT activities and of in-house performance thereon. As one example, it would seem difficult to justify the outsourcing of the world-class imaging system for processing land records, financial claims and voter registration. In-house performance probably could not be bettered and the system would seem to be a critical one, best managed in-house. But overall in this case there was little sense of the factors that should inform IT sourcing decisions.

Our own work suggests that the low risk route is to outsource those IT activities that are commodities, that do not give competitive edge or represent a distinctive superior competence, that are technically mature, understood and stable, not highly integrated, and for which the vendor can achieve economies of scale and has superior technical expertise to support (Lacity *et al.*, 1996; see also Chapter 8). In the IRS case failure came from outsourcing development projects with low technology maturity. Feeny *et al.* (1997) suggest that such projects require an "in-sourcing", partnership approach where external vendors work together with in-house staff as resources under internal management to achieve mutual learning in areas for which the business and technical objectives are none too clear. The IRS seemed to be moving to such a view by late 1996, but, in our view, the outsourcing at WCC would probably result in a replication of the earlier failures at IRS.

Retained IS capabilities

One tendency in public sector IT outsourcing has been to move to a "residual" IT organization, reducing in-house staff to basically a contract management/monitoring and governance function (Willcocks and Currie, 1996; Reynolds and Willcocks, 2007). Elements of this were observable in the IRS and WCC cases. By contrast, research by Feeny and Willcocks, (1998) and Willcocks and Craig (2007) suggests that an IT function needs to have nine key in-house capabilities. Relationship building and business systems thinking assist the elicitation and delivery of business requirements. Designing technical architecture and technology fixing ensure technical supply while external supply is managed through informed buying, contract monitoring, contract facilitation and vendor development capabilities. Additionally there needs to be a governance capability, traditionally fulfilled, or at least overseen, by the CIO. In the WCC case proposals made in November 1996 included the elimination of 109 IT jobs through privatization. Our analysis, based on research at WCC, is that the prime factor here was economic, and the staff selection process had little to do with retaining or building the key in-house capabilities identified above. In practice the decision would have resulted in a model closer to a "residual" than a "key capabilities" IT function. The issues are even clearer in the IRS case. Earlier outsourcing contracts failed, on our analysis, because of weaknesses or omissions in all nine capabilities identified above. In particular the IRS lacked in-house relationship building and business systems thinking capabilities, technical supply capabilities and informed buying/monitoring/facilitation capabilities. Various reports had also highlighted lack of project management capability in the IRS business generally, which added to the problems. These points were widely recognized in evidence presented to the Commission to Restructure the IRS in January 1997.

Even so, most of the remedies focused on rectifying the deficiencies on technical expertise/management before outsourcing. As a major example a new CIO was appointed in 1996, basically for his technical management capability. However his governance role at the IRS meant that he would also need to deal with non-IT managers and employees in the IRS, with the IRS commission and its members, and with senior government figures as well as external suppliers. Our own finding has been that when a governance role becomes so complex it needs to be shared. For example when IT outsourcing represents more than 20% of the IT budget the informed buying capability needs to take on a governance function as well (Feeny and Willcocks, 1997).

Finally, before outsourcing once more, the IRS definitely needed to build up its ability to manage external suppliers. A useful comparison is the UK Inland Revenue (IR) that "totally" outsourced its IS to EDS in 1994 on a ten-year contract (Willcocks and Kern, 1997). The UK IR retained an in-house contract management team covering 14 disciplines as well as a relationship management capability at strategic and operational levels. One additional capability they bought in was an external outsourcing consultant with a "watching brief" to anticipate trouble points and suggest ways of avoiding them. This proved eminently useful because the four in-house capabilities tasked with managing external supply had not been built up to a sufficient level of high performance even in 1996, some two years into the contract. It is by addressing such issues, and by building such capabilities that the IRS would be more likely to achieve greater success in any further outsourcing contracts.

Conclusions

In some respects following the UK lead, privatization through IT outsourcing was an increasing feature in US public administration in the mid-1990s. However, our two cases indicate that outsourcing IT poses a complex set of issues in public sector contexts. In the two cases, at least, the promise sought from outsourcing – that IT problems could be handed over to external vendors who could necessarily achieve cost reductions and/or superior performance – had either failed, or was yet, to be delivered upon.

Our analysis pointed to four critical areas that emerged from the cases – distinctive difficulties associated with public sector contexts; weaknesses in evaluation practice; the criteria used for IT sourcing decisions; and the importance of retaining nine specific sets of capabilities and skills where the external IT market is used to any degree. For the four areas we compared the case histories against our earlier and later research findings. It was clear that the political overlay, the preferences for privatization, the attitudes toward and lack of knowledge about IT amongst senior politicians, together with cost pressures in US public administration adversely affected practice in the other three areas identified. On evaluation practice, this was clearest in the WCC case where better practice was being actively short-circuited. In the IRS case evaluation practice and IT sourcing decision making had weaknesses, revealed by the failure of two outsourcing contracts. The more recent effort was being channelled into improving these areas.

However, both cases revealed continued weaknesses in retained capabilities – in WCC there seemed no detailed analysis of what was required, while, in the IRS case the analysis was stronger on technical supply and management, much weaker on delivering capabilities to support the governance, business and external supply facing tasks. The danger revealed by the case histories was of IT outsourcing decisions being driven by public sector factors and exigencies that undermined IT outsourcing's ability to deliver the very thing it was supposedly designed to achieve, namely an improved business-focused IT service at lower cost. The subsequent acceleration of IT outsourcing in the UK and USA public sectors and the mixed record of these efforts across the 1998–2008 period would suggest that the lessons learned from these 1990s case presented here and in Chapter 6 are as urgent and as relevant as ever.

References

Collins, T. (1996) "Whitehall Smothers Privatization Report", *Computer Weekly*, February 29, 1, 29.

Cordella, A., Willcocks, L. and Mola, L. (2008) ICTs, Marketization and Bureaucracy In the UK Public Sector: Critique and Reappraisal. Paper in the *Second Global Sourcing Conference*, Val D'Isere, France, March.

Currie, W. and Willcocks, L. (1996) "The New Branch Columbus Project at Royal Bank of Scotland: The Implementation of Large-scale Business Process Re-engineering", *Journal Of Strategic Information Systems*, 5, 4, 202–224.

Dunleavy, P., Margetts, H., Bastou, S. and Tinkler, J. (2007) *Digital Era Governance*, Oxford University Press, Oxford.

Feeny, D., Earl, M., and Edwards, B. (1997) "Organizational Arrangements for IS: The Roles of Users and Specialists", in Willcocks, L., Feeny, D. and Islei, G. (eds) *Managing IT as a Strategic Resource*, McGraw Hill, Maidenhead.

Feeny, D. and Willcocks, L. (1998) "Rethinking the IS Function: Capabilities and Skills", in Currie, W. and Galliers, R. (eds) *Rethinking MIS*, Oxford University Press, Oxford.

Government Executive (1996) "Information Technology Guide: Systems Integration/ Outsourcing", *Government Executive*, 28, 4, 16a.

Hassell, N. (1994) "Testing Market Testing", *Management Today*, May, 38–42.

Lacity, M. and Hirschheim, R. (1993) *Information Systems Outsourcing: Myths, Metaphors, and Realities*, Wiley, Chichester.

Lacity, M. and Hirschheim, R. (1995) *Beyond the Information Systems Outsourcing Bandwagon*, Wiley, Chichester.

Lacity, M. and Hirschheim, R. (1996) "The Role of Benchmarking in Demonstrating IS Performance", in Willcocks, L. (ed.) *Investing in Information Systems: Evaluation and Management*, Chapman and Hall, London.

Lacity, M. and Willcocks, L. (1996) *Best Practices in Information Technology Sourcing*. Oxford Executive Research Briefing, Templeton College, Oxford.

Lacity, M. and Willcocks, L. (2001) *Global Information Technology Outsourcing: Search for Business Advantage*, Wiley, Chichester.

Lacity, M. and Willcocks, L. (2009) *Information Systems and Outsourcing: Studies in Theory and Practice*, Palgrave, London.

Lacity, M., Willcocks, L. and Feeny, D. (1996) "The Value of Selective IT Sourcing", *Sloan Management Review*, 37, 3, Spring, 13–25.

Linowes, D. (1996) "The Rationale for Privatization", *Executive Speeches*, April/May, 10–13.

Minoli, D. (1994) *Analyzing Outsourcing*, McGraw Hill, New York.

Mintzberg, H. (1996) "Managing Government, Governing Management", *Harvard Business Review*, May–June, 75–83.

National Audit Office (2006) *Department of Health – The National Programme for IT in the NHS. HC1173*, HMSO, London.

Peters, T. (1996) *Collection of Current Papers*, distributed to the participants of "In Pursuit of Wow" Conference, St Louis, MO, October 17.

Pettigrew, A. (1990) "Longitudinal Field Research on Change: Theory and Practice", *Organizational Science*, 1, 3, 267–292.

Reynolds, P. and Willcocks, L. (2007) "Building and Integrating Core IS Capabilities in Alignment with Business: Lessons from the Commonwealth Bank 1997–2007", *ICIOS Conference*, Heidelberg, May 29–30th.

Samuelson, R. (1995) *The Good Life and Its Discontent: The American Dream in the Age of Entitlement*, Times Books, New York.

Walsham, G. (1995) "Interpretive Case Studies in IS research: Nature and Method", *European Journal Of Information Systems*, 4, 2, 74–81.

Willcocks, L. (1994) "Managing Information Systems in Public Administration: Issues and Prospects", *Public Administration*, 72, 1, 13–32.

Willcocks, L. (1996) *Contracting Out Information Technology in Public Service Contexts: Research and Critique*. Rotterdam School of Management Report No. 296, Erasmus Universiteit, Rotterdam.

Willcocks, L. and Craig, A. (2007) *The Outsourcing Enterprise 4 – Building Retained Core Capabilities*, Logica, London.

Willcocks, L. and Currie, W. (1996) Information Technology Outsourcing in the Public Sector: Towards the Contractual Organization? *OXIIM Research and Discussion Paper RDP 96/8*, Templeton College, Oxford.

Willcocks, L. and Fitzgerald, G. (1994) *A Business Guide to Outsourcing Information Technology*, Business Intelligence, London.

Willcocks, L., Fitzgerald, G. and Lacity, M. (1996) "To Outsource IT or Not? Recent Research on Economics and Evaluation Practice", *European Journal Of Information Systems*, 5, 143–160.

Willcocks, L. and Lacity, M. (2006) *Global Sourcing of Business and IT Services*, Palgrave, London.

Willcocks, L., Lacity, M. and Fitzgerald, G. (1995) "IT Outsourcing in europe and the USA: Assessment Issues", *International Journal Of Information Management*, 15, 5, 333–351.

Wysocki, B. (1996) "States May Well Find Easy Days Are Over", *The Wall Street Journal*, November 4, A1.

8
Analyzing IT Outsourcing Decisions: Size, Interdependency and Risk

Wendy Currie and Leslie Willcocks

Introduction

In this chapter we bring together a number of threads running through previous chapters, and focus on distinguishing between four types of IT sourcing decision: total outsourcing; multiple supplier sourcing; joint venture/ project sourcing; and insourcing. To illustrate each type, detailed case histories are used where we analyze the reasons why specific IT sourcing decisions were adopted, and provide comment on the outcomes. Here we consider total outsourcing at the London Stock Exchange; multiple supplier sourcing at ICI plc; joint venture/project sourcing at CRESTCo Ltd; and insourcing at Royal Bank of Scotland.

A critical part of outsourcing is the work done upfront in defining and designing the arrangement – what we call configuration (see Chapter 11). Any client organization has in play some fundamental sourcing options. But the option chosen shapes the sorts of problem the organization will need to deal with, the risks that need to be mitigated (see Chapter 6), the type of contract required (see Chapter 3), the resources and capabilities needed, relationship issues (see Chapter 4), and the type of supplier required (see Chapter 13). Against a 1990–2008 background of a fast expanding market, ever more sourcing options, and a growing number of suppliers offering a broadening range of services it has become vital not only to choose an appropriate sourcing option (see Lacity and Willcocks, 2009), but also to have the necessary maturity and precise capability to service the management requirement and mitigate the risks associated with that choice. In this chapter we investigate illustrative examples of sourcing choices, their implications and the management issues that arose subsequently in each of the outsourcing arrangements.

Research methodology

This chapter is based upon a larger empirical research study conducted by the authors into IT sourcing decisions in Europe and the USA (Currie and

Willcocks, 1997). The key research objective was to elicit information on three distinct questions that emerged from analyzing the international outsourcing marketplace as it was in 1997. First, "Is it possible to discern distinctive types of IT sourcing strategies pursued by a range of private and public (federal) sector organizations?" This question was generated from existing literature on IT sourcing with some contributions focusing upon "total outsourcing" and others on "selective sourcing". In identifying different approaches to IT sourcing, a typology was developed which generated a second research question: "why do some organizations pursue one type of IT sourcing strategy as opposed to another?". A third question also considered the risks associated with each type of IT sourcing decision. Clearly, organizations pursuing a "total outsourcing" approach would encounter different problems from those adopting a less ambitious approach. Building on the work on risk in Chapter 6, we therefore asked: "Do some forms of IT sourcing pose greater risks for the client organization than others?" To this end, we were concerned with risk mitigation from the client rather than supplier perspective. We developed a typology linking scale of IT sourcing with client/supplier interdependency, and the results of the subsequent field work confirmed there were distinctive types of IT sourcing decisions pursued by the various organizations.

The research methodology consisted of interviews with IT directors and managers in over 20 organizations. Interviews usually lasted over an hour, although some respondents agreed to further interviews where more information was needed. A semi-structured questionnaire was used which comprised over 40 questions. The unit of analysis was the IT function within these organizations, and the IT sourcing strategies they used, either from an external provider or in-house (from a large, self-contained IT department). Different organizations were selected to illustrate the four distinct approaches: total outsourcing; multiple sourcing; specialist/project sourcing and insourcing (retaining an in-house IT function, with the option of buying in external resources to operate under in-house management). It is important to stress that each type of IT sourcing decision should be treated as a heuristic device, that is unlikely to be found in its pure form in any organization. For example, whilst total outsourcing was adopted by some organizations, they may also enter into selective sourcing arrangements which are a variant of the multiple supplier approach (for example BP Exploration – see Kern and Willcocks, 2001).

Four types of IT sourcing decision

We consider four major types of sourcing decisions revealed by our research: total outsourcing; multiple supplier sourcing; joint venture/project sourcing; and insourcing IT where IT activities are managed in-house. Table 8.1 summarizes the key characteristics of each of these forms of IT sourcing. Whilst some organizations select only one type, e.g., total outsourcing, others enter into several types of sourcing arrangements. For example, a financial services company with a large centralized in-house IT department undertaking most of its IT work in-house may also outsource specific IT applications development projects to specialist suppliers (Buck-Lew, 1992). Alternatively, another financial services company may seek to enter into multiple/selective sourcing contracts with a range of external IT suppliers – for example ABNAmro bank in 2005 (Oshri *et al.*, 2007). In doing so, it may seek to reduce its internal IT facility over time. In this context, the company may consider these relationships to be "strategic alliances" or "strategic partnerships" (see Chapter 4). The four types of IT sourcing decision are now discussed in detail.

Total Outsourcing. This approach was adopted by a small minority of our sample organizations including the 1993–2003 Inland Revenue/Electronic Data Systems (EDS) deal, the 1990s London Stock Exchange/Andersen Consulting arrangement, and the British Aerospace/CSC ten-year outsourcing

Table 8.1 The Rationale Behind Four Approaches to IT Sourcing Decisions

Total Outsourcing	Multiple Supplier Sourcing
• Develop "partnership" with single supplier • Sign long-term contract with supplier • Focus on core business • IT perceived as a service/support function • Reduce IT costs • Share risk/reward with supplier • Eliminate IT (problem) function • Access to managerial/technical expertise • Retain strategic control	• Create competition between suppliers • Standardize/coordinate operations • Focus on core business • Formulate framework agreement • Nurture an alliance of suppliers • Develop short-term contracts with suppliers • Suppliers given management responsibilities • Transfer fixed costs to variable costs • Retain strategic control

Joint Venture /Strategic Alliance Sourcing	Insourcing
• Take 49% share ownership of IT supplier • IT supplier may be new or existing company • Differentiation of core competencies between client and IT supplier • Shared risks and rewards • Develop sector specific knowledge • Generate new business opportunities • Access to specialist technical expertise • Retain control and influence over outsourcing	• IT is seen as core business • High level of in-house technical expertise • Centralized IT department • Inadequate supplier/market conditions • Synergy between business/technology • Lack of trust about supplier motivation • Manage contractors as permanent staff • Retain up-to-date technical expertise • Manage peaks and troughs of IT work

contract (Currie and Willcocks, 1997). Huber (1993) also discusses total outsourcing in his Harvard Business Review article, which analyzed the case of Continental Bank and their contract with IBM. Total outsourcing is where an organization chooses to outsource as much as 70–80% of its IT facility, usually to a large single supplier. These contracts have been usually between five and ten years. As discussed in Chapter 4, a common assumption underpinning total outsourcing deals is the nurturing of a "partnership" between client and supplier. This is sometimes called a "strategic alliance". This notion is treated with skepticism in some quarters of the outsourcing literature that found, especially for the early 1990s, the stress falling on making a large profit by the supplier organization at the expense of the client (Lacity and Hirschheim, 1993; also Lacity and Willcocks, 2001). Nonetheless it has been and continues to be presented by many practitioners and academics as a viable working possibility. In this chapter, as in previous chapters, we prefer to apply the phrase "strategic alliance" to situations of major shared risk and reward (see Table 8.1).

Our research found that part of the rationale for total outsourcing was to enable the client to concentrate on its core business activities, thus leaving the supplier to manage the IT facility. Quinn and Hilmer (1994) reinforce this. This usually involves the transfer of a significant proportion of IT staff from the client organization to the supplier. The client receives a large payment for IT assets (hardware, software, networks, databases, etc) from the supplier and, in doing so, removes the burden of having to manage and control what it perceives to be a non-core "service" activity. Concerns about relinquishing strategic IT systems to the supplier may be overcome when the client realizes that "Just because an IT activity is business-critical doesn't mean that all its elements have to be kept in-house". In this context, the strategic versus commodity argument evaporates (Lacity *et al.*, 1995). But as we shall see below, large scale IT outsourcing engenders significant risks to the client, particularly where the lines between strategic and operational activities are unclear. Here, we consider total outsourcing at the London Stock Exchange, weigh some of the opportunities and pitfalls of outsourcing to a large single supplier, and pose questions about the long-term viability of this arrangement.

Multiple Supplier Sourcing. Most of the organizations in our sample entered into IT sourcing arrangements with a variety of suppliers. ICI adopted the view that IT should be "business-led and business-managed". As such, it was important to remember that outsourcing was a "commercial relationship" and not simply a partnership based only on trust and cooperation. GrandMet, who developed tight contracts with their suppliers to ensure that service level agreements (SLAs) were met, shared this view. Part of the rationale for multiple supplier sourcing has been discussed by Cross (1995) who analyzed the situation at British Petroleum Exploration (a company also researched by the authors of this chapter – see Currie and Willcocks, 1997. See also Chapter 4). This company negotiated a framework agreement with its suppliers who outlined the procedures and policies of how each party would work together. Contracts were not expected to exceed five years duration. Suppliers were encouraged to form an alliance and compete with each other for business with the client. The difference between total outsourcing (above) and multiple suppliers sourcing is significant. First, the client organization tends to safeguard against being dependent upon a single supplier that may ultimately control all its IT assets. Second, multiple supplier sourcing encourages competition and innovation by ensuring that contracts are short term and liable for renewal not necessarily with the same supplier (or combination of suppliers). Third, this approach enables the client to concentrate on its core business activities in that the suppliers management and provide IT services. Fixed costs become variable costs as the client reduces its in-house IT staff and instead purchases a portfolio of IT services from selected suppliers. The client intends to retain strategic control of IT, although significant management responsibilities are transferred to supplier organizations.

Interviews with IT managers suggested that multiple supplier sourcing was adopted to avoid the inevitable risks of using only one supplier. However, some companies have experienced difficulties of managing and coordinating different suppliers (see below and Chapter 4). ICI negotiated outsourcing contracts on the basis of "competitive and selective" outsourcing. One component of contracting out selected IT services is that fixed costs become variable costs as the client reduces its in-house staff through purchasing a portfolio of IT services from multiple suppliers. The client intends to retain strategic control of IT, although significant management responsibilities are transferred to supplier organizations. We illustrate multiple suppliers sourcing by considering the case of ICI plc. IT outsourcing was undertaken by this company partly as a result of the 1990s de-merger with Zeneca, and partly to reduce and restructure the IT infrastructure.

Joint Venture/Strategic Alliance Sourcing. An organization enters into a joint venture with a supplier on a shared risk/reward basis. This may involve selecting an existing IT supplier or helping to create a new company to which work can be outsourced. Sometimes an organization may take shared ownership in an existing IT supplier or vice versa. An example being discussed in early 1998 was the UK Post Office where it was considering setting up a specialist IT supplier who would also offer its products and services to the external marketplace. XChanging's contracts with BAE and the London Insurance Market begun in 2001 and detailed in Chapter 13 are also examples of such joint ventures. In another example, CRESTCo Ltd was an independent company set up by the Bank of England to design, implement and maintain the Crest electronic settlement system. Given the demise of the Taurus project in 1993, City of London institutions funding this project in conjunction with the London Stock Exchange sought an alternative approach to developing a large-scale information system in-house with significant help from management consultant. Instead, CRESTCo Ltd was set up with the strict brief of developing a much more scaled-down version of the Taurus system.

Whereas the budget for the Taurus project fell somewhere in the region of £75–100 million (with some estimates claiming an overall cost of up to £400 million), the Crest system was given a budget of about £35 million (Currie, 1997).

The key advantage of the joint venture/strategic alliance sourcing approach is to reduce the risks of single supplier or multiple suppliers outsourcing contracts. Here, the organization may own a large share in an IT supplier and will therefore be able to influence its strategy and planning processes. It will also gain access to specialist managerial and technical skills, which it may not have in-house. Such an approach delineates the core competencies of both organizations in question. On the one hand, the organization seeking the joint venture with an IT supplier will be able to retain its own core competencies by obtaining this resource elsewhere (see Chapter 2). On the other hand, the IT supplier, which may be a small company looking to develop a partnership with a larger company (not necessarily in the same business) will be able to concentrate on its own core competencies of supplying IT services and also benefit from additional funding and support.

Part of the rationale for joint venture/project sourcing is to mitigate the risks associated with single and multiple supplier outsourcing deals. By entering into a joint venture, an organization can control the activities of the supplier company and share risk and reward. In this chapter we consider the joint venture between the Bank of England and CRESTCo Ltd, as part of a strategy to retain control over the development of the Crest equity settlement system to replace the failed Taurus project. Chapter 13 continues this discussion but in the context of business process outsourcing.

Insourcing. An organization opts to retain a large centralized IT department and insource management and technical capabilities according to the peaks and troughs of IT work. Contractors may be given employment contracts between three months and a year, although there are many examples of them staying with an organization for several years. The Royal Bank of Scotland hired as many as 40% of contractors to work on some IT projects (Currie and Willcocks, 1996), and, amongst our sample organizations, this was also done at Eagle Star Insurance. Although IT outsourcing was fast increasing throughout the 1990s in all sectors including central government, financial services, and manufacturing a significant proportion of private and public sector organizations still retained a large in-house, often centralized, IT department. Some of these organizations remained deeply skeptical of the division between the business and technology functions by suggesting that IT should instead be perceived as part of, not separate from, the business. In our case studies, this was apparent in the UK Post Office and Eagle Star Insurance in that technical innovation was perceived as critical to the future of the business and not something which could easily be transferred to an external supplier. In some cases we found in-house technical capability equal to, if not greater than in supplier organizations. Here the judgment was that to outsource a large proportion of the IT facility would not achieve material benefits, for example access to new skills or cheaper labor.

Scale of IT sourcing decisions and client/supplier dependency

The academic and practitioner literature on IT outsourcing has been concerned broadly with two related issues. The first is the scale and growth of IT outsourcing and the service market over the 1990–2010 period. Admittedly this has been impressive, seeing outsourcing move from a fad to a routine tool of management though not without its management difficulties (for example, Lacity and Willcocks, 1996, 2000; a compendium of papers on this topic appears in Willcocks and Lacity, 2009). The second is a concern for the actual experiences of organizations entering outsourcing arrangements and the debates surrounding their related advantages and disadvantages (Lacity and Hirschheim, 1993; Willcocks and Lacity, 1998, 2006, 2009). In this section we consider the literature in relation to the second issue by examining the four types of IT sourcing decision in the contexts of the scale of IT sourcing and client/supplier interdependencies.

In Figure 8.1 the scale of IT market use refers to the percentage of IT work done by external supplier(s); resources attributed to the contract(s) (financial, staff, technology, etc) and length of contract(s). Large scale total outsourcing carries with it the greatest interdependency between client and supplier. Unlike multiple/selective sourcing, total outsourcing deals are usually with

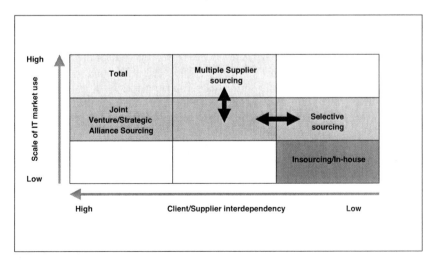

Figure 8.1 Comparing Types of IT Sourcing Decisions

one large single supplier, the success of which therefore depends upon the development of a successful partnership between the two parties. Multiple/ selective sourcing, on the other hand, is a strategy that intends to create an alliance of suppliers who compete with each other for business with the client. Interdependency between the client and supplier is reduced, although the client may be faced with problems of lack of coordination and logistical issues as commissioning and managing the various contracts takes precedence over providing the IT services. A variant of multiple supplier/selective sourcing is selective sourcing. This type of sourcing is relatively low risk as the client organization carefully selects one or several IT supplier(s) but for specific, discrete contracts. This type of sourcing arrangement removes some of the coordination problems associated with managing multiple suppliers (Straub *et al.*, 2008). To this end, it represents a halfway house between multiple sourcing and insourcing.

In the case of joint venture/strategic alliance sourcing, it is a common problem that IT applications development work invariably goes over time and budget. Numerous examples of this problem have been well documented in the literature (Currie, 1994, 1996ab; Sauer and Willcocks, 2007). The decision to outsource a large scale IT applications development project to an external provider tends to increase client/supplier interdependency given that the outcome is almost entirely dependent upon the supplier's ability to deliver a fully functional system. Failure to do so can create innumerable problems for the client organization as was the case at the London Stock Exchange in 1993, the London Ambulance Service and Wessex Health Authority (Currie, 1995) and more recently in, for example, the National Health Programme for IT (Sauer and Willcocks, 2007). To reduce these risks, some organizations choose instead to retain an in-house IT department and insource technical capability in the form of contractors (project managers and programmers, etc). But while this reduces client/supplier interdependency, there is no guarantee that an in-house IT department, even with contractors being managed internally as permanent staff, will produce more effective IT projects.

What emerges from this discussion is that risks are associated with all forms of IT sourcing decisions. It therefore becomes important to build on the work in Chapter 6 and consider in some detail the case histories of specific IT sourcing decisions. The following section discusses the case histories of four types of IT sourcing decisions, beginning with total outsourcing. The purpose of including these examples is to demonstrate the importance of contextualizing IT sourcing decisions by market, business sector and managerial/technical capabilities and skills. As Chapter 11 will argue, management capability applied in specific contexts shape levels of success in outsourcing, and the search for a universally applicable set of best practices may well be simplistic.

Case histories of IT sourcing decisions

Empirical research for this study was carried out in the winter of 1996/97 and involved a series of interviews with key decision makers on IT sourcing, usually the IT director or business operations manager. All interviews were taped and the transcripts were sent to the interviewee for validation. In some cases, material had to be edited for reasons of confidentiality. However, the results do not detract from the key research objective of this chapter – to discern different IT sourcing strategies across a range of organizations. The following case studies are analyzed at some length to provide a more detailed picture of IT sourcing strategies pursued within the UK.

"Total" outsourcing at the London Stock Exchange (LSE)

Context and overview

The Stock Exchange approached outsourcing through the signing of a five-year single supplier deal in 1992 with Andersen Consulting. When the Exchange decided to outsource the operation of a large part of its IT, it was spending approximately £55 million per annum on running its systems. This figure was rising by 20% a year. This was considered excessive; moreover it was also used predominantly to run legacy systems that were in need of upgrading or replacement. Outsourcing at the Exchange needs to be placed within a wider business context taking into account the "big bang" of 1986 and other fundamental changes within the financial services sector during this time.

Early days: 1985–92

During the 1980s and 1990s, the Exchange underwent major rationalization with the reduction of several layers within the organization hierarchy. During this period, the LSE re-evaluated technology infrastructure and the provision of IT services. One major objective was not to allow technology to become a straight jacket on the business but instead develop a technology architecture that was both flexible and effective. Up to 1992, the cost of providing IT services had been increasing with a corresponding decrease in user satisfaction with the existing systems. The technology infrastructure was both fragmented and complex, and the users were finding the systems increasingly difficult to operate. Information dissemination was a natural by-product of trading, and it was important to be able to respond quickly to regulatory changes within the marketplace. Part of the rationale for outsourcing was to gain access to technical capabilities and skills that would help develop the technical architecture to enable the Exchange to compete in a global and high tech marketplace.

At the time of signing the single supplier outsourcing deal in 1992, there were some reservations and philosophical objections to this strategy from varying quarters of Exchange staff. At the time, large-scale outsourcing deals were relatively uncommon. Given that IT was at the heart of the Exchange's activities, there were serious concerns about outsourcing such a resource to an external supplier. As part of the outsourcing contract, 300 IT staff from the Exchange transferred to the supplier's payroll. The Exchange retained ownership of the systems. Neither the ill-fated Taurus system, nor the Talisman system formed part of the outsourcing deal.

Post-1992

Between the late 1980s and early 1990s, the Exchange initiated a number of changes to the IT infrastructure. Old systems were being phased out with new ones coming on board. In 1996, the Sequence system at the LSE went live. The overall budget for the program was £85.7 million and it was delivered at £81 million. This was (and is) unusual for large-scale computer projects. The development of the software was about £35 million. A further £9 million was for migration software to link old systems to new systems during the four phases of delivery. About £23 million was spent on hardware (central hardware, customer testing service hardware and alternate site hardware). The rest of the budget was used in delivering the system (testing, and delivering services in four phases).

The reasons for the success of the Sequence system were given as follows. First, the Exchange took a clear view about what the system was intended to achieve in terms of business objectives. Key questions asked were: What are the major business requirements for the system? How can the business and technical parameters be fixed throughout the design and implementation stages? These parameters became fixed from the outset, partly because changing business requirements inevitably lead to confusion and problems in the development and implementation stages of technical projects. The Exchange became well aware of this problem during the Taurus project. So, other than two changes that were anticipated during the development phase of the project – (one being forced upon the Exchange by the introduction of the ISD – Investment Services Directorate at the beginning of this 1996, and the other with the launch of the AIM market) – no other changes were permitted. Second, the Exchange applied its expertise of the market and customer management to provide an interface to deliver the program of change. Through two separate arrangements, a large external supplier was brought in to design the system to meet business requirements, and later deliver the system into live service. This supplier was not expected to enter into further sub-contracting relationships with other suppliers, particularly since the Exchange also procured computer equipment and services from other suppliers for activities such as networking and applications.

The Exchange imposed a lot of discipline across the businesses including development and delivery schedules relating to the different phases of the project. Regular meetings were held by senior managers to track the progress of the project. The Exchange claims these meetings were based upon "open reporting". So if there was a problem, people were encouraged to discuss it openly and constructively.

During the peak of the development phase of the project, there were about 350 people involved, 150 of which were in the development team. The remaining people were divided between the business teams within the Exchange. They were either full-time or part-time staff or others who were seconded to the project for a specified period of time. For example, whereas customer relations staff were full-time, legal and finance staff were engaged on the project for part of their time. There was a further 80 staff dedicated to service delivery. According to one spokesperson, large-scale IT projects are only successful if proper discipline is imposed upon the team. She said this was also important for outsourcing. She offered the following insights in respect of the outsourcing strategy pursued at the Exchange:

> "It is probably optimising your future investment in the particular part of the business you are outsourcing, where you still probably maintain or heighten your control of how you use the committed investment and future investment. Why, because in order to outsource you have to be very clear as to what that part of the activity contributes to your business, what you are seeking from that activity. So you have to be very specific about what you expect, either in terms of service levels, investment return or whatever, in the area of the business you outsource as you go through that outsourcing period. It also requires for you to manage your supplier. So again the business has to become far more attuned and astute about the management of that supplier and therefore the services that they give you. It also enables you then to sit back and think through what you want out of future investment. There are a number of things there. You optimise the investment; you gain better control; and if you have chosen your supplier correctly for what you want to achieve, you then introduce yourself to a range of expertise and skills that you would probably not have if you did it in-house."

The single supplier outsourcing deal at the Exchange emerged from initial meetings between senior management and the supplier in late 1991 to early 1992. The LSE board eventually accepted the supplier's proposals, and this process took about four months to complete. At the signing of the out-sourcing contract the IT budget was about £55 million and rising by 20% per annum. One of the reasons for IT outsourcing to a major supplier was significant cost reduction (see Chapter 2). Cost savings were achieved on a risk-reward basis. As the supplier worked to rationalize the Exchange's IT activities, staff numbers and therefore costs fell. At least 150 people employed to operate the service were displaced leaving a total of 200. In parallel, the commitment was made in 1993 to develop the new trading and information systems, allowing the Exchange to operate at a much lower rate. By 1997 the annual IT bill, not just for trading and information, but all of the IT services, was £36 million, and fell again over the next few years. The targets set by the Exchange were to reduce this figure by another 20%–25%, with the cost savings shared between LSE and supplier. The following comments were made by an LSE respondent to describe the relationship with the supplier:

"We are on the outsourcing side (rather than insourcing) because all of the people are now employed by the supplier. So, if you like, I have a service management or supply management relationship with the supplier. But it is worth saying we did more than just outsourcing. Definitely in the arrangements that we have in place, there is a sharing of the risk and therefore, it requires both parties to work together. We had to take some very interesting business decisions in order to clear some of the ground for the supplier to start rationalising the services. Without those business decisions, they would not have been able to do some of the rationalisation. So it was much more of a sort of co-sourcing, but they have had the responsibility to deliver, but I have equally had the responsibility for providing the framework for which they can carry on and deliver. We have seen our cost base come down dramatically over the years."

The Exchange employed an IT director who dealt directly with the supplier. Other suppliers were also used for a range of work such as applications development, support and maintenance, and networking and telecoms. The IT director reported to the director of business operations. Contact with the major supplier was on a weekly basis and sometimes daily depending on the issues which needed discussing. Given the size of the contract, a partner from the supplier organization spent most of his time at the Exchange. Commenting on the concept of "partnership" in an outsourcing context in addition to the advantages and disadvantages of the contract, our spokesperson said:

"Certainly we have taken a partnership approach here. We have to share in the risk and reward. The disadvantage that could occur is that the business does not manage the relationship it has created. If any business is thinking of doing this arrangement, it has to think through quite clearly, why it wants to do it, what it expects from it, and how it is going to manage it, and make sure it develops enough resources to manage the situation. As you probably know, it is very easy for the supplier to manage the client."

Moreover, commenting on the future of the outsourcing suppliers:

"They will rationalise their activities. At some point, they will have to stop and actually look for efficiency gains in their own business. In the second generation of these sorts of arrangement, people are thinking through what can be commoditised, and how this can be done. Some suppliers are now sub-contracting. I think that the major outsourcing firms will have to sit back and think about it."

Whilst the Exchange was satisfied with its total outsourcing arrangement with Andersen Consulting, key questions remained over the long-term future of this relationship. Although the contract was for five years duration, our spokesperson did not address the issue of switching costs, in the event of moving to another supplier, or bringing back the IT facility in-house. It appeared from the discussions that short-term imperatives, such as cost cutting and downsizing, tended to outweigh long-term considerations of future benefits. Indeed, once rationalization had been achieved, it was difficult to see how the Exchange would further benefit from the outsourcing deal, and how the supplier would offer a value-added service. These questions tended to remain unanswered, or, in some minds, were not addressed at all.

Multiple supplier sourcing at ICI plc

Context and overview

ICI went through a major transition from the early 1980s to the late 1990s, and this was both business and technology led. As at 1997, this transition was still taking place facilitated, in part, by an outsourcing arrangement described as *"selective and competitive sourcing"*. By tradition, ICI had a fairly active involvement with IT. It grew up originally in the more technical side of the company in the post-war years of the 1950s and 1960s as computing emerged from the engineering and production environment and then broadened into the commercial area with the automation of payroll and commercial systems. One result was an information technology capability which grew up initially from the various separate divisions of the company, each owning and managing its own data center, telecoms network and associated IT activities. When the company made a major thrust into continental Europe and set up ICI Europa, this situation was repeated with the new company having its own data center, telecoms network and software facility. This was once more the situation in North America, with the acquisition of another company. So by the early 1980s, the entire technical resource was fragmented right the way through the company.

1980–90 – a period of restructuring

Under the latter days of Sir John Harvey Jones as CEO in 1981/82 there was an effort to restructure business and technical activities. A debate was emerging about how best to organize these activities for cost effectiveness, efficiency and rationalization. This resulted in setting up a central monopoly based at Wilmslow in the United Kingdom, initially called Central

Management Services. The monopoly was given powers in mainframe computing and wide area telecoms. What followed was a ten-year period when that central monopoly created an effective global telecoms network by integrating those networks. It was still an area of monopoly telecoms suppliers (with British Telecom in the UK and others operating abroad), where raw bandwidth was purchased, i.e., leased lines. But then ICI built up its own network of switching technology to load that capacity and give it a wider range of services. For example, ICI had the capability for a customer in Finland to make a telephone call to the company and receive a reply from Belgium long before this type of service was available on the open market. This provided the company with a telecoms network that consolidated the major data centers since it established the standard principle of distant independent computer charges enabling those closure of a number of the smaller data centers by merging them into larger ones. In addition, through a coherent electronic messaging and document capability which, although partly based on IBM mainframe and partly based on DEC, using a transfer system called Electronic Document Transfer (EDT), the whole company could effectively be linked up.

These changes were perceived in a positive light during the 1980s, and they generated greater shareholder value. Such change was top management-led. There was a degree of opposition from the businesses as they felt a marked loss of technical autonomy. Yet the Board took the view that there was real benefit in merging these activities. During this time, the businesses still retained significant IT budgets and they had to pay to this IT "monopoly" since it was not paid for centrally. Coupled with this, software was largely specified and developed by the businesses even though it was run on central mainframes. There was a certain amount of shared software, i.e., pan-Continental European distribution and accounting systems, but totally different systems in the UK, including quite significantly different ones between the businesses, and different ones in North America.

The 1990s and beyond

In the early 1990s, the central group that had generated significant shareholder value in the 1980s became too large and too technical in its approach. It tended to see itself as setting the IT agenda for the entire company. By 1992, there were about 1,300 people in corporate IT (telecoms, mainframe, systems development, etc). Monopoly conditions within corporate IT tended to restrict the autonomy of the various business units from making their own IT-enabled business decisions. Structural problems also faced corporate IT, particularly with the de-merger plan. These issues suggested a radical rethink facilitated by the opportunities to source IT services from the market.

In 1992, corporate IT services were paid for by the businesses who had little choice in the matter. They were unable to go to the external marketplace for IT services as this was not permitted. A situation was reached where the group had significant technological excellence. However, the businesses were unhappy because they believed that corporate IT services were not responsive to their requirements. Many felt this group was simply pursuing its own technical agenda and, in doing so, passing costs onto the various businesses. A concrete example of this was where the 45 people from the 1,300 strong staff in corporate IT were engaged in "blue sky technical work" like voice recognition. Questions could be asked about the feasibility of doing voice recognition development work in a chemical company, especially when this technology could be procured from the marketplace.

Internal de-regulation of IT services

The concerns from the businesses about the role of corporate IT services coincided with other wide ranging strategic changes at ICI, such as the de-merger of Zeneca. In mid-1992, ICI announced it would take its pharmaceutical, crop protection and speciality chemicals businesses and create a totally separate company. So in the process of achieving this objective, ICI had to break up all those corporate groups and locate them into one of two much smaller groups – ICI and Zeneca. The major structural changes that were occurring to reduce costs and rationalize business services created an opportunity to re-visit the role of corporate IT.

Selective and competitive outsourcing

Rationalization and downsizing resulted in a loss of 400 of the 1,300 jobs in corporate IT. These job losses were across the hierarchical scale from managers to technicians. Given the split between ICI and Zeneca, a strategy was formed to split the telecoms network giving each company a much smaller facility. This was a critical activity within ICI, but to divide it internally would cost about £5 million. This option was considered too expensive for each of the two businesses to undertake. An outsourcing arrangement was therefore considered as an alternative and cheaper option. Senior managers at ICI went to the marketplace and offered British suppliers the opportunity to compete for the contract to split the telecoms network. At the actual time of the de-merger in 1993, ICI had already signed a contract with Zeneca that stated that by the end of 1994, the split would be complete. So for the period between 1993 and 1994 ICI continued to sell services to Zeneca on a transitional basis. In the autumn of 1993, the outsourcing document was developed, and tested throughout the marketplace at a fairly high level.

Selecting the suppliers

A short list of three major supplier groups was drawn up: Racal Network Services, a combination of BT and MCI, and a combination of Cable and Wireless and AT&T. In the following spring of 1994, they were given the bidding document. This document, written by ICI with the help of its legal team, clearly specified what the company wanted from the supplier. The competitive bidding process was undertaken throughout the spring and summer of 1994 with the three potential suppliers. The ultimate contract was eventually won by Racal Network Services who paid ICI and Zeneca £3m to take over the telecoms network. Senior management at both companies considered this to be a preferable outcome than paying £5 million themselves to split the network. This move also cut tariffs by 20% because ICI's telecoms network facility was merged with the larger outfit of the supplier. This was an additional benefit from outsourcing. Twenty employees transferred to Racal under the terms of the deal.

A world-class datacenter

As a consequence of the de-merger with Zeneca, ICI was left with a world-class data center in the United Kingdom and a much smaller one in Holland. Zeneca ended up with its own data centre. The UK data center was full scale, purpose built and world class, which ran with about 350 MIPs. But it had the capability of running between 8–900 to 1,000 MIPs. The Dutch data center by comparison was situated on the 4th floor of an office building and was much smaller. ICI had a total of about 400 staff associated with those two data centers including a large software group that was doing development and maintenance work.

When the company looked at the business use of this corporate resource, it came to the view that it was in decline as the individual businesses were increasingly re-evaluating their own business processes. They were modernizing, streamlining and implementing new off-the-shelf software packages like SAP that ran on midrange machines. This required smaller capacity. As time went on, they were moving off the mainframe onto stand-alone machines. ICI was therefore faced with several options. The first was to wait while the use of the data center went into marked decline, resulting in staff redundancy, re-deployment or re-skilling. The second was to convert the data center into a standalone business with its own profit and loss account. The third was to find an external supplier to manage the data center for ICI. Weighing the three options carefully resulted in the decision to go out into the marketplace with a bidding document.

An alternative supplier selection strategy

On this occasion, ICI's strategy was somewhat different from the traditional approach to outsourcing. The traditional strategy was to go to about 12–15 suppliers and request information from each one in turn. This was believed to be a waste time and energy. So instead, the company employed the help of consultants to review the marketplace. The potential field was narrowed down to a list of about four suppliers who were judged to be able to offer the required standard of service. They were then invited to present their case in December 1994. They were presented with an analysis that basically outlined the existing resource of datacentre and people. Suppliers were informed that financial projections showed that the business use of this resource would reduce over time. However, the supplier would only be guaranteed a sum of money based upon ICI's assessment of how this service would be used over time, that is the cash flow associated with the historic mainframe legacy system that was moving into decline.

Risk and reward – the key to success?

Potential suppliers were told that any deal was incumbent on them taking over the data center and all the people associated with it. They were not expected to make anyone redundant, nor should they close the data center at some point in the future. Instead, they were expected to generate new business using that resource so, as ICI's business use continued to decline, this would be offset by new customers. Should the suppliers agree to operate under these conditions, they were told they would have the right to be on the bid list every time ICI went outside to tender. With this proviso, the four companies agreed to bid on that basis. A company called Philips/Origin won the contract (see Chapter 4) and they took responsibility for 400 people in the data center as from 1 February 1996. This company paid £4.5 million for the facility and transferred all the staff on a no redundancy/no liability deal under TUPE conditions. In conjunction, a five-year deal was signed purely for the legacy systems together with the promise that the supplier would be on the bid list if other business went outside. Not all the IT budget was outsourced since this contract only covered the existing legacy systems. Senior management structured the debate in two ways:

1. All staff transferring to the supplier would come under TUPE legislation (i.e., they would be given the same terms and conditions, excluding pension rights, as before);
2. Should the supplier wish to make anyone redundant, they would have to finance this themselves.

Evaluating the advantages and disadvantages of corporate IT outsourcing against the above contracts demonstrated that, on balance, ICI over the next few years had a positive experience. Coupled with these decisions, outsourcing was also undertaken by some of the businesses. For example, the decorative paints business (Dulux) in Europe outsourced its IT resource as part of a much broader deal with CSC involving business process re-engineering. Similarly, in North America, Melinex plastics film business signed an outsourcing deal with EDS in 1995. Here, the supplier ran the existing systems on DEC mainframes and invested significant effort in developing new systems to help the film business get closer to its customers.

Evaluating outsourcing from a client perspective

Evaluating the experiences of outsourcing within ICI, both at the corporate level and in the various business areas, management believed that a wide range of ICI expertise existed for commissioning and managing IT outsourcing contracts. But any experience of outsourcing should not be examined in isolation of the wider business imperatives. As such, the two corporate IT outsourcing contracts were driven by very different market, business and technological conditions existing in a given time period. The de-merger of ICI and Zeneca initiated the first contract. This involved outsourcing the telecoms network in Europe and the UK. Here, the key question was posed: Given that we have to split the telecoms network, what is the most effective way of doing so?

In the second outsourcing contract, the data center and the people associated with it, were all part of a declining asset in terms of cost and business use. Here, the key question was: Is there a strategic partner in the marketplace who would wish to run a large database and thereby reduce costs? Given there was an active marketplace from which these services could be purchased under competitive conditions, ICI believed it was more effective to outsource this facility.

By adopting a strategy of selective and competitive outsourcing, the company preferred using multiple suppliers who would compete for business rather than a single supplier as in the case of the London Stock Exchange, above. The company perceived outsourcing to be a complex commercial relationship between client and supplier, and best negotiated by people with a business rather than technical background. In their assessment, the risks in having more than one outsourcing contract were not as great as for single supplier deals. It was also easier to select specific IT activities for outsourcing, such as the data center and telecoms network, rather than contracting out all of them to one supplier. However, as ICI managers admitted, managing the relationship with any number of suppliers invariably poses problems over contracting, logistics and coordination. In response, some have tried a different model for outsourcing, namely joint venture/project sourcing, which we will now discuss.

Joint venture project sourcing at CRESTCo Ltd

Context and overview

This case history offers a different slant on IT outsourcing in that a specialist company was set up with a clear objective to develop a large-scale computer system. CRESTCo Ltd was created in 1994 to "establish, design, construct, acquire, own, manage and operate, or, in whole or in part, arrange for the management and operation of, the CREST settlement system in accordance with the principles and requirements published by the Bank of England" (CRESTCo Ltd. Memorandum and Articles of Association, October 1994).

CRESTCo was set up as an independent company, owned by a consortium of 69 firms across the UK. Unlike other large-scale computer system development projects undertaken within organizations, the CREST system was the core activity of CRESTCo Ltd, with all its employees working toward a common goal. Coming three years after the failed Taurus computer project (abandoned in March 1993), the CREST system went live in the summer of 1996 (notwithstanding some teething problems). Part of the success of the CREST system was that applications development work and outsourcing activities formed part of a clearly defined business strategy from the outset.

A joint venture approach to systems development

The CREST equity settlement system began operations just three years after the Board of the Stock Exchange announced it was abandoning the Taurus computer project. The CREST system was the new computer system released by CRESTCo Ltd in the summer of 1996. CRESTCo Ltd was the company set up by the Bank of England to run the CREST system. With the implementation of CREST, securities were progressively dematerialized from paper records into an electronic format. The first transactions were settled using CREST one month following its implementation. The transition was scheduled to culminate in April 1997 when the Stock Exchange's Talisman settlement system was decommissioned, some 17 years after it first began operating. CREST marked a new phase in strategic IT developments for the securities industry. It put the industry on a new platform that could support wholesale changes in the way it operated. Examples included links from CREST to other international settlements systems, or using CREST to handle other instruments such as unit trusts. Many of its international competitors in the US and elsewhere already had paperless settlement systems (Willcocks and Hindle, 2004).

CREST had three major advantages over Talisman. First, it eliminated the everyday risks of settlement. A certificate moved through an average of 25 pairs of hands each time it was traded. It could get lost or mis-filed. It may also be lost through transportation. Second, it allowed a reduction in financial risks. The biggest risk in settlement was that the investor who bought a share would go out of business before money was paid. The longer the delay between the transfer of shares and payment – known as the settlement cycle – the greater the risk. The London market had already moved to a shorter cycle, in which trades were settled five days after the transaction, a system known as T + 5. CREST enabled London to move to T + 3 by autumn 1997, and already allowed the same day transfer of cash and shares. A reduction in settlement time was in line with other world markets. Third, it lowered the overall cost of settlement. The system itself required about £35m in income a year to break even (including network costs) compared with Talisman's £65m in revenue. Although Talisman included some settlements services not available on CREST, it still cost nearly twice as much when services were properly compared.

Unlike the Taurus system that was managed by the London Stock Exchange, the responsibility for CREST shifted to the Bank of England. Whereas the Stock Exchange struggled to accommodate all the interests of its members and ended up with a "requirements creep" problem, the Bank of England set up a task force which was given two months to originate the CREST proposal. The new proposal was a "descoped" version of Taurus, since the task force specified a much simpler systems architecture. The task force learned the lessons from Taurus by creating highly structured functional and technical specifications. In turn, they excluded some of the more ambitious aims of Taurus that were politically contentious. For example, unlike Taurus, where shareholders would be forced to relinquish their paper share certificates, this became optional under CREST. However, paper backed transactions were more expensive, particularly for the small shareholder (private investor). The key functions of the CREST are outlined below:

- CREST will respond to electronic messages from members to transfer stock between accounts;
- It will authenticate the messages and compare the instructions input by the buyer and the seller – and match them;
- On settlement day, it will check the availability of stock and cash in the CREST members' accounts, and move the stock from the seller's account to the buyer's. The buying member's bank will be instructed to pay the selling member's bank and will be unconditionally obliged to do so;
- CREST will notify the stock's registrar who will commit to register valid transfers within two hours of the electronic transfer within the system;
- The contents of each member's accounts on the register, and in CREST, will be a mirror image of each other.

Source: Documentation from CRESTCo Ltd.
(See also, *Financial Times*, Survey on IT, 3.7.96, p. 8).

The business strategy for the CREST computer project was finalized in May 1994. Software development was completed in December 1995. The development process was audited by both the Bank of England's internal auditors and Price Waterhouse. During this period, CRESTCo Ltd grew from six employees of the Bank of England, working on the Bank's premises, to a staff of more than 120 with offices in the City of London.

The total cost of developing the CREST system was £30m. The annual operating costs were estimated to be £18m. Any surplus in profit would be passed on to the users. The decommissioned Talisman system gave the Stock Exchange an income of £55m a year. The securities industry stood to see its processing costs fall dramatically. CREST was financed through the private sector, with 69 member firms contributing £12m in equity, and a £17m borrowing facility. Full control of the project remained with the Bank of England, until completion of development when the system was handed over to the shareholders. Details of all transactions were transmitted directly from CREST to the Stock Exchange to allow it to police the market and ensure that trades and settlement data married up. Shareholders in Crestco were able to dictate future enhancements, as they eventually came to control the company.

Joint venture project sourcing by the Bank of England as witnessed in the development of CRESTCo Ltd was, in part, a reaction against the failure of the Taurus project managed by the London Stock Exchange. CRESTCo Ltd was set up with the primary aim of developing the CREST equity settlement system. Unlike other large-scale computer projects, the CREST system had a clearly defined technical and business specification, budget and delivery date. Although there were some delays in the implementation of the CREST system, these problems were hardly insurmountable. One advantage of this type of IT sourcing was the Bank of England's ability to retain control over the activities of CRESTCo Ltd. This would not have been the case if the project had outsourced to an independent supplier. In some respects, joint venture/project sourcing is a hybrid between external and internal IT sourcing.

Subsequently, and partly endorsing the sourcing approach adopted, CREST merged with Brussels-based Euroclear in 2002, and by mid-2004 was dealing with over 5 million transactions a month in over 7,000 securities, moving over £400 million of cash daily, serving over 270 users acting for over 35,000 corporate and individual users (Willcocks and Hindle, 2004).

Insourcing at Royal Bank of Scotland

Context and overview

The final IT sourcing decision discussed here is insourcing. This means that an organization either chooses to do all its IT work in-house using its own permanent staff or combines this with external contractors hired for short-term periods to work on specific IT projects, under internal management control. The use of contractors occurs widely in private and public sector organizations throughout the major economies. In the UK the IT contractor market has thrived over the years where many IT professionals chose to become freelancers instead of working permanently for one employer. This was particularly attractive in the "internet bubble" years of 1996–2001. In 1997 we found length of contract as usually between three months and a year, but in some cases IT contractors were having their contracts renewed for several years. Organizations use contractors for a variety of reasons including: a desire to access scarce technical skills; dissatisfaction with external suppliers; a wish to retain control over projects; and the opportunity to manage the peaks and troughs of projects.

Bank objectives

Many organizations seek to hire contractors for in-house, large scale IT projects that occur from time to time. One such example was the Columbus project at Royal Bank of Scotland. Unlike the CREST system discussed above, IT sourcing for the Columbus project was largely through the hiring of external expertise. This was in the form of large and small IT consultancy firms, in addition to hiring contractors from IT recruitment consultancies. One of the bank's objectives was to demonstrate its own innovative capabilities and skills in large-scale project management. The Columbus project was perceived by senior management as a major innovation that would enhance the bank's overall competitive position in a cutthroat industry. Key objectives of the Columbus project were:

• Become best bank in UK by 1997;
• Change from account-based to customer-based service;
• Provide a "seamless service" to customers;
• Create a mini bank at each branch;
• Develop specialist mortgage centers (mortgage shops);
• £200 million profit improvement by 1997;
• Fully exploit new technology;
• Reduce/eliminate credit card fraud;
• Over £100 million committed to developing new technology.

As a consequence of London Stock Exchange "big bang" in 1986, the stock market crash in 1987, and the UK financial services act which effectively deregulated the British financial services industry, the Royal Bank faced intense competition in the late 1980s and early 1990s, particularly from other banks, building societies, and insurance companies. Coupled with this, the deep economic recession, mounting bad debts (£1.1 billion bad debt provisions were made between 1991/92 – FT, 1995), lack of underlying profit and costs of 63% of income all provided the impetus to embark on the Columbus project in 1992 (Oram and Wellins, 1995). Senior management at the bank conceded that lifetime customer loyalty could no longer be guaranteed. Indeed, customers were becoming more in tune with the range of financial services offered by competitors, and were becoming fickle in their choice of financial institutions (Currie and Willcocks, 1997). The Columbus project was launched with the support of a Change Management Group (CMG). According to a corporate report published by the bank, Columbus was intended to transform the bank into *"the best retail bank in the UK by 1997"*, and this would be achieved by implementing major changes to structures, products, services, job titles and roles, training policies, technology and marketing/ sales. A summary of the key strategic objectives of the

Columbus project, as detailed by senior managers in 1992, is outlined below:

- Branch Banking Division (BBD) to be organized around three customer streams – retail, commercial and corporate;
- New managerial roles to be introduced network-wide during 1995;
- Each branch to have ready access to specialist centers and knowledge without having to house all the traditional back office functions;
- Five branches to test the New Branch Design;
- Well over £100m committed to developing new technology;
- Human resource policies and processes to be designed to reflect the new organization.

Implementing the changes

The Columbus project team was set up to identify how these changes could be achieved. According to senior managers, it was crucial that line management were the focus for building the New Bank. Comments made by senior managers in the business units and Technology Division during 1992 and 1993 stressed that, in spite of millions of pounds invested in new technology, few tangible benefits had arisen in the business units. Yet Columbus was intended to be more than simply a large scale IT project. It was described as a major re-engineering project conceptualized and planned by senior executives with the aim of revolutionizing the entire bank.

Interviews with IT managers at the bank confirmed that in conjunction with a large in-house IT department, other forms of IT sourcing were being used. For the most part, the bank tended to outsource, where appropriate, specific IT projects to specialist suppliers. From an industrial relations perspective, this form of IT sourcing was less contentious than other large-scale forms of IT sourcing. Specialist/project sourcing and insourcing, involving hiring contractors as a resource to be managed, was essentially short term; whereas total outsourcing and multiple supplier outsourcing was long term and posed more threats to unionized bank staff with permanent (secure) employment. Indeed, the conservative nature of the bank suggested that introducing major change was not easy, especially if it was perceived to denigrate existing career structures and employment patterns. However, interviews with senior managers in the business units and Technology Division pointed to increasing the proportion of IT work undertaken by external suppliers. Yet no final policy had been introduced. This obviously had implications for the future size and scope of the in-house IT department.

Unlike the London Stock Exchange and Continental Bank (Huber, 1993) which chose a total outsourcing approach, Royal Bank tended to value the capabilities and skills of its large in-house IT function and did not therefore adopt the rhetoric that IT was just a commodity or a service. Having said that, the growing use of external contractors at project manager level and not just analyst and programmer levels, tended to suggest that contracting-out of IT services was a growing trend.

Discussion and conclusion

Empirical research on four distinct IT sourcing strategies in UK organizations suggests that complex market, business, technical and political considerations influence IT sourcing decisions (Currie and Willcocks, 1997; Lacity and Willcocks, 2009). However, as Chapter 2 made clear, the decision to outsource is one that is usually taken on the premise that an external supplier offers a more efficient and cost-effective service than the in-house team. In many cases, client organizations become dissatisfied with in-house IT service provision and are encouraged by supplier rhetoric offering a streamlined service at lower cost. For example, total outsourcing at the London Stock Exchange was initiated by international changes in the market and the need to become more competitive. Large outsourcing suppliers had already undertaken work with the Exchange, and this was stepped-up with the signing of a five-year deal with a single supplier. Outsourcing was accompanied by rationalization at the Exchange, resulting in many job losses and further dismantling of the IT infrastructure. The dangers of this approach have been by now well documented in the literature on total outsourcing deals (see Willcocks and Lacity, 2006). Indeed, the very act of total outsourcing makes it difficult, if not impossible, to bring IT back in-house should the contract run into difficulties. On the other hand, multiple suppliers outsourcing, adopted by ICI, was intended to encourage selective and competitive outsourcing. This strategy mitigates the risks associated with total outsourcing, although the task of managing and coordinating multiple contracts can be time consuming, as many have found to the present day (Lacity and Willcocks, 2009). At ICI, suppliers were carefully selected according to their specialist knowledge. Judging from the experience of these contracts, the company retained control and received a more efficient service.

The desire to retain control over a large-scale IT project was a significant factor in the Bank of England's decision to set up CRESTCo Ltd. Faced with the history of the failed Taurus project, the City did not wish to witness another high profile project failure. To this end, joint venture/project sourcing was a viable alternative to the high risks associated with total outsourcing or multiple supplier sourcing. Interestingly, the experience of Taurus had perhaps colored the view of the Bank of England against using a large, single supplier. CRESTCo Ltd was therefore staffed by Bank of England staff with suppliers being kept at arms length. Similarly, Royal Bank of Scotland had retained a large in-house IT department and managed most of its IT applications development projects in-house (with permanent and contract staff). Whilst the Royal Bank of Scotland used a range of IT suppliers, it tended to prefer multiple supplier sourcing and had recently signed a contract to outsource the cheque processing service.

One of the salient points arising from our empirical research is the tendency of organizations to develop short-term solutions and thereby overlook potential long-term problems. Companies entering into total and multiple suppliers outsourcing arrangements tended to concentrate on their own strategic objectives rather than assess the long-term impact of dealing with a supplier organization. Indeed, once rationalization of the client's IT infrastructure was undertaken, the returns from low margin work would encourage the supplier to seek new income streams from the contract. This was likely to be done by offering the client strategic support and advice on new directions in the business-technical interface. This could pose serious threats to the client's ability to retain control of strategic decision making in vital areas of its business activities.

As the outsourcing services market has expanded and organizations have looked to increase their portfolio of outsourced IT services, it has become increasingly important for client organizations to be more adept at understanding and predicting the strategic priorities and positioning of their suppliers, and at making sourcing choices they can manage effectively. Whilst our research makes a contribution to our understanding of the strategies behind different types of IT sourcing, thus meeting the research objectives of this study, client strategies do evolve over time according to changes in the IT sourcing marketplace, their own learning, and changes in their capabilities. Indeed by the mid-2000s, Willcocks and Lacity (2006) could build a learning curve to show the evolution of a client organization's changing objectives, and maturing ability to manage outsourcing across four phases, namely "hype and fear", "cost focus", "quality focus", and "value-added". Our conclusion from the present chapter and that later study is this – client organizations have a proliferation of choices they can make but the key to success is "being smart in their ignorance", that is, learning to take up only the sourcing choices they and their supplier(s) have the maturity and capability to deliver on.

References

Buck-Lew, M. (1992) "To Outsource or Not?", *International Journal of Information Management*, 12, 1, 3–20.

Cross, J. (1995) "IT Outsourcing: British Petroleum's Competitive Approach", *Harvard Business Review*, May/June, 94–102.

Currie, W. (1994) "The Strategic Management of Large Scale IT Projects in the Financial Services Sector", *New Technology, Work and Employment*, 9, 1, 19–29.

Currie, W. (1995) *Management Strategy for IT*, Pitman, London.

Currie, W. (1996) "Outsourcing in the Private and Public Sectors: An Unpredictable IT Strategy", *European Journal of Information Systems*, 4, 4, 226–236.

Currie, W. (1996) "Direct Control or Responsible Autonomy: Two Competing Approaches to the Management of Innovation in Information Systems", *Creativity and Innovation Management*, 5, 3, 190–203.

Currie, W. (1997) "Computerising the Stock Exchange: A Comparison of Two Information Systems", *New Technology, Work and Employment*, 12, 4, September.

Currie, W. and Willcocks, L. (1996) "The New Branch Columbus Project at Royal Bank of Scotland: The Implementation of Large-scale Business Process Re-engineering", *Journal of Strategic Information Systems*, 5, 3, 213–236.

Currie, W. and Willcocks, L. (1997) *New Strategies in IT Outsourcing: Major Trends and Global Best Practice*, Business Intelligence, London.

Huber, R.L. (1993) "How Continental Bank Outsourced its Crown Jewels", *Harvard Business Review*, January/February, 121–129.

Kern, T. and Willcocks, L. (2001) *The Relationship Advantage: Information Technology, Sourcing and Management*, Oxford University Press, Oxford.

Lacity, M. and Hirschheim, R. (1993) "The Information Systems Outsourcing Bandwagon", *Sloan Management Review*, Fall, 35, 1, 73–86.

Lacity, M. and Willcocks, L. (1996) Best Practices in Information Technology Sourcing. Oxford Executive Research Briefing, 2, Templeton College, Oxford.

Lacity, M. and Willcocks, L. (2000) *Inside IT Outsourcing: A State-Of-Art Report*. Executive Research Report, Templeton College, Oxford.

Lacity, M. and Willcocks, L. (2001) *Global IT Outsourcing: Search for Business Advantage*, Wiley, Chichester.

Lacity, M. and Willcocks, L. (2009) *Information Systems and Outsourcing: Studies in Theory and Practice*, Palgrave, London.

Lacity, M., Willcocks, L. and Feeny, D. (1995) "IT Outsourcing: Maximizing Flexibility and Control", *Harvard Business Review*, May/June, 84–93.

Oram, M. and Wellins, R.S. (1995) *Re-engineering's Missing Ingredient: The Human Factor*, Institute of Personnel Development, London.

Oshri, I., Kotlarsky, J. and Willcocks, L.P. (2007) "Managing Dispersed Expertise in IT Offshore Outsourcing: Lessons from Tata Consultancy Services", *MISQ Executive*, 6, 2, 53–65.

Quinn, J.B. and Hilmer, F.G. (1994) "Strategic outsourcing", *Sloan Management Review*, Summer, 43–55.

Sauer, C. and Willcocks, L. (2007) "Unreasonable Expectations – NHS IT, Greek Choruses and the Games Institutions Play around Mega-Programmes, in Sauer, C. and Willcocks, L. (eds) NHS Special Issue, *Journal of Information Technology*, 22, 3,Introduction.

Straub, D., Weill, P. and Schwaig, K. (2008) "Strategic Dependence on the IT Resource and Outsourcing: A Test of the Strategic Control Model", *Information Systems Frontiers*, 10, 2, 195–211.

Willcocks, L. and Hindle, J. (2004) *From The Eye of The Market 1 – The London Insurance Market: Modernization Or Muddle?*, XChanging, London.

Willcocks, L. and Lacity, M. (eds) (1998) *Strategic Sourcing of Information Systems*, Wiley, Chichester.

Willcocks, L. and Lacity, M. (2006) *Global Sourcing of Business and IT Services*, Palgrave, London.

Willcocks, L. and Lacity, M. (2009) *Research Studies in Information Technology Outsourcing: Perspectives, Practices and Globalization*. Volume 1 – Making IT Outsourcing Decisions; Volume 2 – Managing Outsourcing Relationships; Volume 3 – Global Outsourcing: Issues and Trends, Sage, London.

9
Information Technology Insourcing: Myths and Realities

Rudy Hirschheim and Mary Lacity

Introduction

As the external services market has evolved, academics have systematically studied a number of important aspects of these IT outsourcing decisions. These studies can be categorized as descriptive case studies and surveys of the current outsourcing practices; surveys of practitioners' perceptions of risks and benefits of outsourcing, studies of determinants of outsourcing, and identification of best practices which distinguish success from failure (Loh and Venkatraman, 1992; Ang, 1993; Willcocks and Fitzgerald, 1994; Clark *et al.*, 1995; Klepper, 1995; Grover *et al.*, 1996, Gurbaxani, 1996; Nam *et al.*, 1996). A detailed review of outsourcing research can be found in Dibbern *et al.* (2004), while Willcocks and Lacity (2009) provide a three volume set of research papers on these topics. In general, research indicates that selective sourcing has always been the norm, in fact, but, as Chapter 8 pointed out, that outsourcing options have become more complex. There are many perceived benefits and risks of outsourcing, but many studies are based on respondents' *perceptions* rather than actual outcomes. Our earlier research on determinants of outsourcing generally showed that companies most likely to outsource on a large scale were in poor financial situations, had poor IT functions, or had IT functions with little status within their organizations (Lacity and Hirschheim, 1993, 1995). To this day there is still considerable debate on whether certain sourcing decisions and practices result in success or disappointment (Lacity and Willcocks, 2009).

Much of the IT sourcing research base covers the motivations and consequences of *outsourcing*, with some coverage also given to *backsourcing* (bringing outsourced activities back in-house – see for example Whitten and Leidner, 2006). But the literature has tended to neglect another important option: *insourcing*. Insourcing is the practice of evaluating the outsourcing option, but confirming the continued use of internal IT resources to achieve the same objectives of outsourcing. The Westchester County case in Chapter 7 provided some discussion of insourcing. We believe that insourcing must be fully explored to complement the growing body of outsourcing research.

Only by understanding the processes and outcomes of both outsourcing and insourcing can a comprehensive understanding of IT sourcing result. This unexplored insourcing option provided the motivation behind our research. Can internal IT departments achieve the same results as outsourcing vendors? If so, why have they not done so in the past? Do IT departments actually reduce costs or improve service after winning an insourcing bid? If so, how did IT departments achieve the results? We conducted 14 insourcing case studies to research these issues. The experiences of case study participants are examined and analyzed. The resulting picture is a rich and varied one involving a number of key decision makers, alternative reasons for choosing insourcing, contrasting outcomes, and varying perceptions of its success or failure. But we also identified a number of common experiences. These similarities and differences across the cases make up the subject matter of this chapter.

This research contributes to the IT sourcing research base by providing evidence that companies need not necessarily turn to outsourcing to improve IT performance. While outsourcing may be a preferred option for some organizations for various reasons, such as returning to core competencies or focusing IT staff on more business-oriented IT activities, our cases show that if cost reduction is the major objective, often times IT managers can replicate a vendor's cost reduction tactics. Insourcing success, however, is predicated on a number of key issues, including aligning the perceptions of and agendas for IT, senior level sponsorship of the decision, and a fair and rigorous evaluation process.

Research method

In order to develop an in-depth understanding of IT insourcing decisions and outcomes, we adopted a multiple case study approach. Our aim was to interview various stakeholders within organizations who were likely to have different views of the insourcing decision, who could provide longitudinal accounts of the decision-making process, who could explain the contexts in which decisions were embedded, as well as the outcomes of the decision.

Data collection

We interviewed 41 participants at 14 companies (See Table 9.1). The choice of the case studies was based on the desire to have a variety of sourcing experiences in terms of degree of financial "success" claimed, primarily assessed *a priori* through the trade press and personal contacts. With this design, we sought to generate insights into best sourcing practices by comparing "successes" and "failures". The organizations studied also represent a wide spectrum of industries. In order to facilitate the discussion, the 14 companies will be referred to by pseudonyms based on their industry type – CHEM1, CHEM2, FOOD1, etc.

Table 9.1 Case Study Profiles

Company Pseudonym and Industry	Participants	Sourcing Decision(S) Scope	Decision Sponsor	Decision Year	Evaluation Process	Size of Company: Annual Revenues/ Annual IT Budget at Time of Decision	Size: IT Head Count	Expected Cost Savings	Cost Savings Achieved
1. CHEM1 Chemicals	1. Manager of IS 2. Manager of DP 3. Network Services Supervisor	Entire IT function insourced	IT Manager	1991	Three external bids	$5 billion/ $17 million	60	No cost savings estimated	No cost savings achieved
2. DIVERSE1 Diversified Product Management	4. Director of Advanced Technology	(a) Entire IT function insourced (b) Apps development outsourced	(a) IT Manager (b) Senior Manager	(a) 1991 (b) 1992	(a) No formal bid process (b) Two external bids	$3 billion/ $30 million	184	(a) No cost savings estimated (b) 20%	(a) No cost savings achieved (b) No, costs rose
3. PETRO1 Petroleum Refining	5. VP of IS 6. Director, Sys Coordination 7. Director, Tech Support 8. Director, World Wide Telecom-munications	Entire IT function insourced	Senior Manager	1988	No formal bid process, approached by vendor	$35 billion/ $240 million	1,800	No cost savings estimated	No cost savings achieved

Table 9.1 Case Study Profiles – *continued*

Company Pseudonym and Industry	Participants	Sourcing Decision(S) Scope	Decision Sponsor	Decision Year	Evaluation Process	Size of Company: Annual Revenues/ Annual IT Budget at Time of Decision	Size: IT Head Count	Expected Cost Savings	Cost Savings Achieved
4. PETRO2 Petroleum Refining	9. Corporate Mgr. Planning 10. Division Manager 11. Corporate Mgr. Technology Development 12. Mgr. Software Strategies 13. Mgr. of Corporate Computing	Entire IT function insourced	Senior Manager	1991	Internal bid and two external bids	$10 billion/ $32 million	134	43%	Yes, achieved within 5 years
5. PETRO3 Petroleum Refining	14. Assistant Treasurer 15. Director of IS 16. Manager of Technical Support	Entire IT function insourced	IT Manager	1990	Two external bids	$3 billion/ $6 million	25	No cost savings estimated	No cost savings achieved
6. DIVERSE2 Natural Gas, and other services	17. Manager of IS 18. VP, Operations 19. Vendor Account Manager 20. VP of Computer Utility 21. Outsourcing Consultant	(a) Entire IT function insourced (b) Entire IT function outsourced	(a) IT Manager (b) Senior Manager	(a) 1988 (b) 1988	(a) No formal bid process (b) One informal external bid	$6 billion/ $100 million	530	(a) 0% (b) 20%	(a) None (b) No, customer threatened to sue vendor

Table 9.1 Case Study Profiles – *continued*

Company Pseudonym and Industry	Participants	Sourcing Decision(S) Scope	Decision Sponsor	Decision Year	Evaluation Process	Size of Company: Annual Revenues/ Annual IT Budget at Time of Decision	Size: IT Head Count	Expected Cost Savings	Cost Savings Achieved
7. CHEM2 Chemicals	22. Manager of DP	(a) Entire IT function outsourced (b) Entire IT function insourced	(a) Senior Manager (b) IT Manager	(a) 1984 (b) 1988	(a) One external bid (b) No formal bid process	$.7 billion/ $4 million	40	(a & b) Savings anticipated but not quantified	(a) No, terminated contract due to excess fees & poor service (b) Savings achieved
8. RUBBER Rubber and Plastics	23. VP of IS	(a) Entire IT function outsourced (b) Entire IT function insourced	(a) Senior Manager (b) IT Manager	(a) 1987 (b) 1991	(a) No formal bid process, one informal external bid (b) No formal bid process	$6 billion/ $240 million	1,000	(a & b) Savings anticipated but not quantified	(a) No, costs rose to 4% of sales (b) Yes, costs fell to 1% of sales
9. RETAIL1 Apparel Manufacturer & Retailer	24. VP of IS 25. Director of IS Administration	Entire IT function insourced	IT Manager	1988	No formal bid process	$2 billion/ $27 million	125	54%	Yes, achieved within four years
10. UNIVERSITY	26. CIO 27. Interfaculty Council Member	Entire IT function insourced	Senior Manager, then CIO	1992	Compare one external bid with one internal bid	$250 million/ $7 million IT	110	20%	Yes, achieved within one year

Table 9.1 Case Study Profiles – *continued*

Company Pseudonym and Industry	Participants	Sourcing Decision(S) Scope	Decision Sponsor	Decision Year	Evaluation Process	Size of Company: Annual Revenues/ Annual IT Budget at Time of Decision	Size: IT Head Count	Expected Cost Savings	Cost Savings Achieved
11. FOOD Food Manufacturer	28. Data Center Director	Entire IT function insourced	Senior Manager	1988	Compare one external bid with internal bid.	$7 billion/ $18 million	80	45%	Yes, achieved within three years
12. TCOM Telecom-munications	29. Manager of IS 30. Internal Lawyer 31. Previous Manager of IS 32. Data Center Manager 33. Facilities Management Director 34. Chair, RFP Team 35. Chair, Internal Bid Team	Entire IT function insourced	Senior Manager	1991	Compare two external bids with internal bid	$.5 billion/ $7 million	39	46%	Yes, achieved within two years
13. ENERGY Energy Company	36. Director of IS Planning 37. CIO	Entire IT function insourced	Senior Manager	1989	Compare three external bids with internal bid	$6 billion/ $60 million	180	25%	Yes, achieved within two years
14. INTL-BANK International Bank	38. Executive VP 39. VP, EDP Control 40. Director, Applications Development 41. Director, Technology Development	Entire IT function insourced	Senior Manager	1989	Never really considered outsourcing	DM557 billion in assets	1,800	20% cost savings through adoption of best practices	Yes

At each case site, we conducted face-to-face interviews with individuals directly involved in the sourcing decision. Each interview lasted from one to three hours. Interviewees included senior business executives and IT managers who sponsored the sourcing evaluations, consultants hired to assist contract negotiations, and IT personnel responsible for gathering technical and financial information pertaining to the sourcing decision. All interviews were conducted in person at the company site. All participants were assured of anonymity so as to promote open discussions.

Interviews followed the same protocol, proceeding from an unstructured to a structured format. During the unstructured portion, participants were asked to tell their "sourcing story". The unstructured format allowed the participants free rein to convey their interpretations. After participants completed their stories, they were asked semi-structured questions designed to solicit information on specific sourcing issues that may have been absent from their previous recollections. These issues included coverage of the scope of the sourcing decision, sponsors of the decision, the sourcing evaluation process, and implementation process. All participants were also asked to assess the decision outcome in terms of their perceptions of "success" or "failure" and why they felt the way they did about the outcome. When participants expressed a viewpoint, they were prompted to provide specific supporting evidence. The evidence consisted of anecdotes as well as documentation such as benchmarking reports, IT budgets, internal bids, outsourcing bids, and bid analysis criteria. In cases where opinions of participants at the same organization differed, we conducted follow-up telephone calls with participants to clarify their positions.

Participants were also asked specific questions about their company and IT department. Pertaining to their company, participants described the organizational structure, the major products and services produced, competition in the industry, financial situation, corporate goals, business successes and failures. Pertaining to IT, participants described IT activity in terms of headcount, budget, chargeback system, size of data centers, user satisfaction, challenges, goals, and reputation.

Data analysis

The interviews were tape recorded and transcribed. The transcribed text was then analyzed using a data analysis process involving the following steps:

1. **Create individual case descriptions.** The transcribed interviews were used to write-up detailed cases. The cases were a compilation of the various interviewees' perceptions about the insourcing decision process and outcome. Each case included the historical details in which insourcing was considered; the key participants in the decision process; their pre-understanding of the sourcing options and apparent values and assumptions; how these values and beliefs were manifest in the actual decision

to insource; the implementation of the decision; and the consequences (results) of insourcing.

2. **Analyze six decision factors across the cases.** Once we had a feel for each individual case, we then scanned across the 14 cases to see what similarities and differences existed. We analyzed six factors across the cases, decision scope, decision sponsor, evaluation process, year of the decision, size of the organization, and decision outcome. These factors were derived from our previous research on outsourcing (Lacity and Hirschheim, 1993).

3. **Employ a rhetorical device to generalize common themes among the cases.** The use of archetypes is employed to condense and simplify a complex subject matter. We are not using archetypes necessarily as an analytical tool (i.e., a way to analyze the data), but rather as a rhetorical device to convey the themes extracted from our analysis of the textual data collected in the case studies.

4. **Identify common lessons across the cases.** While these archetypes capture the differences among insourcing approaches, we also sought to characterize common elements, or lessons to be learned from the body of research. These common lessons describe stakeholder attitudes, perceptions, and behaviors that are based on implicit assumptions about IT sourcing.

Four archetypes of insourcing

The issues associated with the choice of an IT sourcing strategy are often murky, hidden behind euphemisms, perceived differently by different stakeholder groups, and generally not easily analyzed. Nevertheless, in trying to explain what we found in our research about these issues we noted certain similarities and differences in patterns and these coalesced around four loosely connected alternatives in the way organizations approach IT insourcing. In the following, we describe these four alternative approaches in terms of *archetypes*. Each archetype is also discussed through an individual case study. It should be noted that these approaches, depicted through the archetypes, are neither as clear cut nor as animated as they are made out to seem. There is overlap and their differences are overstated for the purpose of effect. They are highly simplified but powerful conceptions of an ideal or character type. The archetypes play an important role in conveying the essential differences that exist in alternative ways organizations approach IT insourcing.

ARCHETYPE 1 – senior executives enable internal IT managers to cut costs

Six of our cases – PETRO2, UNIVERSITY, FOOD, TCOM, ENERGY, and RETAIL1 – reflect this archetype. It begins when external pressures threaten the organization causing senior management to search for ways to reduce costs, including IT costs. Under this scrutiny, senior executives question the value of rising IT expenditures and mandate that IT managers cut costs. IT managers counter that costs are high because users resist their cost reduction tactics. Senior management despairs at the gridlock and formally invites outsourcing vendors to submit bids. IT managers rally, requesting they be allowed to compete with vendor bids. They argue that senior management's outsourcing threat serves to empower IT managers because they can convince users that IT cost will be cut – either by them or by an external vendor. By replicating a vendor's cost reduction tactics, internal IT managers prepared internal bids that beat vendor bids. Once these bids were awarded to the internal IT managers, they succeeded in meeting – or in some cases exceeding – their bid proposals, resulting in a successful financial outcome. A description of one of the cases – PETRO2 – serves to demonstrate this theoretical archetype.

PETRO2. PETRO2 – a *Fortune 100* conglomerate of petroleum, natural gas, and chemicals companies – ran into severe financial difficulties in the late 1980s. Senior management responded by cutting costs through the sale of assets, reduced headcount, and budget cuts. In this climate, senior management began to scrutinize the rising costs of IT – where was the value from these IT expenditures? The corporate manager of IT planning explains:

> All they (senior management) see is this amount of money that they have to write a check for every year. Year after year after year. Where is the benefit? MIS says, "Well, we process data faster than we did last year." They say, "So what?" MIS says, "Well, we can close the ledger faster." And they say, "So what? Where have you increased revenue? All you do is increase costs, year after year after year and I am sick of it. All I get are these esoteric benefits and a bunch of baloney on how much technology has advanced. Show me where you put one more dollar on the income statement."

Internal IT managers repeatedly tried to reduce costs by consolidating their three data centers, but business unit managers refused, perceiving that the new consolidated center would not effectively cater to their needs. For example, one of the business unit leaders declared:

> If it cost $5 million more dollars to have this in my business unit and be able to control it and make it responsive to my needs it's worth $5 million dollars to me.

Only after senior management initiated an outsourcing evaluation did IT managers convince senior managers and users that they could match a vendor's offer:

> The IT management said that there is no reason we should be excluded from the party. You cannot assume, it's not fair to say that we'll just do what we've been doing. We ought to have the same freedom to make deci-

sions that outsourcers are making. So IT management in each of the divisions caucused. We put together a team. – Corporate Manager of Technology

This team prepared an internal bid based on severe cost reductions, including data center consolidation. This bid beat two external bids. The internal IT department was awarded the bid and subsequently consolidated the data centers, installed automation in the tape libraries, re-organized the work flows, standardized software, and instituted a new chargeback system that curtailed excessive user demands. These tactics reduced headcount by 51% resulting in a 43% cost reduction, thus deeming the insourcing project a financial success. The corporate manager of technology attributes the success to senior management's empowerment of the IT staff:

This is critical: this is the first time someone handed a MIS guy a stick. In the past, if a company came in and said, "I want this new piece of software, I need it." Bingo, we went out and bought it. That doesn't happen anymore. In fact the opposite happens. They couldn't just go buy something for their special needs, we wouldn't pay for it.

ARCHETYPE 2 – IT managers terminate failing outsourcing contracts

Our second archetype – exemplified by CHEM2 and RUBBER – also resulted in a financial insourcing success, but the route to success was very different. In these two companies, senior managers had previously outsourced over 80% of the IT budget and engaged in long-term contracts. Due to poorly negotiated contracts, however, IT costs rose and service levels dropped. The senior IT managers assembled a case to terminate the outsourcing contract and rebuilt the internal IT organization. Senior executives and users supported the IT managers' proposals. After an initial investment, IT costs dropped and service levels improved as a result of insourcing. Here is what happened at CHEM2.

   CHEM2. Senior executives at CHEM2 decided to outsource the entire IT department in 1984 after a leveraged buyout left the company debtridden (Decision 1, CHEM2-a). After analyzing three vendor bids, senior executives signed a seven-year, fixed price contract with the only vendor they perceived as capable of handling their information needs. The contract stipulated that the vendor would provide the same level of service that CHEM2 received from the internal IT department in 1984. During the first month into the contract, the vendor charged CHEM2 for many services senior executives assumed were covered in the contract. Excess charges were not the only problem. The manager of information technology noted that the vendor's goal was to maximize profits, therefore, the vendor failed to introduce new technology (without a stiff excess fee), the vendor reduced staff and over-worked remaining employees, and the vendor siphoned the best talent to woo other customers:

> I think you find with outsourcing that any innovation in technology comes from your own people, requirements from users on your staff. But basically the [outsourcing vendors] just crank it. And so we were operating old software...You pay for them to learn your business, then they move those people to court other companies in your industry. They transfer skills to get new business, now the learning curve is yours to pay for again. – Manager of IT

The manager of IT accumulated the evidence of rising IT costs and decreased service levels to convince senior management and users to terminate the contract. Senior management bought into the proposal, even though the vendor tried to keep the contract:

> I opened up negotiations early, to renegotiate the contract to get me out...It's like when you were a little kid. Two weeks before Christmas, you suddenly cleaned up your act and behaved a whole lot better...But I think they [senior management] had an awful lot of feedback from the users that they didn't like the systems. In other words, they were not supported in the manner that they needed to be supported to run the business. Also the issues of quality came up, customer service, no new technology. – Manager of IT

The manager of IT put together a plan to rebuild the internal IT department, which included purchasing a new machine, buying packaged software, and hiring back 40 analyst programmers from the outsourcing vendor. After an initial investment, the IT manager conveyed that users are happier with the service and that his current IT budget is less than the fixed price contract, indicating a successful financial outcome.

ARCHETYPE 3 – IT managers defend insourcing

Archetype 3 was the first time in which insourcing resulted in financial failure in that no cost savings (or service improvements) occurred. In these cases, exemplified by CHEM3, DIVERSE1, PETRO3, and DIVERSE2, IT managers took charge of the outsourcing evaluation for a number of "political" reasons, such as proving efficiency, justifying new resources, or trying to enhance their reputation as a business person (see Chapter 2). They used the outsourcing evaluations to confirm to senior management the legitimacy of continued sourcing through the internal IT departments. In three cases, these cursory evaluations eventually backfired, senior managers firing IT managers or eventually outsourcing. In the remaining case, the company merely proceeded as is.

PETRO3. The Director of Information Services initiated an outsourcing investigation after users consistently complained to senior management about the lack of service in the applications area. The Director of IS explained that user demands far exceeded his current resources, leading to a large applications backlog. He explains:

> I said, "I cannot get any support from you in how to allocate these resources. And we cannot be the traffic cop in this whole process because it is not right." I said, "I'm trying to satisfy everybody and it's not working." – Director of IS

His investigation consisted of inviting several vendor bids – not for applications, but for the data center, a function he knew was performing well. After the bids were analyzed, the Director of IS drafted a letter to the chairman of the board explaining that continued insourcing cost less than outsourcing. The Director of IS explains the outcome:

> I had their attention now. And so some of the people who were bashing us backed off. Their group executives now tell their users, "Back off, they are doing the best that they can."...So did it help? Since then, I've been to two officer meetings, so I guess it did.

Although a political victory, there was no change in IT costs:

> As a result of having done this study, there is no difference now than if we had not done the study...It really came down to an exercise. We did not try to make outsourcing work. What we were really trying to do was to come up with the justification for why we shouldn't outsource. – Manager of Technical Support

ARCHETYPE 4 – senior executives confirm the value of IT

Archetype 4 indicates the case where the insourcing decisions did not result in significant reduction in IT costs, but the insourcing decisions were still considered a success because companies re-validated and further legitimated internal sourcing. In the two companies that exemplify this approach – PETRO1 and INTL-BANK – senior IT executives had full support from senior management. Each has implemented organizational structures and processes to demonstrate the cost effectiveness of its IT departments.

PETRO1. In the mid-1980s, PETRO1, one of the world's largest petroleum companies, suffered severe financial difficulties which forced senior management to find ways to cut costs. An outsourcing vendor, cognizant of the situation, called the CEO and offered to purchase his IT assets, hire his IT staff, and reduce his current IT costs while still maintaining service levels. The CEO called his direct subordinate, the VP of IT, and told him to draft a letter to the vendor, declining the offer. The VP of IT conveys this conversation with the CEO:

> He says, "I'm not interested in letting other people, '– that's the CEO talking –' have access to our data. I don't have to go outside for use of our data, so prepare a letter back to the chairman of [the outsourcing vendor] and say we appreciate your offer but at this time we consider our information technology as part of the strategic work that we have."

When the VP of IT asked how the CEO could readily dismiss the vendor's offer without further analysis, he explained how he had spent 30 years educating and demonstrating to senior managers the value of IT. For example, he convinced the CEO to "invite" all new general managers to attend a week-long executive computer class which focused on IT-enabled business achievement. He abandoned the general allocation chargeback system in favor of unit pricing and compared these prices with vendor offerings to demonstrate his cost-efficiency:

> If you start billing your customers as a controlled expense is it not anticipated that users will say, "Hey could I get this done cheaper elsewhere?" Wouldn't it be nice to be able to answer that question before it was asked?

His IT department even became an outsourcing vendor by providing IT services to external customers. Although external customers represent only 10% of the IT budget, the VP of IT explains that this creates a marketing mentality among his staff to be both cost-efficient and service-oriented. The VP of IT also participated on two top executive committees – The Corporate Research Committee and the Operating Committee. These committees set corporate strategy and allocate large amounts of resources. His high profile contributed to the quick dismissal of the vendor's outsourcing proposal:

> So I think the concept of your IT person being part of the management of the company – not just a technician sitting on the sidelines – is something that keeps you from outsourcing.

Table 9.2 offers a summary of the four archetypes and classifies the 14 cases.

Table 9.2   Insourcing Archetypes and Case Classification

Sponsor / Financial Outcomes	Senior Managers Sponsor Insourcing Decision	IT Managers Sponsor Insourcing Decision
Significant Reduction in IT Costs	**Archetype 1** *Senior managers enable IT managers to reduce costs, typically by creating an RFP and inviting both internal and external bids.* PETRO2 UNIVERSITY FOOD TCOM ENERGY RETAIL1	**Archetype 2** *IT managers terminate failing outsourcing contracts. These outsourcing experiences were so disastrous that no formal evaluation process was needed to confirm the termination decision.* CHEM2 RUBBER
No Change in IT Costs	**Archetype 4** *Senior managers confirm the value of IT without a formal bid process because their support and faith in IT is traditionally strong.* INTL-BANK PETRO1	**Archetype 3** *IT managers defend insourcing. Even apparently "rigorous" evaluations were perceived as biased against outsourcing.* CHEM1 DIVERSE1 PETRO3 DIVERSE2

Discussion

Prior to our data collection, our conception of insourcing "success" and "failure" was equivalent to financial outcomes of the process, i.e., insourcing "successes" were companies that achieved cost savings of at least 20%, while insourcing "failures" were companies that achieved little or no cost savings. Remembering that, as Chapter 2 showed, while organizations may have many objectives for outsourcing, cost savings invariably figure somewhere in their requirements (see also Willcocks and Lacity, 2006). In our research design, we selected "successes" and "failures" to ascertain: After outsourcing evaluations re-confirmed insourcing as the preferred sourcing strategy – why did some companies achieve dramatic savings (and thus success) while others merely continued "as is?"

Based on our analysis – which led to the four archetypes – we re-conceptualized our notions of "success" and "failure" along stakeholder lines. In the majority of cases, our original conception of cost-savings as the primary criterion for success only captured the perceptions of senior executives, whom we concluded perceived IT as a cost to be minimized. In cases of extreme cost-cutting – up to 54% in one company – senior executives deemed the insourcing decision as a *success*, but users perceived it as a *failure*. Unlike senior executives who focused on cost, users primary criterion for success was service excellence. Because service degradation accompanied severe cost cuts due to the cost/service trade-off, users were most displeased with the insourcing outcomes in the majority of cases. And IT Managers' perceptions of insourc-ing *success* and *failure* were even more complex – many IT Managers hoped that the insourcing projects would raise the status of IT in the eyes of senior management, but remain disappointed on this front.

Thus, we assume a stakeholder interpretation of success and failure. We have categorized these stakeholders into three main groups: senior management, business unit managers and users, and IT managers. As we discuss, each stakeholder group sets a different *expectation* for IT performance, and as such, holds different *perceptions* of IT performance and the effects of insourcing.

Senior management's expectations of IT performance: minimize costs. In all but two of the participating companies – PETRO1 and INTL-BANK – senior executives focused on one dimension of IT performance: cost efficiency. These senior executives were frustrated with the rising costs of IT and questioned the value of IT expenditures. Because of the questionable value of IT, many senior executives viewed IT as a commodity – a necessary cost of doing business. As such, senior executives' IT performance expectations focused on cost minimization, i.e., provide the "commodity" function as inexpensively as possible. We have already seen a number of quotes in the context of the individual cases. Other illustrative quotes from our participants capture senior management's perception of IT:

They are always telling us our processing for payroll is too damn expensive. Then when you say, "Well have you looked outside?" "Oh yes, we beat the heck out of them." So our costs are too high but they can't get it any cheaper. – Director of IT Administration at RETAIL1

The Board could care less about IT. They treated it like they treated the heat or electricity. – CIO of UNIVERSITY

There was a feeling that this was a rat hole to pour money down. – The Data Center Manager at FOOD describing his senior management's perceptions of IT

One of the questions I asked was, "How do you view IT, Mr. President, particularly in the operational center, as an asset to your corporation? Of potential value?" For the most part, business people don't see it that way.

They see it as cost. – The IT Manager at TCOM describing the President's view of IT.

I think I got the feeling that there was an intolerance by our management about having a big computer operation. It was viewed as a big boat anchor even though it was a vital service. And they kept asking questions if there were other ways to do this... – Director of IT, PETRO4

Based on these and other quotations in the transcripts, we conclude that senior management in all but two of the participating companies – PETRO2 and INTL-BANK – viewed IT as a cost to be minimized. Furthermore, these senior executives perceived that their current sourcing strategies had failed to meet this major objective, as "evidenced" by the rising costs of IT. In the six companies illustrating archetype 1, senior managers were pleased that the outsourcing evaluation served to mobilize internal IT managers to cut costs. In archetype 2, senior management cancelled outsourcing contracts and brought the function back inside when costs for IT increased through outsourcing. In archetype 3, IT costs did not decrease and led to senior management questioning the value of IT.

We believe that senior management's perceptions of IT as a cost to be minimized are tied, in large part, by accounting for IT as an overhead, which only serves to highlight the costs, and not the value of IT investments. For example, one VP of IT noted that his CEO kept asking him why IT budgets were rising when budgets in all the other functional units were falling. The VP of IT responded that marketing costs dropped 10% partly because IT implemented a new credit card system and that transportation costs dropped because IT automated 16 truck-refueling systems. Prior to the outsourcing evaluations, all but two participating companies – PETRO1 and INTL-BANK – accounted for IT in this way, thus contributing to our understanding of why these senior executives sent the mandate to IT Managers: *Cut IT Costs.*

Users' view of IT: service excellence. Unlike senior management, users did not view IT as a commodity; IT is not a sack of cement, but must be custom-tailored to meet their idiosyncratic business requirements. As such, users set service excellence as their major expectation for IT performance. For example, users generally demanded customized software, a local staff of dedicated analysts and programmers, excess IT resources "in case they are needed", sub-second response time all the time, 24-hour help, information centers, training, etc. At PETRO2, for example, users demanded their own local data centers and did not want to consolidate to save money at the corporate level. Recall the declaration of one business unit leader, *"If it cost $5 million more dollars to have this in my business unit and be able to control it and make it responsive to my needs it's worth $5 million dollars to me."*

At FOOD, users in each business unit demanded custom-tailored soft-ware – even when standard packages were more cost efficient. For exam-ple, different business units chose different packages for word processing, electronic mail, fourth generation languages, and spread-sheets. From the business unit perspective, it made more business sense to use packages with which users were familiar rather than incur the inconvenience and expense of learning a standard package. As the data center manager explains, users were generally pleased with IT:

> These people never complained about service or price. They were big users, in many ways, they were a perfect customer. They had only a couple things a week they cared about. And we had it hardwired, execute those two things routinely with no trouble. The rest of the week, they didn't care what we did to them. They were the perfect customer.

In summary, participants consistently reported users set service excellence as the primary expectation for IT performance.

IT manager's view: caught in the middle. Juxtaposed to senior manage-ment's cost reduction mandates were users pleas for service excellence. This leads to a "cost/service" dilemma, which can be depicted as a matrix high-lighting realistic verses unrealistic IT performance expectations. Because of the cost/service trade-off, IT can be realistically expected to perform in one of two boxes at a given point in time: IT can provide a premium service for a premium cost *or* IT can provide a minimal service for a minimal price. If organizations perceive that a given IT function is a critical contributor, then IT can be realistically expected to perform in the *Differentiator* quadrant. As a differentiator, service excellence supersedes cost efficiency. If organizations perceive that a given IT function is merely a utility, IT can be realistically expected to perform in the *Commodity* or low cost producer quadrant. As a commodity, IT can be expected to deliver a standard service at a minimal cost.

But in our case companies, senior executives were demanding cost cuts while users were demanding service excellence. IT managers were expected to perform the near impossible: provide a Rolls Royce service at a Chevrolet price – to be *Super Stars*. IT managers could not simultan-eously satisfy both stakeholder groups because the "best practices" associ-ated with one objective are in direct conflict with the "best practices" prescribed for the other objective. In general, the *differentiator* quadrant calls for decentralization, customization, and encouraged user demand. The *commodity* quadrant calls for centralization, standardization, and curtailed user demand. The result: neither stakeholder group was satisfied and began to perceive that IT provided poor service that cost too much – IT was a *Black Hole* (See Table 9.3).

Implications for practice

We believe that outsourcing evaluations often result from the frustrations caused by different stakeholder expectations and perceptions of IT performance. This belief is based on an analysis of what IT managers can *realistically* achieve versus what senior executives and users *expect* them to achieve. Different stakeholder perspectives set unrealistic performance expectations for IT managers, leading to frustration, loss of faith in internal IT management, and hopes that outsourcing vendors will provide the solutions. While outsourcing can lead to a reduction in IT costs, this reduction often comes at a price: reduced service. Moreover, since it is known that most of the cost savings come from the implementation of key cost reduction strategies such as data center consolidation, unit-cost chargeback systems, standardized software, etc. rather than economies of scale, internal IT departments should be able to reduce costs on their own. And indeed they did.

However, while IT managers can theoretically implement cost reduction strategies, internal politics often prevent them from doing so. This is why *senior executives need to allow IT managers the ability to submit internal bids in competition with external vendors.* The outsourcing threat may overcome political obstacles and allow IT managers the freedom and power to propose and implement drastic cost cuts. If senior executives merely compare external bids with current costs, they may allow the vendors to "pick the low lying fruit." That is, vendors may make drastic cost cuts but absorb most of the savings themselves, merely passing some benefit to customers in the form of modest price cuts. Users, on the other hand, who have been used to service excellence from IT must now realize that such premium service comes at a price – it is not a free good. Implementing outsourcing or insourcing helps focus users' attention on the cost/service trade-off. IT managers, for their part, need to make visible the cost/service trade-off and work for a consensus on what level of service IT should provide for a given cost.

In conclusion, we wish to offer this sobering thought: even if insourcing is chosen over outsourcing, and the expected cost savings are realized, there is

Table 9.3   IT Cost/Service Trade-Off

Cost / Service	Low Cost	High Cost
Service Excellence	***Super Star*** Senior management's and users' expectations about IT	***Differentiator*** Users' underlying wishes about IT
Minimal Service	***Commodity*** Senior management's underlying beliefs about IT	***Black Hole*** Senior management's and users' perceptions about IT

no guarantee it will be perceived as "successful" due to the very different expectations held by the various stakeholders. Success is related to who is doing the evaluating.

References

Ang, S. (1993) *The Etiology of Information Systems Outsourcing*, PhD Dissertation, Department of Information and Decision Sciences, University of Minnesota, USA.

Clark, T., Zmud, R. and McCray, G. (1995) "The Outsourcing of Information Services: Transforming the Nature of Business in the Information Industry", *Journal of Information Technology*, 10, 4, 221–237.

Dibbern, J., Goles, T., Hirschheim, R. and Bandula, J. (2004) "Information Systems Outsourcing: A Survey and Analysis of the Literature", *Database for Advances in Information Systems*, 34, 4, Fall 2004, 6–102.

Grover, V., Cheon, M. and Teng, J. (1996) "The Effect of Service Quality and Partnership on the Outsourcing of Information Systems Functions", *Journal of Management Information Systems*, 12, 4, 89–116.

Gurbaxani, V. (1996) "The New World of Information Technology Outsourcing", *Communications of the ACM*, 39, 7, 45–47.

Klepper, R. (1995) "Outsourcing Relationships", in Khosrowpour, M. (ed.) *Managing Information Technology Investments in Outsourcing*, Idea Group Publishing, Harrisburg, PA, pp. 218–243.

Lacity, M. and Hirschheim, R. (1993) *Information Systems Outsourcing: Myths, Metaphors and Realities*, Wiley, Chichester.

Lacity, M. and Hirschheim, R. (1995) *Beyond the Information Systems Outsourcing Bandwagon: The Insourcing Response*, Wiley, Chichester.

Lacity, M. and Willcocks, L. (2009) *Information Systems and Outsourcing: Studies in Theory and Practice*, Palgrave, London.

Loh, L. and Venkatraman, N. (1992) "Diffusion of Information Technology Outsourcing: Influence Sources and the Kodak Effect", *Information Systems Research*, 334–358.

Nam, K., Rajagopalan, S., Rao, H. and Chaudhury, A. (1996) "A Two-Level Investigation of Information Systems Outsourcing", *Communications of the ACM*, 39, 7, 36–44.

Whitten, D. and Leidner, D. (2006) "Bringing Back IT: An Analysis of the Decision to Backsource or Switch Vendors", *Decision Sciences*, 37, 4, 605–621.

Willcocks, L. and Fitzgerald, G. (1994) *A Business Guide to Outsourcing Information Technology*, Business Intelligence, London.

Willcocks, L. and Lacity, M. (2006) *Global Sourcing of Business and IT Services*, Palgrave, London.

Willcocks, L. and Lacity, M. (2009) *Research Studies in Information Technology Outsourcing: Perspectives, Practices and Globalization*. Volume 1 – Making IT Outsourcing Decisions; Volume 2 – Managing Outsourcing Relationships; Volume 3 – Global Outsourcing: Issues and Trends, Sage, London.

10

Contracts, Control and "Presentation" in IT Outsourcing

Thomas Kern and Leslie Willcocks

Introduction

Adoption by some of the largest international corporations has seen outsourcing become a key component of the information technology management agenda. Critical to this agenda is the formulation of comprehensive contracts. For this, legal experts and/or advisors can be consulted, but enforcement depends very much on client and vendor account managers. In this chapter a theoretical analysis of the contract contrasted with empirical data from client and vendor post-contract management practice revealed that the contract has a number of purposes beyond its sole legal nature, outlining a number of control dimensions both parties aim to enforce. Here we present findings from 13 organizations on the role of the outsourcing contract in ensuring control over the client's outsourcing destiny (for this subject see also Chapters 3 and 11).

Research has shown that the client-vendor relationship is indeed more complex than a mere contractual transaction-based relationship (Kern, 1997; Kern and Willcocks, 2001; Klepper, 1994, 1995; McFarlan and Nolan, 1995; Willcocks and Cullen, 2006; Willcocks and Kern, 1997; Willcocks and Lacity, 2009, especially Volume 2). A major complexity is the near impossibility of presentation[1] of future requirements in long-term deals such as outsourcing, due to the volatility of information technology and the likely changes in user and company requirements. Thus suggestions have been made that the client-vendor relationship has to include relational contract and/or partnering dimensions (Kern, 1997; Poppo and Zenger, 2002; Willcocks and Kern, 1997; Willcocks and Cullen, 2006 – see also Chapters 3 and 4). By the mid-2000s, partly induced by broader international regulatory pressure on corporate governance, the importance

---

[1]"to make or render present in place or time; to cause to be perceived or realized as present" (Macneil 1974a).

of establishing a broader framework for IT governance has been stressed (Weill, 2004). However, research and industry practice has clearly shown that a central focus has to remain on the contract and hence its enforcement in the post-contract management stage (Lacity and Hirschheim, 1993, 1995; Lacity and Willcocks, 2009). A neglected area in research to this day is discovering and explaining which contractual dimensions are eventually operationalized. Such information would allow practitioners to better understand and prescribe the contractual dimensions of the client-vendor relationship. Moreover, we conjecture that these dimensions essentially define the client company's and to some extent the vendor's, control agenda over whether the major objectives of the outsourcing arrangement are being achieved. Pilot analysis of two IT outsourcing contracts revealed a number of dimensions that pervaded the post-contract management agenda. In each case the client attempted to maintain control through two detailed contractual clauses/ schedules, acting essentially as a third party judicial entity. By control we mean the process by which the client company initiates activities to assure contractually agreed terms are by the vendor(s) company delivered in full and according to expectations and objectives: *"Control, in other words, is aimed at ensuring that a predictable level and type of performance is attained and maintained"* (Child, 1984, p. 136).

In this chapter we analyze the role of the contract in IT outsourcing to elucidate the post-contract management agenda. This agenda essentially prescribes the operationalization of the contract and the control dimension in IT outsourcing. Drawing upon two precedent contracts, we highlight the clauses actually being used. Next, we present findings from an exploratory research study into the client-vendor relationship that reveals how organizations attempt to enforce the contract. The ensuing discussion identifies five different purposes of the contract in the client-vendor relationship, which allow us to infer that a number of contractual dimensions also define the control agenda for the client in the post-contract management stage.

The IT outsourcing contract

The contract in outsourcing has been described as a mechanism that establishes the balance of power between the client-vendor (Lacity and Hirschheim, 1993). Contracts essentially have to be as "airtight" as possible (Lacity and Hirschheim, 1993; Fitzgerald and Willcocks, 1994abc; Saunders *et al.*, 1997), because research has shown that vendors tend to refer to it as their chief source of obligation (Lacity and Willcocks, 2009). Vendors, however, would prefer to see the contract as a working document (*cf.* EDS lawyers Hartstang and Forster, 1995), giving them flexibility to suggest improvements and new services. Clearly, this is in the interest of most vendor companies for their goal is one of profit margins.

An IT outsourcing contract tends to be more complicated than other business contracts, resembling as it does a *"hybrid between an asset purchase and sale agreement, and a sale/leaseback agreement, in that there is a sale of assets or transfer of operations, transfer of employees, and a lease back to the customer of the information technology services that were divested"* (Halvey and Melby, 1996, p. 43). This legal complexity is evident in the detail and in the time typically invested in negotiating agreement. Third party legal experts have for quite some time emphasized the need for comprehensive contracts, not only because it is their livelihood, but also because it basically becomes a reference point specifying how the client and vendor relate (Fitzgerald and Willcocks, 1994b; Lacity and Willcocks, 2009). The table in the Appendix summarizes the main clauses of an outsourcing agreement as specified by legal experts (Burnett, 1998, 2008; Clifford-Chance, 1997; Halvey and Melby, 1996; Klinger and Burnett, 1994; Mayer *et al.*, 1996).

Nature of the outsourcing contract

As previously discussed, the outsourcing contract is unlike other service contracts because of the nature of what is being contracted for and the length of the contracts. This makes it extremely difficult to presentiate service provision or any other exchanges that may be needed in the future. Outsourcing contracts, and indeed most long-term contracts have a tendency to be incomplete, which raises the possibility of opportunistic behavior by the vendor (Williamson, 1975; Hart, 1995). Macneil (1974b, 1980) in turn proposes to alleviate the incompleteness and presentation situation through a relational, as opposed to a transactional, contract. However, there is evidence that, despite Macneil's theorem, most effective outsourcing contracts are essentially neither completely transactional nor relational but mainly transactional intertwined with relational aspects (Currie and Willcocks, 1997; Lacity and Hirschheim, 1993; Willcocks and Cullen, 2006; Willcocks and Kern, 1997). Actual operationalization of the written letter of any contract requires procedures that Macneil (1974ab) prescribes to the relational contract (e.g., extensive cooperation). In this chapter we will focus solely on the transactional aspect of how the contract is enforced, which we identify as determining the con-trol agenda. In the following sections we first discuss control, before looking at the post-contract management agenda in outsourcing. The analysis of two pro-forma precedent contracts elicits the dimensions which pervade post-contract management and further defines the "transactional" level of the client-vendor relationship (or "contractual" as we have termed it elsewhere – see Kern and Willcocks, 2001).

The concept of control

Control is a complex issue that has received considerable attention in the literature. Table 10.1 lists some important contributions. Anthony's (1965) contribution in particular is often referred to, and well known for its distinction between strategic planning, management control and operational control. Strategic planning is defined as the process of deciding on the objectives of the organization, on changing these objectives, on the resources used to attain these objectives and on the policies that are to govern the acquisition, use and disposition of these resources. Anthony distinguishes strategic planning from the more management and operational control issues like Child (1984) does. Management control is defined as the process by which management assures that resources are obtained and used effectively and efficiently in the accomplishment of organizational objectives, whereas operational control focuses more on the actual efficient and effective performance of activities. Child (1984), Eisenhardt (1985), Hofstede (1981) and Ouchi (1979) define the context of control in organizations and outline a number of characteristics that lend themselves to defining a typology. Boland (1979) and Orlikowski (1991) are useful for revealing how control has been applied in the context of information management.

Three common dimensions can be identified according to Fischer (1993) that describe a useful typology for analyzing control in IT: focus of control (directed at whom or what), measures of control (degree of control), and process of control (means of enforcing control). Using this typology as an underlying guide, the next section presents the post-contract management agenda as the focus of control, before looking at the process of control in the empirical findings. The subsequent discussion will then allude to the degree of control in outsourcing.

Post-contract management in IT outsourcing

The greatest challenge that client companies face following the signing of the contract is the achievement and enforcement of agreed terms.

Table 10.1 Overview of Important Control Literature

Author & Year	Control context
Anthony (1965)	Management control process
Boland (1979)	Control versus control over
Child (1984)	Control use in organizations
Eisenhardt (1985)	Control as part of organizational design
Hofstede (1981)	Typology of management control
Orlikowski (1991)	Impact of IT on control in organizations
Ouchi (1979)	Typology of control

A number of stipulated terms will always be integral to driving the outsourcing venture forward for both sides. For the majority of client organizations we can assume they are service levels and costs (i.e., payments), whereas for the vendor it is clearly payment (i.e., profits). This control agenda defined by the contract is an integral part of post-contract management. By 2000, based on over ten years of drawing up outsourcing contracts, several law firms had developed pro-forma precedent contracts. Here we analyze these and related sources to establish templates against which to assess our case histories and also briefly look at the often elusive concept of control.

To enforce the contract, the appointed client managers and/or residual IT group are held accountable for the management and delivery of all products and services related to the outsourcing venture (Fitzgerald and Willcocks, 1994ac; Cullen and Willcocks, 2003). Related to this task will be the conjoint rationalization and implementation of the vendor's processes for service changes, charges, and general financial and operational management of the contract, as well as approval of any special projects that may arise. Appointing duties and responsibility in the post-contract stage is critical, as effective management necessitates continuous communication between the responsible persons to ensure services, payments, and extra requirements are met, and conflicts resolved. In our sources we found the post-contract management agenda for the client to cover the issues detailed in Table 10.2.

For the client to accomplish this management agenda, an effective communication and operations structure has to be established in each organ-

Table 10.2   Post-contract Management Agenda (adapted from Halvey and Melby, 1996)

1. Setting and/or approving IT strategy, architectural directions, and business improvements;
2. Insuring user service objectives and customer satisfaction targets are achieved;
3. Insuring quality and continuous improvements;
4. Setting and changing priorities to insure objectives of the business are met;
5. Being the focal point for determination and translation of all new business requirements necessitating vendor action;
6. Resolving disputes that arise;
7. Overseeing the vendor's performance as specified in the agreement;
8. Monitoring overall service quality and continuous improvement initiatives;
9. Assuring proper charges and billing for the services rendered;
10. General contract administration and amendment control; and
11. Involvement in allocating new managers in vendor company to handle the account.

ization and between both parties. McFarlan and Nolan (1995, p. 22) suggest interfaces have to occur at multiple levels: *"At the most senior levels, there must be links to deal with major issues of policy and relationship restructuring, while at lower levels, there must be mechanisms for identifying and handling more operational and tactical issues. Both the customer and outsourcer need regular, full time relationship managers and coordinating groups lower in the organisation to deal with narrow operational issues and potential difficulties."* To ensure the various interfacing points on the vendor's side matches the client's operational and management style, they should ensure mutual involvement in selecting key vendor personnel.

Contract operationalization and control

We undertook a closer analysis of some of the key clauses and schedules in a UK (Clifford Chance, 1997) and a North American (Halvey and Melby, 1996) precedent contract. The following contractual issues, for analytical purposes classified under each type of interaction, were found to demarcate the transactional focus of the post-contract management agenda.

A. Service exchanges

The most important part of every outsourcing agreement is the description of the services the vendor has to supply (Klinger and Burnett, 1994; Burnett, 2008). Therefore, the service requirements have to be as detailed as possible to avoid disputes over service scope. Services are typically described in a series of exhibits, i.e., schedules. The following give an indication of what exhibits might cover:

- Architecture and product standards (services delivered according to these standards);
- Company critical services (non-achievement may result in liquidated damages);
- New technology environment (new products/services and migration plan);
- Security services (data and/or physical security services);
- Value-added services (e.g., risk/reward sharing, marketing, and others).

B. Service enforcement and monitoring

To enforce services, performance standards and service levels have to be established and agreed for each service the vendor has to provide. Service levels typically include response times, processing priorities, systems availability used to provide services, and percentages for processing errors (Halvey and Melby, 1996). In some cases clients want to streamline the service levels through the joint efforts of the parties after the contract has been signed. In these circumstances, but also when all service levels have been specified, it is essential that the client monitors the service levels and possibly benchmarks them against previous and/or best-in-class service levels. The vendors non-achievement of service levels is often directly tied to liquidated damage provisions, giving clients a powerful leverage and control mechanism. Typical clauses and exhibits for service enforcement and monitoring are:

- Application development measure procedures (allows client to monitor development);
- Benchmarking (the client can compare at any time services with other services of third parties);
- Customer satisfaction survey (to be carried out by the vendor at certain intervals and reported to the client);
- Performance reporting requirements (reports on service performance to be provided by the vendor in intervals).

C. Financial exchanges

For the vendor to provide the services according to the agreement, the client will be charged a base fee with respect to the base services provided. Fees allocated to these base services need to be as exact as possible to avoid any confusion and dispute. Any additional services outside the previously agreed service scope (e.g., overtime, additional volume of services) will be charged according to agreed price rates. Similarly, details of fees payable to the vendor for services above baseline (e.g., hourly, daily, weekly, monthly) should also be covered to give the client flexibility. The timing of the payments has to be agreed, but they depend largely on the client's approval. The following are typical clauses and schedules:

- Base fees (fees payable for base services);
- Expenses (previous agreement on expense budget);
- Incremental fees (fees payable for additional services above baseline);
- New service fees (fees payable for new services out of services scope).

D. Financial control and monitoring

To ensure the client has some level of control over the costs, appropriate means to monitor the fees charged by the vendor need to be agreed. Burnett (2008) suggests the client must have the right to audit and request verification of the charges put forward by the vendor at any time. Additionally, the client can enforce liquidated damages in circumstances of non-performance of service levels. Other suggested means included:

- Audit (access to financial information and charges);
- Liquidated damages (for failing to meet service levels);
- Open book accounting (vendor keeps an open book of costs and charges accessible by the client);

- Price lists (list or catalogue of prices of different services, hardware, software and technology that the client can request from the vendor).

E. Key vendor personnel

Of fundamental importance to the client will be to know who is responsible for certain services, areas, or technology in the vendor company, and vice versa. The precedent contracts suggest that key vendor employees will be explicitly listed in the contract as remaining with the account for specified time periods, or equivalent staff made available (Clifford Chance, 1997). The client should have approval rights over vendor employees and their length of involvement with the account. Furthermore, the vendor has to disclose to the client how it will structure its organization to be able to respond to their needs. Both the key contact points and the structure are fundamental to ensure communication. The contract will address these under the following terms or schedules:

- Supplier personnel and key employees;
- Vendor account management team structure.

F. Dispute resolution

Typically the contract will give guidance on an informal resolution mechanism to deal with disputes. If disputes cannot be resolved in the first instance, the contract describes an escalation procedure and the appropriate persons, groups, or committees to contact. As a final resort a neutral third party advisor or even a judgment is suggested in the contract to resolve a dispute:

- Dispute resolution (details of procedures for resolution).

G. Change control and management

Finally, to ensure the contract allows for flexibility to cater for changes in user and company requirements, the contract specifies change procedures the client can initiate formally. For this a change request has to be issued detailing the changes required from the vendor. This will most likely affect pricing arrangements, and possibly take effect with a time delay. The agreed procedures will be specified in a schedule referred to something like:

- Change control procedures.

The analysis revealed that service exchanges, service enforcement and monitoring, financial exchanges, financial control and monitoring, and change control and management circumscribe the nature of the ongoing transactional processes between both parties. Secondly, it identifies in the vendor company the key contact points and provides an overview of the account management teams organizational structure describing some of the structural factors of the client-vendor relationship, whereas the dispute resolution method describes some of the skills the managers handling the relationship must have. Combined, these arrangements will come to bear upon the client-vendor relationship and describe the focus of the control agenda in post-contract management.

Field studies

Findings from the research portray in detail those issues that play a crucial part in client attempts to control their outsourcing arrangements. Our analysis suggests that maintaining control over the outsourcing venture through contractual means has been seen as particularly important. The general concern following hand-over was loss of control and over-dependency on the vendor. Clients were thus keen to affirm their control in the venture, through a number of different contractual dimensions and considerations. Although we recognize that our study focuses on a small and geographically distinct sample where a particular set of contracting practices apply at a particular moment in time, in the light of subsequent research (see Cullen and Willcocks, 2003; Lacity and Willcocks, 2009) a number of learning pointers emerge that are perennially applicable to outsourcing contract management.

Research approach

In the late 1990s we undertook research into client and vendor relationship practice in 13 organizations based in the United Kingdom. Using a semi-structured interview protocol a series of interviews were undertaken with a range of participants, including lawyers, IT managers, contract managers, account executives, general managers, and support managers in both customer and vendor organizations. Questions addressing the contract, post-contract management, relationship management, the nature of the working relationship and the evolution of a relationship were posed, with a strong emphasis on what characteristics influenced the operationalization of the contract. These are some of the key questions asked:

- What role does the contract play in the relationship? Have you had to refer, enforce it, or use it in anyway in the relationship so far?;
- Could you describe the state of the relationship? What operational difficulties have you encountered?;
- What were some of the major milestones, achievements and/or developments in relationship? Examples?;

- Are you achieving your expectations and outsourcing intentions? Why not?;
- What are the upcoming challenges for the relationship?

While we made no judgment as to whether the 13 contracts were successful or otherwise, we did need to be in a position to assess whether specific contractual practices were experienced as essential, helpful or otherwise. The interviews were scheduled for one hour but in many cases lasted anywhere up to three hours. All of the interviews were tape-recorded and transcribed, after which the responses from the client and the vendor companies were grouped together into subject categories by applying a "data display" method (Miles and Huberman, 1994). The resulting checklist matrices of subject categories were then classified into areas of agreement and commonality, and into sets of disagreement and problems. The areas of agreement that illustrated a within-group similarity (Eisenhardt, 1989) identified those variables which underpinned the outsourcing relationship, and also provided the means for further subjective cross-case analysis. In some cases it was possible to cross-case analyze a client company's response with its respective vendor company's response. The interviews formed the basis for a number of case studies, which were corroborated by the collection and the ensuing analysis of relevant documentation, including internal memos, company information, minutes of meetings, and outsourcing contracts. Tables 10.3, 10.4, and 10.5 present an overview of the companies interviewed, clients' perceptions of their relationship focus, and subjective third party ratings of the partnering capabilities of the vendor companies interviewed. The following tables are constructed from interview responses, as indicated.

Findings

The contract

Contracts were found to stipulate at length the terms and obligations the vendor and the client had to fulfill. Its ultimate function was explained as its legal nature, allowing the client and/or vendor to produce the contract in court, in cases of, for example, dispute or termination (*Solicitor, Service A*). This legal nature of the contract[2] – in the United Kingdom – made it near impossible to include non-legalistic terms such as trust, cooperation and so on in the contract (*Partner, Service A*). The vendor could not commit to these terms contractually because they could not know what the client's requirements were. In essence then, the contract outlined the bare bones of the deal

---

[2]North American contracts on the other hand can include goodwill gestures, and relationship important notions such as trust, cooperation, etc., in the contract and exhibits, i.e., schedules (*Partner, Service A*).

Table 10.3 Client Companies

Client Company & Interviewee	Industry	Annual Turnover	Origin	Outsourced	Start of deal	Length of deal	Size of deal transferred	No. of people transferred	Relationship Focus (1997)[3]	Customer of Vendor Company
Client A Business Support Manager	Retailing & Stores	£780mn (1995)[1]	British	Total	1993	10 years	£1bn	120	Transactional/ Relational	**Vendor B**
Client B Group IS Manager	Chemicals manufacturer	£10bn (1996)[2]	British	Selective (Europe) 1. Telecoms network 2. Data center, software support & legacy systems 3. Desktop systems & phones	1. 1994 2. 1995 3. 1997	1. 3 years 2. 5 years 3. 4 years	1. <10mn 2. £75mn 3. £40mn	1. <10 2. 400 3. <10	1. Transactional 2. Relational 3. To recent	1. **Confidential** 2. **Vendor B** 3. **Confidential**
Client C Management Services Manager	Property Investment & Development	£472mn (1995)[1]	British	Selective 1. Hardware & software maintenance 2. Legacy system, & software development	1. 1993 2. 1995	1. 4 years 2. 3 years	1. £2.5mn 2. £10mn	none transferred	1. Relational 2. Transactional	1. **Confidential** 2. **Confidential**
Client D Economic Analyst	Aerospace Manufacturer	£3.5bn (1995)[2]	British	Total & major business process reengineering programmes	1996	10 years	$900mn	850	Relational	**Vendor A**

Table 10.3 Client Companies – *continued*

Client Company & Interviewee	Industry	Annual Turnover	Origin	Outsourced	Start of deal	Length of deal	Size of deal transferred	No. of people transferred	Relationship Focus (1997)[3]	Customer of Vendor Company
Client E MIS Executive	Motor Car Manufacturer	£397mn (1995)[2]	British	Selective 1. Software development & IT operations	1. 1992	1. 5 years	1. <0.5mn	1. 12	1. Transactional	1. **Confidential**
				2. Systems integration	2. 1992	2. <3years	2. <05mn		2. Transactional	2. **Vendor B**
				3. Global networking	3. N/A	3. 3 years	3. £1mn		3. Transactional	3. **Confidential**
Client F IT Coordinator	Electronics Manufacturer	£270mn (1995)[1]	Japanese	Selective legacy & operating systems	1994	5 years	£2.5mn	none transferred	Transactional/ Relational	**Vendor D**
Client G Corporate IT Adviser	Oil, Gas, & Nuclear Fuels	£453mn (1995)[2]	Dutch/ British	Selective & Total (Global) 1. desktop computing, networking, & others	1. N/A	1. <1 year	1. <20mn	1. <10	1. Transactional	1. **Others**
				2. Total	2. 1993	2. 3 years	2. <20mn	2. <10	2. Transactional/ Relational	2. **Vendor A**

[1] United Kingdom Turnover; [2] Total including other subsidiaries; [3] Findings from research in 1997 rated according to Macneil (1974a) distinction between transactional and relational.

Table 10.4 Vendor Companies

Vendor company & Interviewee	Origin	Employees (Globally)	Annual Turnover (Global)	Business or Service areas	Explicit Relationship view	Partnering capabilities[1]
Vendor A – Managing Director & Programme Director	American	approx. 70,000	£12,4bn (1995)	Consulting, Systems Development, Systems Integration, Systems Management, & Process Management	Yes	3
Vendor B – European Strategic Director	American	approx. 50,000	£4,2bn (1996)	Management Consulting/Professional Services, Systems Integration, Outsourcing	No	2
Vendor C – Partner	American	38,000	£4,2bn (1995)	Consulting, Business Process Management, Outsourcing, Change Management, Strategic Management	No	3
Vendor D – Executive Director (UK)	British/ French	27,000	£1,8bn (1996)	IS and business process management, project services, products, consulting, and education & training	Yes	3
Vendor E – Business Director & Principal Consultant	French/ British	9,400	£678mn (1995)	IT consulting, systems integration, products and outsourcing	No	4

[1] Meta Group Inc.'s (1996) global rating of IT vendors on a scale of 1 to 5; (1 is best). Partnering capabilities entail the "ability to partner at various levels" including megadeal alliances and project-specific partnerships.

Table 10.5 Outsourcing Advisor

Outsourcing Advisor & Interviewee	Origin	Employees (Globally)	Annual Turnover (Global)	Business or Service areas	Specialist Area
Service A Solicitor & Partner	British	approx. 5,000	approx. <£5mn	Financial, Corporate, Commercial, & Litigation Matters	IT Outsourcing Contract Development

"...which is the formal structure of the relationship on which you might actually rely if it all collapsed and you had to seek legal redress" (Partner, Service A).

The contract was found to build the foundation, on which the ensuing client-vendor relationship was then based (*Business Director, Vendor E; Managing Director, Vendor A*).

"It defines how you are going to work more than anything else, but you then still have to make it work. This is just paper, it's people that make things work. This gives them the guidelines, the stepping stones, the structure..." (Management Service Manager, Client C).

For *Group IS Manager Client B* getting the contract, i.e., the foundations right was vital, because a badly formulated contract could lead to frustration, and in some circumstances – as Client A experienced – to costly renegotiations, and eventuate in possible failure.

The contract's role in the post-contract management stage was also found to be one of guidance. During this stage, managers implementing the venture used the contract as a management guide to operationalize the contract. The *Manager* from *Client C* explained the use of the contract in the beginning as essential for

"...bedding down the exact processes. We are still doing things for the first time and therefore it gets referred to in the sense of this is how we thought we would do it, how does that actually match up to what we are doing, what's the next step, what's missing, shall I just check that I'm doing this right. So it's being referred to in that way, but it's not being referred to in an adversarial way." It is used as a vehicle for describing the relationship and getting rid of ambiguity (European Strategic Director, Vendor B).

The contract and its schedules defined the level of control and the responsibility and expectations of each side (*Managing Director, Vendor A*). In most situations the contract gave the client ultimate control through the possibility of invoking early termination via exit clauses (according to *MIS Executive, Client E; Business Director, Vendor D*). Seldom were these invoked though, as they could introduce new cost factors (e.g., switching), a loss of time and result in a break down of services. Consequently:

> "although we legally have the option to do that [terminate] the much more practical solution is to learn your lessons and to renegotiate the contract to address the things that you think you would like to be better." (Business Support Manager, Client A)

This seemed to be an approach a number of customers adopted. Termination is really the last resort (*MIS Executive, Client E*).

Interestingly though, the *IT Coordinator* from *Client F* and the *Manager* from *Client A* explained they did not find the contract that important. In fact, as the *Manager* at *Client A* explained

> "...the existing contract is treated the way many companies treat a strategy document, you don't really want a strategy process (where) you produce a document and stick it on the shelf and never read it again. Occasionally we get the contract out and we refer to what it actually says. ... And if we get the contract out we've failed in our ability to manage the situation."

Similarly, the *Coordinator* at *Client F* explained:

> "if we ever have to go back to the contract then the out-sourcing deal has failed. The contract is there to actually protect us as a company but to have to invoke anything within the contract means you have failed to negotiate with the supplier. And really it's not something we want to do lightly."

The reason being that in most situations if you operate an outsourcing venture solely by the contract the ensuing relationship could go dangerously wrong, because the contract does not adjust according to possible changes. The outcome of a contract may become totally inflexible, and to actually specify the relationship in any detail over that length of time of the contract is really outside of reality (as explained by *MIS Executive, Client E*). Therefore, the only way flexibility was found to be attainable was through agreeing specific contractual change procedures.

Flexibility and changes

In essence, the legal nature of the contract does not exactly allow for flexibility. Therefore, the contract is

> "...drafted as a long term commitment, and pricing takes into account the changes in some way, shape or form." (Client C)

In other words, the contract requires renegotiation or amendment if major parts were to be changed, but for service or technological requirement changes there are procedures available in the contract that cater for these. As the partner from (*Service A*) explained there were

> "very detailed change control procedure because clearly you know that technology is going to change. It is the most difficult thing to provide for, you need to encourage the suppliers to come up with changes, because you want them to be proactive. But then you also want the strategy to stay with the customer so they can actually determine whether the changes go with their objectives. ... But it is difficult. You can't prescribe what's going to happen all you can do is provide provisions in the contract to point people in the right direction and give them flexibility as far as possible." (Partner, Service A)

According to the *Client* and *Vendor* companies, change procedures were commonly initiated in two steps. Upon realizing changes in the business require alterations in the services delivered by the IT function or system, Clients would issue a request for change with the vendor company. This change request stated in detail the requirements, and the vendor would then present the exact specification and costs for the new services and/or products. In some situations vendors would actually propose change, as services may have become defunct or services were duplicated (*Executive Director, Vendor D*). The second step was for the Client to formally sign-off the proposed changes and their price, so that the Vendor could arrange for them to be implemented. However, change management and control were found in practice very problematic as Clients were uncertain on many occasions whether they had catered for all eventualities (*Solicitor, Service A; Management Services Manager, Client C and Corporate IT Advisor, Client G*).

Post-contract management

The findings from client and vendor companies revealed that essentially the post-contract management agenda was concerned with enforcing the contract and achieving the stipulated terms. Interviewees corroborated this finding by suggesting that control over the vendor and vice versa was enforced through the following five contractual dimensions:

- Financial control and monitoring;
- Penalty payments;
- Monitoring of service levels and/or products;
- Performance measurements; and
- Selection of key interface points.

Financial control and monitoring

Clients and *Vendors* suggested that everything in the contract at the end of the day wound down to a financial consideration:

> "...the case where we do stick firmly to the contract primarily is when it comes to money. If we are duty bound to pay something or if we are not

bound to pay for something, we either will or won't depending on what it says. ... I think we are softer on service where we are looking for flexibility, but hard-nosed on cost issues where we are very precise." (Business Support Manager, Client A)

However, this was not to say that other stipulated terms in the contract would be disrespected. It was just emphasized that the profit margins and payments to be made would always be closely monitored and scrutinized by both parties (*Manager, Client A; Director, Vendor E*). It was one of the key areas where control was emphasized. For example, the *Economic Analyst* from *Client D* explained that in their contract with *Vendor A* every change initiative and/or major service delivery improvement was cost benefit analyzed. And the way that was measured was usually pounds over a period of time (*Economic Analyst, Client D*).

To be able to undertake such an assessment, you needed complete access to the costs and pricing strategy of your vendor (*Executive Director, Vendor D*). In other words as *Clients* explained, you needed an open book arrangement. Essentially, this arrangement gave the client a lot of control over where the vendor actually made money. This was apparent in *Client A's* objective:

"the new arrangement should make it clearer how Vendor B make their money. We don't want them to go out of business, we don't want them to have such a bad deal that they walk away from it. But we do want to understand, and we have in the past understood them, where we think they make their money, but it will be clearer with the open book arrangement. The deal was always set up that we would save costs in the first few years and they would make more money in the later years of the contract. And it could well be that they weren't sure that those costs ... were going to be generated in the first few year of the contract. So they may feel they've lost money in the first couple of years." (Manager, Client A)

However, when the vendor suggested an open book arrangement because the problem or issue could not be settled through a fixed price, the client subsequently gave the vendor control over large profit margins. This was exemplified by the *Director's* (*Vendor D*) explanation of an open book arrangement:

"If you want to out-source that kind of situation then the other way of doing it is ... [by] an open pricing arrangement. In other words I say to you I don't know how much this is going to cost, you don't know either, and what we will do is put sufficient people and hardware in and we will write all the costs of those down and you can look at those and make sure you are happy that we are not putting enough people on that problem. It's open. We will agree in addition to that cost that we can charge you a certain figure, a certain percentage, or a certain amount of money. ... So I would rather say we will do that and in addition we will charge you £50,000 a month for our management, for our profit, for our margin. And we will look together at the cost of doing this and then our total charge would be those costs plus our management charges."

Clearly, this latter arrangement would give the vendor significant to total control over the costs and possible services they would deliver at the end of the day.

Another means for controlling the costs was through the introduction of a competitive benchmarking process (*Partner, Service A*). This was found to be an important contractual contingency (*Solicitor, Service A*). It protected customers where prices increased, while the quality of services decreased. It also allowed customers to compare prices and services against competitors and request the vendor to match industry "best practice". This seemed especially appropriate for commodity processes such as basic computing or telecommunications. To ensure cost control:

> "you continually set your suppliers of the commodity services at each others throat, demand that they keep to a certain international standard, and request lower and lower prices the whole time." (Group IS Manager, Client B)

Cost control was crucial for the client to have, since the motivation of the vendor was always to make a profit (*Principal Consultant, Vendor E; European Strategic Director, Vendor B; Executive Director, Vendor D; Partner, Vendor C*). In some cases such as total outsourcing deals, before the vendor could actually make a profit they would have to recuperate the initial premium payment, and only then would the vendor begin to make a profit from the deal:

> "So premium payment may be say £30M. or what number it might be, but how do you pay for it? You pay for it by charging them back for it. You squeeze a bit more to actually pay for some of that money. Therefore you are putting a tighter squeeze on the situation as you go along." (Partner, Vendor C)

Penalty payments

In the event of a client not receiving the quality of services for the value of the money, it was suggested that that would be a just cause for enforcing penalty payments or in extreme cases early termination of the contract (*MIS Executive, Client E*). Penalty payments were described by clients as a formalized means of control, to ensure, for example, that target deadlines are met (*Management Services Manager, Client C*).

However, requesting penalty payments and enforcing them unilaterally may damage the overall relationship. It was suggested that a mutual understanding of the reason for enforcing penalty payment was necessary, to avoid reoccurrence and to ensure the client-vendor relationship moved forward. It seemed to play a similar role to early contract termination, it being seen as the last resort for enforcing control over service delivery.

Monitoring of service levels and/or products

Another key control factor was the monitoring of services and their delivery. These were very carefully monitored as services were in many cases the main part of the deliverables for which the client contracted the vendor (*Group IS Manager, Client B; Management Services Manager, Client C; Solicitor, Services A*). In most deals services were explicitly detailed in the service level agreement (SLA), which outlined what client companies expect as their basic service requirements. For example *Client E* stressed that they had very detailed SLAs including specific availability targets, response times, outages, and so on for their service requirements. The SLAs essentially defined the chief (hard) measure:

> "If we are not actually getting the SLAs, then it is our right not to pay. We are paying for a quality service and that's what we specified in the SLA and if the SLA is not achieved, then in my view the contract stresses that we should pay less." (MIS Executive, Client E)

The importance of service level agreements in the contract was emphasized by both client and vendor companies. The UK *Managing Director* from *Vendor A* described this importance as a level of control it gave both parties and the extent to which the SLAs defined each others responsibilities and the clients expectations. The *Executive Director* from *Vendor D* endorsed this view and further explained that:

> "… a service level agreement really expresses what the customer wants and what's important to him. Because what a customer would say normally is I want 99% availability of service. When you get down to the service level agreement, they might well say actually this system we want 99.5% availability and this one we would be happy with 75% or 50%. You actually really get down to what they want in a detailed sense. That then enables you to measure whether you are billing them for that service. So it helps the relationship, because when the customer says your service is no good you can say well that's pretty strange because according to my statistics we hit every one of these service levels."

It thus became a control factor through which both parties were found to assert their power.

Performance measures

To ensure services and/or products were delivered according to expectations and agreement, clients and vendors operated an array of hard and soft performance measurement methods. Depending on the outsourcing intent, clients focused their performance measures on cost reductions, services delivery, service improvement, specific projects, new technology, user satisfaction and others. In the majority cases *Clients* and *Vendors* explained they measured a range of the former, to address both business and user measures:

"You have got to be able to put together an analysis that is partly people's subjective reaction to what's going on, partly objective measures of where their contribution has been ... And it's a combination of those different measures all coming together that allows you to do it. You must have some very hard measures in there, more of those hard measures that are output oriented the better." (Group IS Manager, Client B)

Thus, *Client B* uses service delivery according to contract, step changes performance measure, return on net assets, and other business measures, such as customer responsiveness, output measures such as On Time In Full (did the customer get everything they wanted in good time) as their main measures. Alternatively, *Client A* employs a scorecard scheme, that allows them to:

"...look at are we on time with the budget, does the user community like the new systems, do the board of directors feel that the new systems are a good thing. This allows us to measure whether our programmes succeed.... So we are trying to more formally set up a tool for measuring the success of the programme, as we don't have anything similar at the moment for the Vendor B relationship." (Business Support Manager, Client A)

Vendors explained their performance measures similarly involved an array of objective and soft methods, including third party auditing. The *Executive Director* from *Vendor D* explained they measured their performance against the SLAs, performed a customer satisfaction survey, undertook an internal quality review of staff and attained an external auditors assessment of specific contracts. Similarly, the *Partner* from *Vendor B*, explained that they used surveys, reviews and external audits to measure success in contracts. Accordingly, the *Director* from *Vendor E* explained:

"...we have every month a service measurement report. So we have a clear statement every month on at least the objective measures. That doesn't tell the whole story because it's the subjective measures which are also very important. So if a customer carries out at their expense a survey every year which measures the subjective satisfaction of all the receivers of the service, both managers and technical people – and that's a useful guide on an annual basis – we also from time to time commission bits of research from a market research organisation who go to our customers and ask them about services, service values, and so forth."

The subjective measures employed in some cases were crucial as they elicited whether the services delivered satisfied the user community. *Clients* explained that sometimes formal measures were achieved as per agreement, but they did not actually satisfy the users' requirements. It was then a matter of adjusting them accordingly, which in many situations the vendor would not undertake without formally increasing costs (*Corporate IT Advisor, Client G*). *Vendor A* employed in *Client D* a contract measurement scheme of customer values and expectations, alongside their objective indicators:

> "So it isn't just a matter of asking the customer are you satisfied or not, we have to understand what his expectation is rather than what his requirement is. Then there are some quite sophisticated measurement systems that we deploy to actually take a particular user, look at all the parameters of interest to him.... It might be reliability, it might be the quality of original thought, empathy, all these sorts of things. And we get the user to identify, first of all what are the dimensions of what you would expect from us, and what is the most important. ... So you get a picture of what he wants and then how he thinks we are measuring up against that. So that's how you measure the soft issues. And we have to do that on a continual basis across all aspects of the relationship. Different people have very different expectations from us." (Programme Director, Vendor A)

User satisfaction was the most common soft measure elicited by both vendor and client companies. Although, extremely difficult to measure and most commonly arrived at by customer satisfaction surveys, it was found to be an important indicator of whether vendors achieve the users service requirements (*MIS Executive, Client E; IT Coordinator, Client F*). *Vendors* found user satisfaction surveys fundamental, because:

> "that's what actually is going to affect our reputation. That's what, if some-one goes through a reference visit, they are not going to tell them that we achieved all these SLA's they are going to tell them whether we are good or not so good. It's going to be perception on a particular subject." (Executive Director, Vendor D)

Interface and/or contact points

The *Clients* explained that in situations where discrepancies about service levels and/or payments arose, they would contact a specific manager in the vendor company. In most cases the *Clients* revealed, they knew the managers in the vendor company quite well because they were involved in selecting them as their contact points (*Management Services Manager, Client C*). In a number of *Client* companies the residual IT group defined the actual contact points. So for example at *Client A*, the remaining five IT managers who handled the outsourcing deal – which included a senior manager in charge of the contract, two middle managers in charge of the headquarters' IT requirements and the overall store systems, and two operational managers in charge of assessing the service levels and delivery, business developments and requirements – were also the main contact points for the vendor. Similarly, at *Client D* a small remaining client team represented the main interface point for *Vendor A* in matters of IT (*Programme Director, Vendor A*). In most instances this interface structure was mimicked by the vendor company:

"There tends to be a matching process where you take the structure of the company that you are going to service provide and take the structure of the customer and kind of match it. So our Managing Director matches with their Managing Director and so on. When you start in terms of building the relationship, you need to have that matching pulled through. To make sure you don't fall over each other." (Business Director, Vendor E)

In some cases, *Vendors* explained, the contact points in the client company interfaced with a number of managers on the vendor side (*Business Director, Vendor D and Programme Director, Vendor A*). This suggested that the client company contact point had a one-to-many relationship:

"It is rarely a simple one to one relationship. In Vendor E's case in every contract there will be two managers contacting the person on the client's side. One will be a service or customer service manager and the other will be a business development manager. These two managers job is to develop business in a very proactive way, and to make sure the service is satisfactory and is on time. So there is a set of relationships for each of these customers." (Business Director, Vendor E)

Client and *Vendor* companies stressed the importance of staffing the interface points. For the *Client* this entailed retaining a group of experienced managers who could effectively handle the vendor (see also Lacity and Willcocks, 2009, Chapter 15 on this topic). This group could then act as a controlling agent. Findings suggested that the IT team took responsibilities for researching and defining the IT function for the business, and for controlling the vendor. To ensure continuation of the relationship between the IT group and the vendor:

"…you have to engage the delivery team. [To do that] most people are expected to stay on a contract for 18 months to 2 years. And some people will stay there longer." (Partner, Vendor B)

Discussion

The findings confirm researchers' insistence over the years on the critical, perennial importance of the contract in outsourcing (Lacity and Hirschheim, 1993; Lacity and Willcocks, 2009; Willcocks and Lacity, 2009 – see also Chapter 3). From our evidence we would suggest that this importance derives from the multiple purposes that are associated with the contract. The study of its enforcement revealed that in post-contract management there were five main ways in which the contractual terms affected or influenced the management of the client-vendor relationship. In the following section we discuss these, and elaborate the control agenda inherent in enforcing the contract. We also point to some perennial principles when it comes to IT outsourcing contracts.

The outsourcing contract

Firstly, **the contract undergirds the IT outsourcing venture in a number of ways**, even though the clients we researched stressed essentially *"it is only paper"*. The document might be termed **the manual** for the deal, outlining the parties' commitments, and the client's expectations. Clearly, it is not the agreement that will make the outsourcing deal work, but the people. However, for the people, it takes on a significant enough role beyond merely a *"strategy document on a shelf"* (*Manager, Client A*); indeed it would appear to be associated with five purposes in post-contract management. Firstly, the contract has a legal function, in the sense that it can be produced in court to explain the arrangements of the deal that were agreed by both parties. Its legal status encapsulates, for example, termination clauses, penalty demands and dispute resolution procedures, that client companies can legally enforce in court. Although companies emphasized that such extreme measures were seldom implemented, they still posed a strong means of putting pressure on the vendor to ensure contractual achievement. The legality of the document allows clients to ultimately wave it as a *"sword and shield"* as the *Solicitor* from *Service A* highlighted.

Secondly, **the contract attempts to presentiate service levels as far into the future representing user and organization requirements**. Of course uncertainty cannot be avoided, only mitigated, due to the nature of the rapid changes in information technology, and likely changes in user and business requirements (Willcocks *et al.*, 1997). To this extent the actioning of presentation as it might be ascertainable in transaction or discrete deals, is not possible in long-term IT outsourcing ventures. This would seem to be the case for most deals, given the fact that on average deals last, as reported by many survey results over the years (see Saunders *et al.*, 1997; Fitzgerald and Willcocks, 1994abc; Lacity and Willcocks, 2001, 2009) somewhere between three to five years. Therefore, it would seem plausible to consider outsourcing contracts more relationally (according to Macneil's description) than transactionally focused, especially when considering the rate at which they become outdated. Of course, building in regular contract reviews and renegotiations terms can restore the transactional focus, and indeed this has been a major feature of more recent trends in contracting (Currie and Willcocks, 1997; Lacity and Willcocks, 2001, 2009).

Thirdly, **the contract assures client control over the outsourcing venture in that it initially defines the obligations and expectations bearing on the vendor.** It also gives the client ultimate control through its legal status (possibility to terminate proceedings). The findings revealed that, as we had theoretically conjectured, client companies affirmed their control via a number of contractual clauses that were later operationalized in the post-contract management stage. These then also became the measures through which the client monitored the vendor'(s) performance and vice versa.

Fourthly, **the contract is to be understood as the "bare bones" of the client-vendor relationship.** It prescribes the start, the length of the venture and through a number of clauses and schedules outlines the structure of the relationship, at least to the point of determining the key interfaces (e.g., interface and/or contact points). It further describes, at least in the start up phase, the exchanges that need to occur to achieve the stipulated terms (e.g., service levels and financial exchanges). Additionally, the contract also prescribes ultimate dissolution and termination of the relationship via exit clauses and schedules.

Fifthly, **the outsourcing contract provides guidance to the managers chiefly involved in the outsourcing venture.** The findings revealed that in the post-contract management stage at least five contractually agreed clauses and/or schedules pervaded the agenda. They comprised some of the reasons for why the client contracted the vendor, and thus described the early objectives both parties aimed to achieve.

Post-contract management and control

As evident, one of the purposes or roles of the contract is its use for the client to assure control over those functions and reasons for which it had essentially outsourced. All client companies interviewed revealed that the base line services, their delivery and costs were some of the key factors over which they affirmed control. For the vendor companies it was clearly stated that payment, i.e., profit was their main goal. The affirmation of both parties' control truly emerged in the post-contract management stage.

Post-contract management essentially is the starting point of "working together". Respondents explained that at this point the client-vendor relationship began to take shape. The early endeavor was the conjoint operationalization of the contract. But with enforcement a number of control issues arose for the client. On a routine basis these were chiefly focused on what the vendor was delivering, the charges incurred, and the effectiveness of the working relationship. Other control issues emerged from the dilemma of presentiation and the possibility that a client, over time, would find the deal unworkable.

It was found that these control concerns pervaded the post-contract management agenda so much so that the client companies invested considerable time to affirm their control. This then provided the basis upon which the client-vendor relationship began to be built. In other words, the control dimensions defined enforcement of the contract, and thus delimited those contractual management issues inherent to the dyad.

It became apparent that a number of contractual dimensions, which subsequently pervaded the post-contract management agenda, specifed early on those activities that the client designated later as their control agenda with the vendor. In part these were management issues, but essentially they can be summarized as the clients' control dimensions. Table 10.6 outlines these findings in line with the control typology adopted.

Looking at these control activities and the purposes of the contract, it would seem one can draw a number of parallels. Firstly, all the control dimensions are enforceable legally in court. Secondly, the service levels agreed and the possibility to adjust requirements through change control, gives the contract presentation flexibility. Thirdly, combining the two would make the contract the controlling factor in IT outsourcing. Fourthly, they define the contractual level of the client-vendor relationship and thus support the notion that they outline the bare bones of the relationship (Davis, 1996; Kern and Willcocks, 2001).

Conclusion

In this chapter we discussed the experiences of 13 organizations with IT outsourcing contracts and their operationalization in the post-contract management stage. The empirical findings corroborated our initial assumptions about which contractual issues were enforced. These were also identified as the control agenda clients employed in the venture to manifest its outsourcing destiny. A number of issues were pointed up, that need consideration prior to outsourcing.

Output, financial, relational, and change issues, and how to retain control over control emerged as requiring careful planning prior to contracting and undoubtedly have to inform any client's outsourcing strategy. Hence it would seem prudent for organizations considering outsourcing to establish a task list for the group of managers selected to handle the deal, that assures firstly, that managers have the greatest control over these and related issues and secondly, that the outsourcing strategy is achieved. This requires the group to have a clear understanding of contractual requirements and the general organizational objectives. In most situations the organizational IT goals will then be mirrored by the outsourcing strategy. Table 10.7 summarizes the issues that need attention prior to outsourcing

Table 10.6 Control Agenda in the Client-Vendor Relationship

Contract	Post-Contract Management	Control (Findings according to participants)	Client's Level of Control	Client Control Dimensions
• Service level agreements & exchanges • Service measurements & monitoring procedures • Penalty clauses for non-performance	• Overseeing the vendor's performance as specified in the agreement. • Insuring user service objectives and customer satisfaction targets are achieved. • Monitoring overall service quality and continuous improvement initiatives.	• Client and Vendor spend considerable time on assuring services are delivered according to agreement. • However, Client has the ultimate responsibility to assure services are deliver and users are satisfied. • For the Vendor, delivery is a necessity as payments are dependent on service level achievement.	High	Output Control
• Financial payments & exchanges • Financial monitoring & assessment	• Assuring proper charges and billing for the services rendered.	• Again, both parties spend considerable time on monitoring and controlling costs. • Clients have the ultimate responsibility to monitor charges raised by the Vendors. • Vendors goal obviously is to make a profit, so this is where one of their core focus will be.	High	Financial Control

Table 10.6 Control Agenda in the Client-Vendor Relationship – *continued*

Contract	Post-Contract Management	Control (Findings according to participants)	Client's Level of Control	Client Control Dimensions
• Dispute resolution procedures • Key vendor personnel	• Resolving disputes that arise. • Involvement in allocating new managers in vendor company to handle the account.	• In cases of dispute the client can raise complaints with senior managers and escalate matters until satisfactorily resolved. Extreme disputes may demand a third party arbitrator. • Client knows and sometimes selects managers appointed on the vendor side. Breakdown of relations may cause clients to request the vendor company to allocate a new manager.	High to Shared with Vendor	Relational Control
• Arrangements for adapting to changing circumstances in the future	• Setting and changing priorities to insure objectives of the business are met.	• Change control and management allow the client to initiate change requests when new requirements arise in the business.	Total	Change Control
• Early termination clause	• *No management agenda.*	• This legal arrangement allows the client ultimately to terminate the contract. Although seldom enforced, it gives the client company a means of putting pressure on the vendor.	Total	Control over Control

Table 10.7   Management Implications – Contractual Issues to Consider Prior to Outsourcing

Control Dimension	Contract	Management Implications (Attention warranted prior to outsourcing)
Output Control	• Service level agreements and exchanges • Service measurements and monitoring procedures • Penalty clauses for non-performance	• Specify in detail service levels and what is expected from the vendor. • Specify both hard and soft performance measures. Best practice suggests appointing additionally an external third party to undertake evaluations. • Specify penalty clauses and use them!
Financial Control	• Financial payments and exchanges • Financial monitoring and assessment	• Make sure the contract details all prices for services. • Ensure you are aware of how vendor prices and charges for services. Best practice suggests an open book arrangement for closest scrutiny. • Predetermine procedures and/or methods for assessing vendor charges.
Relational Control	• Dispute resolution procedures • Key vendor personnel	• Include clear escalation procedures with specific people or positions to approach in the vendor firm and third party arbitrators. • Strongly, request the vendor to commit its account management team for at least two years. • Include clauses that enable you to partake and veto appointments.
Change Control	• Arrangements for adapting to changing circumstances in the future	• Assure contractual change management and procedures are specified. • Define pricing mechanism that apply for future change requirements and services. • Specify the possibility for future renegotiations of services and prices.
Control over Control	• Early termination clause	• Include exit clause and the procedures for termination. • Specify the length of assistance vendor has to provide following termination.

to ensure strategic alignment of the outsourcing deal with the clients overall business objectives.

Controlling occurs at different intervals in the post-contract management stage. Clearly, daily and weekly interactions involve output and financial controls and sometimes relational and change control. However, relational and change control occur infrequently and control over control may only be enforced in complete breakdowns or by the last resort of putting pressure on the vendor. In the client-vendor relationship therefore, one could expect output, financial, relational and change control to essentially define the contractual level. We can assume that the critical relationship factors such as cooperation, communication, and trust will develop on back of the contract and the enforcement of these control dimensions – a process that, from separate research, Lacity and Willcocks (2001) saw as an effective mode of building both control and relationships.

Finally, the present study possesses a number of limitations in terms of sample size and geographical distinctiveness. Due to the rather small sample further studies need to look at expanding and verifying our findings. However, it has to be said, the details of outsourcing contracts and their operationalization have not been a notable theme in the academic literature (see Dibbern *et al.*, 2004; Willcocks and Lacity, 2009). Also the distinctiveness of legal systems and hence contracting across countries and continents, may give rise to a number of additional issues that are unique and country specific to contract management practice. Thus we suggest further research is needed into the post-contract management agenda to elaborate in detail the tasks client managers need to perform prior to outsourcing to assure the greatest possible success of their deal. We suggest that these will revolve strongly around the control dimensions identified in this chapter.

References

Anthony, R.N. (1965) *Planning and Control Systems – A Framework For Analysis*, Harvard Business School Press, Boston.

Boland, R.J. (1979) "Control, Causality and Information Systems Requirements", *Accounting, Organisations and Society*, 4, 259–272.

Burnett, R. (1998) *Outsourcing IT: The Legal Aspects*, Aldershot, Hampshire, Gower Publishing.

Burnett, R. (2008) *Outsourcing IT: The Legal Aspects*, Aldershot, Hampshire, Gower Publishing. Revised edition.

Child, J. (1984) *Organisation: A Guide to Problems and Practice*, 2nd edn, Harper and Row Publishers, London.

Clifford-Chance (1997) *Outsourcing Agreement Precedent*, Clifford Chance, London.

Cullen, S. and Willcocks, L. (2003) *Intelligent IT Outsourcing*, Butterworth, Oxford.

Currie, W. and Willcocks, L. (1997) *New Strategies in IT Outsourcing: A Study of Best Practices and Emerging Trends in Europe and the USA*, Business Intelligence, London.

Davis, K.J. (1996) *IT Outsourcing Relationships: An Exploratory Study of Interorganisational Control Mechanisms*. Unpublished DBA Thesis, Graduate School of Business Administration. Harvard University, Boston.

Dibbern, J., Goles, T., Hirschheim, R. and Bandula, J. (2004) "Information Systems Outsourcing: A Survey and Analysis of the Literature", *Database for Advances in Information Systems*, 34, 4, Fall 3, 6–102.

Eisenhardt, K.M. (1985) "Control: Organisational and Economic Approaches", *Management Science*, 31, 2, 134–149.

Eisenhardt, K.M. (1989) "Building Theory from Case Study Research", *Academy of Management Review*, **14**, 4, 532–550.

Feeny, D.F. and Willcocks, L.P. (1997) *The IT Function: Changing Capabilities and Skills*, Working Paper Oxford Institute of Information Management, Oxford.

Fischer, S. (1993) "The Paradox of Adoption and Routinisation in Technology Management", *Malaysian Journal of Management Science*, 2, 1, 3–20.

Fitzgerald, G. and Willcocks, L. (1994a) Contracts and Partnerships in the Outsourcing of IT, *15th International Conference on Information Systems*, Vancouver, Canada, ICIS.

Fitzgerald, G. and Willcocks, L. (1994b) *Information Technology Outsourcing Practice: A UK Survey*, Business Intelligence, London.

Fitzgerald, G. and Willcocks, L. (1994c) *Outsourcing Information Technology: Contracts and Client/Vendor Relationships*. Oxford Institute of Information Management. RDP94/10: 1–20. Templeton College, Oxford.

Halvey, J.K. and Melby, B.M. (1996) *Information Technology Outsourcing Transactions: Process, Strategies, and Contracts*, John Wiley and Sons, New York.

Hart, O.D. (1995) "Incomplete Contracts", *NBER Reporter*, **5** (Summer) 18–24.

Hartstang, S. and Forster, K. (1995) *Der Outsourcing Vertrag. Outsourcing in der Informationstechnologie: Eine strategische Management-Entscheidung.* J. Berg and H. Gräber. Frankfurt, Campus Verlag: 60–81.

Hofstede, G. (1981) "Management Control of Public and Not-for-profit Activities", *Accounting, Organisations and Society*, 2, 193–211.

Kern, T. (1997) The Gestalt of an Information Technology Outsourcing Relationship: An Exploratory Analysis, *International Conference on Information Systems*, Atlanta, Georgia.

Kern, T. and Willcocks, L. (2001) *The Relationship Advantage: Information Technology, Sourcing and Management*, Oxford University Press, Oxford.

Klepper, R. (1994) "Outsourcing Relationships" in Khosrowpour, M. (ed.) *Managing Information Technology with Outsourcing*, Idea Group Publishing, Harisburg, Penn.

Klepper, R. (1995) "The Management of Partnering Development in IS Outsourcing", *Journal of Information Technology*, 10, 4, 249–258.

Klinger, P. and Burnett, R. (1994) *Drafting and Negotiating Computer Contracts*, Butterworths, London.

Lacity, M.C. and Hirschheim, R. (1993) *Information Systems Outsourcing: Myths, Metaphors and Realities*, John Wiley and Sons Ltd., Chichester.

Lacity, M. and Hirschheim, R. (1995) *Beyond the Information Systems Outsourcing Bandwagon: The Insourcing Response*, Wiley, Chichester.

Lacity, M. and Willcocks, L. (2001) *Global Information Technology Outsourcing: Search for Business Advantage*, Wiley, Chichester.

Lacity, M. and Willcocks, L. (2009) *Information Systems and Outsourcing: Studies in Theory and Practice*, Palgrave, London.

Macneil, I.R. (1974a) "Commentary: Restatement (Second) of Contracts and Presentiation", *Virgina Law Review*, 60, 4, 589–610.

Macneil, I.R. (1974b) "The Many Futures of Contracts", *Southern California Law Review*, 47, 691–816.

Macneil, I.R. (1980) *The New Social Contract: An Inquiry into Modern Contractual Relations*, New Haven, Yale University Press.

Mayer, Brown and Platt (1996) *Information Technology Outsourcing: Legal Issues Information*, Chicago, Illinois.

McFarlan, F.W. and Nolan, R.L. (1995) "How to Manage an IT Outsourcing Alliance", *Sloan Management Review* (Winter), 4, 9–23.

Miles, M.B. and Huberman, A.M. (1994) *Qualitative Data Analysis*, 2nd edn, SAGE Publications Inc, California.

Orlikowski, W. (1991) "Integrated Information Environment or Matrix of Control? The Contradictory Implications of Information Technology", *Accounting, Management and Information Technology*, 1, 9–42.

Ouchi, W.G. (1979) "A Conceptual Framework for the Design of Organisational Control Mechanisms", *Management Science*, 25, 9, 833–848.

Poppo, L. and Zenger, T. (2002) "Do Formal Contracts and Relational Governance Function as Substitutes or Complements?", *Strategic Management Journal*, 23, 4, 707–725.

Saunders, C., Gebelt, M. and Hu, Q. (1997) "Achieving Success in Information Systems Outsourcing", *California Management Review*, 39, 2, 63–79.

Weill, P. (2004) "Don't Just Lead: Govern: How Top Performing Firms Govern IT", *MIS Quarterly Executive*, 3, 1, March, 1–17.

Willcocks, L. and Cullen, S. (2006) *The Outsourcing Enterprise 2 – The Power of Relationships*, Logica, London.

Willcocks, L.P. and Kern, T. (1997) "IT Outsourcing as Strategic Partnering: The Case of the UK Inland Revenue", *Proceedings of the Fifth European Conference in Information Systems*, June, Cork, Ireland.

Willcocks, L., Feeny, D. and Islei, G. (eds) (1997) *Managing IT as a Strategic Resource*, McGraw Hill, Maidenhead.

Willcocks, L. and Lacity, M. (eds) (2009) *Research Studies in Information Technology Outsourcing: Perspectives, Practices and Globalization*, Sage, London. Three volumes.

Williamson, O.E. (1975) *Markets and Hierarchies: Analysis and Antitrust Implications, A Study in the Economics of Internal Organization*, New York, The Free Press.

Appendix IT Outsourcing Contract: Essential Clauses and Issues

Clauses, i.e., Terms and Conditions	Brief outline
1. Parties and Term	The companies and length of contract.
2. Definitions	Explanations and definitions of wording.
3. Supporting documentation	Any documentation clarifying the clients and vendors intentions and objectives, and that can be helpful for dispute resolution (e.g., RFP).
4. Asset transfer	Transfer of assets and employees to vendor.
5. Base services, i.e., service supply and testing	Description of services to be delivered to the vendor.
6. Performance standards, i.e., service level agreement	Description of the service levels vendor is expected to provide.
7. Service & equipment location(s)	The actual physical locations of services and security issues.
8. Additional services and projects	Any other services or projects the client may need or is considering.
9. Service management and contract monitoring	Both parties endeavor to achieve the terms stipulated in the contract.
10. Disaster recovery and security	Backup and emergency services and other security concerns.
11. Obligations & responsibilities of the client	Client should make all reasonable efforts to ensure achievement of the contract.
12. Benchmarking	Method for monitoring vendor's performance.
13. Vendor personnel	Overview of vendors key employees for contract.
14. Payments	Describes the base charges and any additional charges for services delivered.
15. Payment schedule	The times of payment for the different services delivered.
16. Taxes	Explains the tax situation.
17. Audits	Financial control and monitoring.
18. Change control and management	Provisions to change services and its management.
19. Dispute resolution	Procedures for dispute resolution.
20. Termination – fees and assistance	Reasons for termination, the fees that may arise when client wishes to terminate the contract, and the length of assistance the vendor shall perform.
21. Proprietary rights	Legal property rights given to the vendor for the length of the contract to deliver services of software and systems.
22. Confidentiality	Confidentiality of information and the effects of breach.
23. Damages	Liquidated damages in the event the vendor fails to meet service levels. Also liability for damages by the client or vendor to the other party when relating to the performance of the contract.
24. Miscellaneous provisions	Numerous other contractual terms and conditions.
25. Appendices	Exhibits, i.e., schedules.

Part III

Studies 2000–2008: From IT to Business Process and Offshore Outsourcing

11
IT Outsourcing Configuration: Defining and Designing Outsourcing Arrangements

Sara Cullen, Peter Seddon and Leslie Willcocks

Introduction

In this chapter, we introduce the concept of information technology outsourcing (ITO) "configuration", defined as: *a high-level description of the set of choices the organization makes in crafting its IT outsourcing portfolio.* From research into 49 ITO arrangements studied over time, we identify seven attributes – Scope Grouping, Supplier Grouping, Financial Scale, Duration, Pricing, Resource Ownership, and Commercial Relationship – as key descriptors of an organization's ITO configuration. Seven further cases tested the relevance of the attributes. The contribution of this chapter is its articulation of the concept of configuration as a taxonomy of ITO structural characteristics, the key attributes, and demonstration that configuration is an important concept for understanding, comparing, and managing ITO arrangements. In particular we detail the rationales for 31 different options in outsourcing, the risks and management issues emerging for each, and how these play out in different combinations in selected, illustrative case studies.

Pervasive adoption of IT has made information technology outsourcing (ITO) a growing multi-billion dollar industry (Cullen and Willcocks, 2003; Lacity and Willcocks, 2009). The market is ever maturing, suppliers and their offerings ever expanding, and technology advancements increasingly enable the separation of management, implementation and operations (Feeny *et al.*, 2005). With "offshoring" attracting increasing attention, the level of ITO activity seems set to grow even larger (Lacity and Rottman, 2007; Rottman and Lacity, 2005 – see also Chapters 14 and 15).

This is in spite of all too frequent failures. Hirschheim and Lacity (2000) found that a large number of contracts were being renegotiated or terminated (see also Chapter 9). Building on past research evidence, Willcocks and Cullen (2005) predicted that large-scale deals involving complex processes and 80% plus of the IT budget, could see a third fail and another third have mixed outcomes. Various commercial publications support this prediction. Earls (2004) reports that a fifth of contracts end prematurely. Deloitte (2005) found that one in four organizations had brought functions back in-house.

Along with mixed success has come mixed advice. For example, Lacity and Willcocks (1998, 2001) and Sambamurthy *et al.* (2001) suggest that "selective" is more successful than "total" outsourcing, the latter being where at least 80% of the IT budget is outsourced to a single supplier. The argument is that suppliers have different core competencies, thus despite the additional overheads from managing multiple contracts and relationships, it is better to use multiple suppliers. Yet Rouse and Corbitt (2003) report that "the probabilities for those engaged in selective outsourcing were statistically no different – for cost savings or for business flexibility".

How is one to interpret such contradictory findings? One possibility is that success has been measured differently (therefore incomparably) in different studies (Hui and Beath, 2002; Lee *et al.*, 2004; Dibbern *et al.*, 2004). Another possibility is that it is a mistake to treat all ITO arrangements as instances of the same phenomenon: outsourcing involves a variety of choices that result in widely differing types and forms of arrangements (Marcolin and McLellan, 1998; Dibbern *et al.*, 2004). Thus conflicting results could be due to comparing "apples and oranges"; or quite different things as if they are the same. In this chapter, we explore the latter explanation. Our thesis is that the expression "IT Outsourcing" is too general a concept for use in making meaningful comparisons of ITO between organizations, or for making generalizations about effective management methods. In essence, our goal is provide the conceptual framework for a theory of management of ITO. The theory being that many major problems in ITO are due to agency issues between the client (principal) and supplier (agent) (Jensen and Meckling, 1976; Williamson, 1985) and that, different types of ITO arrangements lead to different types of agency problems that require different types of management (see also Chapter 8).

To understand why all ITO is not homogeneous, consider the following two organizations. One is a manufacturing firm, MAN; the other a national service provider, SERV. Both operate nationally, have annual revenues from $2–$5 billion, and started ITO over eight years ago for similar reasons – cost savings. But their configurations are very different.

In 1998, MAN entered into an arrangement with a sole supplier in a 3+2[1] $10M p.a. fixed-price deal. It sold its IT assets and data center to the supplier at a high price, agreeing in return to pay high rates for IT services, and

---

[1]"3+2" means that the initial contract term was for three years with the option to extend it for another two. Outsourcing-specific terms such as 3+2, fixed price, etc., are later.

transferred its data center staff. Five years later, it backsourced[2] its IT assets and awarded two separate contracts, thereby saving 70% of the original contract's value. By contrast, SERV entered into a series of labor contracts with various suppliers whose job was to provide programmers. SERV's contracts were for five years with a combined estimated value of $30M per annum, unit-priced at specified labor rates per hour.

The main issues for MAN in its ITO deal were the sale of assets, transfer of staff and contracted costs greater than market prices. Ultimately, the main issues for SERV were around the extent to which suppliers were expected to provide project management and methodologies, when the suppliers believed they were only to provide "bodies". The point of these examples is that although both describe their activities as outsourcing, the nature of their arrangements and the issues they faced were very different, thus any comparison requires a deeper understanding of the intentional and structural differences.

With examples like this in mind, the question posed in this chapter is: *How can one best describe an organization's high-level structural approach to IT outsourcing in a manner that provides insight into the choices open to management when structuring an ITO deal?* To answer this question, we introduce the concept of an organization's *ITO configuration*. Broadly, configuration is a high-level description of the set of structural choices made in crafting IT arrangements. Reviewing an organization's configuration is like looking out from a vantage point over the buildings of a city and saying: "We have one deal over here, the tall, thin, brown one. We have another deal over there, the long, fat, blue one", and so on. Each building is like an individual deal. Zooming in one any one building, the deal can be described in enormous detail, e.g., by the contract, service level agreements, governance arrangements, etc. Configuration considers the "zoomed out" view.

Note also that an organization's configuration is not static. Just as a city's skyline changes over time, so its ITO configuration changes over time. Reconstruction, via refinements and renegotiations, is continuous and ongoing. Further, the next generation deal(s) are rarely reconfigured the same as those they replace. The configuration perspective presented here focuses on "coherent clusters of characteristics" (Mintzberg and Lampel 1999, p. 25) from the client organization's perspective, as in Lee *et al.* (2004). It does not represent the supplier's view, albeit widely recognized as missing in the ITO literature (Hui and Beath, 2002; Dibbern *et al.*, 2004) – although such a concept might very well be applied from that perspective. For that reason, the supplier's structural characteristics (i.e., if the supplier "offshores" some of the work, or if service delivery occurs through several related entities rather than a single entity) are not captured – nor is this the intent.

---

[2]That is, brought the outsourced IT assets back in-house – see also Chapter 9.

Why is ITO configuration so important to the client organization? Configuration matters because an organization must make many structural choices in constructing its ITO portfolio and deals. As discussed in Chapter 8, different choices make certain goals more achievable than others, and involve different risks. Configuration matters because different configurations require different lifecycle planning and management approaches (Cullen *et al.*, 2005). Lastly, configuration matters because mismanaged structure has been shown to be responsible for some of the greatest relational problems in ITO as attested by Kern and Willcocks (2001).

The set of configuration attributes presented here helps to make the most important management choices and their consequences visible. Our conviction is that where managers make informed and comprehensive choices in structuring their ITO arrangements, they will achieve better outcomes. A taxonomy of ITO configuration possibilities, derived from researched cases studied longitudinally, provides a comprehensive definition of the choices available, and the risks and management issues associated with each such choice, as they have emerged from our study of practice.

Overview of the configuration concept

Our configuration model was derived from research by the lead author who participated as a senior outsourcing consultant in 49 ITO outsourcing projects in Australia during 1994–2002 (Figure 11.1). The model is based on systematic analysis of the related working documents (plans, contracts, reports, evaluations, correspondence, presentations, minutes, reviews, audit findings and regular interaction and discussion with participants). Structural attributes were synthesized and harmonized, and then categorized by the first author, who had detailed, first-hand knowledge of the cases. Working iteratively through the 49 cases, the model was refined to ultimately include seven key attributes that capture the essence of the structures of the different arrangements.

To test that the identified attributes were important, and indeed necessary, for understanding and managing ITO, two additional steps were taken. First, an early version of the model (Cullen and Seddon, 2004) was tested by the three authors, using a series of cases, which led to further refinement of the model and, ultimately, the version presented in this chapter. Second, seven additional case studies were conducted during 2003 and 2004, in five different industries. Details of these cases are provided in the section headed "Testing ITO Configuration" below.

The configuration model

As most organizations source IT services from several suppliers under differing arrangements (Cullen and Willcocks, 2003; Lacity and Willcocks, 2009), we use the term "portfolio" to describe the collection of ITO deals in force at

1994	1995	1996	1997	1998	1999	2000	2001	2002
1. Logistics JV	8. Consumer products maker	12. Federal gov't	18. Defence	26. State gov't	33. Federal gov't cluster	39. Diversified manufacturer	45. Funds manager	48. Service provider
2. Petroleum	9. Electrical utility	13. Medical products	19. Federal gov't	27. State gov't	34. Bank	40. State gov't	46. Airline	49. Gas & electric utility
3. Stock broker	10. Insurer	14. Federal gov't	20. State gov't	28. Transport	35. Electric utility	41. Telco equip manufacturer	47. Insurer	
4. Bank	11. State gov't cluster	15. Electric utility	21. Federal gov't	29. Water utility	36. State gov't	42. Travel company		
5. Bank		16. Consumer products	22. Telecom	30. Industrial products	37. University	43. Telecom		
6. State gov't		17. University	23. Federal gov't	31. University	38. Insurer	44. University		
7. State gov't authority			24. Miner	32. Logistics				
			25. Miner					

Figure 11.1 Cases in Order of Chronology

any one time. Just as a stock-market portfolio is the set of all investments, real and financial, owned by an individual or organization, so an organization's ITO portfolio is the set of ITO contracts in force at any one time. Based on the 49 theory-building cases detailed in Figure 11.1, we identified seven attributes that were key to understanding and describing the structure of an organization's ITO portfolio. As shown in Figure 11.2, these are: (1) Scope Grouping, (2) Supplier Grouping, (3) Financial Scale, (4) Pricing Framework, (5) Duration, (6) Resource Ownership, and (7) Commercial Relationship.

Each attribute has several options, e.g., fixed, unit-based, or cost-based pricing for the Pricing framework. In a large complex ITO portfolio, different options may be chosen for different deals, and within a given deal, the configuration attributes may have any number of options present. We believe these attributes provide a helpful way of disaggregating the complexity of many ITO portfolios, providing comprehensiveness in defining the parameters of any IT outsourcing arrangement, and also insights into the rationale, risks, and management issues of the different choices.

In a chapter such as this, it is not possible to discuss all 49 cases used in deciding that the seven attributes identified in Figure 11.2 emerged as the key ones for describing both individual deals and the overall portfolio. This detailed discussion appears in Cullen (2005). However, below we provide one illustrative case from the 49 that instantiates the seven attributes for both the individual deal and the overall portfolio. Detailed discussion of

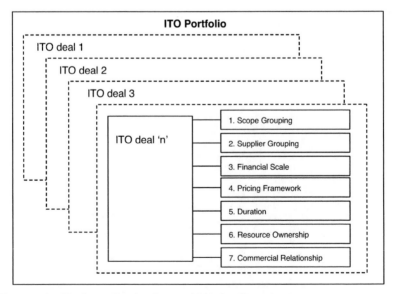

Figure 11.2   The Seven Key Attributes of ITO Configuration

the facets and options available for each of the seven attributes, their risks, and the management implications of each option, is presented in the subsequent section.

Case example

SOE1 is a state-owned enterprise with annual revenue of around AUD $1 billion. The initial outsourcing deal was negotiated in 1994, and it was the only one in the portfolio at that time. SOE1 outsourced [1][3] all its IT to [2] a single prime supplier (the supplier, however, had to subcontract 70% of the work due to their lack of infrastructure, thereby becoming a prime contractor). This was [3a] moderately large at A$20M p.a., with [3b] 100% of the IT budget outsourced under a [4] a 5+5 year[4] [5] fixed-price contract. Resource ownership [6] had the supplier owning the assets and supplying and managing labor. The facilities ownership was split in that SOE1 owned the helpdesk facilities and the supplier subcontracted the data center. As noted above, this was intended to be [7] a "partnering" deal in which the supplier replaced the IT department in its entirety. Problems arose because it was dealt with in practice as distinctly arms-length. By transferring all IT staff from CIO on down, SOE1 was left with no in-house IT expertise and IT was stagnant for five years. SOE1 was unable to gain access to, or control, the majority of its IT costs because the prime contractor did not pass on the requirement to the subcontractor for full cost disclosure. Furthermore, the quality of services delivered was well under market benchmark metrics. SOE1 was unable to renegotiate the subcontract and suffered under this configuration for the full five years. Near the end of the first term, SOE1 hired a new CIO, who reconfigured the sourcing arrangements. He [1] re-scoped services into three groups (distributed services, mainframe, and applications) which were contracted out to [2] three different best-of-breed suppliers. As with the first contract, this group of contracts was [3a] moderately large, with [3b] almost 100% of the IT budget outsourced. Each of the three contracts had a different duration [4] – one 3+2 years, one 6+3+3 years, and one evergreen.[5] Pricing [5] was hybrid in all three contracts, combining fixed-price and unit-priced elements. Resource ownership [6] changed so that each supplier provided and managed the entirety of the resources (facilities, assets and labor). Each contract was arms length [7]. The attributes of the two generations are summarized in Table 11.1.

---

[3]The numbers in square brackets [...] correspond to the seven configuration attributes.
[4]A "5+5" year deal means that the initial contract term was for five years with the option to extend it for another five. The motivational consequences of choosing a 5+5 year deal instead of, say, a ten-year deal, are discussed in the next section.
[5]Evergreen deals have no expiry; rather the contract continues until either party invokes its termination rights (see later in this chapter).

Table 11.1   Comparison of Configurations and Outcomes in the SOE Case Study

Attribute	1st Generation, 1994	2nd Generation, 1999
1. Scope grouping	Total (whole-of-IT)	Total (whole-of-IT), but backsourced strategy
2. Supplier grouping	Sole supplier (which turned into a Prime supplier)	Three "best of breed" – mainframe, distributed operations, and application
3. Financial scale	AUD $20M p.a. (100% budget)	AUD $25M p.a. (100% budget)
4. Pricing framework	Fixed price	Hybrid: combination of fixed and unit
5. Contract duration	5+5 year terms	3+2 years; 6+3+3 years; evergreen
6. Resource ownership	Supplier owned all assets. SOE1 provided the facility for help desk	Each supplier "owned" all facilities and labor with their service scope, and some assets. SOE1 directly leased bulk of assets.
7. Commercial relationship	Arms-length, but described as "partnering"	Arms-length

At the end of year one of the 2nd generation portfolio, cost savings were good and service quality was adequate for two of the three deals (these were adjudged successful). The third was less successful from a service view, but had yielded the greatest cost savings (which made the CIO, but not his users, very happy). The CIO attributes the greater success of the second-generation to changes in configuration. Particularly important changes included the move (1) from a prime contractor to best-of-breed; (2) from a commercial relationship that assumed partnering to explicit arm's length deals; (3) to hybrid pricing; and (4) to SOE1 owning the bulk of the assets.

Prior research concerning ITO configuration

The above example shows that changing ITO configuration led to marked improvements in outcomes from ITO outsourcing. Given its apparent importance, it is surprising, however, that the notion of configuration has been little discussed in the literature. Of course, there has been much discussion of concepts like selective outsourcing (Lacity and Willcocks, 1998, 2001; Sambamurthy *et al.*, 2001), which is an aspect of Attribute 1 – Scope Grouping. Further, as shown in Table 11.2, in various papers, various prior researchers have discussed the importance of all seven attributes. But with the exception of papers by Lee *et al.* (2004) and Dibbern *et al.* (2004), none

Table 11.2   Literature Supporting the Configuration Attributes

Attribute	Supporting Literature
1 Scope	Millar (1994), Earl (1996), Lacity and Willcocks (1998, 2001), Cullen and Willcocks (2003), Lee *et al.* (2004), Dibbern *et al.* (2004)
2 Supplier Grouping	Williamson (1985), Cross (1995), Currie (1998), Klepper and Jones (1998), Lacity and Willcocks (1998, 2001), Gallivan and Oh (1999), Dyer (2000), Humphry (2000), Hui and Beath (2002), Cullen and Willcocks (2003), Dibbern *et al.* (2004)
3 Financial Scale	Loh and Venkatraman (1992), McFarlan and Norton (1995), Lacity *et al.* (1996), Klepper and Jones (1998), Willcocks *et al.* (2002)
4 Pricing Framework	Currie (1996), Klepper and Jones (1998), Domberger *et al.* (2000), Cullen and Willcocks (2003)
5 Contract Duration	Earl (1996), Lacity and Willcocks (1998), Klepper and Jones (1998), Knolmayer (2002), Cullen and Willcocks (2003), Lee *et al.* (2004), Dibbern *et al.* (2004)
6 Resource Ownership	Williamson (1985), Ang and Beath (1993), Loh and Venkatraman (1995), Klepper and Jones (1998), Currie (1998), Lee *et al.* (2004), Dibbern *et al.* (2004)
7 Commercial Relationship	Millar (1994), Cross (1995), Drucker (1995), McFarlan and Norton (1995), Ang and Cummings (1997), Venkatraman (1997), Currie (1998), Klepper and Jones (1998), Lacity and Willcocks (1998), Cullen and Willcocks (2003), Dibbern *et al.* (2004)

of these studies has drawn attention to the huge range of options available, nor their management consequences, when constructing an ITO portfolio.

This is beginning to change. In their recent paper, Lee *et al.* (2004) frame their discussion of ITO configuration around three dimensions: degree of integration, allocation of control, and performance period. Their "degree of integration" is comparable to a combination of our Scope (services outsourced) and Financial Scale (proportion of the function outsourced). Their "allocation of control" corresponds to a combination of our Pricing Framework (manner of compensation), Resource Ownership (authority and residual rights), and Commercial Relationship (complementary resources). Their "performance period" corresponds to our Duration, although their description revolved around whether the contract was long, medium, or short term rather than how duration was structured.

Likewise, Dibbern *et al.*'s (2004) deal-level taxonomy is analogous to our configuration concept. Their "degree" is comparable to a combination of our *Scope* and *Financial Scale* (extent of outsourcing), "mode" to *Supplier Grouping* (one or multiple suppliers), "ownership" to *Resource Ownership* (limited in their case to wholly owned, partially owned or externally owned), and "timeframe" to *Duration* (in terms of short vs. long term). Pricing is not discussed. Nor is the notion of commercial relationship made explicit in their taxonomy, albeit relationships were discussed at length in the research.

The seven configuration attributes

Attribute #1: scope grouping

Scope Grouping describes <u>what</u> services are provided to <u>whom</u>, and <u>where</u>. The three facets are Service, Recipient and Geographic, as summarized in Table 11.3. Any combination of service, recipient, and geographic scope may be in effect for a given portfolio, as well as in a complex deal.

Service Scope describes the nature of the work, aligned with the traditional segmentation of an IT function (i.e., applications development, network management, data center). Researchers encourage organizations to think of themselves as a collection of services that provide value (e.g., Quinn *et al.*, 1990). The portfolio-view of service scope breaks out IT into a segmentation model (such as Figure 11.3), while the deal level focuses on service scope within a given deal. Each firm may outsource different services. Some, for example, may outsource nearly everything, whilst others perform selective outsourcing of, say only the helpdesk. Furthermore, firms outsource services to varying degrees. For example, technology supporting helpdesk, or the whole help desk service.

Recipient Scope refers to the groups (i.e., divisions, strategic business units, subsidiaries) that have been identified to receive specific ITO services. This is particularly applicable to decentralized organizations which allow business units to elect to participate in outsourcing initiatives. BHP Billiton, the world's largest diversified resources company, has different service specifications regarding its different businesses depending on their requirements, although all services are provided by one ITO supplier. An outsourcing contract tailored to the various recipients in an organization has been described as "creative contracting" by Lacity and Willcocks (1998) whereby specialist contractual provisions are created to meet particular recipient needs.

Geographic Scope refers to the physical locations that have been identified to receive particular ITO services (e.g., state, national, international regions). Geographic scope is often complex for global firms (Dibbern *et al.*, 2004). For example, in 2005 Ericsson outsourced IT infrastructure across the world, but each region chose its own supplier. Pasminco, a global mining company, found that its chosen supplier could not provide services in all its locations, thus it selectively configured scope to match the regional capabilities of the supplier.

Table 11.3 Scope Grouping Facets

Facet	Options	Rationale	Risk	Management Issues
What Service (functional service bundles)	**Service Scope** 1. Entire service scope	• Conducive to a sole or prime supplier	• Maintaining knowledge and control	• Retaining appropriate core competencies • Providing strategy and direction • Providing management focus and time
	2. Selected scope	• Conducive to best-of-bread and/or panels	• Integration of end-to-end processes and outcomes	• Total cost of ownership (TCO) management • Detailed performance metrics that aggregate to overall service metrics
Whom Recipient (business unit that receive services/s)	**Recipient Scope** 1. All business units	• Organizational consistency and standardization • Potential scale economies	• Unique needs not met cost-effectively	• Getting buy-in from business unit management • Tailoring agreement to meet unique needs while keeping necessary items standard
	2. Business unit self select	• Accountability and ownership	• Integration between units	• Extensive contract flexibility rights (e.g., to merge or eliminate business units, move under a prime)
Where Geographic (physical locations that receive service/s)	**Geographic Scope** 1. All geographies	• Consistency and standardization • Potential scale economies	• Inconsistent regional market capabilities	• Getting buy-in from regions • Tailoring agreement to meet unique needs while balancing the need for standardization
	2. Geography self select	• Accountability and ownership	• Integration between regions	• Extensive contract flexibility rights (e.g., to merge regions, "chop and change" scope, move under a prime)

278

IT Service/Activity	Not formally considered or N/A	Considered & Rejected Outsourcing	Considering Outsourcing	Partially Outsourcing	Fully Outsourcing	Number of Respondents
Mainframe & Data Centre Operations						
Hardware Support & Maintenance	12%	4%	6%	34%	45%	228
Systems Implementation	24%	3%	4%	60%	9%	227
Applications Development	26%	10%	4%	42%	19%	228
Applications Support & Maintenance	27%	10%	5%	44%	14%	228
Systems Integration	43%	9%	5%	32%	10%	227
Operations & Facilities Management	33%	18%	9%	21%	19%	228
Disaster Recovery	40%	9%	12%	20%	18%	228
Client/Server and Desktop						
Hardware Support & Maintenance	11%	6%	7%	43%	34%	229
Systems Implementation	20%	9%	6%	58%	8%	232
Applications Support & Maintenance	19%	11%	7%	50%	13%	233
Applications Development	27%	9%	5%	45%	13%	233
Systems Integration	39%	11%	7%	36%	7%	231
Operations & Facilities Management	38%	15%	11%	22%	14%	230
Disaster Recovery	44%	11%	10%	24%	11%	232
IT Management and Support						
Education & training	15%	3%	5%	58%	19%	232
Help desk	36%	22%	13%	9%	19%	233
Asset Management	63%	11%	7%	13%	6%	230
IT Strategic Planning	65%	21%	1%	13%	0%	231
Communications						
Network services between & beyond premises (WAN Services)	9%	3%	7%	37%	44%	233
Cabling & infrastructure in premises	17%	5%	5%	35%	38%	231
Operations & facilities mgmt	31%	14%	10%	20%	24%	231
LAN services	36%	16%	10%	18%	20%	233

Figure 11.3 Service Scope in Australia

Table 11.4 Supplier Grouping Options

Option	Rationale	Risks	Management Issues
Sole Supplier (one supplier)	• Sole accountability • Potential to pass on economies • Streamlined contracting costs and processes • End-to-end key performance metrics	• Monopolistic supplier behaviors • Compromise quality where the supplier is not best of breed (in services, industries or geographic locations)	• Extensive contract flexibility rights due to the dependence on supplier • Independent expertise to avoid solution channeling and ensure value for money (quotes are market values)
Prime Contractor (Head supplier that sub-contracts)	• Single point of accountability • Allows best-of-breed subcontracting • Streamlined, but a bit more complex, contracting costs and processes • End-to-end KPIs	• Prime must be expert at subcontracting (selection, management, disengagement) • Client may desire different subcontractors • Client often required to resolve issues between the prime and subcontractor(s) • Primes and subcontractors often encroach "territories"	• Contract ensuring various rights over the subcontracting (access, selection, veto, etc) • Compliance auditing ensuring the prime passes obligations to the subcontractors • Oversight ensuring all parties are operating as an efficient and united front
Best of Breed (Two or more suppliers)	• Greater control • Flexibility to chop and change • Promotes competition and prevents complacency	• Attracting the market for small "slices" of work • Keeping suppliers interested, giving management focus, and allocating staff • Interdependent services and contracts • Integration complexity • Tracing accountability	• Designing interdependent contracts between independent suppliers • Multi-party interface and handover management • End-to-end process management is more difficult • Multiple lifecycle management
Panel (preferred suppliers)	• Buy services and assets when required • Promotes ongoing competition • Prevents complacency	• Attracting the market when panel is a pre-qualification and does not guarantee work • Adding new panel members or wanting to use suppliers not on the panel	• Panel bidding process for work • Ongoing ranking of panel members based on performance • Managing and evaluating the total program

Attribute #2: supplier grouping

Supplier Grouping refers to the decisions made regarding how many suppliers provide the outsourced services. Though not addressed in Lee *et al.*'s (2004) model, Gallivan and Oh's (1999) foremost conclusion was that managers must be aware that there are more options than the traditional dyad (one buyer, one seller). As shown in Table 11.4, our research of the 49 cases identified four options: *Sole Supplier, Prime Contractor, Best-of-Breed,* and *Panel.*

Our characterization of supplier groupings utilizes Williamson's (1985) three forms of governance – "independent", "market" and "network" which is richer than the ITO literature that tends to treat supplier grouping as either sole or multiple suppliers (Currie, 1998) and does not recognize the structural variability possible in the multiple supplier concept. Williamson's "network" structure attempts a stable network of suppliers, which is characteristic of our *Sole Supplier, Prime Contractor* and *Best-of-Breed* options. The reason for this increased granularity of network structure types, is to emphasize that supplier networks may take various forms, and their requisite management differs. Note that *Best-of-Breed* is a network, but one that operates akin to Williamson's "market" structure based on interchangeable, loosely coupled suppliers. In a *Panel* there is a list of preferred suppliers in continuous competition. This is the independent structure, in which interactions are many and brief.

Sole Supplier is a network of two parties, or a simple dyad (Gallivan and Oh, 1999), where a single supplier provides the entire scope, from a portfolio view, or a particular scope, from a deal view. This is preferred to achieve sole accountability and seamless service, but results in compromised service quality in certain areas, as the supplier is rarely preeminent in all areas (Cullen and Willcocks, 2003). While it may lower communication costs (Dyer, 2000), switching barriers expose this option to opportunistic supplier behavior (Hui and Beath, 2002). See also Chapter 4 for further discussion.

Prime Contractor arrangement is another choice of network, with many supplier interfaces to the organization being under the control of the head contractor. This well recognized form of "supply chain" contracting was absent in Gallivan and Oh's (1999) taxonomy, and varies from Lacity and Willcocks' (1998) "multi-sourcing" whereby several suppliers are contracted under one contract without a lead supplier. In the prime contractor option, there is one head supplier that is accountable, and contractually liable, for the entirety of the contract but who uses any number of subcontractors to deliver all or part of the scope. The subcontractors have expertise, or operate in regions, that the prime does not, or are mandated by the organization (often to support local industry). This was the preferred approach of the Australian Government in requiring major suppliers to subcontract work to local firms as part of an industry development initiative (Humphry, 2000). Even though companies like BP Exploration and DuPont have not found suppliers managing each other to be a productive arrangement (Cullen and Willcocks, 2003), alliance networks such as prime contracting, enabling two or more suppliers to offer services as a package, were predicted by Klepper and Jones (1998) to be one of outsourcing's long-term trends. They also note, however, that this arrangement requires contract provisions that limit what can be subcontracted, to which firms, and how the subcontractors will be controlled.

Best-of-Breed is a network, but as indicated, one that operates akin to Williamson's "market" structure based on interchangeable, loosely coupled suppliers. A *Best-of-Breed*, or "multi-vendor" (Gallivan and Oh, 1999; Dibbern *et al.*, 2004), approach is where the organization has any number of suppliers, and thus the firm is, in effect, the "head contractor". This has been the lower risk option of 75% of UK and 82% of US organizations (Lacity and Willcocks, 2001, 2009). The benefits and problems with this option relate to the competition element – it is difficult to manage suppliers that may be competing with one another, but the competitive tension also yields continuous improvement and cost effective benchmarking (Cross, 1995; Currie, 1998).

In a *Panel* there is a list of preferred suppliers in continuous competition. This is the independent structure, in which interactions are many and brief. Typically, work is not guaranteed and each supplier competes on a regular basis for various contracts or "work orders" over a defined period. This is often the case for applications development, hardware purchasing, and consulting as the work tends to be periodic and the requirements vary with each initiative. Figure 11.4 shows that the preferred supplier approach (panel) is the most widely used in Australia and least common was the "best of breed" approach espoused in the literature. See also Chapter 8 for a discussion of supplier options.

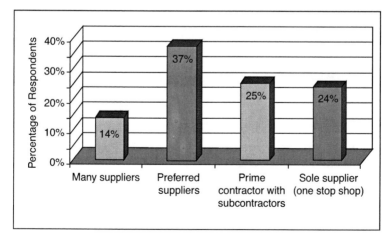

Figure 11.4   Supplier Grouping in Australia

Table 11.5 Financial Scale Components

Facets	Option	Rationale	Risks	Management Issues
Relative (% ITC spend outsourced)	Large relative scale	• Enable focus on core business • Speed of change, if contracts are flexible	• High risk and impact on organization and stakeholders • Consumes significant management resources • Knowledge retention	• Integration of processes and deliverables into the organization • Management of ITO must be a core competence
	Small relative scale	• Retain operational knowledge • Manageable within existing functions • Outsource tasks, not functions	• Management responsibility "bolted on" to an individual's existing role. • Expertise and/or attention may be absent.	• Ensuring risks are managed, since the dollar value is low and can be overlooked • Ensuring those responsible know how to manage ITO
Absolute (p.a. value)	Large absolute scale	• Attract many suppliers and/or large suppliers	• Winner's curse (supplier bids too low to make a profit) • Supplier may have superior experience and take advantage of an inexperienced firm	• Getting expertise superior, or at least equal, to the suppliers/(s) • Minimizing costs overruns
	Small absolute scale	• Target small suppliers and be an important client • Can be approved within lower ranks	• Subcontracting may be required • Need to get the market's attention • Often receives scant attention from either or both parties • Lots of "little" deals can quickly add up to large relative scale	• Managing the overall small-scale deals as a portfolio

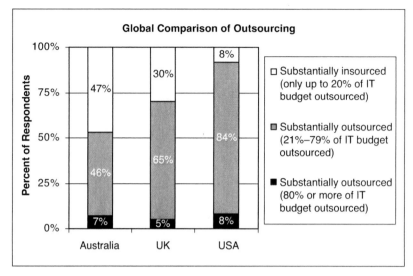

Figure 11.5   Percentage of IT Expenditure Outsourced

Attribute #3: financial scale

Financial Scale indicates the degree of outsourcing performed in financial terms. It describes the financial value to the organization using *Relative* (Loh and Venkatraman, 1992) and *Absolute* dimensions, as well as its financial value within the industry using the absolute dimension. These two facets of Financial Scale are described in Table 11.5.

Looking at the average ITC (IT and communications) budget, Willcocks *et al.* (2003) surmised that by the end of 2001 approximately 30% of average corporation's IT costs were outsourced and predicted that this would double by 2005. Other sources, as shown in Figure 11.5, suggest over half of organizations are outsourcing at least 20% of their IT budgets.

Outsourcing 80% or more of the ITC budget is deemed total outsourcing (Lacity *et al.*, 1996). Total outsourcing is very high risk if not done appropriately, and the stakes are high (Cullen and Willcocks, 2003 – see also Chapter 4). Klepper and Jones (1998) noted that total outsourcing requires considerable time, effort and money analyzing the deal and executing the contracting process; they further note that small scale outsourcing attracts few suppliers and little attention once won.

Attribute #4: pricing framework

Early ITO deals were typically fixed price, but today there are many more options (Cullen and Willcocks, 2003; Lacity and Willcocks, 2009). The Pricing Framework describes the method by which the payment to the supplier(s) is calculated. Our analysis of the 49 cases identified three basic

Table 11.6   Pricing Options

Option	Rationale	Risks	Management Issues
Lump sum, fixed price (single consolidated fee)	• Potential to lock in cost • Predictable costs within the specified volume bands • Explicit financial goal	• Misinterpretations over what is "in" and "out" of scope • Negotiating requirement changes • Lose track of individual cost drivers, when lumped into one sum • Difficult to reduce price when lesser volumes are required • Portion of the fixed price relates to the supplier's risk in terms of the volatility of cost to supply.	• Forecasting against fixed price limitations such as volume constraints • Explicit scope definitions required, and agreeing charges for "out-of-scope" work • Unbundling lumped prices to assess cost drivers or benchmark
Unit Pricing (Price per specific transaction unit	• Ability to "chop and change" services • Volume discounts • Can reduce costs by reducing demand • Can track unit costs • Assists charge-back	• Premium if supplier does not have a base guaranteed workload • Exceeding budget as supply is effectively "unlimited", particularly if there has been pent up demand or latent demand created	• Demand tracking and management, as price is directed related to usage
Cost Based Pricing (At cost plus a management fee or % mark up)	• Full knowledge of costs • Retain knowledge of operations • Can track unit costs, in particular when calculating TCO (total cost of operations)	• Costs are known, but in the control of the supplier • Costs incurred prior to scrutiny, can only correct future behavior, not recoup past "losses" • Supplier is reliant upon directions and does not have an inherent motive to reduce cost	• Understanding of cost drivers and market prices • Directing supplier's efficiency • Auditing and benchmarking costs and efficiency

options: *Lump-Sum Fixed, Unit, and Cost Based* (Table 11.6). Pricing combinations, or hybrids, are more common today than any pure form, particularly with mature outsourcing organizations. Currie (1996) recognized the fixed and unit options only, and a hybrid, using a minor variant of terminology; Klepper and Jones (1998) recognize all three forms of pricing alternatives, as well as the hybrids. Otherwise, the ITO literature is surprisingly silent on pricing constructs given that different pricing structures have such strong motivational impacts on supplier behavior.

Lump-sum Fixed Price represents a single sum contract (e.g., $2 million p.a. to operate a call center). Fixed price contracting can be effective where demand levels and the cost to supply are both highly predictable – otherwise the price will be anything but fixed. As was found in many cases, the quoted fixed price was rarely the one paid, as volumes fluctuated and controversial "out-of-scope" services attracted additional fees (Cullen and Willcocks, 2003).

Unit Priced contracts charge a price per a specific transaction unit (e.g., $13 per call). This is the utility form of outsourcing, whereby the organization only pays for what is used. Issues arise over the need to guarantee a minimum base load in order to cover any permanent resources the supplier requires, the organization's ability to forecast demand, and the degree of volume discounts available (Cullen and Willcocks, 2003).

Cost Based (cost plus) contracts have the supplier pass through its costs plus provisions for profit via a percentage mark up (e.g., cost plus a 3% markup) or a fixed management fee (e.g., cost plus $1 million p.a.). This approach has value when the demand needs to be flexible and the cost to supply are uncertain, but has a high overhead due to the oversight needed to verify that "best cost" was achieved, particularly if the supplier's margin is a percentage of cost, thus motivating the supplier to increase costs in the absence of mitigating controls (Cullen and Willcocks, 2003).

Attribute #5: duration

The duration reflects the agreed length of the contract, including extensions, for which we have defined three basic options: *Single Term, Evergreen,* or *Rollover* (Table 11.7).

Conflicting advice over long- versus short-term contracts abounds. Earl (1996) believes the uncertainty involving IT and the requirement to experiment in its application precludes having long-term contracts. Klepper and Jones (1998) argue that long-term contracts enable the supplier to learn about the organization and for the parties to establish mutual trust. Lee *et al.* (2004) note that in certain cultures, like Korea, longer-term contracts are a reflection of the value that the culture places on long-term relationships. However, all these studies assume a *single term*, which has not been the norm for some time. Single term deals are fixed-duration contracts which expire on a specified date and do not provide for extensions.

Table 11.7   Duration Options

Option	Rationale	Risks	Management Issues
Single term (fixed one-term)	• Can be aligned to life of assets or other contracts	• Often results in a retender, even if the supplier has performed well	• Preparing for end of contract
Rollover (extendable)	• Pre-set conditions for extending the contract past the initial term • Motivates the supplier to do well to get the extension	• Client tends to retain absolute rollover discretion, thus is not guaranteed • Rollovers occur with no competitive tension	• Assessing the rollover conditions as well as the current market conditions (to decide if a retender is warranted)
Evergreen (in perpetuity)	• Never "out of contract"	• Complacency in either or both parties	• Continuous assessment of contract

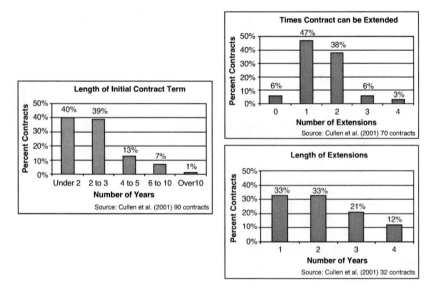

Figure 11.6   Duration in Australia

The norm as at 2009 is *rollover* contracts, which have a fixed initial term and extension options (typified in Figure 11.6). Rollovers offer a measure of security for the supplier, as well as a measure of flexibility for the firm. The extension(s) can be either automatic whereby the contract continues until the parties agree otherwise, or optional whereby the contract ends unless the extension is agreed (Cullen and Willcocks, 2003). Repeated contracting has substantial benefits in lowering contracting and governance costs (Klepper and Jones, 1998).

Less common, but popular in some organizations is the use of *evergreen* contracts. Evergreen deals have no expiry, rather the contract continues until either party invokes its termination rights. Knolmayer (2002) recognized this form with regard to the hiring of freelance personnel on a day-to-day basis.

To go back to the debate on short- vs. long-term contracts, any of the duration structures can be any length. For example, a single-term deal could be for one or ten years, an evergreen deal could end after one year or go on for ten years, and a rollover could be any number of years (e.g., a 3+2+2) deal could be three, five or seven years depending upon whether the extensions are taken up. The key is balancing certainty for the supplier, in order to provide price discounts or amortize set-up costs, and flexibility for the organization to change their requirements. Then it is a matter of designing contractual provisions and governance appropriate for the chosen duration form. As Dibbern *et al.* (2004) note, the costs incurred in actually managing a contract tend to be independent of the length of the contract, rather it has more to do with the duration structure in context of the overall configuration.

Attribute #6: resource ownership

Dibbern *et al.* (2004) make special mention that the frequent approach of conceptualizing scope grouping and resource ownership as one construct is not appropriate; the evidence suggests it is more appropriate to treat these two attributes separately, because different forms of resource ownership have very different management implications.

Resource ownership describes which party controls and/or owns the various service delivery resources (assets, facilities and labor). Ownership is

	Party "Owning" the Resource (S = supplier, C = client)												
Resource	S	C	S	C	S	C	S	C	S	C	S	C	S
Assets (e.g. hardware, software)	✓		✓			✓	✓			✓		✓	✓
Facilities (e.g. office site, data center)	✓			✓	✓			✓	✓			✓	✓
Labor (direct and/or management)		✓	✓		✓			✓		✓	✓		✓
	Infra-structure		Onsite		Service & Facility		Asset Buy-in		Facility Host		Labor Buy-in		Total Owner-ship
	Type of Resource Ownership												

Figure 11.7   Resource Ownership Alternatives between the Parties

Table 11.8 Resource Ownership Options

Options	Rationale	Risks	Management Issues
Infrastructure (asset & facilities)	• Access to facilities and technology without capital investment • Pay for required capacity • Potential for volume discounts	• Potential switching costs • Often requires commodity or standard type asset use (vanilla solutions) • Contract length tends to reflect asset life, not business plan cycle	• Capacity planning • Ensuring security and disaster recovery at supplier • Ensuring asset refreshment is at market standards and prices
On-site (labor & assets)	• Co-location promotes interaction and understanding • Greater degree of confidentiality • Can observe supplier's staff • More seamless services	• No economies of scale from shared facilities with other clients • Supplier's staff adopt the culture of client rather than the supplier's	• Support, maintenance, and security of facilities • Maintaining a professional and effective relationship
Service and facility (facilities & labor)	• Assets are able to ported to alternative supplier or back in-house at minimal cost • No novation of software licenses or asset leases required	• Ensuring assets are maintained in accordance with warranty • No economies of scale from shared assets with other clients	• Relationship management • Ongoing performance and compliance reviews • Ensuring security and disaster recovery at supplier
Buy-in (assets only)	• Direct control of service delivery and outcomes • Pay for required assets • Can incorporate competition for each buy-in round via panel	• Supplier has little accountability other than to meet specifications	• Asset specification, implementation, integration and management

Table 11.8 Resource Ownership Options – *continued*

Options	Rationale	Risks	Management Issues
Facility host (facility only)	• Direct control of service delivery and outcomes • No need to support and maintain purpose built facility	• Network link to host – another potential node fault • Limited physical access to site	• Network management • Ensuring good security and disaster recovery at supplier
Labor (workforce and/ or management)	• Access to skill base and expertise • Lower switching costs, if specialized organizational knowledge not required	• Service outcome accountability difficult to separate between parties • Providing clear directions to the supplier • Site accommodation and access for supplier staff	• Auditing of supplier timesheets
Total (Whole-of-IT)	• Greater focus on "core" business • Access to facilities and technology without capital investment • Centralized support • End to end performance metrics • Less integration issues	• Loss of control • Over-dependence on the supplier • High exit barriers and disengagement costs • Significant transition requirements • Extensive rights required in contract	• Relationship management • Ongoing performance and compliance reviews • Maintaining and obtaining knowledge without ongoing direct experience • Ensuring viable termination options and sourcing alternatives • Auditing internal controls at supplier

not literal; it identifies the party holding facility or asset leases, for example, or the party holding the labor agreement with contracted staff. Thus, our use of resource ownership is more a hybrid of residual right theory and TCE (transaction cost economics). TCE is concerned with the investment of the "owner", while residual rights theory is focused on the excise of control. Figure 11.7 names the seven ownership alternatives that can exist in any given deal. Table 11.8 is the summary of rationale, risks and issues related to each combination.

The degree of asset specificity (Williamson, 1985; Ang and Beath, 1993; Klepper and Jones, 1998) plays a key role in this resource ownership decisions. If a resource is specific to a place, or if necessary knowledge is unable to be separated from specific people, or if a competitive advantage is due to a certain asset or configuration of all the resources – the switching costs become immense and the client can be subject to a holdup by the supplier (Williamson, 1985). There is very little in the ITO literature on various forms of resource ownership other than the notion of "facility sharing" (Currie, 1998) which we have expanded beyond purely the facility to include all the key tangible resources including assets and labor.

Attribute #7: commercial relationship

The commercial relationship summarizes the high-level organization-to-organization nature of relationship structure. Dibbern *et al.* (2004) identify the need for better descriptions of inter-organizational relationships, as the literature is inconsistent and vague. Our analysis of the 49 cases identified the four options as *Arms-length*, *Value-add*, *Co-sourced*, and *Equity* (Table 11.9).

Arms-length is where the deal is between unrelated parties characterized by mutually exclusive accountabilities. It is the form of contracting known as a "market relationship" (Klepper and Jones, 1998).

Value-add is where the parties have a combination of arms-length services as well as shared business initiatives. Millar (1994) describes value-added outsourcing as where the supplier is able to add value to the activity that could not be cost effectively provided in-house. Klepper and Jones (1998) describe this as an "intermediate" relationship characterized by complex work and substantial benefits. Lacity and Willcocks (1998, 2001) characterize value-added outsourcing when the parties combine to market new products and services. Under these arrangements, although there is typically one contract, there are distinct and unique components which have different obligations and remuneration approaches (Cullen and Willcocks, 2003). A leading example, which goes beyond value-adding to the IT function toward value-adding to the enterprise, is the arrangement between South Australia and EDS, whereby EDS must put back 10% of its outsourcing revenue into the state's economic growth (Dibbern *et al.*, 2004).

Table 11.9 Commercial Relationship Options

Options	Rationale	Risks	Management Issues
Arms-length (independent parties)	• Distinct accountabilities • Transparency	• Can result in a more adversarial approach	• Delivery of accountabilities
Value-add (shared business initiatives)	• Ability to derive greater mutual value from the relationship	• The value-added component can get left behind in the need to deliver the "core contract" • The risk/reward sharing of potential initiatives are often good concepts rarely worked out in advance and are difficult to implement	• Delivery of accountabilities plus planning and executing initiatives
Co-sourced (integrated resources and accountabilities)	• Both parties contribute valuable expertise • Co-location facilitates shared commitment of field staff • Client tends to maintain directional control	• Shared accountability decreases "answerability" • Often means client bears majority of risk • Disengagement turmoil	• Establishing and ensuring shared values when supplier wants profit and the client wants to control costs • Cost savings and overrun sharing
Equity (related entities)	• Shared governance and often board representation • Can facilitate the transition – asset, facility and staff transfers • Both parties receive a return on investment if profitable	• Partners with different agendas – supplier to make profit and client to have low cost • Unwinding equity to cancel contract or vice versa • Makes use of alternative suppliers politically difficult and could be contractually prevented	• Managing the contract as well as the entity or equity investment • Ensuring a balance of political, economic and legal power such that one party is not more dominant than the other

The *Co-sourced* approach, referred to as "cooperative outsourcing" by Millar (1994), is where both parties provide a mix of service labor and assets, and have integrated accountability. Often, these involve co-location of staff and management. The co-sourcing, as well as the equity model described below, have been identified (Drucker, 1995; McFarlan and Nolan, 1995) as major vehicles for business growth, where the parties pair complementary strengths to undertake ventures that neither may have had independently.

Equity relationships are where the parties have some form of shared equity, which is akin to the terms "cross-equity" (Venkatraman, 1997) and "equity-holding" outsourcing (Lacity and Willcocks, 1998), but not the "joint ventures" definition of Dibbern *et al.* (2004) which refers only to joint equity in an IT function spun off by the client organization – see for example Chapter 13. The organization may have an ownership stake in the supplier's entity, the supplier in the organization, or both in each other. Alternatively, they may have shared, but rarely equal, equity in joint venture. On occasion, it may be a related entity providing services to other related entities (e.g., a wholly-owned shared-service subsidiary), although that particular relationship structure has been deemed insourcing by Ang and Cummings (1997). In the-mid 1980s, the equity option was introduced by EDS when it took equity stakes in three large clients, Continental Airlines, First City Bank, and Enron (Dibbern *et al.*, 2004). The approach of the organization taking equity in the supplier proved quite popular in the 1990s. Examples included Delta Airlines in AT&T, Swiss Bank in Perot Systems, Telstra in ISSC/IBM GSA, and Commonwealth Bank in EDS (Cullen and Willcocks, 2003; Dibbern *et al.*, 2004). Most subsequently terminated the equity holding parts of their deals (Lacity and Willcocks, 2009).

Note that "partnering" (Klepper and Jones, 1998; Kern and Willcocks, 2001) is not defined as an option. Partnering is a term expressing a trust-based relationship that parties attempt to engender, not description of the relationship structure (see also Chapters 3 and 4). Trust, and the ability to rely on the other party not behaving opportunistically, is sought in all forms of commercial relationships. Support for excluding a partnering option as a discrete structure is provided by Lacity and Hirschheim (1993) and Hancox and Hackney (1999) who found partnering descriptors were fallacious and at odds with the actual contractual relationship. Rather, "partnering" described negotiation techniques, power balancing, and a collection of intangible characteristics such as compatible cultures.

Testing ITO configuration

In the preceding pages, we have argued that one possible reason for the mixed success and conflicting advice in ITO research is that not all outsourcing is the same. Just as it is not enough to know that a medical patient is sick – because different forms of sickness require different treatments – so it is not enough to know the client firm is involved in outsourcing – because different ITO configurations require different management. This led us to examine the 49 case studies (summarized in Figure 11.1) looking for key differentiators of ITO types that required different types of management. The results of that analysis, including the management issues raised by different configuration choices, have been summarized in Tables 3.9. In essence, these seven tables provide the beginnings of a contingency theory of management of ITO. The theory is that different configuration choices require different management. The purpose of this section is to test whether these seven key attributes are, indeed, important.

Methodology

Tests of the importance of the seven key attributes in classifying different types of outsourcing were conducted using seven additional case studies. These case studies were conducted during 2003 and 2004 in five different industries. They involved contracts signed between 1999 and 2001, with dollar values ranging from AUD $1 million to $133 million per year. The lead author had no prior association with any of the companies in these cases. In each firm, detailed semi-structured interviews totaling 34 hours were conducted with the CIO and the top contract manager by the lead author at the headquarters of each firm. (Two managers per organization were interviewed to reduce reliance on a single source of evidence. The interview questions are attached in Appendix A). The interviews were digitally recorded, manually recorded on the questionnaire form, and then coded into a database. In addition, documents such as contracts, correspondence, and performance evaluations were used to substantiate the interviewee's statements and perceptions.

Results

The following tables summarize the ITO configurations of these seven organizations. Tables 11.10–11.12 are portfolio-level descriptions of Scope, Supplier Grouping, and Financial Scale. Table 11.13 shows all seven attributes for the major deal within each case.

The diversity of these ITO configurations at both the portfolio level and deal level in these seven cases is striking. No case was the same. Each organization had chosen different configuration attribute options. At the portfolio level, Table 11.10 shows a very wide variety of IT services being fully or partially outsourced, Table 11.11 shows a wide mix of choices about supplier groupings, and Table 11.12 shows that the value of outsourcing ranged from $40M up to $400M and the relative percentage of the IT budget was between 10% and 80%. At the individual deal level (where questions were asked about the most important deal in the portfolio), Table 11.13 again shows a wide range of choices. Given this diversity of choices, it is hardly

Table 11.10 Test Cases – Scope Configuration (Portfolio)
(Black areas are insourced)

	Case 1: MAN1	Case 2: SERV1	Case 3: MIN1	Case 4: GOV1	Case 5: GOV2	Case 6: CON1	Case 7: MAN2
Applications							
Development	Full	Partial	Partial	Partial	Partial		
Implementation	Full	Partial	Partial	Consid'g	Partial		
Support & maintenance	Full	Partial	Partial		Partial		
Operations							
Mainframe & servers	Full	Partial	Partial			Full	Full
Data networks (LAN/WAN)	Full	Partial	Partial	Partial		Partial	Full
Desktop	Full		Partial			Full	
Voice networks	Full	Partial	Partial	Partial		Partial	Full
Other		Partial		Full			
Management & Support							
Disaster recovery	Full	Partial	Partial			Partial	Full
Helpdesk	Full	Partial	Partial	Consid'g		Full	
Procurement	Partial		Partial			Partial	
Strategic planning				Partial	Partial		
Systems integration	Full	Full	Partial	Partial	Partial	Partial	
Training	Full	Full	Partial		Partial		Full
Other		Partial			Partial		

Table 11.11 Test Cases – Supplier Grouping (Portfolio)

	Case 1: MAN1	Case 2: SERV1	Case 3: MIN1	Case 4: GOV1	Case 5: GOV2	Case 6: CON1	Case 7: MAN2
# ITO contracts	3	40	12	30	225	12	6
Supplier Grouping							
Sole Supplier	90%		65%	42%	5%	50%	
Prime Contractor						40%	
Best of Breed Suppliers	10%	30%	15%	16%	5%	10%	100%
Multiple Common Suppliers		70%					
Panel			20%	41%	90%		

Table 11.12 Test Cases – Financial Scale Configuration, AUD (Portfolio)

	Case 1: MAN1	Case 2: SERV1	Case 3: MIN1	Case 4: GOV1	Case 5: GOV2	Case 6: CON1	Case 7: MAN2
Annual IT expenditure	$50M	$200M	$400M	$120M	Not tracked	$70M	$40M
% outsourced	80%	35%	55%	61%	10%	60%	25%
Value of outsourcing	$40M	$70M	$220M	$73M	Not tracked	$42M	$10M

Table 11.13 Test Cases – Configuration (Deal)

		Case 1: MAN1	Case 2: SERV1	Case 3: MIN1	Case 4: GOV1	Case 5: GOV2	Case 6: CON1	Case 7: MAN2
(1) Scope Grouping	Service	Whole of IT	Apps development	Whole of IT	Apps development	Note books	All IT except networks & apps	Data center facility, equip, & ops
	Recipient	Parent and subsidiaries	Parent, all units, all subsidiaries	All units, all spin offs	All schools	Parent	Parent and subsidiaries	Parent, subsidiaries optional
	Geographic	National	National	Global	State	State	National	National
(2) Supplier Grouping		Sole	Best of Breed	Prime	Prime	Sole	Sole	Sole
(3) Financial Scale	Relative	80%	15%	33%	26%	Not tracked	23%	25%
	Absolute	$40M	$30M	$133M	$31M	$1M	$16M	$10M
(4) Pricing Framework		Fixed	Unit	Hybrid	Unit	Fixed	Fixed	Fixed
(5) Contract Duration (years)		Fixed (5)	Fixed (5)	Rollover (7+1+1)	Rollover (3+3)	Fixed (1)	Rollover (6+TBD)	Rollover (3+2)
(6) Resource Ownership		Supplier – all	Supplier – labor	Supplier – all	Supplier – labor	Supplier – labor	Supplier – all	Supplier – all
(7) Commercial Relationship		Arms-length	Co-sourcing	Value-add	Arms-length	Co-sourcing	Value-add	Arms-length

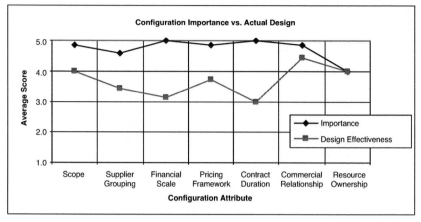

Figure 11.8   Configuration Design Gap

surprising that "one size fits all" advice in the past, on how to manage ITO has been ineffective.

A small amount of quantitative information was collected in the interviews. Using a five-point Likert scale, each interviewee was presented with the information in Tables 11.3–11.9 and for the most important deal in their portfolio, asked (a) about the importance of choosing the configuration option that best suited their management goals, and (b) how appropriate their own organization's choices had been. Results are shown in Figure 11.8, where scores have been averaged across the 14 interviewees. For each of the seven configuration attributes, the upper line shows the importance of getting that configuration choice right, and the lower line shows how effective the organization's actual choices had been. We make two observations about Figure 11.8. First, the scores for importance are all very high; the experienced ITO executives and managers in these cases thought all seven attributes of configuration were very important. Second, the gap between the importance score and effectiveness is an indication that knowledge of the information presented in Tables 11.3–11.9 is sorely needed. No single individual would have configured their deal exactly the same way "had they only known" the implication of the choices.

Conclusion

In the past 20 years, ITO has moved from being a relatively straightforward concept to one that is a complex aggregation of multiple options and permutations (Dibbern *et al.*, 2004; Willcocks and Lacity, 2009). In this chapter, we have argued that because ITO arrangements can be so different, it is a mistake to treat them all as instances of the same phenomenon. We therefore introduced the concept of "configuration" to describe comprehensively the combination of attributes that gives each outsourcing deal, and the ITO portfolio, its distinctive structural traits. In essence, configuration is the starting point for a contingency theory of management of ITO. It is expected that the theory will be built around the proposition that most major problems in ITO are due to agency issues (Jensen and Meckling, 1976; Williamson, 1985) between the client (principal) and supplier (agent) and that different types of ITO arrangements lead to different types of agency problems that require different types of management. It is our belief that if managers are presented with sound, straightforward explanations of the structural choices and related risk and management implications, they will be able to make better decisions, manage appropriately, and achieve better outcomes.

The configuration model we have presented is an instructive way of dis-aggregating structural attributes to provide insight for management as to the rationale, risks and issues inherent in each of the different choices available, and what management must do to make an ITO configuration work. Results from interviews in the seven test cases reinforced that all seven configuration attributes were very important things to get right and the configuration choices their organizations had made were less than optimal. Furthermore, although the model presented here is based on 56 cases from Australia, because the agency issues that cause so many prob-lems for ITO clients and suppliers are common to organizations across the world, it is expected that the framework will be useful in understand-ing outsourcing management in countries with similar economic develop-ment (e.g., North America and Europe). In particular it will be interesting to see other researchers explore further whether particular combinations of options are associated with greater or lesser degrees of ITO success – some-thing we did not find in our own 56 cases.

In fact, while there will inevitably be demand for prescriptions as to the "best ways" of configuring ITO arrangements, and indeed the "best ways" of managing them our study suggests there are no easy answers. The mix of intent, the context for which the deal is being configured, and how well the deal is actually resourced and managed, invariably combine in unique ways, making each total configuration specific to its circumstances. What seems to be critical, therefore, is for a management to have clarity regarding the configuration attributes and how they fit together to meet their specific needs given the prevailing context and resources that can be applied. Also critical is for a management to understand the 31 options available to them and the risks and management issues inherent in each, and in their different combinations. It is our hope that our development of the configuration concept, and our insights into the risks and management issues inherent in each of the options identified, will lead to more effective management and research into outsourcing in the future. We believe the configuration approach to understanding ITO, in all its complexity, is highly promising.

References

Ang, S. and Beath, C. (1993) "Hierarchical Elements in Software Contracts", *Journal of Organizational Computing*, 3, 3, 329–361.

Ang, S. and Cummings, L.L. (1997) "Strategic Response to Institutional Influences on Information Systems Outsourcing", *Organizational Science*, 8, 3, 235–256.

Cross, J. (1995) "IT Outsourcing at British Petroleum", *Harvard Business Review*, May–June, 94–102.

Cullen, S. (2005) *Outsourcing IT and Services: Research Into Lifecycle, Configuration and Success*, PHD Thesis, University of Melbourne, Melbourne.

Cullen, S. and Seddon, P.B. (2004) "Configuration: An Important Concept for Understanding IT Outsourcing", *Pacific-Asia Conference on Information Systems*. Summer, Hong Kong.

Cullen, S. and Willcocks, L.P. (2003) *Intelligent IT Outsourcing: Eight Building Blocks to Success*, Elsevier, Chichester.

Cullen, S., Seddon, P.B. and Willcocks, L.P. (2005) "Managing Outsourcing: The Lifecycle Imperative", *MIS Quarterly Executive*, 4, 1, April, 229–246.

Cullen, S., Willcocks, L.P. and Seddon, P.B. (2001) *Information Technology Outsourcing Practices in Australia*, Deloitte Touche Tohmatsu, Sydney.

Currie, W.L. (1996) "Outsourcing in the Private and Public Sectors: An Unpredictable IT Strategy", *European Journal of Information Systems*, 4, 4, 226–236.

Currie, W.L. (1998) "Using Multiple Suppliers to Mitigate the Risk of IT Outsourcing at ICI and Wessex Water", *Journal of Information Technology*, 13, 169–180.

Deloitte (2005) *Calling a Change in the Outsourcing Market*. Deloitte Development LLC, http://www.deloitte.com/dtt/cda/doc/content/us outsourcing_callingachange.pdf April.

Dibbern, J., Goles, T., Hirschheim, R. and Jayatilaka, B. (2004) "Information Systems Outsourcing: A Survey and Analysis of the Literature", *ACM Data Base*, 35, 4, 6–102.

Domberger, S., Fernandez, P. and Fiebeg, D. (2000) "Modelling the Price, Performance and Contract Characteristics of IT Outsourcing", *Journal of Information Technology*, 15, 2, 107–118.

Drucker, P. (1995) "The Network Society", *The Wall Street Journal*, March 29, A14.

Dyer, J. (2000) *Collaborative Advantage: Winning through Extended Enterprise Supplier Networks*, Oxford University Press, New York.

Earl, M. (1996) "The Risks of Outsourcing IT", *Sloan Management Review*, 37, 3, 26–32.

Earls, A. (2004) "End of the Affair: Bringing Outsourced Operations Back in-house", *Computerworld*, May 31, p. 35.

Feeny, D., Lacity, M. and Willcocks, L. (2005) "Taking The Measure Of Outsourcing Service Providers", *Sloan Management Review*, 46, 3, 41–48.

Gallivan, M.J. and Oh, W. (1999) "Analyzing IT Outsourcing Relationships as Alliances among Multiple Clients and Vendors", *Proceedings of the 32nd Annual Hawaii International Conference on Systems Sciences*. HICSS, Hawaii.

Hancox, M. and Hackney, R. (1999) "Information Technology Outsourcing: Conceptualizing Practice in the Public and Private Sector", *Proceedings of the 32nd Annual Hawaii International Conference on Systems Sciences*. HICSS, Hawaii.

Hirschheim, R.A. and Lacity, M.J. (2000) "The Myths and Realities of Information Technology Outsourcing", *Communications of the ACM*, 43, 2, 99–107.

Hui, P.P. and Beath, C.M. (2002) "The IT Sourcing Process: A Framework for Research". Working Paper, University of Texas at Austin, Texas.

Humphry, R. (2000) *Review of the Whole of Government Information Technology Outsourcing Initiative*, Commonwealth of Australia, Sydney, December.

Jensen, M.C. and Meckling, W. (1976) "Theory of the Firm: Managerial Behavior, Agency Costs and Ownership Structure", *Journal of Financial Economics*, 4, 305–360.

Kern, T. and Willcocks, L.P. (2001) *The Relationship Advantage: Information Technologies, Sourcing, and Management*, Oxford University Press, Oxford.

Klepper, R. and Jones, W.O. (1998) *Outsourcing Information Technology Systems & Services*, Prentice Hall, New Jersey.

Knolmayer, G. (2002) "Cybermediaries Supporting the Management of Independent Workers: A Case Study of Extended Outsourcing Relationships", in Hirschheim, R.A., Heinzl, A. and Dibbern J. *et al.* (eds). *Information Systems Outsourcing: Enduring Themes, Emergent Patterns, and Future Directions*, Springer-Verlag, New York.

Lacity, M.C. and Hirschheim, R.A. (1993) *Information Systems Outsourcing: Myths, Metaphors, and Realities*, Wiley, New York.

Lacity, M. and Rottman, J. (2007) *The Offshore Outsourcing of IT Work*, Palgrave, London.

Lacity, M.C., Willcocks, L.P. and Feeny, D. (1996) "The Value of Selective Sourcing", *Sloan Management Review*, Spring 13–25.

Lacity, M.C. and Willcocks, L.P. (1998) "An Empirical Investigation of Information Technology Sourcing Practices: Lessons from Experience", *Management Information Systems Quarterly*, 22, 3, September, 363–408.

Lacity, M.C. and Willcocks, L.P. (2001) *Global IT Outsourcing: In Search Of Business Advantage*, Wiley, Chichester.

Lacity, M. and Willcocks, L. (2009) *Information Systems and Outsourcing: Studies in Theory and Practice*, Palgrave, London.

Lacity, M., Willcocks, L. and Feeny, D. (1996) "The Value of Selective IT Sourcing", *Sloan Management Review*, 37, 3, Spring, pp. 13–25.

Lee, J-N., Miranda, S.M. and Kim, Y-M. (2004) "IT Outsourcing Strategies: Universalistic, Contingency, and Configurational Explanations of Success", *Information Systems Research*, 15, 2, 110–131.

Loh, L. and Venkatraman, N. (1992) "Determinants of Information Technology Outsourcing: A Cross-Sectional Analysis", *Journal of Management Information Systems*, 9, 1, Summer, 7–24.

Loh, Lawrence and Venkatraman, N. (1995) "An Empirical Study of Information Technology Outsourcing: Benefits, Risks, and Performance Implications". *Proceedings of the 16th International Conference on Information Systems*, Amsterdam 277–288.

Marcolin, B.L. and McLellan, K.L. (1998) "Effective IT Outsourcing Arrangements", *Proceedings of the 31st Annual Hawaii International Conference on System Sciences*. HICSS, Hawaii, 654–665.

McFarlan, F.W. and Nolan, R.L. (1995) "How to Manage an IT Outsourcing Alliance", *Sloan Management Review*, 4, 9–23.

Millar, V. (1994) "Outsourcing Trends", *Proceedings of the Outsourcing, Cosourcing and Insourcing Conference*, University of California-Berkeley, California.

Mintzberg, H. and Lampel, J. (1999) "Reflecting on the Strategy Process", *Sloan Management Review*, 40, 3, 21–30.

Quinn, J.B., Doorley, T. and Paquette, P. (1990) "Beyond Products: Services-Based Strategy", *Harvard Business Review*, March–April, 58–67.

Rottman, J. and Lacity, M. (2005) "Twenty Practices for Offshore Outsourcing", *MISQ Executive* 3, 3, 117–130.

Rouse, A.C. and Corbitt, B. (2003) "Revisiting IT Outsourcing Risks: Analysis of a survey of Australia's Top 1000 organizations", *14th Australasian Conference on Information Systems*, Perth, 1–11.

Sambamurthy, V., Straub, D.W. and Watson, R.T. (2001) "Information Technology Managing in the Digital Era", in Dickson, G.W. and DeSanctis, G. (eds) *Information Technology and the Future Enterprise, New Models for Managers*, NJ: Prentice Hall, 281–305.

Venkatraman, N. (1997) "Beyond Outsourcing: Managing IT Resources as a Value Center", *Sloan Management Review*, 38, 3, 51–64.

Willcocks, L.P. and Cullen, S. (2005) *The Outsourcing Enterprise: A CEO Agenda Briefing*, LogicaCMG, London.

Willcocks, L. and Lacity, M. (2009) *Research Studies in Information Technology Outsourcing: Perspectives, Practices and Globalization.* Volume 1 – Making IT Outsourcing Decisions; Volume 2 – Managing Outsourcing Relationships; Volume 3 – Global Outsourcing: Issues and Trends, Sage, London.

Willcocks, L., Petherbridge, P. and Olson, N. (2003) *Making IT Count: Strategy, Delivery, Infrastructure*, Butterworth Heinemann, Oxford.

Williamson, O.E. (1985) *The Economic Institutions of Capitalism: Firms, Markets, Relational Contracting*, The Free Press, New York.

Appendix A   Structured Interview Questions
Sourcing Decisions (refer Table 10)

Please tick the best description of your organization's sourcing decision	Fully outsourced	Partially outsourced	Considering outsourcing	Rejected outsourcing	Not considered	N/A
Applications						
a. Development	O	O	O	O	O	O
b. Implementation	O	O	O	O	O	O
c. Support & maintenance	O	O	O	O	O	O
d. Other _____	O	O	O	O	O	O
Operations						
a. Mainframe & servers	O	O	O	O	O	O
b. Data networks (LAN/WAN)	O	O	O	O	O	O
c. Desktop	O	O	O	O	O	O
d. Voice networks	O	O	O	O	O	O
e. Other _____	O	O	O	O	O	O
Management & Support						
a. Disaster recovery	O	O	O	O	O	O
b. Helpdesk	O	O	O	O	O	O
c. Procurement	O	O	O	O	O	O
d. Strategic planning	O	O	O	O	O	O
e. Systems integration	O	O	O	O	O	O
f. Training	O	O	O	O	O	O
g. Other _____	O	O	O	O	O	O

Supplier grouping (refer Table 11)

How many IT outsourcing contracts does your organization currently have?   _____# contracts

Percent covered by supplier structure (in terms of outsourcing spend)

a. Sole Supplier – one supplier without any subcontracting   _____%
b. Prime Contractor – one supplier that subcontracts   _____%
c. Best of Breed Multiple Suppliers – several suppliers   _____%
d. Panel – pool of suppliers "on call"   _____%
e. Other _____   _____%
          100%

Expenditure (refer Table 12)

What is the approximate total annual IT expenditure (in millions)?	$_____ IT spend
What percent of the IT expenditure is currently outsourced?	_____% outsourced

Appendix A   Structured Interview Questions – *continued*
Sourcing Decisions (refer Table 10)

Deal-Level Configuration (refer Table 13)

(1) Service Scope: what services are in the scope of this contract?

Applications		Operations		Management/Support	
a. Development	○	a. Mainframe & servers	○	a. Disaster recovery	○
b. Implementation	○	b. Desktop	○	b. Helpdesk	○
c. Support & maintenance	○	c. Networks – Data (LAN/WAN)	○	c. Procurement	○
d. Other _____	○	d. Networks – Voice	○	d. Strategic planning	○
		e. Other _____	○	e. Systems integration	○
				f. Training	○
				g. Other _____	○

Recipient Scope: what business groups are in the scope of this contract? _____

Geographic Scope: what is the geographic coverage of this contract? _____

(2) Supplier grouping: what predominant supplier structure does the contract have in place?
a. Sole Supplier
b. Prime Contractor
c. Best of Breed Suppliers
d. Panel
e. Other _____

(3) Financial Scale: What is the approximate per annum value of the contract?
$_____ pa

(4) Pricing framework: what price structure is the contract predominately using?
a. Fixed lump sum price
b. Unit price
c. Cost based (actual cost + markup or + management fee)
d. Other _____

(5) Duration
a. What is the initial term of the contract? _____ years
b. How many times can the contract be rolled over (extended)? _____ occasions
c. For what length of term? ____ year terms

(6) Resource ownership structure: what resource ownership split is in place?

	Organization	Supplier(s)	Other
a. Who owns the data center facilities?	○	○	○ _____
b. Who owns the IT assets?	○	○	○ _____
c. Who owns the service delivery labor?	○	○	○ _____

(7) Commercial relationship: what predominant relationship structure is in place?
a. Arms-length – separate resources and equity
b. Value-add – arms-length with significant strategic initiatives (i.e. joint R&D, joint marketing)
c. Co-sourcing – commingled resources between the separate parties
d. Shared equity – the separate parties own equity in each other
e. Joint venture – the parties own shared equity in a separate service delivery entity

12
IT Outsourcing Success: A Framework for Assessing Intentions and Outcomes

Sara Cullen, Peter Seddon and Leslie Willcocks

Introduction

This chapter proposes and demonstrates the usefulness of a new conceptualization of information technology outsourcing (ITO) success. Based on results from three ITO surveys conducted during 1994–2000, a review of the literature, and data from 49 in-depth ITO cases, it is argued that although some organizations may, at times, seek outcomes from outsourcing similar to other organizations, fundamentally what each firm seeks from outsourcing is different. Accordingly, it is argued, studies that recognize the idiosyncratic and changing nature of outcomes sought are likely to offer greater insight into what comprises successful outsourcing. Developing this idea, the chapter proposes an ITO outcomes framework consisting of a list of 25 goals that organizations frequently pursue when outsourcing IT. The list reflects most goals pursued by most organizations, but only some of these goals are expected to be applicable to any given organization at any given time.

Our key argument is that ITO success should be assessed by, first, asking organizations to nominate the outcomes that were/are most important to them at various times in the life of the contract, then second, gauging the extent to which each organization has achieved its nominated outcomes during the period when those outcomes were being pursued. The usefulness of the framework is assessed using seven in-depth case studies and a 2007 survey with responses from 56 large organizations. The results from these 63 organizations show that (a) all 25 goals were considered "applicable" by at least 20% of these organizations, (b) no organization set out to achieve all 25 goals, (c) the goals pursued changed with time, and (d) no important goals were missing (except, perhaps, relationships). It is therefore suggested that the instrument presented in Appendix A is a useful tool for future research into ITO success.

Despite over decade of research into ITO, the dependent variable for much ITO research, ITO success, is surprisingly under-researched. In their comprehensive reviews of the literature, Hui and Beath (2002) and Dibbern *et al.*

(2004) attribute disparate conclusions on ITO success, at least in part, to the lack of an accepted success construct. Supporting this view, Lee *et al.* (1999, 2004) – who used the Grover *et al.* (1996) instrument to measure ITO success – suggest that metrics of success need further development: *"As outsourcing grows in complexity, researchers need to develop more sophisticated metrics to assess the success of outsourcing ventures"*.

One of the key issues concerning the ITO success construct is whether a certain outcome, e.g., cost savings, is desirable and therefore applicable to every outsourcing initiative, or whether ITO success is so idiosyncratic that one must assess it against each organization's own, different, criteria. Dibbern *et al.* (2004), for instance, argue that ITO is such a complex phenomenon that *context* plays a much more significant role in ITO than in other areas of IS success measurement. They further argue that expectations, and their realization, are critical to any research into ITO success and are more closely tied to predefined criteria and actual results. Echoing this view, Lacity *et al.* (1996) report that the criteria that drove an organization's perception of success varied between organizations, and elsewhere Lacity and Willcocks (2001) explicitly recognize that outcomes are more appropriately assessed relative to each organization's goals rather than assuming that all organizations want the same things to the same degree (e.g., cost savings).

Unrecognized in most of the literature is that outcomes sought from outsourcing have a temporal dimension, as well as varying from organization to organization. Only two studies by King and Malhotra (2000) and Hui and Beath (2002) explicitly recognize the temporal nature of an organization's outsourcing goals. In both these studies, short-term outcomes were defined as operational, mid-term as tactical and learning, and long-term as strategic. However, associating a particular outcome to a time-period for benefit realization does not recognize the fact that organizations' operational, tactical, and even strategic goals for outsourcing may change over the life of the contract.

In response to these three concerns, i.e., prior researchers' arguments that (a) further work is required to refine the ITO success construct, (b) what constitutes ITO success may differ from organization to organization, and (c) organizational goals for ITO change over time, the objective of this study is to provide a comprehensive framework for conceptualizing and assessing ITO success. To demonstrate the contribution of our framework, we compare it to what we regard as the best instrument currently available for measuring ITO success, namely that of Grover *et al.* (1996).[1] We identify some difficulties with their framework and provide a solution to those difficulties in the form of the new instrument in Appendix A. The contributions of this study are the new conceptual framework; the evidence that different organizations do seek

---

[1]In July 2007, Google Scholar reported 164 citations to the Grover *et al.* (1996) paper.

different outcomes from outsourcing; the evidence that these goals change over time; the insight that satisfaction is a valid perceptual measure of ITO success because it draws on the respondent's goals, not on some researcher's pre-defined list; and the ITO Success measurement instrument presented in Appendix A that is constructed around these insights. Use of the new conceptual framework proposed in this study will, we hope, help future researchers build better theories to explain why some outsourcing projects are more successful than others.

New conceptual frameworks correspond to what Gregor (2006) calls Analysis theories. Gregor's criteria for evaluating Analysis theory are as follows:

> If any classification system is developed, implicit claims are that the classification system is useful in aiding analysis in some way, that the category labels and groupings are meaningful and natural, and that hierarchies of classification are appropriate (most important divisions are shown at the highest level). The logic for the placement of phenomena into categories should be clear, as should the characteristics that define each category. In addition, important categories or elements should not be omitted from the classification system, that is, it should be complete and exhaustive. A previous classification system could be revised as new entities come to light, or some preferable way of grouping or naming categories is identified. A judgement as to the degree to which the theory satisfies these criteria allows one to assess the contribution to knowledge. (p. 264)

In this study, we attempt to satisfy all the above criteria for making a successful contribution to an Analysis theory of ITO Success measurement. In addition, however, the current study offers more than just a *taxonomy* of different possible types of outcome from IT outsourcing. Our framework also embodies the important insight that not all organizations pursue all possible outcomes listed in the framework. This means that in assessing ITO success, each respondent must first indicate which goals were important to his/her organization at the time of interest, then ITO success should be evaluated in terms of the achievement of *those* goals, not the achievement of all possible goals.

To present our case for the validity and usefulness of this new ITO success framework, we proceed as follows. First, the framework is presented and justified in Section 2. Second, in Section 3, the usefulness of the framework is assessed using data from (a) seven in-depth case studies conducted during 2003 and 2004, and (b) 56 responses from a 2007 survey of large organizations with ICT outsourcing contracts. Finally, some further justification of the framework is presented in the Discussion section, Section 4, along with a discussion of the generalizability of the empirical findings from Section 3.

A framework for assessing ITO success

Table 12.1 contains what we claim is a comprehensive (25-point) list of the most commonly intended outcomes from ITO. It represents a collective view of the goals of many organizations (as opposed to any single organization). As mentioned earlier, a research instrument for assessing ITO success based on this framework is presented in Appendix A.

The method proposed for using this instrument is to:

a. ask interviewees or survey respondents which of the 25 possible outcomes are (i) applicable to their organization, (ii) initial primary intended outcomes, (iii) current primary intended outcomes, and (iv) future primary intended outcomes;
b. ask them to identify any other primary intended outcomes not in the list of 25;
c. ask them to score on a Likert scale the extent to which those outcomes have been achieved; and
d. if comparison with ICTO success in other organizations is intended, calculate an average score for intended outcomes at the relevant time in the life of the contract.

The rationale for using the above method for measuring ITO success is that the success of an organization's outsourcing endeavors should be assessed against its own goals for the project, not in terms of some researcher-assumed goals. By contrast, our benchmark nine-item instrument from Grover *et al.* (1996) (a) assumes that its nine items are applic-able in *all* situations, and (b) does not ask about outcomes such as obtaining value for money, cost savings, and improved service quality, that (i) have been argued by authors such as Domberger (1998) and Domberger *et al.* (2000) to be fundamental reasons for outsourcing, and (ii) are the goals most frequently checked by respondents to our survey (reported below) as goals applicable to their organizations. Since a respondent's *Satisfaction with ITO* will be assessed against whichever goals are important to that respondent, we accept that any sensible question about satisfaction with ITO, such as Grover *et al.*'s question 9: "We are satisfied with our overall benefits from out-sourcing", will always yield a valid perceptual indication of ITO success (no matter which goals the organization has decided to pursue, nor how much such goals have changed since the inception of the deal). What distinguishes our measure is that we do not accept that it is valid to assume that the eight remaining questions in the Grover *et al.* (1996) instrument are always applicable to all respondents.

Table 12.1 ITO Outcomes and References[2]

Value for Money	Other Research Studies that have Discussed this Goal
1. Demonstrable value for money	Fowler and Jeffs (1998), McAulay *et al.* (2002), Hui and Beath (2002)
2. Market price under internal cost	Mylott (1995), Apte and Sobol (1997), Klepper and Jones (1998), Fowler and Jeffs (1998), Lacity and Willcocks (2001), McAulay *et al.* (2002), Dibbern *et al.* (2004)

Improved Financial Results	
3. Ongoing cost reduction	Apte and Sobol (1997), Lacity and Willcocks (2001), McAulay *et al.* (2002), Lee *et al.* (1999, 2004)
4. Stabilize and predict costs	Mylott (1995), **Grover et al. (1996) Q.6**, Apte and Sobol (1997), Klepper and Jones (1998), Hurley and Costa (2001)
5. Means of financing assets	Apte and Sobol (1997), Klepper and Jones (1998)
6. Convert capital to operating expense	Cross (1995), Mylott (1998), Klepper and Jones (1998), Lacity and Willcocks (2001), Hurley and Costa (2001), Lee *et al.* (2004)
7. Aggregate total demand for economies	Mylott (1995), **Grover et al. (1996) Q.4&5**, Klepper and Jones (1998), Fowler and Jeffs (1998)
8. Cash for sale of assets	Mylott (1995), McFarlan and Nolan (1995), Klepper and Jones (1998), Lee *et al.* (2004)
9. Reduce staff numbers	Mylott (1995), Fowler and Jeffs (1998), McAulay *et al.* (2002)
10. Rationalize/consolidate assets	Fowler and Jeffs (1998), Lacity and Willcocks (1998)
11. Remedy for poor performance	Cullen (2004)

Improved Operations	Other research studies that have discussed this goal
12. Improve service	Fowler and Jeffs (1998), Domberger *et al.* (2000), Lacity and Willcocks (2001), Hurley and Costa (2001), McAulay *et al.* (2002), Dibbern *et al.* (2004)
13. Obtain services not available internally	Klepper and Jones (1998), McAulay *et al.* (2002)
14. Improve discipline/accountability	Lacity and Willcocks (2001)
15. Obtain better/more expertise	Mylott (1995), **Grover et al. (16) Q.2&3**, Apte and Sobol (1997), Klepper and Jones (1998), Fowler and Jeffs (1998), Lacity and Willcocks (2001), Hurley and Costa (2001), McAulay *et al.* (2002), Lee *et al.* (2004)

[2]Items in bold correspond to those in Grover *et al.*'s (1996) ITO success measure [16], discussed later.

Table 12.1   ITO Outcomes and References *– continued*

Value for Money	Other Research Studies that have Discussed this Goal
16. More flexible work practices	Fowler and Jeffs (1998), McAulay *et al.* (2002)
17. Align resource supply to demand/ minimize capacity gap	Cheon *et al.* (1995), Mylott (1995), Apte and Sobol (1997), Klepper and Jones (1998), Hurley and Costa (2001), Lee *et al.* (2004)
18. Obtain better/more technology	Mylott (1995), **Grover *et al.* (1996) Q.7&8**, Apte and Sobol (1997), Klepper and Jones (1998), Fowler and Jeffs (1998), Hurley and Costa (2001), McAulay *et al.* (2002), Lee *et al.* (2004)
19. Standardize technology	**Grover *et al.* (1996) Q.5**, Lacity and Willcocks (2001), McAulay *et al.* (2002)
20. Standardize services	Lacity and Willcocks (2001), McAulay *et al.* (2002)

Strategic Outcomes	Other research studies that have discussed this goal
21. Concentrate on core business	Quinn and Hilmer (1994), Mylott (1995), **Grover *et al.* (1996) Q.1**, Fowler and Jeffs (1998), Quinn *et al.* (1990), Klepper and Jones (1998), Hurley and Costa (2001), Lee *et al.* (2004)
22. Refocus internal IT staff on high value/strategic activities	**Grover *et al.* (1996) Q.1**, Apte and Sobol (1997), Klepper and Jones (1998), Fowler and Jeffs (1998), Lacity and Willcocks (2001), McAulay *et al.* (2002), Lee *et al.* (2004)
23. Contribute to business	Klepper and Jones (1998), Hurley and Costa (2001), Lacity and Willcocks (2001), Hui and Beath (2002)
24. Access to best practices, new developments	Mylott (1995), Klepper and Jones (1998), **Grover *et al.* (1996) Q.3&8**, Fowler and Jeffs (1998), Lacity and Willcocks (2001), McAulay *et al.* (33)
25. Industry development	Lacity and Willcocks (2001)

Developing the 25-point list of possible intended outcomes

The following process was used for developing the list of possible intended outcomes in Table 12.1. First, the framework builds on answers to questions on ex-ante goals and ex-post outcomes from outsourcing in a series of three surveys on ITO conducted in 1994, 1997, and 2000 (described in

Cullen *et al.*, 2000, 2005). During the course of those surveys, the list of outcomes evolved from seven in the 1994 survey, to 15 in 1997, to 21 in 2000. Each successive survey incorporated lessons from open items from the prior surveys (e.g., respondents were always invited to suggest additional outcomes sought not in the lists provided) and new ideas from the literature. For instance, the 2000 survey had been compared and reconciled with the 12 goals from the Lacity and Willcocks (2001) survey.

Second, the list of 21 commonly pursued ITO outcomes from the 2000 survey was refined into 25 by the lead author, based on (a) a review of the literature, and (b) a thorough analysis of 49 case studies of ITO projects. With respect to these case studies, the lead author had participated as a senior outsourcing consultant in 49 ITO projects spanning 51 countries during 1994–2002, and had detailed first-hand knowledge of the 49 cases. (A list of the types of organization and year of each project is documented in Cullen, 2004). Working documents reviewed for each project included plans, contracts, reports, evaluations, correspondence, presentations, minutes, reviews, and audit reports. The process involved scanning these documents for each of the 49 projects looking for additional outsourcing goals not already covered in the framework.

Third, to ensure that we built on the insights of prior researchers, the 25 outcomes were compared to goals and outcomes reported in the ITO literature. For each of the 25 possible outcomes identified in this study, prior studies that have discussed that outcome are summarized in the right-hand column in Table 12.1. Not all studies used the same terms, so there is not an exact one-to-one mapping, but the underlying concepts are similar. In particular, we tried to identify indicators of ITO success that were not in our list. As one might expect, Table 12.1 shows that although no prior study has reported all 25 outcomes, each outcome other than the eleventh (remedy for poor performance) has been discussed in at least one study by prior researchers.

Finally, as with the Grover *et al.* (1996) study which grouped items into the three categories, the 25 outcomes were grouped into what we think are four conceptually distinct categories. According to Gregor (2006) in an Analysis-theory paper: *"The logic for the placement of phenomena into categories should be clear, as should the characteristics that define each category"*. We compare our categorization scheme to that of Grover *et al.* (1996) in Table 12.2. Grover *et al.*'s three categories correspond almost exactly to the three most important "primary reasons for outsourcing" reported by Saunders *et al.* (1997, p. 70), namely, technological considerations, cost savings, and strategic considerations. The reason for advancing our alternative to Grover *et al.*'s and Saunders *et al.*'s categorization is that, as Domberger (1998) suggests, outsourcing is only worth doing if the net cost to the client organization drops as a result of outsourcing, subject to the proviso that there is no drop in service quality. This suggests that two key constructs in assessing ITO success are *service quality* and *cost*.

In our framework, the first construct, success in meeting the client organization's *service* goals is assessed using the group of questions headed "Improved Operations" in Table 12.1. Meeting such service goals seems to be a more fundamental objective than achieving Grover *et al.*'s (1996) and Saunders *et al.*'s (1997) "Technological benefits", which are (one hopes) a source of improved service outcomes. Second, success in meeting the client organization's *cost* goals is assessed using the group of questions headed "Improved Financial Results" in Table 12.1. This is similar to Grover *et al.*'s (1996) Economic success category (and Saunders *et al.*'s (1997) Cost Savings, but it also includes the notion of improved financial control, which does not necessarily imply cost savings. Third, our "Value for money" category then assesses the organization's success in balancing these service and cost objectives. There is no counterpart for this "value for money" construct in the Grover *et al.* instrument, but it has been mentioned by Fowler and Jeffs (1998), McAulay *et al.* (2002), and Hui and Beath (2002). If one wanted a single measure of ITO success, Value for money would seem to be a good candidate. Finally, our "Strategic" category is very similar to that of Grover *et al.* (1996); it is concerned with whether outsourcing helps the client organization to focus on its core business.

In short, based on the process summarized above, it is argued that the 25-point ITO outcomes framework in Table 12.1 provides a comprehensive summary of most types of benefits that organizations have typically sought to achieve from ITO. The final list is not intended to represent all possible goals that every organization may have for ITO – only those that were

Table 12.2   Comparing Success Categories in this Study with Those from Grover *et al.* [16]

Outcome Categories Proposed in this Study		Grover *et al.*'s (1996) ITO Success Categories	
Category	Definition	Category*	Definition (p. 93)
Value for money	Value for money	Economic	"utilize expertise and economies of scale" "to manage its cost structure"
Improved Financial Results	Cost reduction and stability		
Improved Operations	Improved service, including access to new and better technology	Technological	"gain access to leading-edge IT"
Strategic focus	Focus on the core business	Strategic	"enable a firm to on its core business"

*Note: This is a conceptual classification, not one backed by empirical evidence. In Grover *et al.*'s factor analysis, reported in their Table 3, p. 102, all eight factors loaded on the one construct.

observed regularly. For example, excluded from the framework was the possible desired outcome of transferring public-sector staff to the private sector. This was a unique and infrequent government-specific goal. Another example possible desired outcome also excluded from the framework was obtaining non-unionized labor. This was only applicable to organizations in a troubled unionized environment.

Different organizations pursue different outcomes from IT outsourcing

In assessing ITO success, it is important to understand that only some of the 25 goals from Table 12.1 are likely to be pursued in any given outsourcing deal. This is particularly apparent when one examines results from the 2000 survey (Cullen *et al.*, 2000) which had 235 responses from large organizations where 17 goals from the 25 in Table 12.1 were included in that survey. As shown in Table 12.3, each of the 17 goals from the 2000 survey was a primary reason for outsourcing for *some* organizations whilst being *not applicable* for others. In short, based on results from both the 2000 survey (and the 49 case studies), it is clear that ITO success measurement *must* recognize that different organizations pursue different goals in different deals. This is why using a "one size fits all" approach to ITO success measurement is inappropriate.

According to Gregor (2006) the contribution of an Analysis-theory paper is assessed by considering the extent to which its new classification scheme is different to, and more helpful than, the old one. To enable such a comparison, the first eight items from the Grover *et al.* (1996) instrument are also shown in column 6 in Table 12.3. (The ninth question, quoted earlier, which asked about overall satisfaction is not considered further because it does not appear in Grover *et al.*'s subsequent analysis, e.g., see their Table 12.3). Comparing columns 1 and 6 in our Table 12.3 it is apparent that there is no clear match in the Grover *et al.* instrument for thirteen questions in column 1, yet as shown in columns 2 and 3, considerable numbers of respondents indicated that these outcomes were of primary or secondary interest to their organizations. For example, there is no clear match in the Grover *et al.* (1996) instrument for question 3 "Ongoing cost reduction", or question 12 "Improve service", or question 13 "Obtain services not available internally", yet as shown in column 2, many respondents indicated that these were primary reasons that their organizations entered into outsourcing contracts. In addition, there are some questions in the Grover *et al.* instrument that are not relevant to some organizations. For example, in response to question 18 "Obtain better/more technology", 41 of 185 organizations that answered this question indicated in column 4 that this was not a primary or secondary goal for their organization, yet Grover *et al.* ask two questions (7 and 8) about this outcome. Likewise, in response to question 21 "Concentrate on core business", 44 of 190 organizations indicated that this was not a primary or secondary goal for their

Table 12.3 Desired ITO Outcomes from the Lead Author's Survey [Anon3] Matching Table 12.1 and Items from the Grover *et al.*'s [16] ITO Success Instrument

Outcome (Numbered to Correspond to Table 12.1)	Primary Reason	Secondary Reason	Not Applic.	Total	Grover *et al.* (1996)
(Column 1)	(Col. 2)	(Col. 3)	(Col. 4)	(Col. 5)	(Col. 6)
3. Ongoing cost reduction	52	57	81	190	
4. *Stabilize and predict costs**					6. We have increased control of IS expenses
6. Convert capital to operating expense	24	45	112	181	
7. *Aggregate total demand for economies**					4. We have enhanced economies of scale in human resources 5. We have enhanced economies of scale in technological resources
8. Cash for sale of assets	3	17	161	181	
9. Reduce staff numbers	25	57	100	182	
10. Rationalize/ consolidate assets	29	40	112	181	
11.Remedy for poor performance	6	21	154	181	
12. Improve service	64	65	56	185	
13. Obtain services not available internally	94	44	54	192	
14. Improve discipline/ accountability	25	69	89	183	
15. Obtain better/ more expertise	115	61	17	193	2. We have enhanced our IT competence 3. We have increased access to skilled personnel
16. More flexible work practices	40	54	88	182	
17. Align resource supply to demand/minimize capacity gap	71	60	53	184	

Table 12.3 Desired ITO Outcomes from the Lead Author's Survey [Anon3] Matching Table 12.1 and Items from the Grover *et al.*'s [16] ITO Success Instrument – *continued*

Outcome (Numbered to Correspond to Table 12.1)	Primary Reason	Secondary Reason	Not Applic.	Total	Grover *et al.* (1996)
(Column 1)	(Col. 2)	(Col. 3)	(Col. 4)	(Col. 5)	(Col. 6)
18. Obtain better/ more technology	69	75	41	185	7. We have reduced the risk of technological obsolescence 8. We have increased access to key information technologies
21. Concentrate on core business	83	63	44	190	1. We have been able to refocus on our core business
22. Refocus internal IT staff on high value/ strategic activities	66	69	51	186	1. We have been able to refocus on our core business
23. Contribute to business	31	61	87	179	
24. *Access to best practices, new developments**					3. We have increased access to skilled personnel 8. We have increased access to key information technologies
25. Industry development	18	30	130	178	

* Item from Table 12.1 *not* included in the 2000 survey, but which matches a question from Grover *et al.* [16]

organization. In proposing the new framework in this chapter, our argument is simply that if an organization does not set out to achieve a particular goal, it does not make sense to evaluate ITO success by asking if they have achieved a good outcome in respect of that non-desired goal.

It is this conditional nature of the various possible outcomes from Table 12.1 that creates difficulties for conventional approaches to instrument development. For example, column 4 in Table 12.3 shows that not all items apply to all organizations. This means it is not possible to use conventional first- or second-generation factor-analytic techniques to refine the list of

25 items into an instrument for measuring ITO success or even to help in grouping them as we have done in Table 12.2. Instead, we had to rely on human judgment to group items that seemed similar under the four headings in Table 12.1, i.e., Value for money, Improved Financial Results, Improved Operations, and Strategic outcomes.

Desired outcomes also change over time

In addition to recognizing that different organizations pursue different goals for ITO in different deals, it is also important when assessing ITO success to understand that the outcomes sought from ITO change over time, even for the one deal. Management may start out with quite ambitious goals for an outsourcing project, encounter problems, then focus on some more targeted, but more achievable, goals for their ITO deal. Since perceptions of success will normally be gauged relative to current goals, it is suggested that in asking managers to identify intended outcomes, care should be taken to distinguish between at least three types of intended outcome, namely: (1) initial primary intended outcomes – the focus at the outset of the deal; (2) current primary intended outcomes – the current focus of the deal; and (3) future primary intended outcomes – the future focus of the deal.

Assessing the completeness of the framework

The preceding section has presented a framework that corresponds to what Gregor (2006) describes as an Analysis theory of ITO success measurement. The framework is the list of 25 types of outcome shown in Table 12.1, grouped into four categories as defined in Table 12.2, plus the argument that because different organizations pursue different goals at different times, ITO success should normally be assessed against the currently sought goals of each individual organization. The usefulness of this theory is assessed empirically in this section. The first half of this section uses seven in-depth case studies as its source of data. The second half uses 56 responses from a survey (plus results from the seven case studies) to extend that assessment to a broader range of organizations.

The cases

A case-study methodology was the technique chosen for our first assessment of both the completeness of the framework in Table 12.1, and the extent to which outcomes sought had changed over time. The questions were: (a) Were any common objectives missing from the list in Table 12.1? (b) Which objectives motivated your organization to engage in outsourcing? and (c) Are those objectives still relevant today? For these case studies, in 2003 we invited 14 of the 100 largest IT-using organizations in one State to participate in the study. Seven of the 14 organizations accepted; each became the subject of a case study. Unlike the 49 ITO case studies used in constructing the ITO-outcomes framework in Table 12.1, the lead author

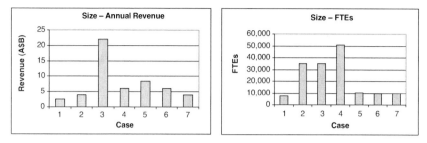

Figure 12.1   Test Cases – Organization Size

had no prior association with any of the organizations in these cases. The seven participating organizations were from five different industries comprising communications and transport services, manufacturing, mining, government and conglomerates of multiple industries. The size of the seven organizations ranged from US$2B to US$22B in per annum revenue and from 7,800 to 51,000 employees as shown in Figure 12.1.

Guided by Lacity and Hirschheim's (1993) observation that much of the ITO literature tends to be over optimistic because the evaluation is often too early in the agreement, i.e., during the "honeymoon period", it was decided to focus on a major contract in each of these seven organizations that had been in operation for at least two years. After discussions with the CIOs at the seven organizations, seven contracts were selected. With the exception of case 6 for which the contract was completed in one year, the contracts had been in operation for no less than two years, and up to five years, at the time of the interviews. Overall, as documented later in Figure 12.2, cases 1 and 7 would probably be called failures. Their average ITO success scores as measured by our instrument were 1.9 and 2.8 out of five, respectively. By contrast, cases 4 and 5 would be considered successes. Their average ITO success scores were 4.1 and 4.5, respectively.

The seven cases involve contracts signed between 1999 and 2001, ranging from US$1 million to $133 million per annum. Using the guidelines of Cullen (2004) for describing key features of such contracts, these contracts are summarized in Table 12.4. Service scope ranged from whole-of-IT to selective services; geographic scope from state-based to global; supplier grouping from panels to sole suppliers; financial scale from large to small; pricing from fixed to unit-based; duration from long to short term; resource ownership from the supplier owning all the service delivery resources to the supplier providing purely the labor component; and commercial relationship structures from arms-length to co-sourcing.

Detailed semi-structured interviews totalling 34 hours were conducted with the CIO and the top contract manager by the lead author at the headquarters of each firm. As explained earlier, the interview questions are attached in Appendix A. Two senior managers per organization

Table 12.4 Configurations of the Seven Test Cases

		Case 1: MAN1	Case 2: SERV1	Case 3: MIN1	Case 4: GOV1	Case 5: GOV2	Case 6: CON1	Case 7: MAN2
(1) Scope Grouping	Service	Whole of IT	Apps development and support	Whole of IT	Note book mgmt	Single app development	All IT except networks & apps	Data center facility, ops, & equip
	Recipient	Parent and subsidiaries	Parent, all units, all subsidiaries	All units, all spin offs	All schools	Parent	Parent and subsidiaries	Parent, subsidiaries optional
	Geographic	National	National	Global	State	State	National	National
(2) Supplier Grouping		Sole	Best of Breed	Prime	Prime	Sole	Sole	Sole
(3) Financial Scale	Relative	80%	15%	33%	26%	Not tracked	23%	25%
	Absolute	$40M	$30M	$133M	$31M	$1M	$16M	$10M
(4) Pricing Framework		Fixed	Unit	Hybrid	Unit	Fixed	Fixed	Fixed
(5) Duration (years)		Fixed (5)	Fixed (5)	Rollover (7+1+1)	Rollover (3+3)	Fixed (1)	Rollover (6+ TBD)	Rollover (3+2)
(6) Resource Ownership		Supplier – all	Supplier – labor	Supplier – all	Supplier – labor	Supplier – labor	Supplier – all	Supplier – all
(7) Commercial Relationship		Arms-length	Co-sourcing	Value-add	Arms-length	Co-sourcing	Value-add	Arms-length

were interviewed to reduce reliance on a single source of evidence. The interviews were digitally recorded, manually recorded on the instrument form (Appendix A), and then coded into a database. In addition, documents such as contracts, correspondences, and performance evaluations were used to substantiate each interviewee's statements and perceptions.

To explore the extent to which intended outcomes for outsourcing change, interviewees at each case organization were first asked to identify which of the 25 ITO outcomes in Table 12.1 (a) were *applicable* to their organization (as potential outcomes that could have been sought), and (b) their organization had pursued as desired outcomes. In addition, they were asked if any desired outcomes were missing from the list. In response to this last question, one additional outcome mentioned in two of the seven cases, was "good relationships with suppliers". This outcome, which is an outcome driver rather than a desired outcome *per se*, is discussed in more detail in the Discussion section below.

As required by the instrument, three timeframes were used for classifying outcomes sought:

1 initial primary intended outcome – the focus at the outset of the deal,
2 current primary intended outcome – the current focus of the deal, and
3 future primary intended outcome – the future focus of the deal.

The degree to which each desired outcome was achieved was assessed on a five-point Likert-type scale:

1 = very poor outcome against expectations
2 = poor outcome against expectations
3 = no perceptible outcome against expectations
4 = good outcome against expectations
5 = very good outcome against expectations

Case study findings

Table 12.5 summarizes outcomes that were judged by the managers in the case study organizations to be *applicable* to their organization (heading "AO"), *initial primary outcomes* sought ("IPO"), *current primary outcomes* sought ("CPO"), and *future primary outcomes* sought "FPO"). A tick/check in the AO column means that the interviewees said that outcome was applicable to their organization. In other words, it would have been meaningful for their organization to try to achieve that goal. A tick/check in any of the three columns to the right of the AO column indicates that the interviewees said that this was a goal of interest to their organization either in the past, now, or in the future. The blacked-out cells indicate outcomes

Table 12.5 Applicable and Intended Outcomes per Case

Outcome Attribute	Case 1				Case 2				Case 3				Case 4				Case 5		Case 6				Case 7		
	AO	IPO	CPO	FPO	AO	IPO	CPO	FPO	AO	IPO	CPO	FPO	AO	IPO	CPO	FPO	AO	IPO	AO	IPO	CPO	FPO	AO	IPO	CPO
Value for Money																									
1. Value for money	✓	✓				✓	✓		✓	✓	✓	✓	✓	✓	✓	✓		✓	✓	✓	✓	✓			✓
2. Price under internal cost	✓	✓							✓	✓			✓	✓	✓				✓	✓	✓			✓	
Improved Financial Results																									
3. Ongoing cost reduction	✓	✓			✓	✓			✓	✓			✓	✓		✓			✓	✓	✓			✓	
4. Cost stability	✓	✓			✓	✓	✓		✓	✓			✓				✓		✓	✓				✓	
5. Financial assets	✓	✓			✓	✓			✓	✓	✓		✓						✓					✓	
6. Convert to operating expense	✓	✓		✓					✓	✓			✓						✓					✓	
7. Aggregate demand	✓	✓							✓					✓					✓						
8. Cash from asset sales	✓	✓						✓	✓										✓					✓	✓
9. Reduce staff	✓	✓		✓					✓															✓	✓
10. Rationalize assets	✓	✓				✓			✓										✓	✓	✓				
11. Remedy for poor performance	✓										✓						✓								
Other						✓			✓	✓															
Improved Operations																									

Table 12.5 Applicable and Intended Outcomes per Case – *continued*

Outcome Attribute	Case 1				Case 2			Case 3				Case 4				Case 5		Case 6				Case 7		
	AO	IPO	CPO	FPO	AO	IPO	FPO	AO	IPO	CPO	FPO	AO	IPO	CPO	FPO	AO	IPO	AO	IPO	CPO	FPO	AO	IPO	CPO
Value for Money																								
12. Improve service	✓	✓			✓	✓		✓	✓			✓	✓	✓	✓	✓		✓	✓	✓	✓	✓		✓
13. Obtain services not available internally	✓	✓					✓	✓	✓			✓	✓	✓	✓	■	■	✓	✓	✓	✓	✓		
14. Improve discipline/accountability	✓			✓	■	■		✓				✓	✓			■	■	✓	✓	✓	✓	✓		
15. Obtain better/more expertise	✓		✓		■	■		✓	✓		✓	✓						✓	✓	✓	✓	✓		
16. Flexible work practices	✓			✓	✓	✓		✓	✓			✓	✓					✓	✓	✓		✓		
17. Scalability	✓			✓	✓	✓	✓	✓	✓			✓						✓	✓	✓		✓		✓
18. Obtain better/more technology	✓	✓						✓				✓				✓		✓	✓	✓		✓		✓
19. Standardize technology	✓							✓				✓				✓	✓	✓	✓	✓	✓	✓		
20. Standardize services	✓							✓				✓				✓	✓	✓	✓	✓	✓	✓		
Other	■	■	■	■	■	■	■	■	■	■	■	■	■	■	■	✓	✓	■	■	■	■	■	■	■
Strategic Outcomes																								
21. Focus on core business	✓	✓			✓	✓		✓	✓			✓	✓					✓	✓	✓	✓	✓		
22. Refocus internal IT staff	✓	✓			■	■		✓	✓			✓	✓					✓	✓	✓	✓	✓		
23. Contribute to business	✓			✓	✓		✓	✓				✓						✓	✓	✓	✓	✓		
24. Access best practice, developments	✓	✓	✓		✓			✓				✓				✓	✓	✓	✓	✓		✓		
25. Industry development	✓	✓			■	■	✓	✓				✓				■	■	✓	✓			■	■	■
Other	✓				■	■		✓		✓	✓	✓				■	✓	✓		✓	✓	✓		✓
Total attributes	24	23	2	8	14	4	7	27	10	4	3	22	5	7	5	9	7	23	10	9	9	25	4	5

Notes:

1. AO = Applicable outcome, IPO = initial primary outcome sought, CPO = current primary outcome sought, FPO = future primary outcome sought. Blacked-out cells mean "outcome not applicable".

2. Case 2 had no current goals. The Case 5 contract had ended, thus had only initial goals. Case 7 had not identified any future goals at the time of the study.

3. "Other" comprises: Case 3: financial – "utility purchasing form" and strategic – "use of the innovation fund"; Case 4: strategic – "technology adoption by users"; Case 5: operational – "risk management"; and Case 6 strategic – "partnering-style relationship", Case 7 strategic – "controlled relationship".

that were judged to be not applicable to the organization in question. They had no tick in the AO column.

As shown in the "Total attributes" row at the bottom of Table 12.5, all 25 outcomes were judged to be applicable to at least one of the seven case organizations, all 25 had been sought by at least one of them, all seven case organizations had changed and reduced the number of outcomes sought, and no two firms had the same portfolio of applicable, initially sought, or outcomes sought now. Furthermore, although the list of 25 possible outcomes is not intended to be fully comprehensive, none of the interviewees at the seven case organizations identified any *common* goals that were missing from the list other than "good relationships with suppliers" (discussed in more detail in the Discussion section below). These findings support our argument that (a) the list of 25 potential outcomes is quite comprehensive, and (b) no single set of outcomes is applicable to all organizations.

In observing the changes to intended outcomes over time in Table 12.5, two trends appear. First, firms more experienced with outsourcing had fewer intended outcomes at the outset. The "first generation" deals (first-time outsourcing) comprised of cases 1, 3, 4, 6, and 7 had an average of 10.5 initial intended outcomes at the outset, nearly twice that of the "second generation" firms which had an average of 5.5. Second, all organizations became more focused over time. As shown in Table 12.5, after the first few years of each deal, there was a general trend to reduce intended outcomes over time. The number of intended outcomes reduced to an average of 4.5 current goals and 6.5 future goals. This suggests that an organization can focus on relatively few outcomes at any given time. It appears that organizations in first-generation deals may be unrealistic at the outset; however within a few years they develop more realistic expectations.

Finally, Figure 12.2 shows that outcomes that were initial intended *primary* outcomes were generally achieved to a greater extent than the outcomes that were not primary goals.

A survey to assess the applicability of the framework

In addition to the above seven case studies, we also used a survey to assess the applicability of the items in the framework in a wide variety of organizations. The questions addressed by the survey were: (a) Is it correct to assume that only some of the outcomes in Table 12.1 are applicable to any one organization, or are some questions applicable to all organizations?, (b) What are the most frequent goals for outsourcing in large organizations, and (c) Do outcomes sought change over time? To answer these questions we sent e-mails containing the URL for a survey to senior IT managers in 1,000 of the country's largest IT-using organizations inviting them to complete a detailed online survey on ICT outsourcing in October 2006. Job titles of these 1,000 senior managers were IT Manager, Director IT, or sim-

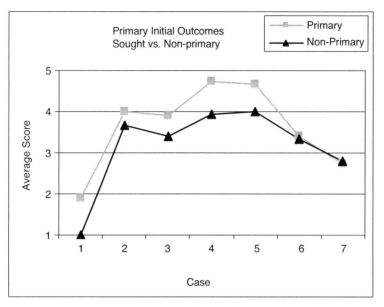

Figure 12.2   Outcomes Achieved – Primary Goals versus Non-Primary Outcomes Achieved

ilar (56%), CIO (18%), General Manager IT (12%). Many of those e-mails were deleted without being read, so we followed up in late October 2006 with a hard-copy version of the survey, then during December 2006 and January 2007 individually telephoned over 900 organizations that had not responded.

The questionnaire included the instrument in Appendix A along with many other questions related to another study. It took approximately 30 minutes to complete. All respondents were offered free copies of a report based on the survey if they completed the questionnaire. Our records indicate that by March 2007, 102 people had started to complete the online version of the survey. However, only 56 completed the full survey. The completed survey response rate is thus only 56/960 = 6%. A response rate of 6% is not as high as we would have liked, but the opinions of these 56 senior IT managers about the outcomes from their largest ICTO contract provide a lot of valuable information, discussed in sections 3.5 and 3.6. The generalizability of these findings is discussed in section 4 below.

Contextual information

In order to make transferability judgments based on the analysis that follows (as suggested by Palmquist, 2004) it is important to understand more about the respondent firms. For that reason, details of the respondents' industries,

Table 12.6   Respondents by Industry

Industry	Count	Industry	Count	Industry	Count
Agriculture, forestry & fishing	1	Government – Federal	5	Media	2
Car Hire	1	Government – State	9	Minerals processing	1
Construction	1	Health & community services	1	Mining	1
Education	3	Health Insurance	1	Trade – Retail	3
Electricity, gas & water	3	Hospitality	1	Transport & storage	3
Finance & insurance	5	Law and Legal	3	Total	56
Government – City/ local	4	Manufacturing	8		

organization sizes, IT budgets, and degree of involvement with IT outsourcing (which was often substantial) are provided in Tables 12.6 and 12.7. From these tables it is evident that respondent organizations (a) are from a wide range of industries and firm sizes, (b) operate in a wide range of different geographic regions, (c) have very different percentages of ICT budget outsourced (both in the country under study and offshore), and (d) typically have fewer than five ICT contracts.[3]

Outcomes applicable, initially sought, and currently sought

Respondents to the survey were presented with the instrument in Appendix A and asked to indicate goals that were applicable, initially sought, sought now, and to be sought, as well as to score outcomes achieved on the five-point Likert scale in Appendix A. Results for the 56 respondent firms have been combined with those from the seven case study organizations (to give a total sample size of 63) and are reported in Table 12.8.[2]

Lessons from Table 12.8 are as follows. First, all outcomes from Table 12.1 were considered "applicable" to at least some organizations. Three outcomes in particular, namely "Demonstrable value for money" (97%), "Improved Operations" (94%), and "Stabilize and predict cost" (86%), were applicable to almost all organizations. Frequent selection of these three items is consistent with the argument presented in the justification of the categories in Table 12.2 that outsourcing is fundamentally a question about value for

---

[3]There appears to have been some respondent fatigue at this stage of the survey, because only 31 of 56 respondents actually checked any outcomes as "currently sought".

Table 12.7 Characteristics of Organizations in the Sample

Organizational Attribute	Attribute Range	Count	Percentage (of the 56 orgs.)
Revenue	$<100M	4	7
	$100–499M	22	40
	$500–999M	7	13
	$1–4.9B	15	27
	$5–20B	7	13
Employees	<1000	12	22
	1,000–4,999	32	58
	5,000–40,000	11	20
Geographic coverage	Local	5	9
	State	19	35
	National	21	38
	Asia Pacific	2	4
	Global	7	13
	No answer	1	2
Annual ICT Spend	$<10M	21	38
	$10–99M	28	51
	$100–999M	6	11

Organizational Attribute	Attribute Range	Count	Percentage (of the 56 orgs.)
Percent ICT spend outsourced	<10%	12	22
	10–49%	34	62
	50–90%	8	15
	No answer	1	2
Percent ICT spend offshore	0%	39	71
	1–9.9%	9	16
	10–20%	4	7
	100%	1	2
	No answer	2	4
Number of ICTO contracts*	1	10	18
	2–4	29	53
	5–15	11	20
	20–120	4	7
	0?	1	2
Number of ICTO suppliers*	2–4	29	53
	5–15	11	20
	20–100	4	7
	0?	1	2

* Number of contracts not equal to number of suppliers

Table 12.8 ICT Outsourcing Outcomes Applicable and Sought
(N=63: 56 responses from the 2007 survey combined with those from the seven cases)

Outcome (Col. 1)	Applicable % (Col. 2)	Initial Primary Outcome Sought (IPO) (Col. 3)	Current Primary Outcome Sought (CPO)* (Col. 4)	Number of Respondents who Scored their Success in Achieving the Outcome (Col. 5)	Mean Outcome Achieved on a Scale of 1=low to 5=high (Col. 6)
Value for money					
1. Demonstrable value for money	97%	44	19	60	3.52
2. Market price under internal cost	70%	33	8	40	3.53
Improved Financial Results					
3. Obtain ongoing cost reduction	79%	32	17	47	3.30
4. Stabilize and predict costs	86%	34	15	50	3.77
5. Means of financing assets	35%	11	3	18	3.78
6. Convert capital to operating expense	37%	12	3	15	3.93
7. Aggregate total demand for economies	59%	23	9	30	3.63
8. Obtain cash for sale of assets	21%	6	1	6	3.32
9. Reduce staff numbers	51%	24	5	27	3.67
10. Rationalize/consolidate assets	40%	12	8	19	3.38
11. Get remedy for poor performance	57%	22	5	34	3.49
Improved Operations					
12. Improve service	94%	42	18	55	3.64
13. Obtain services not available internally	84%	38	13	50	3.77
14. Improve discipline/accountability	63%	20	12	34	3.12
15. Obtain better/more expertise	84%	40	11	50	3.42
16. Allow more flexible work practices	48%	15	7	25	3.12

Table 12.8 ICT Outsourcing Outcomes Applicable and Sought – *continued*
(N=63: 56 responses from the 2007 survey combined with those from the seven cases)

Outcome (Col. 1)	Applicable % (Col. 2)	Initial Primary Outcome Sought (IPO) (Col. 3)	Current Primary Outcome Sought (CPO)* (Col. 4)	Number of Respondents who Scored their Success in Achieving the Outcome (Col. 5)	Mean Outcome Achieved on a Scale of 1=low to 5=high (Col. 6)
17. Align resource supply to demand/ minimize capacity gap	55%	21	7	26	3.73
18. Obtain better/more technology	70%	29	6	40	3.62
19. Standardize technology	65%	27	7	35	3.88
20. Standardize services	71%	32	8	41	3.82
Strategic					
21. Concentrate on core business	79%	38	10	44	3.61
22. Refocus internal IT staff on high value/ more strategic activities	73%	29	14	42	3.50
23. Contribute to business (i.e. joint R&D, joint commercialization)	43%	11	8	20	3.04
24. Access to best practices, new developments	70%	29	11	36	3.31
25. Industry development	48%	13	7	21	3.10

* Possibly due to respondent fatigue, only 31 of 56 survey respondents answered this question

money. Second, based on the scores in column 6, some outcomes, such as "standardizing technology", "standardizing services", and even "concentrating on the core business" appear to be much more achievable than others, such as "accessing best practices" and "obtaining ongoing cost reduction". The value of working with the list of outcomes presented in this chapter (Table 12.1 and Appendix A) is that it opens the researchers' and respondents' minds to this range of possible benefits. Without the list, many of these possible benefits may not be considered. Finally, the scatterplot in Figure 12.3 (which only shows the 26 organizations that reported non-zero numbers of *both* initial and current primary outcomes sought) shows that the number of reported primary outcomes sought by these 26 organizations certainly changed with time. If the number of primary outcomes sought had not changed, the dots in Figure 12.3 – each representing a single organization – would all lie on the straight line shown sloping upwards from the origin. They don't.

Averaged outcomes-achieved scores compared to overall satisfaction

Although the scores on the individual items are often of more interest than any overall average measure, researchers often seek to compare ITO

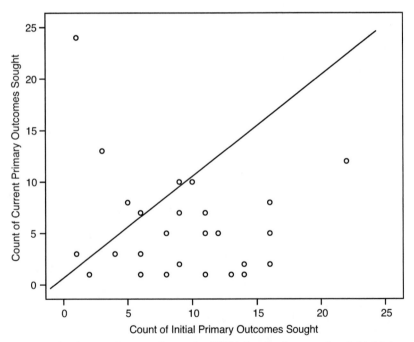

Figure 12.3   Current Primary Outcomes (CPO) Sought Compared to Initial Primary Outcomes (IPO) Sought for the Survey Respondents that Reported Non-Zero CPO *and* IPO

success across organizations. If one has access to data like that summarized in Table 12.8, the best way to compare overall ITO success would seem to be to compare averages of perceived success in achieving intended outcomes. The question is, "Are such averages useful for comparing ITO success across organizations?"

As indicated earlier, overall satisfaction is likely to be a valid measure of ITO success because each respondent will intuitively compare success against the goals relevant to his/her organization. This means that one way to assess the validity of average outcomes-achieved scores is to compare them to overall measures of satisfaction. For that reason, two questions related to satisfaction were included in Appendix A.

Table 12.9 reports average overall satisfaction (Overall Satisfaction), satisfaction with the service provider(s) (Sat. with supplier), *applicable* outcome scores (Mean Outcome), primary outcome initially sought scores (Mean IPO), and primary outcomes currently sought as reported by the 63 respondents. As noted earlier, only 31 of the 56 survey respondents checked any outcomes as "currently sought". Their mean Outcomes-achieved scores for outcomes currently sought are considerably lower than those for outcomes overall, which could explain why they have become a focus of management attention.

Spearman correlation coefficients between the various measures are shown on the right of Table 12.9 (together with the number of observations used for calculating each correlation coefficient). No statistical tests of significance have been calculated because it is not clear that the sample is representative of the population of all large organizations in the country with ITO contracts. The correlation coefficients show that the first five measures are highly correlated.[4] These high correlations suggest that all five measures are tapping similar constructs. This, in turn, provides preliminary evidence that averages of the outcomes-achieved measures for individual items selected by the respondents (i.e., Mean Outcome and Mean IPO) are likely to be useful measures of ITO success. The lower mean score for Mean Primary Outcomes currently sought (CPO) and lower correlations between this and the other measures suggests that there is something different about outcomes currently sought that could be worth investigating in future research.

Discussion

Idiosyncratic nature of outcomes sought

As suggested already, the results in the previous section demonstrate that organizations outsource for different reasons. Future discussions of

---

[4]If the sample were judged to be representative, SPSS says that all correlations reported in Table 12.9 are significantly different from zero at $p<0.001$, except for the correlations with Mean CPO, two of which are only "significant" at $p<0.05$.

Table 12.9 Means and Spearman Correlation Coefficient for Satisfaction with IT Outsourcing, Value for Money, and Mean Outcomes Scores

(N=63: 56 responses from the 2007 survey combined with those from the seven cases)

	Mean	Std. Dev	Spearman Correlation Coefficients (and Number of Observations)					
			Overall Satisfaction	Sat with Supplier	Value for Money	Mean Outcome	Mean IPO	Mean CPO
Overall Satisfaction	3.42	0.96	1.000	.830	.689	.768	.752	.576
N			61	61	58	61	56	30
Sat with supplier	3.43	1.02	.830	1.000	.716	.687	.765	.430
N			61	62	59	62	57	31
Value for money	3.56	1.01	.689	.716	1.000	.767	.723	.631
N			58	59	59	59	55	30
Mean Outcome	3.65	0.69	.768	.687	.767	1.000	.913	.725
N			61	62	59	62	57	31
Mean IPO	3.75	0.72	.752	.765	.723	.913	1.000	.458
N			56	57	55	57	57	26
Mean CPO	3.26	0.99	.576	.430	.631	.725	.458	1.000
N			30	31	30	31	26	31

Overall Satisfaction: Overall, how satisfied is your organization with this contract?
Sat. with supplier: How satisfied is your organization with the outsourcing suppliers(s)?
Value for money: Outcome-achieved score for Demonstrated value-for-money
Mean Outcome: Mean of all the respondent's outcome-achieved scores, equally weighted
Mean IPO: Mean of outcome-achieved scores for primary outcomes initially sought, equally weighted
Mean CPO: Mean of outcome-achieved scores for primary outcomes currently sought, equally weighted

outsourcing success or outcomes must recognize this fact. For example, it is not valid to assume that all organizations seek cost savings when they outsource. As shown in Table 12.8, row 3, cost saving was not an applicable objective for 21% of organizations studied. For such organizations, it does not make sense to assess ITO success by asking about cost savings. Consequently, any study of ITO success at the firm level requires a more detailed deconstruction of what success means for that organization. Furthermore, as demonstrated in the case studies (see Figure 12.2), intended outcomes are achieved to a greater degree than those that were not. This emphasizes, again, that understanding the unique nature of an organization's desired outcome portfolio is vital for assessing ITO success.

As explained above and Figure 12.3, not only did each firm have its own suite of desired outcomes, but these changed over time. In other words, an organization's definition of success is not static. The goal posts are always moving. The original intent of the deal may not reflect the current or future intent. Any discussion regarding success must therefore also be explicit about periods during which specific outcomes were sought.

Techniques driving success and failure of IT outsourcing

The fact that any one firm has achieved any given outcome or group of outcomes, does not automatically mean that that same outcome or group of outcomes is achievable by any other firm that outsources its IT. Various explanations were offered by managers in the case study organizations for their outcomes, both successes and failures. These explanations provide quite rich insights into the case organizations and the way managers in those organizations think about both outsourcing success and failure.

For example, case organizations 2, 4, 5, and 6 reported that they had realized good value for money, but each attributed it to a different reason. Case 2's management attributed their success to offering suppliers a "take it or leave it" deal *"give me as much labor as I need for an hourly rate of 10% more than what it costs me in-house"*, case 4's to competitive tendering, case 5's to the fixed-price nature of the contract, and case 6's to the long-term duration of the contract. One might infer then, that such techniques represent successful methods for achieving value for money. However, the techniques that worked for these organizations were also identified as reasons for failure in other cases. For example, case 5's fixed-price configuration was also adopted by case 1. However, in case 1, this action caused the supplier to go bankrupt and was a poor value-for-money outcome, *"we didn't know the risk of the supplier not getting additional clients and the sustainability of their business"*. Case 6's long-term duration solution was also adopted by case 7. However, case 7 had a poor value-for-money outcome because the price for services in this case was higher than market rates (the second-generation deals with three new suppliers, not just one, achieved 70% cost savings over the first-generation deal).

Exploring the causes of *poor* outcomes led to a similar conclusion about the variability of reasons for those outcomes. Cases 1 and 4 which realized very poor results in terms of being able to refocus internal IT staff on strategic activities again attributed their outcomes to different causes. In an excellent example of Kern *et al.*'s (2002) Winner's Curse, case 1's management had chosen a new-entrant supplier that had priced its services too cheaply to make a profit and case 1's CIO and IT team became focused on managing disputes with the service provider rather than managing IT, *"I was not the CIO for nine months, three days and four hours"*. This was not the reason for case 4's inability to refocus IT staff. Case 4 became focused on *"micro-management of the users"* in helping the users adopt the purchased technology because management had under-scoped the work outsourced and left out key areas that were not assigned to either party. IT staff had to carry out these activities on a reactive basis, meaning that desired refocusing was not achieved.

Do these two cases mean that choosing a vendor that is not going to make money on the deal, or under-scoping the work and the retained IT organization, are causes of failure? In these two cases is the answer yes, but in other cases the answer is no. For example, like case 1, case 5 also chose a supplier that underbid the fixed price. However, case 5's supplier was able to absorb the cost overruns and deliver a successful application, thereby winning substantial future work and becoming *"our number one preferred developer"*. case 5 never set out to refocus IT staff, so that outcome was not relevant to it, but nor did it have to reallocate any staff to the "firefighting" as did cases 1 and 4. Finally, as stated earlier, case 4 did not fully scope the work nor design carefully the retained organization. Neither did case 3, but management there have been able to rescope and reshape the contract every day since signing, and it has been able to refocus IT staff well, *"we have no worker bees anymore, we focus on strategy, business analysis, architecture, and relationship management"*.

In short, single-factor explanations of success as well as failure are too simplistic. In different contexts, techniques that drove successful outcomes in some cases led to failure in other cases. In addition, factors that led to failed outcomes in some cases yielded good results in others. For these reasons, the wide range of success advice and prescriptions appearing throughout the literature must be viewed as highly conditional – not only in terms of the success constructs the author(s) have adopted, but also in terms of the contextual situation of each of the organizations involved.

Is "relationship with supplier" an outcome?

As mentioned earlier, a question that arose during the conduct of the case studies was whether the relationship between the parties is an outcome or a means to obtain desired outcomes. The framework in Table 12.1 does not explicitly recognize quality of the relationship as an outcome, yet many practitioners and researchers argue that the key to success in outsourcing is good working relationships (see for example [Alborz *et al.*, 2005; Kern and Willcocks, 2002; Lacity and Willcocks, 2000ab]). In terms of specific studies: Dibbern *et al.* (2004) note that success might only occur if accompanied by partnering-style behaviors; Grover *et al.* (1996) report that what they called "partnership" – a combination of two behaviors (supplier problem notification and the parties helping each other) and two perceptions (supplier is trustworthy and the working relationship is happy) by the client organization – was a major factor in explaining variance in perceptions of outsourcing success; and Corbett (2005) argues that outsourcing relationships replace many of an organization's traditional assets – people, technologies, facilities, methods, and know-how, and that the relationship becomes a asset itself requiring ongoing investment. Based on these and similar studies, the importance of the relationship in achieving ITO success is indisputable.

The question is, however, whether relationship goals should be treated as, say, a fifth category of outcomes in Tables 12.1 and 12.2 or as, say, a variable moderating or mediating other factors such as use of selective sourcing that are posited to be drivers of ITO success. Within this study, at least two of the seven case study organizations had made achieving a better relationship a distinct goal, albeit not at the outset of the deal. An example goal from one organization was as follows: "*better change management and communications, recognize and manage the fact that different businesses and countries have different relationships, having the vendor take a decision and take a risk*". Further, in the survey, respondents were asked "What importance to you attach to the relationship between the parties in this contract?" All 56 respondents chose to answer this question. On a scale from 1=low to 5=high, their mean score for the Importance of the Relationship was a very high 4.70 (s.d. 0.60). Thus although relationship goals are not benefits from outsourcing *per se*, future studies should at least consider the merit of adding relationship-type goals to the 25-point list.

Generalizability of the findings from this study

The response rate for the survey discussed in Section 3 was very low, so it is important to assess the extent to which the results from this study are generalizable to (a) all large organizations in the country studied, and (b) the rest of the world. Seddon and Scheepers (2006) argue that the key to drawing generalizable conclusions from any survey with less than a 100% response rate is to demonstrate – through argument – that the sample is *representative,* in terms of the factors of interest in the study, of the population of interest.

As explained earlier, 46 of 102 respondents started but did not complete the online survey. Their initial responses (captured on the survey website) are compared to the 56 organizations that completed the survey in

Table 12.10   Key Statistics for Organizations that Completed the Survey Compared to Those That Did Not

	The 56 Complete Responses to the Survey	The 46 Firms that Started but did not Complete the Survey	Difference in Means, Independent Samples t-statistic	Significance (2-tailed)
Average Revenue	$2.0 billion	$2.1 billion	0.375	0.709
Average Employment	3,600	4,600	0.776	0.442
Average ICT spend	$44 million	$41 million	–2.177	0.033*
Average % of ICT budget outsourced	29%	14%	–3.047	0.003**
Average % of outsourcing budget offshore	3.2%	1.6%	–0.775	0.440
Average number of outsourcing contracts	7.5	3.8	–1.365	0.176
Average number of outsourcing suppliers	6.5	5.4	–0.268	0.790

*=p<0.05;   **p<0.01

Table 12.10. The independent-samples t-test (equal variances not assumed) shows that ICT spend and the percentage of ICT expenditure outsourced are significantly higher for the firms that completed the survey.[5] Assuming that non-respondent firms are more like those who failed to complete the survey, this suggests that managers of organizations more involved in outsourcing were more motivated to complete the time-consuming survey (it took many respondents 30 minutes to complete). The inference we draw from Table 12.10 is that the findings reported in this study are likely to be more representative of organizations that make more intense use of ICT and of ICT outsourcing than those that do not.

Armed with this information, how generalizable are the claimed contributions of this study, first, to all large organizations in the country studied, and second, to other large organizations in developed economies? The five claimed contributions of this study and comments on their generalizability are summarized in Table 12.11. The analysis in Table 12.11

---

[5]Inferential statistics (p-values) are meaningful here because the question is whether these two samples could be random samples drawn from the same population. For average % of the ICT budget outsourced, the tests show that this is highly unlikely.

Table 12.11 Generalizability of Claimed Contributions of this Study from the 63 Organizations Studied to All Large Organizations within Country X*

Claimed Contribution	Comment on Generalizability
1. The new conceptual framework.	Generalizable: It seems unlikely that other organizations with fewer outsourcing contracts would have more or very different desired outcomes.
2. The evidence that different organizations do seek different outcomes from outsourcing.	Generalizable: If these 63 organizations have such different mixes of goals it seems unlikely that organizations with fewer outsourcing contracts would all have similar goals.
3. The evidence that these goals change over time.	Generalizable: If the goals of the seven case study organizations have changed, and the outcome scores for the 31 organizations scoring current primary intended outcomes in Table 12.9 are so different, it seems unlikely that other organizations' goals would not also change.
4. The insight that satisfaction is a valid perceptual measure of ITO success because it draws on the respondent's goals, not on some researcher's pre-defined list.	Generalizable: This was an insight based on logic, not data. It does not depend on the sample of data collected. It provides the justification for the argument that the correlation tests reported in Table 12.9 provide useful information.
5. The ITO Success measurement instrument based on the above insights.	This contribution is generalizable because the contributions above are generalizable.

* Country name suppressed to maintain anonymity during the review process

suggests that the results from this study *are* likely to hold true for all large organizations that outsource ICT in the country studied. Further, where other countries have similar institutional settings, we would also expect the claimed contributions of this study to apply there as well.

Conclusions and directions for future research

This chapter has focused on the measurement of outsourcing success. It builds on earlier work discussed in Chapter 2. Its primary contribution is the evidence that different organizations seek different outcomes from outsourcing and that these change over time. It follows that although ITO success may validly be assessed by asking questions about overall satisfaction[6] – and possibly about achievement of the four broad sub-goals in

---

[6]As explained earlier, satisfaction is an acceptable measure because the respondent in each organization may be assumed to use his or her organization's own set of goals when assessing satisfaction.

Table 12.1 (Value for money, Improved Financial Results, Service Delivery, and Strategic Outcomes), which seem to apply to most organizations – any attempt to assess ITO success in terms of more detailed criteria, such as cost savings or focusing on core business, requires identification of the different criteria relevant to each organization for each different contract at the time of the study.

The 25 outcomes proposed in Table 12.1 represent a convenient catalogue of frequently sought outcomes from ITO. Questions about the achievement of those that are relevant can be framed in terms of past, present, and future outcomes sought as well as assessed in terms of negative, null, and positive outcome realization as shown in Appendix A. In using such an instrument it is important to understand that organizations refine their desired outcomes from their ITO deals over time. Thus while original outcomes sought may be met, longitudinal studies need to consider the achievement of different outcomes at different times.

Looking forward, future research might seek to explain *why* organizational goals for ITO change, and whether there is merit in including questions about the relationship between ITO client and vendor as an indicator of ITO success, as suggested for example by Willcocks and Lacity (2009). Further progress in understanding outsourcing and the drivers of ITO success also seems likely through studying interdependences between intended outcomes. Although Dibbern *et al.* (2004) did not find any study in this area, preliminary work carried out by Rouse *et al.* (2001) found associations between cost reduction and strategic benefits, and service and strategic benefits. In addition, Dibbern *et al.* (2004) called for intensive research in the area of balancing multiple outsourcing outcomes and multiple stakeholder expectations (see also Chapter 9). Assessments of success are also likely to be different depending on who is surveyed and their expectations – in this study, CIOs, IT managers, and contract executives. What happens when different stakeholders are examined (i.e., users, business managers, supplier personnel) and the conflicting expectations that may surface, offers an interesting research path. Hirschheim and Lacity (1998, 2000, see also Chapter 9) found that achieving multiple stakeholder goals is elusive, if not unrealistic, and involves many trade-offs.

These and many more research opportunities can be explored on a consistent and comparable manner once a reasonably complete ITO success construct becomes sufficiently tested and adopted. It is hoped that this research has contributed to that goal.

References

Alborz, S., Seddon, P.B. and Scheepers, R. (2005) The Quality of Relationship Construct in IT Outsourcing, *Proceedings of the Ninth Pacific Asia Conference on Information Systems* (PACIS), pp. 1118–1131.

Apte, U. and Sobol, M. (1997) "IS Outsourcing Practices in the USA, Japan and Finland: A Comparative Study", *Journal of Information Technology*, 12, 4, 289–304.

Cheon, M.J., Grover, V. and Teng, J.T.C. (1995) "Theoretical Perspectives on the Outsourcing of Information Services", *Journal of Information Technology*, 10, 4, 209–210.

Corbett, M. (2005) "Outsourcing: Just the End of the Beginning", in Brudenall, P. (ed.) *Technology and Offshore Outsourcing Strategies*, Palgrave, London, x–xiii.

Cross, J. (1995) "IT Outsourcing at British Petroleum", *Harvard Business Review*, May–June, 94–102.

Cullen S. (2004) *Outsourcing IT and Services: Research Into Lifecycle, Configuration and Success*", PHD Thesis, University of Melbourne, Melbourne.

Cullen, S. Seddon, P. Willcocks, L. and Rouse, A. (2000) *A Survey of Australian IT Outsourcing Practices*, Deloitte Touche, Melbourne.

Cullen, S., Seddon, P. and Willcocks, L. (2005) "Managing Outsourcing: The Lifecycle Imperative", *MISQ Executive*, June, 229–246.

Dibbern, J., Goles, T., Hirschheim, R. and Jayatilaka, B. (2004) "Information Systems Outsourcing: A Survey and Analysis of the Literature", *ACM Data Base*, 35: 4, 6–102.

Domberger, S. (1998) *The Contracting Organization: A Strategic Guide to Outsourcing*, Oxford University Press, Oxford.

Domberger, S., Fernandez, P. and Fiebeg, D. (2000) "Modelling the Price, Performance and Contract Characteristics of IT Outsourcing", *Journal of Information Technology*, 15, 2, 107–118.

Fowler, A. and Jeffs, B. (1998) "Examining Information Systems Outsourcing: A Case Study from the United Kingdom", *Journal of Information Technology*, 13, 111–126.

Gregor, S. (2006) "The Nature of Theory in Information Systems", *MIS Quarterly*, 30, 3, 611–642.

Grover, V., Cheon, M.Y. and Teng, J. (1996) "The Effect of Service Quality and Partnership on the Outsourcing of Information Systems Functions", *Journal of Management Information Systems*, 12, 4, Spring, 89–116.

Hirschheim, R.A. and Lacity, M.C. (1998) "Reducing Information Systems Costs through Insourcing: Experiences from the Field", *Proceedings of the 31st International Conference on System Sciences*, Hawaii, 644–653.

Hirschheim, R.A. and Lacity, M.C. (2000) "The Myths and Realities of Information Technology Outsourcing", *Communications of the ACM*, 43, 2, 99–107.

Hui, P.P. and Beath, C.M. (2002) *The IT Sourcing Process: A Framework for Research*. Working Paper, University of Texas at Austin, Texas.

Hurley, M. and Costa, C. (2001) *The Blurring Boundary of the Organisation: Outsourcing Comes of Age*, KPMG Consulting, Sydney.

Kern, T. and Willcocks, L.P. (2002) "Exploring Relationship in Information Technology Outsourcing: The Interaction Approach", *European Journal of Information Systems*, 11, 1, 3–19.

Kern, T., Willcocks, L. and Heck, E. (2002) "The Winner's Curse in IT Outsourcing: Strategies for Avoiding Relational Trauma", *California Management Review*, 44, 2, 47–69.

King, W.R. and Malhotra, Y. (2000) "Developing a Framework for Analyzing IS Outsourcing", *Information & Management*, 37, 323–334.

Klepper, R. and Jones, W.O. (1998) *Outsourcing Information Technology Systems & Services*, Prentice Hall, New Jersey.

Lacity, M.C. and Hirschheim, R.A. (1993) *Information Systems Outsourcing: Myths, Metaphors, and Realities*, Wiley, Chichester.

Lacity, M.C. and Willcocks, L.P. (1998) "An Empirical Investigation of Information Technology Sourcing Practices: Lessons from Experience", *MIS Quarterly* 22:3, 363–408.

Lacity, M.C. and Willcocks, L.P. (2000a) *Inside Information Technology Outsourcing: A State of the Art Report*, Templeton College, Oxford: Templeton Research, Oxford.

Lacity, M.C. and Willcocks, L.P. (2000b) "Relationships in IT Outsourcing: A Stakeholder Perspective", in Zmud, R. (ed.) *Framing the Domains of IT Management Research: Glimpsing the Future through the Past*, Pinnaflex, California.

Lacity, M.C. and Willcocks, L.P. (2001) *Global Information Technology Outsourcing: Search for Business Advantage*, Wiley, Chichester.

Lacity, M.C., Willcocks, L.P. and Feeny, D. (1996) "The Value of Selective Sourcing", *Sloan Management Review*, Spring, 13–43.

Lee, J-N. and Kim, Y-G. (1999) "Effect of Partnership Quality on IS Outsourcing Success: Conceptual Framework and Empirical Validation", *Journal of MIS*, 15, 4, 29–61.

Lee, J-N., Miranda, S.M. and Kim, Y-M. (2004) "IT Outsourcing Strategies: Universalistic, Contingency, and Configurational Explanations of Success", *Information Systems Research*, 15, 2, 110–131.

McAulay, M., Doherty, N. and Keval, N. (2002) "The Stakeholder Dimension in information Systems Evaluation", *Journal of Information Technology*, 17, 241–255.

McFarlan, F.W. and Nolan, R. (1995) "How to Manage an IT Outsourcing Alliance", *Sloan Management Review*, Winter, 9–23.

Mylott, T.R. (1995) *Computer Outsourcing: Managing the Transfer of Information Systems*, Prentice Hall, New Jersey.

Palmquist, M. (2004) "Introduction to Generalizability and Transferability", Website: http://writing.colostate.edu/guides/research/gentrans/pop2a.cfm (viewed June 2007).

Quinn, J.B., Doorley, T. and Paquette, P. (1990) "Beyond Products: Services-Based Strategy", *Harvard Business Review*, March–April, 58–67.

Quinn, J.B. and Hilmer, F.G. (1994) "Strategic Outsourcing", *Sloan Management Review*, 35, 4, 43–55.

Rouse, A., Corbitt, B. and Aubert, B. (2001) "Perspectives on IT Outsourcing Success: Covariance Structure Modelling of a Survey of Outsourcing in Australia", Working Paper, Montreal: *École des Hautes Études Commerciales de Montrèal*, March.

Saunders, C., Gebelt, M. and Hu, Q. (1997) "Achieving Success in Information Systems Outsourcing", *Californian Management Review*, 39, 2, 63–79.

Seddon, P.B. and Scheepers, R. (2006). Other-settings Generalization in IS Research, *Proceedings of the 27th International Conference on Information Systems*, 1141–1158.

Willcocks, L. and Lacity, M. (eds) (2009) *Research Studies in Information Technology Outsourcing: Perspectives, Practices and Globalization*, Sage, London, three volumes.

Appendix A Interview Questionnaire and Survey Instrument

Indicate the outcomes achieved to date in section A and, in column B, the primary outcomes sought	A. Outcomes Achieved						B. Primary Outcomes Sought		
	N/A	Very poor	Poor	None	Good	Very good	Initially sought	Sought now	To be sought
Value for Money									
1. Demonstrable value for money	○	○	○	○	○	○	—	—	—
2. Market price under internal cost	○	○	○	○	○	○	—	—	—
Improved Financial Results									
3. Obtain ongoing cost reduction	○	○	○	○	○	○	—	—	—
4. Stabilize and predict costs	○	○	○	○	○	○	—	—	—
5. Means of financing assets	○	○	○	○	○	○	—	—	—
6. Convert capital to operating expense	○	○	○	○	○	○	—	—	—
7. Aggregate total demand for economies	○	○	○	○	○	○	—	—	—
8. Obtain cash for sale of assets	○	○	○	○	○	○	—	—	—
9. Reduce staff numbers	○	○	○	○	○	○	—	—	—
10. Rationalize/consolidate assets	○	○	○	○	○	○	—	—	—
11. Get remedy for poor performance	○	○	○	○	○	○	—	—	—
12. Standardize technology	○	○	○	○	○	○	—	—	—
13. Standardize services	○	○	○	○	○	○	—	—	—
Other _____	○	○	○	○	○	○	—	—	—

Appendix A   Interview Questionnaire and Survey Instrument – *continued*

Indicate the outcomes achieved to date in section A and, in column B, the primary outcomes sought	A. Outcomes Achieved						B. Primary Outcomes Sought		
	N/A	Very poor	Poor	None	Good	Very good	Initially sought	Sought now	To be sought
Operational									
14. Improve service	○	○	○	○	○	○	___	___	___
15. Obtain services not available internally	○	○	○	○	○	○	___	___	___
16. Improve discipline/accountability	○	○	○	○	○	○	___	___	___
17. Obtain better/more expertise	○	○	○	○	○	○	___	___	___
18. Allow more flexible work practices	○	○	○	○	○	○	___	___	___
19. Align resource supply to demand/ minimize capacity gap	○	○	○	○	○	○	___	___	___
20. Obtain better/more technology	○	○	○	○	○	○	___	___	___
Other ____	○	○	○	○	○	○	___	___	___
Strategic									
21. Concentrate on core business	○	○	○	○	○	○	___	___	___
22. Refocus internal IT staff on high value / more strategic activities	○	○	○	○	○	○	___	___	___
23. Contribute to business (i.e. joint R&D, joint commercialization)	○	○	○	○	○	○	___	___	___
24. Access to best practices, new developments	○	○	○	○	○	○	___	___	___
25. Industry development	○	○	○	○	○	○	___	___	___
Other ____	○	○	○	○	○	○	___	___	___

Overall satisfaction: On a scale of 1 to 5 (1=very dissatisfied, 5 = very satisfied):

	1	2	3	4	5
Overall, how satisfied is your organization with this contract?	○	○	○	○	○
How satisfied is your organization with the outsourcing suppliers(s)?	○	○	○	○	○

13
Business Process Outsourcing: The Promise of the Enterprise Partnership Model

David Feeny, Leslie Willcocks and Mary Lacity

Introduction

In this chapter we report our research into Business Process Outsourcing (BPO). Using case studies, we assess initial progress and challenges to 2005, then update developments to 2008. As is reflected in these cases, by 2001 the outsourcing of so-called IT-enabled back office support processes was beginning to be seen as a viable strategy by many large corporations, fuelling forecast revenue growth of 10%–15% per annum in a market already estimated then as worth nearly a quarter of that of IT outsourcing (Lacity and Willcocks, 2001). Figures for BPO are, for many reasons, notoriously difficult to arrive at accurately, but in a review of several studies Willcocks and Lacity (2006) suggested that in 2006 the market could have been as big as $US80 billion and would grow at a forecast 10–12% over the next five years.[1]

The service provider for all four of the BPO deals we study here is Xchanging, a company founded in 1998 specifically to address the BPO market. Its approach is based on the vision and prior learning of its founding CEO, and is distinctive in a number of respects. *Firstly*, in sharp contrast to the "move to low cost labor" logic of "offshore" BPO, Xchanging sought to invest to improve the cost and quality of its clients' processes through the application of seven business competencies. By 2008 it had also embraced nearshore and offshore options to offer a global service, with some 22% of Xchanging staff on-site, 60% nearshore and 18% offshore in India and Malaysia. *Secondly*, it operates a well-defined model of phased implementation to address what it sees to be changing success factors over the life of a contract. *Thirdly*,

---

[1]By way of comparison, IDC (2007) forecasts offer different figures, suggesting for 2007–11 a 14.3% growth rate in BPO revenues per annum, with the human resource, finance and accounting and procurement markets globally estimated as $US36 billion in 2007. Obviously much depends on how such estimates are calculated.

In the Enterprise partnership deals we have studied, Xchanging claims to work in true partnership with its clients, including financial partnership rather than "fee for service" arrangements. By end of 2007 it had seven such partnership deals but had also developed and delivered additional offerings to clients, including more traditional outsourcing, systems and software products, straight-through processing and business support.

In this chapter we focus only on the four original BPO enterprise partnerships, namely:

- An HR Services Partnership with BAE SYSTEMS providing services to the client's 150,000 employees and dependents, worth £250 million over ten years;
- A subsequent ten-year Partnership with BAE SYSTEMS to manage £800 million of procurement in indirect spend categories;
- An Insurance Services Partnership jointly formed with Lloyd's of London and the Insurance Underwriters Association, to settle more than £20 billion of business each year within a network of some 180 companies;
- A subsequent Claims Services Partnership with Lloyd's of London, to manage more than 250,000 claims per year to a combined value of £8 billion.

In our analysis we evaluate this Xchanging "enterprise partnership" model against some of the key issues identified during our years of research into the related field of IT outsourcing (see earlier chapters. Also Lacity and Willcocks, 2009) Specifically, in that IT domain we have long since learned to be sceptical of the rhetoric of "partnership" (see also Chapter 4); we have consistently experienced client frustration at the lack of supplier innovation and added value as the deal proceeds (see also Chapter 2); we have identified the value of using a range of sourcing arrangements to address the specific business role and needs of each activity (see also Chapters 8 and 11).

While recognizing that the contracts studied were still in their early years at the time of our research between 2001 and 2005, we report a number of findings:

- In all four cases there had been major changes to the service provided, resulting in significant improvements to cost and/or quality. In each case it seemed clear that these improvements would not have been achieved "in-house", without outsourcing;
- The "Enterprise Partnership" model of Xchanging did indeed produce a partnership dynamic, a very different set of motivations and behaviors to those common in traditional fee-for-service arrangements;

- Through its investment in competencies and its mechanisms for continuing client involvement, the Xchanging model incorporated promising and distinctive means for achieving change and improvement on a sustainable basis – throughout the life of the contract;
- The Xchanging Enterprise Partnership model has been particularly suited to the outsourcing of services when service excellence is important, as well as cost; when the existing service has not been a priority for management attention, as is commonly the case within back office functions of large corporates; when the service can benefit from new technology infrastructure, but has not been seen as a priority candidate for internal investment.

In summary, we conclude that Xchanging did indeed bring to the BPO market a distinctive model of engagement. When measured against the familiar shortcomings of previous models of outsourcing, we find the Xchanging model providing some new and more convincing answers – the promise of a "better way".

Business Process Outsourcing (BPO) research

By the early 2000s the outsourcing of business processes – particularly of so-called back office support processes – had become a major phenomenon and prominent topic in many corporate boardrooms. At one stage Gartner Group had forecast double digit annual growth for BPO and a world market worth as much as $234 billion by 2005. The June 2002 announcement by Procter & Gamble that they were negotiating BPO contracts worth $1 billion a year was the largest and latest "blue chip" endorsement of the concept, following major Human Resource outsourcing contracts placed in 1999–2001 by the likes of BP and Bank of America (both described in Willcocks and Lacity, 2006). Many commentators saw BPO as the "next big thing".

Potential beneficiaries on the supply side included both new and familiar names. The well-established providers of IT outsourcing were increasingly targeting BPO: for example, Accenture chairman Joe Forehand reported in January 2002 that 50%–60% of his company's new business pipeline was in the area of BPO; at much the same time EDS claimed to have more than 22,000 employees dedicated to BPO, supporting nearly 4,000 clients in 29 countries. These were joined by new specialist BPO companies such as EXULT, the beneficiary of the HR Services contracts placed by BP and Bank of America. And below the mega-contract level there was the burgeoning growth of "offshore" specialists – BPO revenues in India for example were said to have increased by 70% in the year of 2004, to $US1.5 billion.

So what are the keys to BPO success? Is the IT outsourcing experience of an Accenture or EDS an advantage, or is BPO significantly different? How important in the overall scheme of things are the low labor costs of offshore providers? What is the learning to date? In this chapter we seek to provide insights into BPO, based on a research study in one of the service providers specializing in this market – Xchanging.

Founded in 1999, Xchanging was simultaneously one of the "new kids on the block", a venture capital backed start-up which is a "pure play" BPO company; and yet an "old hand". Xchanging's founder, David Andrews, was the Andersen partner in charge of setting up an early BPO accounting services deal for BP in 1990. On the original Xchanging Board sat John Bramley – the initiator of that accounting services deal when BP Exploration's Finance Head. Among his team of seasoned executives was John Attenborough – a key colleague of Andrews in implementing that deal and a number of subsequent ones. Together they claimed to have developed, through a decade of experience, a distinctive and superior model of BPO.

For the research we had access to both client and provider personnel in Xchanging's four existing "Enterprise Partnership" deals. We brought to the research study our extensive prior experience in the field of IT Outsourcing – between us we had by 2001 researched more than 350 IT outsourcing deals of all shapes and sizes, and our findings had appeared in prominent publications.[2] Based on that experience we particularly wanted to explore whether the Xchanging approach to BPO successfully addressed what we had found to be three recurring difficulties in other models of outsourcing:

1. **The Lack of Partnership** between client and provider. All the early large IT outsourcing deals were loudly proclaimed as "Strategic Partnerships" – but in reality they were structured as win/lose relationships and performed accordingly (see also Chapters 2 and 4). Typically, the client muscle ensured that contracts were initially skewed in their favor; but massive potential switching costs allowed the vendor to exploit changing business and technology contexts to reap the future rewards. Even shared risk/reward deals in the IT outsourcing field have typically struggled as the interests of the client (better/cheaper services) have diverged over time from the goals of the vendor (to concentrate on gaining additional external revenues). *Did the Xchanging deals demonstrate real evidence of successful partnership? Were client and service provider experiencing creation and sharing of new value, which could not have been achieved without the deal? Were forward goals being successfully aligned?*

2. **The Lack of Sustainability.** A common experience in IT outsourcing has been that the vendor has indeed reduced costs on baseline services,

---

[2]Our outsourcing publications from 1993–2001 are listed in Lacity and Willcocks (2001) *op. cit.* They included 12 books and 50 refered journal and conference papers.

but at the expense of the service quality experienced by end users – that there was no "added magic" from the vendor. Even more regularly have we heard the client complain that there has been "no innovation", that they are experiencing a period of "mid-contract sag" in which the vendor has lost energy and enthusiasm. In the IT domain we have found that the client needed to retain in-house a range of "core capabilities" to effectively manage the evolution of the function in line with the needs of the host business (Feeny and Willcocks, 1998). *What were the prospects for continuing success for the different stakeholders over the 10-year life of the Xchanging deals? Could service quality and service cost improve simultaneously? And continue to do so? What stimulus was required to ensure success over time?*

3. **The Lack of Fit between homogeneous provider solutions and heterogeneous client contexts and needs.** In the IT outsourcing domain, we see increasing recognition by businesses that no single provider – or single contracting form – is appropriate across their whole range of IT activity. Selective IT sourcing, always the major trend, has become increasingly prevalent from 2002–08, though the notion has often seen multiple supplier outsourcing mistaken for the selective sourcing principles we ourselves observed as effective (Lacity *et al.*, 1995; Lacity and Willcocks, 2001, 2009). *Does the domain of business process outsourcing exhibit different characteristics? Did the Xchanging model represent a credible generic approach to service provision for a whole range of back office functions and processes? In a wide variety of businesses and industry sectors?*

We found that each of the four Xchanging Partnership deals provided a rich picture of BPO experience; each has also been documented as a separate case study (see Willcocks and Lacity, 2006; Willcocks *et al.*, 2003; Lacity *et al.*, 2003), with its own specific findings. In this chapter we look across the case studies for a composite understanding of the Xchanging approach – in theory and in practice. And we assess the overall evidence that Xchanging has developed a distinctive and convincing model of Business Process Outsourcing.

Research scope and methodology

The research study gave us access to the Xchanging company's first four major deals:

- An HR Services Partnership with BAE SYSTEMS which provides services to the client's 150,000 employees and dependents, worth £250 million over ten years;

- A subsequent ten-year Partnership with BAE SYSTEMS to manage £800 million of procurement in indirect spend categories;
- An Insurance Services Partnership jointly formed with Lloyd's of London and the Insurance Underwriters Association, which settles more than £20 billion of business each year within a network of some 180 companies;
- A subsequent Claims Services Partnership with Lloyd's of London, which manages more than 250,000 claims per year to a combined value of £8 billion.

For each of these deals we interviewed a cross section of stakeholders. These included the key executives from the client and on the Xchanging team; sample users of the service being provided; representatives of those who had transitioned from the client to Xchanging as part of the deal. A total of 38 interviews were conducted in late 2001 and first half of 2002. We conducted additional follow-up interviews with key players across the 2002–05 period. In addition we had access to a range of documentation, including contractual documents, partnership business plan material, Xchanging Methodology Manuals. We also looked back from 2008 to report on subsequent events and results.

Several things became increasingly clear as we progressed through the research. Firstly, that Xchanging had a very well-defined business model which pervaded the thinking of all those that we met. Secondly, there was an integrated logic underpinning the different components of the business model and defining how they interacted. Thirdly, the business model was an experience-based model; the presence and development of each component could be traced back to specific formative experiences of the founding CEO and his executive team. In short, understanding the structure and origins of the Xchanging business model was central to any understanding and evaluation of the BPO activity covered by this research. Therefore it is important to overview the historical evolution of the model, before providing evidence of its influence on the deals studied and evaluating potential contribution to successful BPO.

The roots of the Xchanging business model

"I said in 1998 I am going to create my own business. I can see how it can be done. I have got the experience to know where the pitfalls are. I hope I can find someone out there who is prepared to back these ideas."
– David Andrews, Founder and CEO of Xchanging

While Xchanging was founded in 1998 and signed its first BPO contracts in 2001, the roots of its business model went back many years. Founder David Andrews was in fact the Andersen (now Accenture) partner asked to set up that firm's outsourcing practice in the mid-1980s; but the early deals were principally for IT facilities management services in competition with the likes of EDS. Andrews dates his critical learnings from the end of the 1980s and the ground-breaking deal for accounting services reached with BP's John Bramley.

Learnings from the BP experience

"I was retired and happy at home doing my gardening for three years, and then quite out of the blue in 1998 I got a phone call from David Andrews. We both shared almost a sense of despair that outsourcing had not gone where it had become apparent to us in the early 1990s it ought to be going. We began to formulate the sort of things a new company might do." – John Bramley, former Finance Director, BP Exploration

As Finance Director in John Browne's management team for BP Exploration, Bramley had issued a challenge to Andersen. Concerned that "every three years or so we built a new accounting system, and diverted a vast amount of everybody's attention away from running the business", he approached his established consultants and advisers. But instead of asking for help in building the next system, he instead requested they provide "a seamless uninterrupted accounting service", doing whatever they needed to do to achieve it. Brought in to lead Andersen's response, David Andrews found that Bramley also had clear ideas about the nature of any deal. It was to be a partnership, not a "black box" contract, with shared benefits beyond initial cost reduction guarantees. There would be a joint BP/Andersen Review Board which had access to detailed information on costs, costs savings, and the margins being achieved. It was a new way of working which was to become the first key element of the Xchanging business model – **Enterprise Partnership**:

"BP taught me how you did Enterprise Partnerships. It was an entirely different way, which I found extraordinarily hard and agonizing. I was betting my career at Andersen, and I was not necessarily seeing the prospect of a profitable arrangement." – David Andrews

Another layer of learning was about the capabilities required to make the deal a success. Firstly there was the understanding of Service:

"In IT outsourcing deals you would create what were called service level agreements, but in fact they were focused on measurement of resources – uptime, response time and so on. BP were very good at defining service in a different and very logical and structured manner, breaking it down into types of customer, classes of service they needed. While we have now taken that a lot further in Xchanging, it was a huge breakthrough at the time. Otherwise we would have run the deal as an accounts department (albeit external), we would not have run it as a service to customers." – David Andrews

Secondly, there was a concentration on process rather than IT:

"Huge breakthrough because I quite deliberately said to BP I don't want your IT. We will do the accounting. You can keep your IT and we will buy what we need from you. What I wanted to do was see what happened if you improved business processes and service without touching the IT. We found we could engineer a huge improvement and do it on the back of the old legacy system which then went on for another seven or eight years before it was replaced." – David Andrews

And, thirdly, there was understanding of people and behavior. Andrews brought in John Attenborough, then running his own consultancy specializing in behavior change, and charged him with creating the required mind set among those transferred from BP's accounting function. John Bramley recalled the impact:

"It was apparent that, through John Attenborough, they knew more than we did at BP about people and behaviour, and they applied that knowledge very successfully. They achieved remarkably quickly, I would say within six months, a really strong sense of purpose and pleasure amongst the people we had transferred. People knew that their business now depended on them; they were not just a back office that nobody wants to bother about." – John Bramley

Ten years later these capabilities – Service, Process, People – formed three of the **Xchanging "Competencies", the second strand of the Xchanging business model.** As we shall see later, there were eventually seven Competencies defined in total, each representing an area of knowledge considered critical to the development of the company's Enterprise Partnership deals.

The power of these early learnings and the insight of John Bramley were to lead years later to that "out of the blue" phone call, and Bramley's subsequent recruitment as a non-executive Director of Xchanging. But as the pioneering BP deal became a visible and notable success, David Andrews was drafted in to lead new challenges where the first learnings were confirmed and new ones achieved.

The London Stock Exchange – and other learning experiences

In the early 1990s the London Stock Exchange (LSE) was widely perceived to be in crisis. While clearly the leading exchange in Europe in terms of trading activity, its operational platform was very slow, fragile and high cost – the consequence it was said of decades in which LSE was run as a "gentlemen's club". There was particular concern that its technology base had fallen well behind that of its international competition. IT infrastructure included five separate data centers and around 200 distributed databases; the track record of systems development was consistently poor, and there was constant speculation about the viability of its planned new settlement system TAURUS. In 1992 LSE Chairman Sir Andrew Hugh-Smith called Andersen Consulting's Managing Partner and requested top level help. David Andrews was made client partner for the LSE.

What started as a strategic consulting assignment quickly took a new path. Andrews proposed a major outsourcing deal in which Andersen would take responsibility for all IT operational and development activity outside of the TAURUS development:

> "I said look, you can send a lion tamer to deal with this jungle but I will probably get trampled to death by elephants or bitten to death by a snake. I am a good lion tamer but this isn't what you need. What you need is to bulldoze down this whole jungle and recreate something. We will get control of it and drive down the cost, and we can use the savings generated to fund replacement of the trading systems." – David Andrews

The initial five-year deal worth £50 millions was signed in April 1992; it reflected the learnings and the open book accounting of the earlier BP deal. And when the £44 million contract to replace trading systems was signed in April 1994, it was indeed seen to be financed by the operational savings which were already being achieved.

The LSE experience added to Andrews understanding of what was required in a Service competency:

> "Whereas at BP we had a single corporate customer, here we had 200 trading houses which we had to get to act as customers. Historically they were acting as bullies, beating up the Stock Exchange every time something went wrong, it was always the Stock Exchange's fault. Now to become a customer and to behave as a customer you have got to have a relationship that enables you to do that. You have got to know what it is you are getting, that you want what you are getting, that you know what the price is, that you know when you have got it. You don't achieve that by saying the response time is so many seconds. We put in place a service agreement which covered service definition, service specification, service

management. Working with LSE Executives Jane Barker and Sir Andrew Hugh-Smith we were able to achieve a customer mindset." – David Andrews

A second major learning from the LSE situation came from Andrews's exposure to component-driven architecture, a technique which Andersen had been developing in some of their largest and most complex systems-build assignments in the USA:

> "The LSE represented a very complex systems environment where you could not replace everything, you had to refurbish legacy, build on legacy, put a superstructure on top. And you could not wait two years for 200 customers to agree on the functionality they wanted. So we said we would build a structure with standard components and roll out functionality very quickly, as requirements became agreed, on a multiple release basis. We took eighteen months to put the component architecture in place, then every six months after that there was a new release of functionality. Later, when I did the Exchange consolidation in Germany, we did it in nine months and three months." – David Andrews

So while the world of systems-build in the late 1990s was becoming dominated by massive and monolithic ERP implementation projects, Andrews was planning a very different approach to what would be Xchanging's fourth Competency – Technology. He had seen at BP the potential to *"sweat the IT legacy asset"*. He had experienced at the LSE the power of component-driven architecture, and of its need for *"very clever people, scientific level people"*. And he had noted that not only customers were delighted by the experience of new releases of functionality every few months; the best IT people were also *"excited by the immediacy of introducing a bit of change every three months"*.

Andrews's commitment to what would become Xchanging's fifth Competency – Environment – was illustrated by an experience in his next role. In March 1995 he became Managing Partner for Andersen Consulting's Western Europe Region. His overall brief was to turn around an unprofitable business. But he also had a more specific problem: he hated the offices he inherited in Paris – and he had long believed in the contribution of workplace environment to business success. He called in another of his previous contacts, an Architect named Andrew Chadwick:

> "David understands that the real estate environment can be a surfboard for the business. He said he wanted new offices; but to stay within budget they would need to be substantially smaller and we would make them work on a space-time or virtual basis. I trawled the Paris market

and came back with two locations. I said to him one of them is extrovert and the other is introvert, and all you have to do is choose. In my view you should take the extrovert building because it fits with your whole ethos. He did, and we created 55 Avenue Georges Cinque. It became famous and every CEO went through the place. We started to get serious business."
– Andrew Chadwick

One more piece of the jigsaw

A final piece of learning from the 1990s seemed to stem more from a synthesis of various strands of experience. It was the **Four Stage Implementation Process, representing the third critical part of the Xchanging Business Model**, alongside Partnership and Competencies. Three ideas come together in the rationale for this approach to implementation:

- The behavioral change model used by John Attenborough recognized that employees transferred as part of a BPO deal would progress from an inevitable **mourning** of their prior roles through four further stages – **forming** cautious views of their new roles, **storming** or confronting to establish their roles in the new organization, **norming** into new patterns of teamwork, and finally **performing** as part of a fully effective team. An effective implementation process involved recognition and proactive management of the individual's needs at each stage of the transition;
- The implementation process must also recognize that the individual customers of what was now an external service must also be proactively managed if they were to successfully transition to a new mindset. This in turn was dependent on detailed service definition;
- In an Enterprise Partnership (rather than a traditional fee-for-service deal) an efficient and effective implementation process was a means of keeping partnership in step, of aligning expectations and rewards through the life of a deal.

The first two points above are well illustrated by the experiences at BP and LSE. The third needs some elaboration. In traditional fee-for-service outsourcing, the customer prepares full and detailed statements of services, costs, and resources; and the supplier verifies those statements in a detailed due diligence process before contracting and taking responsibility for the service. For a major outsourcing deal this is a time consuming process which can delay for up to a year the service transition. Furthermore, the end-point of the process is typically a legal document running to hundreds of pages, a document which is extremely difficult to understand, monitor, and enforce. All of this is a consequence of misaligned incentives: both parties are well aware that from the moment of contract this will be a zero-sum win/lose situation, and each is seeking to maximize their starting position in what is often a strongly adversarial process.

As Andrews and colleagues realized from the BP deal onwards, in a true Partnership relationship aligned incentives made possible a very different process. They devised a new four phased implementation approach which not only recognized the need to manage transition in transferees and service users, but also captured the objectives and expectations of the partner organizations over time:

- As soon as a Letter of Intent was signed, the partnership entered a *Preparation* phase in which, in parallel with contract negotiations, a first level mapping of the "as-is" service and process was achieved. This provided the information base for creation of the Business Plan which the Enterprise Partnership would pursue;
- With the signing of the contract, the Partnership moved into *Realignment*. While service may show some improvement in cost and/or quality through implementation of quick and obvious opportunities, the main emphasis was on service stability during successful induction of the transferees; and on detailed due diligence through creation of a full service definition and service specification. These two sets of activity were crucial in establishing the sought-for trust and behaviors in both transferees and service customers, required for the success of the Partnership. The Realignment

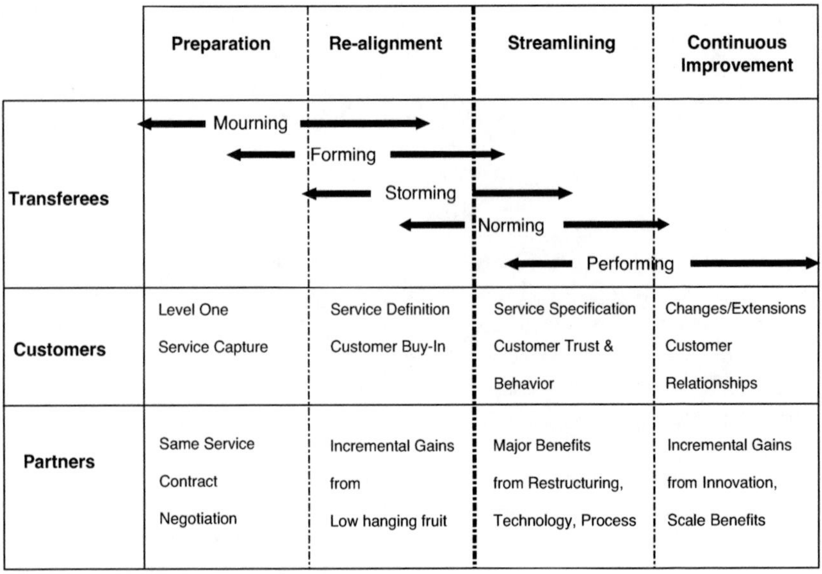

	Preparation	Re-alignment	Streamlining	Continuous Improvement
Transferees	← Mourning →	Forming →	Storming →	
		← Forming →	← Norming →	
		← Storming →	← Performing →	
Customers	Level One	Service Definition	Service Specification	Changes/Extensions
	Service Capture	Customer Buy-In	Customer Trust & Behavior	Customer Relationships
Partners	Same Service	Incremental Gains	Major Benefits	Incremental Gains
	Contract	from	from Restructuring,	from Innovation,
	Negotiation	Low hanging fruit	Technology, Process	Scale Benefits

Figure 13.1   Four Phases of Implementation

phase concluded with the sign-off of the detailed service definition. The Win/Win structuring of an Enterprise Partnership allowed any resultant re-basing of costs to be absorbed into a revised business plan;

- The planned major improvements in service cost and quality were then implemented during the *Streamlining* phase, at a time when both transferees/service providers and customers had become prepared for them. The Partnership could operate on a viable financial basis because benefits were being passed on to the client business as and when they were being achieved, within an open book operating regime;
- Future benefits in the final phase of *Continuous Improvement* were seen to depend on the Partnership's success in further service and process innovation, targeted at both existing and additional end-user customers.

Figure 13.1 provides a conceptual summary of the logic of the implementation model. The three strands of Enterprise Partnership, Competencies, and Phased Implementation comprise the business model which Andrews laid out in his business plan for his new company, Xchanging.

Creating the Xchanging company

When he founded Xchanging in 1998 David Andrews was convinced that the market for business process outsourcing was set for major expansion, and that, through his experiences, he had identified an approach that was superior to currently prevailing offerings. Xchanging's target would be the "back office" functions and processes of major corporations, the "cinderella" activities which typically had suffered from years of relative under-investment and ad-hoc expansion. But for Xchanging to succeed with such clients it needed the resources to back its ideas. Andrews embarked on a search to find a financial backer who would share his ambition to turn Xchanging into a globally significant business. He succeeded when General Atlantic Partners, the leading US-based private equity investment firm, agreed to an investment of £50 million.[3] With GA's backing, Andrews could then set out to recruit the top level team that would turn Xchanging's business model into operational reality.

His first objective was to find a leader for each of Xchanging's identified Competencies. The individuals selected would each provide a combination of thought leadership and proven implementation experience. To head the People Competency, he had to look no further than John Attenborough; similarly Andrew Chadwick was retained to set up the Environment Competency. Others were recruited through a search process which started with

---

[3]The £50 million was later increased to £60 million. GA announced a further £50 million investment in Xchanging in November 2002.

an identification of where the target competency was most likely to be world class. For example, Andrews looked to the consumer products sector to find a Practice Director for the Service Competency; he recruited Bryony Moore who had held senior marketing posts in Black & Decker and Braun Electric, followed by consulting assignments in such firms as Johnson & Johnson and Sara Lee. Similarly, GE Corporation was identified as having the best understanding of process improvement, leading to the recruitment of Paul Ruggier from GE Capital to set up the Process Competency. In each of them Andrews recognized the combination of qualities he was seeking:

> "Within two minutes of speaking to Bryony, I knew that this person just lived and breathed customer service and knew what needed to be done......I had not known the story of GE's adoption of the Six Sigma methodology for process improvement. The passion that Paul Ruggier communicated to me said that I wanted that man." – David Andrews

1999 also saw the first recruitment of someone earmarked to be CEO of an Xchanging Enterprise Partnership:

> "I knew I needed people who were top class operators. I knew I didn't want consultants but people who had the intellectual horse-power of consult-ants. Richard Houghton was a Harvard Business School Baker Scholar, spent five years with McKinsey, then a Divisional Chief Executive at Caradon. The pedigree is phenomenal." – David Andrews

The search for a Commercial Director – the person who would be responsible for embedding Xchanging's Partnership concepts in contracts negotiated with clients – provides one more example of Andrews's approach to recruitment:

> "You have got to have someone who is superbly competent in shaping and concluding deals. I said to myself, after a number of false starts, the only place to go for this is investment banking. As soon as Adele Brown came on board from Lazards, all of a sudden our ability to put together interesting deals professionally to the marketplace changed." – David Andrews

As the team came together, one priority was to capture in detail the Xchanging approach, to start building the intellectual property in the form of manuals for each Xchanging competency. The other task of course was to win some business! Inevitably this represented something of a roller-coaster ride for a start-up company, with disappointments along the way.

But by the beginning of 2002 Xchanging had in place the four contracts which we have had the opportunity to research:

- An HR Services Partnership with BAE SYSTEMS to provide services to the client's 150,000 employees and dependents, worth £250 million over ten years. Essentially, the "transactional" HR activity was transferred to Xchanging, the "strategic" HR activity was retained within BAE SYSTEMS;
- A subsequent ten-year Partnership with BAE SYSTEMS to manage £800 million of procurement in indirect spend categories;
- An Insurance Services Partnership jointly formed with Lloyd's of London and the Insurance Underwriters Association, which settled more than £20 billion of business each year within a network of some 180 companies. The respective settlement offices of Lloyd's and the IUA – known as the Lloyd's Policy Signing Office (LPSO) and the London Processing Centre (LPC) – were transferred to Xchanging;
- A subsequent Claims Services Partnership with Lloyd's of London, which managed more than 250,000 claims per year to a combined value of £8 billion.

The Xchanging business model in action: evidence from the research

The anatomy of partnership

All four of the deals studied were structured as "Enterprise Partnerships", the first implication of this being that each resulted in the creation of a new Business Unit within Xchanging. They were respectively called Xchanging Human Resource Services (XHRS), Xchanging Procurement Services (XPS), Xchanging Insurance Services (XIS), and Xchanging Claims Services (XCS). The Xchanging company had full operational control of each business unit, and appointed its Chief Executive and management team. The contractual framework for each of these Enterprise Partnerships was similar and included the following features:

- **Financial accounting**. "Profits" of the business unit were shared between Xchanging and its Client Partner, usually on a 50/50 basis. Profits were generated through cost efficiencies achieved on baseline services; through introduction of new services, which were priced at an agreed mark-up over cost; through sale of services to third parties. Accounting was on an open book basis;
- **Baseline service guarantees**. While details vary, there were commitments on cost and quality improvements over time. For example, in the XHRS deal, BAE SYSTEMS were guaranteed minimum levels of cost savings in the early years; the contract also committed XHRS to improve baseline service to "world class upper quartile" performance by the end of year five;

- **Human resources.** All those responsible for service provision within the client partner transferred to the Enterprise Partnership on agreed terms. Xchanging became responsible for their employment and benefit costs, and for any redundancy costs incurred. Xchanging committed to assign some of its key talent into the partnership;
- **Investment.** Xchanging committed to a minimum level of investment into the partnership, for identified purposes. For example, the XIS contract identified £15 million of investment in various categories; within the XHRS contract £17 million were committed, primarily for the implementation of a new technology base;
- **Governance.** The contract established joint governance bodies for the partnership: a Board of Directors; a Service Review Board; and, if a significant technology investment was committed, a Technology Review Board.

The simplicity of means embodied in these arrangements has a remarkable elegance to anyone who has waded through the waist-deep documentation of more typical major outsourcing deals. It reflects the ability, within a partnership deal, to defer detailed due diligence to the post-contract Realignment phase; and to focus instead on what was required to deliver the performance ambitions of the contract. This goes back to the diagnosis by Andrews and Bramley of what would enable a superior model of outsourcing:

> "First a mechanism for maintaining active involvement from senior management, on both sides...". – John Bramley

The governance provisions established the mechanism for the involvement of both sides. Within them, the **Service Review Board** (SRB) was familiar from that of the BP accounting services deal. Each Enterprise Partnership had an SRB with equal membership from Xchanging and the client partner. It met regularly to monitor performance of existing services, and to sign off on the specification and pricing of any proposed new ones. It had contractual powers to impose financial penalties if persistently poor service performance was being experienced. It also had a crucial role in the sign-off of detailed service definition, specification, and baseline cost which marked the end of the Realignment phase. Kim Reid who, as HR Director for BAE SYSTEMS Customer Solutions and Support Group, was one of the client-side members of the XHRS Service Review Board saw the Board as one of the instruments of partnership:

> "If this was a traditional customer/supplier relationship I think you would get the customer blaming the supplier for not delivering a service. For me the partnership means that the accountability for delivering service into

the business is mine. I have to make sure it is delivered as a seamless service so that myself and my other HR Directors will not say 'this went wrong because XHRS did this'. If something goes wrong it is because we did it. It is very much a partner type relationship." – Kim Reid

The joint **Board of Directors** established for each Enterprise Partnership took governance arrangements a step beyond Andrews's previous experience. The idea was triggered by his perception that client management attention begins to wane once an outsourcing deal has progressed beyond its early stages:

"Could I get sponsors to continue to turn up for meetings? Well maybe, but it was hard work. So when we formed Xchanging we put enterprise partnership into a standard commercial structure. It's a breakthrough because you have got rules there. You have got rules like you have a Board of Directors and you have non-executive Directors, and they have to turn up for meetings. And you have certain duties as Board Members, you have to act in the best interest of the business whether you are from the outsourcer or the client. That is a big mindset change, but business people who have worked in public companies and served on Boards understand that, of course they do. I think it is the last brick in the governance wall." – David Andrews

While the real test of this idea would not come until later years of the partnerships, it is easy to see its symbolic power. For example, the first Annual Report of XHRS was introduced by non-executive Chairman Tony McCarthy – whose "day job" was Group HR Director of BAE SYSTEMS.

The Enterprise Partnership structure was not the only business format offered by Xchanging. In particular, each of the Enterprise Partnership business units was charged with pursuing external clients for their services, with several "wins" scored for XCS and XIS in 2002/03, and many since for these and the procurement arm. The logic of such deals was that they added economies of scale to each of the businesses, to the potential advantages of all parties. While detailed study of these "add-on" deals was beyond the scope of our research, the documentation we saw showed that in the 2001–05 period these additional external clients experienced most of the elements of the Xchanging business model – four phases of implementation, deployment of Xchanging's Competencies, establishment of joint Service Review Boards. However, there were two important contractual differences:

- These clients did not have representation on Boards of Directors, since no new business unit, or Board, was being established;

- For the same reason, the new clients received guarantees on service costs but did not share in any further cost efficiencies achieved.

Our overall understanding of Xchanging's emerging practice, confirmed by looking at subsequent deals from 2006–08, is that a "partnership ethos" was embedded in their approach to all deals; but the level of client participation in governance and profits varied pragmatically as a function of the size and complexity of the deal.

Competencies – "the DNA of Xchanging"

When David Andrews first assembled his business plan for Xchanging, the business model featured five Competencies that would be critical to success – in the areas of **People, Service, Process, Technology, Environment.** Richard Houghton's recruitment alerted Andrews to a sixth – **Sourcing** – based on Houghton's own experience of the impact of highly professional procurement skills while at Caradon. Finally, the need identified in the business plan for strong program management skills was translated into establishment of a seventh Competency – **Implementation.** Collectively these Competencies came to known as the "DNA of Xchanging". By permeating the activity of every Xchanging deal they would deliver the second requirement of a superior approach to business process outsourcing:

> "...coupled with that joint senior management involvement, supporting that really, the availability within the supplying company of the necessary range of skills, some of which were deficient in previous outsourcing models." – John Bramley

Our research confirmed the centrality of Competency deployment to the Xchanging approach. The following sections include some of the many examples we experienced.

The People Competency in action

The People Competency Manual captured the tool set which John Attenborough built up over the years to take transferees progressively from **Mourning** through the stages of **Forming, Storming,** and **Norming** to **Performing** as "champion teams". It provided for each stage guidance to management on what would be appropriate and inappropriate behaviors; the tools most relevant to helping individuals through that stage; and a standardized format for assessing individual progress.

For the transferees, who had previously been working far from the spotlight within corporate back offices, it represented a new level of management attention. Alan Bailey, himself a management transferee from BAE

SYSTEMS, recalled the impact of the XHRS launch event which marked the start of the Forming stage:

> "So these guys had never been talked to like that before, and it's exciting for them because they are profit generating, not the overhead cost we had always been referred to in the past." – Alan Bailey

The momentum was then increased through a series of three-day induction sessions, which all transferees attended within six weeks of the contract being signed:

> "The transferred employees had seen Xchanging's management team, because we all went to these things, did Q & As, stood on the stage and answered all their questions, Richard Houghton [XHRS CEO] did all of them, he was committed to doing these. The employees hadn't seen that before. They had been in an area where they didn't see the management very often, didn't get access to them and then all of a sudden, this is an enthusiastic team that they are now seeing and they were part of it, they went back buzzing." – Alan Bailey

The People Competency operated on the basis that a great deal of potential resided in people buried in back offices. One key to the future success of the partnership business was to find ways to release their energy, talent and commitment:

> "I have a fundamental belief that inside each of these vertical back office functions if you just screw the lid off and put some water in, people just go oomph and grow". – John Attenborough

We found that those transferred at the management level were the first to experience this sense of new potential. From BAE SYSTEMS, Alan Bailey and colleague David Bauernfeind were revelling in their roles as members of the XHRS executive team. Darren Fisher, transferred from Lloyd's into the XCS executive team, spoke of a similar effect:

> "One of the reasons for the behavioural change I think is that the whole silo thing has quite rightly been broken down, and people have been given different responsibilities to what they had in Lloyd's. If you had asked me six months ago if the management team could gel and blend and operate the way it does, I would have said there was no way. I think we all feel much more empowered than we felt before." – Darren Fisher

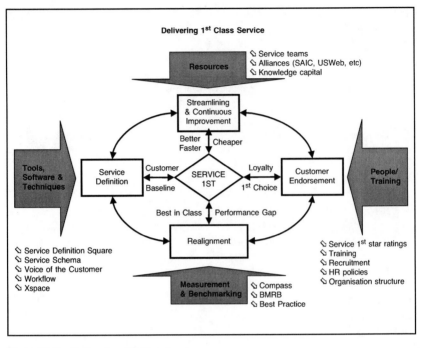

Figure 13.2   Delivering 1ˢᵗ Class Service
Source: Xchanging Service Manual, 2004

The Service Competency in action

Bryony Moore, recruited as Practice Director of the Service Competency, faced the challenge of establishing the formal tool set for her area, of translating her accumulated personal learning into documented best practice. The Service Competency Manual shows (Figure 13.2) a four pronged approach to the achievement of "First Class Service".

The critical start point is the creation of a detailed Service Definition, a task which Bryony Moore led personally on secondment to the executive team of the XHRS partnership.

> "In BAE SYSTEMS which had just gone through this massive merger, they have got over 70 sites. On each of those sites, there are often multiple BAE SYSTEMS businesses, a history of conjoined businesses and different cultures; and everybody thought that their bit of HR was different from everybody else's. We now have one operating HR Service specification for the whole of the BAE SYSTEMS in the UK. Now, that has taken a huge amount of relational work in doing workshops, because all we have done is capture the 'as-is'. It is not about us telling them what they are going to get; the

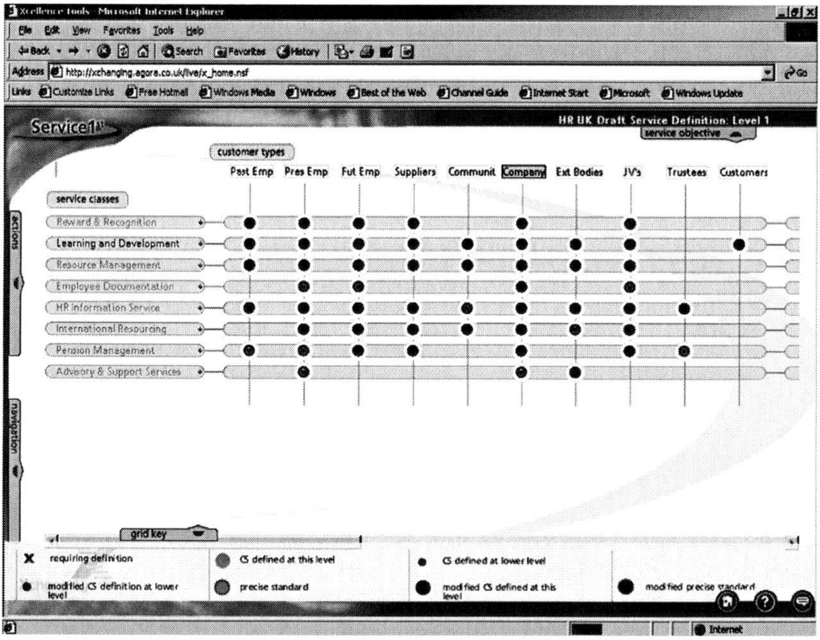

Figure 13.3 The XHRS Service Definition Site (2005)

process of service definition is to define the 'as is', what has historically been done until today so that we can get a stake in the ground." – Bryony Moore

Using a web-based tool developed by Xchanging, the team mapped more than 400 specific services within eight categories:

- Reward and Recognition;
- Learning and Development;
- Resource Management;
- Employee Documentation;
- HR Information Services;
- International Resources;
- Pension Management;
- Advisory and Support Service.

The completed service definition showed for each service which of the ten stakeholders within BAE SYSTEMS were the target customers: current employees, past employees, future employees, the company, BAE SYSTEMS' suppliers, BAE SYSTEMS' customers, the community, external governing bodies, joint ventures, and trustees. Once approved, it made available online as a common reference point (Figure 13.3).

Creation of a detailed service definition served multiple purposes. It was a key component of the due diligence which, in the Xchanging model, was completed after the contract was signed. It established for the Service Review Board the base for future measurement and progress toward the achievement of external benchmarks of world class service quality – the second prong of the Service Competency model. And the extensive exposure to customers which its creation required was critical to the building of trust:

> "In an organization like BAE SYSTEMS, the way they do business and protect the interests of their business is they are very detailed, and it is very much by consensus and there has to be approval and support from all parts of the business. They don't take anything on trust. You have to prove yourself every step of the way. And also HR, historically here, has not delivered in a lot of areas. Therefore, I must manage the people and we have had to work very hard to show them that they can trust us, that we will deliver on our promises, that we do understand what is required, that we will focus on what is important to them." – Bryony Moore

At this stage the Service Competency had prepared the ground for the third element of the Service model, restructuring to a new organization in the Streamlining phase of implementation (see Figure 13.1). In the case of XHRS this involved the creation of seven Service Streams, each operating as a mini service business; and the appointment of five Customer Relationship Managers, aligned to the major business groupings of BAE SYSTEMS. A further training program helped all transferees to move from a "back office" to a "front office" mindset, the fourth strand of the model:

> "The area that I can have the biggest impact during streamlining is on training and changing the mind of our own people to give them a practical way of operating differently. We said it is very different working for a service organisation where HR is the core business, not a back office function. We have to get everybody up to a certain standard and the pace at which we are going to work is much faster and tougher than you are used to, the standards and attention to detail are absolutely primary and therefore, the Service Xcellence training is a first step in that direction. And most of them already have a pretty good understanding and they found this most enjoyable, most instructive, very helpful, and very practical." – Bryony Moore

Kim Reid, HR Director for BAE SYSTEMS Customer Solutions and Support Group, provided a favorable report on the Service progress being made by XHRS:

> "I guess some of my colleagues wouldn't say this but I do think that the service from a process, control point of view has improved extraordinarily.

I think Xchanging really does have the right processes in place, they really know what they are doing on that. Some of the transformation that I have seen in some of the people that are in XHRS, especially the customer relationship managers, one or two of them, they never would have interacted with the business in the way that are doing now, they have become a lot more professional. They are a lot more understanding of what drives a business, understanding of cost base and how you actually get value out of a business, so that's been quite a nice surprise to see that happen and to see that happen so quickly."– Kim Reid

The Process Competency in action

Paul Ruggier saw the creation of Xchanging's Process Competency as *"an opportunity to take the best of my learnings from Procter & Gamble, Texaco, and GE, and do it the way I felt was right."* One step was to bring together a best practice methodology and tool set for process improvement under the label CMADIS – Contracting projects, Measuring data, Analyzing data, Developing solutions, Implementing solutions, and Sustaining benefits. While CMADIS incorporated tried and tested tools from his Six Sigma experience, he wanted to extend previous methodologies in three of these stages: projects would be "contracted" rather than merely "defined"; and he brought new emphases and ideas to the implementation and sustaining stages. He then identified as particularly important to the Xchanging approach the full time assignment of people from within the business:

> "In the past, we have all been there, you have had your process improvement project but you have also had your day job to worry about. We take people full time from the business and train them, I think that is the key. Nobody knows the business better than those actually doing it." – Paul Ruggier

The XIS partnership business, to which Ruggier himself was seconded, provided the clearest evidence of the Process Competency in action. During the pre-contract Preparation stage for XIS, Ruggier carried out extensive process analysis. Based on this work, he was able to advise that an XIS business plan which called for 50% cost reduction over five years was realistic. Working with Adrian Giles – another external recruit experienced in Six Sigma techniques – he identified 37 projects that could be tackled immediately. At the same time he was selecting potential project leaders from those who would transfer from the client side.

When the XIS contract was signed in May 2001, six of these transferees were assigned full time to process improvement work. They received intensive training in the CMADIS methodologies and became certified "Black Belts" within the generic language of Six Sigma (see Figure 13.4).

In June 2001 the Black Belts were handed their projects. Each was required to complete within three months, without required technology change; and each was to deliver £200,000 of cost savings. They succeeded. Whereas the XIS business plan had a Year 1 objective of saving 16 full time jobs, the first wave of process work identified a headcount reduction of 84 people – equivalent to a £2 millions annual saving in a £7 millions cost base. The team moved on to a second wave of projects, continuing to reflect the Ruggier approach:

> "You do 'bite size' projects that you can get results from in three months. You analyse the process at level 4 where it becomes actionable. You take people from the businesses, train them thoroughly in the techniques and let them do process improvement full time – full time people, full time results. Six Sigma is also enormously useful as a discipline, and a benchmark to measure process performance against...also choosing the right people for Black Belt training – people willing to challenge existing paradigms, intelligent, analytical skills, influencing and conflict resolution skills, respect in the organisation." – Paul Ruggier

The Process Competency's approach of selecting transferees from the "grass roots" of the business and training them as Black Belts fitted very well with Attenborough's belief – cited earlier – that those "buried within back offices" often have great inherent development potential. The Black Belts we interviewed were clearly excited by their experiences:

> "At first I was reticent about coming forward. But it has been the first time I have been able to go through a whole process and implement something that makes a – significant is too small a word for it – a fundamental change to the business. You do feel good about it!" – John Morris

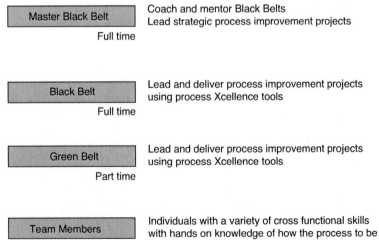

Master Black Belt
Full time
Coach and mentor Black Belts
Lead strategic process improvement projects

Black Belt
Full time
Lead and deliver process improvement projects using process Xcellence tools

Green Belt
Part time
Lead and deliver process improvement projects using process Xcellence tools

Team Members
Part time
Individuals with a variety of cross functional skills with hands on knowledge of how the process to be improved works and functions

Figure 13.4   Xchanging's Six Sigma Infrastructure

"I was quite cynical about whether a very small team of no status could go in and influence change. But here we could influence our Managing Director to make a change from the strategy he set out. I have never been in that position before. And it is interesting now because people treat me differently, they talk to me differently." – Barbara Chandler

But they also recognized the role of the methodology in what they had been able to achieve:

"I think the CMADIS cycle has been what has made the difference.."
"Without the rigour of the CMADIS process I very much doubt we would have achieved this in the time we have achieved it."
"CMADIS is very, very powerful. The rigour in the approach is very, very powerful."

The Technology Competency in action

Practice Director for the Technology Competency was Steve Bowen, who joined Xchanging after a ten-year career in Accenture where he described himself as having been *"focussed on technology architectures, big architectures."* He shared David Andrews's belief in the power of component driven architectures, and welcomed the challenge of shaping Xchanging's technology capability:

"You very rarely get the opportunity to have a free reign, to drive technology the way you believe it should be driven unconstrained by the specifics of a client assignment. The essence of the brief was quite simple: Xchanging had to be able to scale as a business without the bottomless pit of money required to re-invent the wheel every time. What we had to do was come up with a technology platform that would be a beating heart at the centre of every partnership business. Invest once and implement many times." – Steve Bowen

At the heart of Bowen's solution was a four box architecture, capturing the generic requirements of any service business (Figure 13.5).

- The Reference box captured the "static" information of the business – for the XHRS business this would include Health and Safety policies, Employment Law, and so on; for XPS, the contracts set up with suppliers; for XCS the policy documents and claim registration requirements. The relevant tools were those of knowledge and content management;
- The second box was labelled Performance because it captured both the detailed Service Definition and the performance data relevant to each service component;
- The Relationship box was the source of information about both customers and suppliers of the service business – the tracking of contacts made, follow-up committed and so on;

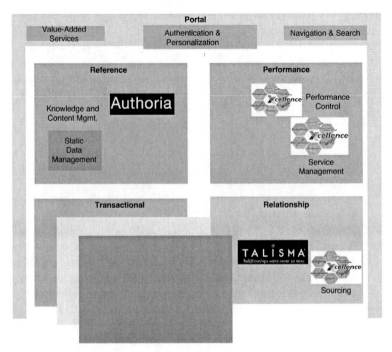

Figure 13.5   Xchanging's Technology Architecture Framework

- The fourth box was the gateway to the transaction systems underpinning the business activity over time – the claims processing systems, the trading platform for procurement for example.

Wrapped around these boxes was the software required to deliver the services through an internet portal – the log-on authentication and personalization, navigation and search, and other value-added services. The architecture was designed to provide a scalable model to support Xchanging's growth over time, and to provide the flexibility of decision making about legacy system replacement which had proven so important, in Andrews's experience.

The first test of the technology approach came in the XHRS business, where provision of an "e-HR" system to end users had been specified as a key requirement by BAE SYSTEMS. The test was passed when XHRS launched the first version of **peopleportal** at the beginning of October 2001, five months after contract signature. Three further releases each provided new functionality over the next five months. The impact was considerable:

> "I think they were absolutely astonished that we delivered on that, I don't think they expected it for one minute." – Richard Houghton, CEO, XHRS

"I think the peopleportal has been the first sign from within the business that something has changed, something has actually happened. I think the first time it was used, it was used for the senior leadership population, we were doing an exercise on pay review so each senior leader within the business (650) of them had access to that people portal. We had a lot of very good feedback, it was very good, the technology was great, it was web based, but we've had some very good feedback but we've also had people who just can't get the hang of using the technology." – Kim Reid, HR Director, BAE SYSTEMS Customer Solutions and Support Group

In the XIS partnership business, the technology competency was presented with a different set of problems. The immediately chal-lenging issue was what to do about inherited outsourcing contracts. XIS CEO John Benjamin reflected ruefully that:

"If I had our time again we would have looked much harder at the IT contracts we had inherited. If IT is 40% of your costs, and you aim to dramatically reduce overall business costs, it gets in the way if you are hemmed in by seven year IT contracts, not negotiated with very much flexibility. You know there are going to be problems if you don't have methods for reconciling change within them."

Clearly these issues had to be sorted before XIS could move on to a higher level IT agenda. In April 2001 Xchanging had headhunted, and seconded to the XIS IT post, David White – a highly experienced IT exe-cutive with a background in large-scale manufacturing, retail, and insur-ance organizations, and in managing the IT aspects of mergers. White got written into the contract with Lloyd's and IUA that if need be, the out-sourcing contracts could be broken, albeit by paying penalties, even though the contracts still had between five–six years to run. This gave XIS some negotiating strength. The way forward, then, was to attack the substantial IT cost base of £12 million a year. This was possible, because, in David White's experience, IT outsourcing suppliers had not always managed their cost base that well, often having inherited their own IT from an inefficient company they had taken over the assets of in a previous deal.

White skilfully leveraged the obligations of the supplier under the contract to benchmark and deliver best practice cost-effective service. On the development contract, in a very short time, he achieved an agreed 28% cost reduction on £5.4 million by attacking variable costs like cus-tomer liaison charges, and inflationary clauses. In the £5.7 million a year Lloyd's facilities management contract, he leveraged the supplier's con-tractual obligation to utilize cost effective mainframe and data warehousing environments to save £1.5 million in the first year. Further savings were targeted for later years.

At the time of the research significant technology investments – based on the same platform – were under development for each of the partnership businesses, under the direction of the "technology solution architect" embedded in each business. Bowen was pursuing a pragmatic mix of external procurement and in-house development by small fast cycle teams. He reflected on what he felt was the distinctiveness of the Xchanging approach:

> "In the classic model consultants will come in and they will start mucking about with your transactional systems. Oh you have got to merge all of these 16 systems into one great big massive system, million man days and we'll charge you a thousand pounds a day. We leave those systems alone – we've implemented this in BAE SYSTEMS while their 28 transactional systems are still out there. We'll take time to figure out what to do with those systems, while we are already delivering value.... I think we do have a unique approach to information architecture, but uniqueness does not last very long. We now tend to rely more on our implementation credentials. As one potential client expressed it, 'you know what you want to do, the speed at which you do it is incredible, you have incredibly bright people working for you, and you are delivering.'" – Steve Bowen

The Environment Competency in action

The Environment Competency was charged with providing a threefold contribution to the success of Xchanging's Enterprise Partnerships:

- To reinforce in the minds of both transferees and Xchanging's service customers that something has changed, that the old back office has become the front office of a service business – the "business surfboard" effect;
- To help build the "look and feel", the brand of the Xchanging company;
- To improve the cost efficiency of Xchanging's real estate.

The potential tension between these elements – particularly the first and the third – was addressed by the techniques developed by Environment Practice Director Andrew Chadwick. Chadwick claimed to have pioneered the use of CAD in architecture, inventing the idea of "organizational modelling" to capture an understanding of how people actually use office space. He combined this with the concept of the non-territorial office to design what he calls the "space time office" – the space you need for the time you need it. Chris Main, who worked with Andrews and Chadwick on the Georges Cinque project and now represented the environment competency on the XCS team, explained that this was not just about "hot desking":

"When we moved into Georges Cinque you actually had to think what do I need for today? Do I need a closed space to meet people in? Do I just need a space where I can work quietly? Do I need an informal area to talk to people? Then you would interact with a reservation system and a group of people who helped on that." – Chris Main

Space time office design delivered Chadwick's philosophy of *"less/better rather than more/mediocre"* real estate. It met the challenge of cost efficiency by moving the business closer to the target of "virtual estate":

"I define virtual estate as the space you need if you could wave a wand and change everything tomorrow and move into the space that fits you. Actual real estate is always bigger than virtual estate. The difference between the two is what I call trapped value." – Andrew Chadwick

By mid-2002, the environment competency had completed three projects for the Xchanging partnership businesses:

• New offices in London's Billiter Street for the management teams of XIS, and Xchanging as a whole;
• A purpose built shared service centre for XHRS in Preston, north west England, which also accommodated XPS staff;
• Offices for XCS in Gallery 6 of the spectacular building created for Lloyd's some years ago by Richard Rodgers.

All these facilities feature shared some common "look and feel" – the same range of furniture, and a distinctive and ubiquitous blue carpeting with the Xchanging logo; but there were significant differences reflecting their separate purposes. For example the Preston building met the low cost objective while simultaneously transporting XHRS transferees from *"the porta-cabins of BAE SYSTEMS at Wharton"* to their own "front office" facilities.

The XCS offices in Gallery 6 on the other hand symbolized the partnership business's presence in the heart of the insurance market. But in marked contrast to the conventional layouts you found throughout the rest of the Lloyd's building, it featured a variety of spaces, shapes, and moods – small cost efficient workstations within an open area, enclosed quiet rooms, a "combination space" modelled on *"the University Common Room where Dons read their newspapers, get their letters from pigeon*

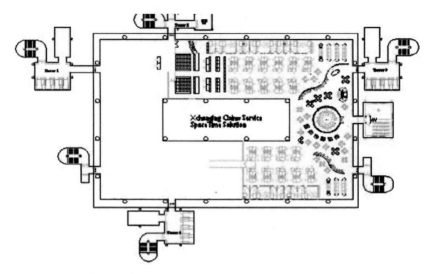

Figure 13.6   The New XCS Offices in Gallery 6 (2004)

holes, and talk about nuclear physics – a space that is informal and formal at the same time". The objective was to allow a choice of environments for meetings with customers, the Brokers and Underwriters who may be dealing with anything from straightforward modest claims to the massive consequences of the attack on the World Trade Towers. Figure 13.6 shows the layout of Gallery 6, one example of the Environment Competency in action.

The Sourcing Competency in action

When Richard Houghton convinced David Andrews of the significance of Sourcing as an additional competency (see Figure 13.7), David Rich-Jones was recruited into Xchanging. His experience included a period in Smith-KlineBeecham, where he created a global purchasing function to manage the company's £7 billions annual spend across 140 countries; as well as corporate purchasing roles in NatWest Bank, and more recently Caradon. However, when Xchanging won the XPS deal to manage procurement of indirect categories for BAE SYSTEMS, Rich-Jones was the obvious person to lead that new Enterprise Partnership. His former Caradon colleague John Doherty joined Xchanging as Practice Director for Sourcing.

The Sourcing Competency brought three sources of leverage to the task of reducing procurement spend:

- The category expertise of the best procurement professionals;
- A set of tools and techniques to support those professionals, including software tools for modeling procurement strategies, and a technology based trading platform;

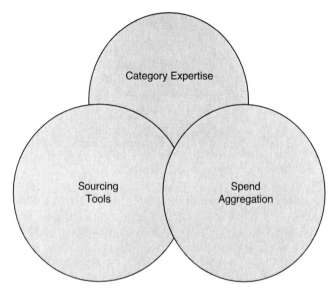

Figure 13.7 The High Level Model of the Sourcing Competency (2003)

• The ability to aggregate demand into volumes more attractive to suppliers.

While these may be familiar ideas, at least in outline, Doherty pointed out that they were not commonly found within Xchanging's target customer domain:

"In a nutshell we are bringing the ideas of strategic commodity management, which hitherto have been typically applied to direct materials or core procurement, into what is normally a fragmented and disparate and neglected area of indirect procurement. We are building specific expertise in a relatively narrow range of commodities, rather than offering ourselves as procurement consultants who can consult on anything." – John Doherty

Not surprisingly, the Sourcing Competency was in the early years most strongly linked with the XPS partnership business, which had taken over the management of seven categories of indirect procurement for BAE SYSTEMS – remuneration and benefits, vehicle fleets, learning and development, non-technical contract labor, stationery, and recruitment. A base-lining process for each category created a definition of standard units that made up that category and their existing costs. Modeling processes identified appropriate strategies for the future management of that category.

Xchanging had three broad strategies for category management:

- An arm's length strategy in which the end user traded directly with Xchanging's chosen supplier, who passed an agreed margin to Xchanging. Stationery procurement, for example, was managed in this way;
- A middle level strategy in which Xchanging actively managed the accounts payable and receivable processes. The vehicle fleet category followed this strategy;
- A "thick involvement" model in which Xchanging acted as a market-maker between multiple customers and suppliers. This was the strategy for the non-technical contract labour category.

A specific example, of vehicle fleet management, showed some of the theory in action. This was a category where BAE SYSTEMS had already achieved a market rate by doing the "simple and obvious things" – aggregating their demand, requesting tenders from multiple leasing companies, selecting a winner who had quoted a monthly lease rate based on all his own costs. Xchanging achieved an improvement on this by first unitizing all the elements of car lease (Figure 13.8); then disaggregating the supply chain to achieve unbundled prices:

"You go to the lease provider and say we don't want you give us a standard quote, we want you to quote for your cost of financing and providing the lease. Similarly you go separately to the car manufacturer, to the maintenance and repair market and so on. It's a procurement technique you

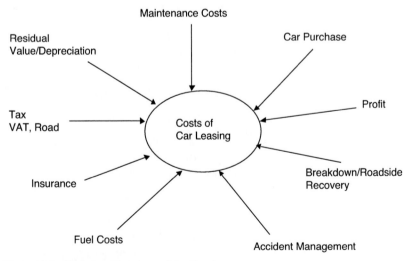

Figure 13.8   The Cost Elements of Car Leasing

would use on core materials, but we are applying it to a non-core area where typically clients do not have the time or energy." – John Doherty

As XPS moved toward the end of a hectic period of base-lining, the Sourcing Competency was starting to promote its contribution to the other partnership businesses.

The Implementation Competency – grit in the oyster?

"A key differentiator of the implementation team is that overall it is agnostic as to whether a particular approach is used or not, or as to the order in which one approach is used relative to another. Whatever is fit for purpose is key. Fitness for purpose overrides dogma, and outcome is more important than process." – Xchanging Implementation Manual, Principles section

The graphic used by Xchanging to introduce its competencies, its "DNA", was the first clue that Implementation was different (See Figure 13.9). It is positioned at the center of the other competencies, its basic role being to orchestrate their impact to best effect within each enterprise partnership. While there was an expectation (Figure 13.10) that Service and People would be the early competency levers, followed by the application of Process and Technology during the Streamlining phase, Implementation was expected to support each Enterprise Partnership CEO in identifying the actual deployment that would yield the most effective business plan. Thus while XHRS followed the "typical" plan fairly closely, Process work

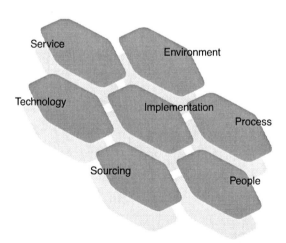

Figure 13.9   Implementation at the Centre of Xchanging's "DNA"

dominated the Realignment phase of XIS, and Environment made an early contribution to XCS.

Xchanging saw its Implementation Competency as bringing together the best traditions of consultancy and operations:

> "The Implementation competency is guided by a healthy paradox. It blends the rigorous project management disciplines exemplified by world-class consultants with the practicality and pragmatism that is only gained through the experience of running operations...The Implementation competency requires intellectual flexibility to vary or reverse a traditional approach according to circumstance...As a result there are no rules, only guidelines." – Implementation Competency Manual, 2003

To achieve their role, Xchanging looked for four personal characteristics in members of the Implementation team:

- The **imagination** to visualize what becomes possible once one or more of the assumptions that guided previous practice is challenged. This imagination is likely to be stimulated by experience of operations and operational performance in other industries and other Xchanging partnerships;
- An **awareness of the potential of new technology**, particularly the power of putting information in the forefront of customer and partner consciousness through internet portal technology;
- Commitment to **rigorous methods and disciplined ways of working,** since Implementation has a central role in driving and directing all of the activities of Xchanging in forming and operating Enterprise Partnerships;

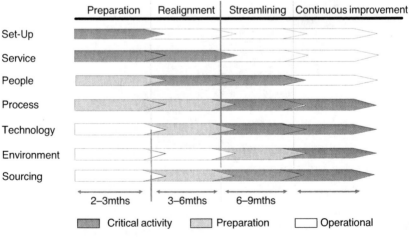

Figure 13.10   Typical Schedule for Competency Deployment Intuitive

- A **control consciousness** to deliver Implementation's responsibility for maintaining and augmenting control over day-to-day operations during periods of radical change; team members must be experts in assessing the risks posed by change initiatives, embedding appropriate controls to the satisfaction of Xchanging and Client management.

The Implementation Competency Practice Director, Mike Margetts, was another who spent his early professional career in Andersen Consulting – but a subsequent job as European Head of Project Services at Credit Suisse First Boston underlined some contrasts that shaped his values:

> "The approach at Andersens was all about structure and being very deterministic about the way things are done. CSFB was an environment where it did not really matter what you were going to do in six months. If you didn't do it in three months then you didn't do it. That was fantastic!" – Mike Margetts

The underpinning philosophy which Margetts looked for in the Implementation Competency reflected this emphasis on speed and results:

> "Implementation is a beacon of pragmatism. I understand best practice, and I do my best not to follow it – I do my best to cut corners from it. It is a difficult thing to systematize that approach, because it is an anti-approach." – Mike Margetts

We experienced in the research a number of examples of pragmatic problem-solving action, particularly in projects to roll-out new technology and new user services in the XHRS partnership to which Margetts was seconded. But the proper measure of the implementation competency's success in action must be a function of enterprise partnership progress toward achievement of goals and milestones.

Progressing the Enterprise Partnerships through four phases of implementation

To re-cap for a moment, the Xchanging approach was to manage each Enterprise Partnership through four phases of implementation. This was seen as a critical and distinctive component of the Xchanging business model, enabling an orderly and successful transition to partnership for the transferees, the end user customers, and for Xchanging's client organization overall. Each of the phases had well defined entry and exit points, and certain key activities:

- **Preparation** started when a Letter of Intent was signed, providing Xchanging with exclusive rights to negotiate a deal. In parallel with negotiations, Xchanging would research and formulate a business plan for the new enterprise. A vision was articulated for the business; the expected role of each Competency in achieving that vision over time was outlined; a five-year financial plan was developed. All this was shared with the client, creating mutual expectations of the partnership. Preparation concluded when the Contract was signed;

- During **Realignment**, the critical implementation level tasks were the induction of transferees into Xchanging, and detailed due diligence through the creation of a full Service Definition. At the same time Xchanging would be progressing projects, in areas such as Process and Technology, for the major change areas identified in the business plan. The external emphasis during Realignment was on confidence building and attitude changing among the customer end users. Service performance levels had to be sustained, and could be incrementally improved where there were obvious opportunities to do so. Realignment was complete when the client signed off on the detailed Service Definition, and on any re-basing which it implied;

- **Streamlining** was the phase of discontinuous and potentially far-reaching change, when the initiatives prepared during Realignment were put into effect. Streamlining was considered complete when all the major building blocks of the new business were seen to be securely in place – the culture, the organization, the physical and technological infrastructure and so on;

- The business then moved into **Continuous Improvement**, lasting for the remaining duration of the contract. The success of the business became dependent on exploitation of the platform created by Streamlining, through innovations in services offered and cost structure to support them, and through the acquisition of new external customers.

Table 13.1 shows the implementation status of Xchanging's Enterprise Partnerships in late 2002. It shows that the first two partnerships – XIS and XHRS – took much longer at the Preparation stage than Xchanging's target of three months. This was attributed to protracted negotiations with Clients who were wrestling with what they saw to be an unfamiliar, and as yet unproven, model. The follow-on deals with each client partner proceeded more smoothly through Preparation. From Realignment onwards, progress was seen to be good, with – most critically – the expectations set by the business plan for each partnership being met. The success of the partnerships in meeting the milestones of their business plans – with evidence that was shared transparently between Xchanging and the client – built the confidence and momentum for further progress.

From the Xchanging perspective, CFO Andrew Bester reported that he found all the enterprise partnership businesses were trading profitably. XIS made a significant profit in its first full year. XCS had won two external

Table 13.1   Progress of Enterprise Partnerships through Implementation Phases

	Xchanging Insurance Services XIS	Xchanging HR Services XHRS	Xchanging Claims Services XCS	Xchanging Procurement Services XPS
Preparation Dates	May 2000– April 2001	June 2000– April 2001	August 2001– October 2001	July 2001– October 2001
Realignment Dates	May 2001– September 2001	May 2001– October 2001	November 2001– February 2002	November 2001 onwards: base-lining by Category
Streamlining Dates	October 2001– August 2002	November 2001 – December 2002	March 2002– December 2002	Transition by Category
Cost Efficiency Examples	– 30% productivity improvement – 25% reduction in contract IT costs	– 33% productivity improvement	– 60% productivity improvement targeted through volume growth	– 12% average cost reduction achieved across categories managed
Service Improvement Examples	"e-repository" service launched	– Four releases of "peopleportal" achieved – Performance improvements in several critical services	– Enhanced Claims Review Service launched – Two new external clients signed – "Claimsportal" implemented	– "Sourcing Workroom" and "Sourcing Portal" implemented – Improved relationships with suppliers

clients, a critical step in their aggressive growth plan. XHRS made a small profit, in line with plan, after the guaranteed first year cost savings were passed to BAE SYSTEMS. XHRS CEO Richard Houghton was confident of "a decent profit" in the second year. Much of the bumpiest ride had been experienced by XPS: the business plan was predicated on BAE SYSTEMS transferring spend equivalent to £80 million/annum in seven identified categories; it became apparent that the actual spend transferred in these categories was closer to £35 million. This challenge to partnership was resolved when BAE SYSTEMS transferred another eight categories, bringing the total rate of spend transferred to £100 million/annum. Since XPS had been successful in winning control of a further £100 millions spend by customers external to the partnership, 2002 was completed on a high note.

As our initial research field work came to an end, comments from senior client-side Executives reflected the challenges involved in change – and their recognition that these BPO initiatives were not simplistic forays into cost reduction:

"There are layers to the prize, I think. I saw our own settlement bureau, LPSO, by itself as a dying organization. So I thought survival was one issue, and my first prize was to avoid that doomsday scenario. The longer term and much bigger prize is the impact that XIS can have on the way the London Market does business. I have been aboard seven years, and when I arrived at Lloyd's people were talking about the need for change. But everybody was kind of sitting and staring at the situation and saying well of course there are obvious benefits to be had here, but they will never be achieved. Creating XIS is the first step towards those being achieved. I think the creation of a single 'quality' organization in the middle of the London market business process will pay enormous dividends in taking the whole London market reform programme forward." – Nick Prettejohn, CEO of Lloyd's

"It has been a challenging year for all concerned. There have been a number of significant achievements such as the creation of a stand-alone company, the launch of the custom-built Service Centre in Preston, the launch of peopleportal, and significant progress in graduate recruitment and international assignments. We also now have, for the first time, a defined HR service specification and associated service metrics, which are reviewed monthly. Yet, as one might expect in such a complex undertaking, much remains to be done... We have learned a lot along the way, and I would like to see XHRS provide an example to BAE SYSTEMS of an entrepreneurial and 'service first' mindset...A great start and I am confident we will see significant further improvements as we continue on our journey to HR Excellence." – Tony McCarthy, BAE SYSTEMS Group HR Director

"The real attraction for us with Xchanging was to use the base that we BAE had established, the volume that we bought, to go and get third party revenue. If we could get a leverage ratio of 3 or 4 to 1, that would give us a much better business opportunity than just driving around internal activity... It has taken a lot longer than we anticipated to do all the base lining and all the legal and contractual work, but once we get active on a category there is good evidence that the benefits are there." – Jim Robinson, BAE SYSTEMS Procurement Director

The Xchanging business model – an assessment

Our research provided an opportunity to assess the benefits of what Xchanging claimed to be a distinctive approach to business process outsourcing. We were particularly interested in evaluating the potential for the Xchanging business model to address what we have found to be three critical issues during many years of research into IT outsourcing:

1. The issue of **partnership** between client and provider. In classic "fee for service" deals there is clearly a divergence of goals between client and provider, a correct perception that "a penny into your pocket is a penny out of mine"; this has obvious implications for attitudes and behaviors

which are particularly problematic in deals of extended duration. However, previous attempts to implement "goal aligned" deals also have a chequered history in our experience;

2. The issue of **sustainability**, the achievement of continuing performance improvement in deals which last five–ten years. We have consistently encountered client disappointment with what they perceive to be lack of innovation by the provider;

3. The issue of **applicability** of providers and their abilities to different client contexts. As the outsourcing market in all its forms continues to develop and grow, we find clients increasingly looking to select "horses for courses".

Whereas our case studies of the individual Enterprise Partnerships each included a number of specific findings, our analysis here focuses on these three central issues.

1. An assessment of partnership, Xchanging-style

The management literature has regularly highlighted the growing importance and attraction of partnership between firms – of "strategic partnerships", "joint ventures", "strategic alliances" and so on (see also Chapter 4). The "Resource Based View" of strategy focuses management on investment in core capabilities, and partnership with external providers to achieve non-core activities; the success of Japanese firms such as Toyota has encouraged adoption of partnership style relationships along the supply chain; increasing globalization has led to a proliferation of alliances around marketing and technology activities. But the literature has also increasingly chronicled the challenge of achieving partnership rather than the many potential reasons for wanting it.

Xchanging opted for a partnership proposition, signalled most obviously by the financial reward sharing arrangements of its Enterprise Partnership contracts. More fundamentally, it seems clear that the deals we studied were creating and sharing value that could not be achieved by either of the parties individually.

From the client perspective, the barriers were those of organizational complexity and lack of corporate priority:

"Everybody was saying there are obvious benefits to be had here, but they will never be achieved." – Nick Prettejohn, CEO of Lloyd's

"The company's priorities are investment in Engineering and in Research and Development, not in good old HR." – Chris Dickson, BAE SYSTEMS HR Director

From Xchanging's perspective, the company had assembled a range of impressive management skills but its intention was not to generate one-off consultancy fees. Partners were needed to provide the large scale activity which could be leveraged by those skills, to create a stream of annuity style revenues and profits:

> "We effectively have been given a 50% financial share plus management control of someone else's inefficient infrastructure." – Andrew Bester, CFO Xchanging

While some might suggest that each party is guilty of settling for a glass that is half empty, we see both client and provider to be consciously acquiring a large glass that is half full – rather than no glass at all. The institutional arrangements of Enterprise Partnerships were convincing in their alignment of goals in pursuit of Win/Win activity. Perhaps more importantly the values and behaviors espoused by key executives within Xchanging were generating a high level of momentum in that activity in the first few years of the organization's history. Many of these individuals had come from a background in consultancy, where the business model honored the mega project. But we consistently encountered – in Implementation, in Technology, in Process – the alternative values of "business benefits, fast and frequently". Within a different business context and incentive structure, they were exploiting their considerable skills to, we perceived, much greater effect for the client.

The powerful impact of the incentive structure got an Enterprise Business off to a good start, but what other aspects of the business model may contribute? Prior literature consistently highlights five factors as key enablers of successful strategic partnerships (Monczka *et al.*, 1998; Mohr and Spekman, 1994):

- The **Trust** that typically comes from a combination of personal relationships and professional credibility;
- A recognition of **Interdependence** in which all parties have a necessary role in achieving success;
- High levels of **Information Sharing** between the parties, including sharing of critical and proprietary information;
- High levels of **Information Participation** through joint planning and goal setting;
- A joint problem solving approach to **Conflict Resolution**.

It is instructive to assess the Xchanging business model, beyond the partnership contracting structure, against these factors. Xchanging's distinctive four phase implementation model seemed to make a particular contribution to the establishment of **trust**. Most notably, the creation of a detailed Service Definition during the Realignment phase involved extensive exposure to end user customers, and the completed definition – available online once approved – reinforced the idea that "we know you, understand you, and know what we are doing". The model allows relationships and trust to be built before the major changes were experienced in the Streamlining Phase. The appointment of Relationship Managers in Streamlining provides a mechanism for keeping that understanding and trust in place.

The Competency model is key to understanding partnership **interdependence**. Uniquely in our experience, Xchanging did not claim special knowledge of the back office activity a client may be seeking to outsource – of HR, claims settlement or whatever. That domain knowledge resided partly in retained client staff, and partly in those transferred to the enterprise partnership. The role of the competencies was to provide the complementary skills that would generate an altogether more effective and efficient service.

Open book accounting was clearly the critical step in **information sharing**; supported by the extensive service performance reporting provided from Streamlining onwards. While Xchanging had full management control of the partnership businesses, the business plan for each was shared with the client at Preparation. The Board of Directors, drawn from both sides, was then charged with onward review and development of the business plan, a forum for joint planning and goal setting – for **information participation** at the highest level.

Finally, the joint Service Review Board provided the formal mechanism for **conflict resolution**. It did not guarantee collaborative problem solving, but as we have seen (Kim Reid quote, p. 13), it seemed to be providing it.

In summary, the evidence from Xchanging's early years was that Xchanging was achieving real partnership in the situations, and that this was no accident. In 2003 we had one reservation for the future – that the acquisition of new clients could start to weaken the goal alignment between Xchanging and its Enterprise Partner clients. But the potential dilemma was already recognized:

> "I think third party business will be of great benefit financially to the partnership. It also brings in new ideas and different ways of doing things and gives the people who are doing the transactional side a different experience and perhaps different ways of doing things. But I guess one of the concerns from people in the business, if Xchanging goes out and wins more third party business, is that going to affect the service? The concern within the business will always be if that happens will the level of service drop. With all the measures that are in place I would find it would be difficult, you would spot the service dropping immediately and the contractual measures would be there to actually reign that back." – Kim Reid, HR Director, BAE SYSTEMS Customer Solutions and Support Group

But it would be churlish to finish this section on that note. By 2003 and through to 2005, the Xchanging business model had passed each test of partnership we had set.

2. An assessment of the potential sustainability of Xchanging enterprise partnerships

By 2003 none of the enterprise partnership businesses had fully moved into the Continuous Improvement phase, nor reached sufficient longevity of duration to experience "mid-contract" sag. On the contrary, all were in periods of intensive activity and excitement. But our experience elsewhere of client complaints of "lack of innovation" has been so consistent that we felt it important at that time to make some attempt to assess the potential sustainability of service performance improvement under the Xchanging business model. What would be the enablers of innovation through the life of the businesses? And how likely were they to be in place? And, from hindsight, what actually happened?

The first key to success, recognized from the outset by David Andrews and John Bramley, was continuing and active client involvement. The governance mechanisms of Boards of Directors and Service Review Boards were designed with this in mind. The announced plan by XHRS to add "local" Service Review Boards to address issues specific to BAE SYSTEMS business units subsequently further extended client involvement and stimulus. Our own prior thinking in this dimension, based on studies of IT outsourcing, has stressed the importance of particular people capabilities on the client side (Feeny and Willcocks, 1998). A combination of these institutional mechanisms and capability strands seemed appropriate, with regular rotation of client "non-executives" who bring a range of skills and perspectives.

Another source of the new perspectives which can trigger innovation is of course the world beyond the partnership businesses. As Kim Reid pointed out in the quotation in the previous section, the acquisition of new external business may introduce new ideas as well as bringing financial benefits from increased scale. In practice this subsequently happened in three of the enterprise partnerships, but not in the BAE HR business. Another pro-active route was for Xchanging to continue its policy of targeting external hires to bring in people who have demonstrated outstanding skills within a different business context – something it subsequently continued to do not least under the pressures of expansion. Both David Andrews and XIS CEO John Benjamin cited the example of Peter George, recruited from Ford to be Operations Director of XIS and seen to be having a "*huge impact*" through the application of his experience in automotive to the partnership business.

This philosophy of looking across industry sectors and companies to find and apply "world class practice" of course underpinned from the start the establishment of the Xchanging Competencies. And the development progress of the Competencies, was in our view most critical to the achievement of sustainability. The gains made by the partnership businesses during Streamlining tended to be associated with the direct efforts of the Competency Practice Directors seconded to that business. Subsequently

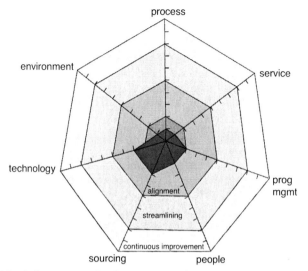

Figure 13.11 A Competency Exploitation Map for Each Partnership Business

the Competency skills had to become pervasive across and within the businesses, paralleling the success of Process's engagement of transferees through the Black Belt scheme. Recognizing this, Xchanging implemented two measurement systems by 2003. The first tracked the development of each competency in five dimensions: codification, training, tools, knowledge capital, organization. The second (Figure 13.11) captured for each partnership the level of exploitation of the competencies within that partnership; it provided an ongoing stimulus for discussions between partnership business CEOs and competency Practice Directors on the available levers for moving the business forward.

Finally, we know the time-honored phrase that "necessity is the mother of invention". The partnership business CEOs knew that Andrews expected them to grow their revenues by 20%–25% per annum, through a combination of service innovation and external sales. The incentives were in place, and a credible infrastructure for continuous improvement was being proactively developed. While there clearly could be no certainty in the absence of empirical data, our assessment, as of 2003, was that Xchanging had an excellent chance of sustaining performance improvement in its partnership businesses.

An assessment of the applicability of the Xchanging business model

We have seen evidence that the Xchanging business model was proving effective across four enterprise partnership businesses. Later evidence from 2005–08 also showed continued success in most of the existing and also in the new enterprise partnership businesses, though, as we shall see,

Xchanging bought out BAE's share of the HR partnership in 2007. These businesses represent a number of "back office" activities, and different client industry settings. Xchanging aimed to expand each partnership by attracting additional clients, and to set up more Enterprise Partnerships over time. Based on the evidence in 2003, what was the overall scope for application of the Xchanging model? And in what contexts was it likely to be most effective? And what happened subsequently? In 2003 we assessed the applicability of the model using a set of frameworks devised from our earlier research experience (Lacity *et al.*, 1996). Our methodology looked from the client perspective at appropriate sourcing strategy, and it was developed in the context of IT sourcing (see Figure 13.12). But, after minor modification, we believe it provides interesting insights into the potential for business process outsourcing, and the distinctive strengths of the Xchanging model.

The process starts with an analysis of **business factors**, an assessment of the contribution the relevant activity makes to the operations and to the market positioning of the overall client business. Does the activity make a "marginal" or a "critical" contribution to business operations? Does it represent a "commodity" to be performed to a required standard? Or a potential competitive "differentiator" whose performance should be maximized? If the answers are "marginal" and "commodity", the logical sourcing strategy will be to minimize cost through competitive tendering, fee-for-service,

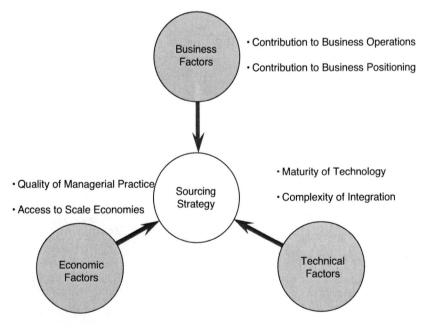

Figure 13.12   A Framework for Sourcing Strategy

and a basic service level agreement. At the other extreme, for "critical differentiators" an external provider is relevant only if it provides the capability to improve performance, and is willing to engage on terms that fully align goals with the client business. In this analysis:

- The settlement service of XIS was probably a "critical" but "commodity" activity for Lloyd's and the IUA. While costs were important, cost reductions must not be achieved at the expense of the quality of the service;
- XCS on the other hand maybe perceived as both "critical" and a potential "differentiator" for Lloyd's. This would support Lloyd's CEO Prettejohn's concern that XCS must be a separate partnership business, focussed on aligning with Lloyd's target competitive positioning;
- A positioning of XHRS as similar to XIS in this mapping illustrates the importance of client executive perception. In many firms transactional HR activity might be seen as a "marginal commodity" whose costs should be minimized. The early misgivings about outsourcing of BAE SYSTEMS line executives demonstrated that they did not share that view. In the words of Tony McCarthy, XHRS is on a journey to service excellence, committed to achieving world class service standards as well as low levels of cost;
- The seven categories of indirect procurement managed by XPS probably occupied a number of positions on the map; the range of three category management strategies supported their ability to respond to this.

Going forward from 2003, the Xchanging model looked to be an attractive option for the outsourcing of what clients perceive to be "critical commodity" activities; the emphasis on service quality as well as cost, and the continuing client engagement are all appropriate in this domain. On the other hand, in the "marginal commodity" domain these same features of the model may represent over-engineering. Finally, the model, with its shared incentive structure, seemed able to operate well for "critical differentiators" such as XCS; but clients would often have both the motivation and the means to operate their equivalent activities successfully in house.

The second analysis, of **economic factors**, looks at the potential to improve the client firm's position through two key drivers of cost – managerial practices and access to economies of scale. This analysis confirmed the logic of Xchanging's targeting of the back office activity of large corporates. As three of the individual case studies – XHRS, XIS, XPS – showed particularly clearly, these can be contexts in which managerial practices are lagging because of insufficient attention; and where the achievement of in-house scale economies is constrained by a legacy of fragmented and dispersed activity. There is a considerable prize to be won, but the question is how:

- In the XHRS and XIS examples, client-side executive management recognized that the *Do-It-Yourself* approach would not be viable because the necessary changes required levels of management attention and investment that would not be available to back office processes. In the XPS context, there had previously been periodic application of in-house management expertise to indirect procurement – but this had still left significant room for further improvement;
- The client-side decision makers also saw *Management Consultancy* projects as an unconvincing option to take. They were seen to represent high up-front costs to achieve one-step rather than sustainable change. There were also concerns about the accountability for and ownership of outcomes; and about lack of skills and knowledge transfer;
- *Fee-for-Service Outsourcing* was recognized as a credible alternative in the competitions that led to XHRS and XIS. It had the advantage for the client of full up front commitment to reduced cost levels; but real uncertainty about longer-term outcomes as business contexts change and the incentives of client and provider diverge. (The challenge posed for XIS by inherited IT outsourcing contracts provided a cameo of the sort of difficulties that can commonly arise);
- The *Enterprise Partnership* model was seen to protect against this difficulty and to promise higher performance – in quality and/or cost – over the longer term. The alignment of incentives allowed the model to address the contrasting demands of the XPS and XCS contexts, as well as the more familiar requirements of XHRS and XIS.

The final leg of our model looks at **technical factors** in the context of the activity. Is the underpinning technology for the activity mature and stable, or are there major opportunities for change in the activity enabled by recent technology developments? And does the technology base for this activity have a simple or complex interface into the wider infrastructure of the firm? To outsource a technologically stable activity which has a simple interface into the rest of the business, the expected course of action is to go regularly to formal competitive tendering: the requirement is easy to specify and switching costs from one supplier to the next should be low. But the context for the four Enterprise Partnerships we studied was very different:

- The effective use of new technology was seen to be a key factor in the future performance of XHRS, XIS, XCS, XPS (and was already, by 2002/03, creating an impact in three of the four). However, it is impossible to identify and specify in advance the full and detailed implications of technology over a five–ten year contractual period. The successful embrace of new technology requires a journey of discovery, and goal-alignment would be a critical factor in ensuring that client and provider progress that journey in harmony;

- In all four deals there was a complex service interface to the client – multiple locations and client entities, classes of user, types of transaction etc. In XIS, for example, there was further complexity in the form of organizational heritages, technical platforms, contractual infrastructures. The chosen provider's (in this case Xchanging's) ability to handle complexity was a critical factor in such situations, for the client knew that there would be large switching costs – in finance, time, and turmoil – in any necessary move to a new provider.

Overall, the analysis, and subsequent developments to 2008, consistently suggests that the Xchanging business model provides a high level of fit with the needs of its declared target market – the back office activities of large and complex organizations. It is seen to be particularly appropriate – a superior model of outsourcing – when the outsourced activities are recognized by the client as critical to business operations. Clients who join an existing enterprise partnership, rather than trigger the creation of a new one, would benefit provided they too valued service excellence above the lowest possible cost base. Thus, in our view, the Xchanging business model had in 2003, and continued to have, in 2008, a significant range of applicability.

Subsequent developments 2005–08

Financially, Xchanging has been notably successful. For 2006 it had revenues of £393.5 million (operating profit £32.3m, share of profit after tax 17.1m), which increased by 19% for 2007 to £468.2 million (operating profit £38.9m, share of profit after tax 22.8m). Revenues were up in all three market segments – Business Lines (cross-industry delivery of e.g., HR, and/or procurement, or finance services), Insurance and Financial Markets, and the group exhibited a strong balance sheet and cash flow. The first half year of 2008 produced a further 20% growth in revenues, and a 39% increase in adjusted operating profit against 2007 first half figures, while Xchanging's share of profit after tax continued to climb.

By end of 2006 Xchanging employed around 3,700 people mainly in UK, Europe and Asia. It had six enterprise partnerships, by this date complemented by a number of 100% owned businesses, operating resources on-site, onshore and through two low cost offshore delivery centers. Each market segment had its own management structure bolstered by shared service delivery in procurement, HR, finance and IT hosting to extract scale benefits and ensure consistency of approach. Clearly the contractual approach and structure had evolved to match the client base Xchanging had compiled. There were some risks in Xchanging's top ten customers accounting for nearly 66% of revenues, so Xchanging had to establish further partnerships and major third party customers to sustain its level of growth. In 2006 it in fact secured a seven-year procurement partnership with National Australia Bank (UK), a partnering deal with University of Birmingham NHS Foundation Trust, a five-year gain-share procurement outsourcing deal with Liberata, and a similar deal with BAE Systems Australia. By March 2007, however, it had bought out the BAE Systems 50% share of the HR and indirect procurement enterprise partnerships, the price being some £57 million. In April 2007 Xchanging became officially listed on the London Stock Exchange and entered the FTSE 250 in June. In November 2007 it won a 400 million euro eight-year partnership contract to deliver business process services and cost savings to Allianz Global Investors.

By 2007 various sources were predicting a compound annual growth rate in the HR, procurement and finance and accounting BPO markets of between 10% and 14.3% (Lacity and Willcocks, 2009; IDC, 2007). Xchanging was well placed to gain more of this business having over 4,200 employees based mainly in seven countries with customers in 34 countries. Its "blue chip" customers included American Express, Deutsche Bank, Aon, Boots, Allianz, ACE, Compass, AXA, BAE Systems, Lloyds/IUA and Tech Mahindra. To capture a variety of customers and their differing needs Xchanging had found it advisable to add four more offerings to its Enterprise partnership model, namely outsourcing (aiming to guarantee sustainable savings), products (seeking to deliver the best solution), Straight Through Processing (optimizing the value chain) and Business Support (applying know-how for results). 2007 turned out to be a good year for Xchanging, expressed not least in its share price. In April 2007 the company was listed at 240p the top of the quoted price range, and raised £75 million of primary capital. It ended the year with a 17% increase in share price since listing and followed up with a 2 pence per share dividend in May 2008.

Conclusions

The first conclusion from our research is that there does seem to be very considerable scope for improving the performance of "back office" activities. We see no reason to doubt that the evidence in our case studies – that such activities commonly lack attention and investment priority – is representative of the wider picture. "Back Office Improvement Potential" deserves to feature more prominently on the executive agenda.

But what is the preferred route to achieving that improvement? One message from our earlier research into IT outsourcing was "never outsource a problem – the rewards will go overwhelmingly to the supplier"; in other words the strong advice for IT was "DIY first, perhaps outsource later". The

BPO research challenges that prescription. Given the competing demands of front line activity and what we have learned about the potential size and complexity of the back office improvement task, DIY is not the convincing first best option here.

Not surprisingly given its scope, the research has not advanced the case for a Management Consultancy solution either. Apart from the concerns expressed about the expense and lack of ownership associated with this option, it does not and cannot address the issue of creating a front office/service mindset in employees who remain within a corporate back office.

So we come to the conclusion that BPO is rightly moving up the corporate agenda, as the route to back office improvement. But which model of BPO? While the familiar fee-for-service model does not align the goals and interests of client and provider over time, there may be many BPO contexts in which it is possible to build in appropriate safeguards. For example, the offshore outsourcing of certain types of Call Center has clearly been successful. Clearly, Xchanging evolved its own model to include more obvious outsourcing arrangements in its offerings, and like almost all other suppliers sought to achieve standardized, low cost delivery for aspects of its operations. It has also sought to leverage its other strengths – products, know-how, streamlining value chains – in order to find new customers and market needs. By 2008 its overall strategy was based on rapid growth and highly efficient production, with growth vital for both economies of scale and globalization of its services. It had strong European expansion and an increasing US and Asian presence.

So what of the enterprise partnership model? Clearly two of the original four were ended in 2007, but the amount paid to buy them out indicates the considerable value they generated to both BAE Systems, the client and the supplier, Xchanging. Moreover, new clients have continued to sign up to the enterprise partnership proposition throughout 2005–08, for example a 12-year EP with Deutsche Bank in 2004/05, a ten-year EP with Aon Limited in 2006, and one with Allianz Global Investors in 2007. It is in the very situations we have researched – of high complexity, technological dependency, and business criticality – that the fee-for-service model looks hardest to manage and least attractive. By contrast, the Enterprise Partnership model is seen to be elegant in its conception and effective in its execution to date – driven people who are consistently recognized as highly capable and highly motivated. For these situations certainly, we judge that Xchanging has indeed developed a "better way".

References

Feeny D. and Willcocks L. (1998) "Core IS Capabilities for Exploiting Information Technology", *Sloan Management Review*, Spring.

IDC (2007) *Worldwide and US Business Process Outsourcing 2007–2011 Forecast. Market Opportunities By Horizontal Business Process.* Doc 208290, September, IDC, New York.

Lacity, M., Willcocks, L. and Feeny, D. (1995) "IT Outsourcing: Maximise Flexibility and Control", *Harvard Business Review*, May–June, 84–93.

Lacity, M.C., Willcocks, L.P., and Feeny, D.F. (1996) "The Value of Selective IT Sourcing", *Sloan Management Review*, Spring.

Lacity, M. and Willcocks, L. (2001) *Global Information Technology Outsourcing: Search for Business Advantage*, Wiley, Chichester.

Lacity, M. and Willcocks, L. (2009) *Information Systems and Outsourcing: Studies in Theory and Practice*, Palgrave, London.

Lacity, M., Feeny, D. and Willcocks, L. (2003) *Transforming Back Office to Front Office: Lloyd's of London and Xchanging's Enterprise Partnership for Insurance Claims Management*, Templeton College, Oxford.

Monczka, R.M., Petersen, K.J., Handfield, R.B. and Ragatz, G.L. (1998) "Success Factors in Strategic Supplier Alliances: The Buying Company Perspective", *Decision Sciences*, 29, 553–577.

Mohr, J. and Spekman, R. (1994) "Characteristics of Partnership Success: Partnership Attributes, Communication Behaviour, and Conflict Resolution Techniques", *Strategic Management Journal*, 15, 135–152.

Willcocks, L. and Lacity, M. (2006) *Global Sourcing of Business and IT Services*, Palgrave, London.

14

Outcomes from Offshore Outsourcing: Evidence from a Client's Perspective

Joseph Rottman and Mary Lacity

Introduction

While Chapters 2 and 12 focused on outcomes across the 1990–2007 period, they drew mainly on evidence from IT and business process outsourcing arrangements. What about outcomes from the relatively newer, and faster growing, phenomenon of offshore outsourcing? In this chapter we report the findings from a Fortune 500 biotechnology company that engaged six Indian offshore suppliers on 21 IT projects during 2003 through 2005. Interestingly, we found mixed results on the success of offshore projects. At the organizational level of analysis, we found evidence that the biotechnology company's offshore strategy to simply replace domestic contractors with cheaper, offshore suppliers was a poor fit with its own social and cultural contexts. This chapter provides further food for thought on offshoring and builds on the 1990s work we carried out represented in Chapter 5, catching up with 21st century developments, and providing insight into practices that work, and future research needs.

India still dominates the offshore outsourcing[1] market

Global IT outsourcing (ITO) has grown from a $12 billion market in 1989 (Krass, 1990; Rothfeder and Coy, 1990) to a $200 billion plus market in 2005 (Willcocks and Lacity, 2006). By the late 2000s the fastest growing segment within the global ITO market was Asia, particularly India. The offshore ITO market (primarily Indian suppliers) conservatively represented about 25% of the global ITO market at $56 billion by end of 2008

---

[1]We define "offshore outsourcing" as outsourcing work to a supplier located on a different continent than the client. We define "near-shoring" as outsourcing work to a supplier located in a different country, but adjacent to the client or on the same continent as the client. We define "offshoring", as moving work from one client location to a client location in a different country.

(E-business Strategies, 2006; Willcocks and Lacity, 2009, volume 3). Forrester, McKinsey and NASSCOM predicted that India alone would grab $142 billion of the ITO market by 2009 (E-business Strategies, 2006; Ross, 2004). Although by the mid-2000s there were reports that India was struggling with high turnover, wage increases, and infrastructure issues associated with rapid growth (McCue, 2005; Srivastava, 2005), evidence suggests that India will continue to be a dominant player in the global ITO market (Carmel and Tjia, 2005; Engardio, 2006; Minevich and Richter, 2005), with China emerging as the next biggest rival (Overby, 2005; Lacity And Rottman, 2007). The July 3, 2006 issue of *BusinessWeek*, for example, listed India's Tata Consultancy Services, Infosys, Satyam, and Wipro among the Global Information Technology 100. Their prospects for continued growth in the world market are strong (Minevich and Richter, 2005; Lacity and Rottman, 2007). Therefore, practitioners and researchers have continued interest in understanding how to successfully engage Indian offshore suppliers.

Many practitioners are struggling with offshore outsourcing of IT work

However, practitioner outlets have been reporting widely varying offshore outsourcing success rates. The following examples reported high success rates with offshore outsourcing:

- A survey of 38 companies in North America and Europe, of which 85% were involved in offshore outsourcing of IT work, found that 89% were satisfied with their offshore outsourcing initiatives (Beal, 2004);
- A DiamondCluster (2005) survey of 210 buyers found that offshore outsourcing satisfaction rates were high, but falling from 79% to 62% between 2004 and 2005.

In contrast, the following practitioner outlets reported low success rates:

- A Gartner survey found a 50% failure rate for offshore outsourcing initiatives (Aron and Singh, 2005);
- A survey of 204 software developers found that 46% viewed the work performed by the offshore teams to be of poor quality and 14% viewed the deliverables from offshore teams to be "unusable or a setback to progress" (Carter, 2006);
- Ventoro's survey of over 5,200 executives from North America and Europe found that nearly 28% of respondents experienced cost *increases* and another 25% did not generate any cost savings with offshore outsourcing (Hatch, 2005).

The root causes of failure were: lack of client preparation, lack of joint client-vendor planning, poor client team morale, miscommunication and cultural barriers, and poor vendor team performance (Hatch, 2005). *CIO*

Magazine reported that savings may not be realized because the transaction costs (vendor selection, transitioning work, layoffs and retention, lost productivity, additional processes, and managing the contract) of offshore outsourcing can be as high as eight times the cost of the offshore labor (Overby, 2003).

Clearly, many practitioners have been struggling to realize expected benefits from offshore outsourcing. As academics, we can provide a better understanding of the practices that affect offshore outsourcing outcomes. We already have a good grasp of domestic outsourcing, in which client and supplier firms are located in the same geographic area. Additionally, we are building a solid base of research on offshore outsourcing (see Appendix A for a summary of IT sourcing research from 1989 to 2006), but there is clearly a need for more academic research (Dibbern *et al.*, 2004).

We aim to contribute to the literature by identifying the project attributes and contextual issues that contributed to project outcomes at a Fortune 500 biotechnology company (hereafter called Biotech[2]). By 2009 Biotech continued to employ approximately 15,000 employees spread across 400 locations in more than 40 countries. Our research in 2005, based on 44 interviews and over 2,000 documents, focused on the IT group at US headquarters. This group comprised about 600 IT workers, of which 400 were Biotech employees and 200 were domestic contractors. Biotech engaged six Indian offshore suppliers on 21 IT projects during 2003 through 2005. The official documents from the Program Management Office (PMO) reported that offshore outsourcing was successful in reducing Biotech's IT costs. But interviews with knowledgeable participants suggested that many projects were not successful in meeting cost, quality, and productivity objectives. Like practitioner reports stated above, many Biotech participants struggled with high transaction costs associated with management of offshore workers on many of their projects.

This research provides an opportunity to understand how clients perceive offshore outsourcing and the challenges and complexities they experience when moving IT work offshore. The overall questions we asked and answer in this chapter are:

"How do knowledgeable participants view project outcomes?"
"Which project attributes explain differences in participants' ratings of project outcomes?"
"How do contextual issues explain offshore outsourcing experiences?"

The chapter is structured as follows. The Research Method describes the data collection methods. The Case Description describes Biotech's

---

[2]We used a pseudonym because participants were guaranteed anonymity of their identities and the identity of their company.

outsourcing journey. The Project Outcomes section describes how participants rated 21 projects. The Project Level Findings section explains the data analysis methods and presents seven project level findings using the participants' project ratings. An Organizational Level analysis then follows, where we interpret contextual issues and presents four findings. The Case Validity section assesses seven validity checks. The chapter concludes with implications for practice and research.

Research method

A pluralistic case study

Most researchers feel compelled to label tightly their case study research using predefined categories based on philosophical assumptions, research methods, or research purpose. Case study labels based on philosophical assumptions include the labels "positivist," "interpretive", or "critical" (Klein and Myers, 1999; Burrell and Morgan, 1979; Benbasat *et al.*, 1987). Case study labels based on research methodology include such labels as "action research", "enthnomethodology", "longitudinal case study", "in-depth case study", or "field interviews" (Greenwood and Levin, 1998; Mumford *et al.*, 1985). Yin (2003) categorize case studies by research purpose using the labels "explanatory", "descriptive", or "exploratory." Furthermore, case study categories have been classified to even finer sub-categories. For example, Denzin and Lincoln (1994) claim six sub-categories of interpretive case research: "post-positivist", "constructivist", "feminist", "ethnic", "Marxist", and "cultural studies".

Recent thinking has argued that such paradigmatic and methodological labels may be forced and artificial. Mingers (2001) argues that it is possible to detach research methods from research paradigms and use research methods both critically and knowledgably within a context. Mason (2001) argues that research does not have to be "either/or." Rather, research can simultaneously pursue both good science, which leads to understanding, and can contribute to practice.

The Biotech case study emerged over a two-year period that involved cycles of data collection, interpretation of data, and participant feedback on data interpretation. From this perspective, the case is "interpretative" in that we attempted to understand phenomena through the meanings participants assigned to them (Orlikowski and Baroudi, 1991; Burrell and Morgan, 1988). As will be shown, different stakeholders have different views on offshore. They did not uniformly share a clear, consistent, objective "reality." The analysis was mostly an iterative process of letting the data drive the story, searching for patterns across the interviews, looking for documents to shed light on the interviews, and re-reading interviews to shed light on the documents. We used prior empirical research on project management and outsourcing to help us look for clues in the data. Thus, although our findings are organized and clearly presented, the process of inquiry was mostly iterative and emergent.

However, the case is also "positivist", in that we had at least one clear research question, we had some *a priori* specifications of constructs and conjectures based on prior research, and we measured constructs (Dubé and Paré, 2003). This positivist aspect becomes evident in the project level analysis and findings. When then interpreted these "hard numbers" from the views expressed by participants. Thus, as Mingers notes, we found it "both desirable and feasible to combine together different research methods to gain richer and more reliable results" (Mingers, 2001, p. 243).

Whether one focuses on the interpretive or positivist aspects of the Biotech case, we believe that the case is "generalizable" in a practical manner (Mason, 2001; Yin, 2003; Lee and Baskerville, 2003). We believe the human capacity to reasonably apply lessons from one context to another is very high. Other researchers, clients, and suppliers will be able to learn from Biotech's experiences and apply them, as appropriate, to their own research and organizational contexts.

Data collection: February 2004 to September 2005

Data was collected in two formal phases and feedback was exchanged in two phases.

Phase I: Five interviews conducted with senior IT managers. During Phase I, we approached Biotech to participate in a study that examined the best practices for managing offshore outsourcing. (See Rottman and Lacity, 2004 for a full description of this project). In February of 2004, we interviewed five people from Biotech – the then CIO (since promoted and replaced by a direct report), three IT Leads who report directly to the CIO, and the Head of the Program Management Office (PMO) which managed all offshore outsourcing activities.

Phase II: Informal interactions and feedback. After those interviews, we met one of the IT Leads, the Head of the PMO, as well as other Biotech employees at various offshore outsourcing events (a users group meeting, an executive outsourcing class, and several sourcing conferences) during Spring and Summer of 2004. We listened to formal presentations by Biotech employees and their offshore outsourcing consultant at a users group meeting. They listened to two of our speeches at a users group meeting and at an executive outsourcing class. Afterwards, Biotech employees provided feedback on our findings and updated us on their offshore experiences. It was clear that the Head of the PMO was questioning whether Biotech was really saving money with offshore, given the additional administrative overhead and anecdotal complaints from Biotech project managers.

Phase III: Forty interviews conducted and over 2,000 documents gathered. In Spring of 2005, the Head of the PMO asked us to systematically assess IT employees' perceptions of offshore outsourcing. He felt that the IT employees would be more honest if they were interviewed by academics and if their identities would not be revealed. He also wanted us to identify the practices that contributed to project outcomes. He said he would allow us access to any people we wanted for interviews. Additionally, he offered us access to any documents pertaining to offshore.

In the Summer of 2005, the authors developed the interview guide (see Appendix B). The interview questions were designed to create a project rating, to investigate potentially important attributes that may contribute to project outcome based on prior research, and to explore new ideas, practices, and experiences with offshore outsourcing.

It is important to note here that the researchers were diligent in confronting their preconceptions of offshoring successes (Klein and Myers, 1999) and in avoiding relating any of the past research cases to the participants of the Biotech case. In order not to bias the participants, the researchers did not offer advice or an evaluation of the current state of Biotech's offshore efforts prior to the interviews. As Klein and Myers (1999) point out, that while prejudices and preconceptions form an base of understanding, they should be set aside "if we are to begin to understand a text or text – analogue" (p. 76).

The lead author then interviewed 40 Biotech employees (including the new CIO who was appointed in February, 2005) and re-interviewed the Head of the PMO. All interviews were conducted face-to-face, tape-recorded, and lasted approximately 90 minutes. Over 1,000 pages of transcription were generated.

Table 14.1 shows the titles of the participants interviewed and the number of participants with that title. The 44[3] participants are all fulltime employees at Biotech. Appendix C shows the organizational chart for IT. Specifically, it shows the six units that report to the CIO (Enterprise Architecture, ERP, R&D, Marketing, Web, and Security), and the reporting structure and titles of participants.

In addition to the interviews, we had access to documents Biotech generated related to their offshore efforts. We examined over 200 statements of work (SOW), over 400 spreadsheets tracking various projects, and all the PMO's presentations relaying the status of offshore projects. We also examined the PMO's extensive database of all offshore contractors, invoices, requisitions, timesheets and disbursements. Additionally, individual participants provided project timelines, supplier correspondence, and code samples.

Phase IV: Findings review and feedback. In September 2005, the Head of the PMO and CIO were independently debriefed on the research find-

---

[3]One participant was interviewed in both Phase I and Phase III, thus we have 44 not 45 participants in all.

Table 14.1   Biotech Participants and Titles

Title of Participant	Number of Participants with this Title	Title of Participant	Number of Participants with this Title
Application Architect	1	Program Lead	2
Architecture Lead	1	Program Services Lead	1
CIO	2	Project Lead	2
Client Systems Team Lead	1	Project Manager	3
Commercial IT Lead	1	Senior Project Manager	1
DBA Project Lead	1	Software Architect	1
DBA Team Lead	2	Team Lead HR Services	1
Development Coordinator	1	Team Lead IT HR	1
Engagement Manager	1	Team Lead SAP	1
IT Lead	4	Team Lead SATT	1
IT Team Lead	7	Team Lead Tech Services	1
Manager Data Management Team	1	Technical Architect	1
Manager IT	1	Technical Lead	2
Offshore Project Coordinator	1	Web Administrator	1
Total		44	

ings. Despite the criticisms of the PMO office and senior management's role in implementing offshore, both accepted the report as accurate. Most of their questions centered on "How can we do this better?"

The next section describes Biotech's offshore journey. We wrote this case description based on the socially constructed "facts" from the interviews and documents.

Case description: BIOTECH's offshore journey

1. The CIO seeks to reduce IT costs through offshore outsourcing

As stated above, Biotech is a Fortune 500 company and a leading provider of biotechnology-based products. According to 10-K (annual) reports, Biotech experienced flat revenues yet increasingly positive net income from 1999 to 2001. According to the CIO, in 2001, senior management was beginning to feel the financial pains of a major litigation, increased competition, and rising costs of inputs. Predicting losses for 2002, senior management sought to cut the budgets of overhead departments.[4] For 2002, the CIO's IT budget was reduced by 5%. *"Doing more with less"* became the CIO's major challenge for 2002.

Senior IT Leads explore offshore outsourcing as a means to reduce IT costs. In Spring, 2002, the CIO tasked the senior IT Leadership Team, comprised of 12 senior IT managers (called IT Leads), to develop a strategy to cope with the tighter IT budget. One of their proposals was to possibly move some IT work offshore. The CIO and IT Leads reasoned that every hour of work done offshore could potentially save the company $40.

The CIO and IT Leads intend to replace domestic contractors with cheaper offshore IT workers. The participants were in agreement pertaining to reasoning behind the projected cost savings. Most of Biotech's IT workforce resides in the corporate IT department on the headquarters campus. The corporate IT department comprises about 600 people, including 200 domestic contractors. The domestic contractors earn hourly wages of about $65. If domestic contractors could be replaced with offshore workers who typically earn $25 per hour, then the CIO and IT Leads reasoned they could save at least $40 per hour. Thus, their number one objective was to reduce IT costs, primarily by replacing some of the domestic contractors with cheaper offshore equivalents. (There was no evidence that the CIO or IT Leads intended to use offshore to replace any Biotech IT employees). According to the CIO:

> "One was simply looking at how much work do we give India? And if you make the assumption that we would be doing that work anyway, it's pretty easy to calculate the cost if you [would] have done it in the U.S. versus doing it in India. It becomes a pretty straightforward calculation."

IT Leads visit offshore clients in the US and suppliers in India. In Summer of 2002, three IT Leads (all of whom we interviewed) pursued their offshore investigation by visiting offshore clients in the US. Convinced by the cost savings they saw in other client organizations, they hired an offshore consultant to serve as a guide to India and to Indian suppliers. They said they selected India as the offshore venue because Biotech already had R&D facilities in Bangalore, India. In that facility, they reasoned, Biotech had full-time IT employees who could potentially play a significant role in managing offshore outsourcing.

In August of 2002, two IT Leads made the trip to India. They found many different approaches to offshore outsourcing (captive centers, joint ventures, fee-for-service), but the bottom line was *"it was quite an advantage from the cost perspective."* – IT Lead

---

[4]Indeed, Biotech suffered an 8% drop in sales in 2002 and experienced net losses. Since 2003, both revenues and profits increased.

Upon returning from India, the IT Leads began to rally senior management support for offshore outsourcing. The CIO approved and created a new Program Management Office for offshore projects. The role of the PMO is to transfer knowledge about offshore contracting, negotiations, and management:

> "The idea was that we could each do individual efforts but if there was a [Program] Management Office, it would make the effort a little bit easier for everybody who wanted to do it. So, if somebody wanted to pursue an offshore project, they didn't have to learn everything from scratch. There's a lot of overhead in terms of contractual work and negotiations that has to be accomplished. So, by putting that in the Program Management Office, everyone can do the project and feel unconstrained by those issues." – IT Lead

The CIO mandates offshore outsourcing. Because offshore outsourcing would likely meet with resistance from the internal IT staff, the CIO implemented the strategy as a mandate:

> "As I looked at rolling this out, I knew we needed a critical mass of projects and people involved and offshoring was not a very popular topic. There was some fear of losing jobs and of losing contractors who are tightly integrated into our design teams. So, if I just waited for volunteers, I might not have reached that mass. So we used a rather heavy hand. I don't know another way to do it." – CIO

New projects would require that at least 15% of the budget be outsourced offshore. In total, the CIO budgeted $6.2 million for offshore during 2003 to 2005.

The Head of the PMO and IT Leads select suppliers. The offshore consultant helped the IT Leads and Head of the PMO identify potential suppliers. During due diligence, the IT Leads and PMO Head narrowed the list of potential suppliers through interviews and supplier presentations. The IT Leads and PMO Head were interested in engaging suppliers with significant science domain knowledge as well as the willingness to participate in small projects during the start-up stage. Two large suppliers decided not to participate due to the small scale of the initial projects. Ultimately, Biotech engaged six Indian suppliers. Two suppliers were large, earning more than $1 billion in revenues in 2005. Four suppliers were small, the largest of which earned less than $150 million in 2005.

2. Biotech launches 21 projects offshore in 2003 to 2005

To kick off the offshore initiative, the CIO and the IT Leads held a town hall meeting for all IT employees. During this meeting, the offshore strategy and the role of the PMO were introduced. IT employees were told that no employee would lose their job as a consequence of offshore outsourcing.

The offshore consultant, in cooperation with the PMO, delivered several cultural awareness training sessions to educate the IT staff on the challenges of managing Indian suppliers. All initial staff members involved in offshore outsourcing (at all levels) attended. To illustrate the purpose of these sessions, the following excerpt from the document "Introduction to Offshore" is provided below:

> "The experience of doing a project offshore is new to [Biotech]. Offshore projects, while presenting important opportunities for cost reduction, also present significant differences to project managers, team members and clients. The purpose of this section is to describe the best practices and resources available to help [Biotech] people become accustomed to working on offshore projects."

These sessions covered Indian economy, culture, music, and educational institutions. Particular attention was paid to the differences between US and Indian cultural norms. The PMO created and distributed an "Illustrated Guide to Offshore" to IT employees.

IT Leads started bringing projects to the PMO in early 2003. The PMO was tasked with coordinating project selection, project management, tactical duties (human resource related tasks for on-boarding of supplier resources, facilitating system account creation, interfacing with Biotech IT security for login IDs, etc.) and tracking all SOWs, invoices, and timesheets. During 2003 and 2004, the PMO and IT Leads met to discuss successes and failures in the offshore initiative and to assess supplier performance. Two small suppliers were identified as poor performers and when the engagements expired, contracts were not renewed.

In all, 14 projects were launched in 2003, six projects in 2004, and one project in 2005. The number of offshore supplier workers peaked in October, 2004 at 68 and as of June 2005, Biotech engaged 35 offshore workers. As of Summer 2005, a total of $4.1 million dollars had been paid to offshore suppliers.

3. Offshore outcomes are unclear

The official word from the PMO: offshore outsourcing is realizing projected cost savings. During the 2003–05 timeframe, the PMO was in charge of reporting on the project status of offshore projects. The PMO created monthly and yearly reports on the total costs of offshore outsourcing. Every document reports a total cost savings. For example, the document titled "2004 IT Offshore Accomplishments", states that as of July 23, 2004, Biotech saved $560,000 with offshore outsourcing. According to the Head of the PMO and the Offshore Project Coordinator, the number is based on multiplying the costs of the offshore hours and comparing this number with what it would have cost had they used domestic contractors. The number does not consider transaction costs, productivity, or quality. Thus, month after month, the PMO documents report that offshore outsourcing is successful in meeting Biotech's cost savings targets.

The burning question: is offshore outsourcing really worthwhile? The Head of the PMO questioned whether these cost savings were realistic. During our first interview with him, he said:

"It is clear that we saved money on a per hour basis, there is no way to argue about that, but did [the offshore supplier] do it as fast as we would do it? The other big complaint came from the project managers: 'Managing offshore projects is really hard....' If I had to count up how hard this is, then we lost money. That is clearly anec-dotal since they don't keep track of how much they spend on domestic project in terms of project management."

Based on our initial five interviews, we understand the PMO's suspicion about the actual outcomes of offshore outsourcing. In addition to the Head of the PMO, one other IT Lead expressed skepticism about the official story that offshore outsourcing was saving Biotech money:

"I wish we had better project and budget metrics. We really don't know how to translate the 'hourly savings' into a real number. I am not sure at the end of the day what our savings would be."

However, two other IT Leads seemed to think offshore outsourcing, in general, was successful. The first quote by an IT Lead claimed that overall economic benefits were met:

"I think the one comment I'll make is, all of our startups were difficult. I don't think there's one startup that happened in that March to July 2003 timeframe that didn't hit some startup issues. But the conversation that I had with leadership here at [Biotech], none of these projects missed any of their deliverables. They all delivered on the date. They all delivered at the economic level we expected. And when I say, pretty much on the dates, we probably had one or two out of 17 that missed a little bit, but I wouldn't call those significant." – IT Lead

The following quote captures what one IT Lead thought about the anec-dotal complaints from project managers:

"If Biotech's project managers work overtime with offshore because they have to come in early or stay late to take a call or have a confer-ence with India, then they mentally count it differently than if they

were just working overtime on some domestic project. That is one complaint we hear often, 'My work day is extended because of offshoring.'"
– IT Lead

The CIO concludes:

"Our offshore experiences have certainly been mixed. I am working with the IT Leads now to do a kind of 'good, bad and ugly' analysis to see where we are and what worked and how we can utilize the offshore model. I think that some of the setbacks were due to the suppliers' shortcomings and some of them were due to how we do business at [Biotech]. We need to understand which were which and go from there."

Thus, there were different opinions as to whether Biotech actually met their offshore objective to reduce IT costs. To move beyond random anecdotes, the Head of the PMO wanted to capture the opinions of all the IT employees involved in offshore outsourcing. We assessed their opinions at a project level so that we could find attributes to help explain differences in project outcomes. The next sections explain the project outcome indicator we used, the attributes we measured, and the overall project level findings.

How participants viewed project outcomes

Measures of project outcomes

Traditionally, practitioners define project success as a project being delivered on time, on budget, with promised functionality (Nelson, 2005; Standish Group CHAOS Report, 2003).[5] At Biotech, there were no formal metrics to uniformly assess project success across the 21 projects, other than to compare offshore expenses with what those hours would have cost if Biotech had used domestic contractors. We created a project indicator of success based on subjective evaluations of the people knowledgeable of the project.

Subjective evaluations are the most common form of IT project evaluation for projects of less than one year duration. For example, Gudea (2005) found that most small and medium-sized IT projects (less than one year to complete) are subjectively evaluated by people involved in the project in a

---

[5]Academics frequently use system use, system adoption, and system diffusion as indicators of success (Jeyaraj *et al.*, 2006). But these measures are more appropriate to assess from users (Nelson, 2005). Because our participants were project managers and team members, they were in a good position to assess budgets, deadlines, and quality of the product.

technical, business, or managerial capacity. In comparison, Gudea found that most large projects (more than one year to complete) are evaluated using hard numbers such as return on investment, payback period, and net present value. This difference in evaluation methods is likely due to the fact that small projects are expensed, whereas large projects must pass through the capital budgeting process.

We asked participants who were intimately involved on a project at various levels (IT Leads, Program Leads, Team Leads, Project Leads, and Architects) to assess the overall success of a project: "Considering the degree to which project objectives were met, budgets and schedules were met, and the quality of the delivered product, what letter grade would you assign the project?"

For each specific project discussed by a participant, the participant assigned a standard US letter grade (A, B, C, D, or F). We used the standard US grading system because it is a common frame of reference for the US participants. Based on the interviews, it was clear that all participants could clearly articulate and defend a letter grade.

Participants' ratings on 21 project outcomes

Among the 21 projects for which participants graded the project outcome, 17 projects had at least two participants independently assign a grade. For four projects, one participant assigned a grade. To calculate the average grade for each project, we converted letter grades reported by participants to numbers. We assigned A = 4, A–/B+ = 3.5, B = 3, B–/C+ = 2.5, C = 2, C–/D+ = 1.5, D = 1, D– = .5, and F = 0. In Table 14.2, we show the 21 projects (labeled A through U), the number of participants that graded the project, the letter grades assigned, the average project rating after converting letters to numbers, and the standard deviation. The overall mean project rating was 1.73 and the median was 1.75 (indicating a grade of between a C and a C–).

In some instances, participants had a shared view of project outcome as evidenced by the similar grades for a project. For example, all five participants independently graded Project D as an "F." Project D entailed Database Administration (DBA) support tasks. The project was managed in the US and delivered by Biotech's captive center in Bangalore. The project deliverables were late and frequently wrong. According to one DBA Team Lead:

> "The project was bloody awful! I had business users demanding, 'Don't send it to Bangalore – they will just screw it up and we will have to redo all the work and it will take five times as long!'"

In other instances, participants had different perceptions of project outcome. Project C provides an example. Project C entailed the visual mapping of DNA to help scientists manage the lineage of traits. Project C was graded by three participants: an IT Team Lead (graded the project a D), a Software

Table 14.2   Participants' Ratings of Project Outcomes

Project	Number of Participants who Assigned a Grade	Letter Grades Assigned by Participants	Average Project Rating Using A = 4, A-/B+ = 3.5, B = 3, B-/C+ = 2.5, C = 2, C-,D+ = 1.5, D = 1, D-, F+ = 0.5 and F = 0	Standard Deviation of Average Project Rating
A	3	C+, D, F	1.17	1.26
B	1	C-	1.50	n/a
C	3	D+, D, A-	2.00	1.32
D	5	F, F, F, F, F	0.00	0.00
E	3	F, C, B	1.67	1.53
F	4	C, B, B, D	2.25	0.96
G	5	A, A, A, B, B	3.60	0.55
H	4	F, F, F, D	0.25	0.50
I	1	D	1.00	n/a
J	2	B, C-	2.25	1.06
K	2	F, D,	0.50	0.71
L	3	A, A, C	3.33	1.15
M	4	C, D, C-, B	1.88	0.85
N	4	C, F, F, F	0.50	1.00
O	3	B+, B+, B+	3.50	0.00
P	3	B, C+, D+	2.33	0.76
Q	9	D, C, D, D, B, B, F, B, B	1.89	1.17
R	2	C+, D	1.75	1.06
S	1	C-	1.50	n/a
T	1	D	1.00	n/a
U	3	C-, B, B	2.50	0.87
	Overall		1.73 (mean) 1.75 (median)	1.02

Architect (graded the project a D+), and a Project Lead (graded the project an A–). One explanation for the divergent views may be that participants viewed different outputs. The IT Team Lead and Software Architect viewed the project outputs directly from the supplier. They defended their grades as follows:

"[The offshore supplier] would send me code that would not compile! I would have to fix the code, submit it to the code repository and then run it. That is the code that feeds the status: the vendor's bad code that we fixed." – Software Architect

"When we would actually get the beginnings of code [from the supplier], I would have to look at it and I remember thinking, 'This is a bunch of crap!' I would have to create the class and sequence diagrams, send them back to the supplier and then re-code before submitting it. For [Project C] it would have been easier to write the code myself." – IT Team Lead

In contrast, the Project Lead viewed the outputs only after the IT Team Lead and Software Architect fixed the supplier's errors. This may explain his higher grade: "*I never talked with the supplier's developers, just the Project Lead for the offshore team…I think it went OK, some issues with code, but in general, I think it went well.*" – Project Lead

Another example of the research model capturing differing perceptions of a projects success is Project N. This project involved the creation of a hand held device to capture field data. It would be used by scientists to record the characteristics (growth rate, condition, etc.) of plants in research facilities. Project N was graded by four participants; three of which gave the project an "F" while the fourth participant gave it a "C". The primary difference in perception in this project was related to the stage in the systems development lifecycle the participants observed. The three participants who gave the project an "F" (two Team Leads and an Application Architect), were tasked with the requirements definition and introductory design phases for the project. Their perceptions of the early phases were quite negative.

According to the Application Architect,

"It was terrible, they (the supplier) couldn't even draw correct UML [unified modeling language] models. They had interfaces deriving from concrete classes, they had associations that are impossible to have. They were meaningless associations. So I started looking at that closer and I realized if you just start replacing all of the aggregation notation with generalization then all of a sudden it makes sense. So what they had done was write UML diagrams, but with the wrong notation. How could a CMM5 firm let this happen?!"

In contrast, the Team Lead who gave the project a "C", took over the project during the later stages of development and was responsible for project completion. He had a more positive opinion.

"I guess it was OK when it was completely executed. Didn't blow our socks off. We had some delays. We could account for some of the delays because of new technology and they (the supplier) had some performance problems, probably comparable to what we would have seen here locally. But, I mean, I remember walking out – okay, done. We got through it. No significant scar tissue. Had some expectations, didn't quite meet them all, it was little late. And cost-wise, maybe a wash. Helped us understand some of the true cost elements of off shoring."

The point is that the research model was sensitive to varying perceptions from the participants on project outcomes. All participants could assign and defend a grade based on their perceptions of reality.

Project level findings

Project level data analysis

Besides assessing participants' views on project outcomes, we needed to determine which attributes might differentiate highly rated projects from poorly rated projects. We used the same data analysis method described in Lacity and Willcocks (1998), namely, to code the documents and transcribed interviews into data categories and map these categories against the project rating. The data categories were selected based on prior research as well as data categories that emerged from the interviews. We examined the following data categories:

1. Size and number of offshore supplier(s) engaged on the project;
2. Project type;
3. Supplier engagement model used on the project;
4. Contract value in terms of dollars paid to the supplier on a project;
5. Project size;
6. Organizational unit within IT managing the project;
7. Year the project was started;
8. Contract type.

Each of these categories is defined and explained below.

1. Offshore supplier: *The number and size of the offshore supplier(s) engaged on a project.* Prior research has found that outsourcing to a single supplier, particularly under circumstances of high asset specificity, is riskier than using more than one supplier (Aubert *et al.*, 1999; Currie and Willcocks, 1998; Gallivan and Oh, 1999; Williamson, 1991; see also Chapters 4 and 8). However, multi-sourcing creates higher transaction costs than outsourcing to a single supplier (Lacity and Willcocks, 2001, 2009). Prior research has used the client as the unit of analysis (Chaudhury *et al.*, 1995; Cross, 1995; Gallivan and Oh, 1999). Thus, these studies addressed the question,

"Did/Should the *client* engage more than one supplier?" At the client level, Biotech multi-sourced by engaging six offshore suppliers. But we viewed this research as an opportunity to ask the question at a project level: "Does the number of suppliers on a *project* matter?"

In addition to single versus multi-sourcing, we also examined the size of the supplier (large versus small). Practitioners and researchers have noted that size of suppliers affects their capabilities (Levina and Ross, 2003; Martorelli *et al.*, 2004; Moore *et al.*, 2004), which, we reason, would affect a project's outcome. On the one hand, large suppliers would likely have better sourcing capabilities, economies of scale, and economies of scope to help them deliver successful projects (Feeny *et al.*, 2005; Levina and Ross, 2003). On the other hand, small suppliers may pay more attention to the client because the client represents a larger portion of their revenues (Feeny *et al.*, 2005). We did not conjecture whether large or small suppliers would have higher success rates, but instead viewed this research as an opportunity to investigate the effect of supplier size on project outcome.

Among the 21 projects, Biotech engaged one small Indian supplier on 12 projects, one large Indian supplier on five projects, and multiple suppliers on 3 projects. In addition, one project used Biotech's captive center in Bangalore.

2. Project type: *Either "new development" or "maintenance/support."*

Prior IT outsourcing research has examined the projects/functions clients outsource. Ang and Straub (1998) examined eight IT functions: IT strategy, IT planning, capacity management, production scheduling, IT human resource management, security management, network management, and PC management. In their sample of 243 US banks, they found that banks more frequently outsourced capacity management and production scheduling than the other six functions. (However, the authors did not analyze which outsourced functions led to higher satisfaction with outsourcing).

Grover *et al.* (1996) assessed the following types of outsourced projects/ functions: Applications development and maintenance, systems operations, telecommunications, end user support, and systems planning and management. In a survey of 188 IT executives, they found that type of project/function affected outcomes (see also Chapter 12). Specifically, outsourcing of systems operations and telecommunications led to increased client satisfaction. They also found that outsourcing applications development and maintenance, end user support, and systems management did not lead to increased client satisfaction.

At Biotech, 15 projects entailed new software development and six projects entailed maintenance and/or support of existing software. We conjectured that the new software development projects would entail more uncertainty, and would thus contribute to lower project ratings, as predicted by transaction cost economics (TCE) (Williamson, 1991). Although Poppo and Zenger (1998) hypothesized a relationship between technological uncertainty and outsourcing satisfaction based on TCE, their survey of 152 clients did not find a relationship. We saw this as an opportunity to examine it again.

3. Supplier engagement model: *The physical location of offshore supplier managers and developers.* This category emerged from the data. Biotech used three supplier engagement models to organize the 21 projects. The cheapest model in terms of hourly wages entailed having all the offshore supplier employees (managers and developers) in India. This model was used on 12 projects. The most expensive model had some offshore supplier managers and developers onsite. This model was used on five projects. The middle model had some offshore developers onsite, but no offshore supplier manager onsite. This model was used on four projects.

4. Contract size: *The value of the contract in terms of actual dollars paid to the supplier(s) for a project.* Practitioners have frequently told us that the more strategic a client account, the more attention the supplier will pay to the account. The two most important determinants of a supplier's perception of a strategic account are current revenues generated from the account and the potential for future revenues generated from the account (Feeny, 2006). We wondered: Does value of the contract matter?

We used actual dollars spent as the indicator of contract value because Biotech closely tracked these figures for each project. Using dollars spent, the contract values ranged between $4,300 and $1,363,098, with a mean contract value of $193,000 and a median contract value of $64,473.

5. Project size: *The size of the project in terms of duration in number of days.* For over 25 years, IT researchers have recognized the relationship between project size, risk, and outcome (Gopal *et al.*, 2003; Keil *et al.*, 2003; Keil and Montealegre, 2000; McFarlan, 1981; Wallace *et al.*, 2004). In general, prior research has found that larger-sized projects are riskier and have lower success rates than smaller-sized projects (Jones, 1994). For example, Carroll (2005) found that small projects (less than six months) had a success rate of 50%, medium-sized projects (six to nine months) had a 40% success rate, and none of the projects in the sample (n = 22) over nine months were successful. Aladwani (2002) in a study of 42 IT projects found that project size negatively affects project planning, which negatively impacts project success. Practitioners and researchers suggest transforming a large project into smaller projects through phased functionality, prototyping, or pilot testing to reduce risk and increase success (Jones, 1994; Standish Group International, 2003; Willcocks *et al.*, 1997).

We wanted to determine the extent to which project size sheds light on Biotech's project outcomes. There are a number of ways to measure project size (lines of code, function points, duration in days or months, dollars spent, and man hours). We used duration of the project in days because Biotech's PMO closely tracked this number. (Biotech did not track total costs of the project, only the costs directly invoiced by the offshore suppliers). Using duration, the project sizes ranged from 11 days long to 1,030 days long. The average project was 350 days long and the median project was 272 days long.

6. Organizational unit: *The organizational unit within IT managing the project.* This category emerged from the data when it became apparent during the interviews that some groups seemed to be experiencing more success with offshore outsourcing than others. At Biotech, six units report directly to the CIO (See Appendix D). Five of these units engaged offshore suppliers for at least one project: Enterprise Architecture, ERP, R&D, Marketing, and Web.

7. Project Start Year: The year the project was started. Based on prior research, we thought that earlier projects would have lower ratings than later projects. For example, Lacity and Willcocks (1998) found that more recent contracts had higher frequencies of success than older contracts. They attributed this finding to learning curve effects. Three research studies on offshore outsourcing also found learning curve effects (Carmel and Agarwal, 2002; Kaiser and Hawk, 2004; Rottman and Lacity, 2006). All three studies found that clients use offshore outsourcing more strategically over time. Biotech launched 14 projects in 2003, six projects in 2004, and one project in 2005.

8. Contract Type: *The type of contact signed with suppliers.* This issue is discussed in detail in Chapter 11. Researchers have found/argued that contract type is an important success factor in IT outsourcing. Contracts have been generally categorized as "classical", "neoclassical", and "relational" (Williamson, 1979). In the context of IT outsourcing, contracts have been categorized as "standard contracts", "detailed contracts", "loose contracts", "mixed contracts", "buy-in contracts", or "partnerships" (Lacity and Willcocks, 1998; Lee *et al.*, 2004) or "fixed price" versus "time & materials" (Gopal *et al.*, 2003; Lichtenstein, 2004), or "stage-by-stage" versus "two-stage" (Richmond and Seidmann, 1993). Lacity and Willcocks (1998) found that detailed contracts had the highest frequency of success. Lee *et al.* (2004) found that outsourcing was more successful when contract type was matched with IT strategy. Gopal *et al.* (2003) specifically studied contracts with an Indian offshore provider. They found that contract choice significantly determined project profit. Lichtenstein (2004) found that customers accept too much risk in contracts, compared to prescriptions from economic theories. Richmond and Seidmann (1993) developed a mathematical model that argues a two-staged contracting process leads to higher business value than stage-by-stage contracting. We wondered, "how does contract type affect project outcomes?" At Biotech, however, we learned that there was no variability in contract type. Among the 21 projects studied at Biotech, 20 were time & materials contracts not to exceed a specified maximum amount. One project was managed through a captive center, which we call offshoring. Thus, we could not assess the affect of contract type on project outcome.

Table 14.3 summarizes the data categories as captured at Biotech.

Table 14.3   Data Categories for Project Level Analysis

Data Category	Data Values	Number of Projects	Percentage of Projects n = 21
Offshore Supplier Size and Number	One Small Supplier	12	57%
	One Large Supplier	5	24%
	Multiple Suppliers	3	14%
	Biotech's Captive Center	1	5%
Project type	New development	15	71%
	Maintenance/support	6	29%
Supplier engagement model	Some supplier managers & developers on-site	5	24%
	Some supplier developers on-site	4	19%
	No offshore supplier managers or developers on-site	12	57%
Contract Value: Actual Dollars Spent	Lesser-valued (Less than $193,000)	14	67%
	Greater-valued (More than $193,000)	7	33%
Project Size: Duration	Shorter (Less than one year)	13	62%
	Longer (Greater than one year)	8	38%
Organizational Unit	Enterprise Architecture	1	5%
	ERP	2	10%
	R&D	10	48%
	Marketing	5	24%
	Web	3	14%
Project Start Year	During 2003	14	67%
	During 2004/2005	7	33%
Contract Type	Time & Materials	20	95%
	Captive	1	5%

Seven project level findings

We cross-tabulated project ratings across seven data categories: (1) offshore supplier size and number, (2) project type, (3) supplier engagement model, (4) contract value, (5) project size, (6) organizational unit managing the project, and (7) project start year.

Because project ratings are numeric, there are several ways to divide the data into categories of "success". We divided the data into two. We categorized individual projects that rated above the mean project rating of 1.73 as the "more successful projects" and projects that rated below the project mean as the "less successful projects". Given the sample contains 21 projects, dividing the data into two categories by mean seemed the most reasonable criterion. (We note that the mean and median are nearly identical and selecting the median would not change results). Because we have provided all the data in Appendix D, other researchers could easily use our data to apply alternative methods from the one we selected, such as dividing data into thirds or using the raw average grades such as A–B projects in one category, C projects in a category, and D/F projects in a category.

Our analysis yields seven project level findings.

1. Overall, participants rated projects that engaged one large offshore supplier higher than projects that engaged one small offshore supplier or multiple suppliers. For this analysis, we cross-tabulated size and number of the offshore suppliers with project rating (see Table 14.4).

Table 14.4 Project Rating vs. Size and Number of Offshore Suppliers

Offshore Supplier Size:	PROJECT RATING:		
	Number of Projects that were Rated *Above* the Mean Project Rating	Number of Projects that were Rated *Below* the Mean Project Rating	Percentage of Projects Rated *Above* the Mean Project Rating
One large supplier (greater than $1 billion in annual revenues)	4	1	80%
Multi-sourced	2	1	67%
One small supplier (less than $150 million annual revenue	5	7	42%
Captive center	0	1	0%

Among the 21 projects, 12 projects engaged one small offshore supplier, five projects engaged one large offshore supplier, one project involved the captive center, and three projects engaged more than one supplier. The two most definitive findings based on this analysis are:

1. Participants rated four out of five projects (80%) that engaged one *large* supplier above the mean project rating.
2. Participants only rated five of the 12 projects (42%) that engaged one *small* supplier above the mean project rating.

The participants provide insights to these findings. According to the participants, a major advantage of the larger suppliers was that they had greater access to experienced IT personnel. An IT Lead with over 25 years with Biotech said:

"[The small vendors] would take forever to find resources with the skills and levels of experience we were needing. The small vendors did not seem to be able to attract and retain good people. That really hurt our projects – it took longer to ramp up and if there was unplanned turnover – we were dead. The larger vendors seemed to have a much deeper bench. Cycling on and off a project was much smoother with the larger vendors and we did not have to spend as much time explaining technologies or methodologies to them. Turnover seemed much less of an issue with the larger vendors."

One Program Lead expressed dissatisfaction with the smaller suppliers. In his experiences, the smaller suppliers lacked the experience to accurately bid and manage projects. He said:

"[The small supplier] just didn't get it. We estimated internally (using offshore rates) that a project we had pegged for offshore should cost about $80,000 and take about six to nine months. The supplier's bid was $40,000 and they estimated it would take four months. I wanted an accurate estimate of the effort and time it would take more so than just trying to get the lowest dollar I could on the project. So I told the supplier they were significantly off in their bid and asked them to resubmit. The second bid came in at $60,000 with a time frame of six months. By this time, we were already running behind schedule and needing to pursue offshore, so we accepted the bid. The supplier ended up spending an additional six months and we ended up fixing a lot of the code and doing the testing ourselves."

Table 14.4 also shows that participants rated two of the three multi-sourced projects above the mean project rating. Because only three projects were multi-sourced, we must be very cautious in deriving conclusions based on this data. However, the Team Lead SAP provided insight into the efficacy of using multiple suppliers on a project:

> "You have to understand what the supplier wants and what the supplier brings to the table and how your project fits in. For example, [a large supplier] should bring in process expertise and great talent, but they aren't interested in my $5000 little project. However, small suppliers are often hungry for business and can bring in specific skills. So, when we gave large, generic chunks of projects to the large vendors and smaller, more specific chunks to the small vendor, it worked pretty well."

2. Overall, participants rated both development and maintenance/ support projects equally. For this analysis, we cross-tabulated project type with project rating (see Table 14.5). Based on prior research, we speculated that new development projects would have more risk and thus lower project ratings than projects involving maintenance or support of existing systems. However, evidence did not support this speculation. Overall, participants rated both development (53%) and maintenance/support (50%) above the mean project rating nearly equally. According to an interview with a Software Architect, it was evident that the type of project did not matter because all the work was new to the suppliers. He said:

> "It really didn't matter the types of work we gave to the supplier. Even for what we considered to be routine, like maintenance, they had to learn the system, the tools and how we worked. Even though it was old to us, it was like new development to the supplier. For example, we have a Lotus Notes database to maintain, it was very difficulty to find Notes experts. They had to learn the system from scratch."

Table 14.5   Project Rating vs. Project Type

Project Type:	PROJECT RATING:		
	Number of Projects that were Rated *Above* the Mean Project Rating	Number of Projects that were Rated *Below* the Mean Project Rating	Percentage of Projects Rated *Above* the Mean Project Rating
New Software Development	8	7	53%
Support and or maintenance of existing software	3	3	50%

3. **Overall, participants rated projects with some offshore supplier employees onsite higher than projects with all supplier employees off-shore.** For this analysis, we cross-tabulated the supplier engagement model with project rating (see Table 14.6). Biotech used three engagement models, entailing different locations (onsite or offshore) of supplier managers and supplier developers.

Table 14.6 shows that participants rated seven of the nine projects (78%) that had some supplier managers and/or developers onsite higher than the mean project rating. In contrast, participants rated four of the 12 projects (33%) that located all the supplier employees offshore higher than the mean project rating.

Table 14.6   Project Rating vs. Supplier Engagement Model

	PROJECT RATING:		
Offshore Supplier Engagement Model:	**Number of Projects that were Rated *Above* the Mean Project Rating**	**Number of Projects that were Rated *Below* the Mean Project Rating**	**Percentage of Projects Rated *Above* the Mean Project Rating**
Some supplier managers and developers on-site	4	1	80%
Some supplier developers on-site but no supplier managers on-site	3	1	75%
No supplier managers or developers on-site	4	8	33%

According to multiple participants, project managers at Biotech were under extreme pressure to keep projects costs low. Because any offshore supplier employee onsite is paid onshore rates (about $65 per hour verses about $25 per hour offshore), project managers were pressured to keep as much of the supplier headcount offshore as possible. However, some participants said that quality suffered when all of a supplier's employees were offshore because they did not understand Biotech's requirements and could not easily communicate with Biotech's IT staff and business users. Several participants concluded that an onsite engagement manager (OEM) and some onsite developers were needed to better understand and communicate requirements and thus ensure quality. According to a Program Lead:

"If this project was to be staffed by domestic contractors, we would have just added two new contractors. However, since we were new to offshore, we priced in an OEM to interface between the business sponsors and the two offshore developers. We realized that all project cost savings was lost, but the OEM helped us improve our processes, interviewed and managed the developers and was responsible for status updates."

Project Q is another example in which participants viewed an onsite engagement manager at critical to success. Project Q required new development of Biotech's SAP systems. According to the Team Lead HR Services:

"SAP is a rather business critical system around here, so we understand the risk. SAP is running our core business functions and it's doing it globally. So we already had the mentality of protecting our environment. And even though the OEM is expensive, they are worth it. They interface between our analysts and the offshore developers and save a lot of time and rework. They help to protect our environment."

4. **Overall, participants rated projects with greater-valued contracts higher than projects with lesser-valued contracts.** For this analysis, we cross-tabulated contract value with project rating. Because the mean contract value ($193,000) is substantially different than the median contract value ($64,473), we analyzed both. Table 14.7 and Table 14.8 show the results. Table 14.7 is based on the *mean* spend as dividing line between greater and lesser-valued contracts. It shows that participants rated 71% of the greater-valued contracts above the mean project rating, compared to 43% of the lesser-valued contracts.

Table 14.7   Project Rating vs. Contract Value using Mean

Contract Value:	PROJECT RATING:		
	Number of Projects that were Rated *Above* the Mean Project Rating	Number of Projects that were Rated *Below* the Mean Project Rating	Percentage of Projects Rated *Above* the Mean Project Rating
Greater-value (greater than $193,000 mean spent)	5	2	71%
Lesser-value (less than the $193,000 mean spent)	6	8	43%

Table 14.8   Project Rating vs. Contract Value using Median

| | PROJECT RATING: | | |
Contract Value:	Number of Projects that were Rated *Above* the Mean Project Rating	Number of Projects that were Rated *Below* the Mean Project Rating	Percentage of Projects Rated *Above* the Mean Project Rating
Greater-value (greater than $64,473 median spent)	7	3	70%
Lesser-value (less than the $64,473 median spent)	3	7	30%

Table 14.8 is based on the *median* spend as dividing line between greater and lesser-valued contracts. It shows that participants rated 70% of the greater-valued contracts above the mean project rating, compared to 30% of the lesser-valued contracts. Thus, contract value mattered. However, none of the participants directly addressed the value of the contract issue during the interviews, so we cannot easily interpret this finding.

5. Overall, participants rated larger-sized projects higher than smaller-sized projects. For this analysis, we cross-tabulated project size with project rating. Our measure of project size is numeric (number of days). We initially used three rules to categorize projects as "larger" versus "smaller." The rules were (1) Gudea's (2005) cut-off of over/under one year in duration, (2) over/under the mean duration of 350 days, and (3) over/under the median duration of 272 days. However, rules (1) and (2) are coincidentally equivalent with our data.

Table 14.9 and Table 14.10 show the results. Table 14.9 is based on the *mean* and *one-year cut-off* as dividing line between longer (larger) and shorter (smaller) sized projects. It shows that participants rated 63% of the larger-sized projects above the mean project rating, compared to 46% of the smaller-sized projects.

Table 14.10 is based on the *median* duration as dividing line between larger and smaller sized projects. It shows that participants rated 70% of the larger-sized projects above the mean project rating, compared to 30% of the smaller-sized projects.

Some of the participants claimed that smaller-sized projects could not meet financial objectives because the transaction costs of dealing with the offshore suppliers swallowed the projected cost savings. Below are some of the quotes supporting this interpretation:

"On the smaller projects, the overhead costs of documenting some of the projects exceeded the value of the deliverables." – IT Lead

"I think we used a shot gun approach with all these little projects. I think they were too small and too scattered to consolidate any savings or even any learning. You had people all over [Biotech] doing little projects and we could not capture any savings or any metrics." – Web Administrator

"A lot of our projects were too small. We had one, maybe one and a half, resources working offshore and the overhead was killing us trying to keep track of what was going on offshore." – Program Lead

Table 14.9 Project Rating vs. Project Size using Mean

	PROJECT RATING:		
Project Duration:	Number of Projects that were Rated *Above* the Mean Project Rating	Number of Projects that were Rated *Below* the Mean Project Rating	Percentage of Projects Rated *Above* the Mean Project Rating
Longer (More than one year)	5	3	63%
Shorter (Less than one year)	6	7	46%

Table 14.10 Project Rating vs. Project Size using Median

	PROJECT RATING:		
Project Duration:	Number of Projects that were Rated *Above* the Mean Project Rating	Number of Projects that were Rated *Below* the Mean Project Rating	Percentage of Projects Rated *Above* the Mean Project Rating
Longer (longer than 272 year)	7	3	70%
Shorter (Less than 272 days)	3	7	30%

Conversely, one IT Team Lead explained that larger-projects allowed Biotech to recover overhead by benefiting from mounting experience:

"The larger projects I did seemed to work a little better. It took quite some time to figure things out, and with the smaller projects, they would end at that point. With the larger ones, we could use the learning and rela-tionships we built for longer periods of time and improve as we went along."

6. **Overall, some organizational units had higher participant-rated projects than other organizational units.** Participants from five of the six units that report directly to the CIO managed at least one offshore project. Table 14.11 cross-tabulates these five units against project rating. Projects managed by the Web and ERP units all scored above the mean project rating. The most interesting finding, however, is that the R&D unit did the most offshore projects, yet participants rated only 30% of projects above the mean project rating.

Table 14.11 Project Rating vs. Organizational Unit

	PROJECT RATING:		
Organizational Unit within Biotech	**Number of Projects that were Rated *Above* the Mean Project Rating**	**Number of Projects that were Rated *Below* the Mean Project Rating**	**Percentage of Projects Rated *Above* the Mean Project Rating**
Web	3	0	100%
ERP	2	0	100%
Marketing	3	2	60%
R&D	3	7	30%
Enterprise Architecture	0	1	0%

The level of domain specific knowledge required by these different units may explain the results. Some participants noted that projects within the R&D area required the supplier to have very specific scientific knowledge, whereas the Web and ERP units required more common knowledge. According to an IT Lead in the R&D area:

"What makes some of this [offshore outsourcing] hard is that we are making up the questions at the same time we are asking the supplier to come up with answers. We are inventing new products with highly scientific processes and foundations. In our area, we are really 'out there' in regards to the kinds of things we are creating."

Conversely, all of the projects in the less scientifically-intense areas of Web and ERP were rated above the mean. A Team Lead SAP explained:

> "A lot of what we do in our area is more generic than in the [R&D] area. The bulk of our work are change requests to our SAP systems. The suppliers are well equipped in the SAP tools like ABAP. Once we accurately explain the specifications and modifications needed to fulfill the change request, the ABAP part is fairly straight forward."

7. Overall, participants rated recent projects higher than older projects. For this analysis, we compared the project ratings for earlier projects that were launched in 2003 against projects that were launched after 2003. Table 14.12 shows that participants rated 43% of the earlier projects above the mean project rating, compared to 71% of the later projects, indicating that organizational learning did occur.

Table 14.12   Project Ratings vs. Project Start Year

	PROJECT RATING:		
Project Start Year:	Number of Projects that were Rated *Above* the Mean Project Rating	Number of Projects that were Rated *Below* the Mean Project Rating	Percentage of Projects Rated *Above* the Mean Project Rating
During 2003	6	8	43%
During 2004 or 2005	5	2	71%

Some participants stated that as projects and engagements matured, the quality of deliverables improved. For example, a Team Lead SAP in the ERP area said,

> "It took us quite some time to figure out how much different working with an offshore supplier was. We are very used to working with domestic contractors in a staff augmentation model. Offshore is different. But, as time went on and the supplier helped to improve our documentation and requirements definition processes, the change requests went more smoothly and our internal SAP consultants were better able to utilize the offshore resources. I am seeing much more bang for my buck now when compared to the beginning."

Organization level findings

From the Case Description section, it is clear that the official word in PMO documents was that offshore outsourcing was meeting Biotech's objective to reduce IT costs. Based on the project ratings from knowledgeable participants, results were obviously mixed, and generally less positive than the "official word." While the previous section focused on project attributes to explain offshore outsourcing outcomes, this section focuses on the broader contextual issues.

Initially, the CIO and IT Leads' strategy was to replace, person-for-person, domestic contractors with offshore IT workers. Participants provided four insights as to why this strategy was a poor fit with Biotech's social and cultural contexts.

1. Strong social networks between Biotech IT employees and domestic contractors could not easily be replicated with offshore suppliers. Although prior research suggests significant differences between contractors and permanent employees (Ang and Slaughter, 2001), this was not evident at Biotech. At Biotech, we learned that domestic IT contractors are treated like Biotech IT employees. They are housed in the same types of cubicles with permanent workers, wear the same identification badges, attend the same meetings, and are tightly integrated into project teams. One reason for the lack of distinction is that Biotech often uses domestic contractor positions as a precursor to fulltime positions. Indeed, among the 44 people we interviewed, ten were previously domestic contractors before becoming fulltime Biotech employees. The following quotation describes the close integration of domestic contractors and Biotech employees:

> "Our culture is totally different from a contract resource point of view. I came from some other companies. I was shocked when I came into [Biotech] to see how the contractors were actually integrated into the scene. I mean, I couldn't tell [who was a contractor and who was a fulltime employee]. Same meetings, you have as many responsibilities as some of the senior managers have here. Some [contractors] have been around sometimes for over a decade. This is a totally different paradigm." – IT Lead

In contrast, the Indian offshore IT workers were obviously treated differently. Despite efforts to integrate the offshore workers into the teams, internal Biotech employees never felt a sense of connection with them. According to an IT Team Lead, *"We even tried bringing over some people from India for team building, and it worked when they were here, but when they went back, the team aspect fell apart."* In addition to the social disconnection, there were technical barriers as well. Due to security concerns and bandwidth constraints, offshore workers were not allowed to access production data or Biotech's internal systems such as the code repository. This hampered development and created obstacles for the offshore workers.

2. Biotech's "sneaker-net" culture among business users, IT employees and domestic contractors could not easily be replicated with offshore suppliers. At Biotech, we learned that requirements analysis is an informal process. Because IT workers reside on the same campus as business users, Biotech's IT employees and domestic contractors typically walk over to meet business users to seek or clarify functional requirements. Thus, the process was called "sneaker-net" by some participants. Like the social networks that facilitate knowledge transfer between IT employees and domestic contractors, there are also social networks that facilitate knowledge transfer among IT employees, domestic contractors, and business users. According to the CIO, *"Here at [Biotech], we have always worked very closely with our contractors and our business sponsors. Tight collaboration is part of our DNA. That makes this offshoring pretty tough."*

Furthermore, the CIO said that requirements are not only informally *gathered*, requirements are also informally *documented*. He said requirements are typically "documented" on white boards or in personal notebooks. A Web Developer corroborated the CIO's statement:

> "A lot of times in our environment, the developers will be involved in requirements, meaning taking their own notes and gathering that under-standing. And that's not something that happened with offshore. We had to retranslate what he had to paper and then translate it to them, and it doesn't work very well. I think in a development environment, it's important that the developers be part of requirements gathering, so that they can understand what it is and why it is."

Biotech's "sneaker-net" culture did not fit well with offshore. Indian-based IT workers did not have access to users to establish the social networks needed to facilitate knowledge transfer. A Project Manager in R&D said:

> "We had no way to get requirements from the user and get them to the offshore team. We could have easily done this project onshore because we know how to go back and forth with the user, but the offshore team just couldn't do it."

In hindsight, an IT Lead acknowledged that Biotech had not thought through the knowledge transfer process: *"We didn't have anything in place that was really allowing us to transfer the knowledge. There was, like, a huge leak."*

3. Biotech's IT managers had more difficulty assessing relevant skills and experiences for offshore suppliers than for domestic contractors. Biotech IT Managers interview domestic contractors in person and contact previous employers to verify résumé claims. In contrast, Biotech IT Managers interviewed offshore workers by phone and relied on the supplier managers to verify qualifications. According to several participants, this process resulted in a poor skills match. For example, according to a Development Coordinator:

> "Our domestic ABAP contractors would have three to five years of ABAP experience and six to ten years of other IT experience. The offshore contractors would come to us as "experienced", but that meant they had two to three years of IT/ABAP experience total. They didn't understand IT projects – let alone the ABAP processes."

One IT Team Lead, stated, *"We never knew if what was on the résumé would actually be what the guy would actually be able to do. The interview process was hit and miss."* Finally, a Software Architect echoed the frustration with inexperienced supplier employees:

> "The supplier would send us a guy with 'five years experience'. But when we worked with him we would realize he really had only one true year of experience. He had done the exact same tasks at five different engagements. So he only had one real year of experience five times."

4. Biotech's project management processes and expectations were often incompatible with offshore suppliers. Despite the cultural awareness training, many participants were unprepared for the cultural differences between US IT workers and Indian IT workers. In the US, domestic contractors are trusted to speak up when deadlines slip or they do not understand requirements or processes. An Application Architect describes the trust he has in his domestic contractor to communicate with him:

> "And I make it clear to my contractors, if you don't understand something, you're in my office, every day. I mean, I got one contractor who is reasonable, $54 bucks an hour, really reasonable guy. He basically comes in my cube, probably, 15 times a day, and that's what we have to do. We've got a couple other guys that are very similar to him and, basically come in all the time for clarification."

In contrast, we heard from many participants that the offshore IT workers could not be relied upon to report that the project was behind schedule or that they did not understand the requirements. The following four quotes serve as evidence about not reporting project delays:

> "When the project was going so far off course, they never really told us that they were behind on deadlines. They always said everything was going well." – Offshore Project Coordinator

"Well, probably the biggest awareness that was raised was their tendency to not want to deliver bad news." – Technical Lead

"An iteration was due on Monday. On Friday the guy [Indian Project Manager] says 'it's fine. A little bit of a stretch, but it is fine'. And on Tuesday he's asking for another two weeks! So they missed it by 100%. They didn't feel like they could tell us if they were going to miss it. This seems to be the modus operandi, dig and dig and spade and spade to get anybody to tell you that things are wrong. Because they just simply won't. They will tell you it is great." – Head of the PMO

One IT Lead summed it up by saying, "*The place could be on fire and they would say, 'Oh it's great, a little warm, but it is great!*"

The following quote addresses the offshore supplier's reticence to express incomprehension:

"You can sometimes be talking with someone and across the table they'll be shaking their head as if they understand and agree with everything you're saying. You find out later that they didn't understand what you were talking about." – IT Lead

During an offshore outsourcing class the second author attended, Biotech's offshore consultant talked about the cultural challenges at Biotech. According to him, Biotech's Indian suppliers view time more fluidly than Westerners. He said, "*If an Indian IT worker knows how to complete a task even though he knows it will be late, then he would view it as unnecessary to contact the customer. He is the expert and the customer should trust that he is professionally completing the task.*"

Epilogue. Like most first-time adopters with offshore outsourcing, Biotech felt the need to rethink its strategy. Biotech planned to migrate the strategic intent of offshore from "IS improvement" to "business impact" (DiRomualdo and Gurbaxani, 1998). According to the CIO, he planned to reduce offshore outsourcing and increase the strategic role of the captive center (offshoring). This may seem illogical given that the project done at the captive center (Project D) was the lowest rated project. However, the CIO believed that he could best serve Biotech by helping his company sell Biotech products to the Indian market. He stated:

"A set of IT Leads and I are heading to Bangalore soon and we plan to put a lot of energy into getting the captive center up to our internal standards. I know the captive center has a 'black eye' with our internal users, but I see our development center there as a lever for increasing our exposure to the Indian markets. If we can get it running smoothly and then expand our headcount and visibility in India, that will help us to market and sell our products in a *very large and growing market. I think* showing the Indian government that we have a commitment to a large development center will go a long way to improving our relationship with India as an important customer to us."

As previously mentioned, three research studies on offshore outsourcing also found that clients used offshore outsourcing more strategically over time (Carmel and Agarwal, 2002; Kaiser and Hawk, 2004; Rottman and Lacity, 2006). Both Carmel and Agarwal (2002) and Rottman and Lacity (2006) found that client organizations initially engaged in offshore outsourcing to reduce costs, and then later used offshore outsourcing more strategically to increase revenues, access new markets, and to create agile sourcing networks (see also Oshri *et al.*, 2008).

Thus far, we have discussed project level attributes and contextual reasons to explain Biotech's experiences with offshore outsourcing. The next section points to learning from Biotech that may be valuable to other practitioners and researchers.

Case validation

While we followed a pluralistic case study approach, all research must demonstrate validity. We adopted Klein and Myer's validity checks because if forced into a label, the case study method is more interpretative than positivist. As shown in Table 14.13, Klein and Myers (1999) principles support the use of interpretive method.

Conclusion – implications for practice and research

Implications for clients

For clients, there are several lessons to be learned from Biotech's experiences.

First, the research suggests that project attributes affect project outcomes. While we are cautious to make definitive prescriptions based on 21 projects, it is clear from this research and other research that clients have control over many project attributes that may affect success (Choudhury and Sabherwal, 2003; Gopal *et al.*, 2003; Krishna *et al.*, 2004; Sabherwal, 1999). Clients can control strategy formulation, supplier selection, size of projects, size of engagements, contract type, project type, and engagement models when considering offshore outsourcing.

Second, the research demonstrates that an offshore strategy must either fit with the organization's norms and practices (DeLong and Fahey, 2000), or the client may have to change norms and practices to achieve offshore success. At Biotech, the "sneaker-net" culture and close social

Table 14.13 Case Evaluation using Klein and Myers (1999) Interpretive Research Principles

Interpretive Field Research Principle	Brief Definition from Klein and Myers (1999)	Sections in the Biotech Case that Demonstrate this Principle
Hermeneutic Circle	"Iterating between considering the interdependent meaning of data and the whole that they form."	Project Level Findings: The data findings were created by cross referencing data categories to the project success indicator. We then asked, what does this finding mean in the larger context of Biotech? The answers emerged from combing the transcribed interviews to interpret the findings in the context of the case as evidenced by interview data.
Contextualization	"Requires critical reflection of the social and historical background of the research setting, so that the intended audience can see how the current situation emerged."	The background to the case explains the circumstances leading to Biotech's offshore journey. The research methods section explains how we became involved in the Biotech case.
Interaction Between Research and Subjects	"Requires critical reflection on how the research materials were socially constructed through interaction between researchers and participants."	Interactions between the researchers and participants entailed multiple phases.
Abstraction and Generalization	"Relating the idiographic details to theoretical, general concepts that describe the nature of human understanding and social interaction."	The abstracted categories used are supplier size and number (one small, one large, multiple and captive center), project type (new development and maintenance/support), engagement model (on- and/or off-site resources), contract value (less than or more than average), project duration (shorter than or longer than average), organizational unit (EA, ERP, R & D, Marketing or Web), Project Start Year (2003 or 2004–05) and Contract Type (Time and Materials or Captive).

Table 14.13 Case Evaluation using Klein and Myers (1999) Interpretive Research Principles – *continued*

Interpretive Field Research Principle	Brief Definition from Klein and Myers (1999)	Sections in the Biotech Case that Demonstrate this Principle
Dialogical Reasoning	"Requires sensitivity to possible contradictions between the theoretical preconceptions guiding research design and actual findings."	Both prior to and during the research, we were cognizant of our own perceptions of Biotech's efforts and purposefully and carefully avoided imparting any value judgments or preconceptions regarding success, engagement models, or project metrics.
Multiple Interpretations	"Requires sensitivity to possible differences in interpretations among the participants."	We showed that stakeholders often have different perceptions of reality concerning offshore. We concluded that the perceptions were largely explained by the information filtering that occurred at different levels in the organization.
Suspicion	"Requires sensitivity to possible biases and systematic distortions in the narratives."	Hopefully, participant suspicion was minimized by the assurance of anonymity and the CIOs encouragement to provide the researchers with an honest assessment. In his words, "the good, the bad and the ugly".

networks between business users, IT employees, and domestic contractors were a poor fit with offshore outsourcing. In some cases, Biotech participants changed the practices in one of two ways:

1. Some Biotech project managers abandoned the "sneaker-net" process in favor of formal documentation of business, technical, and procedural requirements. Participants pursuing this option generally agreed that it facilitated knowledge transfer. According to a Technical Architect:

> "They [the offshore supplier] improved our internal processes. They all have been documenting procedures and processes. Now, we've got it so proceduralized that we've anticipated 90% of the questions."

But participants also complained that it significantly increased their project overhead. As previously noted, one IT Lead said: *"On the smaller projects, the overhead costs of documenting some of the projects exceeded the value of the deliverables."* A Software Architect in R&D said: *"We severely underestimated the amount of time and work it took to get the offshore team to understand first the needs of the users, then the tools we were using and then finally the capabilities we were shooting for."*

2. Some participants brought supplier managers and developers onsite to build social networks. Among the 21 projects, Biotech brought offshore supplier employees onsite for nine projects, of which seven scored above the mean project rating. Again, the benefit of this practice is that it facilitates knowledge transfer from user to offshore IT worker. Participants said it was worth the extra cost. In describing the Onsite Engagement Manager used in the marketing unit at Biotech, a Team Lead said:

> "He is talented, he knows his technology, is a good systems analyst and has good relationships with the team offshore. He's the one right now making a very cohesive environment. I think if we did not have a link there, we would be hurting. We have never had a situation where we've missed our deadlines for deliverables."

The drawback of this practice is that it increases costs.

Third, the research suggests that clients need robust measures to monitor and manage offshore outsourcing programs. Biotech's simple formula for calculating cost savings (cost of hours offshore versus what the hours would have cost onshore) disseminated the message that offshore outsourcing was successful. The PMO's official word that offshore was "successful", put pressure on participants to support senior management's "successful" agenda. As one Software Architect said, *"You didn't want to tell them [senior management] the bad news too much. Because, this was their baby and you didn't want to say, "You have a terribly ugly baby!"* Metrics that capture productivity, quality, process improvement, supplier compatibility, and organizational learning are needed to carefully manage offshore outsourcing.

Implications for suppliers

First, it is evident that offshore suppliers must also address the knowledge transfer issue. Offshore suppliers often rely heavily on Capability Maturity Model (CMM) processes to ensure that business requirements are properly documented (Adler *et al.*, 2005). However, if their clients are operating at CMM levels of two or below, the relationship may struggle with the issues experienced at Biotech. Suppliers may have to help clients improve their CMM processes, or be flexible by finding ways to fit into the client's requirements analysis processes.

Second, offshore suppliers must also protect knowledge after it is transferred. Because of increasing employee turnover rates (McCue, 2005; Srivastava, 2005), Indian suppliers in particular must have good knowledge management processes. Some participants at Biotech said that supplier turnover was a problem because when supplier employees left, they took the hard-earned, client-specific knowledge with them. An IT Lead said:

> "And the other thing, too, is their turnover rates. So those five-year guys on the offshore team, they're already looking to move. They're not looking to move to a technical lead or architect or programming. And the opportunity is there. So, personally for them, it's a great opportunity, they could move at five years. And, so we can't even keep them on the offshore team."

Suppliers must find innovative ways to capture tacit knowledge by using, for example, video repositories, interactive training modules, mentoring and shadowing to grooming replacements (Rottman, 2006).

Third, for some offshore suppliers, it is evident that poor communication remains a major impediment to project outcomes. Both this study and prior studies cite the improvements needed in the communication between users, internal IT staff, and offshore suppliers. For example, Carmel and Tjia (2005) identified 17 practices for improving cross-cultural communication, such as talking to expatriates, and remembering the six R's – repeat, reduce, rephrase, reiterate, review, and recap.

Implications for research

The Biotech research and review of the offshore outsourcing literature in Appendix A suggests several areas in which academics can provide a significant contribution.

First, the Biotech research suggests that offshore outsourcing can be used as a rich context for studying how social networks facilitate knowledge transfer of business requirements. For example, the work of Nahapiet and Ghoshal (1998) may be tested further in the offshore outsourcing of IT work context. They argue that social capital (such as social networks) helps to create intellectual capital (such as understanding user requirements). They also posit that organizations have an advantage over markets in creating and sharing of intellectual capital. Some work on this appears in Oshri *et al.* (2008). Thus, maybe domestic contractors at Biotech are not inherently different than offshore IT workers, but that domestic contractors were essentially insiders. We have one anecdote that suggests that offshore IT workers can essentially become "insiders" over time. A quote from an Indian Project Lead who has been a fulltime Biotech employee for four years sums up the need for a greater understanding of the social networks in knowledge transfer:

"Communication was a real issue – even for me and I am from Mumbai. I found it hard during the conference calls to understand what they were saying, especially during the interviews and code reviews. And when we would send emails back and forth, I thought, 'What are they trying to say, I don't understand where they are coming from.' It would take two or three extra emails, just to make sure we were talking about the same things."

From a review of the offshore outsourcing literature, several fruitful avenues of research include:

More research on under-examined offshore destinations, particularly China, Philippines, South and Central American countries. If analysts are correct in predicting high growth in global IT outsourcing and the wage inflation occurring in India, we need a better understanding of country and supplier capabilities beyond India.

More research on practices for managing offshore projects and how these practices compare to projects outsourced domestically. Among the 22 offshore outsourcing studies, four studies besides this chapter have examined offshore outsourcing from the project level (Choudhury and Sabherwal, 2003; Gopal *et al.*, 2003; Krishna *et al.*, 2004; Sabherwal, 1999). Although our chapter makes a contribution on this front, more data is needed to understand the generalizability of our results. For example – do many other clients have the same success rates with new development and maintenance/support?

Large sample surveys to provide a better understanding of the offshore phenomena, and to test and develop theories. As Appendix A notes, most researchers studying offshore are not yet using or testing theories, with the exception of a few people. Researchers study new phenomena, like offshore outsourcing, first with case studies. But as a criticalmass of adopters builds, large sample surveys become feasible. We believe enough clients have adopted offshore outsourcing to pursue larger sampling.

More macro-economic studies are needed to inform the public debate on offshore outsourcing. Data collected by government agencies may be viewed as partisan. For example, there is considerable debate about the accuracy of the Department of Commerce's report, *An Overview of Workforce Globalization in the U.S. IT Services and Software, U.S. Semiconductor and the U.S. Pharmaceuticals Industries* (Democratic Caucus, 2006). To respond to anti-offshore rhetoric, we need "objective" data to determine the economic effects of offshore outsourcing. As Kofi Annan, 2001 Nobel Peace Prize winner notes: *"It has been said that arguing against globalization is like arguing against the laws of gravity."*

References

Adler, P., McGarry, F., Talbot, W. and Binney, D. (2005) "Enabling Process Discipline: Lessons from the Journey to CMM Level 5", *MIS Quarterly Executive*, 4, 1, March, 215–227.

Aladwani, A. (2002) "IT Project Uncertainty, Planning, and Success", *Information Technology & People*, 15, 3, 210–237.

Ang, S. and Slaughter, S. (2001) "Work Outcomes and Job Design for Contract Versus Permanent Information Systems Professionals on Software Development Teams", *MIS Quarterly*, 25, 3, September, 321–350.

Ang, S. and Straub, D. (1998) "Production and Transaction Economies and Information Systems Outsourcing – A Study of the U.S. Banking Industry", *MIS Quarterly*, 22, 4, 535–552.

Applegate, L. and Montealegre, R. (1991) "Eastman Kodak Organization: Managing IS Through Strategic Alliances", *Harvard Business School Case* 9–192–030, Boston.

Aron, R. and Singh, J. (2005) "Getting Offshoring Right", *Harvard Business Review*, 83, 12, December, 135–143.

Aubert, B., Dussault, S., Patry, M. and Rivard, S. (1999) "Managing Risk in IT Outsourcing", *Proceedings of the 32nd Annual Hawaii International Conference on System Sciences*, 685–691.

Barney, J. (1991) "Firm Resources and Sustained Competitive Advantage", *Journal of Management*, 17, 1, 99–120.

Barney, J. (1999) "How a Firm's Capabilities Affect Boundary Decisions", *Sloan Management Review*, 40, 3, Spring, 137–145.

Beal, B. (2004) "Survey Shows Satisfaction with Offshore Outsourcing", February 10, available on http://searchcio.techtarget.com/originalContent/0,289142,sid19_gci 949702,00.html last accessed 7/16/06.

Benbasat, I., Goldstein, D. and Mead, M. (1987) "The Case Research Strategy in Studies of Information Systems", *MIS Quarterly*, 11, 3, 369–386.

Blau, P. (1964) *Exchange and Power in Social Life*, Wiley, New York.

Bruno, G., Esposito, G., Iandoli, L. and Raffa, M. (2004) "The ICT Service Industry in North Africa and Role of Partnerships in Morocco", *Journal of Global Information Technology Management*, 7, 3, 5–26.

Burrell, G., and Morgan, G. (1979) *Sociological Paradigms and Organizational Analysis*, Heinemann Educational Books, New Hampshire, (reprinted 1988).

Carmel, E. (2006) "Building Your Information Systems from the Other Side of the World: How Infosys Manages Time Zone Differences", *MIS Quarterly Executive*, 5, 1, March, 43–53.

Carmel, E. and Agarwal, R. (2002) "The Maturation of Offshore Sourcing of Information Technology Work", *MIS Quarterly Executive*, 1, 2, June, 65–77.

Carmel, E. and Tjia, P. (2005) *Offshoring Information Technology: Sourcing and Outsourcing to a Global Workforce*, Cambridge University Press, Cambridge.

Carroll, J. (2005) "The John Carroll Research Survey Results", *Project Management Institute*, available on http://www.pmi.org/Prod2/groups/public/documents/info/pp_carroll.pdf, last accessed 7/18/06.

Carter, T. (2006) "Cheaper's Not Always Better", *Dr. Dobb's Journal*, February, available on http://www.ddj.com/184415486, last accessed 7/18/06.

Chaudhury, A., Nam, K. and Rao, H. (1995) "Management of Information Systems Outsourcing: A Bidding Perspective", *Journal of Management Information Systems*, 12,2, Fall 131–159.

Choudhury, V. and Sabherwal, R. (2003) "Portfolios of Control in Outsourced Software Development Projects", *Information Systems Research*, 14, 3, September, 291–314.

Cocheo, S. (2004) "The Dobbs Effect", *ABA Banking Journal*, 96, 5, May, 32–38; 65.

Cross, J. (1995) "IT Outsourcing at British Petroleum", *Harvard Business Review*, 73, 3, May–June, 94–102.

Cullen, S., Seddon, P. and Willcocks, L. (2005) "Managing Outsourcing: The Life Cycle Imperative", *MIS Quarterly Executive*, March, 4, 1, 229–246.

Currie, W. and Willcocks, L. (1998) "Analyzing Four Types of IT Sourcing Decisions in the Context of Scale, Client/Supplier Interdependency, and Risk Mitigation", *Information Systems Journal*, 8, 2, April 119–144.

DeLong, D., and Fahey, L. (2000) "Diagnosing Cultural Barriers to Knowledge Management", *Academy of Management Executive*, 14, 4, 113–127.

Democratic Caucus, Committee on Science, U.S. House of Representative (2006) "Globalization and the American Workforce: What Did the Technology Administration Really Say?", July 24, available on http://sciencedems.house.gov/investigations/investigations_detail.aspx?NewsID=1167, last accessed 8/2/2006.

Denzin, N. and Lincoln, Y. (1994) "Introduction: Entering the Field of Qualitative Research", in Denzin and Lincoln (eds) *Handbook of Qualitative Research*, Sage, Thousand Oaks, pp. 1–17.

DiamondCluster *2005 Global IT Outsourcing Study*, available on http://www.diamondcluster.com/Ideas/Viewpoint/PDF/DiamondCluster2005OutsourcingStudy.pdf, last accessed 7/10/06.

Dibbern, J., Goles, T., Hirschheim, R. and Bandula J. (2004) "Information Systems Outsourcing: A Survey and Analysis of the Literature", *Database for Advances in Information Systems*, 34, 4, Fall, 6–102.

DiRomualdo, A. and Gurbaxani, V. (1998) "Strategic Intent for IT Outsourcing", *Sloan Management Review*, 39, 4, Summer, 67–80.

Drezner, D. (2004) "The Outsourcing Bogeyman", *Foreign Affairs*, 83, 3, May/June, 22.

Dubé, L. and Paré, G. (2003) "Rigor in IS Positivist Case Research: Current Practices, Trends, and Recommendations", *MIS Quarterly*, 27, 4, December, 597–635.

Dutta, A. and Roy, R. (2005) "Offshore Outsourcing: A Dynamic Causal Model of Counteracting Forces", *Journal of Management Information Systems*, 22, 2, Fall, 15–36.

E-business Strategies "Offshoring Statistics: Dollar Size, Job Loss, and Market Potential", http://www.ebstrategy.com/Outsourcing/trends/statistics.htm last accessed on 07/12/06.

Ein-Dor, P. (2004) "IT Industry Development and the Knowledge Economy: A Four Country Study", *Journal of Global Information Management*, 12, 4, Oct–Dec, 23–49.

Eisenhardt, K. (1989) "Agency Theory: An Assessment and Review", *The Academy of Management Review*, 14, 1, Jan, 57–76.

Ekeh, P. (1974) *Social Exchange Theory: The Two Traditions*, Harvard University Press, Boston.

Engardio, P. (2006) "The Future of Outsourcing", *BusinessWeek*, (3969), January 30, 50–58.

Feeny, D. (2006) "Managing IT Suppliers", presentation to UK Cabinet Office representatives, Said Business School, Oxford University, United Kingdom, February 28.

Feeny, D., Lacity, M. and Willcocks, L. (2005) "Taking the Measure of Outsourcing Providers", *Sloan Management Review*, 46, 3, Spring, 41–48.

Feeny, D. and Willcocks, L. (1998) "Core IS Capabilities for exploiting Information Technology", *Sloan Management Review*, 39, 3, Spring, 9–21.

Fjermestad, J. and Saitta, J. (2005) "A Strategic Management Framework for IT Outsourcing", *Journal of Information Technology Case and Application Research*, 7, 3, 42–60.

Gallivan, M. and Oh, W. (1999) "Analyzing IT Outsourcing Relationships as Alliances among Multiple Clients and Customers", *Proceedings of the 32 Annual Hawaii International Conference on Systems Sciences*, 1–15.

Gopal, A., Sivaramakrishnan, K., Krishnan, M., and Mukhopadhyay, T. (2003) "Contracts in Offshore Software Development: An Empirical Analysis", *Management Science*, 49, 12, December, pp. 1671–1683.

Greenwood, D. and Levin, M. (1998) *Introduction to Action Research: Social Research for Social Change*, Sage Publications, Thousand Oaks.

Grover, V., Cheon, M. and Teng, J. (1996) "The Effect of Service Quality and Partnership on the Outsourcing of Information Systems Functions", *Journal of Management Information Systems*, 12, 4, Spring, 89–119.

Gudea, S. (2005) "IT Project Valuation Survey", posted on the Project Management Institute Website, http://www.pmi.org/prod/groups/public/documents/info/pp_soringudea.pdf, viewed 6/1/06.

Hall, J. and Liedtka, S. (2005) "Financial Performance, CEO Compensation, and Large-Scale Information Technology Outsourcing Decisions", *Journal of Management Information Systems*, 22, 1, Summer, 193–222.

Hatch, P. (2005) *Offshore 2005 Research*, Ventoro, Ver 1.2.5, January 22.

Homans, G. (1961) *Social Behavior: Its Elementary Forms*, Harcourt Brace Jovanovich, New York, (revised 1974).

Huber, R. (1993) "How Continental Bank Outsourced its Crown Jewels", *Harvard Business Review*, 71, 1, 121–129.

Jeyaraj, A., Rottman, J. and Lacity, M. (2006) "A Review of the Predictors, Linkages, and Biases in IT Innovation Adoption Research", *Journal of Information Technology*, 21, 1, 1–23.

Jones, C. (1994) *Assessment and Control of Software Risks*, Prentice-Hall, Englewood Cliffs, NJ.

Kaiser, K. and Hawk, S. (2004) "Evolution of Offshore Software Development: From Outsourcing to Co-Sourcing", *MIS Quarterly Executive*, 3, 2, June, 69–81.

Keil, M. and Montealegre, R. (2000) "Cutting Your Losses: Extricating Your Organization When a Big Project Goes Awry", *Sloan Management Review*, 41, 3, Spring, 55–68.

Keil, M., Rai, A., Mann, J. and Zhang, G. (2003) "Why Software Projects Escalate: The Importance of Project Management Constructs", *IEEE Transactions on Engineering Management*, 50, 3, 251–261.

King, W. (2004) "Outsourcing and the Future of IT", *Information Systems Management*, 21, 4, Fall 83–84.

Klein, H. and Myers, M. (1999) "A Set of Principles for Evaluating Interpretive Field Studies in Information Systems", *MIS Quarterly*, 23, 1, 67–94.

Krass, P. (1990) "The Dollars and Sense of Outsourcing", *Information Week*, (259), February 26, 26–31.

Krishna, S., Sahay, S. and Walsham, G. (2004) "Managing Cross-Cultural Issues in Global Software Outsourcing", *Communications of the ACM*, 47, 4, April, 62–66.

Lacity, M. and Hirschheim, R. (1993) *Information Systems Outsourcing: Myths, Metaphors and Realities*, Wiley, Chichester.

Lacity, M. and Rottman, J. (2007) *The Offshore Outsourcing of IT Work*. Palgrave, London.

Lacity, M. and Willcocks, L. (1998) "An Empirical Investigation of Information Technology Sourcing Practices: Lessons from Experience", *MIS Quarterly*, September, 22, 3, 363–408.

Lacity, M. and Willcocks, L. (2001) *Global Information Technology Outsourcing: Search for Business Advantage*, Wiley, Chichester.

Lacity, M. and Willcocks, L. (2009) *Information Systems and Outsourcing: Studies in Theory and Practice*, Palgrave, London.

Lee, A. and Baskerville, R. (2003) "Generalizing Generalizability in Information Systems Research", *Information Systems Research*, 14, 3, September, 221–243.

Lee, J., Miranda, S. and Kim, Y. (2004) "IT Outsourcing Strategies: Universalistic, Contingency, and Configurational Explanations of Success", *Information Systems Research*, 15, 2, June, 110–131.

Levina, N. and Ross, J. (2003) "From the Vendor's Perspective: Exploring the Value Proposition in Information Technology Outsourcing", *MIS Quarterly*, 27, 3, September, 331–364.

Lichtenstein, Y. (2004) "Puzzles in Software Development Contracting", *Communications of the ACM*, 47, 2, February, 61–65.

Loh, L. and Venkatraman, N. (1992) "Determinants of IT Outsourcing: A Cross-Sectional Analysis", *Journal of Management Information Systems*, 9, 1, 7–24.

Martorelli, W., Moore, S., McCarthy, J. and Brown, A. (2004) "Indian Offshore Suppliers: The Second Tier", Forrester Research Report, July 14, available on http://www.forrester.com/Research/Document/Excerpt/0,7211,34847,00.html, last viewed 6/1/06.

Mason, R. (2001) "Not Either/Or: Research in Pasteur's Quadrant", *Communications of the AIS*, 6, 16, March.

Matloff, N. (2004) "Globalization and the American IT Worker", *Communications of the ACM*, 47, 11, November, 27–30.

Matsumoto, H. (2005) "Global Business Process/IS Outsourcing to Singapore in the Multinational Investment Banking Industry", *Journal of Information Technology Case and Application Research*, 7, 3, 4–24.

McCue, A., (2005) "Outsourcing Flops Blamed on Tunnel Vision", Silicon.com, published on ZDNet News: June 22. Available on http://news.zdnet.com/2100-9589_22-5757832.html

McFarlan, F.W. (1981) "Portfolio Approach to Information Systems", *Harvard Business Review*, 59, 5, September–October, 142–150.

McFarlan, F.W. (2005) "Globalization of IT-Enabled Services: An Irreversible Trend", *Journal of Information Technology Case and Application Research*, 7, 3, 1–3.

Miles, R. and Snow, C. (1978) *Organizational Strategy, Structure and Processes*, McGraw Hill, New York, revised 2003 by Stanford University Press, Stanford.

Minevich, M. and Richter, F. (2005) "Top Spots for Global Outsourcing", *CIO Insight*, 1, 51, March 5, 55–57.

Mingers, J. (2001) "Combining IS Research Methods: Towards a Pluralist Methodology", *Information Systems Research*, 12, 3, 240–259.

Moore, S., Martorelli, W. and Brown, A. (2004) "Indian Offshore Suppliers: The Market Leaders, April 8, Forrester Research Report, http://www.forrester.com/Research/ Document/Excerpt/0,7211,34181,00.html viewed 6/1/06.

Mumford, E., Hirschheim, R., Fitzgerald, G. and Wood-Harper, A. (1985) (eds) *Research Methods in Information Systems*, North Holland, Amsterdam.

Nahapiet, J. and Ghoshal, S. (1998) "Social Capital, Intellectual Capital, and the Organizational Advantage", *Academy of Management Review*, 23, 2, 242–265.

Nair, K. and Prasad, P. (2004) "Offshore Outsourcing: A SWOT Analysis of a State in India", *Information Systems Management*, 21, 3, Summer, 34–40.

Nash, J. (1951) "Non-Cooperative Games", *The Annals of Mathematics*, 54, 2, 286–295.

Nash, J. (1953) "Two-person Cooperative Games", *Econometrica*, 21, 128–140.

Nelson, R. (2005) "Project Retrospectives: Evaluating Success, Failure and Everything in Between", *MIS Quarterly Executive*, 4, 3, September, 361–372.

Orlikowski, W. and Baroudi, J. (1991) "Studying Information Technology in Organizations: Research Approaches and Assumptions", *Information Systems Research*, 2,1, 1–28.

Oshri. I., Kotlarsky, J. and Willcocks, L. (eds) (2008) *Outsourcing Global Services: Knowledge, Innovation and Social Capital*, Palgrave, London.

Overby, S. (2003) "The Hidden Costs of Offshore Outsourcing", *CIO Magazine*, 16, 22, September 1.

Overby, S. (2005) "It's Cheaper in China", *CIO Magazine*, 18, 23, September 15.

Oza, N. and Hall, T. (2005) "Difficulties in Managing Offshore Software Outsourcing Relationships: An Empirical Analysis of 18 High Maturity Indian Software Companies", *Journal of Information Technology Case and Application Research*, 7, 3, 25–41.

Pfannenstein, L. and Tsai, R. (2004) "Offshore Outsourcing: Current and Future Effects on American IT Industry", *Information Systems Management*, 21, 4, Fall, 72–80.

Pfeffer, J. (1994) *Managing With Power: Politics and Influence in Organizations*, Harvard Business School Press, Boston.

Pfeffer, J. and Salancik, G. (1978) *The External Control of Organizations: A Resource Dependence Perspective*, Harper and Row, New York, reprinted by Stanford University Press, Stanford, 2003.

Poppo, L. and Zenger, T. (1998) "Testing Alternative Theories of the Firm: Transaction Cost, Knowledge-based, and Measurement Explanations for Make-or-buy Decisions in Information Services", *Strategic Management Journal*, 19, 853–877.

Porter, M. (1985) *Competitive Advantage: Creating and Sustaining Superior Performance*, The Free Press, New York.

Richmond, W. and Seidmann, A. (1993) "Software Development Outsourcing Contract: Structure and Business Value", *Journal of Management Information Systems*, 10, 1, Summer, 57–72.

Rogers, E. (1983) *Diffusion of Innovations*, The Free Press, New York.

Ross, C. (2004) "Services Market Sizing Update: 2003 to 2008", Forrester Research Report, April 27.

Rothfeder, J. and Coy, P. (1990) "Outsourcing: More Companies are Letting George Do It", *BusinessWeek*, 3181, October 8, 148.

Rottman, J. (2006) "Successfully Outsourcing Embedded Software Development", *IEEE Computer*, 39, 1, January, 55–61.

Rottman, J. and Lacity, M. (2004) "Twenty Practices for Offshore Sourcing", *MIS Quarterly Executive*, 3, 3, September, 117–130.

Rottman, J. and Lacity, M. (2006) "Proven Practices for Effectively Offshoring IT Work", *Sloan Management Review*, 47, 3, Spring, 56–63.

Sabherwal, R. (1999) "The Role of Trust in Outsourced Relationships", *Communications of the ACM*, 42, 2, Feb, 80–86.

Srivastava, S. (2005) "Could Rising Wages Diminish India's Outsourcing Edge?" News Report, Siliconeer, Jan 21, 2005. Available on http://news.pacificnews.org/news/view_article.html?article_id=167d1c86c1d28e7607c942fd9891938e, last accessed 7/01/06.

Standish Group International (2003) CHAOS Chronicles V3.0, 2003. Available on http://www.standishgroup.com/chaos/toc.php, last accessed 7/17/06.

Teng, J., Cheon, M. and Grover, V. (1995) "Decisions to Outsource IS Functions: Testing a Strategy-Theoretic Discrepancy Model", *Decision Sciences*, 26, 1, January/February, 75–103.

Wallace, L., Keil, M. and Rai, A. (2004) "How Software Project Risk Affects Project Performance: An Investigation of the Dimensions of Risk and an Exploratory Model", *Decision Sciences*, 35, 2, Spring 289–321.

Whang, S. (1992) "Contracting for Software Development", *Management Science*, 38, 3, 307–324.

Willcocks, L. and Lacity, M. (2006) *Global Sourcing of Business and IT Services*, Palgrave, United Kingdom.

Willcocks, L. and Lacity, M. (eds) (2009) *Research Studies in Information Technology Outsourcing: Perspectives, Practices and Globalization*, Sage, London, Three volumes.

Willcocks, L., Feeny, D. and Islei, G. (eds) (1997) *Managing IT as a Strategic Resource*, McGraw Hill, London.

Williamson, O. (1975) *Markets and Hierarchies*, The Free Press, New York.

Williamson, O. (1979) "Transaction Cost Economics: The Governance of Contractual Relations", *Journal of Law and Economics*, 22, 2, October, 233–261.

Williamson, O. (1991) "Comparative Economic Organization: The Analysis of Discrete Structural Alternatives", *Administrative Science Quarterly*, 36, 2, June, 269–296.

Yin, R. (2003) *Case Study Research: Design and Methods*, Third Edition, Sage, Thousand Oaks.

Zatolyuk, S. and Allgood, B. (2004) "Evaluating a Country for Offshore Outsourcing: Software Development Providers in the Ukraine", *Information Systems Management*, 21, 3, Summer, 28–33.

Appendix A: Prior research on IT sourcing

We found two literature reviews on IT sourcing. Dibbern *et al.* (2004) published an extensive review of the academic IT sourcing literature based on 84 studies published between 1991 and 2000. Fjermestad and Saitta (2005) examined 30 articles published between 1991 and 2005. Thus, we refer readers to these journal articles for a more extensive review of the IT sourcing literature.

Research published between 1991 and 2000. The first published outputs from academic research appeared in 1991, which documented companies pursuing large-scale *domestic* IT outsourcing (Applegate and Montealegre, 1991; Huber, 1993). More quantitative research and multiple-case studies followed, focusing on why firms outsource (Loh and Venkatraman, 1992) and how firms benefit (or do not benefit) from IT outsourcing (Lacity and Hirschheim, 1993; Whang, 1992). Between 1994 and 2000, at least 79 other academic studies were published. Overall, we learned *why* firms outsource (mostly to reduce costs, access resources, focus internal resources on more strategic work),[6] *what* firms outsource (mostly a portion of their overall IT portfolio), *how* firms outsource (mostly by formal processes), and IT outsourcing *outcomes* as measured by realization of expectations, satisfaction, and performance (Dibbern *et al.*, 2004). Overall, we know that client readiness, good strategy, good processes, sound contracts, and good relationship management are key success factors (Cullen *et al.*, 2005; Feeny and Willcocks, 1998; Teng *et al.*, 1995; Willcocks and Lacity, 2006). These overall findings were guided by nine theories, in descending order of frequency

Table 14A.1   Theories Used in IT Sourcing Articles Examined by Dibbern *et al.* 2004

Theories	Number of Papers Using this Theory (% of papers using this theory)	Foundational Readings
Transaction Cost Economics	16 (19%)	Williamson 1975, 1979, 1991
Strategic Management Theories	14 (17%)	Miles and Snow, 1978; Porter, 1985
Agency Theory	10 (12%)	Eisenhardt, 1989
Social Exchange Theories	7 (8%)	Blau, 1964; Homans, 1961; Ekeh, 1974
Resource based Theories	6 (7%)	Barney, 1991, 1999
Game Theory	4 (5%)	Nash, 1951, 1953
Resource Dependency Theory	3 (4%)	Pfeffer and Salancik, 1978; Pfeffer, 1994
Innovation Diffusion	2 (2%)	Rogers, 1983

[6]Besides these rational reasons, some studies find personal agendas dominating large-scale outsourcing decisions (Hall and Liedtka, 2005; Lacity and Hirschheim, 1993).

found among the 84 publications studied by Dibbern *et al.* (2004). (See Table 14A.1). Dibbern *et al.* (2004) concluded that researchers should focus on neglected areas, including offshore outsourcing.

Research on Offshore Outsourcing of IT Work. Table 14A.2 summarizes 22 publications that specifically address offshore outsourcing of IT work.

Four publications are editorial, arguing for (Drezner, 2004; King, 2004; McFarlan, 2005) or against (Matloff, 2004) the overall benefits of offshore outsourcing. The 2004 editorials were particularly important to combat negative press about offshore outsourcing during the US Presidential Race (see for example Cocheo, 2004, on the "Lou Dobbs Effect").

As may be indicative of the emerging phenomenon of offshore outsourcing, most researchers are using case studies (13 publications). Three publications entailed single case studies on client firms (Kaiser and Hawk, 2004; Matsumoto, 2005; Rottman, 2006). All three studies show a gradual escalation of offshore outsourcing. The message is that relationships take time to develop.

Two publications were based on single case studies on supplier firms (Carmel, 2006; Gopal *et al.*, 2003). Carmel (2006) used a case study at Infosys to identify practices for managing time zone differences. Gopal *et al.* (2003) used a case study, entailing 93 projects at a large Indian supplier, to differentiate successful from unsuccessful projects. They found that requirements uncertainty, project team size, and resource shortage explained contract choice, which in turn explained project success.

Eight studies involved multiple case studies/interviews (Bruno *et al.*, 2004; Carmel and Agarwal, 2002; Choudhury and Sabherwal, 2003; Krishna *et al.*, 2004; Oza and Hall, 2005; Rottman and Lacity, 2004, 2006; Sabherwal, 1999). These studies were primarily used to look at practices to help ensure outsourcing success. With the exception of Choudhury and Sabherwal (2003) and Sabherwal (1999), publications based on case studies were not explicitly theory driven.

Five publications used secondary data to look at IT service industries overall (Pfannenstein and Tsai, 2004) or in specific developing countries (Bruno *et al.*, 2004; Ein-Dor *et al.*, 2004; Nair and Prasad, 2004; Zatolyuk and Allgood, 2004). In general, these papers found that the following factors facilitate the development of IT service industries in developing countries: research and development budgets, technological infrastructure, available capital, partnerships with multi-nationals, number of educated IT workforce, low labor costs, tax incentives, political stability, and high literacy rates. One study used a simulation to explore the causal foundation of the growth in offshore outsourcing (Dutta and Roy, 2005).

Table 14A.2 Research on Offshore Outsourcing of IT Work

Research Publication	Empirical Base	Findings
1. Bruno *et al.* (2004)	Secondary sources and six case studies to compare the software industries in Algeria, Egypt, Morocco, and Tunisia.	Partnerships between multinational firms and indigenous firms are important success factors in developing countries.
2. Carmel and Agarwal (2002)	13 case studies of client firms sending IT work offshore.	Most clients follow a progressive stage model of offshore outsourcing.
3. Carmel (2006)	Case study on the Indian supplier, Infosys.	Practices to manage time zone differences.
4. Choudhury and Sabherwal (2003)	5 case studies, including 3 cases that entailed offshore outsourcing of IT work to India and Columbia.	Outsourced projects frequently began with simple controls that required additional controls to improve performance.
5. Drezner (2004)	Viewpoint.	Argues the benefits of offshore outsourcing to counter the political backlash.
6. Dutta and Roy (2005)	Simulation.	Causal foundation for growth in offshore outsourcing of IT work.
7. Ein-Dor *et al.* (2004)	Secondary sources to compare the software industries in Israel, Finland, Singapore, and New Zealand.	Developed and tested a model of eight independent variables that affect IT industry success within a country.
8. Gopal *et al.* (2003)	Case study of an Indian Supplier. Used data on 93 projects to identify the determinants of contract choice.	Requirements uncertainty, project team size, and resource shortage explain contract choice, which in turn explains project success.
9. Kaiser and Hawk (2004)	Case study of a financial services company outsourcing IT work to an Indian supplier.	Documents how the relationship progressed over eight years from a small pilot to strategic co-sourcing.
10. King (2004)	Viewpoint.	Argues that overall, offshore outsourcing benefits IT.

Table 14A.2 Research on Offshore Outsourcing of IT Work – *continued*

Research Publication	Empirical Base	Findings
11. Krishna *et al.* (2004)	Unspecified number of case studies of clients offshore outsourcing IT work to Indian suppliers.	Best practices based on choice of projects, managing the relationship, staffing, and training.
12. Matloff (2004)	Viewpoint.	Argues that exporting IT jobs and importing IT workers harms US IT workers, US firms and the broader economy.
13. Matsumoto (2005)	Case study of a global bank that set up a global support center in Singapore.	Staged process of moving work offshore; Competitive advantage of Singapore.
14. McFarlan (2005)	Editorial Preface.	Identifies five emerging issues in global IT sourcing.
15. Nair and Prasad (2004)	Secondary sources to use a SWOT analysis of Kerala (a state in India).	Kerala is well placed to compete based on infrastructure, language proficiency, IT, and costs. But other weaknesses must be addressed.
16. Oza and Hall (2005)	Interviews with 18 Indian software firms.	Main difficulties with offshore outsourcing of IT work are cultural differences, expectation mismatch, language differences, loss of control, job loss and transition.
17. Pfannenstein and Tsai (2004)	Secondary sources to provide an overview of the status of offshore IT outsourcing.	Summarized the statistics, benefits, costs, and risks of offshore IT outsourcing.
18. Rottman and Lacity (2004)	Interviews with 27 people (US customers, offshore suppliers, and consultants).	Practices for managing offshore outsourcing of IT work.
19. Rottman (2006)	Case study of a large US manufacturer outsourcing embedded software to three Indian suppliers.	Practices for using offshore outsourcing for strategic projects.

Table 14A.2 Research on Offshore Outsourcing of IT Work – *continued*

Research Publication	Empirical Base	Findings
20. Rottman and Lacity (2006)	Interviews with 159 participants in 21 client organizations, ten supplier organizations, and nine advisory organizations.	Practices for managing offshore outsourcing of IT work.
21. Sabherwal (1999)	Studied 18 IT projects, of which 16 projects the supplier was located in a different country than the client.	Found a relationship among governance structure (contract), trust, and performance.
22. Zatolyuk and Allgood (2004)	Secondary sources used to examine the software industry in the Ukraine.	Found that the Ukraine has significant advantage to compete.

Appendix B: Interview guide

Participant data:

- Job title
- Length of time in current position
- Where are you in the organizational chart?
- Previous positions and organizations

Please begin by telling us your offshore outsourcing story – why did your organizational unit initiate an offshore project, who was involved, what process did you go through, how did your internal organization react, how did you manage the supplier, who was the business sponsor, and what was the outcome?

Expected Benefits of Offshore Outsourcing <u>per project</u>: (lower costs, better service, meet short term IT demand, experience gained with offshore outsourcing, etc.)

Actual Benefits of Offshore Outsourcing <u>per project</u>: (lower costs, better service, meet short term IT demand, experience gained with offshore outsourcing, etc.)

For each offshore project you worked on, please describe:

Quality of Offshore Outsourcing:

How did you analyze and protect the quality of the deliverables (code, test scripts, documentation etc.)?

What mechanisms in the contract or processes did you use to protect quality?

Compare the quality of individual projects with the quality of domestically sourced projects.

Did you witness quality differences from the different suppliers?

Project Metrics: What metrics were in place for quality control of offshore project deliverables/milestones? SLAs? Defect rates? Submission rates? Unit /IT Acceptance/User Acceptance Tests?

Project Outcome of Offshore Outsourcing:

Perceptions of Success/Failure

How measured

Considering the degree to which project objectives were met, budgets and schedules were met, and the quality of the delivered product, what letter grade would you assign the project? (A–F):

Costs of Offshore Outsourcing:

A major driver of offshore outsourcing is lower salaries in offshore venues. How do the labor costs compare with your in-house labor costs ($ per hour for job category)?

To what degree were labor cost savings offset by higher transaction costs associated with RFP process, contract negotiations, travel expenses, communication costs, and managing projects from a distance?

Describe major transaction costs and how those costs were measured.

Governance of Offshore Outsourcing Projects:
Contract:
- What are the contract terms as far as baseline services, service level requirements, and penalties for non-performance?
- What do you perceive as the strengths and weaknesses of the contract?
- How many pages is the contract?
- What differences did you see in the projects from various contract models and sizes?

Infrastructure: Organizational structure, tools, and processes.
- How do you govern the supplier's activities?
- Project Scheduling and Tracking
- Did you have to create special tools, such as data repository, to coordinate supplier activities?
- Configuration Management (keeping track of modules and sections of code)
- Work Flow automation system
- What differences did you see in the projects from various engagement models?

Problem Recognition and Resolution:
- How would you characterize your relationship with the supplier?
- What is going well?
- Have you had any disputes with the supplier? How were they resolved?
- Have you ever been charged for services you assumed were covered in the contract?

Extent to which you encountered problems with:
- Cultural differences
- Time Zone differences
- Language differences
- Strange Foreign Work-Hour Regulations
- High Employee Turnover in Supplier organization
- Difficulties in Arranging Visas
- Other legal/government difficulties

- An offshore unit's lack of domain knowledge
- Unreliable Telecommunications Infrastructure

Evaluation Process of Offshore Outsourcing:
- Who in your organizational unit became the most avid champion of offshore outsourcing?
- Offshore outsourcing can be a threat to domestic employees. What organizational members were opponents of offshore outsourcing and how were their oppositions addressed?
- What was senior management's perception of offshore?
- What is the general atmosphere at Biotech concerning offshoring?
- What is the plan for future projects and offshore?

Supplier Selection:
- What was included in the RFP?
- Which suppliers were invited to respond? Why were they selected?
- What was your organization's selection criteria?
- Which suppliers worked on the projects you are familiar with?

Practices and Capabilities Needed for Offshore Outsourcing Success
- You now have some experience under your belt concerning offshore outsourcing. If you had it to do all over again, what would you do differently?
- What are the lessons you learned concerning the best and worst practices for offshore outsourcing?
- What capabilities do you need in-house to make sure offshore outsourcing is a success?

442

Appendix C: Organizational chart of Biotech's corporate IT department

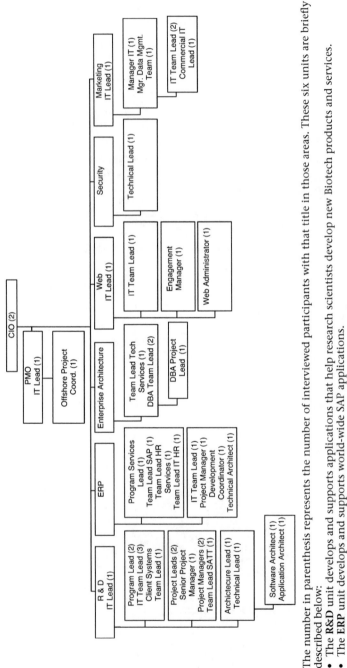

The number in parenthesis represents the number of interviewed participants with that title in those areas. These six units are briefly described below:

- The **R&D** unit develops and supports applications that help research scientists develop new Biotech products and services.
- The **ERP** unit develops and supports world-wide SAP applications.
- The **Enterprise Architecture** unit supports Biotech's worldwide IT infrastructure.
- The **Web** unit develops and supports web-based products for customers and employees.
- The **Security** unit is in charge of all IT security.
- The **Marketing** unit develops and supports applications that assist employees (like sales reps) and customers with existing Biotech products and services.

Appendix D: Biotech offshore projects

Project Letter	Generic Name	Offshore Supplier Used	Project Type	Engagement Model	Contract Size	Duration in Days	Organizational Unit	Start Year
A	3-D DNA Modeling	Small	New Development	Zero On-site	$4,300.00	11	R&D	2003
B	Automated Software Testing	Small	New Development	Zero On-site	$132,701.00	251	R&D	2004
C	CAD DNA	Small & Large	New Development	Zero On-site	$485,089.00	894	R&D	2003
D	Captive DBA	Captive Support	Maintenance /	Zero On-site	$35,686.00	121	Enterprise Architecture	2003
E	Crop Production Support	Small & Large	Maintenance / Support	OEM & Developers On-site	$575,505.10	761	Marketing	2003
F	Customer Incentive Program	Large	New Development	OEM & Developers On-site	$65,958.00	277	Marketing	2003
G	Data Staging Repository	Large	Maintenance / Support	OEM & Developers On-site	$59,008.00	327	ERP	2005
H	Digital Library	Small	New Development	Zero On-site	$204,812.50	633	R&D	2003
I	Distributor Wholesale Compensation	Large	Maintenance / Support	Zero On-site	$7,890.00	32	Marketing	2003
J	End to End Key Product Support	Large	New Development	Developers On-site	$218,418.00	272	Marketing	2003
K	Information Tracking System	Small	New Development	Developers On-site	$31,800.00	227	R&D	2003
L	Inventory	Large Support	Maintenance / on-site	OEM & Developers	$5,376.00	42	Marketing	2003
M	Lotus Notes	Small Support	Maintenance /	Zero On-site	$111,041.00	382	Web	2004

Appendix D: Biotech offshore projects – *continued*

Project Letter	Generic Name	Offshore Supplier Used	Project Type	Engagement Model	Contract Size	Duration in Days	Organizational Unit	Start Year
N	Mobile Product Evaluation	Small	New Development	Zero On-site	$43,000.00	76	R&D	2003
O	Next Generation Intranet	Small	New Development	Developers on-site	$287,135.00	627	Web	2003
P	R&D Business Support	Small	New Development	Developers on-site	$332,618.50	656	R&D	2004
Q	SAP	2 Large & 1 Small	New Development on-site	OEM & Developers	$1,363,098.51	1030	ERP	2003
R	Technical Career Path	Small	New Development	Zero On-site	$10,600.00	42	R&D	2004
S	Temporary Labor	Small	New Development	Zero On-site	$15,225.00	416	R&D	2004
T	Volunteer Website	Small	New Development	Zero On-site	$10,000.00	30	R&D	2003
U	Web Integration	Small	New Development	Zero On-site	$64,473.00	246	Web	2004
21					$4,063,734.61			

15

Offshore Outsourcing, Strategy and the Role of Social Capital

Joseph Rottman and Mary Lacity

Introduction

As evident in Chapters 5 and 14, decision makers often rationalize offshore outsourcing by comparing hourly rates for domestic and offshore workers. This approach is dangerous because it assumes domestic and offshore workers are equivalent "factors of production." Once engaged in offshore outsourcing, senior executives are often disappointed. Many complain that offshore suppliers do not understand their business, deliver late, and produce poor quality work. In reality, the problems are not caused primarily by the supplier – they are primarily caused by the client's naïve focus on only costs and failure to invest properly in the relationship.

One of the best ways to improve overall value is to invest in social capital. Social capital is defined as *"the advantage created by a person's location in a structure of relationships. It explains how some people gain more success in a particular setting through their superior connections to other people."*[1] Social capital is simply the idea that knowledge and resources are exchanged, work gets done, and value is created through social relationships. In the context of outsourcing – *who* the supplier knows in the client organization is the key to ensuring *what* value the supplier delivers. Conversely, *who* the client knows in the supplier organization is the key to ensuring *which* supplier resources will be devoted to the client's account to ensure value. Research suggests that once social capital is built, many benefits follow. These benefits include increased efficiency, more cooperative behavior, higher levels of trust, less need for costly monitoring, and most importantly – increased innovation (Nahapiet and Ghoshal, 1998).

In this chapter, we explain how practitioners can invest the *right amount* of social capital to ensure that they get overall value from offshore outsourcing. If clients invest too little in social capital, they will not get

---

[1]http://en.wikipedia.org/wiki/Social_Capital

the value they seek. At a minimum, clients must invest in social capital by:

- Laying the foundation for trust (called the relational dimension of social capital);
- Creating shared language, codes, and systems of meaning among parties (called the cognitive dimension of social capital);
- Designing social linkages among people (called the structural dimension of social capital).

However, there is one important caveat: if clients invest too much in social capital, they will erode cost savings. For example, if clients bring all the supplier employees on-site to build close relationships, the travel costs and onshore rates would cancel out the cost benefits of outsourcing. Another risk of excessive investment in social capital is the transfer of too much intellectual property to the supplier. Clients must find the right balance in transferring the knowledge the supplier needs to know verses protecting its intellectual assets. Furthermore, clients must find ways to protect the social capital investment in the face of supplier turnover (Oshri *et al.*, 2008). Of course, these dilemmas and challenges are inherent in more domestic forms of outsourcing and are essentially about developing productively the relationship dimension of outsourcing arrangements, as discussed in different contexts in Chapters 3, 4 and 13. Here we look at offshore outsourcing and the practices for investing "the right amount" of social capital are illustrated through the case of a US Manufacturing company. Among the 24 US client firms we studied, US Manufacturing leveraged social capital the best. Its social capital investment yielded the most strategic results from offshore outsourcing. US Manufacturing's suppliers helped to build innovative products faster and cheaper than in-house provision alone. However, before achieving a strategic advantage with offshore outsourcing, US Manufacturing failed in its initial offshore initiatives because managers only focused on costs and ignored the social dimensions of outsourcing. After diagnosing the causes of its initial failures, US Manufacturing remedied the supplier relationships by investing the right amount of social capital. These social capital practices are:

Lay the foundation for trust:

1. Assure the internal IT staff that offshore outsourcing will not result in layoffs;
2. Demonstrate how offshore outsourcing will enhance internal IT career paths.

Create shared language, codes, and systems of meaning among parties:

3. Indoctrinate the supplier employees into the client's world of language and meaning through co-training;
4. Indoctrinate internal employees into the supplier's world of language and meaning by elevating internal CMM/CMMI processes to better match suppliers' processes.

Design social linkages between client and suppliers:

5. Know the suppliers' key power players;
6. Build strong ties with on-site supplier managers;
7. Engage multiple suppliers to broaden the social network.

Require suppliers to protect social capital investment through succession planning:

8. Require suppliers to have shadows for key supplier roles;
9. Require supplier employees trained on-site to train supplier employees offshore.

Protect intellectual property:

10. Divvy intellectual property across multiple suppliers.

While some of the practices to build social capital have been discussed during the Biotech case in the previous chapter, the entire feel of these practices was different at the US Manufacturing site. In comparison to Biotech, US Manufacturing exemplified how clients can shift their view of offshore suppliers as "external providers" to offshore suppliers as "integral partners", – for practitioners seemingly one of the holy grails of most forms of outsourcing (Willcocks and Craig, 2009 – see also Chapter 4).

The next section provides an understanding of US Manufacturing's business and why management wanted to offshore outsource IT work.

US Manufacturing's background and offshore engagements

In 2009 US Manufacturing was a Fortune 100 manufacturer of industrial equipment with over 75,000 employees spread across 20 countries. The successful social capital practices highlighted in this chapter were centered within US Manufacturing's Six Sigma certified Software Center of Excellence (SCE). At the time of the study the SCE at US Manufacturing employed approximately 150 people and had an annual IT development spend of approximately \$32 million. The members of the SCE were responsible for the development and deployment of embedded software[2] systems that were highly integrated into US Manufacturing's core products.

To understand US Manufacturing's offshore journey, we interviewed senior managers within the Software Center of Excellence, including the Manager of the SCE, a Six Sigma Blackbelt and the Engineering Supervisor. Additionally, we interviewed ten people who worked for US Manufacturing's largest supplier in Bangalore, India.

US Manufacturing's first attempt with offshore outsourcing

The Software Center of Excellence began its offshore journey in late 2000 with the hope of taking advantage of the lower labor costs available offshore. With the primary goal of saving money on development costs, they engaged one large Indian supplier to work on several projects.

One project involved integrating a new Global Positioning System (GPS) steering system into one of their larger product lines currently in production. This project required the offshore supplier to design and create the embedded software intended to control the steering systems and interface with the GPS satellites. The project involved new software tools, new interface systems and new processes for both the SCE and the supplier. For this project, all the supplier employees were located offshore to take greatest advantage of the labor rates. Primarily due to the fact that knowledge transfer was an afterthought, this project failed to produce any of the deliverables outlined in the statements of work. The project was ultimately pulled back in-house and completed well behind schedule and over budget. According to the engineering supervisor:

> "It didn't succeed. We would get something back and it didn't do what we wanted it to do and we would have to redo the whole thing. We weren't very good at being outsourcers and the model of throwing a document over the wall and having a supplier magically give us what we want in the end – it didn't and doesn't work."

The GPS project was indicative of the many failures US Manufacturing encountered which were related to social capital and knowledge transfer. Looking back, the manager of the SCE and his staff underestimated the need for extensive domain knowledge transfer about US Manufacturing's

---

[2]Embedded software is software that is embedded in mechanical parts on pieces of equipment to provide task-specific functions. Embedded software is found in many devices, such as thermostats, cell phones, cars, and elevators.

products, processes, and markets, as found for example by Oshri *et al.* (2007a). According to the SCE manager:

> "We had to realize that our Indian vendors did not understand embedded software or even the equipment we manufacture. They didn't even know what our product looked like!"

Tacit knowledge cannot be transferred through documents

The first attempt showed US Manufacturing that they were not successful in transferring knowledge to the supplier. US Manufacturing needed to transfer specialized coding skills and manufacturing domain knowledge. Concerning specialized coding skills, US Manufacturing's embedded software development requires skills not readily available in the offshore space. The "rules" for traditional software do not apply to embedded software. For example, requirements for response time, speed, power consumption and correctly interfacing with the external environment are much greater for embedded software. Concerning the manufacturing domain knowledge, successful creation of embedded software requires an intricate and detailed knowledge of the equipment that will house and interact with the software. Such rich knowledge cannot simply be transferred by passing documents from the client to the suppliers. Rather, the offshore suppliers needed to see the equipment and understand how the software they were building worked.

Discouraged, but hopeful, US Manufacturing tries again. Despite the failures, US Manufacturing did see some promise in offshore development. While the projects themselves were not completed, SCE managers noticed that code quality improved over the life of the projects. They were confident that the offshore developers might be able to reduce the project backlog if US Manufacturing was able to better share knowledge and expertise with the suppliers. The SCE managers decided to move forward with the offshore model, even though one said: "*I must admit, it was a tough sell.*"

US Manufacturing's second attempt with offshore outsourcing

In January 2004, the SCE used the lessons it learned and re-launched its offshore effort. SCE managers chose different suppliers in round two and used better practices to build social relationships to facilitate knowledge transfer.

The client selected suppliers with better capabilities. The supplier selection and engagement process was much different in round two for US Manufacturing. The failures in round one showed US Manufacturing that it was critical to find offshore suppliers with at least some embedded software expertise. They also needed partners willing to invest in a long-term relationship. In round two, US Manufacturing selected two large Indian suppliers that had already exhibited some expertise in the embedded software market, primarily in the automotive industry. In addition, they selected a boutique firm that specialized in embedded software in the manufacturing market. This prior experience with the embedded software development process was a critical success factor that was overlooked in round one. The SCE Manager said:

> "We really didn't understand how different we (embedded software development) were until we saw the failures in round one. We now know that our vendors need a very specialized skill set and we now know how to identifyand test for those skills. We are much better at vendor selection and talent assessment."

Even though suppliers had some knowledge of embedded software, the SCE still had to train suppliers about their unique embedded software practices. For example, US Manufacturing has a unique way of wiring electronic control units which contain the embedded software.

On-site visits acclimatized offshore suppliers to SCE people and processes. The second attempt focused on building closer relationships with suppliers. This time, nearly half of the suppliers' delivery teams spent time on-site at US Manufacturing's headquarters prior to working on the outsourced projects. According to the Manager of the SCE:

> "What we saw was the benefit and real value of actually bringing those people here for a short time to bring them up to speed. Let them see how an application works and work right next to the team doing the development. That is the real benefit to the teaming aspect."

Intensive face-to-face training and shadowing exchanged tacit knowledge from client to supplier. Beyond the offshore supplier delivery teams' short visits to the US, some higher-level offshore supplier employees were given extensive training. The training sessions were delivered by US Manufacturing's architects and project leads to the suppliers' project leads as well as to US Manufacturing's internal IT employees ready for the next phase in their career development. Essentially, these two groups were trained together as peers.

Once trained, the supplier employees who held leadership roles would typically remain on-site at US Manufacturing for six to 18 months. SCE managers did not want to migrate the trained supplier employees offshore too soon because it would create a talent and knowledge vacuum on-site and sever many professional and personal connections that were created. SCE managers also used these on-site supplier employees to educate the next batch of supplier employees. The next group of supplier employees would come over from India and shadow the incumbent supplier employees for three and six months. While this approach was expensive, the two on-site supplier employees were able to (a) establish common frames of reference and (b) transfer social relationships and connections to the new employee. Additionally, because the new supplier employee was trained by the incumbent supplier employee, US Manufacturing's architects and project leads were free to engage in higher level activities. Once the incumbent supplier employees migrated offshore, they then transferred the knowledge obtained during their on-site time to the offshore employees.

Short visits by supplier delivery teams and face-to-face training/workshadowing for supplier project leads were successful in building the social capital necessary for knowledge transfer. However, these practices were costly. The hourly onshore rates were three to four times higher than offshore rates. SCE managers had to be careful about not completely eroding cost savings with these practices. At the time of our interviews, the suppliers provided about 15 people on-site and 35 people off-site. The SCE's ultimate goal was to have a 20/80 ratio of supplier employees onshore versus offshore. This ratio would provide the near perfect balance between the costs and benefits of establishing relationships for knowledge transfer.

The outcome of round 2: lower costs, better quality, higher value. As of 2006, US Manufacturing paid the two large suppliers and one boutique firm about $3.4 million, or 10% of the SCE's annual budget. The three engagements were all increasing in dollar value and headcount.

Thus far, SCE managers saw offshore outsourcing as a success. The suppliers were helping US Manufacturing to develop embedded software quicker and cheaper than in-house provision. The manager of the SCE summarized round two by stating:

"I think we are now doing it right and the data we are gathering support that idea. Our vendors are not only providing a lower cost talent pool, but they are helping us strategically. We keep looking for ways to increase the engagements. Our costs are down, productivity is up, and the quality is as good, if not better than what we can do in house."

Evidence of increased value from offshore outsourcing could be found in the detailed metrics US Manufacturing maintained to track the offshore engagements. As an example of their detailed metrics, consider the costs for one large project comprised of three teams. Figure 15.1 shows the costs per activity for the three teams: the in-house project team, a large supplier team, and the small supplier team. The project was started in July, 2003 and ended July, 2004. The average cost per activity for the internal team remained constant over this time period, about $800 per activity. The large offshore supplier team initially had the highest costs per activity – around $14,000 per activity. The costs were initially high because of the investment in social capital (visits, training, and shadowing). But benefits of this investment rapidly emerged, as evidenced by the severe decline of costs per

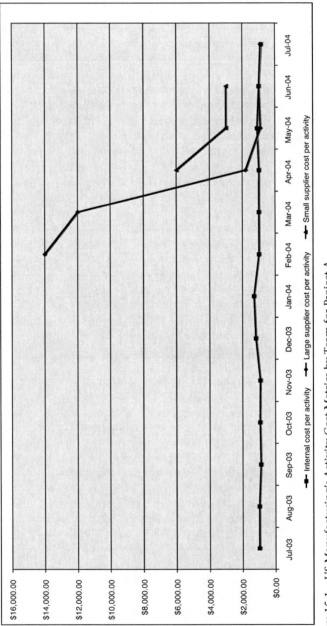

Figure 15.1 US Manufacturing's Activity Cost Metrics by Team for Project A

453

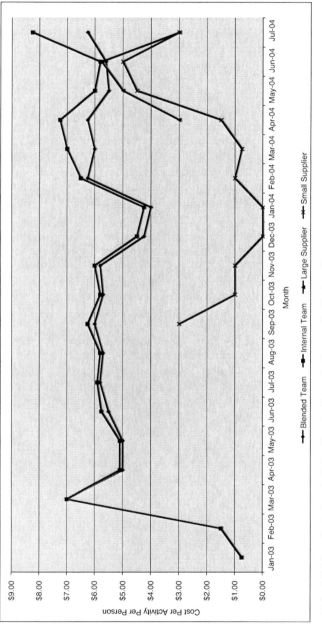

Figure 15.2 US Manufacturing Activity Cost by Team by Person for Project B

activity to $800 within four months. The small supplier team only had a three-month assignment, but the data also show a rapid decline in costs per activity from $6,000 to $3,000.

Whereas Figure 15.1 tracks costs per activity per team, Figure 15.2 tracks cost per activity per team per person. This figure shows the four teams on Project B: (1) the internal team, (2) a large supplier team, (3) the small supplier team and (4) a blended team comprising both internal and offshore employees. Among these four teams, the team consisting of only internal staff had the highest cost per activity! The smallest supplier team had the lowest costs, partly because they initially charged only offshore rates for onshore employees. The blended team (comprising both internal and external employees) had lower costs per activity per person than the internal team, but higher costs than offshore supplier teams.

These metrics not only helped the SCE manage the engagement and understand the costs structures, they also motivated the team. According to the Manager of the SCE:

> "We can't wait for the next month's metrics to come out and see where the points are. We are seeing real cost benefits to the supplier's people coming on board and making real contributions to the tasks and projects!"

Practices for building and protecting social capital

The US Manufacturing case provides an opportunity to explore how clients can invest the right amount of social capital to ensure offshore outsourcing success. For US Manufacturing, investing in social capital was the best way to transfer knowledge, and knowledge transfer was the best way to ensure value. In this section, we discuss practices that build social capital by (1) laying the foundation for trust, (2) creating shared language, codes, and systems of meaning and (3) designing social linkages among parties. Next, we suggest a further practice that requires the supplier to protect the social capital investment through succession planning. The final practice shows clients how to transfer knowledge to suppliers while still protecting intellectual property.

Practice 1 – lay the foundation for trust

Research has shown that workers will not share tacit knowledge without trust (Finnegan and Willcocks, 2007; Inkpen and Tsang, 2005; Lin, 2007). Furthermore, a lack of trust may lead to *"competitive confusion about whether or not a network firm is an ally"* (Inkpen and Tsang, 2005). In the context of offshore outsourcing, client IT staff must be willing to share their knowledge with offshore supplier employees. People are only willing to share knowledge if they believe that overall benefits of sharing outweigh the risks. US Manufacturing laid a foundation for trust through the following two practices.

a) Assure the internal IT staff that offshore outsourcing will not result in layoffs. US Manufacturing, like most of the US client firms we have studied, were using offshore outsourcing to "do more with less." US Manufacturing did not intend to reduce internal headcount through outsourcing, but planned to use offshore outsourcing to reduce the immense backlog of work. This message was strongly communicated to the internal IT staff, which assuaged their fears and made them more willing to cooperate with offshore suppliers. In addition, this message was shared with offshore suppliers so they did not have to worry about replacing US workers.

At US Manufacturing, the plans to explore offshore outsourcing were met with optimism and relief by the internal staff of the SCE. Facing a three-year backlog and a flat staffing forecast, employees welcomed the possibility of a decreased workload. According to the manager of the SCE:

> "My people were tired of working 60 hour weeks. We communicated that offshore was a way to better manage our project pipeline since we were not going to add a bunch of expensive North American resources to meet the demand and then lay them off later, we had to find other ways of being able to add flexibility to our workforce. And so they are not worried about losing their job. They just see this as a way of getting back to some kind of normal 40 to 50 hour workweek, and even more importantly, as a way for them to move up in their level of responsibility."

Once the internal IT staff's fears were assuaged, they willingly worked with offshore suppliers. For example, according to the engineering supervisor:

> "I was amazed at how open our developers were with the supplier's team. Once they realized that the quicker they [the offshore team] were up to speed, the sooner they could share the load, there was no 'turf' to protect, or 'secrets' to keep."

While the lesson to share this positive message seems obvious, in other US client firms we have studied, senior managers decided to keep experiments with offshore outsourcing "low key" even when no layoffs were planned. We found that secrecy *always* resulted in the internal IT staff panicking and sabotaging the experiments by being uncooperative.

b) Demonstrate how offshore outsourcing will enhance internal IT career paths. US Manufacturing realized that if their second attempt was to succeed, internal IT employees needed to understand how offshore outsourcing would affect their career paths. On the surface, offshore outsourcing is often touted as allowing internal IT staff to focus on more interesting, higher-value work. This was certainly true at US Manufacturing because higher-value roles such as architects, project managers, and data base administrators would always remain in-house. But in reality, low-level tasks (such as routine programming) are used to train future project managers. So how will those managers gain their skills and expertise if offshore suppliers are now doing routine work?

SCE managers answered this question by creating a clear vision for IT career paths. From past experience, SCE managers knew that about one third of programmers are promoted to higher value roles. So, for example, if SCE managers projected that they would need five architects in three years time, they hired 15 new programmers internally. Even though these internal programmers cost more than offshore equivalents, the SCE managers knew they needed to provide entry level experiences to groom future IT leaders:

> "We have made the business case to management that even though internal programmers are not as cost efficient as sourced programmers, we need to maintain a certain level of expertise internally."

As suggested by this practice, the SCE needed an accurate forecast of future IT needs. To accurately predict the human resources (HR) demand required significant knowledge of the HR environment, past HR trends and the current staffing constraints. US Manufacturing created an intricate staffing model based on the current and past project staffing data, the current internal talent pool and the projected demand.

The staffing plan was openly communicated to both internal IT staff and suppliers. By communicating the plan with internal IT staff, US Manufacturing's developers were not worried that they were "building their own guillotines" by working closely with the suppliers' teams. Instead, trust was established and enhanced by the internal employees seeing a clear and obtainable career path. By communicating the plan with offshore suppliers, the offshore suppliers could better plan for its staffing needs and better predict its future revenue generation. Such predictability enabled suppliers to stop selling and start working. According to the manager of the SCE:

> "Initially, the suppliers seemed to have one eye on the current project and one eye on what is coming next. Once we were able to share our forecasts with them, the attention turned to the current tasks."

The open communication of the vibrant internal career path and long-term commitment to suppliers laid the foundation for trust among the parties. Both sides saw the benefit of the relationship. As predicted by theory, the atmosphere of trust contributed to the free exchange of knowledge between committed exchange partners (Inkpen and Tsang, 2005; Lin, 2007). Trust is but one prerequisite for knowledge transfer. Another prerequisite is creating shared language, codes, and systems of meaning.

Practice 2 – create shared language, codes, and systems of meaning among parties

Effective communication requires that parties not only share common languages and codes but that language and codes are interpreted through a shared schema (Nahapiet and Ghoshal, 1998). In the context of offshore outsourcing, the "common language" of software development is often only superficially understood between clients and suppliers. For example, clients and suppliers may share the terms "functional requirements", "statements of work", and "code testing" but the meaning of those terms may be vastly different among parties. To a client, "functional requirements" may mean documenting high-level business processes which are immersed in the client's idiosyncratic business jargon. To a supplier, "functional requirements" may mean detailed, technical programming specifications.

Both clients and suppliers must interpret language similarly, but this is not easy. We have witnessed many clients and suppliers clinging to their own interpretations with awkward translations to bridge the gaps. For example, many of the suppliers we have studied were committed to the Software Engineering Institute's Capability Maturity Model (CMM). When US clients passed their own versions of functional requirements to offshore suppliers, the first thing the offshore suppliers did was to translate the US requirements into its CMM formats. The translations were then sent back to the client for validation. Such iterations were wasteful and expensive. Two practices avoid this issue by creating shared language, codes, and systems of meaning.

a) Indoctrinate the supplier employees into the client's world of language and meaning through co-training. One of the best ways to create shared language, codes, and systems of meaning it to provide shared experiences. US Manufacturing did this by co-training new internal employees and supplier employees who would serve as project leads. Both sets of stakeholders took facility tours and training classes on engine architecture, production software, equipment simulation products, operating guides for various lines of equipment, quality assurance processes and an overview of all of the various manufacturing products and platforms. They were introduced to various software development tools, the development environment and embedded development tools. For the supplier employees located offshore, the classes were recorded and streamed to India. According to the manager of the SCE:

> "We couldn't ship an engine or a piece of large equipment over to India, so we did the next best thing: we videotaped many equipment pieces in action and showed what the *ECUs [*Electronic Control Units*]* were designed to do."

The result of co-training was that both internal and offshore supplier employees understood US Manufacturing's business and IT development terms. Both sets of employees now spoke the same language.

Furthermore, they understood the context of the language – both sets of employees understood the manufacturing process and how the SCE developed software for key parts. For this lesson, US Manufacturing primarily indoctrinated the offshore employees into its world of language and meaning.

While training obviously facilitated knowledge transfer about US Manufacturing's products and processes (the cognitive dimension of social capital), an additional benefit surfaced: team members became friends. According to the manager of the SCE:

> "I mentioned that our strategy is to bring some of their folks here onsite to be trained in our processes. We did not plan on this, but it turns out that through the course of bringing them here for that training they get to be friends with and get to know all of the people here and the people here get to know them. So when they go back to India they're not some nameless face that's just working on software. They're friends of the people who are here. They know them and trust them to some degree, and there are relationships that have been built that it turns out are important, or add to the success of that kind of work."

b) Educate the client employees into the supplier's world of language and meaning by elevating internal CMM processes to better match suppliers' processes. In this lesson, US Manufacturing became indoctrinated in the suppliers' world of language and meaning. The SCE managers understood that the suppliers had more mature software development processes. They sought to improve their own process maturity by learning from suppliers' superior CMM capabilities. By agreeing on the same processes, work transitions were smoother. According to the manager of the SCE:

> "That's actually another reason why we're trying to climb the CMM ladder ourselves is so we have enough structure in our organization that we can exploit, we can use other suppliers to do work for us and get predictable results. Not that it's their fault, but if we know that we have to improve our process act. During our first trip offshore the likelihood that we could successfully manage external work was very low, and so we are now climbing up that ladder and are better at managing ourselves and now we can more successfully manage outsource labor."

Practice 3 – design social linkages

Thus far we have discussed building social capital by laying the foundation of trust and creating a shared system of language, codes, and meaning. One missing element goes to the heart of social capital: designing social linkages. Clients must consider which employees in both the client and supplier organizations need to establish social ties (Oshri *et al.*, 2007b).

There are two types of social ties to ponder: strong ties and weak ties. Strong ties require people to spend a considerable amount of time together and are characterized by emotional intensity, and intimacy (Granovetter, 1973). Strong ties between people increases trust, knowledge exchange, learning, environmental adaptation, and technical performance (Kale *et al.*, 2000; Larson, 1992; Rosenkopf and Nerkar, 2001). The downside is that strong ties require high levels of investment. In contrast, weak ties[3] are typically equivalent to acquaintances – people who have met face-to-face and understand the knowledge and resources each possesses. According to Granovetter (1973), weak ties have one remarkable strength: they are much more likely to transmit new, relevant information than a strong tie! The reasoning is that a weak tie is more likely to generate a non-redundant connection between different social circles. The classic example of this phenomenon is a job search. If a person seeking employment only shares this desire with her strong network ties, it is unlikely her close friends have relevant job opportunities. When this desire is disseminated through weak ties, information spreads rapidly to other people in other social networks who are much more likely to have relevant employment opportunities.

In the context of offshore outsourcing, SCE managers had to determine which client and supplier employees needed strong ties and which needed only weak ties. SCE managers could not afford to build strong ties between all SCE and supplier employees because of the high costs of travel, lodging, and onshore rates. They built weak ties with the offshore delivery teams and supplier senior management from the large suppliers. They built strong ties to the suppliers' project leads and engagement managers. In addition, SCE managers built strong ties to the senior partners at the small Indian supplier. These relationships are discussed below.

a) Know the suppliers' key power players. One of the fundamental benefits of social capital is that network ties provide access to resources (Nahapiet and Ghoshal, 1998; Oshri *et al.*, 2007a). For clients, a considerable challenge is building close relationships with the supplier's key power players to ensure that the best resources are devoted to the client's account. For example, one CIO we talked to said she could not get the right resources on her account. After continual frustration with the supplier's appointed liaison, she repeatedly tried to call the supplier's CEO. He never called her back. Then she got creative. She discovered that the supplier worked closely with a strategy professor at Harvard. She called that professor and he immediately called the supplier's COO on her behalf. The COO met with her, solved her problem, and the relationship significantly improved.

---

[3]Weak ties can also occur between people who never met but have a third person with whom they have a strong tie in common. In theory, the strength of a tie is formally defined as a *continuum* (Granovetter, 1973). In the offshore outsourcing context, we are treating the strength of a tie as categorical variable with values "strong" and "weak."

The opportunity to know the supplier's key power players is largely a function of the supplier's size. For suppliers the size of a Wipro or Infosys, their top managers cannot possibly build close relationships with all their clients. In many instances, clients may never even meet the supplier's senior management. One advantage of selecting a smaller supplier is a greater opportunity to build closer relationships with top management. At US Manufacturing, its engagement with the small, specialized supplier showed the advantage of establishing strong ties with the supplier's leadership team.

The small supplier was founded by senior managers from an embedded software division at a large Indian supplier. These entrepreneurs realized that in order to grow their new company, their approach needed to focus on responsiveness and high quality talent. US Manufacturing built and nurtured strong relationships with the principal partners of the small supplier and leveraged these connections to gain access to the supplier's top talent. In addition, the small supplier was willing to invest its own money in the relationship by charging off-site rates for the on-site training at US Manufacturing headquarters. This investment improved the supplier's own domain knowledge while showing a commitment to US Manufacturing. According to the manager of the SCE:

> "It is great dealing with the managing partners at [small supplier]. They know our offshore history and we know their goals for growing their firms. We can call them and talk directly with decision makers about talent levels, ramp up needs, upcoming projects etc. Those relationships helped improve our training models (especially costs) and they have an engagement with a premier client to help market their embedded software skills."

So how can clients build relationships with senior executives from large suppliers? One of the best ways is to visit the supplier delivery team offshore. The supplier delivery team can often arrange for visiting clients to meet their own senior managers. When the manager of the SCE finally made the trip to Bangalore, the supplier delivery team arranged meetings with supplier senior managers. Beyond the value of finally establishing ties to the large supplier's top executives, he developed much closer ties to the supplier's delivery teams. He said:

> "I can't believe I waited two years to meet the people I have been only e-mailing and seeing in video conferences! What a difference this trip has made. Now, I know my team. I should have done this at the very beginning. I now have faces, and more importantly personalities, to go with names and titles. This trip was worth every penny."

b) Build strong ties with on-site supplier managers. Our research found that offshore suppliers working on client sites were often viewed with fear and even contempt. For example, the program managers at one Fortune 100 firm witnessed the internal IT staff's open hostility toward offshore supplier employees. US Manufacturing made a concerted effort to welcome and integrate the offshore supplier employees who would remain on-site for up to six months. Long engagements away from home can leave these workers feeling alienated and lonely. The managers of the SCE invited offshore supplier employees to social events such as birthday parties and happy hours. The effort to increase the social ties between internal and supplier employees paid dividends at US Manufacturing. The line between "us and them" blurred. The suppliers' employees (both on and offshore) were viewed by US Manufacturing employees as team members and they all shared in the successes and challenges of the projects. According to the Group Project Manager at one of US Manufacturing's large Indian suppliers:

> "Of all of our embedded systems clients, [US Manufacturing] has worked the hardest to make our employees feel very much part of the team at [US Manufacturing]. Our customer satisfaction ratings from [US Manufacturing] show the value of this integration. Our employees have internalized the mission and values of [US Manufacturing]. It is a highly coveted assignment to work on the US Manufacturing account."

c) Engage multiple suppliers to broaden the social network. The SCE within US Manufacturing distributed work among three suppliers (two large and one boutique). While maintaining engagements with multiple suppliers did increase transaction costs, the benefits included protection of intellectual property and the creation of a competitive environment to keep costs low and quality high. The use of multiple suppliers also created larger social networks, thus increasing US Manufacturing's ability to both create social capital and manage knowledge transfer. While it may seem counter-intuitive that increasing the number of suppliers would increase the social capital within teams, the SCE found that exposure to divergent engagement models, suppliers with different work processes and styles, and suppliers with unique expertise, broadened the outlook of the internal employees. Specifically, internal teams were able to enhance their own skill sets and increase their levels of expertise and confidence by working with developers from multiple suppliers. The manager of the SCE concluded:

> "In our first try, we only used one vendor and we did not learn much from them and they did not help us. When we spread work out [across suppliers], our processes improved as did the exposure of our internal people to multiple viewpoints. It also helped us to 'keep alive' multiple vendors – we were spreading the development around."

Practice 4 – require suppliers to protect social capital investment through succession planning

The practices to build social capital require a significant financial investment for clients. Clients must ensure that their investment is protected in case of unscheduled supplier turnover. Two practices can help.

a) Require suppliers to have shadows for key supplier roles. Employee turnover can have a destabilizing effect on a social network. As Inkpen and Tsang (2005) found: *"personnel turnover affects intracorporate knowledge sharing, which often takes place through formal or informal exchanges on an individual basis. Maintaining a stable pool of personnel within a network can help individuals develop long-lasting interpersonal relationships".* To mitigate the risks associated with supplier employee turnover, the SCE managers required suppliers to overlap key people, like project leads, at the client site. Depending on the role, the required shadowing period was three to six months. This overlap period had two major social capital and knowledge transfer benefits. First, the knowledge transfer was done predominately between the supplier's employees, thus freeing up the SCE's valuable architects and leads. Second, the incumbents were able to ease the impending transition by introducing their replacements to US Manufacturing's business units and staff and subsequently transferring more social aspects of the arrangement. This helped to maintain the social contacts and connections that were created during the engagement. According to the engineering supervisor:

> "Once we started overlapping the liaisons, our customers felt much better about rolling people off the project. The outgoing liaisons made

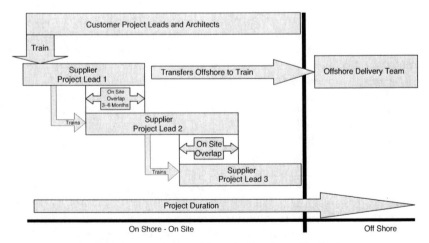

Figure 15.3   US Manufacturing's Use of Supplier Employee Shadowing

our job much easier since they took their initial training and subsequent learning and were able to convey it to their replacement much, much better than we can."

Figure 15.3 shows the relationship between the supplier's on-site projects leaders and the offshore team.

b) Require supplier employees trained on-site to train supplier employees offshore. While the engagement contracts between US Manufacturing and its suppliers did not specifically detail the cost structures and/or penalties for unplanned turnover, both US Manufacturing and its suppliers realized the risks associated with turnover. As mentioned earlier, US Manufacturing needed to ensure that the resources invested in on-site training could be protected in the event of unplanned turnover. According to the manager of the SCE:

"I know [the supplier] will experience turnover, but they will be responsible for transferring the training from one person to another. For example, let's say that we got ten people from [the supplier] working on this domain. When those ten people return from our training, I expect that [the supplier] will actually add other people to the team and train them. The net number will still be ten, but it may be different people as they have other people moving into other roles. As long as they are retaining and passing on that domain knowledge to the new people, that's great. We don't expect those ten individuals to stay tied to this domain forever. We just expect them [the supplier] to now be shepherds of the training we gave them and be able to transfer that to the new folks that they want to add to that team."

While the informal agreements helped to alleviate some fears associated with lost domain expertise in the suppliers' teams, US Manufacturing acknowledged that risks still existed. They were building formal remediation methods into the future contracts. According to the Engineering Supervisor:

"We're trying to build enough domain knowledge in those suppliers in the areas they work in that if one or two guys leave it's not a problem, but we know if the whole team left then we're in big trouble. We would have to go retrain a bunch. So, we are working with them now to protect that investment by working with the suppliers to prevent that and structuring the contracts to address the issue if it happens."

In other companies we studied, clients required suppliers to reimburse training costs if supplier employees did not remain on the account for a certain period of time. From the client perspective, this is a best practice for protecting investment in social capital, although suppliers will likely resist.

Practice 5 – protect intellectual capital

Due to significant amounts of product and process knowledge the suppliers needed to successfully develop software, the SCE chose to co-train both internal and supplier developers. However, the co-training of internal employees with supplier employees creates significant trade secret and intellectual property risks. The amount of information passing from the client to the supplier can lead to a divulging of proprietary intellectual property or an unbalanced relationship with one supplier. US Manufacturing used the following practice to balance the need to transfer knowledge to suppliers against the need to protect its intellectual assets.

a) Divvy intellectual property across multiple suppliers. Whereas earlier Practices addressed the use of multiple suppliers to increase the social network, this Practice focuses on the use of multiple suppliers to protect intellectual property. Considering the proprietary nature of the software the SCE developed, US Manufacturing faced an interesting problem: how to

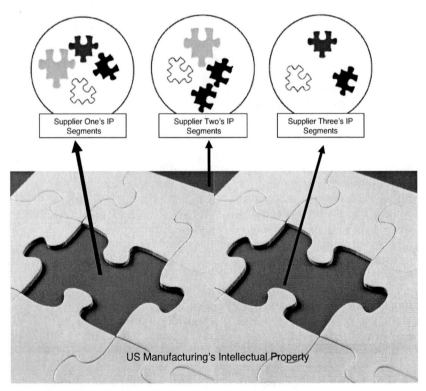

Figure 15.4   Intellectual Property Divided Among Suppliers

transfer enough knowledge to enable successful product development while protecting their trade secrets. To mitigate this risk, the SCE (1) unitized projects into small segments of work and (2) dispensed these segments among three offshore suppliers to effectively distribute the intellectual property. They viewed their intellectual property as a puzzle. By distributing small pieces among three suppliers, no one supplier can assemble the puzzle on their own (see Figure 15.4).

The first part of the practice involved the unitization of tasks to be sourced. US Manufacturing segmented large projects into smaller, well–defined tasks. These tasks were typically five to seven business day activities that had clearly defined objectives and requirements. While the transactional overhead of this strategy was considerable, the Manager of the SCE claimed the transaction costs were more than recouped by such close monitoring:

> "In our first round [the failed attempt at offshore sourcing], projects were allowed to creep and the only people who saw the creep were the accounts payable people on our end and the accounts receivable people at the supplier. Now, each task has an owner and we watch the projects from a functional perspective, not an accounting perspective. By using this strategy, we are seeing much less re-work and the quality has improved considerably!"

The second part of the strategy involves multi-sourcing. While maintaining engagements with multiple suppliers did increase transaction costs and management overhead, the benefits included protection of intellectual property and the creation of a competitive environment to keep costs low and quality high.

Conclusion – social capital as a business asset

Many managers like to call their outsourcing deals "strategic." In reality, much of outsourcing is still about cost reduction in back-office services (see Introduction and Chapter 4). For us, the term "strategic outsourcing" is restricted to circumstances for which suppliers play a key role in helping clients deliver innovative products to the market faster and cheaper than competitors (see also Chapter 8). Under that definition, US Manufacturing is using its offshore suppliers strategically.

As the US Manufacturing case illustrates, strategic use of outsourcing requires a considerable social investment in suppliers. Clients must establish trust, created shared language and meaning, and design social ties. However, we have shown that building social capital requires significant financial resources and time before benefits are realized. Consequently, clients must approach offshore outsourcing as a long-term commitment with carefully selected suppliers in order to earn a return on that investment.

Most importantly, social capital must be viewed as a business asset (Oshri *et al.*, 2007ab). While friendships among client and supplier employees are pleasant, the real purpose of social capital is to add business value. Social capital enables knowledge and resource exchanges that add value in terms of increased efficiency, better quality, and more innovation. As earlier chapters of this book attest, because work gets done through people, relationships matter. A more comprehensive account of how these issues play out in offshore outsourcing contexts is given in Lacity and Rottman (2007).

References

Finnegan, D. and Willcocks, L. (2007) *Implementing CRM: From Technology To Knowledge*, Wiley, Chichester.

Granovetter, M.S. (1973) "The Strength of Weak Ties", *American Journal of Sociology*, 78, May, 1360–1380.

Inkpen, A. and Tsang, J. (2005) "Social Capital Networks and Knowledge Transfer", *Academy of Management Review*, 30, 1, 146–165.

Kale, P., Singh, H. and Perlmutter, H. (2000), "Learning and Protection of Proprietary Assets in Strategic Alliances: Building Relational-Specific Capital", *Strategic Management Journal*, 21, 217–237.

Lacity, M. and Rottman, J. (2007) *The Offshore Outsourcing of IT Work*, Palgrave, London.

Larson, A. (1992) "Network Dyads in Entrepreneurial Settings: A Study of the Governance of Exchange Processes", *Administrative Science Quarterly*, 37, 76–104.

Lin, C. (2007) "To Share or Not to Share: Modeling Tacit Knowledge Sharing: Its Mediators and Antecedents", *Journal of Business Ethics*, 70, 411–428.

Nahapiet, J., and Ghoshal, S. (1998) "Social Capital, Intellectual Capital and the Organizational Advantage", *Academy of Management*, 23, 2, 242–266.

Oshri, I., Kotlarsky, J. and Willcocks, L.P. (2007a) "Managing Dispersed Expertise in IT Offshore Outsourcing: Lessons from Tata Consultancy Services", *MISQ Executive*, 6, 2, 53–65.

Oshri, I., Kotlarsky, J. and Willcocks, L.P. (2007b) "Global Software Development: Exploring Socialization in Distributed Strategic Projects", *Journal of Strategic Information Systems*, 16, 1, 25–49.

Oshri. I., Kotlarsky, J. and Willcocks, L. (eds) (2008) *Outsourcing Global Services: Knowledge, Innovation and Social Capital*, Palgrave, London.

Rosenkopf, L. and Nerkar, A. (2001) "Beyond Local Search: Boundary-Spanning, Exploration, and Impact in the Optical Disk Industry", *Strategic Management Journal*, 22, 287–306.

Willcocks, L. and Craig, A. (2009) *The Outsourcing Enterprise 5 – Step Change: Collaborating to Innovate*, Logica, London.

16
Creating Global Shared Services: Sourcing Lessons from Reuters

Mary Lacity and Jim Fox

Introduction

In this final chapter of a book about sourcing options we examine an approach that is often mooted, and quite often practised, but remains very under-researched. Sometimes shared services is considered as an advanced, more efficient way of retaining IT and other back-office functions in-house. On other occasions, we have seen it used as a half-way house toward potential commercialization, or to outsourcing – following the oft-quoted advice of getting your own house in order before outsourcing, and not outsourcing problems and the "low lying fruit" (i.e., easily reduced costs) (Lacity and Willcocks, 2001, 2009). Creating shared services requires a coordinated integration of four change programs: business process redesign, organizational redesign, technology enablement, and sourcing redesign. If managed properly – shared services reduce costs, improve services, and can even generate revenues. However, surveys show that many executives fail to achieve the promised results. In this last chapter, we present the lessons Reuters learned during a five-year journey to create global shared services within their finance organization. Lessons address the right transformation approach, how to identify processes for shared services by analyzing the costs, attributes and readiness of process activities, and getting business unit clients and internal staff to cooperate and embrace the shared services initiative.

According to Accenture, shared services is defined as *"the consolidation of support functions (such as human resources, finance, information technology, and procurement) from several departments into a standalone organizational entity whose only mission is to provide services as efficiently and effectively as possible"* (Accenture, 2005). Organizations create shared services to dramatically reduce costs, improve services, and even to generate revenues. Early adopters of shared services boasted enormous benefits. General Electric – recognized as the first leader of shared services – implemented shared financial and accounting services in 1984 and reported a 30% staff reduction. DEC followed the year after by creating shared financial services, reducing the finance staff by 450 and reported annual savings of $40 to $50 million (Davis, 2005).[1]

Although IT has not adopted shared services as widely as finance and accounting, more recent reports indicate that IT shared services is growing at a faster rate.[2] Indeed, successful management of IT shared services was described in Andriole (2007) as among the seven habits of effective CIOs. Studies have shown, however, that not all organizations achieve the full benefits they expect from shared services. IBM, for example, found that the results of shared services have been "mundane rather than magical" among a survey of 210 senior managers.[3] Another study of 140 executives in North America and Europe found that *expected* benefits exceeded *actual* benefits in the majority of cases. Thirty-three percent of respondents reported no cost savings. Among the 67% who reported cost savings, the average cost savings was 14%.[4] Furthermore, the average time to fully implement shared services was two years in Europe and twice that long in North America. Given the long implementation times and obvious risks of achieving only mundane outcomes, how can senior executives realize the full potential of shared services? Based on a case study at Reuters, we found that shared services require senior managers to manage four programs of change.

Conceptualizing shared services as four programs of change

Creating shared services is not merely a matter of *consolidating* back offices – we call that *centralization*. Rather, shared services are best conceptualized as the orchestration of four change programs: business process redesign, organizational redesign, technology enablement, and sourcing redesign (Roberts *et al.*, 2003; see also Figure 16.1).[5] Business process redesign specifies *what*

---

[1]This article provides a history of shared service organizations in the United States, Europe, and Asia: Davis, T., "Integrating Shared Services With the Strategy and Operation of MNEs", *Journal of General Management*, Winter 2005, 31, 2, 1–17.
[2]Alsbridge Consulting, "Shares Services: Can You Be an Internal Outsourcer?" webinar on Oct 18, 2007. However, in the government sector, the Accenture report (*op. cit.*) found that more shared service centers exist for IT than for finance.
[3]IBM Business Consulting Services, "Finance shared services and outsourcing." http://www-935.ibm.com/services/uk/bcs/pdf/g510-6143-finance-shared-services.pdf
[4]AT Kearney Report, "Success Through Shared Services." AT Kearney, New York http://www.atkearney.com/shared_res/pdf/Shared_Services_S.pdf
[5]Many other *MISQ Executive* articles provide rich insights into individual programs of change and change management. Two excellent articles on organizational redesign are Chan, Y., "Why Haven't We Mastered Alignment? The Importance of the Informal Organization Structure", 1, 2, June 2002, 97–112. and Agarwal, R. and Sambamurthy, V. "Principles and Models for Organizing the IT Function", 1, 1, March 2002, 1–16. Because a global ERP system is one of the key enablers of shared services, other relevant articles include Brown, C. and Vessey, I. "Managing the Next Wave of Enterprise Systems: Leveraging Lessons from ERP", 2, 1, March 2003, 65–77 and Soh, C. and Kien Sia, S. "The Challenges of Implementing 'Vanilla' Versions of Enterprise Systems", 4, 3, September 2005, 373–384.

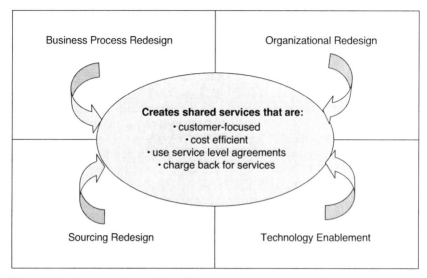

Figure 16.1　Conceptualizing Shared Services as Four Programs of Change

business processes the organization will perform. The main goals of business process redesign are to standardize processes around best practices, to reduce costs, and to improve controls. Organizational redesign specifies *where* business processes will be performed. The goal of organizational redesign is to locate staff based on value of the services they provide; high-touch, high-value services are typically located close to internal customers while standard services are moved to shared service facilities. Sourcing redesign specifies *who* performs the business processes. Sourcing options include a mixture of in-house provision and outsourcing. Enabling technologies are used to implement the newly designed business processes and to coordinate work across different organizational units and across sourcing partners.

Organizations must also determine the best sequence for these change programs. As we saw in Chapter 13, some organizations like BAE Systems and Lloyds of London outsourced first and let the supplier lead the transformation initiative. In the Reuters case, the sequence for creating shared financial services was iterative and involved two overlapping phases. Phase I took place from 2001 to 2004. First business process redesign, organizational redesign and enabling technologies led to the creation of six regional shared service organizations. However, before the completion of Phase I, senior executives required an additional 33% cost savings to help improve profitability. Reuters' finance managers initiated a second round of transformation, this time focusing on organizational redesign, business process redesign, and sourcing redesign. They erected a new captive center in Bangalore and outsourced specialized financial services to third party suppliers. Over five years, the two phases of transformation resulted in a reduction the finance staff by 47% while increasing service (as evidenced by user surveys) and increasing controls. Reuters has since won a number of shared services awards for Best New Shared Service Organization, Best Use of Technology for Shared Services, and Best Shared Services Leader.[6] Thus, these programs of change resulted in better services, increased cost controls and compliance, and lower costs.

As the Reuters case shows, these change initiatives – if managed correctly – result in shared service organizations that function as a business within a business. Great shared service organizations breed high-performers focused on customer service excellence. They use service level agreements to align expectations and to define responsibilities between internal clients and the back office providers. Finally, about 60% of shared service centers charge internal customers for services based on usage (Cecil, 2000; Webster, 2007), although we found that Reuters did not.[7]

Creating shared services is thus about radical transformation, requiring a tremendous amount of change management to achieve success. In this chapter, we present detailed, actionable practices learned from Reuters. We explain the choices Reuters made and the lessons they learned.

Phase 1   business process redesign, organizational redesign and technology enablement

In the late 1990s, Reuters faced a number of environmental and internal changes. The proliferation of the Internet commoditized some of Reuters' core content. For example, companies were buying information from Reuters and widely distributing it over the Internet, thus eroding their revenues. Increased competition in both the European and US markets were causing prices to fall. Internally, rapid organic growth and growth through acquisitions created redundant backoffices resulting in high costs and integration concerns. Increased profitability became the primary charge of Reuters' senior management team.

In the area of finance, Reuters' finance leaders were concerned about Reuters' ineffective finance operating model and relatively high costs – which exceeded 2.3% of revenues. At that time, best-in-breed financial costs were approximately 1.5% of revenues. How could finance costs be reduced? In 2001, the CFO aimed to significantly reduce finance costs by standardizing finance policies for global delivery (business process redesign), implementing standard, global ERP and workflow systems (technology enablement), and

---

[6] Awards were sponsored by the IQPC (International Quality and Productivity Center).

[7] Usage-based chargeback proponents argue that it motivates shared services staff to remain competitive, stimulates internal customers to think before they consume, and provides a way for shared services to generate revenue for further improvements. Usage-based chargeback opponents argue that it creates too much administrative burden and can create conflicts between shared service organizations and internal clients. See also Ross, J., Vitale, M. and Beath, C. "The Untapped Potential of Chargeback", *MIS Quarterly*, 23, 2, 1999, 215–238.

Business Process Redesign:	Organizational Redesign:
Major Activity: create standard processes for global delivery **Major Challenge:** business acceptance **Major Lessons:** 1. Coach, don't police 2. Solicit clients for innovations	**Major Activity:** move end-to-end processes to six new, client-focused regional service centers **Major Challenge:** retaining finance staff **Major Lesson:** 3. Envision the future for retained employees
	Technology Enablement: **Major Activity:** implement single instance of a global ERP system **Major Challenge:** Timing **Major Lesson:** 4. Invest in enabling technology first

Figure 16.2   Phase I Transformation Programs

moving a significant amount of work from the decentralized business units to six new regional service centers (organizational design). Each change program encountered challenges and Reuters learned key lessons (see Figure 16.2). Through the three change programs described below, Reuters reduced the financial service staff by 35% and reduced financial costs from 2.3% of revenues to 1.8% of revenues.

Business Process Redesign. Reuters' main BPR activity was to reduce the number of idiosyncratic business processes by creating global finance policies and standard business processes. In addition to reducing costs, another major reason for the business process redesign was to prepare for the new organizational design. Reuters needed to standardize processes in order to relocate some of them from the decentralized business units to new regional service centers.

Prior to Phase I, Reuters had nearly 600 finance processes. After the redesign, Reuters reduced the number of finance processes to 359. Among the 359, 279 were truly global standards and only 80 were localized business processes. Key controls standards were concurrently implemented under the new global template. Although key controls added challenges to the implementation, they later served as the foundation for the Sarbanes-Oxley (SOX) program and other process standardization initiatives.

The major challenge of BPR was getting business unit clients to accept the changes caused by the re-engineering of business processes. The purchasing activities within the source-to-payment process were the most difficult to change. For example, the finance team in charge of the redesign needed to implement unfavorable policies such as "no purchase order, no payment" to nearly 2,000 employees with purchasing authority. Local business units preferred to buy from their local suppliers even though some of the suppliers had no warrantee. In some cases, controls were ineffective and there was little accountability for spend. In many other areas, such as allowable travel and entertainment, policies varied widely by country. For example, some countries paid for family support costs when employees traveled for business. Some countries had generous but expensive health club policies. Reuters learned two valuable lessons to get business unit clients to accept the business process changes:

Lesson 1   Coach – don't police – business unit clients. Rather than coerce the business unit clients to accept the changes, the finance team acted as coaches. Coaches evangelized the vision set by the "owners" (in this case the CEO, Corporate CFO, and Business Unit CFOs). As coaches, the finance team constantly conveyed the message, "This is your unit's vision – we are here to help." If users were caught violating the new procedures – such as bypassing the new policies to procure on their own – users were coached, not policed. The "offender" was gently reminded of the vision and rules. Once coached on the sidelines, the users played by the new rules.

Lesson 2   Solicit innovations from business unit clients. The finance team fostered a culture that valued change by creating awards for best, continuous improvement. Any Reuters' employee could submit ideas, but the finance team found that the best ideas came from the business unit clients, not from their internal team members. For example, in the editorial division, business clients had difficulty sending new employees to training because they were remotely located. In particular, the editorial employees needed to understand Reuters' travel and entertainment policies, procedures, and technology. The editorial division suggested that finance put a training video on the shared services website. The video was filmed inexpensively by a member of the finance staff. The video explains the T&E policies and shows employees how to use the technology to submit expense forms. The finance team gave awards to employees for ideas – like the video training – that significantly reduced costs and increased service. The awards were very visible and prominent, thus serving as a positive motivator of behavioral change.

Organizational Redesign. Reuters' main organizational redesign activity was to move as many end-to-end processes as possible from the decentralized business units to the new regional service centers. The idea was that the new regional service centers would be client-focused and house subject matter experts.

Prior to the organizational redesign, Reuters' finance employees were located in 25 countries and supported business clients located in 90 countries. The finance employees reported in one of three organizations:

1. Corporate finance. 11% of the finance employees worked in the corporate finance group at London headquarters. Their roles included financial reporting, internal audit, group treasury, group tax, and reporting to the Audit Committee;

2. **Decentralized business units.** 81% of the finance employees worked in decentralized business units in 25 locations. They supported all the financial processes such as strategic analysis, business planning, financial management, investments, budgeting and forecasting, and payroll;

3. **Non-integrated subsidiaries.** 8% of the finance employees worked in independent subsidiaries. In 2001, these independent businesses were completely separate from the corporate finance group and were thus outside the scope and control of the shared services initiative.

The finance team in charge of creating regional shared services estimated that half of the work in the decentralized business units provided direct value to the business or was required to remain local, including strategic analysis, budgeting and forecasting, performance management and financial reporting, statutory and tax accounting, payroll, and project investment management and analysis. These processes were not initially moved to the regional service centers. However, the finance team estimated that the other half of their work provided only indirect value. These activities included purchasing, payables, cash application and management, account entries and reconciliations. Many of these processes were moved to regional service centers.

The six regional service centers were located in London, New York (later moved to St Louis), Amsterdam, Buenos Aires, Nicosia (in Cyprus) and Singapore. The choice of locations was based on balancing close physical proximity to internal customers against low cost provision. The London service center, although an expensive location, was needed to closely support Reuters' London headquarters. St Louis and Buenos Aires were low cost areas that supported Reuters' operations in the Americas. Amsterdam supported European operations, Singapore supported Asian operations, and Nicosia supported Reuters' emerging markets.[8] Reuters learned one important lesson during this initial organizational redesign:

Lesson 3   Envision the future for retained employees. During Phase I, some finance employees did not want to move from the business units to the regional service centers. Some members of the financial staff simply did not want to re-locate. Other members of the financial staff perceived the changes in their roles as deskilling from client-facing services to transaction processing. In the end, about 60% of the staff in the regional service centers was new hires.

In hindsight, the shared services team felt that they should have proactively articulated the vision and career paths for the financial staff to

---

[8]In an analysis of 150 articles on nearshoring, the balance between proximity advantage and lower costs was the main reason stated for nearshoring over offshoring in 60% of the publications. See Carmel, E. and Abbott, P. "Why 'Nearshore' Means that Distance Matters", *Communications of the ACM*, 50, 10, October 2007, 40–46.

prevent so much resistance. The feared deskilling did not occur. Quite the contrary occurred because the resultant culture in these regional centers was strong and the financial staff relished their expanded roles of servicing more clients across more business units. During Phase II, senior finance leaders did not repeat this mistake. Senior leaders identified early in the process which employees would remain at Reuters and more clearly envisioned career paths for retained staff in the finance organization (see also Chapters 14 and 15).

Technology Enablement. The newly designed business processes and organizational structure were enabled by a number of technologies. The most important activity in technology enablement was the migration to one single instance of Oracle ERP across all of Reuters. Oracle was implemented first in the United Kingdom in 2000. Reuters hired a management consulting firm to help Finance and Human Resource functions rollout Oracle and launched the shared service initiative. The consulting firm brought in a team of 25 people and was instrumental in defining the shared service operating model and supported the IT function in the global installation of Oracle. Most of the installation was completed by December 2002.

Besides the ERP system, Reuters also invested in systems for invoice scanning, approval workflow, and electronic employee expenses. These technologies helped Reuters create a more paperless office and enable geographical independence. Reuters also customized existing systems to enable language transition workflow. This application reduced the risk around language dependency.

Reuters also custom built four applications. Two applications – electronic invoice uploads from major suppliers and accounts receivable cash application automation – were built to reduce error rates. Reuters also custom built a helpdesk logging and workflow application to track incidents across geography and functions. Finally, Reuters built an automated straight-through processing and approval of payments to ensure security and control. The role of these technologies certainly enabled the business process and organizational redesigns during Phase I. Concerning the timing of enabling technology *vis-à-vis* other change programs, the Reuters' case offers the following lesson:

Lesson 4 Invest in enabling technology first. Reuters found that technology was a critical enabler of its regional shared services. In particular, Reuters discovered that their best initial investment was the global, single-instance ERP system. As one manager said, *"This is worth investing in before anything else."* The global ERP system drove process standardization and was the "engine" of the regional shared services. Its role during Phase II was even more important, because the now stable technology platform could be replicated in the new Indian captive center.

We note that this lesson is counter to the lesson flagged in Chapter 13 and in some of our other research (Lacity *et al.*, 2003). There, we described how BAE Systems redesigned business processes before technology enablement. BAE Systems' transformation partner – Xchanging – believed that technology should follow business process redesign. At Reuters, the global ERP system was started before the business process standardization. The timing gave the finance team additional leverage to convince business clients to accept the standard global policies. Because the global ERP system was imminent, business clients would need to follow the new policies as embedded in new ERP system.

The finance team was proud of the results emerging from their three transformation programs. They were well on their way to meeting their objectives of reducing finance costs while simultaneously increasing controls and service levels. The celebration, however, was short-lived because Reuters faced a financial crisis.

Deciding how to deliver an additional 33% savings

In 2002, for the first time since Reuters went public, Reuters recorded a pre-tax loss of £493 million.[9] Revenues also dropped by 2%. Early in 2003, the company announced a formal three-year program to achieve total cost savings of £440 million. From the finance organization, senior management mandated an extra 33% cost savings over two years with no lapse in control or service levels. The senior finance leaders brainstormed on how to deliver the additional savings given they were nearly done Phase I. One possibility was outsourcing.

The senior finance leaders initially tried to attract a supplier to move their regional financial services to India and to continue supplying services once the move was completed. A few suppliers did show interest but they required significant upfront management fees. In the end, the leaders worried that an outsourcing supplier would not be able to manage the global complexity and eliminated fee-for-service outsourcing as a viable option.

Next, the senior finance leaders considered commercialization. Because Reuters considered its financial service support as best-in-class, the finance leaders were very excited about the possibility of exploiting this asset, much like Procter & Gamble did when they sold their shared service operations. However, Reuters faced the problem that its shared services operation was too small to excite a serious buyer. While Procter & Gamble is a $40 billion company and had a few thousand people in its shared service center, Reuters is only a $4 billion company with a few hundred people in its shared services.

With large scale outsourcing and commercialization eliminated as viable options to achieve the savings, the finance leaders thought that another

---

[9]In January 2008, £493 million pounds sterling = $US971 million.

organizational redesign – this time more aggressive – could deliver the savings. They were also open to selective outsourcing. By January 2004, the senior finance leaders narrowed the choices down to three options.

Option 1: consolidate six regional service centers into one "transaction center of excellence." This option would migrate the work from six regional service centers (London, Nicosia, Singapore, St Louis, Amsterdam, Buenos Aires) all to a Center of Excellence. The team considered locating the Center of Excellence in Singapore due to its lower cost structure and opportunity for scale. Locating the Center of Excellence in one of Reuters' existing centers offered the added benefit of moving quickly enough to meet the team's two-year time requirement. But the team questioned whether Singapore's costs were low enough to meet the aggressive 33% targeted cost savings.

Option 2: nearshore from six regional service centers to three. This option entailed moving financial support services from higher-cost regional service centers to existing nearby lower-cost regional service centers. Work from London and Amsterdam would be moved to Cyprus, work from St Louis would be moved to Buenos Aires, and work from Singapore would be moved to India. The team questioned whether Buenos Aires and Cyprus had enough local resources to accommodate more services. Other risks included higher inflation, lower tax incentives, and less political stability than other destinations.

Option 3: redesign regional service centers, erect a captive center, and engage outsourcing partners. This option would entail moving some higher value work that remained in the decentralized business units to the six regional service centers, and moving many of the standardized processes now in the regional service centers to a lower cost captive center located offshore. Selective use of outsourcing partners would fill in gaps in Reuters' capabilities. This option became a candidate because the Director of Shared Services began to question whether Option 1 (consolidate six regional service centers to Singapore) would just be a half-way step to an eventual move to China or India. Clearly, Singapore's prices were higher than these two alternative destinations. Independent of finance, other units within Reuters were looking at Bangalore and Bangkok. As the finance leaders further considered this option, they quickly narrowed the location of the captive center to Bangalore. They selected Bangalore because of available talent and because they thought they could piggyback off another Reuters' presence in that city. This option entailed multiple moves and needed closer inspection.

The total financial benefits versus the costs for each option are found in Figure 16.3. The cost assessment was comprehensive and included technical, communications, administrative, employee package, training, travel, and capital outlays. The outcome of this analysis showed that Option 3 would generate the most savings ($6.5 million) and would have the fastest payback period (2.03 years). But, as a reader of Chapters 6 and 8 would ask, what about the risks?

	Consolidate six regional service centers to one transaction center of excellence	Near-shore from six regional service centers to three	Redesign regional service centers, erect a captive center, and engage outsourcing partners
One time investment	$10 million	$10.8 million	$13.5 million
Total Savings	$3.2 million	$2.9 million	$6.5 million
Payback Period	3.05 years	3.75 years	2.03 years

Figure 16.3   Financial Assessment of Shared Services Options

Risk Factor	Consolidate six regional service centers to one transaction center of excellence	Near-shore from six regional service centers to three	Redesign regional service centers, erect a captive center, and engage outsourcing partners
Systems/Communications	2	8	6
Location Stability	1	5	3
Eggs in one basket (1 location)	8	4	7
E2E Process Control	6	3	7
Time Zone Support	5	2	3
Language Coverage	5	2	7
Business Case Delivery	3	7	4
Scale Opportunities	3	6	3
Continuous Improvement	3	6	3
Flexibility/Agility	2	3	2
Strength of Governance	3	5	2
	3.727	4.636	4.272

Figure 16.4   Risk Assessment of Shared Services Options

The shared service team rated 11 risks for the three options on a scale from 9 (indicating high risk) to 0 (indicating low risk). The result of this analysis is found in Figure 16.4. The least risky option was Option 1. The riskiest option was Option 2.

The three options were presented to a meeting attended by the executive sponsor of shared services, the Director of Shared Services, and the shared service leaders in late January 2004. The mood of the room was that it was an election year (US and UK Elections) and the media and popular sentiment were very anti-offshoring. The Director of Shared Services said the move to India is inevitable a few years from now, so he lobbied that Reuters should *"take the higher risk, do it once, do it right."* The vote was taken. The group selected Option 3 and the CFO approved the recommendation. A shared services team was created to manage a second phase of transformation.

Phase II: organizational redesign, business process redesign and sourcing redesign

During Phase II, Reuters launched three transformation programs, the most challenging of which was organizational redesign (see Figure 16.5). The shared services team needed to reconceptualize the organization yet again. This time, the six regional shared services would further exploit its subject

Business Process Redesign:	Organizational Redesign:
Major Activity: ensure processes work in new organizational design **Major Challenge:** linkages across multiple delivery channels **Major Lesson:** 7. Reassemble processes to ensure seamless end-to-end delivery	**Major Activity:** decide which processes to move where **Major Challenge:** move enough processes to obtain savings without sacrificing service or controls **Major Lessons:** 5. Locate greyzone activities to regional centers 6. Analyze processes at the activity level
Sourcing Redesign: **Major Activity:** erect new captive center and outsource to fill gaps in internal capabilities **Major Challenge:** transitioning work **Major Lessons:** 8. Keep transition managers until stability has been obtained 9. Make sending end accountable for migration	

Figure 16.5   Phase II Transformation Programs

matter expertise by assuming more customer-facing responsibilities. Thus even more processes would be moved from the decentralized business unit into the six regional service centers. In addition, the highly standardized transactional processes would be moved from the six regional services to a new captive center in India. The organizational redesign prompted changes to business process flows. Although the policies, controls, and standards remained the same, the shared services team had to ensure seamless end-to-end delivery (business process redesign). In addition, the new organizational design left gaps in some areas, requiring Reuters to engage partners in selective outsourcing (sourcing redesign). Thus, a tremendous amount of work was moved around the organization. After Phase II, the decentralized finance staff in the business units decreased by 44%, the finance staff in the six regional service centers decreased by 61%, and the captive center hired 174 new people. The net result from Phase II was a decrease in finance staff by 18% and cost savings within $100,000 of the targeted $6.5 million. Each transformation program is discussed below.

Organizational Redesign. The new organizational design required moving more processes from the decentralized business units to the regional service

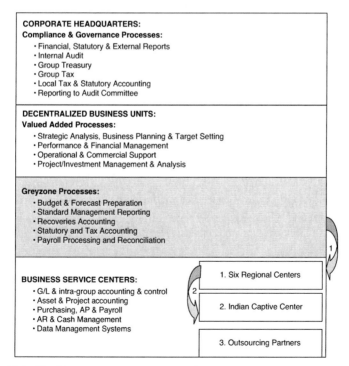

Figure 16.6 The New Finance Operating Model

centers (see arrow 1 in Figure 16.6) and moving the standardized processes in the six regional service centers to a new captive center in India (see arrow 2 in Figure 16.6). The idea was that the six regional service centers would be downsized, but remaining staff would focus on higher value-added processes that require specialist client knowledge. The Indian captive center would provide the standardized, transactional processes that have already been automated and optimized in terms of having low error rates. Reuters learned two lessons concerning the organizational redesign in Phase II.

Lesson 5: Locate "greyzone" activities to customer-focused service centers. Although Reuters had already moved many business processes from the decentralized business units to the six regional service centers during Phase I, senior finance leaders thought many more processes could be moved. The regional service centers were earning a reputation for excellent customer service and were regularly recognized by internal client surveys for enhanced user experience, improved self-service functions, and improved quality of information. Thus, they were ready for more client-focused work.

The shared service team decided to move processes that were non-strategic but still required specific customer knowledge – the so called "greyzone" activities (see arrow 1 in Figure 16.6) – to the regional service centers, now redesigned to assume more responsibility for certain controllership services. The greyzone included activities such as preparing baseline budgets and forecasts, creating standard management reports, and standard accounting functions such as recoveries, statutory, tax and payroll processing. The regional service centers also do processes that required physical proximity to customers, processes that required specialist knowledge, and processes that frequently change. However, despite the increased responsibility for "higher value" work, the overall headcount in the six regional service centers declined by 61% because many processes were moved from the six regional service centers to the new captive center in India (see arrow 2 in Figure 16.6).

Deciding which activities to move from the regional services centers to the captive center in India required a more detailed level of analysis. While end-to-end processes could be moved from the decentralized business units to the six regional service centers because of the client expertise, the shared services team could not move entire processes from the six regional service centers to the Indian captive center. They could only move the standard, low-valued transactional activities *within* processes to the Indian captive center. The next lesson provides a way to analyze candidates for shared services at the *activity* level. Here – processes are pulled apart and component activities are examined by costs, attributes, and readiness.

Lesson 6   Analyze costs, attributes and readiness of process activities to identify contenders for shared services. The shared services team assessed costs, attributes, and readiness *at the activity level*. Finance processes at each of the six regional service centers were inventoried, including the major activities within each process. The team was open to the idea that activities within a

Process 1: Activity 1.1, 1.2, 1.3, 1.4, 1.5...
Process 2: Activity 2.1, 2.2, 2.3, 2.4, 2.5...
Process x: Activity x.1, x.2, x.3, x.4, x.5...

COST:
Which activities provide opportunities
to reduce costs?

Process 1: Activity 1.1, 1.2
Process 2: Activity 2.1, 2.3, 2.4
Process x: Activity x.1, x.2, x.3, x.6

ACTIVITY ATTRIBUTES:
Which activities are suited for shared
services?

Process 1: Activity 1.2
Process 2: Activity 2.1, 2.3
Process x: Activity x.2, x.3, x.6

READINESS:
Which activities
are ready to be
moved to shared
services?

Process activities for shared services

Figure 16.7   Process Analysis at the Activity Level

process could be sourced in different locations. For example, the regional service center might work with a purchasing agent in the business unit to decide what server to buy from which supplier, but India might key the requisition form. In order to decide which location should provide which activity, the shared services team assessed the costs, attributes, and readiness of activities through a set of conceptual funnels (see Figure 16.7).

The first funnel tested activities for costs: can moving this activity from the regional centers to India save us money? Enough volume of work had to justify the extra transaction costs of moving an activity. The second funnel tested for activity attributes: is this activity suited for shared services? The specific criteria used were the extent to which the activity is repetitive and transactional, has few touch points with internal customers, is highly structured and rules-based, uses standardized inputs, outputs, and technology, has low material business impact on internal customers, is independent of third parties, requires simple skills, and is either language neutral (only requires a one-time translation of forms) or local language independent (does not require extensive oral or email communications). The shared services team also assessed whether it was legally possible to relocate the activity. This analysis funneled about 80% of the activities within the 279 processes to go through the next assessment step.

The third funnel tested for process readiness: could this activity be moved? Activities that were ready were well documented, stable, optimized (low error rates), had common service levels, were technology ready, and were politically acceptable to move. The team also had to ensure that the sequencing of activities made sense. For example, they did not want a process that resulted in a sequence of activities "onshore, offshore, onshore, offshore, onshore." This assessment eliminated about 40% of the remaining activities within the 279 processes.

The activities that remained in the regional services centers included purchasing and call center activities. The shared services team knew that purchasing was the most politically sensitive process, so they had to be careful which purchasing activities would transfer and when. The shared services team also kept the call center activities within the six regional service centers because they believed they needed stability in the first line of communication between internal customers and shared services. The call centers would also serve as the best mechanism for spotting trouble and identifying opportunities for continuous improvement.

Once activities within a process were mapped to their optimal source, the process had to be reassembled to ensure a seamless end-to-end delivery.

Business Process Redesign. The shared services team did not intend to change any of the business process policies or standards, but the movement of activities within the processes to new sourcing locations affected the process flows. For example, India was going to key in invoices, but what happens when they get an invoice written in Swedish? The Indian captive center did not have Swedish language support. In this example, the language translation would reside in a business unit administrative function. That staff would translate the invoice from Swedish to English before sending it to India for keying. Reuters had to redesign all the flows to ensure end-to-end delivery:

Lesson 7   Reassemble activities to ensure seamless end-to-end delivery. Because different activities within a finance process could be sourced by three types of service centers (regional, captive, or outsourced), the shared services team had to build solid controls and interfaces across service centers and to/from business clients. Each process was fully documented, including the process name, process reference, author, service imperative, SOX control requirements, process narrative, and all process activities. The processes were fully diagrammed showing inputs, automated process steps and sub-steps, manual process steps and sub-steps, control process steps and sub-steps, decision points, and outputs. Clear lines of responsibility were drawn around the diagrams, indicating the duties of each party. Service levels described the quality and timeliness of outputs. In addition, the detailed process flows were used for training Indian new hires and the outsourcing partners.

Sourcing Redesign. Concurrent with the organizational redesign, the shared services team was busy overseeing the new global captive center in India. Reuters purchased a new facility in Bangalore and used their internal

IT department to build and implement the entire technology and communications infrastructure within four months. Reuters hired a new manager to lead the captive center in Bangalore in July 2004. He had tremendous experience because he spent three years establishing a 300 person captive center for a Fortune 500 company. Unlike other applicants who managed captive centers with 1,500 or more people, this man knew how to efficiently and effectively manage a smaller center.[10] Reuters also hired 150 employees at a pace of 30 per month. To attract good people, Reuters promised that employees would work normal hours, unlike many US-centric Indian support centers.[11] Also, Reuters offered slightly higher than market rates. Once hired, the Indian employees were fully trained via courses delivered on-site in India as well as travel to Reuters' locations in cities around the world for knowledge transfer. New hires shadowed the workers they would replace for two to four weeks to learn about business processes, clients, technology and procedures. Once training was complete, the captive center began providing standardized transactional processes, optimized processes, structured processes, automated processes, processes with low error rates, and processes that would benefit from economies of scale.

The outsourced partners. Reuters needed a number of outsourced partners to enable the new financial operating model. Reuters selected one major outsourcing partner, several specialty partners, and expanded relationships with their existing banking partners. Reuters selected the major outsourcing partner to provide services for statutory accounting and tax and filing that could not be moved across borders. Reuters leveraged this partner's truly global presence to provide country-specific processes rather than trying to retain and develop deep functional expertise in specialized areas throughout the world. For example, Reuters couldn't afford to retain specialized staff versed in local Finnish tax law, but the outsourcing partner could. This outsourcing partner took over the responsibilities for the work of approximately 40 fulltime equivalents. The partner either hired Reuters' staff or leveraged their existing staff to fulfill Reuters' needs.

In addition to the major outsourcing partner, specialty partners were engaged to perform very specific processes like scanning, facilities administration, and local taxes. The shared services team also expanded existing relationships with banking partners to ensure that global shared services could handle payment transactions across borders and across partners. Because sourcing redesign changes *who* performs certain business processes,

---

[10]According to research done by Gunn Partners, "it takes roughly 100 people to make a shared services center worthwhile" and beyond 600 people, "size becomes counter productive." Cecil (2000) *op. cit.*
[11]Only nine employees worked the night shift.

the transition of work to different people requires special care and attention. Reuters learned two important lessons:

Lesson 8   *Keep transition managers until stability has been obtained.*
At Reuters, part of the estimated cost savings for global shared services came from less management. The power players on the shared services team knew they were planning for their own redundancies. The Senior Vice President of the Americas Shared Services said:

> "We actually did put our business case to management and said, 'you don't need the same level management layer you have today. You need a strong management layer in India, and you need the solid customer center management layer on shore, but you don't need us.'"

In September of 2004, senior management wanted the plan accelerated by three months to capture an additional $500,000 in savings. As a result, some members of the shared services transformation team were moved to other programs or left the company prior to stabilization of the new service model. This decision accelerated the cost savings but at the price of a loss of focus. The shared services transformation team had always envisioned that the captive center would be staffed with supervisors who acted as process experts and who would be responsible for the execution and quality of service delivery. However, the new manager hired to run the captive center had a different vision aligned more with the Indian business culture. He organized the captive center so that supervisors were primarily responsible for managing the staff and for allocating work to the staff.

Initially, the captive center suffered from the lack of grooming of subject matter experts. For example, when payments were missing, it required a significant amount of client knowledge to find and reconcile errors. Initially, the Indian staff couldn't perform these duties so the six regional services centers took them back. Over time, however, the regional service center staff groomed the Indians to better perform these tasks, and the processes were eventually moved back to India. Initially, the captive center also experienced higher than expected staff turnover. Reuters had to hire 24 more people in India than anticipated to provide a buffer for turnover and because the new workers were not as experienced or as efficient as the displaced financial staff. But because Indian employees were so much cheaper to hire, the additional headcount did not significantly erode the anticipated savings.

Lesson 9   *Make the sending end accountable for successful migration.*
In many organizations, companies find it difficult to solicit cooperation from employees targeted for redundancy. Reuters was very careful to treat redundant employees fairly and found a way to ensure that the redundant employees were accountable for the success of the migration. First, Reuters gave employees plenty of notice. The decision was made to officially announce the downsizing of the regional centers to the employees in March 2004.

The employees were told that the team did not know exactly who would be impacted, but that everyone would know by July 31, 2004. Some employees would be included in the succession and some employees would be given severance packages. Some employees had 18 months advance notice that they would no longer have a job at Reuters.

Second, Reuters built into the retention package a requirement that the employee facilitate and sign off on the transfer of their work. Part of this responsibility was letting the new Indian workers or third party supplier workers shadow them in their daily jobs. In order to receive their full redundancy benefits, the person from the sending site had to agree that their shadows were ready to take over the process:

> "If you remember nothing else from the transition process, remember this: let the people that are giving away the work give it away. Make them responsible for it. They know the job the best and most will enjoy the process of teaching what they do everyday." – Programme Transformation Leader

Conclusion – moving up the learning curve

Reuters' two phases of transformation took nearly five years (2001 to 2006). In the end, Reuters achieved its vision for effectively and efficiently delivering financial services through global shared services. The finance staff remaining in the decentralized business units focused on strategic finance activities. The six regional service centers focused on finance activities that required close proximity to customers, specialist local knowledge, and non-optimized processes that would have high error rates without special care. The Indian captive center efficiently delivered the highly standardized finance activities. The outsourcing partners filled critical gaps in Reuters' capabilities.

Reuters' finance leaders met their 33% mandate for cost reductions within $100,000 of the target number – significantly more than the average cost savings of 14%[12] most companies seemed to be achieving. The cost savings came primarily from staff reduction. The senior finance leaders were successful because they were committed to the vision of global shared services, dedicated the right resources, and most importantly, managed well the four programs of change. In addition to the lessons specific to the four programs of change – business process redesign, organizational redesign, technology enablement, and sourcing redesign – there are two other high-level lessons relevant to the Reuters' case:

Lesson 10   Integrate within silos before integrating across silos. Reuters is similar to several companies we have studied in that top management

---

[12]AT Kearney Report, *op. cit.*

mandated cost reductions from each back office director simultaneously. Back office directors frequently meet the mandate by creating shared service organizations and by implementing other cost reduction tactics *within their own functional silos*. Given that all the directors share the cost reduction mandate, it is logical to question: should companies create shared service organizations across functional silos to gain better efficiencies? The answer is not simple. The amount of change management required *within* the functional silos is enormous. Trying to coordinate *across* functional silos would require agreeing on locations, addressing vastly different client needs, different types of work, and different types of capabilities. This is why Reuters, and other companies we have studied, erected shared services within silos first.

Although this chapter focuses on financial services, other functional areas within Reuters – most notably IT and HR – were also making drastic changes at the same time. For example, IT Product and Software development was erecting centers in Bangkok and Hong Kong as Finance was moving to Bangalore. For the IT department, Hong Kong was a good base due to the high quality of available IT talent and close proximity to major exchanges that IT supported. In 2006, IT Product and Software Development erected another captive center in Beijing. By 2007, 40 employees worked in that facility, which was predicted to grow to a few hundred by 2009/10. The next logical step was integration of shared services across functions. By 2007, Reuters was expanding its presence in Bangalore by off-shoring some analysis and procurement. Some organizations – such as Procter & Gamble – eventually unify most back offices into one global shared services organization.

Lesson 11   Consider a blended transformation approach. The creation of shared services requires major capabilities to manage large-scale change, re-orient staff, redesign processes, technology enable, establish and enforce standards, and re-organize. Senior managers must consider the right approach towards transformation. In Lacity *et al.* (2003) we discussed five approaches for creating shared services: (1) do-it-yourself, (2) hire management consultants to manage the change, (3) fee-for-service outsourcing, (4) joint ventures for commercialization, and (5) transformational outsourcing through enterprise partnerships (see Chapter 13). We found that many senior managers were not willing to make an upfront investment in shared services to pursue the "do-it-yourself" option. This is why many senior executives use outsourcing options to create shared services because suppliers often make the upfront investment on behalf of the client.

Rather than pick one approach, Reuters selected a blended approach that relied primarily on "do-it-yourself", supplemented with management consultants to help with the global ERP implementation, and fee-for-service outsourcing for global coverage of country-specific processes. Blending approaches is becoming recognized as a "best practice", as found in IBM's survey of 210 senior finance managers. The benefit of a blended approach is access to the "best of breed" source for the myriad of capabilities needed to create shared services. The caveat, of course, is that the additional transaction costs associated with coordinating work across parties can be significant (see earlier chapters). In retrospect, Reuters found that the benefits of a blended approach outweighed the costs.

Since its financial losses in 2002, Reuters significantly improved its financial health, reporting both positive revenue growth and positive operating profit from 2003 to 2006. The 2006 annual report indicated revenues of £2.57 billion (a 7% increase from 2005) and £256 million in operating profit (a 24% increase from 2005). In May 2007, the boards of Reuters and Thompson announced a proposed merger, subject to approval by shareholders and the relevant regulatory authorities. Such mergers are never simple affairs, and tend to raise further questions about how to design and implement sourcing strategy for IT and other back office functions.

References

Accenture (2005) *Driving High Performance in Government: Maximizing the Value of Public-Sector Shared Services,* Accenture, Chicago.

Andriole, S. (2007) "The 7 Habits of Highly Effective Technology Leaders", *Communications of the ACM,* 50, 3, March, 67–72.

Cecil, B. (2000) "Shared Services: Moving Beyond Success", *Strategic Finance,* 81, 10, April, 64–75.

Davis, T. (2005) "Integrating Shared Services With the Strategy and Operation of MNEs", *Journal of General Management,* Winter, 31, 2, 1–17.

Lacity, M.C. and Willcocks, L.P. (2001) *Global Information Technology Outsourcing: Search for Business Advantage,* Wiley, Chichester.

Lacity, M. and Willcocks, L. (2009) *Information Systems and Outsourcing: Studies in Theory and Practice,* Palgrave, London.

Lacity, M., Willcocks, L. and Feeny, D. (2003) "Transforming a Back-Office Function: Lessons from BAE Systems' Enterprise Partnership", *MISQ Executive,* June.

Roberts, B., Jarvenpaa, S. and Baxley, C. (2003) "Evolving at the Speed of Change: Mastering Change Readiness", *MISQ Executive,* 2, 2, September, 58–73.

Webster, D. (2007) "Financial Management and Shared Services", *The Journal of Government Financial Management,* 56, 2, Summer 2007.

Index